F. E. Thompson

A syntax of Attic Greek

F. E. Thompson
A syntax of Attic Greek
ISBN/EAN: 9783337730239
Printed in Europe, USA, Canada, Australia, Japan
Cover: Foto ©ninafisch / pixelio.de

More available books at **www.hansebooks.com**

OF

ATTIC GREEK

BY

F. E. THOMPSON, M.A.

LATE ASSISTANT MASTER AT MARLBOROUGH COLLEGE
AUTHOR OF 'HOMERIC GRAMMAR' & 'ELEMENTARY GREEK SYNTAX,' ETC

NEW IMPRESSION

LONGMANS, GREEN, AND CO.
39 PATERNOSTER ROW, LONDON
NEW YORK AND BOMBAY
1898

CONTENTS.

§ 1-13. *Introduction to the Simple and Compound Sentence, and Definitions of Terms.*

The Statement, Question, and Petition, Subject, Copula, and Predicate, page 1—The Predicate and its Supplementary Adjuncts, or Supplementary Predicates, 2—The Object, Direct and Remote, 5—The Predicate, Attributive or Epithet, and Apposition, 5—Simple and Compound Sentences, 5—Principal and Subordinate Sentences, 6—Co-ordinate Sentences, 7—Classification of Subordinate Sentences into : *A.* Substantival. *B.* Adverbial. *C.* Relative, 7—Oratio Recta, 10—Oratio Obliqua, 10—Sub-direct and Sub-oblique, 11—Virtually Oblique, 11.

PART I.

SYNTAX OF THE SIMPLE SENTENCE.

CHAPTER I.

§ 14-34. *Subject and Predicate—Attributive and Apposition.*

The Subject, page 12—The Copula, 12—Omission of the Copula, 12—Subject and Predicate of the Infinitive in the Accusative, and in the Nominative, 13—Subject and Predicate of the Infinitive in the Genitive and Dative, 13—Omission of the Subject, 13—The Predicate, 14—Peculiarities in the Agreement of Subject and Predicate, 15—Neuter Plural and Verb Singular, 15—Neuter Plural and Verb Plural, 15—Adjective-Predicate in Neuter Singular with Plural Subject, 15—Schema Pindaricum, 16—Agreement of Predicate with several subjects, 16—ὅδε, οὗτος, ἐκεῖνος, as Subject and Predicate, 18—Peculiarities of Number, Singular, Dual, and Plural,

18—The Dual Number, 19—The Plural used for the Singular, 21—The First Person Plural used of a Singular Subject, 22—Peculiarities of Person, 22—Supplementary Predicates, 22—Peculiarities in the construction of the Attributive or Epithet, 23—Peculiarities of Apposition, 24.

CHAPTER II.

§ 35-66.   *The Article.*

Origin and Development of the Article, page 27—Survivals of the older usages of ὁ, ἡ, τό, and ὅς, ἥ, ὅ in Attic Greek, 28—The Article in Attic Greek, 29—The Article with Participles, 31—The Article with Numerals, 31—Fluctuating Use and Omission of the Article, 31—With Objects of external nature, 32—With material objects, 32—With familiar places, things, and persons, 32—With abstract and other words, 32—With names of arts, trades, and sciences, 33—The Article with proper names of persons and places, 33—With geographical names, 33—The noun-making power of the Article, 34—The Article distinguishes the Subject from the Predicate, 36—The Article with the Predicate, 37—Position of the Article : *A.* The Predicative Position. *B.* The Attributive Position, 37—Position when a Genitive follows, 39—Predicative Position when used, 40—Attributive Position when used, 41—Words which vary their meaning according to the position of the Article, 41—Oblique or Dependent Predicates, 43—Idiomatic Phrases with the Article, 46.

CHAPTER III.

§ 67-77.   *Pronouns.*

Personal Pronouns, page 47—Possessive Pronouns, 48—Reflexive Pronouns, 49—Demonstrative Pronouns, 51—The Pronoun αὐτός, 53—Interrogative Pronouns, 56—Relative Pronouns and Attraction, 57—Attraction, 58—Miscellaneous instances of Attraction, 59—Indefinite Pronouns, 61.

CONTENTS.

CHAPTER IV.

§ 78-126. The Cases.

Preliminary note on the cases, page 64—*The Nominative*, 65—*The Vocative*, 66—*The Accusative*. Preliminary Note, 66—1. The Internal Accusative, 67—2. The External Accusative, 67—Conspectus of the Internal Accusative, 67—The Internal Accusative, 68, including :—(*a.*) Accusative of Respect, 69—(*b.*) Accusative of Space and Time, 70—(*c.*) Accusative of Motion, 71—(*d.*) Accusative of the Object and Predicate in agreement or in apposition with the Object, 71—Double Accusative, 71—The External Accusative, 74—Verbs which take an External Accusative, 75—*The Genitive* 78—Preliminary Note on the Genitive, 78—Possessive Genitive, 79 —Genitive of Material or Contents, 80—Genitive of Amount, 81—Genitive of Plenty or Want, 82—The Partitive Genitive (so called), 83—Genitive of Connection, 86—Subjective and Objective Genitive, 90—Genitive of Time and Place, 91—Genitive of Value, 92—Causal Genitive, 93—Genitive with Verbs of Judicial Proceedings, 95—Genitive Absolute, 96—Genitive with Comparatives, 97—Genitive with Verbs containing a Comparative Notion, 97—Genitive of Separation, 98—FREE AND MISCELLANEOUS USES, 100—Genitive with Compound Verbs, 100—Double Genitive, 100—The Epexegetical Genitive, 100—Genitive of the Agent (so called), 101—Free use of the Genitive of Connection, 101—The Genitive with Adjectives and Adverbs, 102—Free use of the Genitive with Substantives, 104—*Preliminary Note on the Dative Case*, 104—Dative of the Indirect or Remoter Object, 105—Miscellaneous examples of the Dative of the Indirect or Remoter Object, 105—Dative of Interest, 106—Free use of the Dative of Interest, 106—Dative of the Possessor, 108—Ethic Dative, 108—Dative of Community or Contact, 108—Dative of the Instrument or Means, Agent, Cause, Measure of Difference, 110—Dative of Circumstance, 113—Dative of Time and Place, 114—List of Verbs which take a Dative, 116—List of Adjectives and Adverbs which take a Dative, 119.

CHAPTER V.

§ 127. *Comparative and Superlative.* Page 120

CHAPTER VI.

§ 128-134.   Voices and Moods.

The Active Voice, page 124—The Middle Voice, 125—The Passive Voice, 130—The Mood, 132—Introductory Note on the Subjunctive and Optative, 132—The Subjunctive in Independent Sentences, 134—The Optative in Independent Sentences, 135—The Imperative, 136.

CHAPTER VII.

§ 135-143.   The Tenses.

Classifications of Greek Tenses, page 138—Time how far observed throughout the Moods, 139—The Kind of Act or State denoted by the Tenses, 140—Ideal division of Tenses, 141—The Present and Imperfect Indicative, 142—The Perfect and Pluperfect Indicative, 144—The Aorist, 145—Note on the Aorist, 148—The Future, 149—Gnomic and Iterative Tenses, 151—The Tenses in the Moods, 152.

CHAPTER VIII.

§ 144-162.   The Three Verbal Nouns.

1. The Infinitive (a Substantive), page 153—2. The Participle (an Adjective), 153—3. The Verbal Adjectives in τος and τεος, 153—Note on the Infinitive, 153—The Infinitive, 153—The Supplementary Infinitive, 154—The Subject before and the Predicate after the Infinitive (commonly called the Accusative with the Infinitive), 157—The Infinitive as a Noun, 160—The Participle, 162—The Participle as an Attributive, 163—The Genitive Absolute, 165—The Genitive Absolute in Greek and Latin, 166—The Accusative Absolute, 167—Verbals in -τεος, 168—Their personal construction, 168—Their impersonal construction, 169—The Supplementary Participle, 169—The Supplementary Participle in agreement with the subject of the Verb : A. With Verbs of Saying and of Perception, 169—B. With Verbs of Emotion, 170—C. With Verbs of Beginning, Continuing, and Ending an Action, 170—D. With Verbs of making

or becoming Manifest, and of escaping Notice, 170—Note on Special Verbs which take this construction, e.g. ἄρχομαι, φθάνω, λανθάνω, etc., 171—The Supplementary Participle in agreement with the Object of the Verb: A. With Verbs of making to cease, finding, detecting, overlooking, 174—B. With Verbs of Perception, 175—The Tenses of the Participle, and time in the Participles, 175—The Future Participle, 176.

PART II.

SYNTAX OF THE COMPOUND SENTENCE.

CHAPTER I.

§ 163-170.   *Substantival Sentences.*

1. *The Indirect Statement*, page 178—2. *The Indirect Question*, 178—3. *The Indirect Petition*, 178—The Indirect Statement, 178 : A. The Infinitive in the Indirect Statement, 178—B. ὅτι and ὡς with the Indicative and Optative in the Indirect Statement, 181—C. The Participle in the Indirect Statement, 186—The Indirect Question, 188—Deliberative or Dubitative Indirect Questions, 190—The Indirect Petition, 191.

CHAPTER II.

§ 171-206.   *Conditional Sentences.*

The Particle ἄν, page 193—Definite and Indefinite Sentences, 194—Conditional Sentences, 195—Distinction of Conditions, 196—Division of Conditional Sentences, 197—Ordinary Conditions, 197—Ordinary Conditions in Greek and Latin, 200—General or Frequentative Examples, 200—The Negatives in Conditional Sentences, 201—Relative Conditional Sentences, 201—Participles in the Protasis, 202—Position of ἄν, 203—Repetition of ἄν, 203—Ἄν with the Future Indicative, 204—Ellipse of the Apodosis, and Ellipse of the Verb, 205—Ellipse of the Protasis, 205—Εἰ and ἄν both in the Protasis, 206—Δέ in Apodosis, 207—Ἐάν seemingly interrogative, 207—Ἄν with the Participle seemingly in Protasis, 208—Conditional

Particles and their Combinations, 208—Examples of Conditional Sentences, εἰ with Indicative in Protasis and Apodosis, 209—(*A.*) Ordinary Present Conditions, 209. (*B.*) Ordinary Past Conditions, 209. (*C.*) Present and Past in Combination, 210—Ordinary Future Conditions, ἐάν (ἤν) with Subjunctive, 210—Less Vivid Future Conditions, εἰ with Optative, 211—Most Vivid Future Conditions, εἰ with Future Indicative, 212—Mixed examples illustrating the connection between and interchangeability of the Subjunctive, Optative, and Future Indicative in Conditional Sentences, 213— The Optative and Indicative with ἄν without a Protasis, 214— Unfulfilled Conditions, εἰ with Historic Tenses of Indicative in Protasis, ἄν with the same in Apodosis, 215—The omission of ἄν in Apodosis with the Indicative, 217—'Εάν (ἤν) with the Subjunctive, and εἰ with the Optative in General or Frequentative Suppositions, 220—Mixed Examples, 222—Examples of the Conditional Participle in a Protasis, 224—Examples of a Conditional Relative Sentence, 225—Relative Conditional Sentences expressing General Suppositions, 226—Examples of Infinitive in Apodosis with ἄν, 226—Examples of Participle in Apodosis with ἄν, 227—Supplementary Note on ἐάν with the Subjunctive, and εἰ with the Optative, 227.

CHAPTER III.

§ 207-224.   *Temporal Sentences.*

"When" in Definite Time (Past), ἐπεί, ἐπειδή (ἡνίκα, ὅτε), page 233—"As soon as," "Directly," in Definite Time, ἐπεί (ἐπειδή), τάχιστα, ὡς, 234—"Whenever," "As often as," in Indefinite Time, ἐπεί, ἐπειδή, ἡνίκα, ὅτε, ὁπότε, (ἐπήν, ἐπειδάν, ὅταν, etc.), 235—"Since" in Definite Time, ἐξ οὗ, 236—"Whilst" in Definite Time, ἕως, ἔστε, ἐν ᾧ, ἐν ὅσῳ, ὅσον χρόνον, ἡνίκα (μέχρι), 237—"Whilst" in Indefinite Time, ἕως, etc., with ἄν and Subj., without ἄν and Opt., 237—"Until" in Definite Time, ἕως, ἔστε, μέχρι ἄχρι, 238—"Until" in Indefinite Time, ἕως, etc., with ἄν and Subj., without ἄν an Opt., 239—The Conjunction πρίν, 240—Πρίν with the Infinitive, 241—Πρίν with the Indicative in Definite Time (Past), 242—Πρίν with the Subjunctive and Optative in Indefinite Time, 242—Πρίν with the Infinitive after Negative Sentences, and with the other Moods after Affirmative Sentences, 243—Ἄν omitted with the Subjunctive, in Temporal and other Subordinate Sentences, 245—Ἄν retained with the Optative, 246—The Subjunctive instead of the Optative or co-ordinate with the Optative in Historic Sequence, 246—The Participle as a Substitute for a Temporal Sentence, 247.

CHAPTER IV.

§ 225-226.   *Concessive Sentences.*

Concessive Sentences, page 249—Note on εἰ καί, καὶ εἰ, etc., 250.

CHAPTER V.

§ 227-239.   (1) *Final Sentences,* (2) ὅπως *with the Future Indicative, and* (3) *Verbs of Fearing with* μή, *etc.*

Final Sentences, page 253—Final Particles with the Subjunctive and Optative, 253—Final Sentences with Past Tenses of the Indicative, 257—Final Sentences with the Future Participle, 258—Relative Final Sentences, 258—Final Sentences with the Infinitive, 259—Ὅπως, ὅπως μή, modal with the Future Indicative, etc.: and Variant Constructions, 259—Elliptical use of ὅπως, ὅπως μή with the Future Indicative, 262—Ὅπως, ὅπως μή with Verbs of Commanding and Forbidding, 262—Verbs of Fearing with μή and μὴ οὐ, 262—Verbs of Fearing, etc., with the Indicative, 266—Note on Dawes' Canon, 267.

CHAPTER VI.

§ 240-244.   *Consecutive and Limitative Sentences.*

Ὥστε with the Indicative and the Infinitive, page 270—Consecutive Sentences in Greek and Latin, 273—Relative Consecutive Sentences, 273—Limitative or Restrictive Sentences, 274.

CHAPTER VII.

§ 245.   *Causal Sentences.*

(*a.*) Causal Particles and a Finite Mood, page 276—(*b.*) Relative Sentences, 278—(*c.*) Participles, 278—(*d.*) Miscellaneous ways, 279.

CONTENTS.

CHAPTER VIII.
§ 246.   *Expressions of a Wish.*   Page 280

CHAPTER IX.
§ 247.   *Relative Sentences*   Page 284

PART III.
PREPOSITIONS, NEGATIVES, ORATIO OBLIQUA, AND FIGURES.

CHAPTER I.
§ 248-252.   *Prepositions.*

Introductory Note on Prepositions, page 286—The Prepositions and their meanings with the three cases, 289—Collected Usages of Prepositions, 289—Prepositions and the cases they go with, 291.

I.—Prepositions with one Case only:
§ 253-255.   (*a.*) *With Accusative only.*
Ἀνά, page 291—Εἰς or ἐς, 292—ὡς, 294.

§ 256-264.   (*b.*) *With Genitive only.*
ἀντί, page 294—ἀπό, 295—ἐκ, ἐξ, 297—πρό, 300—ἄνευ, 301—ἕνεκα, ἕνεκεν, 301—ἕκατι, 301—χωρίς, 301—Old Cases used as quasi-Prepositions with the Genitive, 302.

§ 265-268.   (*c.*) *With Dative only.*
ἐν, page 302—σύν, 305—Note on σύν and μετά, 306—ἅμα, ὁμοῦ, etc., 306.

II.—Prepositions with two Cases.
§ 269-272.   *With Accusative and Genitive.*
διά, page 307—κατά, 310—ὑπέρ, 314—μετά, 316.

III—Prepositions with all three Cases.
§ 273-278.
ἀμφί, page 317—ἐπί. 319—παρά, 328—περί, 332—πρός, 336—ὑπό, 341.

CHAPTER II.

§ 279-310.   *The Negatives.*

Introductory Note, page 345—Οὐ Privative, 346—Οὐ and μή with Adjectives, Participles used as Adjectives, Adverbs, and Substantives, 348—Οὐ and μή with Participles, 350—Οὐ and μή with the Infinitive, 351—Οὐ and μή with Direct and Indirect Statements, 354—Οὐ and μή with Indirect Statements in the Participle, 354—Οὐ and μή with Direct Questions, 355—Οὐ and μή with Deliberative Questions, 356—Οὐ and μή with Indirect Questions, 356—Οὐ and μή with Indirect Petitions, 357—Οὐ and μή with Conditional Sentences, 358—Οὐ and μή with Concessive Sentences, 359—Οὐ and μή with Causal Sentences, 359—Οὐ and μή with Consecutive and Restrictive Sentences, 360—Οὐ and μή with Temporal and Local Sentences, 361 —Οὐ and μή with Final Sentences, etc., 361—Οὐ and μή with Relatives, 362—Μή with Wishes, 364—Μή and Μὴ οὐ with the Infinitive, 365—Μὴ οὐ with the Participle, 368—Μή and μὴ οὐ with the Subjunctive, 369—Οὐ μή with the Subjunctive and Future Indicative, 371—Further examples of οὐ μή with: *A*. Subjunctive, 372—*B*. Future Indicative, 373—Repetition of the Negative, 375—Οὐδείς, μηδείς, οὐδέν, μηδέν, etc., 376—Μή with Oaths and Assertions, 378 —Μή where οὐ might have been expected, 378—Miscellaneous instances showing the power of οὐ to make a downright Negative Statement, 379—Note on μή, μὴ οὐ with the Infinitive and Participle, 380—Note on μή and μὴ οὐ with the Subjunctive, 382—Note on οὐ μή with the Subjunctive and the Future Indicative, 382.

CHAPTER III.

§ 311-327.   *Oratio Obliqua.*

Introductory, page 387—Rules for Sub-direct Clauses in Oratio Obliqua, 389—Types of Sub-direct Clauses in Historic Sequence, 390—Rules for Sub-oblique Clauses in Oratio Obliqua, 392—Types of Sub-direct and Sub-oblique Clauses in the Obliqua, 393—The Apodosis in the Participle in Oratio Obliqua, 395—Relative Sentences in Oratio Obliqua, 395—Some real examples of Oratio Obliqua analysed, 396 —The Infinitive, and ὅτι or ὡς with Finite Moods in Sub-direct Sentences of Oratio Obliqua, 398—Assimilation of Optatives, 402 —Non-Assimilation, 403—Examples of Mixed Graphic and strict Obliqua, 404—Virtual Oratio Obliqua, 404—Past Tenses of the Indicative in Oratio Obliqua, 405—Apparently Abnormal Obliqua, 406—Long Speeches in Obliqua, 407.

CHAPTER IV.

§ 328-347.   *Figures of Rhetoric, etc.*

Alliteration, page 410—Anakoluthia, 411—Antiptosis, 412—Asyndeton, 413—Binary Structure, 413—Brachylogy, 414—Zeugma and Syllepsis, 415—Constructio Praegnans, 415—Brachylogy of Comparison, 416—Catachresis, 416—Ellipse and Aposiopesis, 416—Euphemism, 417—Hypallage, 418—Hyperbaton, Chiasmus, Hysteron Proteron, 418—Litotes, 419—Oxymoron, 420—Periphrasis, 421—Pleonasm, 421—Prolepsis or Anticipation, 422—Puns, 422.

English Index, . . . - . . . Page 425

Greek Index, ... 428

Table of References, ... 434

PREFACE.

SOME explanation, perhaps apology, is necessary for publishing a new Greek Syntax, when so many similar books by really great Greek scholars are in use. My object has been to write a Greek Syntax arranged on the analytical method, *i.e.* by sentences, simple and compound; to attempt for Greek what Dr. Kennedy's invaluable Grammars have done for Latin. Dr. Donaldson's once well-known Greek Grammars are so arranged : they are the works of a very able man and a ripe scholar, but no one would now accept the local theory of the Cases, or the treatment of Conditionals as set forth in them.

I may perhaps be allowed to explain how I came to write this Syntax, and the plan adopted in it, as the book, such as it is, is not a mere compilation from other Grammars. I have for many years been in the habit of jotting down marginal references to constructions. When three years ago it was suggested to me that I should draw up a Greek Syntax, I began by writing out these examples, under their different headings. I thus had an outline of rules with many hundred examples, an outline which has not been materially departed from. I then read or re-read several books bearing on the subject. I need hardly say that my views had to be modified on several points of principle, and still more of detail. With regard to the examples I do not suppose that I have used or referred to one quarter of the original supply. For several of my own, again, I have substituted others, either because these latter were so familiar as to have acquired vested rights with teachers and learners or because they were handier. My original outline began with Homeric instances, but, as I proceeded, I cut these out, and confined myself solely to Attic, chiefly because it was represented to me that, when boys write Greek Prose or Iambics, they have such a fatal perversity for bringing in an Epic word or construction. I need hardly say that, when I read Mr. Monro's masterly *Homeric Grammar*, I felt exceedingly glad that I had suppressed my own attempt to deal with so difficult a subject. A monumental Greek Grammar should of course begin with Homer, and end certainly not before the Hellenistic period, proceeding with the grand march of the historic method. In a book meant for boys or undergraduates the object would, I think, be most practically secured by adding appendices, Homeric, Hellenistic, and so forth. But this suggestion need not be discussed here.

The analysis which I have followed is, with some variations, the logical method made familiar by Dr. Kennedy's Latin Grammars. For instance, I begin the Introduction with a piece of formal logic: the Proposition contains three parts, Subject, Copula, and Predicate. Had I introduced Homeric examples, I should have probably commenced with the Verb (ἵστη-σι, δίδω-σι, Predicate + Subject), connecting the thought with the form, and have attempted to trace thence the gradual growth and development of the Sentence. Indeed I might have begun earlier with the blunt, but perfectly intelligible expression of judgment: νήπιος, *fool* (Predicate only). But though the historical method is unquestionably more scientific, yet I deliberately adopted the logical for several reasons, chiefly because teachers and boys are already familiar with it in learning Latin: a double advantage, for there is thus no new method to acquire, and Greek and Latin can be worked together.

But, whichever method we pursue, it is equally unwise and impossible to be rigidly consistent. Take the Cases, for instance. The Nominative is used both as Subject and as Predicate. The Accusative and Dative qualify a Verb, and so may be regarded as supplementary Predicates. The Genitive qualifies a Substantive, and thus is Adjectival or Attributive : but it may also qualify a Verb, and so becomes a supplementary Predicate. It would however be absurd to split up the Cases, and range their uses under different Chapters. When we come to the Compound Sentence one of two courses is open : either (1) to treat all the usages of the Moods together, giving one chapter to the Indicative, another to the Optative and so on; or (2) to take the different kinds of Subordinate Sentences, and show how they are expressed by the different Moods. Most Grammars adopt the former method, and there is much to be said for it, the same, it might appear, as for the Cases. This method brings together the different usages which often vary so slightly, and shade off into one another; it makes the learner see that there are not so many distinct Optatives, but one Optative. But experience convinces me that the method of sentences is incomparably the most practical and easily remembered, while in the hands of a careful teacher the unity of each Mood may constantly be pointed out. It is far easier for a boy to learn how to express the different kinds of Temporal Sentences by treating them all together than by dividing them among the Moods. All grammars do this for Conditional Sentences, and why not for other kinds of Subordinate Sentences which are almost equally difficult? However, in order to supplement the plan adopted in the text, I have in the Index given a full register of the uses of each Mood. I have to a considerable extent adopted Dr. Donaldson's theory of Predicates with some change of nomenclature. His division into Primary, Secondary, and Tertiary suggests three progressive and co-ordinate stages, whereas a Secondary Predicate is simply an extension and part of the whole Predicate, and a Tertiary Predicate is nothing but an ordinary Predicate (Adjective or Participle), not in the Nominative Case. I prefer therefore the terms Supplementary, and Oblique (or Dependent). But whatever names we use, I believe that there is nothing which gives the learner a greater grasp of a Greek passage than a thorough assimilation of this doctrine of Predication. Take the Participle for instance, one of the commonest forms of supplementary Predicates, in a Platonic paragraph, *e.g.*, the Carpenter who is out of sorts and calls in the Doctor, or the Parable of the Captain and the mutinous Crew: a knowledge of the exact force of the Participle in qualifying the main Predication is essential towards picking our way through the paragraph, and rendering the Greek into adequate English.

To come to details. The treatment of the Cases must be unsatisfactory, in far abler hands than mine. The usages of the Accusative and Dative fall easily enough under fairly distinct heads. But the Genitive seems a wilderness of cross-divisions. I do not see how it is possible to assign its usages to the two distinct heads of Connexion (Genitive), and Separation (Ablative). To take only one case: who shall decide whether the Genitive of Value and Price is the true Genitive denoting Connexion, or an Ablative denoting Exchange, *i.e.* Separation? Comparative Syntax often is quite powerless to help us. Thus the Greek Genitive Absolute seems unquestionably to be, as Krüger pointed out long ago, a real Genitive denoting "the sphere within which," and so the Class, (e.g. θεοῦ διδόντος, within the sphere of divine providence); but in Sanskrit the Absolute Case is the Locative, in Latin it is Circumstantial, i.e. Instrumental, in Old English it was originally a Dative, and subsequently a Nominative, in German a Genitive. I have with misgivings retained the familiar but unsatisfactory " Accusative of Respect;" it is anyhow as intelligible as Professor Goodwin's "Accusative of Specification."

The Aorist requires more courageous treatment than it usually receives, if we are anxious to render Greek into correct and idiomatic English, and *vice versa*. The Aorist-Stem denotes an act *single, complete*, and *summed up*. In the Indicative this act belongs to the past, whether occurring a thousand years ago, or a moment ago. When the past is not recent, the Aorist is translated by the English past tense, ἦλθον, *I came*. But, when the act is recent and bears on the present, the Greeks could use the Aorist where we use a *Perfect*, e.g. Od. v. 172, νῦν δ' ἐνθάδε κάββαλε δαίμων, *but now a god hath cast me on this shore:* Luke v. 26, εἴδαμεν παράδοξα σήμερον, *we have seen strange things to-day*. Again, where the act has occurred, a moment ago, the Greeks often used the Aorist where we use a *Present*. Familiar instances occur in the Tragedians, ἐπῄνεσα,[1] *I commend;* ἥσθην,[2] *I am pleased;* ἐδεξάμην,[3] *I hail*. Once more the *gnomic*

---

[1] Soph. *Ai.* 536.   [2] *Phil.* 1314.
[3] *Elektr.* 668. Similarly ἀπέπτυσα, ὤμωξα, ξυνῆκα, etc., etc.

or *iterative* Aorist is represented by the English *Past, Perfect,* or *Present Tenses.* And lastly in *similes* we must translate the Aorist by a *Present,* e.g. *Il.* v. 161, ὡς δὲ λέων θορὼν ἄξῃ, *as a lion springeth and breaketh.* So far with regard to Principal Sentences. In Subordinate Sentences our rendering must be still more elastic, as we shall see if we have to turn into Greek the following : *when I come, have (am) come, shall come, shall have come,* ἐπειδὰν ἔλθω : *if I had known,* εἰ ἔγνων : *when they had gone,* ἐπειδὴ ἀπῆλθον : *I do not believe what you have said,* ἃ ἔλεξας; not necessarily ἃ εἴρηκας (in past Obliqua *what he had said,* the Pluperfect in English, but the Aorist still in Greek).

Thus, startling as the statement seems, the Greek Aorist is translateable into almost every English tense except the Imperfect.[1] Mr. M. Arnold's dictum is as wise as it is witty: "the Aorist was made for man, and not man for the Aorist."

---

[1] Our English narrative Past Tense is by no means parallel with the Greek Aorist. It often is the idiomatic and correct equivalent for a Greek (or Latin) Imperfect, *i.e.* it is *descriptive* as well as *narrative.* A few minutes' attention to any ordinary conversation, or almost any page of a standard author, would prove this, *e.g.* MACAULAY, *History of England,* vol. i. ch. 2. (fin.):—"Still, however, the contest continued. He [Charles] *assured* the Duke of York that Halifax should be dismissed from office, and Halifax that the Duke should be sent to Scotland. In public he *affected* implacable resentment against Monmouth, and in private *conveyed* to Monmouth assurances of unalterable affection." A boy set down to translate these tenses into Greek would probably use the Aorist, because he has been required to translate the Greek Imperfect by a clumsy, often unnecessary and

In dealing with the Moods I have probably (p. 133) expressed myself too unhesitatingly that the Optative cannot be a past form. Its Secondary endings, and the possible loss of the separable augment, make it at least conceivable that the Optative was originally past. If this were so, a past form would (as in Hebrew, I believe) be used to denote a wish.

I could not treat the Prepositions briefly, and did not wish to do so. Nothing seems to me more conventional than to pick out two or three uses of πρός for instance, and to make the learner believe that these are the dominant and typical usages. Such a course seems to me a great snare. I do not believe that the use of the Prepositions can be taught in a few formal lessons, they must be gradually acquired, like those of the Particles, by constant observation.

In the Oratio Obliqua I have introduced the two technical terms, *Sub-direct* and *Sub-oblique*. Personally, I prefer names to periphrases when dealing with facts of constant recurrence, and I do not find the pupil puzzled. But the teacher need not employ the terms if he objects to them: the treatment of the chapter does not depend on the terms.

I had prepared a chapter on Particles, but have sup-

---

unidiomatic, periphrasis, "he was affecting," "kept on conveying," etc. Much more correctly T. K. Arnold of old taught us on p. 1 that "the dog *howled* all night" required an Imperfect in Latin.

pressed it, as the book already has outrun its intended length.

It only remains for me to acknowledge my special obligations, to authors and to friends.

Of books, besides old guides such as Jelf and Donaldson, Liddell and Scott, I have found the following most useful :—

(1) Krüger's *Griechische Sprachlehre*. This is, all round, the most useful Greek Grammar I know. It is a vast treasury of well-chosen instances covering the whole range of so-called classical Greek Literature. Even if you do not always agree with his arrangement or conclusions, Krüger always furnishes ample materials for induction. In substituting a better example for the one which I had originally noted, I have found Krüger incomparable.

(2) Madvig's *Syntax of the Greek Language, especially of the Attic dialect*. It would be impertinent in me to praise this well-known work by the great scholar. There seems to be nothing at second-hand in it.

(3) Goodwin's *Moods and Tenses*, and *Greek Grammar*. The first-named book by this accomplished scholar is of the greatest value. He has revolutionised the treatment of the Conditionals; his treatment of Final and semi-Final Sentences is hardly less striking. I have ventured to embody the substance of two of his papers in the *Journal of Philology* in a note on ἐάν and εἰ.

(4) Curtius's *Student's Greek Grammar, and Elucidations to the Greek Grammar*. Both books are most instructive; the great philologer's Syntax is singularly vigorous, fresh, and suggestive.

(5) Notes on Constructions in Mr. A. Sidgwick's *Introduction to Greek Prose Composition*. Most practical and incisive.

(6) Riddell's *Digest of Platonic Idioms*, in his edition of the *Apology*. I must record my great gratitude to this lamented author. No book that I know of bearing on Greek Syntax is so suggestive: no Greek scholar of our time seems to me to combine, in so marked a degree, fine taste, subtlety, and sound judgment.

I wish also to express my gratitude for the help afforded in Professor Jebb's editions of the plays of Sophocles and selections from the Attic Orators.

I have sparingly alluded to books of reference, and then only to such as are easily procurable, such as Professor M. Müller's *Essays*. It would be useless to refer boys, or most undergraduates (I suppose), to Delbrück's *Syntaktische Forschungen* for the comparative treatment of Greek Syntax, and the probable evolution of usages and constructions. But while the latter part of this Grammar was in the press, Mr. D. B. Monro published his long looked-for *Homeric Grammar*. It is a book with which every teacher of Greek should be thoroughly familiar, and to parts of which he may conveniently refer his pupils for the origin and explanation of Greek constructions. Mr. Monro has kindly permitted me, in my Index, to refer to certain paragraphs in his work.

I have to thank several friends for much help. Mr. A. Sidgwick has been kind enough to go through the whole of the proofs. I am deeply sensible that in so doing he has most materially added to any value which this book may possess. I have also to thank two old friends for reading through some chapters with me, and giving me the advantage of their views,—Professor Butcher of Edinburgh, and Mr. F. Storr of Merchant Taylors. And, lastly, I am much indebted to several of my colleagues here for help and sympathy.

Some little slips, such as wrong accents, have inevitably escaped several pairs of eyes. They, however, can be easily rectified, and will cause no serious harm. If any one who may use this book cares to point out more important errors, I shall be extremely grateful.

F. E. THOMPSON.

COTTON HOUSE, MARLBOROUGH.
August 1883.

NOTE.

The book is practically divided into—

I. An Elementary Syntax.
II. An Advanced Syntax.

The following distinctions have (with a few unimportant exceptions) been observed :—

In I. 1*stly*, The type is large.
    2*ndly*, The headings are in Italics.
    3*rdly*, The name of the author is given without reference to line or chapter, etc.

II. 1*stly*, The type is small.
    2*ndly*, The headings are in thick black type.
    3*rdly*, Reference is given to the line or chapter, etc., of the author quoted.

INTRODUCTION TO THE SIMPLE AND COMPOUND SENTENCE, AND DEFINITIONS OF TERMS

§ I. *THE STATEMENT, QUESTION, AND PETITION.*

A SENTENCE assumes three forms—(1) the Statement (*Enuntiatio*); (2) the Question (*Interrogatio*); (3) the Petition, *i.e.* a command, request, prayer, or wish (*Petitio*).

A sentence, *logically considered*, connects (positively or negatively) two distinct conceptions. Thus in the sentence, "The rose is sweet," the conceptions of a certain flower and a certain quality are connected positively. Two conceptions are connected negatively in the sentence, "The nightshade is not wholesome." A sentence, *logically and fully expressed*, may be represented by the formulas—*A* is *B*; *A* is not *B*. A sentence therefore necessarily consists of three parts, neither more nor less :—

(1) The *Subject, i.e.* that of which the statement is made;
(2) the *Predicate, i.e.* the statement made of the Subject;
(3) the *Copula, i.e.* the connecting or disconnecting link,—*is* (when the sentence is positive), *is not* (when it is negative).

These three parts are not always present in language. The finite verb contains in itself a complete sentence—στρατηγῶ, *I am general.* The Copula is frequently omitted, being contained in the verb, or understood—Ξέρξης βασιλεύει, *Xerxes is king;* ἀγαθὸς ὁ ἀνήρ, *The man is good.* Logically expressed, these sentences would be—Ξέρξης ἐστι βασιλεύς, ὁ ἀνήρ ἐστιν ἀγαθός.

A

The Statement, Question, and Petition differ from one another simply in the relation of the Predicate to the Subject. Thus we may say, "The door is shut" (Statement); "Is the door shut?" (Question); "Shut the door" (Petition). In the Statement we say that the Predicate is applicable to the Subject; in the Question we ask if the Predicate is applicable to the Subject; in the Petition we request or command that the Predicate may be applicable to the Subject. Whatever remarks are here made with regard to a sentence apply equally to each of its three forms, the Statement, the Question, and the Petition.

§ 2. *THE PREDICATE AND ITS SUPPLEMENTARY ADJUNCTS.*

The Predicate is the whole statement made of the Subject, whether that statement is short and simple, or long and composite. It may be short and simple, consisting of one word, as in the examples given above—

Subject.		Predicate.
Ξέρξης		βασιλεύει,
ὁ ἀνήρ	(sc. ἐστιν)	ἀγαθός,

or it may be a composite expression made up of many words—

Subject.	Predicate.	
ὁ παῖς	χαίρει	ὑπερφυῶς.
The boy	rejoices	exceedingly.
οἱ Ἀθηναῖοι	ἀπῆλθον	τριταῖοι.
The Athenians	departed	on the third day.

THE PREDICATE AND ITS ADJUNCTS.

Subject.	Predicate.
(*You.*)	τίνος διδάσκαλοι | ἥκετε; *To be whose teachers | are you come?*
(*Thou.*)	ἴλεως | αὐτῶν κλύε. *Do thou hear them mercifully.*
He	ἐμοὶ πικρὸς | τέθνηκεν. *is dead, a source of grief to me* (i.e. *his death is grievous to me*).
αὕτη ἡ στρατία *This army*	ἔξεισι | ὄνειδος τῇ πόλει. *will march out (so as to be, or, and will be), a disgrace to the state.*
Thou	ἐπεξέρχει | θρασύς. *advancest in boldness.*
I	ἀγανακτῶ | ἀναμνησθεὶς ἐμαυτοῦ. *am vexed when I recollect my own conduct.*
κρύσταλλος *Ice*	ἐπεπήγει | οὐ βέβαιος. *had frozen not so as to be solid.*
ἡ δύσμορος	εἰς θανόντων ἔρχομαι κατασκαφάς | ἔρημος πρὸς φίλων, | ζῶσα.
I, most unhappy maid,	*am descending to the cavernous chambers of the dead, | forlorn of friends, | while living still.*

Compare two Latin instances—

| Corpora | infinita \| iactantur. |
| *Atoms* | *are tossed about \| in unlimited quantity.* |

4 SIMPLE AND COMPOUND SENTENCES.

SUBJECT.	PREDICATE.
Saxa	paullatim | anima mollia | caluerunt.
Stones	*gradually waxed warm with the softness of life* (ita ut mollia fierent, *so as to become soft*).

Instances may be found on any page of a book in any language. The first point to notice is that the whole expression constitutes the Predicate. The second point to notice is that, on analysing such compound Predicates as the above, there is a word (generally a verb, but it may be a noun or participle), which by itself, if all the rest were away, might stand as a simple Predicate, and that this simple Predicate is further extended or qualified by an adjunct or adjuncts. Thus in the sentence, οἱ 'Αθηναῖοι ἀπῆλθον τριταῖοι, ἀπῆλθον τριταῖοι is the Predicate: ἀπῆλθον alone as a Predicate would, with its Subject, have made a complete sentence; but ἀπῆλθον is extended by stating the time of departure. There may be many supplementary adjuncts which swell out the Predicate. It is most important in Greek to notice them, and discover their special force, for they often convey the real pith and gist of the predication, denoting *manner, degree cause, time, condition, purpose, the anticipated result,* etc. etc.

In Greek, adverbs, adjectives, and participles (sometimes substantives) constantly occur as supplementary adjuncts,[1] or, as they will be called throughout this book, *Supplementary Predicates*.

---

[1] Dr. Donaldson called these supplementary adjuncts secondary Predicates. Thus he would have said that ἀπῆλθον was the primary Predicate, and τριταῖοι the secondary.

§ 3. THE OBJECT, DIRECT AND REMOTE.

The *direct Object* is that which is immediately acted on by a transitive verb. The *remote* or *remoter Object* is that to which the direct object is transferred, or that which is interested and concerned in the verbal action. Δώσω δέκα μνᾶς, *I will give ten minae*. Here μνᾶς is the *direct object*. Δώσω δέκα μνᾶς τῷ διδασκάλῳ, *I will give ten minae to the teacher*. Here τῷ διδασκάλῳ is the *remoter object*.

§ 4. PREDICATE, ATTRIBUTIVE OR EPITHET, AND APPOSITION.

The following instances will show the difference between a Predicate and an Attributive:—ὁ ἀνὴρ (ἐστιν) ἀγαθός, *the man is good*—ἀγαθός, *good*, is a *Predicate*: ὁ ἀγαθὸς ἀνήρ, *the good man*—ἀγαθός, *good*, is an *Attributive*. The Predicate gives new information of the Subject, the Attributive uses information assumed to be known already, and thus forms one notion with a Substantive. *Apposition* does not form one notion with a Substantive, but is a further description appended to a Substantive, *e.g.* χρόνος, ὁ κοινὸς ἰατρός, σε θεραπεύσει, *Time, the common physician, will heal thee.*

§ 5. SIMPLE AND COMPOUND SENTENCES.

Αὐτὸς στρατηγῶ, *I myself am general*, is a *Simple Sentence*. Νικίας ἔφη, *Nikias made a statement*, again, is a Simple Sentence. But if we join the two together, thus—

6 SIMPLE AND COMPOUND SENTENCES.

Νικίας ἔφη αὐτὸς στρατηγεῖν, *Nikias stated that he himself was general*, we have a *Compound Sentence*. A Compound Sentence is thus a sentence consisting of two (or more) sentences compounded into one. Logically, *i.e.* so far as thought goes, there is no difference between a Simple and a Compound Sentence. Each is an expression containing the three necessary elements of a sentence, *i.e.* Subject, Copula, and Predicate ; *e.g.*—

Νικίας (Subject)   ἔφη (Copula and Predicate).
αὐτὸς (Subject)   στρατηγῶ (Copula and Predicate).
Νικίας (Subject)   ἔφη αὐτὸς στρατηγεῖν (Copula and Predicate).

For the last sentence, so far as thought goes, simply amounts to this : *Nikias | stated something.*

Χαιρεφῶν, εἰς Δελφοὺς ἐλθών, ἤρετο εἴ τις εἴη ἐμοῦ σοφώτερος.

Chaerephon, going to Delphi, asked if any one were wiser than I.

Here we have three sentences compounded into one, of which Χαιρεφῶν is the Subject, and the rest is the Predicate, with the Copula contained in ἤρετο. So far as thought goes, it amounts to saying, *Chaerephon | asked a question on a certain occasion.*

§ 6. *PRINCIPAL AND SUBORDINATE SENTENCES.*

In every Compound Sentence there must be one on which the rest depend in construction. Such a sentence is called the *Principal Sentence.* Those which depend in construction on it are called *Subordinate Sentences*. Thus, in the first example above, Νικίας ἔφη is the Principal Sentence, αὐτὸς στρατηγεῖν is the Subordinate Sentence. The dependence of the latter on the former is easily shown; if we remove Νικίας ἔφη, then αὐτὸς στρατηγεῖν cannot stand alone as a sentence. In the second sentence, Χαιρεφῶν ἤρετο is the Principal Sentence; the dependent question, εἴ τις εἴη ἐμοῦ σοφώτερος, and the temporal participial sentence, εἰς Δελφοὺς ἐλθών, are the Subordinate Sentences.

§ 7. CO-ORDINATE SENTENCES.

Co-ordinate Sentences are of the same rank, *i.e.* construction, as those to which they are joined. Thus, if a sentence is co-ordinate with a Principal Sentence, it is a second Principal Sentence: if with a Subordinate Sentence, it is Subordinate, and of the same nature (whether an Indirect Statement, Question, Petition, Adverbial or Relative Sentence). (See below.)

δέομαι καὶ παρίεμαι ὑμῶν μήτε θαυμάζειν μήτε θορυβεῖν.
I beg, and entreat you, neither to wonder, nor to interrupt.

Here καὶ παρίεμαι is co-ordinate with the Principal Sentence δέομαι, and therefore is a second Principal Sentence: while μήτε θορυβεῖν is co-ordinate with the Subordinate Sentence θαυμάζειν (an Indirect Petition), and therefore is Subordinate, and an Indirect Petition.

§ 8. CLASSIFICATION OF SUBORDINATE SENTENCES.

Subordinate Sentences are classified according to the relation in which they stand to the Principal Sentence.

8 SIMPLE AND COMPOUND SENTENCES.

Let the three following groups be taken.

A. PRINCIPAL. SUBORDINATE.

(a) 1. οὐ ῥᾴδιόν ἐστι ταῦτα μαθεῖν.
   It is not easy *to learn this.*

 2. Νικίας ἔφη στρατηγεῖν.
   Nikias said *that he was general.*

(β) 1. ἄδηλόν ἐστιν εἰ ταῦτα ξυνίης.
   It is uncertain *whether you understand this.*

 2. οὐκ οἶδα ὅστις ἐστί.
   I do not know *who he is.*

(γ) 1. περιηγγέλλετο πανστρατιᾷ βοηθεῖν.
   Orders were being sent round *to march in full force.*

 2. δέομαί σου ταῦτα μαθεῖν.
   I beg you *to learn this.*

B. κατέγνωκάς μου ἀδίκως.
   You have condemned me *unjustly.*

 κατέγνωκάς μου διότι χρυσὸν ἔλαβες.
 You have condemned me *because you took a bribe.*

 εὐτυχήσεις ἢν ταῦτα ποιήσῃς.
 You will be fortunate *if you do this.*

C. ἀνέλαβον τὰ ποιήματα ἃ ἐποίησε Σοφοκλῆς.
 I took up the poems *which Sophocles composed.*

In group **A** it will be seen that the Subordinate Sentence supplies (1.) the Subject, (2.) the Object of the Compound Sentence. Now the chief function of a Substantive is to express the Subject or the Object. Such Subordinate Sentences as those in group **A** are therefore called *Substantival Sentences*.

In group **B** the Subordinate Sentence is a supplementary Predicate to the Principal Sentence (see above, § 2). Now an Adverb is the type of a Supplementary Predicate. Subordinate Sentences of this group are therefore called *Adverbial*. They are Conditional (the Protasis or Condition), Concessive, Final, Modal, Consecutive, Limitative, Temporal, Comparative.

In group **C** the Subordinate Sentence stands like an Attributive or Epithet to the noun (ποιήματα) in the Principal Sentence. That noun is the antecedent to the relative, and the relative sentence is used like an adjective used *attributively*. Subordinate Sentences of this group therefore are generally called Adjectival Sentences. This, however, as we shall soon see, is too narrow a use of the term, and too inadequate a name for Relative Sentences. It would be better simply to call them Relative Sentences.

For with regard to Relative Sentences a fundamental distinction must be noticed. Some are (1) Attributive, others again are (2) virtually *Adverbial*.

(1) Attributive (or really Adjectival):—

ἀνέλαβον τὰ ποιήματα ἃ ἐποίησε Σοφοκλῆς.
I took up the poems which Sophocles wrote (or *the Sophoclean poems*).

(2) Virtually Adverbial:—

τίς οὕτως εὐήθης ὅστις ἀγνοεῖ ;
Who is so simple that he does not know?

Here the Relative Sentence ὅστις ἀγνοεῖ = ὥστε ἀγνοεῖν ;

§ 9. We thus arrive at the following Classification and Table of Subordinate Sentences :—

A. SUBSTANTIVAL.

The Subordinate Sentence is the Subject or Object of the Principal Sentence, whether
- α. Indirect Statement.
- β. Indirect Question.
- γ. Indirect Petition.

B. ADVERBIAL.

The Subordinate Sentence like an Adverb is an adjunct of the Predicate.
1. Introduced by a Subordinate Conjunction (such as εἰ, ἐπειδή, ὥστε, etc. etc.).
2. Introduced by a Relative.

C. RELATIVE.

The Subordinate Sentence is either an Attributive, or is equivalent to an Adverbial Sentence (see **B** Adverbial, 2).

§ 10.   *ORATIO RECTA.*

By *Oratio Recta* is meant the words of a person given at first-hand, as from his own lips.

δώσω ἃ ἔχω.   *I will give what I have.*
τί λέγεις ;   *What do you mean ?*
κόπτε τὴν θύραν.   *Knock at the door.*

§ 11.   *ORATIO OBLIQUA.*

By *Oratio Obliqua* is meant the words or thoughts of a person given at second-hand, by some one else.

ἔφη δώσειν ἃ ἔχοι.
He said he would give what he had.

ἠρόμην αὐτὸν τί λέγοι.
I asked him what he meant.
εἶπε τῷ παιδὶ κόπτειν τὴν θύραν.
He told the boy to knock at the door.

§ 12. SUBDIRECT AND SUBOBLIQUE.

A Subordinate Sentence is *Subdirect* when it depends on a Principal Sentence in the *Recta*.

PRINCIPAL.   SUBDIRECT.
δώσω   ἃ ἔχω.

It is *Suboblique* when it depends on a Principal Sentence which itself is Subordinate.

PRINCIPAL.   SUBDIRECT.   SUBOBLIQUE.
ἔφη   δώσειν   ἃ ἔχοι.

In this last example δώσειν is subordinate to its Principal Sentence ἔφη, but it is the Principal Sentence to ἃ ἔχοι. See further under *Oratio Obliqua*.

§ 13. VIRTUALLY OBLIQUE.

A Subordinate Sentence is said to be *virtually Oblique* when it alludes to the words or thoughts of another, the actual verb of saying or thinking on which it depends having to be mentally supplied from the context.

ἐκάκιζον τὸν Περικλέα ὅτι οὐκ ἐπεξάγοι.
They were abusing Pericles because (so they said) he did not lead them out.

A verb like ἔλεγον is contained in ἐκάκιζον.

CHAPTER I.

SUBJECT AND PREDICATE.
ATTRIBUTIVE AND APPOSITION.

§ 14. The Subject is (*a*) a noun, or pronoun, or (*β*) the equivalent of a noun:

(β) οἱ ἀγαθοί, *the good;* τὸ δίκαιον, *justice;* τὸ δεδιέναι, *fear;* ὁ φεύγων, *the defendant;* τὸ δεδιός, *fear;* οἱ νῦν, *the present generation.*

§ 15. The Copula is a verb which merely serves as a link to join the Subject and Predicate, without containing in itself the predication.

The commonest Copulas are εἰμί and γίγνομαι. Many others, however, serve as Copulas, ὑπάρχω, πέφυκα, καθίσταμαι.

Note. Other Copulas are ὀνομάζομαι, καλοῦμαι, φαίνομαι, τυγχάνω, and κυρῶ (even without a participle), κλύω and ἀκούω (*I am called,* or, *spoken of*), πέλω *in poetry.*

εἰμί, expressing existence, may be more than a copula; it may be a predicative verb, *e.g.* ἔστι θεός, *there is a God.*

§ 16. *OMISSION OF THE COPULA.*

The Copula is often omitted in Greek, in fact, wherever the distinction between Subject and Predicate is clearly marked without it:

τό μαντικὸν γένος φιλάργυρον. SOPH. *Antig.*
The tribe of seers is covetous.

ἐχθρῶν ἄδωρα δῶρα κοὐκ ὀνήσιμα. SOPH. *Antig.*
Giftless the gifts of foes, and profitless.

And sometimes the Copula, in a freer way, is omitted in dependent clauses where we might have expected it to be expressed:
ἕως ἔτ' ἐν ἀσφαλεῖ, φυλάξασθε. DEM. 19. 26.
While you are still in safety, be on your guard.
ἕως sub. ἔστε.
Cf. EUR. *Hipp.* 659. THUC. i. 91. 1.

§ 17. SUBJECT AND PREDICATE OF AN INFINITIVE.

The Subject and the Predicate of an Infinitive are in the Accusative.

But the Subject and Predicate of an Infinitive are in the Nominative when they refer to the Subject of the Principal Verb.

The same two rules apply to the Subject and Predicate of a Participle.

For further rules, and for examples, see Compound Sentence, Indirect Statement.

§ 18. The Subject and Predicate of the Infinitive (or Participle) may be in the Genitive or Dative, if the principal verb governs either of those cases.

ᾐσθόμην αὐτῶν οἰομένων σοφωτάτων εἶναι. PLAT. *Ap.* vi.
I noticed that they fancied they were the wisest of mankind.
The subject to εἶναι is omitted, σοφωτάτων is the Predicate.
παντὶ προσήκει ἄρχοντι φρονίμῳ εἶναι. XEN. *Hip.* 7. 1.
It behoves every ruler to be prudent.

The Subject and Predicate, however, in such a construction may stand in the Accusative.

ξυμφέρει αὐτοῖς φίλους εἶναι. XEN. *Oik.* ii. 23.
It is expedient for them to be friendly.
Cf. XEN. *Hell.* iv. 8. 4.

§ 19. Omission of the Subject.

The Subject is omitted in the third person in a great number of indefinite phrases and impersonal verbs.

(a) In terms of the *weather*, or *natural phenomena*. The Subject is a vague indefinite agent (*e.g.* Ζεύς, ὁ θεός). ὕει, *it rains;* νίφει, *it snows;* βροντᾷ, *it thunders;* ἀστράπτει, *it lightens;* χειμάζει, *it is stormy;* συσκοτάζει, *it grows dark;* ἔσεισε, *there was an earthquake.*

Sometimes the agent is expressed—ὕει μὲν ὁ Ζεύς. ALCAEUS, *Fragm.*

(b) The Subject is not expressed when the action alone is worth noticing, and the Subject is well known. σαλπίζει, *the trumpet sounds* (*i.e.* ὁ σαλπιγκτής σαλπίζει, *the trumpeter sounds the trumpet*); σημαίνει (sc. ὁ κῆρυξ, or ὁ σαλπιγκτής), *the signal is given;* κηρύσσει (ὁ κῆρυξ), *proclamation is made;* ἀναγνώσεται (ὁ γραμματεύς), *the reading will follow.*

(c) Passive Verbs—λέγεται, *it is said;* εἴρηται, *do.*; παρεσκεύασται, *preparation has been made.* Cf. Latin, *itur, ventum est.*

Active Verbs—ὡς λέγουσιν, *as men say, as they say;* φασί, *it is said;* οἴονται, *people think.* Cf. Latin, *ferunt, tradunt.*

τίς, τίνες, ἄνθρωποι, in phrases like the last, may be expressed (like the French *on*)—*e.g.* ἤν τις ἀδικῇ, *if one commits injustice.*

(d) Ordinary impersonal verbs and expressions—εὖ ἔχει, μέλει, etc.

Note. The Latin rule that only transitive verbs which are followed by an accusative in the active can be personal in the passive does not hold in Greek. Thus we may say—

κατηγορῶ Σωκράτους, *I accuse Socrates;* and
Σωκράτης κατηγορεῖται, *Socrates is accused.*
πιστεύομεν Σωκράτει, *we believe Socrates* (Socrati credimus); and
Σωκράτης πιστεύεται, *Socrates is believed* (Socrati creditur).

§ 20. *THE PREDICATE.*

The Predicate is usually contained either (1) in *a Verb*, or (2) *an Adjective or Participle.* In the former case the

Predicate agrees with the Subject in *number* and *person*; in the latter case in *number, gender,* and *case.*

(1) ἐνικήθησαν οἱ Ἀθηναῖοι.
The Athenians were defeated.

(2) ἡ ἀλήθεια ἐστιν ὀρθή.
Truth is straightforward.

In the former case the Copula is contained in the inflection of the verb. In the latter the Copula is expressed or understood.

§ 21. Peculiarities in the Agreement of Subject and Predicate.

A neuter plural Subject takes a verb singular.

τὰ ἀνδράποδα ἀπέφυγε, *the slaves escaped.*
τὰ καλὰ τὴν ψυχὴν εὐφραίνει, *good deeds gladden the soul.*

§ 22. A plural verb with neuter plural Subject occurs rarely (chiefly in Thucydides, Xenophon, and Plato). In such cases (often when *persons* are implied) the *distributive* character of the noun is brought out. Thus in Thuc. i. 58, there are two readings,—τὰ τέλη ὑπέσχετο and ὑπέσχοντο. If ὑπέσχετο, Thucydides is following ordinary usage: if ὑπέσχοντο, he is thinking of the persons (the magistrates promised).

ἐνταῦθα ἦσαν τὰ Συεννέσιος βασίλεια. XEN. *An.* i. 2. 23.
There were the (several) *palaces of Syennesis.*

Obs. The phrase δόξαν ταῦτα, *When it had been thus resolved,* which occurs as well as δόξαντα ταῦτα, follows in the participle the construction of δοκεῖ ταῦτα.

§ 23. An Adjective-Predicate in the neuter singular may be used with a plural Subject. The Predicate sums up collectively the character of the Subject.

καλὸν ἡ ἀλήθεια καὶ μόνιμον. PLAT.
Truth is noble and abiding.

ἔρωτες κακὸν μέγα. EURIP.
Loves are a great curse.

Note. Cf. Eur. *El.* 1035; Ar. *Ecc.* 236; Plat. *Phaed.* 242 (μαντικόν τι ἡ ψυχή). The stock quotation is from Hom. *Il.* ii. 204, οὐκ ἀγαθὸν πολυκοιρανίη, εἷς κοίρανος ἔστω, *No good thing the rule of the many, one ruler be there.*
Compare with this the use of the phrases, πάντα εἶναι, *to be all in all* (*i.e.* of prime importance); τὰ πρῶτα εἶναι, *to be the head and front of*; πάντ' ἦν 'Αλέξανδρος, *Alexander was everything, all in all.* Dem. 23. 120.

§ 24. In the poets, and in Plato, a singular verb is occasionally found with a plural Subject. From the occurrence of this construction in Pindar it is called the *Schema Pindaricum.*

ἔστι γὰρ ἔμοιγε βωμοί. Plat. *Euthyd.* 302.
I have altars.

The verb generally comes first in this construction.

Cf. Pind. *Frag.* 344; Pyth. x. 7; Eurip. *Ion*, 1146; *Helen.* 1358; Aesch. *Pers.* 49. Compare in French, "il est cent usages;" and Bacon, *Advancement of Learning*, II. ii. 7, "a portion of the time wherein there hath been the greatest varieties." Shakspere, *Macbeth*, v. iii. "*Serv.* There is ten thousand — *Mac.* Geese, villain? *Serv.* Soldiers, sir." In some cases, however, the apparent singular in English is a real dialectic plural.

§ 25. Agreement of the Predicate when there are several Subjects.

The Dual Subject is considered separately.

(1) The first case is where the Subjects are *persons*. Here (*a*) *with regard to number*, the Predicate may be either correctly plural, or singular in agreement with one prominent subject; (*b*) *with regard to gender*, the masculine is preferred to the feminine; (*c*) *with regard to person*, the first is preferred to the second, the second to the third.

καὶ ἡ γυνὴ καὶ ὁ ἀνὴρ ἀγαθοί εἰσιν. Plat. *Men.* 73.
Both the wife and the husband are good.

ἴσως ἀναβήσεται Φίλιππος καὶ 'Αντιγένης καὶ ὁ ἀντιγραφεύς.
Dem. 22. 38.
Perhaps there will appear Philip, and Antigenes, and the controller.

εἶδον νέους καὶ νέας ὁμιλοῦντας ἀλλήλοις. PLAT. *Leg.* 835.
I saw young men and women associating together.
ἐγὼ καὶ οἱ ἄλλοι πρέσβεις περιήλθομεν. DEM. 129. 72.
I and the other envoys went round.
σύ τε Ἕλλην εἶ καὶ ἡμεῖς. XEN. *Anab.* ii. 1. 16.
You and we are Greeks.
You are Greek, and (so are) *we.*

Observe the emphatic position of the verb when it is in the singular.

(2) The second case is where the several Subjects are *things*. Here (*a*) *with regard to number*, we frequently find the Predicate *in the singular*, in agreement with one prominent Subject; frequently also *in the plural*; (*b*) *with regard to gender*, the Predicate, when plural, is generally *neuter*, when singular it agrees with the prominent Subject.

τῶν κακῶν ἡ στάσις καὶ ὁ πόλεμος αἴτιός ἐστιν. DEM.
Sedition and war are the cause of our troubles.
λήθη καὶ δυσκολία καὶ μανία πολλάκις εἰς τὴν διάνοιαν ἐμπίπτουσιν. XEN. *Ap.* iii. 12. 6.
Forgetfulness, and discontent, and madness often attack the mind.
τὸ ὑγιαίνειν καὶ τὸ νοσεῖν ἀγαθὰ ἂν εἴη.
                                    XEN. *Ap.* iv. 2. 36.
Health and sickness might be blessings.

The singular Predicate is not unknown in English:

Destruction and unhappiness *is* in their ways. Ps. xiv. 7.
So great an affinity *hath* fiction and belief. Bacon, *Advancement of Learning*, i. 4. 8.

(3) The third case is where, in the Subjects, there is a combination *of persons and things*. Here the person will generally *in gender* over-ride the thing; *in number*, as before, both *singular* and *plural* are used.

ἐπύθετο τὸν Στρομβιχίδην καὶ τὰς ναῦς ἀπεληλυθότα.
                                    THUC. viii. 63. 1.
He heard that Strombichides and his fleet had sailed away.
ἡ τύχη καὶ Φίλιππος ἦσαν τῶν ἔργων κύριοι.
                                    AESCHIN. 12. 181.
Fortune and Philip were masters of circumstances.

Great variety is allowable where there is a plurality of Subjects. The leading principles only have been indicated in the above rules.

With disjunctives, ἤ—ἤ, οὔτε—οὔτε, the Predicate generally agrees with the nearest Subject.

§ 26. The demonstrative pronouns ὅδε, οὗτος, ἐκεῖνος, when used as Subjects to a Predicate, or as Predicates to a Subject, either (1) are assimilated to the gender and number of their subject or predicate, or (2) are in the neuter singular or plural.

(1) ἐκεῖνός ἐστιν ἔλεγχος μέγιστος. Lys. 16. 6.
This is the strongest proof.

οἶμαι ἐμὴν ταύτην πατρίδα εἶναι. Xen. *Anab.* iv. 8. 4.
I think that this is my country.

Cf. Verg. *Aen.* vi. 129, hoc opus, hic labor est.

(2) τοῦτ' εἰσὶν οἱ λόγοι. Dem. 8. 7.
The statements are these (come to this).

οὐ λόγων κόμπος τάδε. Thuc. ii. 41. 1.
This is no boastful talk.

Cf. the use of τάδε: οὐκ Ἴωνες τάδε εἰσιν, Thuc. vi. 77. 1. *These are not Ionians, we have no Ionians here.* Cf. Eur. *Androm.* 168.

Also cf. τί, ὅτι, (interrogative):—δημοκρατίαν οἶσθα τί ἐστιν; *Do you know what democracy is?* δουλεύομεν θεοῖς ὅ τι ποτ' εἰσίν οἱ θεοί. Eur. *Or.* 418, *we are slaves to gods, whate'er these gods may be.*

So the phrase τοῦτο ἀληθῆ λέγεις, *what you say is true.*

§ 27. Peculiarities of Number—Singular, Dual, and Plural.

(a) *The singular is used for the plural* (a) with *collective nouns*, (b) with *nouns of material*, (c) with *nouns denoting nationality*, (d) in several *military expressions*, etc.

(a) ὁ ἐχθρός, *the enemy ;* ὁ πέλας, *one's neighbour.*

(b) κέραμος, *tiles ;* πλίνθος, *bricks ;* ἄμπελος, *vines ;* ἐσθής, *clothes.*

(c) ὁ Ἰλλύριος, the Illyrians, ὁ Χαλκιδεύς, the Chalcidians (cf. the Latin Poenus, Romanus). But sometimes, as in Latin, of the general, king, or prince.

(d) ὁ ἵππος, the cavalry; ἀσπίς (= ὁπλῖται), hoplites, heavy-armed infantry.

(β) A collective noun singular (πλῆθος, γένος, στράτευμα, etc.) may agree with a plural predicate. Often there is a mixture of singular and plural.

μέρος τι ἀνθρώπων οὐχ ἡγοῦνται θεούς. PLAT. Leg. 948.
A portion of mankind do not believe in gods.

τὸ στράτευμα ἐπορίζετο σῖτον, κόπτοντες τοὺς βοῦς καὶ ὄνους.
XEN. Anab. ii. 1. 6.
The army provided itself with food by cutting up the oxen and asses.

§ 28. The Dual Number.

1. The Dual is a kind of plural, an unnecessary kind. It is not used in Aeolic, and it has disappeared in Modern Greek. The agreement between a dual subject and its verb or adjective is irregular. We may say that the strict dual agreement is adhered to only where the idea of duality (of there being a pair of things) is prominent.

The first person dual does not exist in the active voice. It is very doubtful whether it occurs in the middle. Il. xxiii. 485, SOPH. Phil. 1079, SOPH. El. 950, seem to be about the only three places, and in all of them the plural may be the correct reading.

νὼ θεασώμεσθα. AR. Av. 664
Let us two see.

(2.) Dual of the Article and of Pronouns.—The feminine dual is defective, especially in the nominative and accusative forms. (See Krüger, p. 235.)

τώ is the regular prose form for all genders, τά is rare in poetry, τοῖν is much commoner than ταῖν.

τώδε is used, not τάδε, but ταῖνδε is used.

τούτω not ταύτα. Both τούτοιν and ταύταιν for the feminine. αὐτώ and αὐτά are both used for the feminine, also αὐτοῖν and αὐταῖν.

20 SUBJECT AND PREDICATE.

ἀλλήλω and ἀλλήλα, ἀλλήλοιν and ἀλλήλαιν are found equally with feminine nouns.

Similarly ἐμώ, μόνω, ματαίω, ἀξίω occur with feminine nouns.

(3) The strict dual agreement is shown in the following examples:

τὼ ἀδελφὼ αὐτὼ ὥπερ ἐγενέσθην ἄμφω ἄπαιδε ἐτελευτησάτην. ISAEUS, 6. 6.
The two brothers themselves who were born both died childless.

Similarly when there are two Subjects :—

ἡδονὴ καὶ λύπη ἐν τῇ πόλει βασιλεύσετον. PLAT. *Rep.* 607.
Pleasure and pain shall reign in the State.

A good instance occurs in SOPH. *El.* 977-985, where the effect is heightened by the dual form.

δύο ἐξ ἑνὸς ἀγῶνος γεγένησθον. ANTIPH. HEROD. 85.
Two trials have been made out of one.

(4) The following miscellaneous instances show the irregularity of agreement both in *gender*, and in *number* :—

ἄμφω τούτω τὼ ἡμέρα. XEN. *Cyr.* i. 2. 11.
Both these days.

κατηγόρησεν ἀμφοῖν τοῖν πολέοιν. IS. xii. 9. 7.
He accused both the states.

τὼ χεῖρε ἃς ὁ Θεὸς ἐποίησεν. XEN. *Ap.* ii. 3. 18.
The hands which God made.

τῶν αὐτῶν δέονται καὶ ἡ γυνὴ καὶ ὁ ἀνήρ. PLAT. *Men.* 73.
The wife and the husband need the same things.

N.B.—δύο agrees with a dual or plural noun, or verb— ἄμφω and ἀμφοῖν, generally with the dual; ἀμφότερος, more commonly with plural than dual.

ἐβούλετο οἱ τὼ παῖδε ἀμφοτέρω παρεῖναι. XEN. *An.* i. 1. 1.
He wished both his sons to be present.

ἀπέθανον οἱ στρατηγοὶ ἀμφότεροι. THUC. v. 74. 2.
Both the generals were slain.

(5) A dual verb is found joined to a plural subject, or several subjects, when the subjects are arranged or contrasted

singly or in pairs. This construction occurs several times in Homer. (*See* Jelf, § 388. 1.)
δυνάμεις ἀμφότεραί ἐστον δόξα καὶ ἐπιστήμη.
PL. *Rep.* 478, B.
Both are faculties, opinion and certain knowledge.
So AESCH. *Eum.* 256, λεύσσετον, of the chorus divided into ἡμιχόρια.

§ 29. The Plural for the Singular is used—

(1) With proper names—οἱ Ἡρακλέες τε καὶ Θησέες, PLAT. *Theaet.* 169, B. Cf. Latin, *Scipiones et Laelii;* English, *Our Burkes and Chathams.* Cf. AESCH. *Ag.* 1439; XEN. *An.* iii. 2. 31.

(2) Very freely with *abstract nouns, i.e.* names of qualities, denoting (as in Latin) instances or kinds of the quality—*e.g.* μανίαι, *fits of madness;* εὔνοιαι, *instances of benevolence;* στάσεις, *instances of revolution;* ἀνδρίαι, *deeds of valour.*
Some words are repeatedly used in this way—βίοι, θάνατοι, *modes or forms of life, death;* ἀκμαί, *prime of life* (flos aetatis); ὕπνοι, *sleep,* etc.

τοῖς μετρίοις ζῆλοί τε καὶ φθόνοι οὐκ ἐγγίγνονται.
PLAT. *Leg.* 679.
Self-controlled persons are not subject to rivalry and envy (or fits of rivalry, etc.).

(3) Terms of weather and time—θάλπη, θερμότητες, *heat;* ψύξεις, *cold;* χάλαζαι, *hail;* ὄμβροι, *rain;* αὐχμοί, *drought;* πάχναι, *frost;* ἐρυσίβαι, *mildew;* μέσαι νύκτες, *midnight,* νύκτες, *hours or watches of the night.*

(4) *Material Nouns*—πυροί καὶ κριθαί, *wheat and barley.*
But here a distinction is commonly made between singular and plural, *e.g.* κρέας, *a piece of meat,* κρέα, *meat;* ξύλον, *a piece of wood, stick, cudgel,* ξύλα, *timber;* ἥλιος, *the sun,* ἥλιοι, *rays of the sun;* ἅλς, *salt,* ἅλες, *salt-works;* λογισμός, *a reckoning,* λογισμοί (also λογισμός), *arithmetic.*

(5) The plural is often used for the singular in poetry to heighten the effect by the vagueness of the expression—αἵματα, φόνοι, *blood* or *bloodshed;* πλοῦτοι, *riches;* θρόνοι, *royalty, royal*

commands; δώματα, *a house;* πύλαι, *a gate;* αὐλαί, *a dwelling;* γλῶσσαι, *the tongue.*

(6) The neuter plural of verbals in -τεος, ἐπιχειρητέα, ἀδύνατα, and πότερα, and many adjectives. See Verbal Adjectives.

§ 30. The First Person Plural is used of a Singular Subject

when (*a*) the author of a book refers to himself; (*b*) especially in the poets, often when a person speaks of himself as acting with or for others.

(*a*) τοῦτο πειρασόμεθα διηγήσασθαι. XEN. *Cyr.* viii. 1. 48.
This we will endeavour to describe.

(*b*) οὐκ ἂν γυναικῶν ἥσσονες καλοίμεθ' ἄν. SOPH. *Ant.* 680.
We should not be called inferior to women.

In PLAT. *Sympos.* 186, B, one physician speaks in the plural as representing the profession.

In tragedy a woman may speak of herself in the plural masculine, sometimes in the singular masculine.

πεσούμεθ', εἰ χρή, πατρὶ τιμωρούμενοι. SOPH. *El.* 399.
We will fall, if fall we must, avenging a father.
(Elektra is speaking).

In EUR. *Hippol.* 1103, the female Coryphaeus speaks of herself in masculine singular.

§ 31. Peculiarities of Person.

The second person singular is used, as in Latin, in an indefinite way like an impersonal expression.

εἶδες ἄν, *you might have seen;* ἡγήσω ἄν, *you would (or might) have thought;* ἡγήσαιο ἄν, *you would think* (credideris).

For peculiarities of the third person, see Omission of the Subject.

§ 32. Supplementary Predicates (*See Introduction*).

Certain adjectives are constantly so used. Such are (*a*) πολύς, ἄσμενος, ἑκών, ἑκούσιος, ἄκων (*invitus*); (*b*) adjectives of number, πρότερος, πρῶτος, δεύτερος, ὕστερος, ὕστατος, δευτεραῖος

SUPPLEMENTARY PREDICATES. 23

(*on the second day*), τριταῖος (*on the third day*); (*c*) words referring to time or place, ὄρθριος, *in the morning;* χρόνιος, *late;* αἰφνίδιος, *suddenly;* σκοταῖος, σκοτιαῖος, *in the dark;* ποσταῖος, *in how many days?*

ὁ 'Ασωπός ποταμὸς ἐρρύη μέγας. THUC. ii. 5. 2.
The river Asopus flowed with a strong stream.
ἀφικνοῦνται αἰφνίδιοι. THUC. viii. 14. 1.
They arrive suddenly.
κακὸς ἑκὼν οὐδείς. PLAT. *Tim.* 86.
No one is deliberately wicked.
σπονδὰς λύουσιν οἱ πρότεροι ἐπιόντες. THUC. i. 123. 3.
The breakers of treaties are the first aggressors.

Observe the following distinctions (Krüger, p. 229) :—

πρῶτος Μηθύμνῃ προσέβαλε.
He was the first who attacked Methymne.
πρώτῃ Μηθύμνῃ προσέβαλε.
Methymne was the first place he attacked.
πρῶτον Μηθύμνῃ προσέβαλε.
His first act was to attack Methymne.

The Greek adjective is more freely used in this way than the Latin, but see Roby, *Lat. Gr.*, 1069.

§ 33. Peculiarities in the Construction of the Attributive or Epithet.

A Substantive is sometimes used as an attributive to another Substantive—

(1) Commonly with ἀνήρ, ἄνθρωπος, γυνή, *e.g.* ἀνὴρ ὁπλίτης, *a heavy-armed soldier;* ἀνὴρ τύραννος, *a despot;* γραῦς γυνή, *an old woman;* ἄνθρωπος πολίτης, *a citizen;* ἀνὴρ Σπαρτιάτης, *a Spartan citizen.* So ἄνδρες 'Αθηναῖοι, ἄνδρες δικασταί, *Athenians, jurymen.*

(2) Many miscellaneous Substantives are thus used as Adjectives, especially in the poets, but some in prose also: ὄλεθρος Μακεδών (γραμματεύς), DEM. 9. 31. 18. 127, *a scoundrel of a Macedonian,* or *a pestilent Macedonian, a pestilent scribe;* ὁπλίτης στρατός, κόσμος, EUR. *Her.* 699, 800. ; γέρων ὀφθαλμός, EUR. *Or.* 529 ; παρθένος χείρ, EUR. *Phoen.* 838 ; λόγος ἔπαινος, PLAT. *Phaedr.* 260, B.

"Ελλην for Ἑλληνικός is often found, e.g. οἱ Ἕλληνες πελτασταί, XEN. An. vi. 5. 26. EUR. Her. 130, στολὴν Ἕλληνα.

καὶ ζῇ τύραννον σχῆμ' ἔχων. SOPH. Ant. 1169.

(3) When there are several attributives to one Substantive the adjectives may be added one after another without conjunctions (Asyndeton).

ἄλλα δόρατα εἶχον παχέα, μακρά, ὅσα ἀνὴρ ἂν φέροι μόλις.
XEN. An. v. 4. 24.

They had other spears, stout, long, such as a man could with difficulty carry.

καί, however, often joins two adjectives, especially πολύς with another adjective, where in English we omit the conjunction, as one combined notion is formed : πολλὰ καὶ χαλεπά, πολλὰ καὶ δεινά, *many difficult things, many dangers;* ἀγαθοὶ καὶ παλαιοὶ νομοθεταί, *good lawgivers of old,* PLAT. Pro. 326. Cf. καλὸς κἀγαθός (καλοκαγαθός), *an aristocrat* (in a political sense), *a perfect character* (in a moral sense).

(4) *An adjective or participle may agree with the sense rather than the form of the word.*

ὦ περισσὰ τιμηθεὶς τέκνον. EUR. Tro. 735.
Oh son, honoured exceedingly.

τὰ μειράκια πρὸς ἀλλήλους διαλεγόμενοι. PL. Lach. 180.
The lads conversing together.

Cf. DEM. 21. 117, κεφαλή, ἐξεληλυθώς. IS. 6. 49, φύσεως, ὅς.

§ 34. Peculiarities of Apposition.

1. *Partitive Apposition* (or Σχῆμα καθ' ὅλον καὶ μέρη, i.e. the figure, or construction, of the whole and its parts).

In this construction the whole comes first, and afterwards in apposition with it are its parts. The noun which contains the whole should strictly be in the genitive, but it is desirable at once to state it as the Subject or the Object of the sentence.

[The really logical construction with the whole in the Genitive is seen here—

τῶν πόλεων αἱ μὲν τυραννοῦνται, αἱ δὲ δημοκρατοῦνται, αἱ δὲ ἀριστοκρατοῦνται. PLAT. Rep. 338.

Of states, some are despotic, others democratic, others aristocratic.]

λῦπαι αἱ μὲν χρησταί εἰσιν, αἱ δὲ κακαί. PLAT. *Gorg*. 499.
With regard to pains, some are good, others bad.
οὗτοι ἄλλος ἄλλα λέγει. XEN. *Anab*. ii. 1. 15.
These men say some one thing, some another.
πᾶσιν ἔργον τι ἑκάστῳ προστέτακται. PLAT. *Rep*. 406.
To all and each some task is appointed.
καθήμεθ' ἄκρων ἐκ πάγων . . .
ἐγερτὶ κινῶν ἄνδρ' ἀνὴρ ἐπιρρόθοις
κακοῖσιν. SOPH. *Ant*. 411.
*We were seated on the hill-top . . .
eagerly provoking each his fellow with bandied threats.*
With a singular whole :—λέγεται ψυχὴ ἡ μὲν νοῦν ἔχειν, ἡ δὲ ἄνοιαν. PLAT. *Phaedr*. 93.

2. A Substantive (with adjuncts) either in the Nominative or Accusative may be in apposition to the verbal action. This is known as the Nominative or Accusative in Apposition to the Sentence.

κεῖνται πεσόντες, πίστις οὐ σμικρὰ πόλει. EUR. *Rhes*. 415.
(Some) have fallen and lie buried, no slight proof of loyalty to the realm.
εὐδαιμονοίης, μισθὸν ἡδίστων λόγων. EUR. *El*. 231.
Blest be thou, the reward of sweetest tidings.
The stock example is—
Ἑλένην κτάνωμεν, Μενελέῳ λύπην πικράν. EUR. *Or*. 1098.
Let us slay Helen, sharp pain to Menelaus (i.e the death of Helen will be a cruel blow to Menelaus).

3. A substantive is very often found in apposition to a preceding pronoun, or pronominal phrase, which draws attention to what follows. Certain idioms of this kind are of the commonest occurrence :

(*a*) τοῦτο, ἐκεῖνο, αὐτὸ τοῦτο, αὐτό preceding a substantive.
ἐκεῖνο κερδαίνειν ἡγεῖται, τὴν ἡδονήν. PLAT. *Rep*. 606.
This it regards as gain (namely) pleasure.
τουτό γε αὐτό, ἡ εὐβουλία. PLAT. *Rep*. 428.
This particular quality, prudence.

In the same way must be explained the usage of ἄλλο τι, ταῦτ' ἄρα, τοῦτο μέν, ἵνα τί, and many other expressions of constant recurrence in Plato.

Some constantly recurring Platonic phrases with αὐτό.

αὐτὸ δικαιοσύνη, *ideal justice*, or *justice in the abstract;* αὐτὸ μέγεθος, *abstract greatness* as opposed to τὸ ἐν ἡμῖν μέγεθος, *concrete greatness.*

(*b*) The numerals, ἕν, δύο, τρία, δυοῖν θάτερον (*one of two*), δυοῖν τὰ ἕτερα, δυοῖν δεῖ θάτερον (*one of two things is necessary*).

δυοῖν δεῖ θάτερον, ἢ πρωτεύειν ἢ ἀνῃρῆσθαι. Is. 6. 89.
One of two things we must do, either be first, or perish.

(*c*) τὸ λεγόμενον (*quod dicunt, quod dicitur*), *as the saying is;* τὸ τῆς παροιμίας (*quod aiunt*), *according to the proverb;* κεφάλαιον (*denique, ad summam*) *to sum up:* σημεῖον δέ, τεκμήριον δέ, *as an instance, in proof of this;* and many others.

τὸ λεγόμενον, κάτοπιν τῆς ἑορτῆς ἥκομεν. PLAT. *Gorg.* 477.
We are come too late for the feast, as the saying is.

Ἀθηναῖοι περὶ δόξης μᾶλλον ἐσπούδαζον ἢ περὶ χρημάτων. τεκμήριον δέ· χρήματα γὰρ πλεῖστα ὑπὲρ φιλοτιμίας ἀνήλωσαν. DEM. 20. 10.
The Athenians used to care more for reputation than money. As a proof of this assertion, they spent vast sums of money for a noble ambition.

(4.) Sometimes a genitive is found in apposition to a genitive which is *implied* in a possessive pronoun or adjective : *e.g.* τὰ ὑμέτερα αὐτῶν for τὰ ὑμῶν αὐτῶν, ὁ ἐμὸς τοῦ ταλαιπώρου βίος, *the life of me, wretched one,* τοῦ ταλαιπώρου agreeing with an ἐμοῦ implied in ἐμός.

ὦ ἄριστε ἀνδρῶν, Ἀθηναῖος ὤν, πόλεως τῆς μεγίστης, etc. (πόλεως in apposition to Ἀθηνῶν implied in Ἀθηναῖος).
PLAT. *Ap.* xviii.
My excellent friend, you an Athenian, a citizen of the greatest city, etc.

Cf. AESCH. *Pers.* 162, where a genitive and a possessive are combined.

CHAPTER II.

THE ARTICLE.

§ 35. Origin and Development of the Article.

ὁ, ἡ, τό (as well as ὅς, ἥ, ὅ) was originally a *demonstrative*. Besides being a demonstrative it supplied the place of the *third personal pronoun*, the *relative*, and the *definite article*.

The first point to bear in mind about ὁ, ἡ, τό, is its essentially *demonstrative* character.

In Homer ὁ, ἡ, τό is a *demonstrative*, both *substantive and adjective*:

(a) Substantive: τῶν νῦν μιν μνήσασα, *of those things now putting him in mind.*

(b) Adjective: φθίσει σε τὸ σὸν μένος, *that thy courage will mar thee.*

It also takes the place of the *third personal pronoun.*

τὴν δ' ἐγὼ οὐ λύσω, but that one (her) *I will not free.*
τοῦ δὲ κλύε Φοῖβος Ἀπόλλων, and *Phoebus Apollo heard that one* (him).

It also does the work of the relative.

ἄνακτι, τὸν ἠύκομος τέκε Λητώ, *to the king, whom fair-haired Leto bare.*

The following examples show the transition in Homer from the demonstrative to the definite article.

ὁ δ' ἔβραχε χάλκεος Ἄρης.
And he, brazen Ares, roared.

Here the noun is in apposition to the demonstrative ὁ.

αὐτὰρ ὁ τοῖσι γέρων ὁδὸν ἡγεμόνευεν.
But he, the old man (or *the old man*), *was leading the way*

ἀλλ' ὅτε δὴ τὴν νῆσον ἀφίκετο.
But when now he came to that (the) island.

τό τε σθένος Ὠρίωνος.
And the might of Orion.

So οἱ ἄλλοι, *the rest;* τά τ' ἐόντα τά τ' ἐσόμενα, *the present and the future.*

The last examples show that the use of ὁ, ἡ, τό as the definite article is to be found as early as Homer.

It must be borne in mind however that such a use of ὁ, ἡ, τό in Homer is exceptional. According to old Greek (Homeric) use, nouns stand without the article as in Latin.

δεινὴ δὲ κλαγγὴ γένετ' ἀργυρέοιο βιοῖο.
And terrible arose the twang of the silver bow.

In Attic Greek prose ἡ κλαγγή, τοῦ βιοῖο would be required. To sum up therefore—

(*a*) ὅς, ἥ, ὅ, originally demonstrative, became the relative (with occasional traces in Attic of its older use).

(*b*) ὁ, ἡ, τό, originally demonstrative, became the definite article (though instances occur in Attic of its use as a demonstrative and as a relative).

(*c*) οὗτος, ὅδε, ἐκεῖνος took the place of ὁ, ἡ, τό, as demonstratives in Attic. The third personal pronoun was in Attic expressed by

(*d*) the oblique cases of αὐτός and (when necessary) in the nominative by the demonstratives.

Obs. The origin and development of the definite article from the demonstrative may be illustrated by English, German, and French.

Thus in English the relatives *who, what, which* were originally interrogatives only. The demonstrative still is constantly used. by us as a relative, *e.g. I know the person* that *you speak of.*

In German *der* is still demonstrative, definite article, and relative.

In French the personal pronoun *il* and the definite article *le* both come from the demonstrative *ille.*

§ 36. Survivals of the older usages of ὁ, ἡ, τό, and ὅς, ἥ, ὅ, in Attic Greek.

I. ὁ, ἡ, τό as a demonstrative :

With μέν and δέ, ὁ, ἡ, τό is freely used in all its cases. ὁ μέν—ὁ δέ, *the one, the other;* οἱ μέν—οἱ δέ, *some, others;* with

τις, ὁ μέν τις—ὁ δέ; τὸ (τὰ) μὲν—τὸ (τὰ) δέ, τὸ δέ τι, *partly;*
τῇ μὲν—τῇ δέ, *this way, that way;* τὸ δέ, *whereas;* τὸν καὶ τόν,
this one and that one; τὸ καὶ τό, *this and that.*

> ἔδει γὰρ τὸ καὶ τὸ ποιῆσαι καὶ τὸ μὴ ποιῆσαι. DEM. 9. 68.
> *We ought to have done this and that, and not to have done the other.*

Cf. SOPH. *Ant.* 557.

Observe the constant use of ὁ (οἱ) μέν at the beginning of a sentence, instead of repeating the noun.

> Ἰνάρως Ἀθηναίους ἐπηγάγετο. οἱ δὲ ἦλθον. THUC. i. 104.
> *Inarus invited the Athenians. So they came.*

II. ὁ, ἡ, τό as a personal pronoun (a rare use).

> καὶ τὸν κελεῦσαι δοῦναι (λέγεται). XEN. *Cyr.* i. 3. 9.
> *And it is said that he ordered.*

Cf. SOPH. *Ant.* 1199.

III. As a relative (a not uncommon use in the tragedians).

> διπλῇ μάστιγι τὴν Ἄρης φιλεῖ. AESCH. *Ag.* 642.
> *With the twofold scourge that Ares loves.*

IV. ὅς, ἥ, ὅ used as a personal pronoun with καί.

> οὐδεὶς ἀντέλεγε· καὶ ὃς ἡγεῖτο. XEN.
> *No one opposed, and so he acted as guide.*

It is rare, except in the common phrase ἦ δ' ὅς.

> ἔστι τις, ἔφην ἐγώ; πάνυ γε, ἦ δ' ὅς. PLAT. *Ap.* iv.
> *Is there any one? said I. Certainly, said he.*

THE ARTICLE IN ATTIC GREEK.

§ 37. Two points must be remembered:

1. The Article is essentially demonstrative.

2. The old usage was to omit the Article with definite objects (see § 35). This old usage survived in many instances, and hence to a great extent the fluctuating use of the Article in Attic.

The Article corresponds generally to the English definite article *the*. It marks off objects as known and definite whether (**A**) individuals or (**B**) classes.

(**A**) The Article denotes individual persons or things which are definite, because—

(*a*) Already known ;

(*b*) Already mentioned ;

(*c*) Distinguished from other objects, often by some accompanying description ;

(*a*) τῶν ἕπτα σοφώτατος ἦν Σόλων. PLAT.
Of the seven sages Solon was the wisest.

(*b*) δουλεύομεν θεοῖς ὅ τι ποτ' εἰσὶν οἱ θεοί. EURIP.
We are slaves to gods, whate'er these gods may be.

(*c*) ὁ πρεσβύτερος ἀδελφός.
The elder brother.

ἡ πόλις ἣν πολιορκοῦμεν.
The city which we are investing.

ἔλαβον τῆς ζώνης τὸν Ὀρόντην. XEN.
They seized Orontes by the girdle.

This last example shows how the Article is used where in English we employ a possessive pronoun.

ἕκαστος τῶν δημιουργῶν τὴν τέχνην καλῶς ἐξειργάζετο. PLAT.
Each one of the artisans (just mentioned) used to practise *his* art well.

Obs. The English article *the* was so used for the possessive in old English. See Bacon's *Advancement of Learning*, ed. Wright ; Glossary—*The.*

(**B**) The Article denotes the whole of a class, with substantives or adjectives, in singular or plural.

ὁ ῥήτωρ, *the (professional) speaker ;* οἱ ἱππεῖς, *the knights ;* οἱ σοφοὶ ἄνδρες, *wise men ;* ὁ φρόνιμος, *the prudent man ;* οἱ πονηροί, *bad men.*

ὁ παῖς πάντων θηρίων δυσμεταχειριστότατον.
PLAT.

A boy (i.e. boys) is of all creatures the most difficult to manage.

§ 38. The Article with Participles.

The article used in this way with a participle has the force of a general statement, e.g. ὁ βουλόμενος, *any one who wishes* (quicunque vult); ὁ τυχών, *any chance comer or person*.

ἅπανθ' ὁ τοῦ ζητοῦντος εὑρίσκει πόνος.
The toil of one who seeketh findeth all.

It is synonymous with the use of πᾶς ὁ (with adjective or participle).

πᾶς ὁ μὴ φρονῶν ἁλίσκεται. MEN. 714.
Every one who does not think is exposed.

§ 39. The Article with Numerals.

The article *may* be used with *cardinal numerals* either to mark a *definite whole*, or the definite parts of a whole, e.g. τὰ δύο μέρη, *two-thirds* (cf. THUC. i. 10 and iii. 15); ἄμφι τοὺς εἴκοσι, *about twenty in all*.

τῶν πασῶν τριήρων τὰς διακοσίας ἡ πόλις παρέσχετο.
The state furnished two hundred of the whole number of ships.

§ 40. Fluctuating use and omission of the Article.

Either (a) The ancient usage has survived when the use of the article had not become established.

Or (b) The word is sufficiently definite by itself from familiar reference, so that it does not need the article.

Or (c) The article is omitted because the vague and general conception of a word, the mere idea of a thing, is entertained apart from its manifestation in a person or event, or its relation to persons, things, and facts.

The equally fluctuating use of the article in English will go far to explain and illustrate the Greek usage.

§ 41. The Article with Objects of external nature.

ὁ οὐρανός, ἡ γῆ, ὁ ἥλιος, ἡ θάλασσα, ὁ ὠκεανός. But also οὐρανός, γῆ, ὠκεανός.

So ἐπὶ θαλάττῃ, *on sea* (sur mer); ὕδωρ ἐξ οὐρανοῦ, *rain from heaven;* περὶ ἡλίου δυσμάς, *at sunset.*

§ 42. The Article with Material objects.

τὸ γάλα, ὁ χρυσός, also γάλα, χρυσός (καθαίρειν χρυσόν, PLAT. *Polit.* 303).

§ 43. The Article with Familiar places, things, and persons.

Here the article is generally omitted according to ancient usage.

ἐκ πόλεως, πρὸς ἄστυ, *to town* (but also πρὸς τὸ ἄστυ); ἔξω Ἰσθμοῦ (and ἐν τῷ Ἰσθμῷ), ἐν ἀκροπόλει.

ἀπὸ δεξιᾶς, ἐξ ἀριστερᾶς, *on the right, on the left;* ἀρχή, τελευτή, εὖρος, μῆκος, βάθος, μῆκος, μέγεθος, ὕψος.

Many military phrases:

ἐπὶ δόρυ, *to the right (spearwards)*; ἐπί or παρ' ἀσπίδα, *to the left (shieldwards)*; ἐπί πόδα, *backwards, facing the enemy.* So στρατός, στράτευμα, στρατόπεδον, κέρας εὐώνυμον, δέξιον, *left wing, right wing.*

βασιλεύς *is* the *(Persian) king;* βασιλεὺς ὁ μέγας, οἱ πρόγονοι, οἱ βασιλέως. So πρυτάνεις, *the Presidents of the Council.*

§ 44. The Article with Abstract and other words.

Here the use is very fluctuating.

ἡ ἀρετή, *virtue;* ἡ ἀνδρεία, *courage;* ἡ δικαιοσύνη, *justice;* ἡ σωφροσύνη, *temperance;* ἡ ἐπιείκεια, *equity.*

But abstract terms often occur without the article. Remark (*c*) above especially applies. In the same section in PLAT. *Rep.* i. 354. we have

οὐδέποτ' ἄρα λυσιτελέστερον ἀδικία δικαιοσύνης,

Never, therefore, is injustice more profitable than justice,

and

λυσιτελέστερον ἄρα ἡ ἀδικία τῆς δικαιοσύνης.

§ 45. The Article with Concrete Words.

So with *concrete words*, the article being omitted either because of the mere idea of the thing or its familiarity: σῶμα, ψυχή, *body, soul;* θεός, *God (no special divinity)*; ἄνθρωπος, *man;* παῖδες καὶ γυναῖκες, *women and children;* πατρίς, *fatherland;* πόλις, *state or country*.

§ 46. The Article with names of Arts, etc.

Names of arts, trades, and sciences do not take the article: μουσική, γυμναστική, *education, mental and physical;* ῥητορική, *rhetoric;* ἀριθμητική, λογισμοί, *arithmetic, numeration*.

Similarly, δόξα, νοῦς, τέχνη, νόμος, *opinion, mind, art, law*.

§ 47. The Article with Proper names of persons and places.

Names of persons and towns do not require the article unless previously mentioned, or spoken of as well known.

Σωκράτης, but ὁ Σωκράτης, either Socrates already mentioned, or the well-known Socrates, *Socrates ille*. So Θῆβαι, αἱ Θῆβαι. Ἀλέξανδος ὁ Μακεδών, Ἀλέξανδρος ὁ Φιλίππου, *Alexander son of Philip*. Also in short business-like notices, Σωκράτης Σωφρονίσκου, Socrates, son of Sophroniscus.

The same rule applies to *names of nations*, but οἱ Ἕλληνες always when opposed to οἱ Βάρβαροι. When nationalities are opposed (as we say "French and English") the article is not used, *e.g.* Ἀθηναῖοι, Λακεδαιμόνιοι (so repeatedly in Thucydides).

οἱ Δημοσθένεις, *orators like Demosthenes* (as we say, our Burkes, our Chathams).

§ 48. The Article with Geographical names.

With geographical names the use and position of the article are extremely fluctuating. The following collocations are generally given as the rule, and may safely be employed.

ὁ Εὐφράτης ποταμός, *the river Euphrates;* τὸ Σούνιον ἄκρον, *the promontory of Sunium;* ἡ Θεσπρωτὶς γῆ, *the land of Thresprotis;* ἡ Δῆλος νῆσος, *the island of Delos;* ἡ Μένδη πόλις, *the city of Mende*.

But the following are given as a caution against dogmatism:
ὁ ποταμός ὁ Εὐφράτης, Ἅλυς ποταμός. THUC.
τὸ Αἰγαλέων ὄρος (*the hill of Aegaleum*); Πάρνης τὸ ὄρος, ἡ Αἴτνη τὸ ὄρος, τὸ ὄρος ἡ Ἰστώνη, τὸ ὄρος τῆς Ἰστώνης, Πίνδος ὄρος (all in Thucydides).
So ἡ Τηθὺς τὸ ὄνομα, τὸ ὄνομα οἱ δαίμονες (PLATO); ὄνομα Ζάγκλη, THUC.
Cf. ἡ Βουλὴ οἱ πεντακόσιοι, *the Council of the Five Hundred*. THUC. viii. 86.

Note. The preposition seems to exercise an influence on the omission of the article. Thus ἐπὶ σκηνήν ἦεσαν, XEN. *An.* vi. 4. 19. ἐπὶ βλάβῃ τῆς πόλεως, THUC. viii. 72. περὶ ἀρίστου ὥραν, THUC. vii. 81. ἐν ἀρχῇ τοῦ λόγου, DEM. 37. 28.

§ 49. *THE NOUN-MAKING POWER OF THE ARTICLE.*

The Article, when prefixed to any word or set of words, makes a noun of the word or words thus brought within its grasp.

(*a*) Adjectives;
>οἱ ἀγαθοί, *good men*, τὸ ἀγαθόν, *the highest good*, summum bonum.
>οἱ πολλοί, *the popular party*, populares.
>οἱ ὀλίγοι, *the oligarchical party*, optimates, optimus quisque.

(*b*) Participles;
>οἱ βουλόμενοι, *all who will*, quicunque vult; οἱ πρῶτοι ἐρχόμενοι, *first-comers*.

Observe the indefinite force which the Article gives to a Participle.

(*c*) Preposition and case;
>οἱ ἐπὶ τῶν πραγμάτων, *the government*.
>τὰ εἰς τὸν πόλεμον, *preparations for war*.
>τὰ ἐφ' ἡμῖν, *what is in our power*.

(*d*) Genitive;
>τὰ τῆς Τύχης, *the dispensations of fortune*; τὰ τῆς

πόλεως (without πράγματα), *the affairs of the state, politics.*

τό τοῦ Θεμιστοκλέους, *the words of Themistocles,* Themistoclis illud.

(e) Infinitives;

τὸ μισεῖν, *hatred;* τὸ ταχὺ λαλεῖν, *rapid talking* (τοῦ ταχὺ λαλεῖν, etc.).

So with a sentence, τὸ ἐμὲ τοῦτο πρᾶξαι.

(f) Adverbs;

οἱ ἐνθάδε, *the living;* οἱ ἐκεῖ, *the dead;* οἱ πάλαι, *the ancients,* οἱ τότε, οἱ νῦν, οἱ οἴκοι = οἱ ἐν οἴκῳ τότε.

ἡ παραυτίκα ἡδονή, *momentary pleasure;* ἡ ἄγαν ἐλευθερία, *excessive liberty.*

Note 1. So with a word or even a letter used *materialiter*, τὸ ἐγώ, *the word I* (similarly in French—le moi est haïssable); τὸ ἄλφα (PLAT. *Crat.* 405), *the letter Alpha.*

ὑμεῖς, ὦ ἄνδρες Ἀθηναῖοι.—τὸ δ' ὑμεῖς ὅταν εἴπω τὴν πόλιν λέγω. DEM. 255. 4.

You, Athenians, and whenever I say you, I mean the state.

ὑπερέβη τὸ καὶ ἐὰν ἁλῷ φόνου. DEM. 23. 220.

He omitted the words, " and if he be convicted of murder."

τὸ γνῶθι σαυτὸν πανταχοῦ 'στι χρήσιμον.

MENANDER, *Fr.* 730.

The adage, know thyself, is useful ever.

Note 2. Instead of repeating a noun it is enough to repeat the Article.

οἱ τῶν πολιτῶν παῖδες καὶ οἱ τῶν ἄλλων (sc. παίδων).
The children of the citizens and those of the others.

Note 3. When two or more terms are joined so closely together as to form one notion, or when they may be brought under one head the article is put only once.

οἱ στρατηγοὶ καὶ λοχαγοί.
The chief officers, namely generals and captains of companies.

ὁ ἥλιος καὶ σελήνη καὶ ἄστρα.
The heavenly bodies, sun, moon, and stars.

§ 50. THE ARTICLE DISTINGUISHES THE SUBJECT FROM THE PREDICATE.

The Subject takes the Article, the Predicate is without the Article.

ὁ μὲν δίκαιος εὐδαίμων, ὁ δ' ἄδικος ἄθλιος. PLAT.
The just man is happy, the unjust man is miserable.

This function of the Article belongs to it in consequence of its demonstrative character. All demonstratives mark the Subject.

ἐν Πέρσαις νόμος ἐστὶν οὗτος.
Among the Persians this is law (*this* Subject, *law* Predicate).

κίνησις γὰρ αὕτη μεγίστη δὴ τοῖς Ἕλλησιν ἐγένετο.
THUC. i. 1.
For this proved to be quite the greatest movement in the Greek world.

The Subject and Predicate, in whatever case they are, can always be detected immediately by the presence of the Article or Demonstrative with the Subject.

ὁ μάντις τοὺς λόγους ψευδεῖς λέγει.
The words which the seer speaks are false.

τοὺς λόγους, Subject; ψευδεῖς, Predicate.

ταύτῃ (Subject) ἀπολογίᾳ (Predicate) χρῆται.
He makes use of this as an excuse.

τοὺς δὲ λόγους μακροτέρους μηκυνοῦμεν. THUC. iv. 17.
We will extend our speech to a greater length.

Obs. With a Superlative Predicate in English we use the Article where Greek does not.

οὗτοι εἰσι πονηρότατοι ἀνθρώπων.
These are the most worthless of mankind.

§ 51. The Article with the Predicate.

Sometimes the Predicate itself is definite, or denotes a class, and in this case takes the Article.

οὗτοι οἱ δεινοί εἰσί μου κατήγοροι. PLAT. *Apol.* ii.
These are those (really) formidable accusers of mine.

§ 52. POSITION OF THE ARTICLE.

A. *THE PREDICATIVE POSITION.*
B. *THE ATTRIBUTIVE POSITION.*

A. The Predicative Position. An Adjective or Participle placed *outside* the Article and its Noun, whether before or after, is a Predicate.

σοφὸς ὁ ἀνήρ
 or
ὁ ἀνὴρ σοφός
} *the man is wise.*

B. The Attributive Position. Any word or set of words placed either (*a*) between the Article and the Noun, or (*b*) after the Noun, with the Article repeated, is an Attributive.

ὁ σοφὸς ἀνήρ, *the wise man.*
ὁ ἀνὴρ ὁ σοφός, do.

The first form is the most natural, and the most common. In the second form the attributive is often used as a further explanation.

τὸ τεῖχος περιεῖλον τὸ καινόν. THUC.
They dismantled the wall, the new one I mean.

Any word or set of words thus placed becomes attributive to the Noun.

ὁ πάνυ Περικλῆς. XEN. *Mem.* iii. 5. 1 (cf. THUC. viii. 1 and 89.)
The consummate Pericles.

ἡ παραυτίκα ἡδονή.
Momentary pleasure.

ἡ ἄγαν ἐλευθερία.
Excessive liberty.

αἱ ἄνευ λυπῶν ἡδοναί.
Painless pleasure.

τὸ τεῖχος τὸ παρὰ τὸν ποταμόν.
The wall alongside the river (the river wall).

ὁ πάντων κάλλιστος καὶ πᾶσι φίλτατος ἀνήρ.
The handsomest and best-beloved man in the world.

Note 1. This attributive or epithet-making power of the Article is shown by the following examples:—

οἱ ὁμολογουμένως δοῦλοι. DEM. 29. 39.
Those who confessedly are slaves.

τὰ τῆς τῶν πολλῶν ψυχῆς ὄμματα. PLAT. *Soph.* 254.
The eyes of the soul of the many.

Σόλων ἐμίσει τοὺς οἷος οὗτος ἀνθρώπους. DEM. 19. 254.
Solon used to hate men such as this person.

ἐν τῷ πρὶν καὶ γενέσθαι ἡμᾶς χρόνῳ. PLAT. *Phaed.* 88 a.
In the time before we came into being at all.

Note 2. When such collocations as the following are found, —ἄνθρωποι οἱ τότε, ἀδικία ἡ ἄκρατος, the Substantive, without the Article, is generally first used in an indefinite way and therefore without the Article; the Attributive follows with the Article as an explanation.

σκεπτέον πῶς ποτε ἡ ἄκρατος δικαιοσύνη πρὸς ἀδικίαν τὴν ἄκρατον ἔχει. PL. *Rep.* viii. 535.
We must consider how pure justice is related to an injustice which is pure (sheer, unmixed).

Note 3. A Predicate may occur *inside* an attributive phrase.

αἱ ἄρισται δοκοῦσαι εἶναι φύσεις. XEN. *Ap.* 4. 1. 3.
Those natures which appear to be the best, or *which appear to be the best natures.*

So especially with ὁ λεγόμενος, ὀνομαζόμενος, καλούμενος.

τὸ Κοτύλαιον ὀνομαζόμενον ὄρος. AESCHIN. 3. 86.
The hill of Cotylaeum as it is called. Mons Cotylaeus qui dicitur.

And regularly οἱ Ἀθηναῖοι καλούμενοι.

§ 53. *WHEN A GENITIVE FOLLOWS, SEVERAL FORMS ARE USED.*

1. ἡ τοῦ πατρὸς οἰκία. } The commonest forms.
2. ἡ οἰκία τοῦ πατρός. }
3. ἡ οἰκία ἡ τοῦ πατρός. Less common.
4. τοῦ πατρὸς ἡ οἰκία. { This form is used when the Genitive has been used just before, or is emphasised.

In accordance with the last position,—τοῦ χωρίου ἡ ἀπορία, THUC. iv. 29; περὶ τοῦ μισθοῦ τῆς ἀποδόσεως. THUC. viii. 85.

Note. Where there are two or more Attributives, some one or other of the above arrangements is employed.

(a) According to the first position—

μεμνῆσθε τῆς ἐν Σαλαμῖνι πρὸς τὸν Πέρσην ναυμαχίας.
AESCH. 2. 74.

(b) According to the third position, which renders the Attributes more distinct—

ἡ σεμνὴ αὕτη καὶ θαυμαστὴ ἡ τῆς τραγῳδίας ποίησις.
PLAT. *Gorg.* 502.

One Attributive, however, is often put after the Article and Substantive.

τὰ ἐκ τῆς Ἰάσου μεγάλα χρήματα διαρπασθέντα.
THUC. viii. 36.

ὁ κατειληφὼς κίνδυνος τὴν πόλιν. DEM. 18. 220.

αἱ πολλὰ βρονταὶ διατελεῖς. SOPH. *O.C.* 1513.

§ 54. THE PREDICATIVE POSITION IS USED BY

(a) οὗτος, ὅδε, ἐκεῖνος.

οὗτος ὁ ἀνήρ
   or   } this man.
ὁ ἀνὴρ οὗτος,

ἥδε ἡ πόλις
   or   } this state.
ἡ πόλις ἥδε,

κατὰ τοὺς νόμους ἐκείνους
   or   } according to these laws.
κατ' ἐκείνους τοὺς νόμους,

(b) ἑκάτερος, ἄμφω, ἀμφότερος.

ἐν ἑκατέρᾳ τῇ πόλει, in each state.
ἄμφω τὼ χεῖρε, both hands.
ἐπ' ἀμφοτέροις τοῖς λιμέσι, off both harbours.

Note. Where there is an Adjective also the usage varies.

ἡ στενὴ αὕτη ὁδός. XEN. *Anab.* iv. 2. 6.
This narrow way.

But ἐκείνη ἡ ὑψηλοτάτη πλάτανος. PLAT. *Phaed.* 229.
That most lofty plane.

(c) ἕκαστος is variable.

ἐν ἑκάστῃ τῇ πόλει   κατὰ τὴν ἡμέραν ἑκάστην
or ἐν ἑκάστῃ πόλει.   or καθ' ἡμέραν ἑκάστην.
In each state.   *Day by day.*

Note. The Demonstratives, especially ὅδε, are often used *in the poets* without the Article.

γυναικὸς τῆσδε. AESCH. *Ag.* 1438.
ξὺν τῇδε χερί. SOPH. *Antig.* 43.

And also in their *deictic* use.

Κρίτων Κριτοβούλου τοῦδε πατήρ. PLAT. *Apol.* xxii
Crito, father of Critobulus, here (in court).

§ 55. THE ATTRIBUTIVE POSITION IS USED BY

(a) τοιοῦτος, τοιόσδε.

ἡ τοιαύτη ἐπιστήμη, *such knowledge*.
ἐν τῇ τοιᾷδε ἀνάγκῃ, *in such a difficulty*.

Note. ὁ τοιοῦτος, *such a person;* ἐν τῷ τοιούτῳ, *in such a case*. The Article is also so used with ποῖος: τῆς ποίας μερίδος; DEM. 246, 10, *of what division?* θέλω σοι τῆς γυναικὸς ἔργα διηγήσασθαι. τὰ ποῖα; XEN. *Oec*. x. 1, *I want to describe to you the deeds of the woman. What deeds?*
So ὁ τοιοῦτος, ὁ τοιόσδε: ὁ τηλικοῦτος, ὁ τηλικόσδε: ὁ τοσοῦτος, ὁ τοσόσδε: *e.g.* ὁ τοιοῦτος ἀνήρ, *such a man;* λαβὲ τὸ τοιόνδε, PLAT. *Phil*. 29, *take a case of this kind*.

(b) *Possessives*, ἐμός, σός, ἡμέτερος, ὑμέτερος, σφέτερος.

ὁ ἐμὸς δοῦλος or ὁ δοῦλός μου (μου ὁ δοῦλος when
My slave, servus meus. [words have preceded].

ὁ ἡμέτερός πατήρ or ὁ πατὴρ ἡμῶν (ἡμῶν ὁ πατήρ).
Pater noster.

Note. ἐμὸς δοῦλος, *a slave of mine, one of my slaves, unus ex servis meis*.

For the position, μου ὁ δοῦλος, see ARIST. *Ach*. 12, *Neph*. 1368, ANTIPH. *Tetr*. B. B. 2, ANDOK. *de Myst*. 50. ὃς ἔχει σου τὴν ἀδελφήν, *who is married to your sister*.

(c) *Reflexives*.

ὁ ἐμαυτοῦ πατήρ, *my own father*.

ὅσα δὴ δέδηγμαι τὴν ἐμαυτοῦ καρδίαν. ARIST. *Ach*. 1.
How oft have I fretted this heart of mine.

Cf. ANDOK. *de Redit*. 10.

§ 56. Words which vary their meaning according to the position of the Article.

(a) πᾶς and ὅλος.

ὁ πᾶς χρόνος = *eternity*. *Apol*. xxxii.

1. πᾶσα πόλις, *every state* (but in plural, πάντες ἄνθρωποι, *all men*).
2. πᾶσα ἡ πόλις, *all the state*.
3. ἡ πᾶσα πόλις, *the whole state, the state as a whole*.
ὁ πᾶς ἀριθμός, *the sum total*.

There seems to be no appreciable difference between 2 and 3.

4. τὰ πάντα μέρη, *all the parts together*.
5. τοὺς πάντας δισχιλίους, *two thousand in all, or all told*.
ξύμπαντες ἑπτακόσιοι ὁπλῖται, *seven hundred heavy-armed all told*.
6. ἐν πάσῃ πολεμίᾳ Σικελίᾳ, *in Sicily altogether hostile*.
7. λύπῃ πᾶς ἐλήλαται κακῇ, SOPH. *Ai*. 275 (cf. *Il*. xi. 65), *he is altogether harassed (all vexed) with ill grief*.

ὅλη ἡ πόλις, }
ἡ πόλις ὅλη, } *the whole state*.

ἡ ὅλη πόλις, }
ἡ πόλις ἡ ὅλη, } *the whole state, the state as a whole*.

ὅλη πόλις, *a whole state*. ὅλαι πόλεις, *whole states*.

(*b*) μέσος, ἄκρος, ἔσχατος.

ἡ μέση ἀγορά, *the central market*.
μέση ἡ ἀγορά, *the centre of the market*.
Forum medium for both in Latin.
ἐπ᾽ ἄκροις τοῖς κώλοις, *at the extremities of the limbs*.
ὁ ἄκρος πολίτης, *the perfect (tip-top) citizen*. DONALDSON.
ἡ ἐσχάτη νῆσος, *the furthest island*.
ἐσχάτη ἡ νῆσος, *the end (or verge) of the island*.

(*c*) αὐτός.

αὐτὸς ὁ ἀνήρ, *the man himself, ipse vir*.
ὁ αὐτὸς ἀνήρ, *the same man, idem vir*.

Note. ἅπας, σύμπας, *all, the whole;* σύμπασα πόλις, ἀρετή, *the state, virtue as a whole,* or *the whole of,* etc. (πᾶς is sometimes so used *in poetry*). Observe the predicative use of πᾶς —

οὐ πᾶν ἀγαθόν ἡδονή ἐστι. PLAT. *Phil*. 27. 28.
Pleasure is not altogether a blessing.

§ 57. Oblique or Dependent Predicates.

An Oblique or Dependent Predicate is simply a Predicate which is not in the Nominative case, but in the Genitive, Dative, or Accusative, most often in the Accusative. This is an exceedingly common construction in Greek, and one which has to be rendered in many different ways into English. The essential point to notice is that the Predicate, in whatever case, is the really important statement, or emphatic word.

The simplest case is where the Accusative is used with Transitive Verbs of making, naming, appointing, deeming, etc.

οἱ κόλακες Ἀλέξανδρον θεὸν ὠνόμαζον.
Flatterers used to call Alexander a god.

οἱ Πέρσαι τὸν Κῦρον εἵλοντο βασιλέα.
The Persians chose Cyrus king (to be king).

ὁ τὸν ἥττω λόγον κρείττω ποιῶν. PLAT.
Who makes the worse reason (appear) the better.

§ 58. Very often the Greek language expresses a *Prolepsis* (*i.e.* an anticipation of the result) by this construction.

παρασκευάσαντες ἐντελῆ πᾶσαν τὴν δύναμιν.
DEM. *Phil.* 1. 9.
Providing all your force so that it shall be complete.
(ὥστε ἐντελῆ εἶναι. Cf. THUC. iv. 17, μακροτέρους.)

Cf. Latin—*paullatimque anima caluerunt* mollia *saxa* (=*ita ut mollia fierent*), JUV. i. 83.

So αὐξάνω τινὰ μέγαν. Cf. AESCH. *Ch.* 262, μέγαν.
So διδάσκω τινὰ ἱππέα (sc. εἶναι), *I teach one to be a horseman.*

§ 59. With the verb ἔχω by an idiomatic usage, similar to the French, the properties of persons or things are described by this construction.

καλοὺς ἔχει τοὺς ὀφθαλμούς.
He has fine eyes, his eyes are fine.
Il a les yeux beaux (so *il a le front large*, etc. etc.)

In such examples, ἔχω (like χρῶμαι with Dative) is merely an alternative for the copulative verb εἰμί. The use of *habeo*

in Latin is parallel; (*e.g.* cum haberet collegam in praetura Sophoclem, Cic. *Off.* 1, *when S. was his colleague in command*).
τὸ σῶμα θνητὸν ἅπαντες ἔχομεν. Isocr. *Phil.* 134.
We all have mortal bodies.

§ 60. Sometimes we must, in translating, make the Oblique Predicate the real Predicate, turning the rest of the sentence into a relative sentence, or using some such device.

ἀξιώσατε διττούς μου τοὺς κατηγόρους γεγονέναι.
Plat. *Apol.* ii.
Consider that my accusers who have appeared fall under two heads.

οὐ γὰρ ἐμὸν ἐρῶ τὸν λόγον, ἀλλ' εἰς ἀξιόχρεων ὑμῖν τὸν λέγοντα ἀνοίσω. Plat. *Apol.* v.
The words which I shall use are not mine: the speaker to whom I shall refer you is trustworthy.

ἱκανὸν παρέχομαι τὸν μάρτυρα. Plat. *Apol.* xviii.
Competent is the witness whom I produce.

οὐ γὰρ βάναυσον τὴν τέχνην ἐκτησάμην. Soph. *Ai.* 1121.
Ay, for 'tis no mechanic art that I acquired. (Cf. *Electra.*)

τοὔργον οὐ μακρὰν λέγεις. Soph. *Phil.* 26.
The task thou settest is not far to seek.

§ 61. Very often, especially in the poets, ὅδε is the subject to an Oblique Predicate. The Predicate is often an interrogative. We may often translate this demonstrative in English by "here," "herein."

ἀπόρῳ γε τῷδε ξυμπεπλέγμεθα ξένῳ. Eur. *Bacch.* 800.
Truly an unmanageable stranger this we have come across.
(ἀπόρῳ Predicate, τῷδε Subject.)

ποίαισι τόλμαις ταῖσδε καὶ φρενῶν θράσει; Soph. *Ai.* 42.
With what hardihood herein, and boldness of soul?
(ποίαισι the Predicate, ταῖσδε the Subject.)
Cf. *Ant.* 1295, τόδε—δεύτερον.

So, like the last—

πόσον ἄγει τὸ στράτευμα;
How many battalions does he bring into the field?

ταύτῃ ἀπολογίᾳ χρῆται. Dem. 49. 63.
He makes this an excuse.

Many excellent instances of the Oblique Predicate occur in ANTIPH. *Tetr.* B. B. 10. 11, 1. a. 2, *Herod.* 1, 9, 11, 16, 18, 84, 93; *Ant.* 1178.

§ 62. Oblique Predicates are found in Latin, but they can be detected only by the emphatic or artificial position of a word.

Omnem crede diem tibi diluxisse *supremum*.
HOR. *Ep.* I. iv. 13.
Live every day as though thy last.

Compare the example below, § 65, ἀφίεσαν τὴν δοκόν, with a line in Propertius—
Fidaque suggesta castra coronat humo. PROP. v. 4. 8.
He enrings a trusty camp by throwing up the soil.

§ 63. Oblique Predicates in the Genitive and Dative.

ἡγούμενοι αὐτονόμων τὸ πρῶτον ξυμμάχων. THUC. i. 97.
At the head of allies who at first were independent.

τούτων τισὶ φύλαξιν ἐχρῆτο.
Some of these he was using as guards.

Cf. SOPH. *Antig.* 556.

§ 64. Free use of the Oblique Predicate.

Sometimes it expresses a mere emphasis.

μεγάλῃ τῇ φωνῇ ἐβόα.
He cried with a loud *voice.*

καταντλήσας πολὺν τὸν λόγον. PLAT. *Rep.* 1. 344.
Having deluged us with a long *sermon.*

§ 65. Sometimes we shall have to translate more freely.

ἀπ' ὀρθῆς καὶ δικαίας τῆς ψυχῆς τὰ πάντα μοι πέπρακται.
DEM. 18. 298.
With uprightness and integrity of heart I have done all (in the uprightness and integrity of my heart).

ἀφίεσαν τὴν δοκὸν χαλαραῖς ταῖς ἁλύσεσι. THUC. ii. 76.
They were lowering the beam by loosening the chains (with the chains loosened).

§ 66. Idiomatic Phrases with the Article.

πολλοί, *many.* οἱ πολλοί, *the many, the people.* Populares.
πλέονες, *more.* οἱ πλέονες, *the majority.* Maior pars.
ὀλίγοι, *few.* οἱ ὀλίγοι, *the oligarchical party or faction.* Optimates, optimus quisque (also οἱ ἀγαθοί, etc.)
ἄλλοι, *others.* οἱ ἄλλοι, *the others, the rest.* Ceteri.

τό (τά) νῦν, τό τήμερον, *the present;* τὸ αὐτίκα, *the present.* (ὁ αὐτίκα φόβος), *momentary terror;* ἡ αὔριον, *the morrow.*

τὸ μέλλον, τὸ ἔπειτα, *the future;* ὁ ἔπειτα βίος (PLAT.), *the life to come.*

τὸ λοιπόν, τὰ λοιπά, *for the future, for the rest.*

τὸ πρίν, τὸ πάρος, τὸ πρόσθεν, *the past or former time* (chiefly poetical phrases); τὸ ἀρχαῖον, τὸ παλαιόν, *of old;* τὰ παρελθόντα, τὰ παρεληλυθότα, *the past* (in prose).

τὸ τότε, ἐν τῷ τότε, *at that time;* ἐν τῷ πρὸ τοῦ, *previously.*

τὸ πρῶτον, *at first;* τὸ τελευταῖον, *at last* (so τὸ δεύτερον, τὸ τρίτον).

τὰ πολλά, *for the most part* (so τὸ πλέον, τὰ πλείω); τὸ μέγιστον, *for the greatest part, or the chief point;* τὰ μάλιστα, *in the highest degree;* ὡς ἐπὶ τὸ πολύ, *for the most part;* τὸ πᾶν, ἐς τὸ πᾶν, *on the whole.*

τὰ τῆς Τύχης, *Fortune and her dealings* (a periphrasis for ἡ Τύχη).

τὰ τῆς πόλεως, *politics.*

ὁ (οἱ) πάνυ, *the excellent,* or *famous;* οἱ πάνυ τῶν στρατιωτῶν, *the pick of the troops;* ὁ πάνυ Περικλῆς, *the admirable Pericles.*

ἐν τοῖς πρῶτοι, *first of all.* Omnium primi.

ἐκ τοῦ ἐπὶ θάτερα, *from the opposite direction;* ἐκ τοῦ ἐπ' ἀριστερά, *from the left.*

οἱ περί, οἱ ἀμφί, οἱ ἀπό, ἐκ. See Prepositions.

CHAPTER III.

PRONOUNS.

§ 67.   *PERSONAL PRONOUNS.*

1st pers., *I, we.*　　ἐγώ, ἡμεῖς.
2d pers., *Thou, you.*　　σύ, ὑμεῖς.
3d pers., *He, she, it, they.* $\begin{cases} 1.\ \text{ἐκεῖνος, οὗτος, } when\ emphatic. \\ 2.\ \text{ὁ μέν—ὁ δέ, οἱ μέν,—οἱ δέ, } at \\ \ \ \ \ beginning\ of\ sentence. \\ 3.\ \text{Oblique cases of } αὐτός. \end{cases}$

The personal pronouns in the nominative are not generally used unless there is a contrast expressed or implied, or more or less of an emphasis.

ἐπεὶ θανόντας αὐτοχεὶρ ὑμᾶς ἐγὼ
ἔλουσα.　　SOPH.
Seeing that when ye died, with my own hands I bathed you.

ἐγὼ σφ᾽ ἀπείργω.　SOPH.
I, even I, withhold him.

σὺ δέ μοι αὐτοὺς κάλει.　ANDOK.
Clerk, summon the witnesses.

Note 1.—σφέ *him, her, it, them* (sing. and pl. accus.) is used in tragedy.

νίν (Doric),　Do.,　do.
μίν (Ionic),　Do.,　do., but only as accus. sing.

Note 2.—ἐμοῦ is more emphatic than μου. When the pronoun is emphatic it is accented, *e.g.* ἐμὲ καὶ σέ, not ἐμὲ καί σε.

§ 68. POSSESSIVE PRONOUNS.

1st pers. my, mine, ours.   ἐμός, ἡμέτερος.
2d pers.   thy, thine, yours. σός, ὑμέτερος.
3d pers.   his, her, its.   Wanting in Attic.

The possessive of the 3d pers. ὅς (ἑός) is Epic : σφέτερος is reflexive (suus). The genitive of αὐτός supplies the possessive to the 3d person.

Besides the possessive pronouns there are the following synonymous usages :—(1) the genitives μου, σου, αὐτοῦ : (2) the reflexive genitives ἐμαυτοῦ, σεαυτοῦ, ἑαυτοῦ : (3) the Article.

Thus, for "I sent my slave," we may write—

1. ἔπεμψα τὸν ἐμὸν δοῦλον, or τὸν δοῦλον τὸν ἐμόν.
2. ἔπεμψα τὸν δοῦλόν μου.
3. ἔπεμψα τὸν ἐμαυτοῦ δοῦλον, or τὸν δοῦλον τὸν ἐμαυτοῦ.
4. ἔπεμψα τὸν δοῦλον.

And so with the other persons, e.g. ἔπεμψε τὸν δοῦλον αὐτοῦ.

After a preceding word the order may be ἥκει μου ὁ δοῦλος, my slave is come; e.g. ἀποδέξασθέ μου τὴν ἀπολογίαν, ANTIPH. Tetr. B. B. 2, listen to my defence.

Note 1. The personal pronoun is sometimes used for the reflexive.

ἐγὼ ὑμᾶς κελεύω ἐμὲ μιμεῖσθαι.   XEN. *Cyr.* viii. 6. 13.
I beg you to imitate me.

And as the subject of an Infinitive, with a reflexive object.

δεῖ ἡμᾶς ἐξετάσαι ἡμᾶς αὐτούς.   PLAT. *Gorg.* 514, A.
We must examine ourselves.

And often in the phrase : μοι or ἐμοὶ δοκῶ (ἔδοξα).

Note 2. The possessives are sometimes used for a genitive, which is usually subjective, but occasionally objective. Thus ἡ ἐμή εὔνοια (=ἡ εὔνοιά μου), *the good-will which I feel*. But also εὐνοίᾳ τῇ σῇ, *from good-will towards thee*: ἡ διαβολὴ ἡ ἐμή, *the prejudice against me*. PLAT.

An adjective in the genitive may qualify a possessive agreeing with the personal genitive implied in the possessive; τἀμὰ δυστήνου κακά, *the woes of me, wretched man*, mea miseri mala. Cf. Latin, mea ipsius culpa; nostros vidisti flentis ocellos. Ov. *Her.* v. 43; (cf. HOR. *Sat.* i. iv. 23).

§ 69. REFLEXIVE PRONOUNS.

1st pers. *of myself, ourselves.* } ἐμαυτοῦ, ἡμῶν αὐτῶν.

2d pers. *of thyself, yourselves.* } σεαυτοῦ, σαυτοῦ, ὑμῶν αὐτῶν.

3d pers. *of him-, her-, it- self, of themselves.* } ἑαυτοῦ, αὑτοῦ { σφῶν αὐτῶν and ἑαυτῶν.

Reciprocal pronoun : ἀλλήλων, *of one another*.

μάλιστα τὴν σαυτοῦ φρόνησιν ἄσκει. ISAEUS.
Above all things cultivate self-knowledge.

καθ' ἑαυτοὺς βουλευσάμενοι τὰ ὅπλα παρέδοσαν καὶ σφᾶς αὐτούς. THUC.
After deliberating apart by themselves, they surrendered their arms and themselves (*their persons*).

Note 1. The separation of the word in the singular makes the expression stronger, especially if αὐτός comes first, *e.g.* αὐτόν με.

καὶ τοὺς παῖδας τοὺς ἐμοὺς ᾔσχυνε καὶ ἐμὲ αὐτὸν ὕβρισεν.
LYS. i. 4.
He disgraced my sons and outraged me myself.

αὐτός often strengthens the reflexives.

καταλέλυκε τὴν αὐτὸς αὑτοῦ δυναστείαν. AESCHIN. 3. 233.
He destroyed his own power.
Ipse suas evertit opes.

Note 2. A reflexive pronoun in a subordinate clause may refer—
1. To the subject of its own clause.
2. To the subject of the principal clause. When so used it is called an *Indirect Reflexive*.

1. Κῦρος πᾶσι παρήγγελλεν καθίστασθαι εἰς τὴν ἑαυτοῦ τάξιν ἕκαστον. XEN.
Cyrus was issuing orders to all that each man should stand quietly in his own rank.

2. ὁ τύραννος νομίζει τοὺς πολίτας ὑπηρετεῖν ἑαυτῷ.
PLAT.
The despot thinks that the citizens are his own servants.

Note 3. As *indirect reflexives* may also be used (1) the oblique cases of αὐτός; (2) the datives οἷ, σφίσι (οὗ and ἕ are very rarely thus used: they are found chiefly in poetry, and in poetical passages of Plato).

(1). οὐχ ἕξειν ὑμᾶς ὅ,τι χρήσεσθε αὐτῷ νομίζει. DEM.
He thinks you won't know what to do with him.

(2) ἔφη εἶναι ἀνδράποδον οἱ ἐπὶ Λαυρίῳ. ANDOK. *de Myst.* 38.
He stated that he had a slave at Laurium.

οἱ Ἀθηναῖοι οὐδὲν σφίσιν ἔφασαν προσήκειν. THUC.
The Athenians maintained that it was no concern of theirs.

Thucydides and Xenophon are partial to this use of οἷ and σφίσι.

Note 4. ἑαυτοῦ, ἑαυτῶν *are sometimes used of the first and of the second person.*

τὰ αὑτῶν ἅμα ἐκποριζώμεθα. THUC.
Let us at the same time furnish all our own resources.

οὐδὲ γὰρ τὴν ἑαυτοῦ σύ γε ψυχὴν ὁρᾷς. XEN.
Why you anyhow do not even see your own soul.
ANTIPH. *Herod.* 11.

Note 5. *The reflexive is sometimes used for the reciprocal* ἀλλήλων.

βούλεσθε περιιόντες αὐτῶν πυνθάνεσθαι; DEM.
Do you wish to be running about and inquiring **one** *of another?*

Cf. S. Luke xxiii. 12, "for before they were at enmity between themselves."

Note.—σφῶν αὐτῶν is also used like suus *and not so, meaning their own men, their own side.*

ὥρμηντο οἱ ἐν Σάμῳ 'Αθηναῖοι πλεῖν ἐπὶ σφᾶς αὐτούς.
THUC. viii. 86.
The Athenians in Samos were bent on sailing against their own countrymen.

So ἡμῶν (ὑμῶν) αὐτῶν partitively.

τὸ τρίτον μέρος ἡμῶν αὐτῶν. THUC. iii. 54. 3.
A third of our own numbers.

§ 70. *DEMONSTRATIVE PRONOUNS.*

This { οὗτος, ὅδε, } So great, so many { τοσοῦτος, tantus, tot. τοσόσδε, }

That ἐκεῖνος, So old, so young (so great) { τηλίκος. τηλικοῦτος. τηλικόσδε. }

Such { τοιοῦτος, τοιόσδε, } talis.

τοῖος is Epic and poetical.

For ἕτερος, see Indefinite pronouns.

ὁδί, οὑτοσί are emphatically deictic forms, *this here;* οὗτος and ὅδε point to something near in space or time; ἐκεῖνος, to something more distant; ὅδε points to something present; οὗτος, to something mentioned, though οὗτος also has the deictic force of ὅδε.

ἡ τραγῳδία ἐστὶ τῆσδε τῆς πόλεως εὕρημα. PLAT.
Tragedy is the invention of this city.

τοῦτ' ἐκεῖν' οὑγὼ 'λεγον. AR.
This is that which I was speaking of.

οὗτος ὄπισθεν προσέρχεται. PLAT.
Here he is coming behind.

τοῦτ' ἐστ' ἐκεῖνο, τοῦτ' ἐκεῖνο = as the saying is, illud quod dicitur.

Note 1.—οὗτος and ὅδε *for first and second person.* ὅδε is often used in poetry of the first person, ἀνὴρ ὅδε is common in Trag. for ἐγώ.

ὅδ' εἴμ' Ὀρέστης, Μενέλεως, ὃν ἱστορεῖς. EUR. *Or.* 374.
I am Orestes, Menelaus, whom thou seekest.
εἰ τὸν νεκρὸν ξὺν τῇδε κουφιεῖς χερί. SOPH. *Ant.* 43.
(Consider) whether thou wilt uplift this corpse together with this my hand.
τίς οὑτοσὶ τίς οὑτοσί; AR. *Ach.* 1048.
Who's this here? i.e. *who are you?*

Note 2.—τάδε, τάδε πάντα, ταῦτα πάντα are used in prose and verse of something near.

οὐκ Ἴωνες τάδε εἰσὶν οὐδὲ Ἑλλησπόντιοι. THUC. vi. 77. 1
The people here are no Ionians or Hellespontines.
Cf. EUR. *Androm.* 168.

Note 3.—οὗτος *and* ὅδε *contrasted.* οὗτος generally refers to what has preceded, ὅδε to what follows. So with all demonstratives in -τος and -δε. But the rule is by no means invariable.

τὸ δὲ οὐκ ἔστι τοιοῦτον ἀλλὰ τοιόνδε μᾶλλον. PLAT.
However, it is not so as you think, but rather as follows.
τοιάδε ἔλεξεν, } *he spoke as follows,* τοσαῦτα } εἰπών, *after*
ἔλεξε τοιάδε, τοιαῦτα
speaking thus, are common phrases in Thucydides.

Note 4.—οὗτος (not ὅδε) and αὐτός (the latter especially in Plato) are the usual antecedents to the relative, like *is* in Latin.

οὗτος *and* ἐκεῖνος *contrasted.* Like *hic* and *ille* in Latin, sometimes, but not always, οὗτος means *this nearer* (i.e. the latter), ἐκεῖνος, *that distant* (i.e. the former), in space or time.

Note 5.—οὗτος and ἐκεῖνος in the neuter, like *hoc, illud* in Latin, often draw attention to and point the coming word or phrase. See Peculiarities of Apposition 3.

They also gather up and emphasise what has preceded.

ἃ ἂν εἴπῃς ἔμμενε τούτοις. PLAT.
Whatever you say, keep to that.

Note 6.—οὗτος, ὅδε, ἐκεῖνος, compared with Latin.

οὗτος often denotes contempt like *iste;* ἐκεῖνος, praise (the famous or illustrious), like *ille*.

οὗτος is the opponent (plaintiff or defendant)=*iste, hic* being the client, οὗτοι, *the judges, the court, or the opposite party*.

οὗτος, as antecedent to the relative=*is* (qui).

οὑτοσί=*hicce, celui-ci, this man here*.

ὅδε is much like *hic, this man here*, marking simply the presence of something, *e.g.* ἀκτὴ μὲν ἥδε, *here is the shore, voici la plage*.

§ 71.   *THE PRONOUN* Αὐτός.

Αὐτός has three usages which must be very carefully distinguished.

1. It is a definitive adjective pronoun, like *ipse*, meaning *self*.
2. With the article, ὁ αὐτός means *the same, idem*.
3. In its oblique cases it is the pronoun of the third person, *him, her, it, them*.

1. Αὐτός in all its cases may mean *self, myself, thyself, himself, herself, itself, themselves*. It has this meaning when it occurs :—

  a. In the nominative case.

  b. In any case in agreement with a pronoun, or with a noun and article when placed outside the article. The pronoun or noun must often be supplied from the context, αὐτός occupying an emphatic position. The pronoun to be supplied may be the indefinite τις.

αὐτοὶ δ' ὅταν σφαλῶμεν οὐ γιγνώσκομεν.   EUR.
Whene'er we trip ourselves we mark it not.

αὐτὸς ἔγωγε ἐτεταράγμην. PLAT.
I myself was quite upset.
αὐτὸν γάρ σε δεῖ Προμηθέως. AESCH.
Thou thyself needest a Prometheus.
αὐτῇ τῇ ψυχῇ θεατέον αὐτὰ τὰ πράγματα. PLAT.
With the soul itself (i.e. *apart from the body) we must behold things in themselves* (i.e. *actual realities*).
ὁ Βρασίδας τῇ Θεσσαλῶν γῇ καὶ αὐτοῖς φίλος ἦν.
Brasidas was friendly to the land of the Thessalians, and to (*the Thessalians*) *themselves.*
Cf. XEN. *Anab.* vii. 8. 22.
οὐχ οἷόν τέ ἐστιν ἀμελῆ αὐτὸν ὄντα ἄλλους ποιεῖν ἐπιμελεῖς. XEN.
It is not possible that one who himself is careless should make others careful.

With a proper name the article is not necessary.
αὐτὸς Σεύθης ἀνέκραγεν. XEN.
Seuthes himself exclaimed.
So αὐτὸς βασιλεύς, *the Great King himself.*

2. ὁ αὐτός, ἡ αὐτή, τὸ αὐτό, and in Attic αὑτός, αὑτή, ταὐτό and ταὐτόν, genitive ταὐτοῦ, etc., means *the same.*
τοὺς αὐτοὺς περὶ τῶν αὐτῶν λόγους λέγουσι. ANTIPH.
They make the same statements about the same things.

3. Αὐτός in its oblique cases only, and never at the beginning of a sentence, is the third personal pronoun, *him, her, it, them.*
ἀποπέμπουσιν αὐτὸν πρὶν ἀκοῦσαι. THUC.
They dismiss him before hearing him.
πολλοὺς αὐτῶν ἀπέκτειναν. XEN.
They killed many of them.
πειράσομαι ξυμμαχεῖν αὐτῷ. XEN.
I will endeavour to help him.
So we should write ξυμμαχεῖν αὐτῇ, αὐταῖς.

THE PRONOUN Αὐτός. 55

Note 1.—Like the Latin *is*, αὐτός (1) recalls a noun which has been mentioned, and (2) it is used, instead of the more usual οὗτος or ἐκεῖνος, as the antecedent to a relative sentence. This second usage is uncommon, except in Plato. In most instances the relative sentence precedes.

(1) ἐτράποντο ἐπὶ τὸν Ξενοφῶντα. καὶ ἔλεγον αὐτῷ.
XEN. *Anab.* vi. 1. 21.
They turned to Xenophon, and said to him.

(2) αὐτὸ οὐκ εἴρηται ὃ μάλιστα ἔδει ῥηθῆναι.
PLAT. *Rep.* 362.
The very point, which above all ought to have been stated, has not been stated.

ἀνέλαβον αὐτὰ ὅσα ὑπῆρχεν ἐπιτήδεια. THUC. vii. 74.
They took with them just whatever was necessary.

Cf. EUR. *Tro.* 662, *I. A.* 1025.

Note 2.—Αὐτός meaning *self* will have to be rendered in many different ways.

(*a.*) *In or by oneself, unaided.*

τὸ χωρίον αὐτὸ καρτερὸν ὑπῆρχε. THUC.
The spot in itself was strong (i.e. *without artificial fortification*).

αὐτὸς ἐποίησα, *I did it myself* (*without help*).

(*b*) *Voluntarily*, sponte.

ἥξει γὰρ αὐτά. SOPH.
Words will come of themselves (*unbidden*).

(*c*) *The great man himself, the Master.*

τίς οὗτος; αὐτός. τίς αὐτός; Σωκράτης.
Who's this? the Master. Who's the Master? *Socrates.*
αὐτὸς ἔφη, *Ipse dixit.*

(*d*) *With Ordinals.*

ἐστρατήγει Περικλῆς τέταρτος αὐτός.
Pericles was general with three others.

(*e*) The neuter αὐτό is used by the philosophers with substantives of all genders to express the abstract idea of a thing: αὐτὸ δικαιοσύνη, *ideal justice*, or *justice in the abstract;* αὐτὴ ἀδικία, αὐτὸ τὸ καλόν, αὐτὸ καλόν constantly in Plato.

In Aristotle αὐτό forms one compound word with the substantive αὐτοάνθρωπος, *the ideal man;* αὐτοαγαθόν, *the highest good*, summum bonum, etc.

§ 72. INTERROGATIVE PRONOUNS.

Who, what (Direct), τίς, τί; (Indirect), ὅστις, ὅτι.
Whether of two (uter) πότερος; ὁπότερος.
How much, how great } πόσος; ὁπόσος.
How many (quantus).
Of what sort (qualis) ποῖος; ὁποῖος.
How old, how great πηλίκος; ὁπηλίκος.

The pronouns in the second column are also relatives. The Direct pronouns are however constantly used instead of the Indirect (see Indirect Question).

σὺ εἶ τίς ἀνδρῶν; ὅστις εἴμ᾽ ἐγώ; Μέτων. ARIST.
What man art thou? (ask you) what man am I? Meton.
See Ach. 106. 959.

Note 1.—ποῖος; is often used in a sarcastic repetition.
οἱ πρέσβεις οἱ παρὰ βασιλέως. ποίου βασιλέως;
The envoys from the King! King quotha! (King indeed!)
So πόθεν, AR. Ran. 1455; Ach. 109; Nub. 366 (a good instance).
Observe that in asking a question the article is generally used with ποῖος when there is no noun.
οἴμαί σε ὁμολογήσειν τὸ τοιόνδε. τὸ ποῖον;
PLAT. Rep. 475, E.
I think you will make the following admission. What admission?
So τὸ τί; ARIST. Batr. 40. Cf. AR. Ach. 418.

Note 2.—Observe the idiomatic use of double interrogatives.
τίς πόθεν μολών σοι μαρτυρήσει; SOPH. Tr. 421.
Who is he, whence comes he, who will bear thee record?
So πῶς τί τοῦτ᾽ εἶπες; PLAT. Soph. 261, C. SOPH. Ant. 40'.

Rarely ὅς is used like ὅστις in a question. ἐγῷδ᾽ ὅς ἐστι,
I know who he is, AR. Ach. 118. The Greeks said οἶδα (αὐτὸν)
ὅς ἐστι or οἶδα τίς (ὅστις) ἐστι.

§ 73. RELATIVE PRONOUNS AND ATTRACTION.

Who	ὅς	(qui)	ὅστις	{ whosoever (quicunque).
Of what sort	οἷος, ὁποῖος	(qualis)	ὅστε	{ (esp. poet.) of such a class, often like ὅστις.
How great, how many	ὅσος, ὁπόσος	(quantus quotquot)	ὅσπερ,	{ the very one, exactly the one who.

What number in a series ὁπόστος (quotus).
How old or how great } ἡλίκος   ὁπηλίκος   ὁπότερος, whichsoever of two.

Obs. ἅττα, Attic (ἅσσα, Ionic) for ἅτινα, *neut. pl. of* ὅστις.
ἄττα, Attic (ἄσσα, Ionic) for τινά, *neut. pl. of* τίς.

§ 74. ὅς, ὅσπερ, ὅστις.

ὅς is definite.

ἔστιν δίκης ὀφθαλμός, ὃς τὰ πάνθ' ὁρᾷ. MENANDER.
There is an eye of justice which sees all things.

ὅστις is indefinite.

ἀνελεύθερος πᾶς ὅστις εἰς δόξαν βλέπει.
CLEANTHES, the Stoic.
Slavish the man whoever looks to fame.

For other usages of ὅστις see Index.

ὅσπερ is particularly definite (περ adds this force to other pronouns and adverbs, *e.g.* ὥσπερ, εἴπερ, ἐπειδήπερ, etc.).

ταυτὸν ἔχουσιν ἁμάρτημα ὅπερ καὶ οἱ ποιηταί.
PLAT.
They are making exactly the same mistake which the poets make.

λυσιτελεῖ μοι ὥσπερ ἔχω ἔχειν. PLAT.
It is good for me to be just as I am.
So ᾗπερ AR. *Ach.* 364. 474.

Note.—οὖν (δή, δήποτε, δηποτοῦν), added to relative pronouns, alters them from relatives, and makes them indefinite. ὁστισοῦν, *any whosoever*; οὐδ' ὁτιοῦν, *not even anything whatsoever*, ne tantillum quidem; ὁποσοσοῦν, *how great soever*, quantuscunque; ὁποιοσοῦν, qualiscunque; ὁποστοσοῦν, quotuscunque; οἱ ὁποιοιδήποτε στρατηγοί, *generals of any sort whatsoever, no matter who*.

§ 75. *ATTRACTION.*

A Relative which would be in the Accusative is often attracted into the case of its Antecedent, if that Antecedent is in the Genitive or Dative. This attraction sometimes, but rarely, takes place when the Relative would have been in the Dative.

χρῶμαι βιβλίοις οἷς ἔχω.
I use the books which I have.
For ἃ ἔχω.
τοῖς ἀγαθοῖς οἷς ἔχομεν κτώμεθα καὶ τὰς ἄλλας.
ISAEUS.
By means of the advantages which we possess we gain our other advantages also.

The Antecedent is often attracted into the clause of the Relative.

χρῶμαι οἷς ἔχω βιβλίοις for χρῶμαι βιβλίοις ἃ ἔχω.
ἀμαθέστατοί ἐστε ὧν ἐγὼ οἶδα Ἑλλήνων. THUC. vi. 39.
You are the most ignorant of the Greeks whom I know.
For Ἑλλήνων οὓς οἶδα.

Note.—The attraction takes place even where the antecedent is omitted.

πρὸς ᾧ εἶχε ξυνέλεγε στράτευμα. XEN. *Hell.* iv. 1. 41.
He was collecting an army in addition to that which he already had.

For πρὸς τούτῳ ὃ εἶχε. Cf. EURIP. *Med.* 753.

Adverbs of place are thus attracted.

διεκομίζοντο ὅθεν ὑπεξέθεντο παῖδας. THUC. i. 89.
They now conveyed across their children from the places where they had sent them for shelter.
For ἐντεῦθεν ... οὗ.

§ 76. Miscellaneous instances of Attraction.

τὴν οὐσίαν ἣν κατέλιπεν οὐ πλείονος ἀξία ἐστιν.
LYS. 19. 49.
The property which he left is not worth more.
ἡ οὐσία, the subject, is attracted into the case of the relative.

So ὃν οἱ θεοὶ φιλοῦσιν ἀποθνήσκει νέος. MEN. 128
(He) whom the gods love dies young.
The demonstrative subject, οὗτος, is omitted.

So πολλοὶ ἀναλίσκουσιν οὐκ εἰς ἃ δεῖ. XEN. *Oik.* 3. 5.
Many spend money on objects which they ought not (to spend it on).
For εἰς ταῦτα εἰς ἅ.

So ἄξω ὑμᾶς ἔνθα τὸ πρᾶγμα ἐγένετο. XEN. *Cyr.* v. 4. 21.
I will bring you where the affair took place.
For ἐκεῖσε ἔνθα.

Several common idioms come under this head of Attraction.

(a) οὐδεὶς ὅστις οὐ (*i.e.* οὐδείς ἐστιν ὅστις οὐ) is declined as one word in Acc. Gen. Dat.
Γοργίας οὐδενὶ ὅτῳ οὐκ ἀπεκρίνετο. PLAT. *Men.* 70.
Gorgias was replying to every single questioner.

In Soph. *Ai.* 725, οὗτις ἔσθ' ὃς οὐ.

(b) θαυμαστὸς ὅσος, ὑπερφυὴς ὅσος are similarly declined, and their adverbs θαυμαστῶς, ὑπερφυῶς.
ὡμολόγησε ταῦτα μετὰ ἱδρῶτος θαυμαστοῦ ὅσου.
PLAT. *Rep.*
He made these admissions with an astonishing amount of perspiration.

ὑπερφυῶς ὡς χαίρω. PLAT.
I am surprisingly glad.
(*i.e.* ὑπερφυές ἐστιν ὥς).

(c) οἷος, and ἄλλος ὅσος, εἴ τις.

ἔλεγε πρὸς ἄνδρας τολμηροὺς οἵους καὶ 'Αθηναίους.
THUC. vii. 21.
He was speaking to bold men like the Athenians.
For οἷοί εἰσι καὶ 'Αθηναῖοι.

ἀνίστη 'Αγριᾶνας καὶ ἄλλα ὅσα ἔθνη Παιονικά.
THUC. ii. 96.
He was raising the Agrianes and all the other Paeonian tribes.

ἐγγυώμεθα ἡμεῖς, ἐγώ, Φορμίων, ἄλλον εἴ τινα βούλεται.
DEM. 20. 100.
Let us promise, I, Phormio, any one he likes.
For ἄλλος τίς εἴ τινα ἄλλον βούλεται.

οἷός τε for τοιοῦτος οἷός τε in the sense of " able," like δυνατός, is exceedingly common.

οἷός τε εἰμὶ ταῦτα ποιεῖν.
I am able to do this.

οὐχ οἷόν τε ἐστίν.
It is not possible; it cannot be.

In the same way, by the omission of the Antecedent, are formed many indefinite pronouns and verbs.

ἔστιν οἵ, commoner than εἰσιν οἵ (*sunt qui*).
ἔνιοι (ἔνι, there are . . . οἵ, those who); ἐνίοτε, *sometimes.*
ἔστιν οὗ, *somewhere;* ἔστιν ᾗ, *in some way;* ἔστιν ὅπως, *somehow.*

The Relative preceding the Demonstrative throws great emphasis on the Demonstrative (as in Latin).

ἃ ποιεῖν αἰσχρόν, ταῦτα νόμιζε μηδὲ λέγειν εἶναι καλόν.
ISAE. 1. 15.
Quae factu turpia sunt ea ne dictu quidem honesta habe.

Observe the phrases: ὃ λέγω, *as I say,* or *as I was saying,* ὅπερ, or ὃ ἄρτι ἔλεγον, ὕπερ εἶπον.

§ 77. INDEFINITE PRONOUNS.

Some, any, A kind or sort of,	τὶς, τὶ	none, nothing,	οὐδείς, οὐδέν (οὔτις) *poet.* μηδείς, μηδέν.
Some (with emphasis),	ἔστιν ὅς ἔστιν οἵ εἰσὶν οἵ	none (emphatic) (less common).	οὐδὲ εἷς. μηδὲ εἷς.
Any whatever,	ὅστις οὖν.		
Some . . . others,	οἱ μέν—οἱ δέ. ἄλλοι—ἄλλοι.		
Each, every, all,	ἕκαστος, πᾶς τις, πᾶς, ἅπας (stronger than πᾶς)		
	σύμπας (*all together*).		
Other, another,	ἄλλος (alius) οἱ ἄλλοι, *the rest*, ceteri.		
One of two (different),	ἕτερος (alter);	neither one nor other	οὐδέτερος. μηδέτερος.

Note 1. πότερος, and its indirect form, ὁπότερος, = *uter, whether, or which of two?* But they may also = *alteruter, one, or either of two.* In this latter sense ποτερός is sometimes written oxytone.

ποιός, *of some sort;* ποσός, *of some size or number* (observe the accents).

ἕτερος should perhaps be classed among Demonstratives, but it is put here in contrast to ἄλλος.

Note 2. Idiomatic uses of τὶς.

(*a*) τὶς means sometimes *many a one.*

μισεῖ τις ἐκεῖνον, ὦ ἄνδρες Ἀθηναῖοι, καὶ δέδιεν.
DEM.
There are those (there are many) who hate him and fear him, Athenians.

(b) It means, like *aliquis*, *some great, some important person, or thing*.

ηὔχεις τις εἶναι, τοῖσι χρήμασι σθένων. EUR. *El.* 939.
Thou wast boasting thyself to be some great one, trusting to thy riches.
Cf. S. Paul, *ad Gal.* ii. 6.
So δρᾶν τι, *to do some great thing.* SOPH. *El.* 305.
Si vis esse aliquis. IUV. i. 74.

(c) It is constantly joined to adjectives, numerals, and pronouns, sometimes to strengthen, sometimes to weaken the expression, in a way for which, in English, we have frequently no equivalent:—

μέγας τις, πᾶς τις, ἕκαστος τις. οὐδείς τις, ὀλίγοι τινές. βραχύ τι, οὐδέν τι, σχεδόν τι, τρεῖς τινες, etc. etc. ποῖός τις; πόσος τις; σχεδόν τι, ἐγγύ τι, οὐ πολλοί τινες, τριάκοντά τινες, τίνες δύο νῆες, THUC. viii. 100.

(d) ἤ τις ἤ οὐδείς—ἤ τι ἤ οὐδέν, *hardly any one, hardly anything*.

οὗτοι μὲν οὖν ἤ τι ἤ οὐδὲν ἀληθὲς εἰρήκασι.
PLAT. *Ap.* 1.
These men then have spoken hardly a word of truth.

(e) τις also covertly alludes to some known person.

ἥδ᾽ οὖν θανεῖται καὶ θανοῦσ᾽ ὀλεῖ τινα.
SOPH. *Antig.* 751.
She then must die, and dying slay another (hers will not be the only death.)

(f) τις = *here and there one*.

τῶν ἐν ὀλιγαρχίᾳ ἀποθανόντων ἴσως τις ἦν πονηρός.
LYS. 30. 13.

Note 3. ἄλλος must often be rendered adverbially, *besides, moreover, as well*, adding as well as opposing. This is very common in Attic.

πέμπτος ποταμὸς ἄλλος. HDT. v. 54.
Yet a fifth river.

Cf. SOPH. *El.* 707; AESCH. *Sept.* 481.

οὐ γὰρ ἦν χόρτος οὐδὲ ἄλλο δένδρον οὐδέν. XEN. *An.* i. 5. 5.
There was no grass, no, nor any tree at all.

Cf. Plaustra iumentaque *alia*. LIV. iv. 41. *Wagons and beasts of burden also.*
And there were also two other malefactors led with him to be put to death. S. LUKE, xxiii. 32.
All these (vices) are portable, with other graces weighed.
SHAKSPERE, *Macbeth*, iv. iii. 90.
ὁ ἄλλος may often be rendered *in general* or *usual.*
παρὰ τὸν ἄλλον τρόπον. ANTIPH. *Tetr.* B. B. 1.
Contrary to my general disposition.

Note 4. πᾶν like *quidvis, quidlibet,* may mean *anything, no matter what.*

οὐδένα δεῖ μηχανᾶσθαι ὅπως ἀποφεύξεται πᾶν ποιῶν θάνατον.
PLAT. *Ap.*
No man should endeavour to avoid death by every means.
τοιαῦτα ἄλλα, cf. *alter idem.* SOPH. *El.* 337.

Obs. τὸ ποιόν, *quality;* τὸ ποσόν, *quantity.*

CHAPTER IV.

THE CASES.

§ 78. Preliminary Note on the Cases.

Greek is developed from a language which had eight cases, or nine, if we regard the separate meanings of the last as belonging to two distinct cases. Of these eight or nine Greek retained only five, although comparative philology shows that traces of the others survived. The work of the lost cases was carried on by the remaining five, as the following table will explain.

INDO-EUROPEAN.	GREEK.
Nominative	Nominative
Vocative	Vocative
Accusative	Accusative
Genitive } Ablative }	Genitive
Dative } Locative } Instrumental } Comitative or Sociative }	Dative

The Greek Genitive and Dative have been called *mixed* cases because they have assumed the functions of the lost cases.[1]

---

[1] The following declension of an Indo-European noun, taken from Schleicher, will show the cases.

Stem VAK (voice, Fοπ(s), voc(s) *i.e.* vox.)

Singular Nom. VAK-s   the voice
         Voc. VAK-   O voice.
         Acc. VAK-am   the voice.
         Gen. VAK-as   of the voice.
         Abl. VAK-at   from the voice.
         Dat. VAK-ai   for the voice.
         Loc. VAK-i   at or by the voice.
         Inst. VAK-bhi } with the voice.
     (and Com.) VAK-a }

The Nominative, Vocative, and Accusative form one group, the Genitive and Ablative a second group, the Dative, Locative, Instrumental, and Comitative (the latter being perhaps another aspect or shade of the Instrumental) a third group.

The Nominative is the case of the *subject*.
The Vocative is the case of the *person or thing addressed*.
The Accusative is the case of the *object*.
The Genitive is the case of the *class* (γένος, genus) *to which a thing belongs*.
The Ablative is the case of *that from which another thing is separated*, the case of *separation*.
The Dative is the case of the *person or thing remotely connected with an action* (the *remoter object*), for *whom or which anything is done*.
The Locative is the case of *the place where an action takes place*.
The Instrumental is the case of *the instrument by which* an action is performed.
The Comitative (or Sociative) is the case of *the accompanying circumstances*.

The details of each case will show that the five Greek cases retain their original meanings, while the *mixed cases* (Genitive and Dative) acquire in addition the meanings of the lost ones. But nearly all the cases, especially the mixed ones, have assumed other shades of meaning and other uses, from analogies which we cannot safely trace now. In treating of any case therefore we may distinguish between (1) its primary and distinct use, (2) its freer, looser use. Attempts to explain and classify the freer uses must necessarily be more or less arbitrary.

§ 79.   *THE NOMINATIVE.*

The Nominative is the case of the Subject, and of the Predicate or Apposition in agreement with the Subject.

    Φίλιππος καθίσταται βασιλεύς.
    Philip is appointed King.

The Nominative is often used for the Vocative.
    ἴθι μὲν οὖν σύ, ὁ πρεσβύτατος. XEN.
    Come then, you, the elder one!

E

οὗτος especially is so used.

ὦ οὗτος Αἴας. SOPH. *Ai*. 89.
What ho! Ajax!

Cf. *Oed. Col.* 1627.

ὁ Ἀπολλόδωρος οὗτος, οὐ περιμενεῖς; PLAT. *Symp.*
Apollodorus, you Sir! stop, won't you?

§ 80. THE VOCATIVE.

In Attic Prose ὦ is generally added.

σκόπει τοίνυν, ὦ Σώκρατες, ἔφη. PLAT.
Consider therefore, Socrates, said he.

μὴ θορυβεῖτε, ὦ ἄνδρες Ἀθηναῖοι. PLAT. *Apol.*
Do not interrupt, Athenians.

The omission of the ὦ makes the address curt, tart, or businesslike, as ἀκούεις Αἰσχίνη; *d'ye hear, Aeschines?*

THE ACCUSATIVE.

§ 81. Preliminary Note on the Accusative.

The Accusative, unlike the Genitive and Dative, is formed with no suffix which in itself gives the case a special application. But it came to denote the object of the sentence, as the Nominative denotes the subject. In speaking of the object, however, we must very carefully distinguish between two distinct significations of the Accusative. Thus ANTIPHON writes, τύπτει τὸν ἄνδρα πληγάς, *he strikes the man blows.* Here πληγάς, *blows*, is already contained in the meaning of the verb τύπτει. This Accusative has been called the *Internal Accusative.* On the other hand, τὸν ἄνδρα, *the man*, is not contained in the meaning of τύπτει. This is called the *External Accusative.* The Internal Accusative is of much freer and wider application than the External, varying from the Cognate Accusative, μάχην μάχομαι, *I fight a fight*, to any word which is substituted for the Cognate Accusative, such as, σπονδὰς ποιοῦμαι, *I make a treaty;* ἐπιστολὴν γράφω, *I write a command;*

THE ACCUSATIVE. 67

πλέω θάλασσαν, I sail the sea ; μέγαλα σφάλλομαι, I am greatly disappointed. The External Accusative is a natural extension, not of the meaning, but of the direction of the verb. The Accusative is naturally associated with a verb, and, when it is not an External Accusative, qualifies the verb almost as an adverb. Thus παῖσον διπλῆν (SOPH. El. 1415), strike a double blow, strike twice ; ἀκὴν ἔσαν, or ἐγένοντο (HOM. Il.) they were or became silence, i.e. silent. Hence the many quasi-adverbs of Accusative form, ἀρχήν, ἀκμήν, πρόφασιν, χάριν, προῖκα, etc., and the wide use of neuter adjectives used adverbially, πολλά, πυκνά, τὸ λοιπόν, etc. Πρῶτον, πρότερόν, again are Accusative forms. Indeed we may say that all Accusatives fall under two heads, either—(1) the Internal Accusative, or (2) the External Accusative.

§ 82. Conspectus of the Internal Accusative.

The Internal Accusative denotes either the *state* or the *operation* of the verb (the state of neuter and passive verbs, the operation of active verbs).

It is either

A. A word kindred in stem or meaning to the verb (the COGNATE ACCUSATIVE), *e.g.*

μάχην μάχεσθαι.
ζῆν βίον.

B. A word substituted for the Cognate Accusative, and limiting or defining the verbal notion.

ψήφισμα νικᾶν, to win, i.e. carry, a measure.

Accusatives of this class denote

(a) That *with respect to which* the state or operation occurs, often the *part affected* (Accusative of RESPECT).

θαυμαστὸς εἶναι τὸ κάλλος, to be remarkable in respect of beauty.
ψυχὴν νοσεῖν, to be ill in mind.

(b) The extent of the state or operation in *degree*, *space*, or *time*.

οὔτε μέγα οὔτε σμικρὸν σοφός εἰμι.
In no degree, great or small, am I wise.

ἀπέχει σταδίους ἑβδομήκοντα.
It is seventy stades distant.
πολὺν χρόνον παρέμεινα.
I waited a long time.

Two further remarks may be made:

(1.) The Accusative follows Adjectives (and Adverbs) as well as verbs, *e.g.*
ἀγαθὸς πᾶσαν ἀρετήν.
ἄτιμοι ἀτιμίαν τοιάνδε.

(2) Adjectives, especially neuter Adjectives and Pronouns in agreement with the Accusative, are freely used instead of the Accusative, which is unexpressed.
μεγάλα κινδυνεύει.
τοῦτο κινδυνεύει.

§ 83. *THE INTERNAL ACCUSATIVE.*

The Internal Accusative is,

A. A word kindred in stem or meaning to the verb. This is called the COGNATE ACCUSATIVE.

τί μόχθον οὐδὲν οὖσα μοχθεῖς; EUR. *And.* 134.
Why, being naught, toilest thou with toil?

ζήσεις βίον κράτιστον ἢν θυμοῦ κρατῇς. MENAND. 186.
Thou wilt live the best life if thou wilt control thine anger.

ξυνέφυγε φυγήν, *he shared the flight*, PL. *Ap.* v.; πόνους πονεῖν, *to undergo labours*, PL. *Ap.* vii.; ἀρχὴν ἦρξα, *I held office*, PL. *Ap.* xx.; ὄνειδος ὀνειδίσαι, *to upbraid with reproaches*, SOPH. *Phil.* 523.

νοσεῖς ἄλγος, *thou art sick with grief*, SOPH. *Phil.* 1326; γραφὴν διώκειν, *to bring an indictment against* (cf. γραφὴν γράφεσθαι, cognate in stem); πόλεμον στρατεύειν, *to engage in war*, THUC. i. 112 (cf. πόλεμον πολεμεῖν and στρατείαν στρατεύειν.)

ACCUSATIVE OF RESPECT. 69

B. A word substituted for the Cognate Accusative, and limiting or defining the verbal notion.

ἕτερον ψήφισμα νικᾷ Δημοσθένης. AESCHIN.
Demosthenes carries a second decree (or measure).

ἠγωνίζοντο στάδιον, πάλην, καὶ πυγμήν. XEN.
They were contending in the race-course, in wrestling, and in boxing.

δίκην ὀφλεῖν, *to lose a law-suit;* 'Ολύμπια νικᾶν, *to win an Olympic victory;* γάμους ἑστιᾶν, *to give a wedding feast,* EUR.; ψήφισμα νικᾷ, *he carries (or wins) a decree,* AESCHIN.

Note. An extension of this Accusative is found in the Poets. This Accusative denotes the *result* of the verbal operation. Practically the verb yields an epithet in agreement with the Accusative.

ἕλκος οὐτάσαι, HOM. *Il.* v. 361, *to stab (and so make) a wound.* Goodwin compares "to break a hole." τροπὰς καταρρήγνυσι, SOPH. *Ant.* 675, *breaks to pieces (and so causes) a rout;* τάκεις οἰμωγάν, SOPH. *El.* 123, *thou meltest a (makest a melting) lamentation;* πεῖραν ἐμώρανεν, AESCH. *Pers.* 715, *he made a foolish attempt;* τέγγειν δάκρυα, PIND. *Nem.* x. 141, *he wetted (i.e. shed wet) tears.*

In SOPH. *Ant.* 973 the passive of this construction occurs. ἕλκος τυφλωθέν, *a blinded wound, i.e. wound inflicted which caused blindness;* the active form would be τυφλοῦν ἕλκος, *to inflict a blinding wound.*

§ 84. ACCUSATIVE OF RESPECT.

An Accusative is constantly joined to a verb, adjective, noun, or even a sentence, to denote that *in respect to which* the state or operation of the verb, etc., takes place. Very often the Accusative denotes *the part affected, e.g.*

κάμνω or ἀλγῶ τὴν κεφαλήν (τὰ ὄμματα, τοὺς πόδας, τοὺς δακτύλους).
I have a pain in the head (eyes, feet, fingers).

βέλτιόν ἐστι σῶμά γ᾽ ἢ ψυχὴν νοσεῖν.   MENAND.
Better to ail in body than in mind.
τυφλὸς τά τ᾽ ὦτα, τόν τε νοῦν, τά τ᾽ ὄμματ᾽ εἶ.   SOPH.
Blind art thou both in ears, and mind, and eyes.
Ἑξακόσιοι τὸν ἀριθμόν, six hundred in number.
Ἕλληνες τὸ γένος (τὸ ὄνομα), Greeks in race (in name).

Compare this Accusative with the Dative of Circumstance.

§ 85. ACCUSATIVE OF SPACE AND TIME.

The Accusative denotes *extension of space and duration of time*.

πλεῖν τὴν θάλασσαν, ANDOK., to sail the sea.
πορεύεσθαι ὁδόν, γῆν, ὄρη, XEN., to travel over a road, land, mountains.

αἱ σπονδαὶ ἐνιαυτὸν ἔσονται.   THUC.
The truce shall be (i.e. last) for a year.

ἀπέχει ἡ Πλάταια τῶν Θηβῶν σταδίους ἑβδομήκοντα.   THUC.
Plataea is seventy stades distant from Thebes.

τὴν τρίτην ἡμέραν εἰργάζοντο καὶ τὴν τετάρτην.
   THUC.
They were working throughout the third day and the fourth.

κέλευθον ἕρπειν, to crawl along a road, SOPH. *Phil.* 1224; ὁδὸν φανῆναι, to appear on a road, SOPH. *El.* 1274; τὴν ὥραν τοῦ ἔτους, DEM. *Phil.* i. 8, during the season of the year.

Note. An Accusative with ordinal numbers means *how long since* or *ago*.

ἐξήλθομεν τρίτον ἔτος τουτί.   DEM. 54. 3.
We came out three years ago

Cf PLAT. *Protag.* 309.

§ 86. ACCUSATIVE OF MOTION.

The Accusative denotes *motion to a place*, without a preposition in Poetry; but in Prose a preposition is required.

οὔπω νενόστηκ' οἶκον.   EUR. *I. T.* 534.
Not yet hath he returned home.

Cf. SOPH. *Ant.* 152, *Phil.* 244; EUR. *Bacch.* 1, 5. Cf. *Julius Caesar—Ere we could arrive the point proposed.*

Very seldom *motion to a person.*   EUR. *Bacch.* 847, 1353.

αἱ νῆες ἀφικνοῦνται ἐπὶ Πύλον.   THUC.
The ships arrive against Pylos.

ἐντεῦθεν ἐξελαύνει εἰς Κολοσσάς.   XEN.
From this place he marches to Colossae.

§ 87. ACCUSATIVE OF THE OBJECT AND PREDICATE IN AGREEMENT OR IN APPOSITION WITH IT.

For this construction, a very common and easy one, see Oblique Predicate.

Verbs of *naming* (καλῶ, ὀνομάζω), *addressing* (προσαγορεύω), *dividing* and *distributing* (νέμω, κατανέμω, διαιρῶ, τέμνω), take this construction both in the active and passive.

καλοῦσί με τοῦτο τὸ ὄνομα.   XEN. *Oik.* 7. 3.
They call me (by) this name.

ὁ Κῦρος τὸ στράτευμα κατένειμε δώδεκα μέρη.
XEN. *Cyr.* 7. 5. 13.
Cyrus divided the army into twelve parts.

ἡ γῆ τὰ αὐτὰ μέρη διανέμεται.   PL. *Leg.* v. 737.
The land is divided into the same parts.

§ 88. DOUBLE ACCUSATIVE.

Certain classes of Verbs in Greek regularly take a double Accusative.

Verbs of:—

asking, i.e. *interrogating*:	ἐρωτῶ, ἠρόμην.
asking, i.e. *petitioning*:	αἰτῶ (and compounds), πράσσω, εἰσπράσσω, πράσσομαι, *I demand, exact.*
concealing:	κρύπτω (ἀποκρύπτω).
teaching:	διδάσκω.
putting on or *off*:	ἐνδύω, ἐκδύω, ἀμφιέννυμι, περιβάλλομαι.
depriving:	ἀφαιροῦμαι, ἀποστερῶ, συλῶ.
saying or *doing anything good* or *ill*:	ἀγαθόν (κακόν, τι, τοῦτο, εὖ, καλῶς, κακῶς), λέγω, ἐρῶ, εἶπον, δρῶ, ποιῶ, ἐργάζομαι (rarely πράσσω).

Similarly: εὐλογῶ, ἐπαινῶ, ψεύδομαι, διαβάλλω, ὑβρίζω, ἀδικῶ, ἀντιποιῶ, βλάπτω, κωλύω, ἀναγκάζω.

οὐ τοῦτό σε ἐρωτῶ. ARISTOPH.
That's *not the question I'm asking you.*

πολλοί με σῖτον αἰτοῦσι, πολλοί δὲ ἱμάτια. XEN.
Many are asking me for food, many for clothes.

ἄλλους ταὐτὰ ταῦτα διδάσκω. PLAT.
I teach others these self-same subjects.

οὐδέν σε κρύψω. SOPH.
Naught will I hide from thee.

ἰδοὺ δ' Ἀπόλλων αὐτὸς ἐκδύων ἐμὲ
χρηστηρίαν ἐσθῆτα. AESCH.
And lo! Apollo's self divesting me
Of garb oracular.

ἀλλήλους τὰ ἔσχατα λέγουσιν. XEN.
They say the most atrocious things of one another.

οἱ μὲν πονηροὶ κακόν τι ἐργάζονται τοὺς ἀνθρώπους,
οἱ δ' ἀγαθοὶ ἀγαθόν. PLAT.
Bad men do harm to others, good men good.

DOUBLE ACCUSATIVE. 73

Note 1. The construction of the Double Accusative is much commoner in Greek than in Latin. Almost any Greek transitive verb can take an Accusative of the External Object, and some one of the many varieties of the Internal Object. The Internal Accusative is often a neuter pronoun, or an adjective agreeing with a suppressed substantive.

Μέλητός με ἐγράψατο τὴν γραφὴν ταύτην. PLAT.
Meletus brought this indictment against me.

In the Passive—

τὰς ἄλλας μάχας, ὅσας Πέρσαι ἡττήθησαν, ἐῶ. ISOCR.
I pass over all the other battles in which the Persians were defeated.

The poets, as might be expected, use great freedom with this construction, from Homer downwards.

χρόα νίζετο ἄλμην. *Od.* vi. 224.
He was washing the brine off his skin.
(He was washing his skin: he was washing off the brine.)

ἀλλ' οὐκ ἐάσει τοῦτό γ' ἡ δίκη σε. SOPH. *Ant.* 538.
Nay, Justice will not suffer thee to do this.

τοιοῦτον θράσος
αὐτή θ' ὁπλίζει. SOPH. *El.* 996.
Thou arm'st thyself in such boldness.

Note 2. In the passive Construction one accusative becomes the subject. *E. g.—*

πολλοὶ ἵππους ἀπεστέρηνται.
Many have been deprived of their horses.

The passive of εὖ, κακῶς, ποιεῖν is not εὖ etc. ποιεῖσθαι but εὖ etc. πάσχειν, and of εὖ etc. λέγειν not λέγεσθαι but ἀκούειν (cf. *bene, male audire*), *e.g.* μεγάλα, εὖ, παθεῖν, πολλὰ κακὰ ἀκούειν.

Note 3. Many of these verbs take other constructions, *e.g.* ἀναμιμνήσκω τινά τινος, αἰτῶ τι παρά τινος, ἀφαιροῦμαί τι τινος ἀγαθὸν ποιῶ σοι. λοιδορεῖν takes an accusative, λοιδορεῖσθαι a dative: μέμφομαι an accus. of thing and dative of person, τουτό σοι; also an accusative of person; also a dative alone of person.

§ 89. *THE EXTERNAL ACCUSATIVE.*

The Accusatives denote the direct object of a transitive Verb.

τὴν μάχην τοὺς βαρβάρους ἐνίκησεν. AESCHIN.
He conquered the barbarians in battle.

μάχην internal Accus., βαρβάρους external Accus.

Note 1. The Accusative depends almost universally on a Verb. But there are few cases in which it depends on a noun (generally a verbal adjective, or a noun of verbal character).

καί σε φύξιμος οὐδεὶς ἀθανάτων. SOPH. *Antig.* 789.
And none of the immortals is able to escape thee.

πόλεμος ἄπορα πόριμος. AESCH. *P. V.* 904.

τὸ πᾶν μῆχαρ οὔριος Ζεύς. AESCH. *Supp.* 594.

Perhaps we may add ἔξαρνοι τὰ ὡμολογημένα, ISAEUS v. 26; ἐπιστήμονες τὰ προσήκοντα, XEN. *Cyr.* 3. 3, 9; Σωκράτης τὰ μετέωρα φροντιστής, PL. *Apol.* II.; unless we regard the accusatives here as accusatives of respect.

The construction is not unknown to Latin—

Quid tibi hanc digito tactio est. PLAUT. *Poen.* v. 5. 29.

Reditum domum in patriam. LIV. xxx. 32.

On this construction see PEILE, *Primer of Philology*, ch. vii. 5.

Note 2. An Accusative stands in apposition not to the object of the verb, but to the state or act jointly denoted by the verb and its object. Very often this Accusative in Apposition has a proleptic force. See *Peculiarities of Apposition.*

αἰαῖ, κακῶν ὕψιστα δὴ κλύω τάδε,
αἴσχη τε Πέρσαις καὶ λιγέα κωκύματα. AESCH. *Pers.* 331.
*Woe! woe! the top of sorrow hear I now,
Shame to the Persians, and shrill lamentations.*

Other instances occur, AESCH. *Ag.* 225, *Cho.* 200, EUR. *Bacch.* 29, 250.

Cf. VERG. *Aen.* xi. 381, Proinde tona eloquium, solitum tibi·

§ 90. VERBS WHICH TAKE AN EXTERNAL ACCUSATIVE.

The following classes of Verbs should be noticed as taking an Accusative of the External Object.

1. Many Verbs of Emotion:

αἰδοῦμαι, *I revere.*
αἰσχύνομαι, *I feel awe or shame in the presence of.*
θαρρῶ, *I feel confidence in.*

ἐκπλήσσομαι, } *I am alarmed*
καταπλήσσομαι, } *at.*
φρίσσω, *I shudder at.* SOPH. *Ant.* 997.

αἰσχύνομαι τὸν πολύυμνον θεόν. EUR. *Ion*, 1074.
I am abashed in the presence of the god renowned in song.

τὸ τοιοῦτον σῶμα οἱ ἐχθροὶ θαρροῦσιν. PL. *Phaed.* 239.
The enemy feel confidence in such a body.

μὴ δύναμιν τῶν Ἀθηναίων καταπλαγῆτε. THUC. vi. 76.
Do not be dismayed at the power of the Athenians.

2. Many Verbs of Motion compounded with Prepositions, such verbs taking the meaning of their kindred transitives.

διαβαίνω, } *I cross.*
διέρχομαι, }
διαπλέω, *I sail across.*
περιέρχομαι, *I go about.*
περιπλέω, *I coast along.*
ἐκδιδράσκω, } *I run away from.*
ἀποδιδράσκω, }

μέτειμι, } *I pursue, go in*
μετέρχομαι, } *quest of.*
ἐκβαίνω, *I exceed.*
ἐξίστημι, *I avoid.*
ὑπερβάλλω, *I cross over surpass.*
ὑφίσταμαι, } *I undertake* (sus-
ὑποδύομαι, } cipio).
ὑποφεύγω, *I avoid, shirk.*

τὰ ἐπιτήδεια ἐκ Σήστου μετιόντες. XEN. *Hell.* ii. 1. 25.
Going in search of provisions from Sestos.

ὑπερέβαλον τὰ ὄρη. XEN. *An.* iv. 4. 23.
They crossed the mountains.

ὅταν οἱ ἄνδρες ἐκβῶσι τὴν ἡλικίαν, ἀφήσομέν που αὐτοὺς ἐλευθέρους. PL. *Rep.* 461.
As soon as the men exceed the prescribed limit of age we shall, I presume, set them free.

οἱ πρόγονοι οὐδένα πώποτε κίνδυνον ἐξέστησαν. DEM. 20. 10.
Our ancestors never shirked any danger.

Cf. VERG. *Aen.* v. 438, vim viribus exit (*i.e.* evitat).

τὸ τοὺς τυράννους εἰσιέναι. DEM. 418. 13.
To act the part of tyrants.

3. Many Compound Verbs, which in their composite form are equivalent to transitive Verbs:

δημαγωγεῖ τοὺς ἄνδρας. XEN. An. vii. 6. 4.
He wins men by popular acts.
τὸν ἑαυτοῦ πατέρα γηροτροφεῖ. DEM. 24. 203.
He nurses his father in his old age.
μὴ τὰ χείρω φιλονεικῆσαι. THUC. v. 111.
Not through contentiousness to choose the worse.
Cf. SOPH. Ant. 994, Schneidewin, w. note.
So οἰκονομῶ (τὸν βίον), *I manage, or regulate.*
συκοφαντῶ (τινά), *I calumniate, or accuse falsely.*
λογοποιῶ (συμφοράς), *I make up tales* (of troubles).
καταναυμαχῶ, *I overpower in naval warfare.*
καταπολεμῶ, *I overpower in war.*

4. Special Verbs.

γελῶ, *I ridicule* (τινά); δακρύω, *I weep for* (φίλους, *friends*), EUR. Frag.
φθάνω, *I anticipate* (τοὺς μέλλοντας, *those who are purposing*).
ζηλῶ, *I emulate* (τοὺς ἀγαθούς, *the good*).
φυλάσσομαι, } *I beware of* (τὸν κύνα, *the dog.*).
εὐλαβοῦμαι, }
ἀμύνομαι, *I defend myself against* (τοὺς πολεμίους).
τιμωροῦμαι, *I take vengeance on* (τὸν φονεύσαντα, *the murderer*).
βιάζομαι, *I force, win by force* (τὸν ἔσπλουν, *the entrance,* THUC. vii. 22).
σιωπῶ, *I pass over in silence* (τὰ δίκαια, *what is right*).
λανθάνω, *I elude the notice of* (τὸν διώκοντα, *the pursuer*).
προθυμοῦμαι, *I promote* (τὴν ξύμβασιν, *the treaty,* THUC. v. 17).

οἱ Ἀθηναῖοι τοὺς τῶν Συρακοσίων ἱππέας ἐφοβήθησαν.
The Athenians were afraid of the Syracusan cavalry.
ἀδύνατα ἦν τοὺς Λοκροὺς ἀμύνεσθαι. THUC. iv. 1.
It was impossible to keep off the Locrians.
τί φυλάξασθαί φημι δεῖν ἡμᾶς; DEM. de Pace iv.
What do I maintain we must guard against?
ὁ Κλεὼν ὑπέφευγε τὸν πλοῦν ... ὑφίσταται τὸν πλοῦν.
THUC. iv. 28.
Cleon was trying to back out of the expedition: he undertakes the expedition.

THE EXTERNAL ACCUSATIVE. 77

5. Ὄμνυμι and expressions *of swearing*, μά, οὐ μά, ναὶ μά, νή.

μὰ Δία, *nay, by Zeus.*
νὴ or ναὶ τὸν Δία, *yea, by Zeus.*
οὐ τὸν Δία, οὐ μὰ τὸν Δία, *nay, by Zeus.*
ὀμωμοκὼς τοὺς θεούς, *having sworn by the gods*, DEM. 301. 1.
οὐ μὰ τὸν Δί’, οὔ (in answers), *No, by Zeus, not,* etc.
οὐ μὰ τὸν Δί’, οὐ μὲν δή, *No, by Zeus, not so indeed.*

Note 1. The poets use great freedom in making Verbs transitive.

τοὺς γὰρ εὐσεβεῖς θεοὶ
θνῄσκοντας οὐ χαίρουσι.
At a good man's death
The gods rejoice not. See PEILE, *Primer of Philology*, p. 131.

So ᾖξεν χέρα, SOPH. *Ai.* 44 (Jebb's note); χορεύω θεόν, *I celebrate the god in the dance*, PIND. *Isth.* i. 7, SOPH. *Ant.* 1152; χορεύειν γάμους, EUR. *I. A.* 1047. So βαίνειν (προβαίνειν) πόδα.

Note 2. An Accusative is found after a compound expression which is equivalent to a Verb. Many accusatives in the poets may be thus explained.

καὶ πάννυχοι δὴ διάπλοον καθίστασαν
ναῶν ἄνακτες πάντα ναυτικὸν λεών. AESCH. *Pers.* 384.
So all night long the captains of ships were keeping afloat (or sailing in and out) *the whole naval host* (διαπ.—καθίστασαν =one verb).

τίν’ ἀεί τάκεις οἰμωγάν ’Αγαμέμνονα; SOPH. *El.*
With what melting lament bemoanest thou Agamemnon?
(τάκεις—οἰμωγάν=one verb.)

εἰ δέ μ’ ὧδ’ ἀεὶ λόγους
ἐξῆρχες (λόγους ἐξῆρχες=προσεφώνεις, Jebb).
SOPH. *El.* 556.
If thou hadst been ever accosting me thus.

Cf. AESCH. *Ag.* 788; SOPH. *O.C.* 583.
See Schneidewin on SOPH. *Ant.* 212.
Cf. TERENCE, *Hauton, Prol.* 41, Mea causa causam hanc iustam esse *animum-inducite.*

Note 3. Poetical and comic use of the Accusative with verbs of looking (an Internal Accusative).

There are many Homeric phrases.

πῦρ ὀφθαλμοῖσι δεδορκώς, *Od.* xix. 446 (looking, *i.e.* flashing fire).

So Ἄρην βλέπειν, δέρκεσθαι, ἀλκὴν ὁρᾶν,
Ἄρη δεδορκότων. AESCH. *Sept. c. Theb.* 553.

Aristophanes is very fond of this idiom.

πρὸς τῶν θεῶν, ἄνθρωπε, ναύφρακτον βλέπεις.
ARIST. *Ach.* 95.
'*fore heaven, fellow, thou look'st an ironclad.*

So βλέπειν νᾶπυ (mustard), ὄμφακας (sour grapes).

Cf. "to look black," "look daggers," and *Hamlet*, "I will speak daggers." "He speaks holiday, he smells April and May," *Merry Wives*, iii. 2.

§ 91.   *THE GENITIVE.*

Preliminary note on the Genitive.

The Greek Genitive is the case of Connexion and its opposite, dis-Connexion or Separation. The Genitive proper denotes the class (γένος) to which a thing belongs. Thus νόμισμα ἀργυρίου, *a coin of silver;* the coin belongs to the class silver. Both in etymology and signification the Genitive is akin to an adjective. (See MAX MÜLLER, *Lectures on the Science of Language*, i. 105; second edition.) The Ablative, on the other hand, denotes that from which a thing is removed. The signification of the lost Ablative has passed into the Genitive. But in the Greek Genitive we can never, perhaps, be sure where we have a strictly Ablative meaning, for as the Genitive denotes Connexion, by a natural law of association, it also denotes the opposite, dis-Connexion, *i.e.* Separation. Further, Connexion (or Relation) is so elastic a conception, that the usages of the Genitive have, by a series of loose analogies, been almost indefinitely extended. This is what we should expect when we consider the popular and unscientific growth of Syntax. It is not possible to tabulate all the usages of the Genitive, or to avoid cross-divisions.

POSSESSIVE GENITIVE.

The Partitive Genitive so-called is a misnomer, due to a confusion of thought. The Genitive denotes the whole, that on which it depends denotes the part. Lastly, as the Accusative essentially depends on a Verb or Verbal notion, so the Genitive essentially depends on a Substantive or Substantival notion.

§ 92.   POSSESSIVE GENITIVE.

The Genitive denotes the Possessor, that to which a thing belongs; with

A. Nouns and Adjectives, οἰκεῖος, ἴδιος (*own, peculiar, or belonging to*); ἱερός, *consecrated to;* and their opposite, ἀλλότριος. These also (ἱερός very rarely) take a Dative.

Nouns, etc.

ἡ τοῦ πατρὸς οἰκία or ἡ οἰκία τοῦ πατρός.
The father's house.

ἡ πόλις ἁπάντων τῶν πολιτῶν κοινή ἐστίν.   ANDOK.
The city is common to all the citizens.

ἱρὸς γὰρ οὗτος τῶν κατὰ χθονὸς θεῶν.   EUR.
Consecrated is that one to the nether gods.

B. Verbs.

οἱ Πέρσαι τὴν Ἀσίαν ἑαυτῶν ποιοῦνται.   XEN.
The Persians are claiming Asia as their own.

τίς ἐσθ᾽ ὁ χῶρος; τοῦ θεῶν νομίζεται;   SOPH. O. C. 38.
What spot is this? To which of the gods is it held sacred (considered to belong)?

Note 1. The Neuter Article with the Genitive is freely used: τὰ τῶν θεῶν, τὰ τῶν Ἑλλήνων (τὰ Ἑλληνικά), *the affairs, concerns, lands, history,* etc., *of the Greeks;* τὸ τῆς ὀλιγαρχίας, *the nature of oligarchy,* or *oligarchy.*

Note 2. In certain familiar phrases there is an ellipse of the word on which the Genitive depends: ἐν Ἅιδου, *in Hades;* ἐς Ἅιδου, *to Hades;* εἰς διδασκάλου, *to the master's* (*sc.* house).

Note 3. The Genitive denotes the person or thing to which something is suitable or becoming (it is a sign of, a mark of, it requires, etc.).

τοῦτο ἔστι παίζοντος. PLAT. *Apol.* 14.
This is (the conduct) of one who is jesting (this is mere banter).
ἔστιν ἄρα δικαίου ἀνδρὸς βλάπτειν καὶ ὁντινοῦν ἀνθρώπων;
PLAT. *Rep.* 1. 335.
Is it the part of a just man to (will a just man) injure any one whomsoever?
πολλῆς ἀνοίας καὶ τὸ θηρᾶσθαι κενά. SOPH. *El.* 1054.
It shows (it is) great madness even to engage in an idle quest.

In expressions of sonship the substantive on which the Genitive depends may be omitted : Σωκράτης ὁ Σωφρονίσκου, Νικίας ὁ Νικηράτου, Θουκυδίδης ὁ Ὀλόρου. More briefly, Μιλτιάδης Κίμωνος. Poet., Διὸς Ἄρτεμις, *Artemis daughter of Zeus;* Ὀϊλῆος ταχὺς Αἴας, *Aias swift son of Oileus.* HOM.

Obs.—This is sometimes called the Genitive of Origin, or Descent, or Source. It is a genitive of the possessor, or of the class, for, as Max Müller points out, it is equally correct to say ὁ υἱὸς τοῦ πατρός, as to say ὁ πατὴρ τοῦ υἱοῦ.

πατρὸς λέγεται Κῦρος γενέσθαι Καμβύσου.
XEN. *Cyr.* 1. 2. 1.
It is said that Cyrus was the son of Cambyses.
So in poetry, φῦναι, βλαστεῖν, τραφῆναί τινος.

§ 93. *GENITIVE OF MATERIAL OR CONTENTS.*

The Genitive denotes the *Material* of which a thing consists, or the *Contents* of a thing.

With Nouns, etc. :—

νόμισμα ἀργυρίου (= νόμισμα ἀργυροῦν).
A coin of silver (Old Eng. adj. *a silvern coin*).
ὁρῶσι σωροὺς σίτου, ξύλων, λίθων. XEN. *Hell.* iv. 4.12.
They see piles of grain, timber, stones.
σῶμα δειλαίας σποδοῦ. SOPH. *Elect.* 758.
A body of pitiable ashes.

B. With Verbs :—

οἱ στέφανοι ῥόδων ἦσαν ἀλλ' οὐ χρυσίου. DEM.
The wreaths were of roses, and not of gold.
θεμέλιοι παντοίων λίθων ὑπόκεινται. THUC.
The substructions were made of stones of all sorts.
Free and poetical uses :—
φωνὴ ὀρθίων κωκυμάτων. SOPH. *Antig.* 1206.
A voice of shrill laments.
πνοὴ φοινίου σταλάγματος. SOPH. *Antig.* 1239.
A gasp of bloody dew.

Expressions such as Ἀθηνῶν πόλις, *the city of Athens* (contrast with "urbs Roma"); Τροίης πτολίεθρον, *the city of Troy*, are poetical.

§ 94. *GENITIVE OF AMOUNT.*

Another aspect of the Genitive of Material is where it denotes the *Amount* of *Space, Time, Money.*

ὀκτὼ σταδίων τεῖχος. THUC.
A wall of eight stades.
τριῶν ἡμερῶν ὁδός. XEN.
A journey of ten days (a ten days' journey).
τριάκοντα ταλάντων οὐσία.
A property of thirty talents.
ἐπιτήδεια τριῶν ἡμερῶν ἔλαβον. XEN. *Cyr.* v. 3. 35.
They took provisions for three days.
γαμεῖν δεῖ ἐπειδὰν ἐτῶν ᾖ τις τριάκοντα. PLAT. *Legg.* 721.
A man should marry when he is thirty years old.
πυραμὶς λιθίνη τὸ μὲν εὖρος ἑνὸς πλέθρου, τὸ δὲ ὕψος δύο πλέθρων. XEN. *Anab.* 3. 4. 9.
A stone pyramid in breadth one plethron, in height two plethra.
χιλίων δραχμῶν δίκην φεύγω. DEM. 55. 25.
I am defendant in a suit involving a thousand drachmae.[1]

---
[1] With the Genitive of Amount may be connected the Genitive of Value.

§ 95. GENITIVE OF PLENTY OR WANT.

With the Genitive of Material may be associated the Genitive after words of Plenty or Want.

A. Adjectives and Adverbs : μεστός, πλήρης, ἔμπλεως, πλούσιος, ἐνδεής, πένης, κενός, ἔρημος, γυμνός, καθαρός, ἅλις.

ποταμὸς πλήρης ἰχθύων. XEN.
A river full of fishes.

τὸ τῆς Λήθης πεδίον κενόν ἐστι δένδρων.
PLAT.
The plain of Lethe is bare of trees.

τύραννος πολλῶν φόβων καὶ ἐρώτων μεστός.
PLAT. *Rep.* 579.
A despot filled with many fears and desires.

So with a Substantive: ἀπορία σίτου, *scarcity of provisions.*

B. Verbs : πίμπλημι, ἐμπίμπλημι, πληρῶ, πλήθω, γέμω, μεστῶ, εὐπορῶ, δέομαι, δεῖ, σπανίζω (κέχρημαι, κεχρημένος, Epic and poetical).

τὰ βιβλία Ἀναξαγόρου γέμει τούτων τῶν λόγων.
PLAT.
The books of Anaxagoras teem with these statements.

ἐσπάνιζον τροφῆς τοῖς πολλοῖς. THUC.
They were in want of provisions for the majority.

παῦσαι, πρὶν ὀργῆς κἀμὲ μεστῶσαι. SOPH. *Ant.* 28.
Peace! ere thou fill me too with wrath.

ὁ παρὼν καιρὸς πολλῆς φροντίδος καὶ βουλῆς δεῖται.
The present occasion requires much thought and counsel

οὐ πόνων κεχρήμεθα. EUR. *Med.* 334.
We have no lack of troubles.

Obs. λέκτρα πίμπλαται δακρύμασιν. AESCH. *Pers.* 100.
Their couches are filled (watered) with tears.

Here the dative of Instrument is used.

Note. The constructions of δεῖ, δέω :—

οὐ πολλοῦ πόνου με δεῖ,
I have no need of much trouble.
ποίας μοι δεῖ φροντίδος; SOPH. *Elect.* 612.
What care need I?
πολλοῦ δέω ἐμαυτόν γε ἀδικήσειν. PLAT. *Apol.* 17.
I am far from intending to wrong myself.

Common phrases with δεῖ are πολλοῦ δεῖ, *far from it;* or, πολλοῦ δέω (personally used), *nothing of the sort;* ὀλίγου δεῖ, *there wants little, all but;* ὀλίγου, (alone) *almost;* ὀλίγου ἐμαυτοῦ ἐπελαθόμην, PLAT. *Apol.* i., *I wellnigh forgot myself (who I was).* So μικροῦ, *within a little, almost.*

ὀκτὼ ἀποδέοντες τριακόσιοι = 292. THUC. iv. 38.
δυοῖν δέοντες πεντήκοντα = 48.

§ 96. *THE PARTITIVE GENITIVE (SO CALLED).*

The Partitive Genitive so called (the Genitive is the whole, the word on which it depends is the part) is used :—

A. With any part of speech denoting participation.

πολλοὶ τῶν 'Αθηναίων.
Many of the Athenians.

τὰ δύο μέρη τῆς στρατιᾶς.
Two-thirds of the army.

'Αθηναίων ὁ βουλόμενος.
Any one of the Athenians who wishes.

τῶν πολεμίων οἱ μὲν ἀπώλοντο, οἱ δὲ ἔφυγιν.
Of the enemy some fell, while others escaped.

τῶν πολιτῶν τις, οὔτις στρατοῦ. SOPH. *Ai.* (twice.)
One of the citizens, no one in the host.

ἀνὴρ τῶν ῥητόρων (ARIST. *Eq.* 423, ἀνήρ = τίς).
One of the speakers; so, δήμου ἀνήρ, *a man of the people* (XEN. *Cyr.* ii. 2. 22).

ἡ ναῦς ἄριστα ἔπλει παντὸς τοῦ στρατοπέδου. LYS.
The ship was the best sailer in the whole squadron.

B. Especially after adjectives denoting participation and their opposites :— μέτοχος, ἀμέτοχος, ἰσόμοιρος, ἄκληρος, ἄμοιρος, ἄγευστος.

μέτοχος ἂν εἴης τοῦ φόνου δράσας τάδε. EUR.
Thou wouldst this bloodshed share shouldst thou do this—(particeps sis caedis).

C. With Verbs, especially with those of giving or taking a share.

μετέχω, μετεστί (μοι), μεταλαμβάνω, I have, or take, a share; μεταποιοῦμαι, I claim a share; μεταδίδωμί (τινι), κοινωνῶ (τίνι), I give a share (to a person, τινί), προσήκει μοι, I have a concern in.

ἀνθρώπου ψυχὴ τοῦ θείου μετέχει. PLAT.
The soul of man partakes of divinity.

οὐ μεταδώσουσι ἡμῖν τῆς ἀρχῆς Λακεδαιμόνιοι.
              HEROD.
The Lacedaemonians will not give us a share in the empire.

οὐδὲν προσήκει μοι τῆς αἰτίας ταύτης. ANTIPH.
I have nothing to do with this accusation (i.e. it does not concern me).

D. Also Verbs of eating, tasting, or drinking, or any Verb denoting participation in a thing :—πίνω, ἐσθίω, γεύω, γεύομαι.

πίνω τοῦ οἴνου, ἐσθίω κρεῶν.
I drink wine, I eat meat.

τῆς γῆς ἔτεμον.
They ravaged (some of) the land.

πέμπει τῶν Λυδῶν.
He sends some (of the) Lydians.

ὅσοι ἔφαγον τῶν κηρίων πάντες ἄφρονες ἐγίγνοντο. XEN.
All who ate of the honeycombs soon became mad.

THE PARTITIVE GENITIVE. 85

The partitive τι may be inserted, cf. ἀπολαύειν τί τινος, *to enjoy some advantage from some source.*

Note 1. Many of these verbs are used transitively and take an Accusative (denoting "an object completely overpowered," J. GRIMM). πίνω οἶνον, λαγχάνω τι, *I attain something*, τινός, *a share of something ;* so πλεῖστον μέρος τινὸς μετέχειν, *to have the greatest part of something* (where μέρος is a whole).

Note 2. Instead of a neuter singular with a partitive Genitive the adjective of certain words (ἥμισυς, πολύς, πλεῖστος, λοιπός) often agrees in gender with the genitive : ὁ ἥμισυς, or ὁ λοιπὸς, τοῦ χρόνου ; τοῦ χρόνου ὁ πλεῖστος, πολλὴ τῆς χώρας (XEN. *Cyr.* iii. 2. 2). Cf. THUC. i. 2, τῆς γῆς ἡ ἀρίστη.

Note 3. Many Adverbs of place are joined with a partitive Genitive : ποῦ γῆς ; ubi terrarum ? πανταχοῦ γῆς, οὐδαμοῦ γῆς· ἄλλοι ἀλλῇ τῆς πόλεως, THUC. ii. 4 ; πηνίκα τῆς ἡμέρας ; *at what time of day ?* πόρρω τῆς ἡμέρας, τῶν νυκτῶν, ὀψὲ τῆς ὥρας.

Many such phrases occur in the poets :—

ποῦ γνώμης ποτ' εἶ ; SOPH. *Antig.* 42.
What is thy purpose ?

ποῦ ποτ' εἶ φρενῶν ; SOPH. *Elect.* 390 (see 404).
What is thy mysterious intent ?

ποῖ λόγων ἔλθω ; SOPH. *Elect.* 1174.
What words shall I utter ?

γαίας ὀρύξας ἔνθα, κ.τ.λ. SOPH. *Aiax* 659.
Hiding it in the earth where, etc.

οἷ μ' ἀτιμίας ἄγεις ; SOPH. *Elect.* 1035.
To what infamy art thou leading me ?

Note 4. The neuter of a pronoun or adjective, or adverb, is not unknown to Greek, but not so common as in Latin (paullum sapientiae, parum sapientiae, aliquid divitiarum, quicquid deorum, etc.). τὶ στασιασμοῦ, THUC. iv. 130 ; ἀμήχανον εὐδαιμονίας, PLAT. *Apol.* ; ἄτοπα τῆς σμικρολογίας, PLAT. *Theaetet.* 175 ; ἐπὶ μέγα δυνάμεως χωρεῖν, THUC. i. 118 ; ἐπὶ πλεῖστον ἀνθρώπων, THUC. i. 1 ; ἐν παντὶ κακοῦ, PLAT. *Rep.* 579 ; ἐν τῷ συμφορᾶς ; SOPH. *Antig.* 1229.

Note 5. The word on which a partitive Genitive depends has often to be supplied :—

ἐμὲ θὲς τῶν πεπεισμένων. PLAT. *Rep.* 424.
Set me down as one of those who are convinced.
Σόλων τῶν ἑπτὰ σοφιστῶν ἐκλήθη. ISOCR. *Antid.* 235.
Solon was called one of the Seven Sages.

§ 97. *GENITIVE OF CONNEXION.*

The following Verbs denoting *Connexion* take a Genitive :—

A. Verbs signifying *to aim at, hit* or *attain, miss.*

στοχάζομαι, *aim at ;* ὀρέγομαι, *reach out towards, strive for ;* τυγχάνω, κυρῶ, ἐφικνοῦμαι, *hit, secure, obtain, attain ;* ἀποτυγχάνω, ἁμαρτάνω, *miss, lose ;* ψεύδομαι, σφάλλομαι, *I am disappointed, balked of.* (*N.B.* κιχάνω generally takes an Accusative.)

B. *Catch hold of, touch, cling to* (*be separated from,* see Gen. of *separation*).

λαμβάνομαι (and compounds with ἐπί, ἀντί), ἅπτομαι, ἐφάπτομαι, θιγγάνω, *I catch hold of, touch, grasp ;* ἔχομαι, *I cling to,* etc. (see examples), ἀντέχομαι, *I cling to, uphold.*

C. *Make trial of, begin, have experience in.*

πειρῶ, πειρῶμαι, *I try, attempt ;* ἄρχω, ἄρχομαι, *I begin ;* ἐμπείρως ἔχω, *I am experienced in.*

D. Verbs of the senses : *hear, smell, taste, touch* (see **B.**), *enjoy.* (But verbs of *seeing* take an Accusative.)

ἀκούω, *I hear ;* ἀκροῶμαι, *listen to, attend lectures ;* ὀσφραίνομαι, *smell* (trans.) ; ὄζω, *smell* (neut.) ; γεύω, *give a taste of ;* γεύομαι, *taste ;* ἀπολαύω, *enjoy.* (The last two verbs more often metaphorically than literally.)

E. *Perceive, understand, remember, forget.*

αἰσθάνομαι, *I perceive ;* πυνθάνομαι, *learn by inquiry ;* ξυνίημι, *understand ;* μιμνήσκομαι, *remember ;* ἐπιλανθάνομαι, *forget.*

F. *Care for, long for, desire, neglect, despise.*

μέλει (μοι), ἐπιμελοῦμαι, I *care for;* πεινῶ, διψῶ, *hunger, thirst after* (literally and metaphorically); ἐρῶ, *love, long for;* ἐντρέπομαι, *respect;* ὀλιγωρῶ, ἀμελῶ, *disregard, neglect;* καταφρονῶ, *despise.*

A. Examples:—

δεῖ στοχάσασθαι διανοίας. ISAEUS.
We ought to aim at intellect.

τοῦ σκοποῦ ἁμαρτὼν τοῦ παιδὸς ἔτυχεν. ANTIPH.
Missing the mark, he hit the child.

ἐφικνεῖται τῆς ἀρετῆς. ISOCR.
He attains unto virtue.

πάντες ὥστε τοξόται σκοποῦ
τοξεύετ' ἀνδρὸς τοῦδε. SOPH. *Antig.* 1033. Cf. 1084.
Ye all, as archers at a mark,
Are shooting at this heart.

τί μοι τῶν δυσφόρων ἐφίει; SOPH. *Elect.* 141.
Why art thou aiming at the insupportable?

φίλης γὰρ προξένου κατήνυσαν. SOPH. *Elect.* 1451.
They met with a kind hostess.

στρατὸς κυρήσει νοστίμου σωτηρίας. AESCH. *Pers.* 793.
The host shall meet with returning deliverance (*i.e.* a safe return).

Obs. ἐπιτυγχάνω, προστυγχάνω, *to come across, fall in with* one, take a Dative.

B. Examples:—

N.B.—λαμβάνω, κρατῶ take an Accusative of the person or thing seized, and a Genitive of the thing seized.

τὸν λύκον τῶν ὤτων κρατῶ.
I get hold of the wolf by the ears.

So ἄγειν χειρός, *to lead by the hand.*

ἔλαβον τῆς ζώνης τὸν Ὀρόντην. XEN. *An.* i. 6. 10.
They seized Orontes by his girdle.

C. Examples :—

Κῦρος ἦρχε τοῦ λόγου ὧδε. XEN.
Cyrus began the conversation as follows (i.e. *was the first to speak*).

Ξενοφῶν τοῦ λόγου ἤρχετο ὧδε. XEN.
Xenophon began his speech as follows.

N.B.—ἄρχειν λόγων, *to be the first to speak;* ἄρχεσθαι λόγων, *to begin one's speech.*

ἀποπειρώμενος ἡμῶν ἐγράψω τὴν γραφὴν ταύτην.
PLAT.
You were making trial of me when you brought this indictment.

D. Examples :—

βροντῆς ἀκούσας μηδαμῶς πόρρω φύγῃς. *Philemon.*
When you hear thunder by no means run away.

τί δῆτα κλάεις; κρομμύων ὀσφραίνομαι. AR.
Why are you weeping then? I smell onions.

So ὀσφραίνεσθαι τῆς τυραννίδος. AR. *Lys.* 619.

εὐθὺς δὲ δείσας ἐμπύρων ἐγενόμην. SOPH. *Ant.* 1065.
Straightway in terror I made trial of burnt-sacrifice.

ὅποι ἂν ἔλθω, λέγοντος ἐμοῦ ἀκροάσονται οἱ νέοι.
PLAT. *Ap.* xxvii.
Wherever I go young men will listen to my words.

Note. With ἀκροῶμαι cf. the use of ἀποδέχομαι (*I accept from, approve*): μὴ ταῦτα ἀποδέχεσθε ᾽Αγυράτου (LYS. 13. 83), *do not accept this statement from* (a Genitive of Separation) *Agyratus.* So ἀποδέχεσθαί τινος λέγοντος. ἀπολαύω τινός (*I enjoy,* literally and figuratively).

ὄζω, *I smell of.*

αὗται μὲν ὄζουσ' ἀμβροσίας καὶ νέκταρος. AR. *Ach.* 196.
These smell of ambrosia and nectar.

Verbs of perception also mean *to hear from,* as well as *to hear.*
τοιαῦτα τοῦ παρόντος ἔκλυον. SOPH. *El.* 424.
Thus much was I hearing from one who was present.

GENITIVE OF CONNEXION.

See *Ai*. 318. So—
εἰδέναι σου πρώτιστα χρῄζω. SOPH. *El.* 668.
Fain would I first and foremost know from thee.
So with a sentence :—
τούτων ἄκουε τί λέγουσιν.
Hear from these men what they say.
But more usually a preposition (παρά, πρός, ἐξ) is added.

E. Examples :—
ἄνθρωπος ὢν μέμνησο τῆς κοινῆς τύχης. MENAND.
Being a man, remember the common lot.
ὀλίγου ἐμαυτοῦ ἐπελαθόμην. PLAT.
I almost forgot myself (who I was).
οὐκ ᾐσθάνοντο προσιόντων τῶν πολεμίων. XEN.
They were not aware of the approach of the enemy.
ἐπύθοντο τῆς Πύλου κατειλημμένης. THUC.
They heard of the capture of Pylos.

F. Examples :—
τί ἡμῖν τῆς τῶν πολλῶν δόξης μέλει ; PLAT.
What care we for the opinion of the world ?
πείθω ὑμᾶς μήτε σωμάτων ἐπιμελεῖσθαι μήτε χρημάτων. PLAT.
I try to persuade you to care neither for the body nor for money.
πεινῶ χρημάτων, ἐπαίνου, XEN. ἀγαθῶν, PLAT.
I hunger after (i.e. *long for*) *money, praise, good things.*
So διψῶ, PLAT. *Rep.* 562 C.
τοῦ θανάτου καὶ κινδύνου ὠλιγώρησε. PLAT.
He disregarded death and danger.

Note 1. μέλει and μεταμέλει take a genitive of thing, and dative of person.
μέλει μοι τούτου.
I care for this, hoc mihi curae est.
μεταμέλει μοι τούτου.
I repent of this ; huius rei me poenitet.

Note 2. Adjectives with these significations are found with the Genitive :—

ἕδραν παντὸς εὐαγῆ στρατοῦ. AESCH. *Pers.* 465.
A throne in full view of all the armada.

ἐπήβολος φρενῶν. SOPH. *Antig.* 492.
Possessed of reason (compos mentis).

Note 3. In the following examples observe the various meanings of ἔχομαι :—

τῶν 'Εννέα ὁδῶν ἐκράτησαν.
They obtained possession of the Nine Roads. THUC.

τῆς μὲν γνώμης, ὦ 'Αθηναῖοι, ἀεὶ τῆς αὐτῆς ἔχομαι. THUC.
I hold, Athenians, to the same unchanged opinion ever.

ἕπονται ἐχόμενοι τῶν ἁρμάτων. XEN.
They follow, coming next to the chariots.

ὁ πληγεὶς ἀεὶ τῆς πληγῆς ἔχεται. DEM. *Phil.* 1. 10.
The boxer who has been struck ever follows the blow.

πάντες κοινῇ τῆς σωτηρίας ἔχεσθε. XEN. *Anab.* vi. 3. 17.
All together provide for your safety.

With ἔχομαι compare the parallel meanings of εἰμί. τῆς αὐτῆς γνώμης εἶναι, THUC. v. 46. τῶν αὐτῶν λόγων εἶναι, PLAT. *Gorg.* 489 (*to keep to the same tale*).

§ 98. *SUBJECTIVE AND OBJECTIVE GENITIVE.*

ὁ φόβος τῶν πολεμίων.
The fear of the enemy.

This Genitive of Connexion is naturally ambiguous. It may mean either (1) the fear which the enemy feels. Here τῶν πολεμίων is *Subjective*, being equivalent to the subject of the verb, and the sentence = οἱ πολέμιοι φοβοῦνται (ἡμᾶς) : or (2) the fear (which we feel) of or for the enemy. Here τῶν πολεμίων is *Objective*, being equivalent to the object of a transitive verb, ἡμεῖς φοβούμεθα τοὺς πολεμίους.

οἱ ἄνθρωποι διὰ τὸ αὑτῶν (Subjective Gen.) δέος τοῦ θανάτου καταψεύδονται, PLAT. *Phaed.* 85 (=αὐτοὶ δεδιότες τὸν θάνατον).
Men, by reason of their fear of death, tell lies.
διὰ τὴν τοῦ ἀνέμου (Subjective) ἄπωσιν τῶν ναυαγίων (Objective). THUC. vii. 34.
In consequence of the wind driving the wrecks into the open sea.

The Objective Genitive represents usually an object in the Accusative or Genitive after a verb, more rarely a Dative.

Acc. διὰ Παυσανίου μῖσος, THUC. i. 96. πόθος τοῦ ἀποθανόντος.

Gen. ἐπιθυμία χρημάτων, ἐπιμελεία τῶν πραγμάτων.

Dat. ἐμμονὴ τοῦ κακοῦ, PLAT. *Gorg.* 479. Cf. ἐμμένειν τῷ κακῷ. πατρὸς τιμωρός κἀμοῦ ταλαίνης, SOPH. *Elect.* 811.

The following may be regarded as free uses of the Objective Genitive :—λύμη βίου, SOPH. *Elect.* 1195, *outrage on life;* δυσμενῶν θήρα, SOPH. *Ai.* 564, *hunting the foe.* So πεῖρα ἐχθρῶν, SOPH. *Ai.* 2, *an attempt on,* or *against, one's enemies;* τὸ τῶν Μεγαρέων ψήφισμα, THUC. i. 140, *decree against the Megarians* (where the preposition περί would have been more usual.)

§ 99. *GENITIVE OF TIME AND PLACE.*

The Genitive denotes the time within which anything takes place. The Genitive is the whole, the time is either indefinite, or recurring. νυκτός, *by night;* τῆς ἡμέρας, *by day;* τοῦ αὐτοῦ θέρους, *during the same summer;* τοῦ λοιποῦ, *for the future;* ἑκάστου ἔτους, *each year;* τρὶς τοῦ ἐνιαυτοῦ, *thrice in the year.*

N.B.—With the Article the Genitive is distributive.

Σωκράτης τὸ αὐτὸ ἱμάτιον ἠμφίεστο θέρους τε καὶ χειμῶνος. XEN.
Socrates wore the same mantle summer and winter.

δραχμὴν ἐλάμβανε τῆς ἡμέρας (or τῆς ἡμέρας ἑκάστης).
He used to receive a drachma a day (each day).

Note 1. τῆς αὐτῆς ἡμέρας or τῇ αὐτῇ ἡμέρᾳ (often with small difference, MADVIG); τοῦ αὐτοῦ θέρους and ἐν τῷ αὐτῷ θέρει (THUC. iv. 133); τοῦ λοιποῦ or τὸ λοιπόν, *for the future*.

So ἄλλης ἡμέρας, SOPH. *El.* 690, *on another day:* οὐ μακροῦ χρόνου, SOPH. *El.* 478, *within no long while:* τοῦ λοιποῦ χρόνου, SOPH. *El.* 817, *for the future:* ἄκρας νυκτός, SOPH. *Ai.* 285, *at dead midnight:* τῆς πάροιθεν εὐφρόνης, AESCH. *Pers.* 182, *during the past night.*

Note 2. The Genitive also denotes the space within which anything takes place (a very rare and poetical, chiefly an Epic, usage).

ἡμερεύοντας ξένους
μακρᾶς κελεύθου. AESCH. *Ch.* 705.
Guests who have been spending the day
On a long journey.

Cf. the Homeric πεδίοιο ἰέναι, πρήσσειν, etc.

Note 3. The ordinary prose Genitive of *place* is either the possessive, or the (so-called) partitive Genitive. Observe that it takes the Article :—

ἐστράτευσαν τῆς Ἀρκαδίας ἐς Παρρασίους. THUC. v. 33.
They marched against the Parrhasians in Arcadia.

Note 4. To the genitive of place, however, belong certain prose usages.

ἐπετάχυνον τῆς ὁδοῦ τοὺς σχολαίτερον προσιόντας.
THUC. iv. 47.
They were hastening on the way those who were advancing slowly.

ἐπορεύοντο τοῦ πρόσω. XEN. *An.* v. 4. 30.
They were marching onwards, forwards.

Cf. προκόπτειν τῆς ἀρχῆς, THUC. iv. 60. ὑπάγειν τῆς ὁδοῦ, etc. προλαμβάνειν τῆς φυγῆς, THUC. iv. 33.

§ 100.   *GENITIVE OF VALUE.*

The Genitive of Value goes with Verbs of *Estimating, Buying,* and *Selling* (cf. Genitive of Amount).

Value or Estimate : ἀξιῶ, *judge worthy;* τάσσω, *rate* or *value;* τιμῶ, *value, assess* (τιμῶμαι).
Buy : πρίαμαι, *I buy;* ὠνοῦμαι, *I buy.*
Sell : πωλῶ, *I offer for sale;* ἀποδίδομαι, *I sell.*

δόξα χρημάτων οὐκ ὠνητή.   ISAEUS.
Reputation is not to be purchased with money.

οὐκ ἂν ἀπεδόμην πολλοῦ τὰς ἐλπίδας.   PLAT.
I would not have sold my hopes for much.

τιμᾶται μοι ὁ ἀνὴρ θανάτου.   PLAT.
My accuser proposes death as my penalty.

χρυσᾶ χαλκείων διαμείβεσθαι νοεῖς.   PL. *Symp.* 218 C.
You are intending to exchange golden for copper.

Note. Verbs of buying more rarely, and only in poetry, take a dative of the price paid. See EUR. *Hel.* 885, *Med.* 233.

Free use of the Genitive of Value.

τίς μεταβάλοιτ' ὧδε σιγὰν λόγων.   SOPH. *El.* 1262.
(Cf. AESCH. *P. V.* 987.)
Who would change thus silence for words?

ἀντίσταθμον τοῦ θηρὸς κορήν.   SOPH. *El.* 571.
A daughter weighed in the balance against a wild beast.

καίτοι ταλάντου ταῦτ' ἔμαθεν Ὑπέρβολος.   ARIST. *Nub.* 876.
And yet Hyperbolus was taught this for a talent.

ἔστι μοι θυγάτηρ γάμου ὡραία.   XEN. *Cyr.* iv. 6, 9.
I have a daughter ripe for marriage.

Under the Genitive of Value may come the Adjectives with their Adverbs :—ἄξιος, ἀνάξιος.

§ 101.   *CAUSAL GENITIVE.*

The Causal Genitive (so called) goes with verbs (and other words) denoting emotion. It is probably a Genitive of Connexion or Relation, meaning *with regard to, in connexion with.*

θαυμάζω, I wonder at or admire; εὐδαιμονίζω, I congratulate; οἰκτείρω, I pity; ὀργίζομαι, I am angry; φθονῶ, I envy or grudge; ζηλῶ, I envy (in good sense) or praise; μακαρίζω, I felicitate; ἄγαμαι, I wonder at, admire.

ζηλῶ σε τοῦ νοῦ, τῆς δὲ δειλίας στυγῶ. SOPH.
I praise thee for thy wit, but for thy cowardice I loathe thee.

εὐδαιμονίζω σε τοῦ τρόπου. PLAT.
I congratulate you on your disposition.

φεῦ, τῆς ἀνοίας ὥς σ' ἐποικτείρω πάλαι. SOPH. *El.* 920.
Fie! how I have been pitying thee this long while for thy folly.

(τῆς ἀνοίας may go with φεῦ.)

θράσους τοῦδ' οὐκ ἀλύξεις. SOPH. *El.* 627.
For this daring thou shalt not escape.

εἴπερ τι κλάεις τῶν 'Ορεστείων κακῶν. SOPH. *El.* 1117.
If thou hast a tear for the woes of Orestes.

Note 1. A similar Genitive is used in exclamations:—

φεῦ τοῦ ἀνδρός, *woe for*, or, *fie on the man!* ὦ Ζεῦ βασιλεῦ τῆς λεπτότητος τῶν φρενῶν, AR. *Nub.* 153, *Royal Zeus! what subtlety of wit!* οἴμοι τῆς τύχης, ὦ μακάριον τῆς φύσεως, etc., σχετλία τόλμης, EUR. *Al.* 741. ὦ τάλαιν' ἐγὼ σέθεν, SOPH. *El.* 1210, *ah, woe is me on thy account.* ὤμοι γέλωτος, SOPH. *Ai.* 367, *ah me for the mockery.* Curtius compares *O des Leides.*

Note 2. Τοῦ, with the Infinitive, denoting the Aim or Purpose of an action (Final), seems to be a Causal Genitive.

Μίνως τὸ λῃστικὸν ἐκ τῆς θαλάσσης τοῦ τὰς προσόδους μᾶλλον ἰέναι αὐτῷ. THUC. i. 4.
Minos used to sweep piracy from the sea for the sake of his revenues coming in to him.

Cf. XEN. *Cyr.* i. 6. 40; SOPH. *Phil.* 197. This construction occurs frequently in late Greek (*LXX.* and *N. T.*)

§ 102. GENITIVE WITH VERBS OF JUDICIAL PROCEEDINGS.[1]

The Genitive is used with Verbs (and words) meaning:

A. *To accuse*: αἰτιῶμαι, διώκω, κατηγορῶ, φεύγω (*I am prosecuted*); ὁ φεύγων, *the defendant;* ὁ διώκων, *the prosecutor.*

So also προκαλοῦμαι, ἐπέξειμι.

B. *To acquit:* ἀφίημι, *I acquit;* ἀποφεύγω, *I am acquitted.*

C. *To condemn:* αἱρῶ, *I convict;* κατακρίνω, καταγιγνώσκω, καταψηφίζομαι (*by vote*), *I condemn;* ἁλίσκομαι, *I am convicted;* ὀφλισκάνω, *I am cast in* or *lose my suit.*

διώκω μὲν κατηγορίας, φόνου δε φεύγω. LYS.
I am prosecuting for libel, but am prosecuted for murder.

πάντες κλοπῆς ἢ δώρων ἑάλωσαν (or ὦφλον).
All were convicted of theft or bribery.

So ἁλῶναι λιποταξίου, ψευδομαρτυριῶν, *to be convicted of desertion, perjury,* passim.

συγγιγνώσκω τινὶ τῆς ἐπιθυμίας. PLAT.
I pardon any one his desire.

γράφεσθαί τινα παρανόμων.
To indict a person for proposing unconstitutional measures.

In the passive :—

τά μου ψευδῆ κατηγορημένα. PL. *Apol.* ii.
The false accusations which have been brought against me.

Note. The case in which the person or thing is put varies greatly. The charge is *generally* in the Genitive, the accused

---

[1] According to Curtius, a Genitive of Cause : perhaps a Genitive of Connexion.

in the Accusative: e.g. διώκω τινὰ φόνου. But with some verbs it is the reverse: κατηγορῶ τί τινος, καταγιγνώσκω (κατακρίνω) φόνον σου. Other verbs take a dative of the person, ἐπισκήπτομαί σοι φόνου, ἐγκαλῶ φόνον σοι. The suit or sentence is in the Accusative. φεύγω δίκην, δικάζω ψήφισμα, Ἔνοχος τοῦ φόνου τοῖς ἐπιτιμίοις, *liable to the penalties for murder.*

§ 103. GENITIVE ABSOLUTE.

The Genitive of a noun with a participle, not connected with the main construction of the sentence, denotes *time, cause, condition,* etc.

θεοῦ διδόντος οὐδὲν ἰσχύει φθόνος,
καὶ μὴ διδόντος οὐδέν ἰσχύει πόνος. MENANDER.
*If God should grant, ill-will availeth naught;
Nor, if he grant not, toil availeth aught.*

ὄντος ψεύδους ἔστιν ἀπάτη. PLAT.
Where is falsehood there is deceit.

The participle alone is sometimes found:—

εἶπον, ἐρωτήσαντος (sc. αὐτοῦ) ὅτι Μάκρωνές εἰσιν.
XEN. *An.* iv. 8. 5.
They said, on his asking them, that they were Macrones.

So ἐξαγγελθέντος, *on its being announced;* ὕοντος, *while it was raining;* συσκοτάζοντος, *when it was growing dark;* τελουμένων εἴποιμ' ἄν, SOPH. *El.* 1334, *when the end is come I will tell thee.* See Participle (Genitive Absolute).[1]

---

[1] It is difficult to decide whether this usage belongs to the Genitive or comes from the lost Ablative. A comparison with Latin seems to favour the latter view. On the other hand, German uses the genitive Absolute (see CURTIUS, *Elucidations* 197, *note*). In old English the Dative was thus used. Each language seems to have proceeded independently in its own way.

§ 104. GENITIVE WITH COMPARATIVES.

The Genitive is joined to Comparatives.

E.g. μείζων τοῦ ἀδελφοῦ, *i.e.* μείζων ἢ ὁ ἀδελφός.
πονηρία θᾶττον θανάτου θεῖ. PLAT.
Wickedness runs more swiftly than death (flees faster than fate).

Note 1. The Greek Comparative, like the Latin, often is rendered into English, "too great," "too good," etc.
κρεῖττον ἦν λόγου τὸ κάλλος τῆς γυναικός.
XEN. *Mem.* iii. 11. 1.
The beauty of the woman was too great for description (lit. *greater than words*).

Note 2. Adjectives in -πλάσιος, -στός take the same construction as Comparatives.
ἐκ φειδωλίας κατέθετο μῖσος διπλάσιον τῆς οὐσίας.
In consequence of stinginess he incurred a hatred double (that of) his property.
πολλοστὸν μέρος ἦν τὰ χρήματα ὧν ὑμεῖς προσεδοκᾶτε.
LYS. 19. 39.
His property was a very little part of what you were expecting.

δεύτερος, *second* (οὐδενός) *to none;* ὕστερος, *later than;* ἕτερος, *other than;* διάφορος, *different from* or *excelling,* similarly take a Genitive; so ὑστεραῖος, προτεραῖος.

§ 105. THE GENITIVE WITH VERBS CONTAINING A COMPARATIVE NOTION.[1]

The Genitive is used with many Verbs which imply *better than, worse than; greater than, less than.*

Such verbs are:—κρατῶ (*I prevail over*), περιγίγνομαι, περίειμι, ὑπερέχω (*am superior to*), διαφέρω, διαφερόντως ἔχω (*excel, differ from*), νικῶμαι, ἡττῶμαι (*am conquered by, inferior to*).

---

[1] The Genitive used with Comparatives may be an Ablative use (cf. Latin), or it may denote a general connexion, "greater in regard to."

Verbs of ruling:—ἡγοῦμαι (also with dative), ἄρχω, τυραννεύω, τυραννῶ, στρατηγῶ.

Many others :— πλεονεκτῶ, μειονεκτῶ, ὑστερῶ, ὑστερίζω, ἐλαττῶ, ἐλαττοῦμαι, λείπομαι.

Many take a dative (τινί) in respect of which the superiority or inferiority is shown.

N.B.—διαφέρομαι, *I quarrel with*, takes a dative.

ἔρως τῶν θεῶν βασιλεύει. PLAT.
Love is king of the gods.

τοῦτο διαφέρω τῶν πολλῶν. PLAT.
In this respect I differ from (or *excel*) *the rest of mankind.*

γυναικὸς οὐδαμῶς ἡσσητέα. SOPH.
We must in nowise yield unto a woman.

γλώσσης μάλιστα πανταχοῦ πειρῶ κρατεῖν. MENAND.
Strive ever chiefest to control thy tongue.

ἄρχοντι προσήκει καρτερίᾳ τῶν ἰδιωτῶν περιεῖναι.
XEN.
A commander should in endurance surpass private men.

§ 106. *GENITIVE OF SEPARATION.*[1]

A Genitive denoting that from which anything is separated is used with many verbs expressing *removal, distance, separation, loosing, delivering,* and the like.

---

[1] The Genitive here is the representative of the Ablative. It is impossible to group the usages of the Genitive under two distinct headings (1) Genitive or Connexion, (2) Ablative or Separation. Many Ablative or Separative uses have already been noticed (*e.g.* Partitive ἀμέτοχος, Connexion ἁμαρτάνω). Any attempt at too rigid symmetry would violently put asunder usages which are closely connected. See *Introductory Note.*

GENITIVE OF SEPARATION.

Such verbs are—διέχω, *I am distant;* χωρίζω, *I separate;* (χωρίζομαι), εἴργω, *I exclude;* ἀπέχω (ἔχω), *I withhold;* στερίσκομαι, *I am deprived of;* ἐλευθερῶ, *I set free;* ψιλῶ, *I strip;* ἀφίστημι (with its intransitive tenses), *I cause to revolt;* παύω, *I make to cease (from);* παύομαι, λήγω, *I cease;* ἀπαλλάσσω, *I deliver from;* ἀπαλλάσσομαι, *I escape;* εἴκω, παραχωρῶ, *I yield;* φείδομαι, *I spare.*

ἡ νῆσος οὐ πολὺ διέχει τῆς ἠπείρου. THUC.
The island is not far distant from the mainland.

Ἑλληνικοῦ πολέμου ἔσχον οἱ Ἀθηναῖοι.
The Athenians desisted from the Greek war.

ζητεῖτε αὐτῶν νυνὶ ἀπαλλαγῆναι. PLAT.
You are seeking now to be set free from them.

μετὰ ταῦτα ξυνέβη Θασίους τῶν Ἀθηναίων ἀποστῆναι.
THUC. i. 100.
After this it happened that the Thasians revolted from the Athenians.

Θησεὺς τὰς Ἀθήνας δεινοῦ προστάγματος ἠλευθέρωσεν.
ISAE. 10. 28.
Theseus delivered Athens from a terrible tax.

εἶπον τῷ Παυσανίᾳ τοῦ κήρυκος μὴ λείπεσθαι.
THUC. i. 131.
They told Pausanias not to leave the herald (see SOPH. *El.* 479).

Similarly with nouns, παυστήρ τῶνδε (πόνων), SOPH. *El.* 384; λυτήρια φόνου, *El.* 447.

Many Adjectives may be brought under this head, as γυμνός, ψιλός, καθαρός, ὀρφανός, ἐλεύθερος : and all words compounded with a privative, ἀμνήμων, ἀμελής, ἄμοιρος, ἄγευστος. Most of these have already been brought under other rules.

ἡ ἐπιθυμία ἀμνήμων τῶν κινδύνων. ANTIPH.
Desire is forgetful of dangers.

εὐχῆς δικαίας οὐκ ἀνήκοος θεός. MENAND.
God is not deaf unto a righteous prayer.

§ 107. Genitive with Compound Verbs.[1]

The Genitive is used with many Verbs compounded with Prepositions, especially ἀπό, ἐξ, πρό, ὑπέρ, κατά. Sometimes the Preposition seems to demand the Genitive, sometimes the signification of the Compound Verb.

Such verbs are ἀποτρέπω, ἐκβαίνω, ἐξίστημι, πρόκειμαι, προτιθέναι, προτιμῶ, ὑπερορῶ (also with Accus.), ὑπεραλγῶ, καταγελῶ, καταφρονῶ, καταγιγνώσκω, and many others.

προστῆναι τύχης, SOPH. *Ai.* 803; ὑπερίστασθαι (ἇς, *in whose defence*), SOPH. *El.* 188.

§ 108.   A Double Genitive.

Sometimes there are two Genitives in the same sentence. In such cases the first generally refers to the agent, the second to the object of his action.

τὰς τῶν οἰκείων προπηλακίσεις τοῦ γήρως. PLAT. *Rep.* 329.
The insults by relations on old age.

διὰ τὸ αὐτῶν δέος τοῦ θανάτου. PLAT. *Phaed.* 85 A.
In consequence of their fear of death.

αὐτῶν Subjective, θανάτου Objective.

τὸ κλεινὸν Ἑλλάδος
πρόσχημ' ἀγῶνος. SOPH. *El.* 682.
The glorious pageant of Greece, consisting in a contest.

Here the Genitives are freer; Ἑλλάδος is possessive, ἀγῶνος epexegetical.

§ 109.   The Epexegetical Genitive.

What is called the Epexegetical (*i.e.* explanatory) Genitive is a free application of the Genitive of Material.

ἀμαθία αὕτη ἡ ἐπονείδιστος ἡ τοῦ οἴεσθαι εἰδέναι ἃ οὐκ οἶδε.
PLAT. *Apol.* xvii.
This culpable ignorance of (which consists in) thinking one knows what one does not know.

---

[1] Some freer and miscellaneous uses of the Genitive are added. They have been brought together at the end of this Section in order not to lengthen previous headings with notes on less common constructions.

ὁ δὲ ἐγκέφαλός ἐστιν, ὁ τὰς αἰσθήσεις παρέχων τοῦ ἀκούειν
καὶ ὁρᾶν καὶ ὀσφραίνεσθαι. PL. *Phaed.* xlv.
*It is the brain which furnishes the sensations of hearing, and
sight, and smell.*

§ 110. Genitive of the Agent (so-called).

In Poetry passive Verbs and passive Verbals sometimes
take a Genitive which practically is like an Agent, and which
in Prose would be expressed by a Preposition with ὑπό, or
some such construction. It is not possible to refer these
constructions to one explanation. Many look like a Genitive
of the source whence, like the old English "of" (*i.e.* off) with
the Agent (ἀπό, *ab*). In some cases it is possible that the
governing word is used like a Substantive on which the
Genitive depends.

ἅπαντα γάρ σοι τἀμὰ νουθετήματα
κείνης διδακτά. SOPH. *El.* 344.
For all these thy admonishings of me are taught by her (*come
from her*).

So πληγεὶς θυγατρὸς τῆς ἐμῆς. EUR. *Or.* 497 (cf. *Electr.* 123).
Smitten by my daughter.

οὕτως ἄτιμός εἰμι τοῦ τεθνηκότος;
ἄτιμος οὐδενὸς σύ. SOPH. *El.* 1214.
= ἀτιμάζομαι πρὸς τοῦ τεθνηκότος.

The connexion of ἄτιμος with words of value may influence
the construction.

And am I thus dishonoured of the dead (i.e. *by the dead*)?
Thou art by none dishonoured.

O. T. 1437 προσήγορος, and cf. *Ai.* 807, φωτὸς ἠπατημένη.

§ 111. Free use of the Genitive of Connexion.

ἡ Κέρκυρα τῆς Ἰταλίας καὶ Σικελίας καλῶς παράπλου κεῖται.
THUC. i. 36.
*Corcyra is well situated for a coasting voyage to Italy and
Sicily.*

παράπλου is a Genitive of Connexion, Ἰταλίας a sort of
Objective Genitive.

τί δὲ ἵππων οἴει ἢ τῶν ἄλλων ζώων; PL. *Rep.* 459 (cf. 470).
What do you think about horses or other animals?

In Plato a Genitive thus introducing a Subject is often thus introduced at the beginning of a sentence; see Riddell, *Digest*, p. 126.

τυφλὸν τοῦ μέλλοντος ἄνθρωπος. PLAT. *Sol.* 12.
Man is blind concerning the future.

ὡς εἴ τις αὐτῶν ἐλπίσιν κεναῖς πάρος
ἐξῄρετ' ἀνδρὸς τοῦδε κ.τ.λ. SOPH. *El.* 1460.
That if any of them hitherto were buoyed up with hopes concerning (centred in) this man, etc.

τοῦ κασιγνήτου τί φῇς; SOPH. *El.* 317.
What say'st thou of (about) thy brother?

Cf. *Antig.* 11; μῦθος φίλων, *news of friends;* cf. *Antig.* 633, 1182, *O. C.* 317.

ἃ δὲ μέγιστ' ἔβλαστε νόμιμα, τῶνδε φερομέναν
ἄριστα. SOPH. *El.* 1095.
But as to the mightiest of ordinances that exist, in respect of these, prospering right nobly.

τῆς μητρὸς ἥκω τῆς ἐμῆς φράσων ἐν οἷς νῦν ἐστιν.
SOPH. *Tr.* 1122.
I am here to tell thee of my mother, what her present plight.

οὐδαμῶς ἐμαυτῆς οὖσ' ἀδείμαντος φίλοι. AESCH. *Pers.* 164.
Being by no means without fear for (concerning) myself, my friends.

The α privative in ἀδείμαντος does not here take a genitive of want or separation (like πέπλων ἄμοιρος, *without a share of robes*). But by a loose analogy common in all language, it may help to account for the use of the genitive.

§ 112. The Genitive with Adjectives and Adverbs.

Partitive, μέτοχος, ἀμέτοχος: ἰσόμοιρος, ἄμοιρος, ἄκληρος, ἄγευστος.

Perception, (ἀκούω): κατήκοος, ὑπήκοος, ἐπήκοος, συνήκοος, ἀνήκοος: ὑπήκοον δεῖ εἶναι τῶν γονέων.
PLAT. *Rep.* 463.

These are also found with the Dative.

τῇ πόλει κατήκοοι ἐγένοντο. PLAT. *Rep.* 499.
They became obedient to the state.

GENITIVE WITH ADJECTIVES AND ADVERBS. 103

Caring for, neglecting, remembering, forgetting, etc.,	ἐπιμελής, ἀμέλης: μνήμων, ἀμνήμων, ἐπιλήσμων. φιλομαθής, fond of learning; ὀψιμαθής, late in learning (serus studiorum).
Experienced in,	ἔμπειρος, ἄπειρος: ἐπιστήμων, τρίβων (versed in).
Aiming at,	δυσέρως (perdite amans), love-sick for; ἐπήβολος (compos), possessed of, or having succeeded in gaining.
Plenty,	μεστός, πλεώς, πλήρης: πλούσιος, ἄπληστος.
Want,	πένης, κενός, ἐνδεής, ἐπιδεής, ἐλλιπής, γυμνός, ψιλός, καθαρός.
Separation,	ἔρημος, ὀρφανός, ἐλεύθερος, ἁγνός (pure from), φειδωλός (sparing of).
Value,	τίμιος, ἄξιος, ὠνητός (purchaseable): ὡραῖος, ripe for (XEN. Cyr. iv. 6. 9).
Comparative notion:— Better, stronger than, and the reverse, Different from,	ἐγκρατής, ἀκρατής, ἀκράτωρ: κύριος, αὐτοκράτωρ. ἄλλος, ἀλλοῖος, ἕτερος, διάφορος, διαφερόντως. μέσος (e.g. ἑνὸς καὶ πλήθους τὸ ὀλίγον μέσον, PLAT. Politicus, 303, A), ἐναντίος τινός, the reverse of a thing; ἐναντίος τινι, opposed to a thing.
Connexion generally, some objective,	ὑπεύθυνος (responsible for a thing, but ὑπεύθυνός τινι, responsible to a person); ὑποτελής (φόρου, 'liable to pay a tribute); ἐπίκουρος, assisting or serviceable against (e.g. ψύχους, cold); τυφλὸς (τοῦ μέλλοντος, blind with regard to the future); συγγνώμων (ἁμαρτημάτων, forgiving of wrongs); κακοῦργος (ἑαυτοῦ), inflicting wrongs on; φιλόδωρος (fond of giving).
Ending in -κός,	πρακτικός, παρασκευαστικός, διδασκαλικός, ποριστικός, κωλυτικός (τῆς ἀρετῆς).
All words compounded with a privative.	ἀπαθής, ἄδωρος, ἀνήκοος, ἀθέατος, ἀγύμναστος, ἄσκενος (unfurnished); ἀτελής (immunis); ἄτιμος, etc. etc.

Others have been given under previous Rules.

§ 113. Free use of the Genitive with Substantives.

A few instances are given to show how the Genitive lends itself to the loosest connexion. Some may be regarded as free Objective Genitives, some as Genitives of Separation, others can only be regarded as Genitives of Connexion.

προsβολή Σικελίας, THUC. iv. 1, *means of approaching Sicily, road to Sicily;* δίκαι πολλῶν ταλάντων, *a lawsuit involving many talents* (cf. Genitive of amount); κράτος τῶν δρωμένων, SOPH. *El.* 85, *victory in our enterprise;* πατρὸς λουτρά, SOPH. *El.* 84, *libations in memory of a father;* ἄρηξις πημάτων, SOPH. *El.* 875, *help in or against troubles* (cf. ἐπίκουρος); πατρὸς τιμωρός, SOPH. *El.* 811, *an avenger whom a father has* (Subjective), *an avenger of a father* (Objective); αἱ τῶν κακῶν συνουσίαι, *intercourse with bad men* (freely Objective); βίᾳ πολιτῶν, *in spite of citizens* (freely Objective); ἀπόστασις τῶν Ἀθηναίων, *revolt from the Athenians* (separation); λύσις θανάτου, *deliverance from death* (separation); ἤθας μύθων, SOPH. *El.* 372, *schooled to words, accustomed to* (cf. ἐπιστήμων, etc.); ἡσυχία ἐχθρῶν, *rest from enemies* (freely Separative); ἀφορμὴ ἔργων, XEN. *Mem.* ii. 7. 11, *means of setting about,* or *stimulus to, deeds.*

THE DATIVE CASE.
Preliminary Note on the Dative.

§ 114. The Dative denotes generally the person or thing more remotely connected with the action than is the Accusative. It thus denotes that to which the direct object is made over or transferred (Dative of the Remoter Object) after verbs and adjectives which seem necessarily to require such a case in order to complete the information they have to give (*e.g.* δίδωμι μισθόν—τῷ στρατιώτῃ. By a natural extension the Dative also denotes the person or thing, affected beneficially or injuriously, interested in the action (Dative of Interest), and can be added at pleasure to any verb whose meaning does not necessarily demand it (*e.g.* οἱ καιροὶ προεῖνται τῇ πόλει, *our opportunities have been let slip, to the injury of the state*). The Dative of Interest includes the Dative of the Possessor, and the Ethic Dative. Next to the Dative of Interest, as akin to it in sense, although probably the use of the case has been transferred from the old Instrumental, may be placed the Dative expressing Contact with or Community, one of the most important and extensive rules belonging to the case. Further, the Dative has inherited the meanings of two lost cases, *first* the Instrumental, including not only the Instrument and Means, but also the Agent, Cause, Measure of Difference, and the accompanying Circumstances; *secondly*, the Locative in its double reference to Place and Time. The Dative of Place, however, is used as a rule only in Poetry; in Prose, to express motion to, not the Dative, but a preposition with the Accusative, is required.

§ 115. *THE DATIVE OF THE INDIRECT OBJECT TO WHOM ANYTHING IS SAID, DONE, OR GIVEN.*

ἡ μωρία δίδωσιν ἄνθρωποις κακά. MENANDER.
Folly bringeth troubles on men.

ἡ γεγενημένη μάχη τῷ βασιλεῖ ἀγγέλλεται. XEN.
The battle which had taken place is reported to the king.

δίδωσι μισθὸν τῷ στρατεύματι. XEN.
He gives pay to the army.

With a substantive—

μὴ ἐξαμάρτητε περὶ τὴν τοῦ Θεοῦ δόσιν ὑμῖν. PL. *Apol.* xviii.
Lest you commit some great error in regard to the gift of the god to you.

§ 116. Miscellaneous examples showing certain verbs which in Greek take a Dative of the Remoter Object.

ὀλιγαρχία τῶν κινδύνων τοῖς πολλοῖς μεταδίδωσι.
THUC. vi. 39.
Oligarchy gives a share of its dangers to the many.

διανέμω χρήματα τοῖς πολίταις.
I distribute money among the citizens.

διαλλάσσει Περδίκκαν τοῖς Ἀθηναίοις. Cf. THUC. ii. 95.
He reconciles Perdiccas with (to) the Athenians.

λαγχάνω δίκην (ἔγκλημα) Δημοσθένει.
I bring a lawsuit (accusation) against Demosthenes.
Demostheni litem intendo.
Ἀχέροντι νυμφεύσω. SOPH. *Ai.* 816.
I shall marry Acheron. (Cf. *nubo* in Latin.)
σὺ δ' εἶκ' ἀνάγκῃ καὶ θεοῖσι μὴ μάχου. EURIP. *Tel. Frag.*
Yield thou to necessity, and war not with the gods.
Cf. SOPH. *Ant.* 718.
εἴκειν τινὶ τῆς ὁδοῦ. HEROD. ii. 80.
To get out of the way for anybody (or *to yield the way to anybody*).

§ 117. *THE DATIVE OF INTEREST, INCLUDING THE DATIVE OF THE POSSESSOR, ETHIC DATIVE, etc.*

The Dative of Interest denotes the person or thing interested in the action (Dativus commodi et incommodi).

πᾶς ἀνὴρ αὑτῷ πονεῖ. SOPH.
Every man labours for himself.
μισῶ σοφιστὴν ὅστις οὐχ αὑτῷ σοφός. MENANDER.
I hate a wise man who is not wise for himself.
καιροὶ προεῖνται τῇ πόλει. DEM. 19. 8.
Opportunities have been sacrificed, to the injury of the state.

Good instances occur in SOPH. *Elect.* 66 (ἐχθροῖς), 496 (ἡμῖν), 979 (ἐχθροῖς), *Antig.* 618 (εἰδότι), DEM. 18. 205 (τῷ πατρί).

§ 118. Free Use of the Dative of Interest.

καίτοι σ' ἐγὼ 'τίμησα τοῖς φρονοῦσιν εὖ.
SOPH. *Ant.* 904 (cf. 25).
And yet I did honour thee in the judgment of the right-minded.
σχεδόν τι μώρῳ μωρίαν ὀφλισκάνω. SOPH. *Ant.* 470.
Belike I incur the charge of folly in the eyes of a fool.

σφῷν μὲν ἐντολὴ Διὸς
ἔχει τέλος δή. AESCH. P. V. 12.
For you (i.e. *so far as you are concerned*) *the hest of Zeus hath ending here.*

οὐδέν εἰμι καὶ τέθνηχ' ὑμῖν πάλαι. SOPH. *Phil.* 1030.
Naught am I, dead to you long since.
(i.e. *you thought me dead.*)

ὑπολαμβάνειν δεῖ τῷ τοιούτῳ ὅτι εὐήθης ἐστι. PLAT.
We must assume in the case of such a person that he is simple.

λαγχάνει τοῦ κλήρου τῇ γυναικί. ISAEUS, 3. 32.
He claims the inheritance in behalf of the woman.
The usual construction would be ὑπὲρ τῆς γυναικός.

στεφανοῦσθαι τῷ Θεῷ. XEN. *Ages.* ii. 15.
To be crowned in honour of the god.

So κείρεσθαί σοι, *to be shorn in honour of thee*, EURIP. *Hip.* 1425.

Note. Several idioms with participles should be noticed:

τῷ πλήθει τῶν Πλαταιῶν οὐ βουλομένῳ ἦν τῶν Ἀθηναίων
ἀφίστασθαι. THUC. ii. 3.
The Plataean democracy did not wish to revolt from the Athenians.

Cf TAC. *Agr.* 18, quibus volentibus bellum erat.

ἡμέραι μάλιστα ἦσαν τῇ Μιτυλήνῃ ἑαλωκυίᾳ ὅτε, κ.τ.λ.
THUC. iii. 29.
Seven days had passed since the capture of Mitylene when, etc.
See Temporal Sentences, § 211.

τῷ μὲν ἔξωθεν ἁπτομένῳ σῶμα οὐκ ἄγαν θερμὸν ἦν.
THUC. ii. 49.
To the outward touch the body was not very hot.

Ἐπίδαμνός ἐστι πόλις ἐν δεξιᾷ ἐσπλέοντι τὸν Ἰόνιον κόλπον.
THUC. i. 24.
Epidamnus is a town on your right as you enter the Ionic Gulf.

So συνελόντι (συντεμνόντι) εἰπεῖν, or simply συνελόντι, *to speak shortly, concisely, in brief, in short*

§ 119. THE DATIVE OF THE POSSESSOR.

Especially with εἰμί, γίγνομαι, ὑπάρχω.

νῆες οὐκ εἰσὶν ἡμῖν.
We have no ships.

ἄλλοις μὲν χρήματά ἐστι πολλά, ἡμῖν δὲ ξύμμαχοι ἀγαθοί. THUC.
Some have plenty of money, but we have good allies.

οὐδὲν ἐμοὶ καὶ Φιλίππῳ.
Philip and I have nothing to do with each other.

τί ἐμοὶ καὶ σοί;
What have I to do with thee? What have we in common?

§ 120. THE ETHIC DATIVE, DENOTING THE PERSON WHOSE FEELINGS SYMPATHISE WITH THE ACTION.

ὦ τέκνον, ἦ βέβηκεν ἡμῖν ὁ ξένος; SOPH.
My child, say (tell me), is the stranger departed?

μέμνησθε μοι μὴ θορυβεῖν. PLAT. *Apol.* xv.
Remember, I pray you, not to interrupt.

πῶς ἡμῖν ἔχεις;
How are you?

ἐγὼ σιωπῶ τῷδε; AR. *Batr.* 456.
What, I hold my tongue at this fellow's bidding?

So, elliptically—

μή μοι μυρίους ξένους. DEM. iv. 19.
Talk not to me of ten thousand mercenaries.

Sometimes a mere interjection expresses the Ethic dative, *e.g.* SOPH. *Elect.* 272, ἡμῖν, *fie on't!*

THE DATIVE OF COMMUNITY OR CONTACT WITH.

§ 121. The Dative of Community or Contact with is words (Verbs, Adjectives, and Adverbs) which denote *likeness* or *unlikeness; agreement* or *disagreement; meeting, encountering, following.*

A. With Verbs.

κακοῖς ὁμιλῶν καὐτός ἐκβήσῃ κακός. MENAND.
If thou associate with the bad, thyself too wilt turn out bad.

Θεῷ μάχεσθαι δεινόν ἐστι καὶ Τύχῃ. MENAND.
'Tis terrible to fight with God and Fortune.

οὐκ ἔφη τὰ ἔργα τοῖς λόγοις ὁμολογεῖν. THUC. v. 55.
He said that their deeds did not correspond with their words.

οὐκ αἰσχρόν ἐστι τοῖς πονηροῖς διαφέρεσθαι.
XEN. *Mem.* ii. 9. 8.
It is not wrong to quarrel with (differ from) bad men.
Contrast the use of διαφέρω with a Genitive.

ἔτυχον προσελθὼν Καλλίᾳ. PLAT. *Ap.* iv. (cf. xviii., ἐντυγχάνω).
I chanced to meet Callias.
So προστυχγάνω, ἐντυγχάνω, ἀπαντῶ, προσκρούω, τινι.

τῷ Ἀλκιβιάδῃ τινὲς ἐς λόγους ἦλθον. THUC. viii. 48.
Certain persons had a conference with Alcibiades.
So διαλέγομαί τινι.

βουλέσθω εὔελπις ὁμόσε χωρῆσαι τοῖς ἐναντίοις.
THUC. iv. 10.
Let him with good heart resolve to close with the foe.
Cf. μάχομαι, πολεμῶ τινι.

χρὴ ἕπεσθαι τῷ νόμῳ. THUC. ii. 35.
One must follow the custom.

B. With Adjectives.

ὁ ἀγαθὸς τῷ ἀγαθῷ φίλος. PLAT.
The good man is dear to the good man.

τοῖς τυράννοις ἀεὶ διάφοροί ἐσμεν. THUC.
We are ever hostile to tyrants.

ἀνθρώποις βλαβερὸν μὲν ψεῦδος, χρήσιμος δ ἀεί ἀλήθεια.
To men falsehood is injurious, truth is ever useful.

Note 1. Constructions of ὁ αὐτός, *idem*:—

a. τοῦτο ταὐτόν (=τὸ αὐτό) ἐστιν ἐκείνῳ.
This is the same as that.
Hoc idem est quod illud.
τὰ αὐτὰ φρονῶ Δημοσθένει (really = οἷς φρονεῖ Δ.)
DEM. 18. 30.
I hold the same opinions as Demosthenes.

b. ταὐτὰ πάσχεις ἅπερ καὶ ἐγώ.
You experience the same as I do.
This is a very common construction of ὁ αὐτός in Demosthenes,
εἴ τις διισχυρίζοιτο τῷ αὐτῷ λόγῳ ὥσπερ σύ.
PLAT. *Phaedr.* xxxvi.
If any one were to affirm positively (with) the same statement as you (that you make).

c. Βουδῖνοι δὲ οὐ τῇ αὐτῇ γλώσσῃ χρέωνται καὶ Γελωνοί.
HEROD. iv. 109.
The Budini do not use the same speech as the Geloni.
Cf. *idem atque* (*ac*) in Latin. This is not so common a construction in Attic.
Brachylogy is very frequent in the construction of ὁ αὐτός.
(ὅταν) εἰσίδω δ' ἐσθήματα
φοροῦντ' ἐκείνῳ ταὐτὰ (=ἅπερ καὶ ἐκεῖνος ἔφερε).
SOPH. *Elect.* 269.
Whene'er I behold him wearing the self-same robes as my dead father (as those of my father).

Note 2. ἴσος, παραπλήσιος, ὅμοιος have the same constructions as ὁ αὐτός.
οὐ καὶ σὺ τύπτει τὰς ἴσας πληγὰς ἐμοί; AR. *Ran.* 636.
Shan't you be beaten with the same number of blows as I?

§ 122. *DATIVE OF THE INSTRUMENT, INCLUDING MEANS, AGENT, CAUSE, MEASURE OF DIFFERENCE.*

The Dative in expressing these meanings has inherited the work of the lost instrumental case.

A. *Instrument* or *Means.*

χρηστὸς πονηροῖς οὐ τιτρώσκεται λόγοις. MENAND.
A good man is not wounded by bad words.

DATIVE OF THE AGENT.

ἔβαλλον αὐτοὺς λίθοις τε καὶ τοξεύμασι καὶ ἀκοντίοις. THUC.
They were attacking them with stones, and arrows, and javelins.

ἔσθ' ὅτῳ ἂν ἴδοις ἢ ὀφθαλμοῖς; PLAT.
Is there anything you would see with but eyes?

Note. χρῶμαι, *I use* (and sometimes νομίζω in the same sense) takes this dative. (Cf. *utor* in Latin.)

χρῶμαι ἀργυρίῳ, βιβλίοις, etc.
I use silver, books, etc.

lit. *I get service done* (*with*), or, *I employ myself* (*with*).

ἀγῶσι καὶ θυσίαις νομίζομεν. THUC. ii. 38.
We use festivals and sacrifices.

Cf. ἀμείβων βαφῇ, a dat. of instrument, AESCH. *Pers.* 319. βίᾳ, *by force* (*per vim*); ἀνάγκῃ, do., are instrumental datives.

B. *Agent* (cf. ὑπό with Gen.).

The Dative denoting the Agent is used in Prose chiefly with the perfect and pluperfect passive. In Homer the same case may refer both to things (Instrument) and persons (Agent). (Compare *Il.* iii. 428 with 436, and see PEILE, *Primer of Philology.*) In Attic, however, the so-called Dative of the Agent oftener appears to be a Dative of Interest.

ταῦτα ἀποτετέλεσταί σοι. XEN.
Those things have been finished by you (? *for you*).

ἐπειδὴ παρεσκεύαστο Κορινθίοις. THUC.
When preparations had been made by the Corinthians (? *for*).

Cf. THUC. iii. 64 (Ἕλλησι). EUR. *Hec.* 1085 (σοι): DEM. 844 1. (τούτῳ).

ἡσσᾶσθαι, νικᾶσθαί τινι, *to be beaten by any one*, are used as well as ἡσσᾶσθαι, νικᾶσθαί τινος, or ὑπό τινος.

Verbals in -τέος regularly take a Dative of the Agent (see Participles).

C. *Cause.* (This may, in some cases, be a Dative of Circumstance.)

εὐπραγίαις οὐκ ἐξυβρίζομεν. THUC.
We do not break out into insolence in consequence of prosperity.

οὐκ εἰμὶ τοῖς πεπραγμένοις
δύσθυμος.   SOPH. *El.* 549.
I am not despondent because of what has happened.
Cf. THUC. i. 95, ἔχθει.

So φιλίᾳ, *through friendship;* εὐνοίᾳ, *through goodwill* (voluntate); ἀγνοίᾳ, *through ignorance;* τῷ μισεῖν, *through hatred* (DEM. 45. 30) ; and φύσει, *naturally.*

ἄνθρωπος φύσει πολιτικὸν ζῷον. ARIST. *Eth.*
Man is by nature a creature adapted to social life.

The Dative of Cause is joined to many verbs expressing Emotion (ἄχθομαι, *I am vexed;* χαλεπαίνω, *I am vexed;* ἀθυμῶ, *I am despondent;* ἥδομαι, *I am pleased;* ἀγάλλομαι, *I exult;* ἐπαίρομαι, *I am elated;* αἰσχύνομαι, *I am ashamed* (also with Accus.), στέργω, ἀγαπῶ, *I am content*). Cf. ἐπί with the Dative after such verbs.

ὁ θεὸς ἔργοις τοῖς δικαίοις ἥδεται. *Philemon.*
God is pleased with righteous deeds.

Λύσανδρος βαρέως ἔφερε τῇ ἀτιμίᾳ. XEN.
Lysander was offended at the affront.

τοῖς σοῖς ἄχεσι καθυβρίζων. SOPH. *Ai.* 153.
Mocking at thy woes.

ἐπαιρόμενος ἢ πλούτῳ ἢ ἰσχύι ἢ ἄλλῳ τῷ τοιούτῳ.
            PLAT. *Rep.* iv. 434.
Elated either by wealth or strength, or some other such advantage.

So χαλεπῶς φέρειν. Both phrases also take the Accus. (EUR. *Med.* 1018).

D. Measure of Difference, especially with Comparatives.

ἕτερος ἑτέρου κεφαλῇ μείζων ἐστί. PLAT.
One man is taller than another by a head (i.e. *is a head taller*).

δέκα ἔτεσι πρὸ τῆς ἐν Σαλαμῖνι ναυμαχίας, etc.
PLAT. *Leg.* 698.
Ten years before the sea-fight at Salamis (*before by ten years*).

τοσούτῳ ἥδιον ζῶ ὅσῳ μᾶλλον κέκτημαι. XEN. *Cyr.* viii. 3. 40.
I live the more pleasantly the more I possess, i.e. *by so much the more pleasantly.*

So πολλῷ, ὀλίγῳ, μικρῷ, μακρῷ (μεῖζον, βέλτιον, etc.). A neuter accusative is also used with comparatives, especially πολύ, ὀλίγον, οὐδέν, μηδέν (ἧττον, μᾶλλον, etc.). See Comparative and Superlative.

§ 123. *THE DATIVE OF CIRCUMSTANCE.*

The Dative expresses the accompanying circumstances.

The Dative has taken on the meaning of the lost Sociative or Comitative Instrumental Case.

In mentioning details of military or naval forces this Dative is constantly used; *e.g.* εἴκοσι ναυσί, πολλῷ στατεύματι, στόλῳ, etc.

ἐφοβοῦντο μὴ μείζονι παρασκευῇ ἐπέλθωσιν. THUC.
They were afraid that they would come against them with a greater force.

οἱ Ἀθηναῖοι ἀτελεῖ τῇ νίκῃ ἀνέστησαν. THUC.
The Athenians retired with the victory incomplete.

κακοῖσιν ὅστις μηδὲν ἐξαλλάσσεται. SOPH. *Ai.* 474.
Whoso knoweth no change in respect of ills.

ἕκτος ἐξ Αἰτωλίας
ξανθαῖσι πώλοις. SOPH. *El.* 705 (see 1343).
*A sixth out of Aetolia
with bright bay mares.*

Cf. SOPH. *Antig.* 589 (πνοαῖς).

Note 1. The preposition which would be used in such a construction, and which is sometimes used, is σύν.

e.g. ἔπλεον ξὺν παντὶ τῷ στρατεύματι. THUC. vi. 62.

Note 2. Many adverbial Datives are thus used: δρόμῳ, *at full speed;* κύκλῳ, *round about;* σιγῇ, *silently;* τούτῳ τῷ τρόπῳ, *in this way, thus;* δημοσίᾳ, *publicly;* ἰδίᾳ, *privately;* πεζῇ, *on foot;* ταύτῃ, *thus;* ᾗ, *in which way;* τῷ ὄντι, *in reality.*

μετά᾽ with Genitive, σύν with Dative, or adverbs proper, are synonymous expressions: *e.g.* σὺν δίκῃ, μετὰ δίκης, δικαίως (for the Dative of Circumstance).

In SOPH. *Ai.* 767, θεοῖς = σὺν θεοῖς, *deo favente.*
In PL. *Apol.* xv. ἐν τῷ εἰωθότι τρόπῳ, *in my usual way.*

Note 3. The use of αὐτός with the Dative of Circumstance is specially to be noticed.

μίαν ναῦν ἔλαβον αὐτοῖς ἀνδράσι. THUC.
They captured one ship, with the men themselves (crew and all).

αὐτοῖς ποιμνίων ἐπιστάταις. SOPH. *Ai.* 27.
Together with the masters of the flocks.

Cf. EUR. *Bacch.* 946, 1134.

σύν and ἅμα are rarely used.

εἵπετο τῷ λοχαγῷ ξὺν αὐτῷ τῷ θώρακι καὶ τῇ κόπιδι.
XEN. *Cyr.* ii. 2. 9.
He was following the captain with breastplate and with bill.

So ἅμα, SOPH. *Antig.* 115.

§ 124. *DATIVE OF TIME AND PLACE.*

The Dative, as representing the defunct Locative, denotes Time when and Place where.

A. *Time.* The Dative denotes a definite point of time when something occurs, in certain phrases without the Preposition ἐν.

It is used chiefly of day, night, month, year, and festivals.

τῇδε τῇ ἡμέρᾳ = σήμερον, τήμερον, *on this day, to-day.*

τῇδε τῇ νυκτί ἀπέθανεν, *he died to-night.*

τῇ προτεραίᾳ, *the day before.* (So τῇ ὑστεραίᾳ, προτέρᾳ, δευτέρᾳ.)

οἱ ἐν Ἰθώμῃ τετάρτῳ ἔτει ξυνέβησαν. THUC.
The (Helots) in Ithome surrendered in the fourth year.

τραγῳδοῖς καινοῖς, DEM. 243. 17, *at the representation of the new tragedies;* ἄθλοισι Πυθικοῖσι, *at the Pythian games,* SOPH. *El.* 49. So Θεσμοφορίοις, τοῖς Ἐπινικίοις, Διονυσίοις, Παναθηναίοις, etc.

So in reckonings of the month: ἕνῃ καὶ νέᾳ, *on the last day of the month* (see Lexicon); Βοηδρομιῶνος μηνὸς τετάρτῃ ἱσταμένου, *on the fourth day of the first decade of Boedromion.*

A prose instance of this Dative of Time occurs in ISOCR. *Evag.* 66.

τίνα εὑρήσομεν τῶν τοῖς Τρωικοῖς χρόνοις γενομένων;
Whom shall we find of those who were born in the Trojan age?

A poetical one in SOPH. *El.* 193.

οἰκτρὰ μὲν νόστοις αὐδά. .
A voice of woe on the return.

Note. As a rule ἐν is added with other expressions, though sometimes it is omitted. Sometimes ἐν is found with the above expressions, except in names of festivals. Ἐν is more likely to be omitted when an adjective is used, *e.g.* ἐν νυκτί, but μίᾳ νυκτί. In Thucydides ἐν is sometimes omitted where we should have expected it, *e.g.* ἐκείνῃ τῇ ἐσβολῇ, THUC. ii. 20, *in this invasion.* So τῇ προτέρᾳ παρουσίᾳ, THUC. i. 128, *during his first stay;* τῇ προτέρᾳ (ἐκκλησίᾳ), THUC. i. 44, *at the former meeting of the assembly.*

χρόνῳ, *in time,* or *at last;* καιρῷ, *in season,* = ἐς καιρόν, (ἐν καιρῷ is extremely rare); χειμῶνος ὥρᾳ without ἐν; οἱ ἐν ὥρᾳ, *men in the prime of life.*

B. *Place.* This use of the Dative without the Preposition ἐν is poetical.

ἔτι μέγας οὐρανῷ Ζεύς. SOPH. *El.* 174.
Still is Zeus great in heaven.

Prose writers, however, use this case with names of towns.

Μαραθῶνι καὶ Σαλαμῖνι καὶ Πλαταίαις. PLAT.
At Marathon, and Salamis, and Plataeae.

N.B.—Μαραθῶνι and Σαλαμῖνι are real Locatives.

So 'Αθήνησι, Θήβῃσι, 'Ολυμπίασι, Πλαταιᾶσι.

Veritable Locatives are οἴκοι, *at home* (domi); χαμαί, *on the ground* (humi); ἄγροισι, *in the country* (ruri); θύρασι, *at the door* (foris); Πυθοῖ, *at Pytho;* 'Ισθμοῖ, *at the Isthmus.*

These are all, except ἄγροισι, used in Prose. In Prose ἄγροις.

§ 125. Lists of Words which take a Dative.

Verbs.

1. Verbs of *telling, promising, advising.*

φημί, *say.*
λέγω, *tell.*
ἀγγέλλω, *report.*
μηνύω, *inform.*
παραινῶ, } *advise.*
συμβουλεύω, }
ὑποβάλλω, *dictate.*
ὑποτίθεμαι, *suggest.*
ὑπισχνοῦμαι, *promise.*

They take an Accusative of the nearer object, *e.g.* ταῦτά σοι παραινῶ, *I give you this advice.*

Obs. κελεύω σε ἰέναι, *I bid you go,* Accus. and Infin.

2. Verbs of *obeying, trusting, and the contrary.*

πείθομαι, *be persuaded by, comply.*
πιστεύω, *trust* (also *intrust*).
ἀπειθῶ, *disobey.*
ἀπιστῶ, *disbelieve.*
ὑπακούω, *serve* (and genitive).
λατρεύω, *serve* (θεοῖς).

Obs. πείθου μοι, *be persuaded by me, hearken to me;* πιθοῦ μοι, *obey me.*

3. Verbs of *helping and hindering.*

ἀμύνω (in Act.), }
ἀρήγω (poet.), } *help.*
βοηθῶ, }
ἐπικουρῶ, *help.*
τιμωρῶ (in Act.), *avenge.*
ὑπηρετῶ, *serve.*
χαρίζομαι, *gratify.*
ἐμποδίζομαι, } *hinder.*
ἐμποδὼν εἶναι, }

For ἀμύνομαι and τιμωροῦμαι see *Middle Voice.*

WORDS WHICH TAKE A DATIVE.

4. Verbs of *being angry with, blaming, threatening.*
ἀγανακτῶ, } *vexed or indignant.*
ἄχθομαι, }
ὀργίζομαι, *angry.*
χαλεπαίνω, *angry, annoyed.*
ἐγκαλῶ, *charge, accuse.*
ἐπηρεάζω, *threaten abusively, or treat despitefully.*

ἐπιτιμῶ, *censure.*
λοιδοροῦμαι, *revile.*
μέμφομαι, *blame.*
φθονῶ, *envy.*
βαρέως φέρω (aegre, graviter, χαλεπῶς φέρω, fero), *I am indignant, annoyed, vexed.*

N.B.—λοιδορῶ Act. takes the Accus.
μέμφομαί τινι, or τί τινι (τίνα or τίνος), *I complain of a person or thing.*
μισῶ, *hate,* takes the Accus.

5. The Impersonal Verbs.

δοκεῖ μοι, *mihi videtur.*
(δοκῶ μοι, *mihi videor.*)
οὔ μοι δοκῶ, *I think not.*
πρέπει μοι, *me decet.*
προσήκει μοι, *it concerns me.*
οὐδέν μοι προσήκει, *nihil ad me attinet.*
δεῖ μοί τινος, *opus mihi est aliqua re,* but δεῖ με ἐλθεῖν.

λυσιτελεῖ μοι, *it is profitable for me.*
μέτεστί μοι τούτων, *I have a share of this.*
μέλει μοι ἀρετῆς, *I care for virtue.*
μεταμέλει μοι τούτων, *I repent of this, poenitet me huius rei.*

6. *Likeness or unlikeness.*
ἔοικα (impers. ἔοικε), *am like.*
ἰσῶ, *make equal.*
ὁμοιῶ, *make like.*

συναλλάσσω τοῦτόν σοι, *I reconcile this man to or with you.*

7. *Agreement, disagreement.*
ἀμφισβητῶ, *dispute.*
ἀπεχθάνομαι, *am odious to, hated by.*
ἐναντιοῦμαι, *oppose.*
ἐπιτίθεμαι, *attack.*
ἐρίζω, *quarrel with.*
ὁμολογῶ, *agree with.*
μάχομαι, *fight.*

πολεμῶ, *at war with.*
στασιάζω, *revolt, rebel, quarrel politically.*
συμφωνῶ, *agree with* (opp. to διαφωνῶ).
συνᾴδω, *agree with* (opp. to διᾴδω).

Like πολεμῶ, διὰ πολέμου ἰέναι τινί, *to be at war with one;* ἐς χεῖρας ἐλθεῖν, or ὁμόσε χωρεῖν τινι, *to come to blows, close quarters, with one.*
ἀμφισβητῶ σοι τοῦ σίτου, *I dispute with you about the food.*

8. Meeting, following.

ἀκολουθῶ, I follow.
ἕπομαι, I follow (also σύν τινι, and μετά τινων).
ἀπαντῶ, meet with, come across.
ἐντυγχάνω, meet with, come across.
προςτυγχάνω, meet with, come across.

προσκρούω, knock up against.
διαλέγομαι, converse with.
ὁμιλῶ, associate with.
πρόσειμι, approach.
σύνειμι, associate with.
ἐπέρχομαι, advance against.
παρατάσσομαι, stand beside in battle.

9. Many verbs compounded with Prepositions, especially with ἐπί, πρός, σύν, περί, chiefly denoting contact. Some have already been given.

ἀντέχω, hold out against.
ἀμφισβητῶ, dispute with.
διάκειμαι
φιλικῶς τινι
(or πρός am friendly dis-
τινα) or posed.
διατίθεμαι or
προςφέρομαι
ἐμβάλλω, throw in.
ἐμμένω, abide by.
ἐμποιῶ, introduce, produce.
ἐπάγω, lead in.
ἐπιστρατεύω, make war on.
ἐπιτάττω, impose.
ἐπιφέρω, bring up or against.
προςβάλλω, put, apply to.
προςτάττω, } apply to.
προςφέρω, }

παραβάλλω, set beside, compare (also τι παρά, or πρός τι).
παρατάττομαι, stand beside in battle.
περιάπτω, fasten round.
περιβάλλομαι, throw round, circumfundere, circumdare, e.g. τῇ νήσῳ τεῖχος, or νῆσον τείχει.
περιτίθημι, place round.
περιπίπτω, fall round or on.
πρόςειμι, come before, e.g. τῷ δήμῳ, address the assembly.
συγχαίρω, rejoice with.
συλλαμβάνω τινί τινος, (τι, or εἴς τι) assist any one in anything.

σύνοιδα, am conscious; ἐμαυτῷ ξυνῄδειν οὐδὲν ἐπισταμένῳ (or ἐπιστάμενος) I was conscious that I knew nothing for certain.
PL. Apol.

ξυνίσασι Μελήτῳ ψευδομένῳ, they are aware that Meletus is speaking falsely (i.e. they know as well as he knows). Ib.

§ 126. Adjectives.

And their cognate Adverbs and Substantives, *e.g.* βοηθός, βοήθεια, πρέπον, πρεπόντως.

Useful, fit, becoming, friendly, like, near, and their contraries.

ἀδελφός (and Gen.), *akin or answering to.*
ἀκόλουθος (and Gen.), *following after, agreeing with.*
ἀλλότριος (and Gen.), *foreign, or different.*
ἀντίστροφος (and Gen.), *corresponding.*
ὁ αὐτός, *the same.*
διάφορος (and Gen.), *different.*
ἔμμονος, *abiding by.*
ἔμφυτος, *implanted.*
ἐπιτήδειος, *suitable.*
ἐχθρός, *hostile.*
εὔνους, *well-disposed.*
δύσνους, *ill-disposed.*
ἴδιος (and Gen.), *private, personal.*
ἴσος, *equal.*
ἄνισος, *unequal.*
ἰσόρροπος (and Gen.), *equally matched.*

κοινός (and Gen.), *common.*
ὅμοιος, *like.*
ἀνόμοιος, *unlike.*
ὁμώνυμος (and Gen.), *called by the same name.*
παραπλήσιος, *similar.*
πίσυνος, *relying on,* fretus.
ἄπιστος, *not to be trusted, or not trusting.*
προσφιλής, *beloved.*
πολέμιος, *hostile.*
σύμμαχος, *in alliance, friendly.*
σύμφορος, σύμφερον, } *expedient.*
ἀσύμφορος, *inexpedient.*
χαλεπός, *difficult, unfavourable,* iniquus.
χρηστός, χρήσιμος, } *serviceable.*
ἄχρηστος, ἀχρεῖος, } *unserviceable.*

Obs. Several take also a Genitive (especially those denoting *correspondency*) sometimes with a slight difference of meaning, for which the Lexicon should be consulted. Compare *par, proprius, similis, alienus*, etc. in Latin.

Adverbs.

ἅμα, *generally temporal.* λοιμὸς ἅμα πολέμῳ, *pestilence at the same time as war.*
ὁμοῦ, *local.* ὕδωρ ὁμοῦ τῷ πηλῷ, *water and mud together.*
ἐφεξῆς, τὰ τούτοις ἐφεξῆς, *what comes next to this.*
ἐγγύς, Dat and Gen. ; see Lexicon.

CHAPTER V.

§ 127. COMPARATIVE AND SUPERLATIVE.

THE Comparative is followed by

A. A Genitive:—

νέοις τὸ σιγᾶν κρεῖττον ἐστι τοῦ λαλεῖν. MENANDER.
Silence is better for young folk than speech.

B. By ἤ:—

κρεῖττον σιωπᾶν ἐστιν ἢ λαλεῖν μάτην. MENANDER.
'Tis better to keep silence than talk idly.

Instead of ἤ the prepositions ἀντί, πρό (with Genitive), or πρός, παρά (with Accusative), sometimes.
ἀντί, SOPH. *Antig.* 182.
πρό, PLAT. *Crit.* 54, B.
πρός, THUC. iii. 37. 1; παρά, THUC. i. 23. 3.

πλέον, ἔλαττον, μεῖον, may omit the ἤ (like *plus, amplius, minus,* in Latin).

ἀπέθανον ὀλίγῳ ἐλάσσους πεντήκοντα. THUC. i. 44. 5.
There fell rather less than fifty.

Instead of πολλῷ with a Comparative marking the measure of difference, πολύ may be used. Thus we may say πολλῷ ἀμείνων or πολύ ἀμείνων, *far, much better.*

Note 1. The Comparative is constantly used, without the other object compared, to denote a degree *too high* or *too low*, a considerable degree or a degree greater or less than usual (*very, rather, somewhat*); not seldom it is used as a matter of idiom, where the Positive would be more natural.

ἐλθὲ μέλος ἀγροικότερον ὡς ἐμὲ λαβοῦσα. ARIST. *Ach.* 675.
Hie thee (Muse), and bring to me a right rural melody (ἀγροικότερον, *countrified*).

μείζοσιν ἔργοις ἐπιχειροῦντες οὐ μικροῖς κακοῖς περιπίπτουσιν. XEN. *Mem.* iv. 2. 35.
By attempting tasks too great they encounter no slight troubles.

τί νεώτερον, ὦ Σώκρατες, γέγονεν; PLAT.
What new thing has happened, Socrates?

οὐ χεῖρον πολλάκις ἀκούειν. PLAT. *Phaed.* 105.
It is no bad thing to hear often.

Note 2. To denote too high or too low a degree, ἢ κατά is used with the Accusative, or ἢ ὡς, ἢ ὥστε with the Infinitive. (Cf. Latin, *quam pro, quam ut, quam qui.*)

εἶδε νεκρὸν μείζω ἢ κατ' ἄνθρωπον. PLAT. *Rep.* 360.
He saw a corpse of superhuman size.

οἱ Ἀθηναῖοι ἐν Σικελίᾳ μείζω ἢ κατὰ δάκρυα ἐπεπόνθεσαν.
THUC. vii. 75.
The Athenians in Sicily had endured sufferings too great for tears.

φοβοῦμαι μή τι μεῖζον ἢ ὥστε φέρειν δύνασθαι ξυμβῇ.
XEN. *Ap.* iii. 5. 17.
I fear that some evil, too great for us to be able to bear, may happen. See EUR. *Bacch.* 840.

The Positive is sometimes so used with ὥστε.

τὸ ὕδωρ ψυχρὸν ὥστε λούσασθαί ἐστιν. XEN. *Ap.* iii. 13. 3.
The water is too cold for bathing.

Cf. THUC. ii. 61. 2; ἐγκαρτερεῖν, without ὥστε.

Note 3. μᾶλλον ἤ (for which πλέον ἤ may be substituted) is used after a Comparative.

αἱρετώτερον ἀποθνῄσκειν μᾶλλον ἢ φεύγειν.
XEN. *Cyr.* iii. 3. 51.
It is more desirable to die than to run away.

δέει τὸ πλέον ἢ φιλίᾳ. THUC. iii. 12.
Through fear more than friendship.

So with a Positive.

ὠνητὴ Ἀθηναιῶν ἡ δύναμις μᾶλλον ἢ οἰκεία.
THUC. i. 121. 2.
The power of the Athenians is purchased rather than their own.

Note 4. Two adjectives or adverbs compared with each other may both be in Comparative.

τὴν εἰρήνην ἀναγκαιοτέραν ἢ καλλίω ὑπελάμβανον εἶναι.
AESCHIN. iii. 69.
They were regarding the peace as inevitable rather than honourable.

So συντομώτερον ἢ σαφέστερον, *curtly rather than clearly.*
Is. 6. 24.

ἰὼ στρατηγοὶ πλείονες ἢ βελτίονες. ARIST. *Ach.* 1078.
Ho! Generals, more numerous than brave.

Cf. Latin—Paulli Aemilii contio fuit verior quam gratior populo. LIV. xxii. 38.
The speech of Paullus Aemilius was more true than acceptable to the people.

Note 5. Both the Comparative and Superlative may be used with a reflexive pronoun to denote a comparative or superlative degree reached by the person himself within his own experience.

πολλῷ χεῖρον ἑαυτῶν λέγουσιν. ANTIPH. v. 7.
They speak much worse than they generally do (much below their real powers, or their average).

ὀξύτατα αὐτὸς αὑτοῦ ὁρᾷ. PLAT. *Leg.* 715, e.
His sight is at its keenest.

Note 6. The Superlative is used, where the Comparative would logically be correct, to denote a supereminent degree of superiority.

κάλλιστον τῶν πρότερον φάος. SOPH. *Ant.* 100.
Light most glorious of all former lights.

Cf. *Antig.* 1212; *Philoct.* 1171.

ἐδέθην παρανομώτατα ἁπάντων ἀνθρώπων.
ANTIPH. *Herod:* 17.
I was thrown into prison in a far more unconstitutional way than ever man was.

Note 7. The Superlative is strengthened by δή, πολλῷ, πολύ:—
μέγιστος δή, *quite the greatest;* πολλῷ, πολύ ἄριστος, *far, much the best.*

ὡς, ὅτι, and οἷον strengthen the Superlative :—
ὡς ῥᾷστα, *as easily as possible* (quam facillime); ὡς or ὅτι μάλιστα, τάχιστα (quam maxime, quam celerrime).
ὅτι ἐν βραχυτάτῳ, *in as short a time as possible*. THUC. iii. 46.
ὡς ἠδύναντο ἀδηλότατα, *as secretly as they were able*.
                                                     THUC. vii. 50.
οἷον ἀθλιώτατον, *in as miserable a plight as possible*.
                                                     ARIST. *Ach*. 384.

Note 8. The phrase εἷς ἀνήρ with a Superlative denotes an unique personal pre-eminence.

εἷς ἀνὴρ πλεῖστον πόνον
ἐχθροῖς παρασχών.   AESCH. *Pers.* 329.
    Wreaking, beyond all else,
    Most mischief to his foes.
(Or, *with his single arm, what one man might*).
Cf. SOPH. *O. T.* 1380; *Ai.* 1340; THUC. iii. 39.

CHAPTER VI.
VOICES AND MOODS.

§ 128. *THE ACTIVE VOICE.*

(1.) The Active Voice includes transitive and intransitive verbs. On the other hand the Middle Voice includes deponent verbs which are active and transitive, such as αἰδοῦμαι τοὺς θεούς, *I reverence the gods;* οἶμαι, *I think.*

(2.) Some verbs are both transitive and intransitive.

ἐλαύνω, *I drive,* and *I ride* (sc. ἅρμα, ἵππον).
ἔχω, *I have,* „ *I am* (with adverbs only).
πράσσω, *I do,* „ *I fare.*
δηλῶ, *I show,* „ *I show myself, am manifest* (sc. ἐμαυτόν).
τελευτῶ, *I end,* „ *I die* (sc. βίον).

So in English *I turn, I join, I move, I change,* etc.

Both transitive and intransitive tenses are found in the same verb.

E.g. ἵστημι, *I set (up);* ἕστηκα, *I stand.*

So φύω, βαίνω, and others.

(3.) Some simple verbs become intransitive when compounded with a preposition.

βάλλω, *I throw.* { μεταβάλλω, *I change.*
{ ἐσβάλλω, } *I rush in, attack,* or
{ ἐμβάλλει, } (of rivers) *flow in.*
κόπτω, *I cut.* προκόπτω, *I make progress.*
φέρω, *I bear.* διαφέρω, { *I differ from, am superior to.*
λείπω, *I leave.* { ἐλλείπω, } *I fail;*
{ ἐκλείπω, } *I die, faint.*

(4.) The Active is sometimes Causative, *i.e.* it means "I get, or allow, a thing to be done," not "I do it myself."

ὁ Κῦρος κατέκαυσε τὰ βασίλεια.
Cyrus had the palace burnt down.

So in Latin—

Verres ad palum alligavit piratas.
Verres had the pirates bound to a post. CIC. *Ver.* iv. 29.

§ 129.   *THE MIDDLE VOICE.*

In the Middle Voice the action of the verb refers in some way or other to *self*. In some verbs, however, the notion of self is so much lost that the Middle differs from the Active only in giving a different meaning to the verb.

The chief uses of the Middle Voice are—

A. Reflexive, { (1.) Directly.
                   (2.) Indirectly.
B. Causative.
C. Reciprocal.
D. The notion of self is so blurred or lost that the Middle must be regarded as giving a new and different meaning to the Active; in some cases there is no Active.

Note. The Aorist Middle is never passive.

The Future Middle is—

(1) sometimes apparently passive, but really middle, *e.g.* λείψομαι, *I will not leave* (σου); λειφθήσομαι, *I shall be left;* ἡ ἀρχή καταλύσεται, *will fall to pieces;* καταλυθήσεται, *be destroyed.*

(2) really passive with certain verbs : τιμήσομαι, *I shall be honoured;* στυγήσομαι, *I shall be hated;* διδάξομαι, *I shall be taught;* στερήσομαι, *I shall be bereft;* ζημιώσομαι, *I shall be fined;* ὠφελήσομαι, *I shall be helped;* ἀδικήσομαι, *I shall be wronged.*

In these cases the Future passive is rarely or never used.

A. *The Reflexive Middle.* $\begin{cases} 1.\ \text{Directly Reflexive.} \\ 2.\ \text{Indirectly Reflexive.} \end{cases}$

(1.) *The Directly Reflexive Middle.* Self is the direct object or accusative.

λούω, *I wash.*   λούομαι, *I wash myself.*
τρέπω, *I turn* (trans.).   τρέπομαι, *I turn* (intrans.), i.e. *I turn myself.*
δηλῶ, *I show.*   δηλοῦμαι, *I show myself.*

The Middle is very rarely used in this way. It is more usual to employ the Active with a Reflexive Pronoun:—

E.g., *I hire out myself,* μισθῶ ἐμαυτόν, not μισθοῦμαι, which means *I hire for myself :* so ἀπέκτεινεν ἑαυτόν, not ἀπεκτείνατο : ἐπαινεῖς σεαυτόν, not ἐπαινεῖ.

(2.) *The Indirectly Reflexive Middle.* Self is the Dative of the Indirect Object, or of Interest.

πορίζω, *I provide.*   πορίζομαι (ὅπλα), *I provide for myself.*
ἀποτίθημι, *I put off* or *away*.   ἀποτίθεμαι (τὸν νόμον), *I put away from myself,* i.e. *disregard.*
     ἀποτίθεμαι ῥᾳθυμίαν, *I put away from myself,* i.e. *I overcome, lazy habits.*
     ἀποτίθεμαι τροφήν, *I put away for myself,* i.e. *hoard* or *store food.*
λούω, *I wash.*   λούομαι τὰ ἱμάτια, *I wash my own clothes* (i.e. *for myself my clothes*).
παρέχω, *I offer* or *present*.   παρέχομαι (δαπάνην), *I furnish my own expenses, from my own resources;* μάρτυρα, *I bring forward a witness for myself, my own witness, in my support.*

The chief notions are—(1.) *for* self.
(2.) *from* self.
(3.) *what belongs to* self.
But the notion of *for* self pervades and easily explains all the uses.

B. *The Causative Middle.*
As the Active means *I cause* or *allow others to do*, so the Middle means *I cause* or *allow others to do something for myself* or *on myself*.

ὁ πατὴρ διδάσκεται τὸν υἱόν.
The father has his son taught.
γράφω, *I write;* γράφομαι τινά, *I get one written down,*
i.e. *I indict.*
Cf. Latin *curo, permitto*, with *ut* and subjunctive, or with Gerundive.

C. *The Reciprocal Middle.* Each agent acts *for self*, and so the action is reciprocal. Verbs compounded with διά especially have this force.
ἀμείβω, *I change.* ἀμειβόμεθα, *we answer each other.*
διαλεγόμεθα, *we converse together.*
διακελεύονται, *they encourage one another.*
διακηρεύονται, *they negotiate by a herald.*

D. See the following Miscellaneous list.

Note. A miscellaneous list of Verbs for reference showing the difference in meaning between the Active and the Middle. In some cases the Reflexive meaning of the Middle is obvious; in some it is dubious; in some it has practically disappeared. For constructions with the Cases the Lexicon must be used.

ἀγάλλω, *I adorn.*   ἀγάλλομαι, *I pride myself, exult.*
ἄγω, *I bring, lead.*   ἄγομαι γυναῖκα, *I marry a wife*
αἴρω, *I take.*   αἱροῦμαι, *I choose.*
ἀφαιρῶ, *I take away.*   ἀφαιροῦμαι τίνα τι, *I deprive a person of something (for my own sake).*

αἴρω, *I take up*.

ἀμείβω, *I change* (trans.).

ἀπέχω, *I keep off, deter*.

ἀποδίδωμι, *I give back*.
(πιπράσκω, *I sell*).
ἀμύνω (see τιμωρῶ).
ἀπαλλάσσω, *I set free*.

ἄρχω (πολέμου), *I am the first of two parties to make (war)*; so with λόγου.
but
ἄρχω, *I rule*.
βουλεύω, *I advise*.

γαμῶ, *I marry (duco)*.

γεύω, *I give a taste of*.
γράφω, *I write down* (cf. τίθημι).
δανείζω, *I put out at interest, lend*.
διδάσκω, *I teach*.

δικάζω, *I decide*.

ἐπείγω, *I urge on, hasten* (trans.).
ἐπιτίθημι, *I put* or *place upon*.
ἔχω, *I have* (neuter, *I am* or *I am able*).
ἐπαγγέλλω, *I proclaim*.

ἐπιψηφίζω, *I put to the vote (of the President)*.

αἴρομαι, *I take on myself, undertake (suscipio), begin, gain*, (Acc.)
ἀμείβεσθαι, *to do by turns, answer, requite*.
ἀπέχομαί τινος, *refrain from, hold aloof from*.

ἀπεδόμην, *I sold*.

ἀπαλλάσσομαι, *I escape, I depart from, I leave off*.
ἄρχομαι (πολέμου), *I begin warlike operations*.

ἄρχομαι (Passive), *I am ruled*
βουλεύομαι, *I deliberate, consider*.

γαμοῦμαι, (1) *I marry (nubo)*;
(2) *I give in marriage, betroth*.
γεύομαι, *I taste*.
γράφομαι, *I get written down, I indict*.

δανείζομαι, *I borrow at interest* (so χρήσασθαι).

διδάσκομαι τὸν υἱόν, *I get my son taught*.
διδάσκομαι ὑπό τινος, *I am taught by a person*.
δικάζομαι (δίκην σοι), *I go to law with you, conduct a case:* especially of the prosecutor, opposed to φεύγειν.
ἐπείγομαι, *I hasten* (intrans.).
ἐπιτίθεμαι, *I attack*, τινί.
ἔχομαι, *I cling to, I come next to, I am eager for* (with Gen.).
ἐπαγγέλλομαι, *I promise, I profess, I denounce*.
ἐπιψηφίζομαι, *I vote, decree by vote (of the Assembly)*.

θύω (*of the priest*), *I sacrifice.*

ἵημι, *I send.*
καταστρέφω, *I overturn.*
κοιμῶ, *I lull to sleep.*
κομίζω, *I transport.*

λαμβάνω τι, *I take.*
λανθάνω, *I escape observation.*

παύω, *I make to cease, I stop* (trans.).
πείθω, *I persuade.*

ποιῶ, *I do or make.*
ποιῶ λόγον, *I compose a speech.*

ὁδὸν ποιῶ. *I make a road.*

προσποιῶ, *I hand over* (trado).
πονηρεύω, *I am wicked.*
πολιτεύω, *I am a citizen.*
σκοπῶ, *I look at, examine.*
σοφίζω, *I make wise, I teach.*

σπένδω, *I pour out a libation.*
τίθησι νόμον ὁ νομοθέτης, *the lawgiver makes a law.*
ὁ θείς, *the mortgager.*

τιμωρῶ τινά τινι, *I punish A for B's satisfaction.*
And so—
τιμωρῶ σοι, *I avenge or assist thee.*
Similarly—
ἀμύνω τί τινι, *I keep off something from B.*

θύομαι (*of the general*), *I get a sacrifice offered, I take auspices.*

ἵεμαι, *I hurry, rush.*
καταστρέφομαι, *I subdue.*
κοιμῶμαι, *I sleep.*
κομίζομαι, *I recover, get back what was lost.*
λαμβάνομαί τινος, *I lay hold of.*
λανθάνομαι, ἐπιλανθάνομαι, *I forget.*

παύομαι, *I cease, stop* (intrans.).

πείθομαι, *I obey.* (πείθου, *be persuaded;* πιθοῦ, *obey.*)

ποιοῦμαι, *I consider.*
ποιοῦμαι λόγον, *I deliver a speech.*
ὁδὸν ποιοῦμαι, *I make a journey.*
ποιοῦμαι σπονδάς, εἰρήνην, συνθήκην, σύμβασιν.
ποιεῖσθαι παῖδας, *to beget children.* Crito, v.
προσποιοῦμαι, *I claim, I aim at.*
πονηρεύομαι, *I behave wickedly.*
πολιτεύομαι, *I act or live as a citizen.*
σκοποῦμαι, *I reflect.* [
σοφίζομαι, *I act the sophist, I quibble, contrive.*

σπένδομαι, *I make a truce.*
τίθεται νόμον ὁ δῆμος, *the people makes laws for itself.*
ὁ θέμενος, *the mortgagee* (also *the depositor in a bank,* etc.).

τιμωροῦμαι τινά τινι, *I revenge myself on A for wronging B.*

τιμωροῦμαί σε, *I wreak vengeance on or punish thee.*

(1) ἀμύνομαί τι, *I defend myself against a thing.*

Hence—
(1) ἀμύνω πόλεμον, *I keep off war.*
(2) ἀμύνω Ἀθηναίοις, *I help the Athenians.*
τίνω δίκην, *poenas do, pendo, luo, I pay a penalty.*
φαίνω, *I show* (trans.).
χρῶ, (1) *I give an oracle.*
(2) *I furnish, lend.*

(2) ἀμύνομαί τινα, *I requite or punish a person,*—τοῖς ὁμοίοις, *with retaliation,* περί or ὑπέρ τινος, *for a certain thing.*
τίνομαι δίκην, *poenas sumo, I exact a penalty or vengeance.*
φαίνομαι, *I appear, am seen.*
χρῶμαι, *I get an oracle given.*
χρῶμαι, *I use.*

Note. An examination of the above list will bring out two points.
1. The Active is often transitive, while the Middle is neuter.
2. The Middle is often used of mental rather than of bodily actions.

§ 130. THE PASSIVE VOICE.

The Syntax of the Passive Voice is much freer in Greek than in Latin.

Thus, besides the constructions noticed in the Notes below, Verbs which take a Genitive or a Dative can be used personally in the Passive, unlike the Latin.

E.g. καταφρονῶ αὐτοῦ, *I despise him.*
καταφρονεῖται ὑπ' ἐμοῦ, *he is despised by me.*
πιστεύουσι τῷ βασιλεῖ, *they trust the king.*
ὁ βασιλεὺς πιστεύεται ὑπ' αὐτῶν, *the king is trusted by them.*
πῶς ἂν ἐπιβουλεύσαιμι αὐτῷ, εἰ μὴ καὶ ἐπεβουλεύθην ὑπ' αὐτοῦ; ANTIPH.
How could I plot against him, unless also I had been plotted against by him?

Note 1. Neuter verbs can form passive participles.
ἄρχω, *I rule;* ἀρχόμενος, *ruled over.*
This is chiefly the case with neuter participles.
τὰ ἠσεβημένα αὐτοῖς (ὑπ' αὐτῶν), *impious acts committed by them.*

τὰ κινδυνευθέντα, *risks run.*
τὰ ἡμαρτημένα, *errors committed.*
τὰ στρατευόμενα, *warlike measures.*
τά σοι πεπολιτευμένα, *your political acts.*

Or with impersonal passives.
παρεσκεύασται, *preparation has been made.*
ἁμαρτάνεται, *error is being committed.*
οὐδὲν ἀσεβεῖται, *no impiety is being committed.*

Cf. Lat. *ventum est, erat; factum est*, etc.

Note 2. Deponent Verbs are those which have no Active Form, *e.g.* δέχομαι, *I receive;* οἶμαι, *I think.* Passive Deponents are those whose Aorist has a Passive (not a Middle form), *e.g.* βούλομαι, *I wish,* ἐβουλήθην. The exclusively Passive forms of Deponents are sometimes Passive not Middle in sense, *e.g.* βιάζομαι, *I force;* ἐβιάσθην, *I was forced.* Even the Middle form of a Deponent may be Passive in meaning, *e.g.* βιάζομαι *I am forced,* or *suffer violence.* In such cases there was an original Active form, *e.g.* βιάζω. See further, JELF, § 368.

Note 3. It will be remembered that the Aorists in -ην and -θην, with their corresponding futures in -ήσομαι, -θήσομαι, are the only Passive forms of a Greek verb. The Middle forms, except the Aorists, and as a rule the Futures, are of course Passive as well as Middle in meaning.

Note 4. The direct object of the Active becomes the subject of the Passive, and the subject of the Active, the agent, is expressed by ὑπό and the Genitive.
ὁ φιλόσοφος διδάσκει τὸν παῖδα.
ὁ παῖς διδάσκεται ὑπὸ τοῦ φιλοσόφου.

The Agent is also expressed, but much less commonly—
(*a.*) By the Dative. See Dative of Agent.
(*b.*) By the Prepositions ἀπό, ἐξ, παρά, πρός. See these Prepositions.

The object of the Active may however remain the object of the Passive, and the dative of the Active become the subject of the Passive. This is an extension of § 130.

οἱ ἐπιτετραμμένοι τὴν φυλακήν, THUC. i. 126, cf. v. 37, ταῦτα ἐπεσταλμένοι, and EUR. *Rhes.* 5. So in English, *I leave him a fortune, He has been left a fortune.*

§ 131. THE MOODS.

Introductory Note on the Subjunctive and Optative.

The Indicative is sharply contrasted with the Subjunctive and Optative.

The Indicative simply and directly makes a statement or asks a question without any qualification.

ὁ βασιλεὺς τέθνηκεν
The king is dead.

πόθεν ἥκεις ;
Where do you come from?

It is commonly said that the Indicative states facts, but the statement need not express a fact actually true; *e.g.* οἱ Πέρσαι ἐνίκησαν τοὺς Ἀθηναίους Μαραθῶνι, *the Persians defeated the Athenians at Marathon.*

The Subjunctive and Optative, on the other hand, make assertions, not as real, but as conceptions present to the speaker's mind.

The Subjunctive and Optative are two aspects of one Mood. In the oldest Greek they represented originally the Willing or Wishing Mood, the Subjunctive being the more peremptory, *Will ;* the Optative, the fainter and more remote, *Wish.* This was soon modified into a second use, the Subjunctive expressing a more vivid, the Optative a fainter, remoter Expectation or Possibility. Hence they soon came to be used in Subordinate Sentences, expressing Purpose, Condition, Indefinite Frequency, etc. And though in Subordinate Sentences the general rule is for the Subjunctive to follow Primary, the Optative Historic tenses, yet there is no such fundamental distinction between the two Moods as to prevent the Subjunctive being used for the Optative, the two Moods sometimes alternating in the same paragraph.

One or two instances from Homer will illustrate the difference between the Subjunctive and Optative :—

Μή σε κιχείω, Il. i. 26, *let me not find thee.*
Μὴ μὴν ἀκλειῶς ἀπολοίμην, Il. xxii. 304, *let me not fall ingloriously.*
οὐκ ἔσθ' οὗτος ἀνήρ, οὐδ' ἔσσεται, οὐδὲ γένηται.
HOM. *Od.* xvi. 437.
Lives not that man, nor e'er will live, nor e'er is like to be (born).

Here the Subjunctive differs from the Future Indicative in stating what is thought likely to occur, not positively what will occur.

ῥεῖα θεός γ' ἐθέλων καὶ τηλόθεν ἄνδρα σαώσαι.
HOM. *Od.* iii. 231.
Lightly a god, an he will, might save thee e'en at a distance.

The Optative gives a more remote representation than the Subjunctive of a future possibility.

Note. The Subjunctive and Optative (with two exceptions to be noticed in the Optative) refer to future time. The reference to the future, however, is more vague in the Optative, so vague that the notion of time is often scarcely apparent in this mood. This, perhaps, may be why the Optative lent itself to a connexion with past tenses in historic sequence. But there is nothing in the form of the Optative, neither its connecting vowel nor its suffixes, which *per se* denotes past time. And the only two usages in which the Optative really refers to past time are: (1) in General Suppositions (see Conditional Sentences); and, (2) in Oratio Obliqua, where occasionally it represents a past tense of the Indicative (see Oratio Obliqua).

The Subjunctive and Optative are both used (1) in Independent, (2) in Subordinate Sentences. Their uses in Subordinate Sentences are given in the Syntax of the Compound Sentence.

§ 132. THE SUBJUNCTIVE IN INDEPENDENT SENTENCES.

The Independent Subjunctive is used :—

A. In Exhortations. First person often with φέρε, ἄγε, ἄγετε, ἴθι (δή or νῦν added).

φέρε δὴ εἴπω πρὸς ὑμᾶς. DEM.
Come now, let me speak before you.

ἀλλ' ἴθι, ἴωμεν.
Come then, let us go (suppose we go).

In SOPH. *Phil.* 300 the 2d Person (μάθῃς).

B. In Prohibitions (with μή).

(a) First person *plural* (singular very rare, cf. EUR. *Hipp.* 567, *Heracl.* 559).

(b) Second and third person with *aorist* subjunctive.

(a) μὴ φοβώμεθα, *let us not be afraid.*
μὴ ἀτελῆ τὸν λόγον καταλίπωμεν. PLAT.
Let us not leave our argument incomplete.

(b) μὴ ταῦτα ποιήσῃς.
Do not do this.
Ne haec feceris.

μηδενὶ συμφορὰν ὀνειδίσῃς. ISOCR.
Taunt no one with a misfortune.

C. In Questions of doubt (Deliberative Questions) with the First Person. βούλει, βούλεσθε (θέλεις, θέλετε in poetry) are often added.

εἴπωμεν, ἢ σιγῶμεν, ἤ τι δράσομεν; EUR.
Are we to (should we, must we) speak, or keep silence, or what shall we do?

τί βούλεσθε δράσω;
Quid vultis faciam?
What would you have me do?
οἴμοι τί δράσω; ποῖ φύγω μητρὸς χέρας; EUR. *Med.* 1271.
Ah me, what must I do? whither escape a mother's hands?

Note 1.—The third person, however, occurs pretty often, especially in Plato and Demosthenes.

πότερον σέ τις τῆς πόλεως ἐχθρὸν ἢ ἐμὸν εἶναι φῇ;
DEM. 18. 124.
Should one call you the enemy of the state, or my enemy?
πόθεν τις ἄρξηται; PLAT.
Where is one to begin?
τί εἴπῃ τις;
What must one say? PLAT. and DEM.
ποῖ τις οὖν φύγῃ;
ποῖ μολὼν μενῶ; SOPH. *Ai.* 403.
Here this τις refers to the first person.

Note 2.—The Subjunctive, expressing a future possibility, common in Homer, is not wholly unknown, though rare in Attic.

οὔτ' ἔστιν οὔτε ποτὲ γένηται κρεῖττον. PLAT. *Leg.* 942.
It is not, nor is it ever likely to get better.

§ 133. *THE OPTATIVE IN INDEPENDENT SENTENCES.*

The Independent Optative is used :—

A. To denote a Wish (without ἄν).

ὦ παῖ γένοιο πατρὸς εὐγενέστερος. SOPH.
Boy, may'st thou prove more fortunate than thy father.

In the first person a wish often conveys an *exhortation*. See Subjunctive in Exhortations.

μὴ ζῴην μετ' ἀμουσίας. EUR.
Let me not live without culture.

In the third person a *command* or *permission* may be conveyed.

ἔρδοι τις ἣν ἕκαστος εἰδείη τέχνην. AR.
Let each man keep to his trade, whate'er he knows.

εἰδείη is assimilated to the mood of principal verb ἔρδοι. Cf. XEN. *An.* iii. 2. 37, ἡγοῖτο (al. ἡγείσθω) : AESCH. *P. V.* 1047, where two Optatives are co-ordinate with preceding Imperatives.

B. In Deliberative Questions. The Optative differs from the Subjunctive in the same questions only in expressing a less vivid and more remote possibility.

τεάν, Ζεῦ, δύνασιν τίς ἀνδρῶν
ὑπερβασίᾳ κατάσχοι ; SOPH. *Ant.* 605.
*Thy power, O Zeus, what mortal man
By o'erstepping might control?*

Cf. AESCH. *Ch.* 392 ; AR. *Plut.* 438 ; SOPH. *O. C.* 170 ; PLAT. *Rep.* 352 C (ἀκούσαις).

Note. Several places, especially in the Tragedians, are quoted where the Optative without ἄν occurs in its Homeric potential sense (e.g. *Od.* iii. 231, quoted before). In most of these places, however, if not all, the reading is doubted. JELF (§ 418, I. A) quotes two passages from PLATO, *Phaedo,* 87 E, ἐπιδεικνύοι—διοίχοιτο, where Heindorf would insert ἄν : and *Rep.* 362 O, ἀδελφὸς ἀνδρὶ παρείη, where τὸ λεγόμενον shows that the phrase is a quotation, probably from the Epic.

§ 134. *THE IMPERATIVE.*

The Imperative is used in Commands, Entreaties, Prayers, and Prohibitions. It denotes future time.

In Prohibitions we must use μή either (1) with 2d Person Present Imperative (continued act), or (2) 2d Person Aorist Subjunctive (single act), thus :—

μὴ κλέπτε, or μὴ κλέψῃς, *do not steal;* but neither μὴ κλέπτῃς nor κλέψον.

AR. *Thesm.* 877 (μὴ ψεῦσον) is a rare exception in Attic.

Μὴ, πρὸς θεῶν, μαινώμεθα, μηδ' αἰσχρῶς ἀπολώμεθα.
                                                XEN.
Let us not, by the gods, be mad, nor die shamefully.

But μή with the 3d pers. Aorist Imperative is admissible both in poetry and in prose.

μηδεὶς ὑμῶν ταῦτα νομισάτω. XEN.
Let none of you think so.

Note 1. For the Infinitive used as an Imperative, see Index.

Note 2. οἶσθ' ὃ δρᾶσον. The Imperative is sometimes used in relative clauses depending on an Interrogative.

ἀλλ' οἶσθ' ὃ δρᾶσον; τῷ σκέλει θένε τὴν πέτραν.
                                                AR. *Av.* 54.
Do you know what to do? Kick the rock with your leg.

οἶσθά νυν ἅ μοι γενέσθω; δεσμὰ τοῖς ξένοισι πρόσθες.
                                                EUR. *I. T.* 1203.
Knowest thou what must be done for me? put chains on the strangers.

Logically it would be ἃ δεῖ γενέσθαι;

And as the Future is used in Greek as an equivalent for the Imperative, we find

οἶσθ' οὖν ὃ δράσεις . . . ὅδησον ἡμῖν σῖτον. EUR. *Cycl.* 133.
Dost know what thou must do? provide us victuals.

The Imperative in Greek is subordinate in the above idioms. As this is impossible in English, we have to substitute a periphrasis. *Do you know what (you must do=do)?*

CHAPTER VII.

THE TENSES.

§ 135. Greek tenses may be classified in two ways.
A. With regard to the *Order of Time*.
B. With regard to the *Kind of Act or State*.

A. ORDER OF TIME.

The Time of a Tense must be either

1. Past (Imperfect, Aorist, Pluperfect).
2. Present (Present, Perfect).
3. Future (Future, Future Perfect).

PRIMARY AND HISTORIC TENSES.

Tenses in Present and Future Time are called *Primary*.
Tenses in Past Time are called *Historic*.

SEQUENCE OF MOODS.

In Compound Sentences the theoretical rule is that—

A Principal Sentence in Primary Time is followed by the Subjunctive in the Subordinate Sentence.

A Principal Sentence in Historic Time is followed by the Optative in the Subordinate Sentence.

This sequence however is purely theoretical; for, as will be seen in the Compound Sentence, a Subjunctive constantly takes the place of an Optative in Historic Sequence.

§ 136. Time how far observed throughout the Moods.

(a) The only mark of Past Time in Greek is the Augment. The distinction between Past and Present therefore is strictly observed only in the Indicative.

Absolute and Relative Time.—The distinctions of Time, however, are observed in the *Optative, Infinitive,* and *Participle,* when these Moods are used in *Indirect Discourse* or *Oratio Obliqua, i.e.* when they represent indirectly the words or thoughts of another. This is most clearly seen in the Indirect Statements and Questions.

ἔφη ταῦτα ποιεῖν—ποιῆσαι—ποιήσειν.
He said that he was doing, did or had done, would do this.

ποιεῖν = ποιῶ in Recta, and therefore is *relatively present ;*
ποιῆσαι = ἐποίησα ,, ,, *relatively past ;*
ποιήσειν = ποιήσω ,, ,, *relatively future ;*

relatively, i.e. to the Principal Verb present, past, and future : but ποιεῖν, ποιῆσαι, ποιήσειν are all *absolutely* past, because ἔφη, the Principal Verb, is past.

ἔλεξαν ὅτι πέμψειε σφᾶς ὁ βασιλεύς.
They said that the king had sent them.
In Recta ἔπεμψεν ἡμᾶς.

ἤρετο εἰ κενὸς ὁ φόβος εἴη.
He asked if his fear was groundless.
In Recta κενός ἐστι ;

ᾔσθοντο τοὺς πολεμίους προσπλέοντας.
They discovered that the enemy were advancing.
Recta, οἱ πολέμιοι προσπλέουσιν.

(b) The *Aorist Participle* denotes an action *past relatively* to the principal verb.

Βοιωτοὶ οἱ ἐξ Ἄρνης ἀναστάντες τὴν Βοιωτίαν ᾤκησαν.
THUC.
Boeotians who had been driven out of Arne settled in Boeotia.

See further however under the Aorist Participle, which in itself does not denote time.

(c) With regard to the *Future in the Moods* it seems always express future time, for

(1.) The *Future Optative* is only used to represent in the Obliqua a Future Indicative of Direct Discourse.

(2.) The *Future Infinitive* is most commonly used after verbs of *saying* and *thinking*, and therefore like the Optative, represents a Future Indicative of the Recta. Whenever the Future Infinitive is used after other verbs, instead of the usual Present or Aorist Infinitive, the idea of futurity still seems to be emphasised, e.g.:—

He delays to do his duty, μέλλει ποιεῖν or ποιῆσαι τὰ δέοντα.
μέλλει ποιήσειν (with emphatic reference to the future).
ἀναβάλλεται is similarly used.

(3.) The Future Participle denotes a future relative to the principal Verb.
συλλαμβάνει Κῦρον, ὡς ἀποκτενῶν.
He seizes Cyrus with the intention of killing him.

B. *THE KIND OF ACT OR STATE.*

With regard to the *Kind of Act* denoted Tenses are divided into

1. Continued (Present, Imperfect).
2. Finished (Perfect, Pluperfect).
3. Indefinite or Single (Aorist Strong and Weak).

1. A *continued Tense* mentions an act as still going on, or in progress, whether in past, present, or future, an act in which the agent is still engaged, *I was writing, I am writing, I shall be writing* (*the letter*).

2. A *finished Tense* mentions an act as one which is perfect, complete, in a finished state, *I have written, I had written, I shall have written* (*the letter*).

3. An *indefinite Tense* mentions the mere act itself, a single act, without any such limitation of its continuance or completion, *I wrote, I write, I shall write* (*the letter*). Hence the Stoic grammarians called such a Tense an Aorist (*i.e.* ἀόριστον or unlimited).

The distinction between the Kinds of Act is observed throughout all the Moods, and is therefore a more universal and abiding distinction than that of Time.

Note. The kind of act is denoted in Greek by the Tense-stem, ΛΥ-, ΛΥΣ-, ΛΥΚΑ-, ΛΕΛΥ-.
The Present Tense-stem (Present and Imperfect Tenses) denotes a continued act.
The Perfect (*i.e.* reduplicated) Tense-stem (Perfect, Pluperfect, and Future Perfect Tenses) denotes a finished act.
The Aorist Tense-stems (Strong and Weak Aorist tenses) denote an indefinite or single act.
The Future is ambiguous, denoting either a continued or an indefinite act.

§ 137. Ideal division of Tenses.

An ideal twofold division of Tenses may be thus constructed, to be read horizontally and vertically.

	Continued.	Finished.	Indefinite.
Present	*I am writing* γράφω, strictly used, scribo	*I have written* γέγραφα scripsi	*I write* γράφω scribo
Past	*I was writing* ἔγραφον scribebam	*I had written* ἐγεγράφη or -ειν scripseram	*I wrote* ἔγραψα scripsi
Future	*I shall be writing* γράψω scribam	*I shall have written* Periphrasis in Active γεγραφώς ἔσομαι scripsero	*I shall write* γράψω scribam

Note. A very rare poetical periphrasis occurs with *Aorist* Participle, σιωπήσας ἔσομαι, λυπηθείς ἔσομαι, SOPH. *O. T.* 1146, *O. C.* 816.

This scheme, however, is purely ideal, and does not correspond to the Greek tenses, however well it corresponds with our analytic English tenses.

In Greek the kind of act, as has been observed already, is denoted by the Present, the Perfect, and the Aorist *Tense-stems:* the Future Tense-stem has to be left out.

The most important distinction is that between a Continued and an Indefinite act.

§ 138. *THE PRESENT AND IMPERFECT INDICATIVE.*

A. The Present Indicative denotes:—

1. An act in which a person is engaged in present time; γράφω, *I am writing now.*

2. An act which is habitual or repeated, or a general truth, without being limited to the present moment.

ῥωμή ἀμαθής πολλάκις τίκτει βλάβην. EUR. *Frag.*
Strength untrained oft brings forth harm.
Vis consili expers mole ruit sua. HORACE.

Note 1. The Present has also certain idiomatic uses of which the following are the commonest:—

(*a*) *The Historic present* denotes a past event. In Compound Sentences it reckons as an historic tense. This historic present seems sometimes equivalent to an aorist (narrative), sometimes to an imperfect (descriptive).

συλλαμβάνει Κῦρον ὡς ἀποκτενῶν. XEN.
He seizes (seized) Cyrus with the intention of killing him.

(*b*) The Present, as it denotes an unfinished act, often denotes an *attempted* act.

τοὺς Λακεδαιμονίους ἀναιρεῖ, τοὺς δὲ Φωκέας σώζει. DEM.
He is trying to destroy the Lacedaemonians, and to save the Phocians.

This is especially the case with δίδωμι, *I offer*, i.e. *try to give*, and πείθω, *I try to persuade*. The present participle also has this meaning.

(c) The Present as a Perfect:—

1. With πάλαι or ἤδη (*all this while, this long while, not now for the first time*), like *iam, iamdudum*, in Latin with the Present.

ἔμοιγε νῦν τε καὶ πάλαι δοκεῖ.   EUR. *Frag.*
I think so now, and I have long been thinking so.

νοσεῖ ἤδη δέκα ἔτη.
He has been ill these ten years.

Esp. in the poets πάλαι may refer to a statement made only a moment ago (as we say hyperbolically—*ever so long ago*). Cf. SOPH. *El.* 676.

2. Certain presents have the force of perfects: ἥκω, *I am come, adsum;* οἴχομαι, *I am gone (quickly)*; νικῶ, *I am victorious;* κρατῶ, *I am victorious;* ἥττωμαι, *I am defeated;* ἀδικῶ, *I have done wrong, I am unjust;* ὄλλυμαι, ἀπόλλυμαι, in Tragedy, *I am lost*, or *undone*.

3. Verbs of hearing and learning, ἀκούω (κλύω, poet.), πυνθάνομαι, αἰσθάνομαι, μανθάνω. ἄρτι is often used with these verbs.

Θεμιστοκλέα οὐκ ἀκούεις ἄνδρα ἀγαθὸν γεγονότα;   PLAT.
Have you not heard that Themistocles proved himself a patriot?

(d) The Present Infinitive and the Present Participle may represent the Imperfect Indicative in English.

οἱ συμπρεσβεύοντες καὶ παρόντες καταμαρτυρήσουσι.
   DEM. *de F. L.* 381. 5.
Those who were his fellow-colleagues in the embassy, and who were present, will bear witness.

B. The Imperfect is the past of the Present. It describes a past action as (*a*) still going on, or (*b*) as going on along with other actions, or (*c*) as frequently recurring.

For (*a*) and (*b*) see Aorist.

c. Σωκράτης ὥσπερ ἐγίγνωσκεν, οὕτως ἔλεγε.   XEN.
Socrates used to speak exactly as he used to think.

Note 2. The Imperfect shares most of the idiomatic uses of the present.

(*a*) The Imperfect of an *attempted act*, like the present of the same.

ἕκαστός τις ἔπειθεν αὐτὸν ὑποστῆναι τὴν ἀρχήν. XEN.
Each one was trying to persuade him to undertake the command.
The *present participle* also often has this sense.

(*b*) When the present has a perfect force its imperfect is a pluperfect. ἧκον, *I had come;* ᾠχόμην, *I was gone;* ἐνίκων, *I had won the victory, I was victorious,* etc.

(*c*) The Imperfect is used for the present when what is seen now to be the case has been in the past inquired about, or sought for, or thought of.

οὐ τοῦτ' ἦν εὐδαιμονία, κακοῦ ἀπαλλαγή; PLAT.
Is not this happiness (*which we were talking about* or *trying to discover*) *deliverance from evils?*
ὅδ' ἦν ἄρα ὁ ξυλλαβών με. SOPH.
This then, I see, is he who seized me (*this was and is*).
To this belongs the famous Aristotelian phrase, τὸ τί ἦν εἶναι

(*d*) In the use of the Imperfects ἔδει, χρῆν, ὤφελον, εἰκὸς ἦν, like the Latin *debebam, oportebat, decebat,* denote what ought to have been done, but what was not done.

οὐδὲν ἄλλο ἔδει λέγειν. DEM.
He need have said nothing else.
Nihil aliud dicere oportebat.
οὐκ εἰκὸς ἦν οὕτως ἐᾶν. SOPH. O. T. 255.
It would not have been right to leave it alone.
Non decebat praeterire.
On these constructions see *Conditional Sentences*.

§ 139. *THE PERFECT AND PLUPERFECT INDICATIVE.*

A. The Perfect denotes an act which is in a finished state. The act must have been begun in the past, but it stands finished in the present. The Perfect therefore is reckoned as a Primary tense. γέγραφα, *I have written, my writing is in a finished state;* δέδεται, *he is in a state of imprisonment.*

Not only in the Subjunctive and Optative, but also in the Indicative, a periphrasis with εἰμί is used for the Perfect. The abiding nature of the result is then emphasized.

εἷς ὅδε μονογενὴς οὐρανὸς γεγονώς ἐστί τε καὶ ἔτ' ἔσται.
PLAT. *Tim.* 31.
This one sole-created heaven hath been created, and shall still endure.

Cf. ἔχω with Aorist Participle.

The Perfect of many verbs is equivalent to a Present: τέθνηκεν, *he is dead;* κέκλημαι, *I am called;* γέγονα, *I am become,* i.e. *I am;* μέμνημαι, *I remember;* οἶδα (σύνοιδα), *I know,* novi. The Pluperfect is then an Imperfect, ἐτεθνήκει, *he was dead,* etc. The Perfect Imperative of such verbs is a simple Perfect.

Note. A great number of Perfects in Homer describe present acts or states: ἄνωγα, βέβριθα, κέκευθα, μέμηλα, μέμονα, ἔρριγα, etc. etc.

B. The Pluperfect is the Perfect carried back to past time. ἐγεγράφη, *I had written, my writing was in a finished state in the past.*

For the Future Perfect, see Future.

The Perfect Imperative (3d singular Middle and Passive) issues a decisive command which is to be executed at once, and there an end.

μέχρι τοῦδε ὡρίσθω ὑμῶν ἡ βραδυτής. THUC. i. 71.
At this point let your slowness find a limit (come to an end).
Hactenus progressa (terminata) esto (finem habeat) vestra tarditas. POPPO.

§ 140.   THE AORIST.

1. The Aorist denotes the mere occurrence of an act in past time. Apart from difference of time the Aorist is always distinguished from the Imperfect (and in the Oblique Moods from the Present) by noticing the mere doing of the act, and not describing the act as in progress. The Aorist has been likened to a point, the Imperfect (and Present) to a line.

Note. As the Aorist notices the mere act or state itself, three aspects of this are observable.

1. *The commencement of the act,* the beginning, not the continuance.

This has been called the *Ingressive or Inceptive Aorist.*

ἐβασίλευσε, *he came to the throne* (ἐβασίλευεν, *he was king*).
ἐπλούτησεν, *he became rich* (ἐπλούτει, *he was a rich man*).
ἐνόσησε, *he fell ill* (ἐνόσει, *he was ill*).

2. *The act as done and over,* not as doing.

ΛΥCΙΠΠΟC ΕΠΟΙΗCΕ denotes the simple fact that Lysippus was the maker of the statue.

ΛΥCΙΠΠΟC ΕΠΟΙΕΙ denotes the labour spent on the making.

ἐδείπνησαν, *they supped,* i.e. *ended supper.*
ἐδείπνουν, *they were at supper.*
νὺξ ἐγένετο, *night came on,* i.e. *it was night.*
νὺξ ἐγίγνετο, *night was coming on,* i.e. *it was twilight.*

3. *The act as instantaneous and momentary,* not as occupying a long time.

ἐγὼ δὲ ἦλθον, εἶδον, ἐνίκησα.
" *Caesar's brag of* '*came, and saw, and overcame.*'" SHAK.

2. The Aorist is *narrative,* the Imperfect is *descriptive;* i.e. the Aorist is used when we merely mention a past act as having occurred, while the Imperfect is used when we wish to describe or paint (so to speak) past acts as still going on.

οἱ μὲν ἀπῆλθον. Κλέανδρος δὲ ἐθύετο, καὶ συνῆν Ξενοφῶντι φιλικῶς, καὶ ξενίαν συνεβάλοντο. XEN. *So they went away. Meanwhile Cleander was engaged in sacrificing, and in friendly intercourse with Xenophon, and they formed a friendship.*

Note 1. Other uses of the Aorist :—

The Aorist is also distinguished from the Imperfect by the mere mention of an act without reference to other acts, while the Imperfect often describes an act as going on side by side with another act.

Παυσανίας ἐκ Λακεδαίμονος στρατηγὸς ὑπὸ τῶν Ἑλλήνων ἐξεπέμφθη μετὰ εἴκοσι νεῶν ἀπὸ Πελοποννήσου, ξυνέπλεον δὲ καὶ Ἀθηναῖοι τριάκοντα ναυσί, καὶ ἐστράτευσαν ἐς Κύπρον, καὶ αὐτῆς τὰ πολλὰ κατεστρέψαντο.
Pausanias was sent out from Lacedaemon by the Greeks as admiral with twenty ships from Peloponnese. The Athenians also accompanied him with thirty ships, and they proceeded to Cyprus, and subdued the greater part of it.

Note 2. The Aorist is used (esp. in Tragedy) where we use a Present. The moment of past time is but an instant before. Something an instant ago has evoked the act.

ἐπῄνεσ' ἔργον καὶ πρόνοιαν ἣν ἔθου. SOPH. *Ai.* 586.
I commend the act, and the forethought thou didst show.
Elect. 668. 677, EUR. *Hec.* 1275, *El.* 248, *Philoc.* 1289, 1314.

ξυνῆκα, *I understand*, and ἥσθην, *I am pleased*, are of constant occurrence.

ἔφριξ' ἔρωτι περιχαρὴς δ' ἀνεπτόμαν. SOPH. *Ai.* 692.
I thrill with love and flutter overjoyed.
Here the act is instantaneous also.

Note 3. English often uses the Pluperfect where Greek uses the Aorist; this is especially the case in Oratio Obliqua:—

οἱ Ἰνδοὶ ἔλεξαν ὅτι πέμψειε σφᾶς ὁ βασιλεύς.
XEN. *Cyr.* ii. 4. 7.
The Indians said that their king had sent them.

Recta ἔπεμψεν, where we should say "*has* sent" (not *sent*). This in Obliqua becomes *had*.
And with temporal and local sentences—

ἐπειδὴ ἐτελεύτησε Δαρεῖος καὶ κατέστη Ἀρταξέρξης.
XEN. *An.* i. 1. 3.
After Darius had died and Artaxerxes had been established in the kingdom.
Quum mortuus esset Darius, etc.

ἐτράποντο ἐς Πάνορμον ὅθεν ἀνηγάγοντο. THUC. i. 92.
They turned towards Panormus whence they had set sail.

Note 4. The Greek Aorist and English Perfect.
Though we have an Aorist in English corresponding to the Greek, yet Greek uses the Aorist even more constantly than English. We use a Perfect sometimes where Greek uses an

Aorist. Thus—*I am shocked if these are the orders which you have given,* δεινὸν ποιοῦμαι εἰ τοιαῦτα παρήγγειλας. Here an act rather than a finished state is denoted, and the Greek Aorist is more correct than the English Perfect. See example above, SOPH. *Ai.* 586, ἔθου would naturally be rendered into English, *thou hast shown.* Again a Gnomic Aorist in Greek may be rendered by an English Perfect.

Note 5. The Aorist Participle generally expresses time prior to its principal verb, but not always so, and, when so, not from its own inherent meaning, but only from its connexion with a principal verb.

Thus γελάσας (οἰμώξας) ἔφη, *With a smile, laugh (sigh) he said.*

εὖ ἐποίησας ἀναμνήσας με. PLAT. *Phaed.* 60.
You did well to remind me.

Here the two acts are contemporary and identical.

So εὖ ἐποίησας ἀφικόμενος. HDT. v. 24.
Cf. Curtius, *Elucidations,* p. 211.

Note 6. The following verbs show the contrast between the Present and the Aorist in the kind of act denoted. It will be noticed that several are Ingressive Aorists.

νοσεῖν, *to be ill.* νοσῆσαι, *to fall ill.*
φεύγειν, *to run away.* φυγεῖν, *to escape.*
φοβεῖσθαι, *to be in fear.* φοβηθῆναι, δεῖσαι, *to take fright.*
πράσσειν, *to be busy about.* πρᾶξαι, *to accomplish.*
γελᾶν, *to be laughing.* γελάσαι, *to burst out laughing.*
ἄρχειν, *to rule.* ἄρξαι, *to obtain dominion or office.*
ἰσχύειν, *to be strong.* ἰσχῦσαι, *to become strong.*
σιγᾶν, *to be silent.* σιγῆσαι, *to become silent.*
ἔχειν, *to have.* σχεῖν, *to obtain.*
φαίνεσθαι, *to appear.* φανῆναι, *to become apparent.*
πολεμεῖν, *to be at war.* πολεμῆσαι, *to begin war.*
bellum gerere. bellum inferre.
βασιλεύειν, *to be king.* βασιλεῦσαι, *to come to the throne.*

Note on the Aorist.

The Aorist is often called the momentary tense. It is doubtful, however, whether momentariness is its essential meaning. We should use the aorist if we translated *The*

Pharaohs built the pyramids, οἱ βασιλεῖς τῶν Αἰγυπτίων ᾠκοδόμησαν τὰς πυραμίδας, though the pyramids, like Rome, were not built in a day. We should equally use it in translating *He burst out laughing*, ἐγέλασε, or *He fell ill*, ἐνόσησε. And again we should use it of such an instantaneous shiver of emotion as is contained in ἔφριξ' ἔρωτι, *I thrill with love*.

The mere mention of the act (or state) itself, without regard to its duration, seems to be the one description of the Aorist which suits it all through. Aorist and indefinite are not very satisfactory words, but they have been retained as familiar, for want of a better. Simple and Isolated have been suggested.

§ 141.   *THE FUTURE.*

The Future denotes an act which will take place hereafter.

Its action is either continued or indefinite (see above).

Note 1. Idiomatic uses of the Future :—

The second person of the Future both affirmatively and negatively resembles an imperative.

(*a*) Affirmatively (either as a statement, or as a question with οὐ Interrogative)— ˙

πρὸς ταῦτα πράξεις οἷον ἂν θέλῃς. SOPH. *O. C.* 956.
Thou wilt do therefore (do therefore) *whatever likes thee.*

οὐχ ἕλξετ', οὐ παιήσετ', οὐκ ἀρήξετε ; AR. *Ly.* 459.

The expression is not so abrupt in form as an imperative. A suggestion is made, or a permission given, which, however, is an unmistakeable Imperative.

(*b*) Negatively with οὐ—

λέγ' εἴ τι βούλει, χειρὶ δ' οὐ ψαύσεις ποτέ. EUR. *Med.* 1320.
Speak if thou wilt, but with the hand thou must touch me never.

Observe (1) that in Euripides οὐ with the Future is a statement, in Aristophanes a question ; (2) that in both passages οὐ with the Future is co-ordinate with an Imperative.

Note 2. A *periphrastic Future* is formed by μέλλω with the Present or Future (more rarely the Aorist) Infinitive.

μέλλω γράφειν, γράψειν (rarely γράψαι).
I am going to write, I mean or intend to write.

μέλλω ὑμᾶς ἄγειν εἰς 'Ασίαν.
I am going to lead you (am on the point of leading you) into Asia.
In Asiam vos ducturus sum.

δεήσει τοῦ τοιούτου εἰ μέλλει ἡ πολιτεία σώζεσθαι.
PLAT. *Rep.* 412.
There will be need of such a ruler if the constitution is to be preserved.

ἔμελλον in the same way is used—
ἔμελλόν σ' ἄρα κινήσειν ἐγώ. AR. *Nub.* 1301.
Aha! I thought I should tickle you.
ἐνταῦθα ἔμελλον καταλύσειν. XEN.
There they were intending to rest.
Ibi deversuri erant.

Sometimes μέλλω, ἔμελλον, means *I am doomed, destined.* πῶς οὐ μέλλω, τί οὐ μέλλω; mean *Why should I not?*

2. The Future Perfect denotes a finished act or state in the Future :—

ἡ πολιτεία τελέως κεκοσμήσεται. PLAT.
Our state shall have been perfectly constituted.

Note. The Future Perfect, like the Perfect, sometimes denotes what will take place instantly.
Compare
κἂν τοῦτο νικῶμεν πάνθ' ἡμῖν πεποίηται. XEN. *An.* i. 8. 12.
If we secure this victory we have done everything.
with
φράζε καὶ πεπράξεται. AR. *Plut.* 1027.
Speak, and it shall be done instanter.

A periphrastic future perfect active is formed with εἰμί—
τὰ δέοντα ἐσόμεθα ἐγνωκότες, κ.τ.λ. DEM. *Phil.* i. 54.
We shall have determined to do our duty.

§ 142. Gnomic and Iterative Tenses.

Almost any tense in Greek, as in English, can express a customary or a repeated act, or a general truth.

1. *The Present—*
ῥωμὴ ἀμαθὴς πολλάκις τίκτει βλάβην. EUR. (See above.)
Strength without science often causeth harm.
Vis consili expers mole ruit sua.

2. *The Perfect—*
πολλοὶ διὰ δόξαν καὶ πολιτ˙κὴν δύναμιν κακὰ πεπόνθασιν.
XEN.
Many have come to trouble (and do come to trouble) in consequence of reputation and political power.
(This perfect alternates with presents in the text.)

3. *The Aorist called Gnomic,* as expressing *a* γνώμη, *sentiment or general truth—*
ἀθυμοῦντες ἄνδρες οὔπω τροπαῖον ἔστησαν. PLAT.
Half-hearted men never yet set up a trophy.
So in English—"Faint heart never won fair lady."
δεινῶν τ' ἄημα πνευμάτων ἐκοίμισε στένοντα πόντον.
SOPH. *Ai.* 674.
And the breath of dreadful winds husheth ever the moaning deep.
The present and perfect, the present and aorist, the perfect and aorist, often alternate in the same paragraph.

4. *The Imperfect and Aorist with* ἄν *denote a repeated act.*
ἀναλαμβάνων οὖν αὐτῶν τὰ ποιήματα διηρώτων ἄν αὐτοὺς τι λέγοιεν. PLAT. *Apol.* ch. viii.
Taking up their poems then I used to ask them (I would ask them) what their meaning was.
εἴ τινες ἴδοιεν πῃ τοὺς σφετέρους ἐπικρατοῦντας ἀνεθάρσησαν ἄν. THUC. vii. 71.
If at any point they saw their own side winning they picked up their courage (as often as this happened).
For an excellent passage see SOPH. *Phil.* 289-297.

§ 143. The Tenses in the Moods.

The distinction previously explained between the Present, the Perfect, and the Aorist, is observed in all the moods,— the Indicative, Imperative, Subjunctive, Optative, Infinitive, and Participle. Some instances are given to show the difference, especially between the Present and the Aorist.

Imperative—

μηδὲν φοβοῦ, *Don't be timid* : μηδὲν φοβηθῇς, *Don't have any fear of this.*

εἴ πῃ ἔχεις ἀντιλέγειν, ἀντίλεγε· εἰ δὲ μή, παῦσαι πολλάκις λέγων τὸν αὐτὸν λόγον. PLAT. *Crit.*
If you have anything to say in objection, say on (at length, in a continued speech), but if not, give over (at once) repeating the same argument.

Subjunctive or Optative—

οὐ τοῦτο πώποτε ἐπείσθην ὡς ἡ ψυχή, ἕως μὲν ἐν τῷ θνητῷ σώματι ᾖ, ζῇ, ὅταν δὲ τοῦτον ἀπαλλαγῇ, τέθνηκεν.
XEN. *Cyr.* viii. 7. 19.
He never believed that the soul, so long as it exists in this mortal body, lives, but that as soon as it is separated from it, it dies (ᾖ denoting continuance, ἀπαλλαγῇ the instant act of death).

Infinitive—

οὐ βουλεύεσθαι ἔτι ὥρα ἀλλὰ βεβουλεῦσθαι. PLAT. *Crit.*
It is no longer the moment to be making up one's mind, but to have it made up.

χαλεπὸν τὸ ποιεῖν τὸ δὲ κελεῦσαι ῥᾴδιον.
It is difficult to do (to be engaged in doing), but easy to command (to say 'do this').

So with the other Moods.

CHAPTER VIII.

THE THREE VERBAL NOUNS.

1. The Infinitive (a Substantive).
2. The Participle (an Adjective).
3. The Verbal Adjectives in -τος and -τεος.

§ 144. Note on the Infinitive.

The Infinitive is, in its origin, a Verbal Substantive in the Dative case. Though subsequently its uses diverged so widely from this limited signification, yet its origin gives us a clue to its different meanings.
Thus—

ὥρα ἀπιέναι would mean *time for going away.*
δυνατὸς γενέσθαι, *able for becoming.*
μανθάνειν ἥκομεν, *we are come for learning.*
παρέχω ἐμαυτὸν τέμνειν καὶ καίειν, *I offer myself for cutting and burning.*
θαῦμα ἰδέσθαι, *a wonder for the viewing.*

For full information consult Professor Max Müller's Inaugural Oxford Lecture.

§ 145. *THE INFINITIVE.*

The Infinitive is a Verbal Substantive denoting action. Compare τὸ ποιεῖν with ἡ ποίησις.
It has therefore points in common both with (1) the Verb, (2) with the Noun.

1. Like the Verb

(*a*) It has *tenses* and *voices*—λύειν, λύσειν, λῦσαι, etc., λῦσαι, λύσασθαι, λυθῆναι.

(*b*) It takes a subject before and a predicate after it.

(c) It governs the same case as its verb.

(d) It is qualified, like a verb, by adverbs, and not like a substantive by adjectives.

(e) It forms subordinate sentences, the indirect statement, a temporal sentence (with πρίν), a final sentence, a consecutive sentence, with ὥστε and ὡς, and in connexion with ἄν it is a substitute for the indicative and optative moods with ἄν. This last use gives it a sort of right to be called a mood.

2. Like a Substantive

(a) It stands as the subject to a verb.

(b) It is declined with the article as a nominative, accusative, genitive, or dative.

(c) It is connected with Prepositions.

§ 146. *THE SUPPLEMENTARY*[1] *INFINITIVE.*

1. The Infinitive supplements the meanings of verbs and nouns (especially of verbs) which in themselves are incomplete.

ἔμαθον τοῦτο ποιῆσαι.
They learned to do this.

οὐ πέφυκε δουλεύειν.
He is not born to be a slave.

Θημιστοκλῆς ἱκανώτατος ἦν εἰπεῖν καὶ γνῶναι καὶ πρᾶξαι.   Lys.
Themistocles was eminently able to speak, to decide, and to act.

Note 1. Sometimes the article is added.
τὸ βίᾳ πολιτῶν δρᾶν ἔφυν ἀμήχανος.   Soph. *Ant.* 78.
I am by nature incapable of acting in defiance of my fellow-citizens. Cf. *Trach.* 545, *O. C.* 442, Aesch. *P. V.* 865.

---

[1] Also called the Complementary, or the Prolate, Infinitive. The term Supplementary seems more simple and intelligible.

The article marks the Infinitive more distinctly as an object. The Infinitive is not always the Supplementary Infinitive, see SOPH. *Ant.* 265.

Note 2. It is impossible to give a complete list of all such verbs. They are fairly the same as in English and in Latin, though this Infinitive is much more extensively used in Greek than in Latin.

The chief verbs perhaps are those expressing—

(*a*) *Wish and desire* (as in Latin), βούλομαι, θέλω, ἐπιθυμῶ.

(*b*) *Caution, fear, shame,* εὐλαβοῦμαι, ὀκνῶ, ὄκνος ἐστί, φοβοῦμαι, δέδοικα, αἰσχύνομαι.

For Verbs of Fearing see also Index.

(*c*) *Intention, determination,* ψηφίζομαι (*I vote*), ἔδοξε, δέδοκται, διανοοῦμαι, ἐν νῷ ἔχω.

So statuo, constituo, with infinitive in Latin.

(*d*) *Ability, capability, fitness,* δύναμαι, οἷός τε εἰμί, ἔξεστι, πέφυκα, as in Latin.

(*e*) *Duty, necessity, compulsion,* δεῖ, χρή, ἀνάγκη ἐστί, ὀφείλω. So in Latin, except that oportet and necesse est in certain senses take a subjunctive.

(*f*) *Custom, habit, chance,* εἴωθα, νόμος ἐστί, ξυμβαίνει, etc. Many of these in Latin, mos est, consuetudo est, contingit, accidit, etc., take ut with subjunctive ; soleo, consuesco, etc., an infinitive.

The adjectives with which this Supplementary Infinitive goes are of a similar meaning, *e.g.* δυνατός, ἱκανός, πρόθυμος, ἐπιτήδειος, ἄξιος, ἀνάξιος, etc.

Sometimes the Greek Infinitive with an adjective corresponds with the Latin adjective and the supine in *u*, *e.g.* χαλεπὸν λέξαι, difficile dictu.

2. The Epexegetical (*i.e.* Explanatory) Infinitive is added to verbs of giving and taking, and to adjectives. This Infinitive further explains the purpose of the verb, or the character of the action, or of the adjective.

ἀνὴρ χαλεπός συζῆν. PLAT.
A difficult person to live with.
παρέχω ἐμαυτὸν τῷ ἰατρῷ τέμνειν καὶ καίειν. PLAT.
I offer myself to the physician to cut and burn (me).

Note 1. Even where the construction is already complete this explanatory Infinitive is sometimes added.
κακὸν οἴομαι ποιεῖν ἃ οὗτος ποιεῖ, ἄνδρα ἀδίκως ἐπιχειρεῖν ἀποκτιννύναι. PLAT. *Apol.* xviii.
It is an evil, I think, to be doing what my opponent is now doing, trying, that is, unjustly to put a man to death.
τῆς σῆς οὐκ ἐρῶ τιμῆς τυχεῖν. SOPH. *El.* 364.
I am not in love with thy honours—to obtain them.

ὥστε with this infinitive and adjectives helps out this explanatory force.
ψυχρὸν τὸ ὕδωρ ὥστε λούσασθαι. XEN. *Mem.* iii. 13. 3.
The water is cold to bathe in.

Obs. This use should be compared with that of the English gerundive (or *to* with the dative of the infinitive), *a house to let, a letter to write,* etc. Both in Latin and Greek the passive infinitive is very unusual, and probably incorrect.

Note 2. The comparative with ἤ, or ὥστε ἤ, and infinitive.
τὸ νόσημα μεῖζον ἢ φέρειν. SOPH. *O. T.* 1293.
The plague is too great to bear.
Pestis maior quam quae (ut) tolerari possit.
μεῖζον ἢ ὥστε φέρειν δύνασθαι κακὸν τῇ πόλει συμβαίνει.
XEN. *Mem.* vi. 5. 17.
A calamity befalls the state too great for it to bear.

Note 3. ὡς, ὥς γε, with the infinitive limit the application.
ἄοπλοι ὡς ἐκ χειρὸς μάχεσθαι. XEN. *Cyr.* vi. 4. 16.
Unarmed so far as fighting hand to hand goes (i.e. *if they come to close quarters*).
εὖ λέγει ὁ ἀνὴρ ὥς γε οὑτωσὶ ἀκοῦσαι. XEN. *Cyr.* vi. 14. 6.
The man speaks well enough just to listen to in this way (i.e. *if that is all you consider*).

THE ACCUSATIVE WITH THE INFINITIVE. 157

To this head belong certain idiomatic infinitives.

ὡς ἔπος εἰπεῖν,
ὡς εἰπεῖν, } so to say.
ὡς ἐπὶ πᾶν εἰπεῖν, speaking generally.
ὡς ἁπλῶς εἰπεῖν,
ὡς συνελόντι   } to speak
εἰπεῖν,   } briefly, concisely.
ἐς τὸ ἀκριβὲς εἰπεῖν, strictly speaking.
ὡς εἰκάσαι, to make a guess.

σὺν θεῷ εἰπεῖν, in God's name.
σχεδὸν εἰπεῖν, almost, so to say, paene dixerim.
ἑκών εἶναι (in negative sentences), willingly. ἑκών is the predicate to εἶναι.
ὀλίγου δεῖν, all but.
κατὰ τοῦτο εἶναι, in this respect.
ὅσον γέ μ' εἰδέναι, so far as I know.

§ 147. The Subject before and the Predicate after the Infinitive (commonly called the Accusative with the Infinitive).

The Infinitive, like other parts of the verb, takes a Subject before and a Predicate after. The Predicate is, of course, in the same case as the Subject. The Predicate may often be the Supplementary Predicate, in which case the Infinitive is, of course, part of the Predicate. The following examples will explain this construction.

INDICATIVE.

Subject.	Verb.	Predicate.
omitted.	εἰμι	Ἀθηναῖος
I	am	an Athenian.
omitted.	ἐπῆλθον	ἄκλητοι
they	advanced	unbidden
Κῦρος	ἐγένετο	πρόθυμος .
Cyrus	showed himself	willing
omitted.	γενοῦ	πρόθυμος
	show thyself	willing
omitted.	ἐγένοιτο	εὐδαίμονες
they	became	happy

THE THREE VERBAL NOUNS.

Infinitive.

	Subject.	Verb.	Predicate.
(ἔφη) *he said*	omitted *that he*	εἶναι *was*	Ἀθηναῖος *an Athenian*
(ἔφασαν) *they said*	omitted *that they*	ἐπελθεῖν *advanced*	ἄκλητοι *unbidden*
(ἔφασαν) *they said*	Κῦρον *that Cyrus*	γενέσθαι *showed himself*	πρόθυμον *willing*
(δέομαι) *I beg*	σου *you*	γενέσθαι *to show thyself*	προθύμου *willing*
(ἐξῆν) *it was permitted*	αὐτοῖς *them*	γενέσθαι *to become*	εὐδαίμοσιν *happy*

1. Predicate in Nominative.

ἐψηφίσασθε ἐξελθεῖν βοηθήσοντες. DEM.
You resolved to march out to the rescue.

2. Genitive.

ἐδέοντο Κύρου ὡς προθυμοτάτου γενέσθαι. XEN.
They were begging Cyrus to show himself as energetic as possible.

3. Dative.

εὐδαίμοσιν ὑμῖν ἔξεστι γίγνεσθαι. DEM.
It is permitted you to become happy.

Note 1. Just as in Latin we may use the Accusative for a Dative, *e.g.* licet esse beatum, for licet esse beato, so in Greek an Accusative Predicate sometimes takes the place of a Genitive or a Dative Predicate.

ἔξεστιν ὑμῖν λαβόντας ὅπλα βοηθεῖν.
For λαβοῦσιν ὅπλα.

ἐδέοντό μου προστάτην γενέσθαι.
For προστάτου.

THE ACCUSATIVE WITH THE INFINITIVE. 159

The explanation is that the mind has inserted the Accusative Subject before the Infinitive, licet mihi me esse beatum, ἔξεστιν ὑμῖν ὑμᾶς λαβόντας ὅπλα βοηθεῖν.

Note 2. The personal passive construction is used in Greek side by side with the impersonal passive followed by the Accusative and Infinitive, the former being the commoner.

ὁ Κῦρος ἠγγέλθη νικῆσαι. XEN.
Cyrus was reported to have conquered.
λέγεται Ἀλκιβιάδην Περικλεῖ διαλεχθῆναι περὶ νόμων.
XEN.
It is said that Alcibiades conversed with Pericles about the laws.

This construction should be compared with the Latin (traditur, fertur, dicitur, existimatur, videtur, creditur, etc., etc., with an Infinitive); *e.g.* existimatur errare, probus esse, *he is thought to be mistaken, to be upright* (*it is thought that he, etc.*) See Zumpt § 607 and *note*. But the Greek construction is much freer, and follows many adjectives.

Certain adjectives, δίκαιος, ἄξιος, *worthy ;* ἐπιτήδειος (*fit*), ἐπίδοξος (*probable*), ἀναγκαῖος (*necessary*), may take either a personal or an impersonal construction with the Infinitive. Thus we may say either δίκαιός εἰμι ταῦτα ποιεῖν or δίκαιόν ἐστιν ἐμέ ταῦτα ποιεῖν, *I am justified in so doing* or *it is right for me so to do.*

Instances of δίκαιος occur in PLATO'S *Apology* ii. 1, *Crito* iv., SOPH. *Ant.* 400.

Note 3. δοκῶ is generally personal :

εὖ λέγειν μοι δοκεῖτε, *I think you speak well.*
Cf. τοῖς πλείστοις ἐδόκουν, *most people thought* (*they seemed to most*).
ἔδοξα ἀκοῦσαι, *I thought I heard.*
δοκῶ μοι τὸν ὄνον ἐξάγειν, *I am determined to lead out the ass.*

The impersonal δοκεῖ τινι is rare : δοκεῖ, ἔδοξε, *it is decreed,* is different. With δοκῶ, δοκεῖ, cf. the use of ἔοικα, *I seem,* varying with ἔοικε, and the Latin, videor mihi, videtur mihi.

Note 4. The Infinitive is used for the imperative in formal or solemn language, in poetry more freely.

(a) In legal orders or official commands.

ἀκούετε λεῴ ... πίνειν ὑπὸ τῆς σάλπιγγος. AR. *Ach.* 1000.
Hear ye, good people all! drink to the trumpet's sound.
With ἀκούετε compare *O yes!*

(b) In prayers.

θεοὶ πολῖται, μή με δουλείας τυχεῖν. AESCH.
Gods of my country, let me not meet with slavery (grant that, etc.).

Examples occur in SOPH. *Elect.* 9, *Ant.* 1080 (where a king speaks), THUC. v. 9, vi. 34.

Note 5. The Infinitive is used in expressions of surprise. (Cf. Lat. 'Mene incepto desistere victam.')

τῆς μωρίας, τὸ Δία νομίζειν, ὄντα τηλικουτονί.
AR. *Nub.* 819

What folly! to think of a man of his years believing in Zeus!

Note 6. The tenses of the Infinitive correspond to the tenses of the Indicative throughout in the *character* of the action (as continued, finished, or indefinite).

They only express distinctions of time when representing the Indicative of the Recta in indirect statements or direct questions.

But the Present Infinitive sometimes represents an Imperfect and not a Present Indicative.

τίνας οὖν εὐχὰς ὑπολαμβάνετ' εὔχεσθαι τὸν Φίλιππον ὅτ' ἔσπενδεν; DEM. *de F. L.* 381. 10.
What vows do you suppose Philip was offering when he was making libations?

This is often the case after ἔφην. So in Latin, memini me dicere means *I remember I was saying* (also accepimus, scribit). See Zumpt, § 589, *note.*

Madvig first pointed out this, § 171. 6, Rem. 1. It is fully discussed in Goodwin, *Moods and Tenses,* p. 15.

§ 148. *THE INFINITIVE AS A NOUN.*

1. The Infinitive, like a Substantive, may stand either as the Subject or the Predicate of a sentence.

THE INFINITIVE AS A NOUN.

Subject.	Predicate.	Predicate.
τὸ δίκην διδόναι	πότερον πάσχειν τί ἐστιν	ἢ ποιεῖν;
To pay a penalty / Paying a penalty	is it { to suffer or suffering	{ to do something? doing. PLATO.

So in English "*to see is to believe,*" *seeing is believing*.

Rarely but sometimes without the article, σωφρονεῖν καλόν, SOPH. *Ai.*, *discretion is a virtue.*

2. The Infinitive with the Article is declined throughout like a Substantive. Its cases then follow the constructions of the Nominative, Accusative, Genitive, and Dative.

Its oblique cases are connected with Prepositions. Unlike ordinary Substantives, however, it (1) can govern the same case as its verb, and (2) can be qualified by an adverb. It corresponds to the Latin Infinitive and Gerund.

Nom. τὸ καλῶς ζῆν, *a noble life*, honeste vivere.
Acc. τὸ καλῶς ζῆν, *a noble life*, honeste vivere (with preposition), honeste vivendum.
Gen. τοῦ καλῶς ζῆν, *of a noble life*, honeste vivendi.
Dat. τῷ καλῶς ζῆν, *for* or *by a noble life*, honeste vivendo.

So διὰ τὸ καλῶς ζῆν, ἐν (πρὸς) τῷ καλῶς ζῆν, ἀντὶ (ἕνεκα) τοῦ καλῶς ζῆν.

Note. (a) Infinitive Nominative:
It is used like the Latin *quod* with Indicative (*the fact* or *circumstance that*).

τὸ Πελοποννησίους αὐτοῖς μὴ βοηθῆσαι παρέσχεν ὑμῖν Σαμίων κόλασιν. THUC. i. 41.
The circumstance that the Peloponnesians did not help them enabled you to chastise the Samians.

(b) The Dative is often a Dative of means, cause, or circumstance, instrument, like the Gerund in -do.

κεκράτηκε Φίλιππος τῷ πρότερος γενέσθαι. DEM.
Philip has succeeded by being foremost in the field.

(c) The Genitive is very often Objective.

ἠπείγοντο πρὸς τὸν ποταμὸν τοῦ πιεῖν ἐπιθυμίᾳ.
                                          THUC. vii. 84.
They were hurrying to the river in their desire to drink (of drinking).

The Genitive of the Infinitive sometimes expresses the aim or purpose (usually in this sense it takes ἕνεκα). The idiom is considered either a genitive of value or a genitive of cause. (See *Causal Genitive*.)

ἐτειχίσθη ’Αταλάντη ἡ νῆσος τοῦ μὴ λῃστὰς κακουργεῖν
τὴν Εὔβοιαν.   THUC. ii. 32 (cf. i. 4).
The island of Atalante was fortified in order that the pirates might not injure Euboea (with a view to their not, etc.).

The construction is not very common, but thoroughly established, in Attic Prose. The only thing in Latin like it is the genitive with the Gerundive, a construction which frequently occurs in Livy : *haec prodendi imperii Romani, tradendae Hannibali victoriae sunt,* xxvii. 9 ; *aequandae libertatis esse,* xxxviii. 50. See Zumpt, § 662, *note* 2.

§ 149.   *THE PARTICIPLE.*

The Participle has three different uses.

A. It is an attributive to a Substantive.

ὁ παρὼν χρόνος, *the present time.*

B. It qualifies the principal Verb of a sentence like a Supplementary Predicate, or Adverbial Sentence.

ταῦτα ἔπραττε στρατηγῶν.
He was doing this while he was general.

C. It supplements the meaning of a verb, the meaning of which would otherwise be incomplete (cf. the Supplementary Infinitive).

(*a*.) The Participle agrees with the Subject.

παύομαι φιλοσοφῶν.
I leave off philosophising.

(*b*.) The Participle agrees with, and is the Predicate to, the Object.

παύω σε φιλοσοφοῦντα.
I make you leave off philosophising.

§ 150. *THE PARTICIPLE AS AN ATTRIBUTIVE.*

A. 1. The Participle when joined to a Substantive corresponds to an Adjective, or more frequently to a Relative sentence.

αἱ Αἰόλου νῆσοι καλούμεναι.   THUC.
The so-called islands of Aeolus (or, the islands of Aeolus, as they are called).

ὁ κατειληφὼς κίνδυνος τὴν πόλιν.   DEM.
The danger which has overtaken the state.

2. The Participle with the Article, when the Substantive is omitted, becomes itself a Substantive.

οἱ λέγοντες, *the speakers.*
οἱ δράσαντες, *the doers.*
ὁ τυχών, *the first-comer.*
ὁ βουλόμενος, *any one who will* (see Article).
οἱ προσήκοντες, *relations,* propinqui.

Note 1. The Future Participle with the Article signifies, in a sort of final sense, *one who is ready, prepared or willing, to do so and so.*

ἡ χώρα ἀγαθὴ ἦν καὶ ἐνῆσαν οἱ ἐργασόμενοι.
XEN. *An.* ii. 4. 22.
The soil was rich and there were people to till it.

Note 2. Many neuter Participles are Substantival.

τὸ σύμφερον, *expediency*, utile, utilitas   With an Adjective in agreement, τὰ μικρὰ συμφέροντα τῆς πόλεως, DEM. *The small interests of the state.*
τὰ δέοντα, *duties* or *duty*, officia.
Thucydides and the poets use a neuter present participle as a Substantive, where an Infinitive would be more usual.
ἐν τῷ μὴ μελετῶντι, *by want of training* (= ἐν τῷ μὴ μελετᾶν).
τὸ δεδιός, *fear* = τὸ δεδιέναι, τὸ θαρσοῦν = τὸ θαρσεῖν = τὸ θάρσος. THUC.
τὸ νοσοῦν = τὸ νοσεῖν = ἡ νόσος.   SOPH. *Phil.* 674.

In the poets οἱ τεκόντες, *parents;* ὁ τεκών, *the father;* ἡ τεκοῦσα, *the mother* (ἡ τίκτουσα also, SOPH.). ὁ ἐκείνου τεκών, *his father*.   τὸ πτοηθὲν σῇ ψυχῇ, *the wild fluttering in thy heart*, EUR. *Bacch.* 1269.

B. The Participle qualifies the Principal Verb like a Supplementary Predicate or an Adverbial Sentence, (Conditional, Temporal, Causal, etc.).

These usages of the Participle are very common in Greek, and are most important to notice. The particles which bring out the special significance of the Participle in each case should be carefully noticed. The different usages are given under the heads of the different sentences in the Compound Sentence. (See *Index*.)

Note 3. The Participle in a Sentence expresses circumstance or manner generally.

The particles οὕτως, τότε, εἶτα, κᾆτα (καὶ εἶτα), ἔπειτα are put before the Principal Verb. The sense hovers between that of time and of circumstance.

To this head belong the phrases (as old as Homer), τί μαθών; τί παθών; in the obliqua ὅτι μαθών, παθών.

τί μαθόντες ἐμαρτυρεῖτε ὑμεῖς; DEM. 45. 38.
What induced you to give evidence ?
τί παθοῦσαι θνηταῖς εἴξασι γυναιξί; AR. *Nub.* 341.
What has happened to (the clouds) that they look like mortal women ?
So τί ἔχων; τί βουλόμενος; PLAT. *Phaed.* 236, E.

All these phrases are periphrases for *why? wherefore?* τί μαθών; *learning what, on what inducement?* denotes an internal motive; τί παθών; *ailing or experiencing what?* denotes an external cause (on what compulsion?).

Note 4. Under this head comes also the peculiar use of ἔχων in colloquialisms.

ποῖα ὑποδήματα φλυαρεῖς ἔχων; PLAT.
What sort of shoes do you keep on chattering about?

τί ληρεῖς ἔχων; lit. *talk nonsense in so behaving.*
Why do you incessantly trifle?

τί κυπτάζεις ἔχων περὶ τὴν θύραν; ARISTOPH.
Why do you keep on poking about at the door?

Note 5. The Participle in a Comparative sense with the Subjective particles ὡς and ὥσπερ, *as if, as though, as thinking.*

δεδίασι τὸν θάνατον ὡς εὖ εἰδότες ὅτι μέγιστον τῶν κακῶν ἐστι. PLAT. *Apol.* xvii.
Men fear death as though they knew for certain that it is the greatest of evils.

§ 151. *THE GENITIVE ABSOLUTE.*

The Genitive Absolute (*i.e.* a Participle agreeing with a Genitive which is not in the main construction of the sentence) is equivalent to an Adverbial sentence, either Conditional, Temporal, Causal, Concessive, or expressing Circumstances generally.

The same particles which accompany the simple Participle (*e.g.* μεταξύ, ὡς, etc.) go with the Genitive Absolute.

ταῦτα ἐπράχθη Κόνωνος στρατηγοῦντος. ISOCR.
These operations were carried out when K. was general.

οὐκ ἂν ἦλθον δεῦρο ὑμῶν μὴ κελευόντων.
I should not have come here if you had not ordered me.

ὡς ὧδ' ἐχόντων τῶνδ' ἐπίστασθαί σε χρή. SOPH. *Ai.*
On the understanding (as knowing) that this is so, thou must form thy judgment (i.e. *thou must know that it is even so*).

Note. The Participle alone, without the Genitive being expressed, occurs (see *Genitive Case, Genitive Absolute*)—

(*a.*) Where the Genitive is easily supplied from context—

οἱ δὲ πολέμιοι, προσιόντων (sc. τῶν Ἑλλήνων mentioned just before), τέως μὲν ἡσύχαζον.
XEN. *An.* v. 4. 16.
The enemy, as they were approaching, for a while were remaining quiet.

Cf. iv. 8. 5, ἐρωτήσαντος (sc. αὐτοῦ).

(*b.*) In certain impersonal expressions—

οὕτως ἐχόντων. XEN. *An.* v. 4. 16.
Such being the case, quae quum ita sint.

ἐσαγγελθέντων ὅτι αἱ νῆες πλέουσι. THUC. i. 116.
On the news arriving that the ships were sailing.

ὕοντος πολλῷ (sc. Διός). XEN. *Hell.* i. 1. 16 (cf. AR. *Vesp.* 774).

Cf. THUC. i. 74 (δηλωθέντος), XEN. *Cyr.* i. 4. 18 (σημανθέντων). Compare the Latin Ablative Past Participle Passive (cognito, edicto, etc.) agreeing with the whole sentence.

The Participle is very rarely omitted.

ὡς ἐμοῦ μόνης πέλας (sc. οὔσης). SOPH. *O. C.* 83.
Since I alone am at thy side.

§ 152. The Genitive Absolute in Greek and the Ablative Absolute in Latin.

Great care must be taken not always to use one where we should use the other. The Greek has a perfect series of active participles, the Latin has no past participle active except in the case of Deponents.

Therefore in Latin we may write—
    His verbis editis egressi sunt.
    So saying they went out.

But in Greek this would be—
    ταῦτα εἰπόντες ἐξῆεσαν,

and not
    τούτων λεχθέντων ἐξῄεσαν,

which would mean *when this had been said* (by others) *they went out*.

Nor, on the other hand, would Latin tolerate such an apparently slovenly structure as the following :—

διαβεβηκότος ἤδη Περικλέους, ἠγγέλθη αὐτῷ.
After P. had already crossed, news was brought him.

In Latin we should write—
Pericli iam transgresso nuntiatum est.

§ 153. *THE ACCUSATIVE ABSOLUTE.*

Instead of the Genitive Absolute the Accusative Absolute is used with Participles of *Impersonal verbs* and certain other expressions.[1]

A. Impersonal Verbs : δέον, ἐξόν, παρόν, προσῆκον, μέλον, μεταμέλον, δοκοῦν, τυχόν, δόξαν or δόξαντα (ταῦτα).

B. Passive Participles used impersonally : προσταχθέν, εἰρημένον, γεγραμμένον, δεδογμένον, προστεταγμένον.

C. Adjectives with ὄν used impersonally ; ἀδύνατον ὄν, αἰσχρὸν ὄν, etc.

The particles ὡς, ὥσπερ (*as though, as thinking that*), etc., may accompany the Accusative Absolute. The Accusative Absolute is equivalent to an Adverbial Sentence, Causal, Temporal, Circumstantial, and especially semi-Temporal and semi-Concessive.

οὐδεὶς ἐξὸν εἰρήνην ἄγειν πόλεμον αἱρήσεται.
No one will choose war when it is in his power to be at peace.

οἱ δὲ τριάκοντα, ὡς ἐξὸν ἤδη αὐτοῖς τυραννεῖν ἀδεῶς προεῖπον.* XEN.
The Thirty thinking it was now in their power to play the despot with impunity, issued an edict, etc.

---

[1] *Obs.*—This is doubtless an Internal Accusative, probably of respect. Compare for instance τὸν αὐτὸν τρόπον with δόξαν ἡμῖν ταῦτα.

οὐχὶ δε ἐσώσαμεν οἷόν τε ὂν καὶ δυνατόν. PLAT.
We did not save you when (though) it was feasible and possible.

δόξαντα ὑμῖν ταῦτα, εἵλεσθε ἄνδρας ἑκατόν. ANDOK.
On coming to this resolution (decree), you appointed a hundred men.

σιωπῇ ἐδείπνουν, ὥςπερ τοῦτο προςτεταγμένον.
                                                                XEN.
They were taking their meal in silence, as though they had been ordered to do so.

For other examples see THUC. i. 126 (ὑπάρχον), viii. 79 (δόξαν). For passive participles see THUC. i. 125 (δεδογμένον), v. 30 (εἰρημένον), v. 56 (γεγραμμένον).

Sometimes a personal verb is found with the Accusative Absolute, but then usually with the subjective particles ὡς, ὥςπερ.

ἔνιοι τῶν ἀδελφῶν ἀμελοῦσιν ὥςπερ οὐ γιγνομένους φίλους.
Some men neglect their brothers under the impression that they do not become friends.
                    XEN. Mem. ii. 3. 3 (quotation shortened).

Cf. *Mem.* i. 2. 20. But XEN. *Hell.* iii. 2. 19 (δόξαντα ταῦτα καὶ περανθέντα), THUC. iv. 125 (κυρωθὲν οὐδέν).

§ 154. *VERBALS IN -τέος.*

Verbals in -τέος imply necessity. They take the same case as the verb to which they belong. The agent is generally in the Dative (but see below). The verbal has two constructions, the Personal and the Impersonal.

§ 155. A. *THE PERSONAL CONSTRUCTION.*

ἀσκητέα ἐστί σοι ἡ ἀρετή.
You must practise virtue.
Colenda est tibi virtus.

§ 156. B. *THE IMPERSONAL CONSTRUCTION.*

Here the verbal is either singular or plural.

ἀσκητέον,
ἀσκητέα,   } ἐστί σοι τὴν ἀρετήν.

ἐπιθυμητέον,
ἐπιθυμητέα, } ἐστὶ τοῖς ἀνθρώποις τῆς ἀρετῆς. DEM.

Men must covet virtue.

Note. The agent, however, in Attic, is fairly often in the Accusative, instead of the Dative.

οὐδενὶ τρόπῳ φαμὲν ἑκόντας ἀδικητέον εἶναι. PLAT. *Crit.*
We maintain that in no way must we deliberately commit injustice.

And the Dative and Accusative are both found together. EUR. *Phoen.* 710, 712.

§ 157. C. *THE SUPPLEMENTARY PARTICIPLE.*

The Supplementary Participle is used, much like the Supplementary Infinitive, to complete the meaning of many verbs and verbal phrases. It agrees either (1) with the Subject, or (2) with the Object of the verb.

§ 158. *THE SUPPLEMENTARY PARTICIPLE IN AGREEMENT WITH THE SUBJECT OF THE VERB.*

The Participle is used with the following classes of Verbs :—

* Verbs marked thus have peculiar usages which are explained in the notes.

A. *Verbs of Feeling and Perceiving* (see Indirect Statement). These verbs differ from the following because they can equally take a finite mood with ὅτι or ὡς, thus showing the substantival character of the construction which they introduce.

B. *Verbs of Mental Emotion.*

χαίρω, ἥδομαι, ἄχθομαι, ἀγανακτῶ (*I am vexed*), χαλεπῶς φέρω (*I am vexed*), μεταμέλομαι, μεταμέλει μοι (*I repent, regret*), ἀνέχομαι (*I endure*), ῥᾳδίως φέρω (*I easily bear*).

χαίρουσιν ἀκούοντες ἐξεταζομένων τῶν ἀνθρώπων.
PLAT.
They like to hear people cross-questioned.

χρημάτων οὐκ αἰσχύνει ἐπιμελούμενος; PLAT.
Are you not ashamed to be devoting yourself to money-making?

ῥᾳδίως φέρεις ἡμᾶς ἀπολείπων. PLAT.
You don't mind leaving us behind (you make light of doing so).

C. *Verbs of beginning, continuing, and ending an action* (including *persevering and growing weary*).

*ἄρχομαι, *ὑπάρχω, φθάνω, διατελῶ, διάγω, διαγίγνομαι (*I continue*), παύομαι, ἀπείρηκα, and κάμνω (*I grow tired*).

τὸν λοιπὸν βίον καθεύδοντες διατελοῖτ' ἄν. PLAT.
You would go on sleeping for the rest of your lives.

οὐ μὴ παύσωμαι φιλοσοφῶν. PLAT.
Never will I give over the pursuit of wisdom.

οὐκ ἀνέξομαι ζῶσα. EURIP.
I will not endure to live.

D. *Verbs of being manifest, being detected (convicted), and of escaping notice.*

*δῆλος εἰμι (δηλῶ, intrans.), *φανερός εἰμι, *φαίνομαι, δείκνυμι, λανθάνω, ἁλίσκομαι (the active form is αἱρῶ).

δῆλος εἶ καταφρονῶν. PLAT.
It is clear that you despise me.

δείξω αὐτὸν ἄξιον ὄντα. DEM.
I will prove that he is worthy.

ἔδειξαν ἕτοιμοι ὄντες. THUC.
They showed that they were ready.

φανεροί εἰσιν ἀγωνιζόμενοι πάντες. XEN.
It is evident that they all are contending.

Πηλέως γὰρ ἄξια
πατρός τ' Ἀχιλλέως ἔργα δρῶν φανήσεται. EUR.
*He shall be seen to do great deeds
worthy of Peleus, and his sire Achilles.*

φονέα ἐλάνθανε βόσκων. HDT.
He was entertaining a murderer unawares.

ἐὰν δὲ ἁλῷς ἔτι τοῦτο πράττων, ἀποθανεῖ. PLAT.
*If you are caught again in this pursuit, you shall die
(if you are convicted of following it any longer).*

So δηλῶ, SOPH. O. C. 556, and Ai. 472, Ant. 20 (in nominative attraction). δείκνυμι (see third example above) may be intransitive, EUR. I. A. 436, THUC. 72. The above verbs, however, have several other constructions, for which see below.

§ 159. Note on Special Verbs.

1. ἄρχομαι takes both the Infinitive and Participle, more usually the Infinitive. The Participle seems to denote, more than the Infinitive, that the act is going on.

ἤρξαντο οἰκοδομεῖν.
They began to build (of the intention).

ἤρξαντο οἰκοδομοῦντες.
They began the building (the act going on).
See THUC. i. 107.

2. ὑπάρχω.

ἐάν τις ἡμᾶς εὖ ποιῶν ὑπάρχῃ. XEN.
If any one first confers a kindness on us.
Otherwise ὑπάρχω is used almost like τυγχάνω.

ὑπάρχει ἐχθρὸς ὤν. DEM.
He is an enemy (to begin with).

3. φθάνω.

(a) ἔφθασε (ἔφθη) ἀφικόμενος.
He was beforehand in arriving.

οὐκ ἂν φθάνοις λέγων (gen. of 2d person).
Make haste, speak—or, *quick, quick speak.* (Lit. *you could
not anticipate (my wish, or your duty) in speaking.*)

The phrase forms an urgent command. Cf. EUR. *Or.* 936, *Alc.* 662, ARIST. *Pl.* 1133.

Cf. λέγε φθάσας, *speak quickly.*
Quin statim loquere !
In the last example φθάνω is in the Participle.
So ἀνέῳξάς με φθάσας. ARIST.
You opened the door before me (got the start of me).
Cf. THUC. iv. 8.

4. ἀνύτω (*I achieve*) is used like φθάνω.
ἄνυσον ὑποδυσάμενος. ARIST.
Look sharp and put your shoes on.
ἀνύσας ἄνοιγε.
Look alive and open the door.

5. αἰσχύνομαι.
αἰσχύνομαι λέγων.
I am ashamed of saying (while I do say).
αἰσχύνομαι λέγειν.
I am ashamed to say (and generally, *I refrain from saying*).

6. ἀποκάμνω.
ἀποκάμνω τοῦτο ποιῶν.
I am weary of doing this.
ἀποκάμνω τοῦτο ποιεῖν.
I leave off doing this through weariness.

7. δῆλός εἰμι. Several constructions.
(*a*) *The personal construction with participle.*
δῆλος ἦν οἰόμενος. XEN.
It was evident that he thought.
The personal construction with ὡς *and participle.*
δῆλός ἐστιν ὥς τι δρασείων κακόν. SOPH. *Ai.*
It is plain that he is craving to do some ill (δρασείω, desiderative).
Cf. SOPH. *Ant.* 242 ; δηλοῖς (verb) ὡς.

(*b*) *The personal and the impersonal construction with* ὅτι *and finite mood.*
δηλοί εἰσιν ὅτι ἐπικείσονται. XEN.
It is clear that they will attack us.

NOTE ON SPECIAL VERBS.

δῆλόν ἐστιν ὅτι παύσομαι. PLAT.
It is evident that I shall give over.

8. φανερός εἰμι, and φανερόν ἐστι : ἀρκῶ (*I suffice*), ἀρκεῖ, *it is sufficient* (SOPH. *Ant*. 547) : ἱκανός εἰμι, ἱκανόν ἐστι, are similarly constructed either with the participle (personally) or with ὅτι and a finite mood.

9. φαίνομαι takes the Participle and the Infinitive.

φαίνεται ἀνὴρ ἀγαθὸς εἶναι.
He seems to be (*is considered*) *a brave man.*
Videtur esse fortis.
The appearance or opinion may be groundless.

φαίνεται ἀνὴρ ἀγαθὸς ὤν.
He shows himself (*proves himself, manifestly is*) *a brave man.*
Cf. *appareo* in Latin.
 Apparebat certamen fore. LIV. *It was evident there would be a struggle.*
 Apparebat utilis. SUET. So ψευδὴς φαίνεται (ὤν omitted).
σημεῖα φαίνεις (=φαίνει) γεγώς. SOPH. *El.* 24.
You show proofs that you are.

10. λανθάνω.

λέληθα ἐμαυτόν εἰδώς. XEN.
I know without myself being aware of it.

HORACE (*Od.* iii. 16. 32) and PROPERTIUS (i. 4. 5) imitate this Greek construction.

 e.g. HOR. *Fallit sorte beatior* = λανθάνει ὀλβιωτέρα οὖσα.
Rarely in Attic λαθών is used participially with a verb = *secretly*, *clam*.

11. τυγχάνω, and (in poetry) κυρῶ.
ἔτυχον προσελθὼν ἀνδρί. PLAT.
I chanced to meet a man.
πρὸς τί τοῦτ᾽ εἰπὼν κυρεῖς ; SOPH. *El.*
Why is it thou speakest thus ?

The notion of chance is often almost lost in both verbs. They often denote mere coincidence in time, *just then*. Both are used sometimes without a participle.

νῦν ἀγροῖσι τυγχάνει. SOPH. *El.*
At this moment he happens to be abroad.

12. οἴχομαι denotes rapidity and completeness.
οἴχεται φεύγων.
Celeriter fugit.
οἴχομαι φέρων.
Celeriter aufero.
οἴχεται θανών.
He is dead and gone.

13. δῆλός εἰμι (above), φανερός εἰμι, λανθάνω are also constructed with ὅτι and finite mood. For λανθάνω ὅτι see PLAT. *Crito*, xii.

14. The Poets use this Supplementary Participle with a great many verbs, *e.g.* verbs implying superiority and inferiority (νικῶ, ἡττῶμαι, ἐλλείπομαι): doing right or wrong (ἀδικῶ, ἁμαρτάνω, εὖ or καλῶς ποιῶ).

§ 160. *THE SUPPLEMENTARY PARTICIPLE IN AGREEMENT WITH THE OBJECT.*

The Participle is the Predicate to the Object.

The Verbs which take this Participle are mostly the active forms of those in the previous rule, but the correspondence is not complete.

A. Verbs of *stopping (making to cease), finding* and *detecting, overlooking* (i.e. *allowing to be done*).

παύω (*I make to cease*, cf. παύομαι), περιορῶ and ἐφορῶ, *I overlook* (περιεῖδον, ἐπεῖδον), but not ἐῶ, δείκνυμι (*I point out*), καταλαμβάνω, αἱρῶ (see ἁλίσκομαι in previous rule), φωρῶ, *I detect, catch, convict.*

γελῶντας ἐχθροὺς παύσομεν. SOPH.
We will check the merriment of our foes.

μὴ περιίδωμεν ὑβρισθεῖσαν τὴν Λακεδαίμονα. ISAEUS.
Let us not look on and see Lacedaemon outraged.

οὐ χαιρήσεις· ἀλλά σε κλέπτονθ' αἱρήσω. ARIST.
You shan't get off scot-free. No, I'll catch you thieving.

CHAPTER II.

§ 171. THE PARTICLE Ἄν.

Ἄν (and the Epic κέν, κέ, Doric κά) were originally *Demonstrative Adverbs* meaning *there, then, so, in that case, perchance, possibly, contingently.* They were Adverbs qualifying the Positive Statement of the Verb. This part of the subject belongs to Philology rather than Syntax.

Ἄν in Attic Greek may be regarded as having practically two distinct uses.

1. It is joined to Verbs, the Indicative (Historic Tenses), Optative, Infinitive, and Participle. It denotes a Condition on which the fulfilment of the verbal action depends.

2. It is joined to Pronouns and Particles with the Subjunctive Mood. Such are ὅς, ὅστις (ὅς ἄν, ὅστις ἄν): ὅτε, ἐπεί, ἐπειδή, πρίν, ἕως, etc. (ὅταν, ἐπάν, ἐπειδάν, πρὶν ἄν, ἕως ἄν): the Conditional εἰ (ἐάν, ἤν): sometimes the Final ὡς, ὅπως, ὄφρα (ὡς ἄν, etc.). In this use ἄν (but not in Final Sentences) makes the meaning of the Pronoun and Particle indefinite, *who-so-ever, when-so-ever, if ever* (in one very common use of ἐάν), though this meaning cannot always be expressed. When Historic Sequence requires a change from the Subjunctive to the Optative ἄν must be dropped, *e.g.* ὅς ἄν βούληται but ὅς βούλοιτο.

§ 172. DEFINITE AND INDEFINITE SENTENCES.

Before dealing with Relative, Conditional, and Temporal Sentences it is most important to understand the difference between a Definite and an Indefinite Sentence.

In the Sentence ταῦτα ἃ βούλονται ἔχουσι, *they have those things which they want*, the antecedent ταῦτα is definite (*those particular and known things*), and the Relative Sentence which follows refers to a definite act. But in the Sentence ἃ ἂν βούλωνται ἔχουσιν, the Antecedent is indefinite and the act is virtually Conditional: *they have whatsoever things they want, anything they want, anything if they want it*. This second sentence in Historic Sequence becomes ἃ βούλοιντο εἶχον. Similarly in the sentence ἐπειδὴ δὲ ὀλιγαρχία ἐγένετο οἱ τριάκοντα μετεπέμψαντό με, *when an oligarchy was established the Thirty Tyrants sent for me*, Socrates is speaking of a definite time (B.C. 404) and of a definite act. But ἐπειδάν ὀλιγαρχία γένηται, *whenever*, or *as often as*, *an oligarchy shall be established*, or *is established*, an indefinite time and act is spoken of. The sentence is virtually conditional again, *if ever*, or *if at any time*, etc., and might be expressed thus, ἐάν ποτε γένηται. In Historic Sequence the sentence would be ἐπειδή γένοιτο.

It will be seen therefore that when the Antecedent is definite the Indicative is used; where indefinite, the Subjunctive with ἄν, or the Optative without ἄν:

e.g. οὓς εἶδεν ἐπῄνεσε, *those whom he saw he praised*.
οὓς ἂν ἴδῃ ἐπαινεῖ, *whomsoever he sees he praises*.
οὓς ἴδοι ἐπῄνει, *whomsoever he saw he used to praise*.

Note. Further instances of—
1. Definite sentences.

Κῦρον μεταπέμπεται ἀπὸ τῆς ἀρχῆς, ἧς αὐτὸν σατράπην ἐποίησε. XEN.
He sends for Cyrus from the province of which he had made him governor.

ἕως ἔξεστιν ταῦτα ὑμῖν ἐπιδεῖξαι θέλω. PLAT.
While it is permitted I desire to explain this to you.

ἐπολιόρκει τοὺς Ἕλληνας μέχρι οὗ ξηράνας τὴν διώρυχα εἷλε τὴν νῆσον. THUC.
He was blockading the Greeks until he drained the ditch and took the island.

2. Indefinite sentences.

ἔξεστι ὅτι ἂν βούληται εἰπεῖν. ANTIPH.
He may say whatever (or anything) he likes.

μέχρι δ' ἂν ἐγὼ ἥκω, αἱ σπονδαὶ μενόντων. XEN.
Until I return let the armistice be observed.

ἕως περ ἂν ἐμπνέω οὐ μὴ παύσωμαι φιλοσοφῶν. PLAT.
So long as I breathe I will never give up philosophy.

κατέστησα δὲ ἐπιμελεῖσθαι εἴ τι δέοι τῷ χορῷ Φανόστρατον. ANTIPH.
I appointed Phanostratus to provide whatever the chorus required.

§ 173. *CONDITIONAL SENTENCES.*

A Compound Conditional Clause consists of two Correlative sentences, one of which contains the Condition, and is called the Protasis;[1] the other contains the

---

[1] Protasis (πρότασις) means Premiss. Apodosis (ἀπόδοσις) means Consequence. The Apodosis is the Principal, the Protasis the Subordinate Sentence. Whether originally a clause with εἰ was a Subordinate Sentence, is a point which need not be discussed in Attic Syntax. How far the Apodosis, as being the Principal Sentence, influences the construction of the Protasis, is an interesting question, which is alluded to under the Oratio Obliqua. Professor Goodwin (*Journal of Philology*, viii. 15, p. 33) strongly maintains the assimilating force exerted by the principal verb on the subordinate verb.

Consequence, and is called the Apodosis. Sucn a clause reduced to its simplest form may be thus expressed:

If A is B, C is D,
or C is D,   if A is B;

i.e. the fulfilment or truth of the Consequence depends on the fulfilment or truth of the Condition. This dependence of the Consequence (the Apodosis) on the Condition (the Protasis) is the essential point of a conditional clause.

§ 174. *DISTINCTION OF CONDITIONS.*

I. The most obvious distinction of Conditions is that of Time. Some refer to the present, others to the past, others to the future. This distinction is universally present in all Conditions.

II. A second distinction concerns the opinion implied as to the fulfilment or non-fulfilment of the Condition. In two forms, and two forms only, the expression in itself conveys information on this point.[1]

III. A third distinction is that between Particular and General Conditions. A Particular Condition refers to a definite act or set of acts: *e.g.* "If the windows up-stairs are

---

[1] There is, as Professor Goodwin tells us, no special form implying that the condition is or was fulfilled. That is to be decided by the context. This is true, though of course a fact may be clearly implied, and in some cases narrated. Such is the case chiefly in past General Suppositions, *e.g.* εἴ τις ἀντείποι, εὐθὺς ἐτεθνήκει, THUC. viii. 66, which is the same as saying, "Every one who spoke against them was at once got rid of." A General Supposition may also be expressed in an Ordinary Past form. Thus, εἴ τι ἄλλο ἐπικίνδυνον ἐγένετο ἁπάντων μετέσχομεν, THUC. iii. 54, which is only a way of saying, "We took part in every danger as it arose." Indeed a fact is narrated here under a conditional form, though not by virtue of the form itself, which need only denote a connexion between Condition and Consequence. With regard to General Suppositions in present time, they may refer to facts, but usually are generalisations from observed facts or habits.

open, the rain is coming in;" "If you receive a telegram send it on to me;" "If he had a five-pound note he would lend it me." A General Condition refers to any act which may occur or have occurred any number of times: "If ever a candidate is convicted of bribery he loses his seat;" "If (ever) he were left to himself he used to waste his time;" "If (ever) he had a shilling in his pocket he gave it to the first beggar he met."

§ 175. *DIVISION OF CONDITIONAL SENTENCES.*

Conditional Sentences accordingly may be divided into:— I. Ordinary Conditions; II. General or Frequentative Conditions. Ordinary Conditions again may be subdivided into A., those with regard to which no opinion is expressed whether the Condition is fulfilled or unfulfilled, probable or improbable, true or false; B., those in which the form of expression implies that the Condition is unfulfilled. There is no form to express an opinion that the Condition is fulfilled. The context alone could suggest this. In General Conditions again no opinion is expressed concerning the fulfilment or non-fulfilment of the Condition. Thus in Ordinary Conditions of the second class alone is any such opinion expressed.

L

§ 176. *ORDINARY CONDITIONS.*

For Real Examples see further on.

A. All that is stated is that a Consequence *did, does,* or *will* follow from a Condition. The expression in itself does not tell us whether the condition was, is, or will be fulfilled. That is beside the question: the stress is wholly on the *if.* The sole difference between the three forms (1, 2, 3) is one of time.

1. PRESENT.[1]
Any Primary Tense of the Indicative.

εἰ ταῦτα ποιεῖς   ἀδικεῖς.[2]
If you do this (strictly   *you are doing wrong.*
if you are doing this)

2. PAST.
Any Historic Tense of the Indicative.

εἰ ταῦτα $\begin{cases} ἐποίεις \\ ἐποίησας \end{cases}$ $\begin{matrix} ἠδίκεις. \\ ἠδίκησας. \end{matrix}$

If you $\begin{cases} \text{were doing this} \\ \text{did this} \end{cases}$ *you were doing wrong.*
you did wrong (aorist, a single act).

3. FUTURE.
To express a Condition in future time there are three forms, differing, but differing only, in distinctness of expression.

(a) The ordinary future form.

ἐὰν (ἢν) ταῦτα $\begin{cases} ποιῇς \\ ποιήσῃς \end{cases}$ ἀδικήσεις.

If you do this (strictly   *you will do wrong.*
if you shall do this)

---

[1] There are endless varieties of present and past conditions, and the two are constantly combined. Present and future may be combined.

εἰ ταῦτα πεποίηκας   ἀδικεῖς, ἠδίκηκας.
If you have done this   *you are doing wrong, you have done wrong* (the Apodosis might be an Imperative).

εἰ ταῦτα δοκεῖ σοι   πλέωμεν.
If you think so   *let us set sail.*

εἰ ταῦτα ποιεῖς   ἀλγήσεις.
If you are doing this   *you will be sorry.*

εἰ ταῦτα ἐποίεις or ἐποίησας   ἀδικεῖς or ἀδικήσεις.
If you were doing, or did this   *you are doing, will do, wrong.*

And so on.

[2] It is hoped that no difficulty will arise from the selection of the verb ἀδικῶ in these special examples. Ἀδικῶ, of course, means, *I am an ἄδικος, a wrong doer*, and also *I do wrong*, or *injure*.

ORDINARY CONDITIONS.

(b) The less vivid future form.

εἰ ταῦτα { ποιοίης   ἀδικοίης ἄν.
           ποιήσειας   ἀδικήσειας ἄν.
If you should do this   *you would do wrong.*

(c) The most vivid future form.

εἰ ταῦτα ποιήσεις   ἀδικήσεις.
If you shall do this   *you will do wrong.*

B. Besides a difference of Time, the form of expression implies that the condition is unfulfilled either in Present or in Past Time. This is implied by the presence of ἄν in the Apodosis, and not by any peculiarity of the Protasis.

1. PRESENT (but see note).

εἰ ταῦτα ἐποίεις   ἠδίκεις ἄν.
If you did this (strictly *if*   *you would be doing*
you were now doing this)   *wrong.*

2. PAST.

εἰ ταῦτα ἐποίησας   ἠδίκησας ἄν.
If you had done this   *you would have done*
                            wrong.

Note.—The Imperfect, however, very often refers to a descriptive, habitual, or continued past.

εἰ ταῦτα ἔπρασσες   ἐθαυμάζομεν ἄν σε.
If you had been acting thus we should have been admiring you.

The Pluperfect denotes a state or condition in the past.

e.g. εἰ ἐλελύμην, *if I had been set free* (*in a state of liberty*).

πάλαι ἂν ἀπολώλη, *I should long ago have been a dead man.*

§ 177. Ordinary Conditions in Greek and Latin.

A.

	Protasis.	Apodosis.
1. Present.	εἰ ταῦτα ποιεῖς *Si haec facis*	ἀδικεῖς. *iniuste facis.*[1]
	εἰ ταῦτα πεποίηκας. *Si haec fecisti.*	
2. Past.	εἰ ταῦτα { ἐποίεις / ἐποίησας *Si haec* { *faciebas* / *fecisti*	ἠδίκεις. ἠδίκησας. *iniuste faciebas.* *iniuste fecisti.*
3. Future.	(*a*) ἐὰν (ἤν) ταῦτα { ποιῇς / ποιήσῃς } *Si haec feceris* (fut. perf.)	ἀδικήσεις. *iniuste facies.*
	(*b*) εἰ ταῦτα { ποιοίης / ποιήσειας *Si haec facias*	ἀδικοίης ἄν. ἀδικήσειας ἄν. *iniuste facias.*
	(*c*) εἰ ταῦτα ποιήσεις *Si haec facies*	ἀδικήσεις. *iniuste facies.*

B.

1. Present (or Continued Past).	εἰ ταῦτα ἐποίεις Si haec faceres	ἠδίκεις ἄν. iniuste faceres.
2. Past.	εἰ ταῦτα ἐποίησας Si haec fecisses	ἠδίκησας ἄν. iniuste fecisses.

II.

§ 178. *GENERAL OR FREQUENTATIVE CONDITIONS.*

These are best taught by real examples. Observe the Apodoses, distinguishing these uses of the Subjunctive

---

[1] The normal Latin equivalents of the Latin of Cicero, Caesar, and Sallust are here given. The variety of Latin forms is far greater than the Greek, and varies more according to the period of the writer. The above are given only as a guide in comparing the two languages, not as an attempt at a full division of the Latin Conditional Sentences.

and Optative (in the Protasis) from their uses in Ordinary Conditions. In the Apodosis any frequentative tense denoting respectively present and past time may be employed.

1. PRESENT (a generalisation true now or for any future occasion).

ἀνὴρ πονηρὸς δυστυχεῖ, κἂν εὐτυχῇ. MENAND.
A bad man is in evil state,
Even if he e'er is fortunate.

2. PAST.

εἴ τις ἀντείποι εὐθὺς ἐτεθνήκει. THUC.
If ever any one spoke against them he was promptly
put to death.

ἐτεθνήκει is, of course, a virtual Imperfect.

§ 179. *THE NEGATIVES IN CONDITIONAL SENTENCES.*

The Negative of a Protasis is μή, of an Apodosis οὐ.

εἰ μὴ ταῦτα ποιεῖς   οὐκ καλῶς ἔχει.
If you are not doing this   it is not well.

For exceptions see the chapter on the Negatives.

Relative Conditional Sentences.

Real Examples are given further on.

As has been explained, a Relative Sentence with an Indefinite Antecedent is equivalent to a Conditional Sentence. Any form of the Protasis with εἰ or ἐάν may be expressed by a Relative Sentence. Both ὅς and ὅστις are used, but ὅστις, as being the indefinite form, is preferred, especially in affirmative sentences. In negative sentences μή is sufficient to show that the Relative is indefinite.

A.

	Protasis.	Apodosis.
1. Present.	ἃ (ἅ τινα) ἔχει = εἴ τι ἔχει.	δίδωσι.
2. Past.	ἃ (ἅ τινα) { εἶχεν ἔσχεν = εἴ τι εἶχε.	ἐδίδου ἔδωκε.
3. Future.	(a) ἃ (ἅ τινα) ἂν ἔχῃ = ἐάν τι ἔχῃ.	δώσει.
	(b) ἃ (ἅ τινα) ἔχοι = εἴ τι ἔχοι.	διδοίη, δοίη ἄν.
	(c) ἃ (ἅ τινα) ἕξει = εἴ τι ἕξει.	δώσει.

B.

	Protasis	Apodosis
1. Present (or Impf. Past).	ἃ (ἅ τινα) εἶχεν	ἐδίδου ἄν.
2. Past.	ἃ (ἅ τινα) ἔσχεν	ἔδωκεν ἄν.

§ 180. Participles in the Protasis.

Any form of a Protasis may be expressed by a Participle. For real examples see further.

A.

	Protasis.	Apodosis.
1. Present.	ταῦτα ποιῶν = εἰ ταῦτα ποιεῖς	ἀδικεῖς.
2. Past.	ταῦτα ποιῶν = εἰ ταῦτα ἐποίεις	ἠδίκεις.
3. Future.	(a) ταῦτα ποιῶν = ἐὰν ταῦτα ποίῃς	ἀδικήσεις.
	(b) ταῦτα ποιῶν = εἰ ταῦτα ποιοίης	ἀδικοίης ἄν.

B.

1. Present (or Imperf. Past)	ταῦτα ποιῶν = εἰ ταῦτα ἐποίεις	ἠδίκεις ἄν.
2. Past	ταῦτα ποιήσας = εἰ ταῦτα ἐποίησας	ἠδίκησας ἄν.

Note. The present participle alone is given (except in **B**. 2). Of course the aorist participle, denoting a single as opposed to a continued act, may be used in any of the forms, while the present participle denotes an imperfect act (*i.e.* an act in progress).

§ 181. Position of ἄν.

ἄν of an Apodosis can never begin a sentence. Its natural position is after its verb, but, as it possesses a power of emphasising the word it follows, it often comes before the verb and after some word which is to be emphasised. Almost any word may be so emphasised, especially an interrogative or a negative.

οὐκ ἂν ἔχοιμί γ' εἰπεῖν ὅτι οὐ προσεῖχον τὸν νοῦν. PLAT.
I could not say that I was not attentive.

πῶς ἄν τις, ἅ γε μὴ ἐπίσταιτο, ταῦτα σοφὸς εἴη; XEN.
How could a man be wise in matters of which he knew nothing certainly?

πολλὴ ἄν τις εὐδαιμονία εἴη περὶ τοὺς νέους.
PLAT. *Apol.* xii.
Great would be the good fortune in the case of the young.

ἆρ' οὖν ἂν με οἴεσθε τοσάδε ἔτη διαγενέσθαι.
PLAT. *Apol.* xxi.
Think you then that I should have lived all these years?
ἄν belongs to διαγενέσθαι.

ἐπιεικῆ ἄν μοι δοκῶ πρὸς τοῦτον λέγειν. PLAT. *Apol.* xxiii.
I think I should be adopting a conciliatory tone towards him.
ἄν belongs to λέγειν and emphasises ἐπιεικῆ.

As in the last two examples ἄν when separated from its verb often comes near οἴομαι, δοκῶ, φημί, οἶδα, so much so as to look as if it belonged to them. But we must be careful to connect the ἄν with its proper verb. οὐκ οἶδα ἄν εἰ, or οὐκ ἄν οἶδα εἰ for οὐκ οἶδα εἰ—ἄν should be especially noticed, *e.g.* οὐκ οἶδ' ἄν εἰ πείσαιμι (EUR. *Med.*), *I know not whether I should persuade him*, where ἄν belongs to πείσαιμι.

§ 182. Repetition of ἄν.

Ἄν is often used more than once in the same sentence. For this repetition there may be two reasons.

1. In a long paragraph, which is complicated by interrupting clauses, ἄν occurs at the beginning. It thus strikes the keynote of the whole so to speak, and gives warning that the whole coming statement is conditional. It occurs again later on near the verb.

2. It may be repeated, more than once, even in a short sentence, if any special word is to be emphasised.

EXAMPLES.

I. In long paragraphs—

ὑμεῖς δ᾽ ἴσως τάχ᾽ ἂν ἀχθόμενοι, ὥσπερ οἱ νυστάζοντες ἐγειρόμενοι, κρούσαντες ἄν με, πειθόμενοι Ἀνύτῳ, ῥᾳδίως ἂν ἀποκτείναιτε. PLAT. *Apol.* xviii.

But you very possibly in annoyance, just like people when they are being roused from a nap, might listen to Anytus, and, with a tap, put me to death, and think nothing more of it.

N.B.—τάχα, *perhaps*, often attaches an ἄν to itself.

In PLAT. *Apol.* xxxii., a good instance. The sentence begins with ἐγὼ γὰρ ἂν οἶμαι—then seven lines later on οἶμαι ἂν recurs, followed by ἂν εὑρεῖν, (all the ἄν's belonging to εὑρεῖν).

II. For emphasis—

οὐκ ἂν ἀποδοίην οὐδ᾽ ἂν ὀβολὸν οὐδενί. ARIST. *Nub.* 118.
I'll not give—no not a copper to any man.

τί δῆτ᾽ ἂν ὡς ἐκ τῶνδ᾽ ἂν ὠφελοῖμί σε; SOPH. *Ai.* 536.
How then, knowing what has happened, could I assist thee?

οὔτ᾽ ἂν κελεύσαιμ᾽ οὔτ᾽ ἄν, εἰ θέλοις ἔτι
πράσσειν, ἐμοῦ γ᾽ ἂν ἡδέως δρῴης μέτα. SOPH. *Ant.* 69.
I would not urge thee, no! nor shouldst thou now Desire to help me, would I have thy help.

Good instances occur in SOPH. *Ant.* 466, 680, 884; AESCH. *Persae*, 431.

§ 183. Ἄν with Future Indicative.

Ἄν with the Future Indicative, Infinitive, and Participle. Many critics have maintained that this construction does not occur in Attic Greek. Many instances have been removed by revision of texts. Mr. Riddell (*Apology*, p. 67, and *Digest*, p. 139) regards the construction as abundantly established, and cites seven instances from PLATO, *e.g. Rep.*

615 D, οὐχ ἧκει, οὐδ' ἂν ἧξει δεῦρο. Other cases are *Apol.* xvii., *Leg.* 719 E, *Symp.* 222 A, etc. Also XEN. *An.* ii. 5. 13, ἂν κολάσεσθε. In *Phaedr.* 227 B, οὐκ ἂν οἴει με ποιήσεσθαι. In *Crito.* xv., οὐκ οἴει ἂν φανεῖσθαι, ἂν with the future infinitive occurs. ἂν occurs with the future participle in PLAT. *Apol.* xvii. (end of chapter), οὐκ ἂν ποιήσοντος. Madvig denies, Krüger defends, the existence of this last construction.

§ 184. Ellipse of the Apodosis, and Ellipse of the Verb.

Ἄν of an Apodosis is sometimes found without its verb. The verb however (an Indicative or an Optative) may be easily supplied from the context.

οἱ δ' οἰκέται ῥέγκουσιν· ἀλλ' οὐκ ἂν πρὸ τοῦ. AR. *Nub.* 5.
The domestics are snoring, but they wouldn't (have been doing so) once. οὐκ ἂν (sc. ἔρρεγκον).

Where two verbs are connected or opposed, it is enough to use ἂν once only, with the first, unless some lengthy complication of clause renders it necessary for the sake of clearness to repeat it, or unless some word is to be emphasised.

οὐδεὶς ἂν ἦν σοι ὃς ἐμοῦ κατεμαρτύρησεν (sc. ἄν).
                                                    ANTIPH. *Her.* 15.
You would have found no one who would have given evidence against me.

τί ἐποίησεν ἄν; ἢ δῆλον ὅτι ὤμοσεν (sc. ἄν); DEM. 31. 9.
What would he have done? Is it not clear that he would have taken an oath?

§ 185. Ellipse of the Protasis.

Sometimes the Protasis, as in all languages, is wholly omitted. It can be easily supplied from the context.

οὐδὲν γὰρ ἂν ἐβλάβην (sc. εἰ ἐτιμησάμην, from what has preceded). PL. *Apol.* xxviii.
I should have received no harm (had I done so and so).

πᾶν γὰρ ἂν κατειργάσω. SOPH. *El.* 1022.
So hadst thou compassed all (sc. εἰ τοιάδε ἦσθα), supplied from a preceding wish.

§ 186. Εἰ and ἄν both in the Protasis.

In several instances εἰ and ἄν are both found in the Protasis (nearly always an Optative). One of the best-known instances is from PLAT. *Protag.* 329 B., καὶ ἐγώ, εἴπερ ἄλλῳ τῳ ἀνθρώπων πειθοίμην ἄν, καὶ σοὶ πείθομαι, *for myself, if I would trust any other man, I trust you.* Here it is considered that ἄν belongs to the verb πειθοίμην, which does double duty, both as a Protasis with εἰ, and also as an Apodosis with ἄν to another unexpressed Protasis, thus : εἰ πειθοίμην, *if I would trust* (*i.e.* πειθοίμην ἄν, *I would trust,* εἰ πίστιν δοίη, *if he should give me his word*). This is an established Attic idiom, e.g. DEM. *Phil.* i. 18, οὗτοι παντελῶς, οὐδ᾽'εἰ μὴ ποιήσαιτ᾽ ἂν τοῦτο, εὐκαταφρόνητόν ἐστι, *it is not lightly to be despised, even if you should not do so* (*do so—if the occasion should arise*). ISOC. *Archid.* 120, εἰ δὲ μηδεὶς ἂν ὑμῶν ἀξιώσειε ζῆν ἀποστερούμενος πατρίδος, προσήκει κ.τ.λ., *if none of you should care to live—if deprived of his country, it behoves you, etc.* In this last example the Second Protasis is given in the participle ἀποστερούμενος, as it is also in DEM. *Meid.* 582, εἰ οὗτοι χρήματα ἔχοντες μὴ προοῖντ᾽ ἄν, *if these men would not spend money—if they had it.*

Other instances occur (perhaps) in AESCH. *Ag.* 930, and *Sept.* 513. See also EUR. *Hel.* 825, DEM. *Meid.* 1206, *de Fals. Leg.* § 190 (with Shilleto's note), ANTIPHON, 6. 29, XEN. *Cyr.* iii. 3. 35 (θαυμάζοιμ᾽ ἄν—εἰ ἂν ὠφελήσειε).

An essential point to notice is that in all these instances (except XEN. *Cyr.* iii. 3. 35) the Apodosis is in the Indicative, generally in the Present, sometimes the Future. The Optative with εἰ and ἄν, therefore, does not denote a remote future supposition except so far as it refers to the unexpressed Protasis. Hence in their notes to AESCH. *Ag.* 930 (reading εἰ πράσσοιμ᾽ ἄν) both Mr. Paley and Mr. Sidgwick consider εἰ πράσσοιμ᾽ ἄν a variant not for εἰ πράσσοιμι, but for εἰ πράξω, translating not, *if I should prosper*, but, *if I have a chance of prospering.*

Jelf (§ 860) and Professor Goodwin (*Moods and Tenses*, 107) compare the Homeric εἰ κεν with the Optative. But in all the Homeric instances an Apodosis with the Optative and κεν is joined, e.g. *Il.* v. 273, εἰ τούτω κε λάβοιμεν ἀροίμεθά κε κλέος ἐσθλόν, *if, in the case given, we should take them, we should win goodly renown.*

In DEM. *Timoth.* 1201. 19, εἰ ἄν occurs with a Past Indicative :

εἰ τοίνυν τοῦτο ἰσχυρὸν ἦν ἂν τούτῳ τεκμήριον, κἀμοί γενέσθω τεκμήριον. Observe the Apodosis in the Imperative: *if this would have been strong evidence for him* (i.e. if he had been able to adduce it), *let it be evidence for me too*. Here, as Professor Goodwin explains (p. 101), the Protasis means : *if it is true that this would have been*, so that reference is really to the present, and only to the past so far as the unexpressed Protasis requires. DEM. *de Cor*. 260. 2, is another instance if εἰ ἐπεχείρησ' ἄν is read; only the Apodosis which follows is τίς οὐκ ἂν ἀπέκτεινε ;

Note. There is no difficulty in connecting an Apodosis with more than one Protasis referring to different times, e.g. DEM. *de Cor*. 274. 28, ἐπεύχομαι πᾶσι τούτοις, εἰ ἀληθῆ πρὸς ὑμᾶς εἴποιμι καὶ εἶπον, *I pray to all these, if I should speak, and did speak the truth before you*.

§ 187.   Δέ in Apodosis.

δέ sometimes introduces an Apodosis as if it were co-ordinate with, or followed, the Protasis. This is instructive as showing that the *logical* importance of the subordinate sentence (Protasis) may assert itself over the *grammatical* importance of the Principal Sentence (the Apodosis). Such cases, however, are very rare in Attic.

εἰ οὖν ἐγὼ γιγνώσκω μήτε τὰ ὅσια μήτε τὰ δίκαια, ὑμεῖς δὲ διδάξατέ με. XEN. *Hell*. iv. 1. 33.

If therefore I know neither what is holy nor what is just, do you then teach me.

Cf. SOPH. *O. T*. 1267; δεινὰ δ' ἦν.

§ 188.   ἐάν seemingly Interrogative.

εἰ is interrogative as well as conditional, but ἐάν is only conditional, and must not be used in Indirect Questions. Where it appears to be interrogative, as in two places cited by Liddell and Scott, it comes after σκόπει or σκέψαι, and clearly means, "if by chance," *e.g.* XEN. *Mem*. iv. 4. 12. σκέψαι, ἐὰν τόδε σοι μᾶλλον ἀρέσκῃ, *consider if perchance you like this better* (si forte tibi placuerit).

§ 189. ἄν with Participle seemingly in Protasis.

A Participle with ἄν must always be in Apodosis. But sometimes examination and explanation are necessary.

πόλλ' ἂν ἔχων εἰπεῖν, σιγῶ.
Though I have much to say, yet I hold my tongue.

ἔχων is a concessive participle, and is itself an apodosis, the sentence being equal to ἔχοιμι ἄν (εἰ βουλοίμην), σιγῶ δὲ (or ἐγὼ ὅς περ πολλ' ἂν ἔχοιμι). ἄν emphasises πολλά.

συθείς τ' ἂν οὐκ ἂν ἀλγύναις πλέον. SOPH. O. T. 446.
If thou speed hence thou wouldst not vex me more.

Here συθείς is itself the Protasis followed by ἄν, which really belongs to ἀλγύναις.

Φίλιππος Ποτίδαιαν ἑλὼν καὶ δυνηθεὶς ἂν αὐτὸς ἔχειν, εἰ ἐβουλήθη, Ὀλυνθίοις παρέδωκεν. DEM. 23. 107.
P. after taking Potidaea, and though he might, if he had wished, have kept it himself, yet handed it over to the Olynthians.

δυνηθεὶς ἄν is the Apodosis (ἠδυνήθη ἄν—εἰ ἐβουλήθη), the participle having a concessive force.

§ 190. Conditional Particles and their combinations.

1. εἰ δὲ μή, *if not, sin minus, sin aliter*, has become so stereotyped a phrase, that it is used where ἐάν δὲ μή would be more correct.

ἐὰν φαίνηται δίκαιον, πειρώμεθα. εἰ δὲ μὴ ἐῶμεν.
PLAT. *Crito* ix.
If it appears right, let us make the attempt; but if not, let us abandon it.

2. ἐάν, εἰ, meaning "if haply" ("in case," "in the event of," "in hope that," "thinking that"). It contains sometimes a virtual oratio obliqua (i.e. the thought of the subject). Cf. *si forte* in Latin.

ἄκουσον καὶ ἐμοῦ, ἐάν σοι ταῦτα δοκῇ. PLAT. *Rep.* 358.
Hear me too, in case you may agree.

πρὸς τὴν πόλιν, εἰ ἐπιβοηθοῖεν, ἐχώρουν. THUC. vi. 100.
They were marching on the city, on the chance of the citizens advancing against them (thinking that they might, etc.).

3. ὥσπερ ἄν εἰ: also written ὡσπερανεί. The phrase is compressed from ὥσπερ ἄν (Apodosis)—εἰ (Protasis), e.g. ὥσπερ ἄν εἰ εἴποι (PLAT. Apol. ix.), *just as if he were to say*, ὥσπερ ἄν ποιοῖτο εἰ εἴποι.

4. πῶς γὰρ ἄν; (sc. εἴη), with a Protasis (εἰ with Optative) omitted. *How would it be, if it were so? How is it possible? How so?*

5. κἄν εἰ: νῦν μοι δοκεῖ κἄν ἀσέβειαν εἰ καταγιγνώσκοι τις Μειδίου τὰ προσήκοντα ποιεῖν. DEM. 21. 51 = καὶ ἄν ποιεῖν—εἰ καταγιγνώσκοι. But κἄν εἰ comes to be used for the simple καὶ εἰ, *even if*.

6. κἄν = καὶ ἐάν.

§ 191. Examples of Conditional Sentences.

(1) Ordinary Present Conditions. (2) Ordinary Past Conditions. (3) Present and Past in combination. *See* § 177 A, 1 and 2.

Observe that the condition may be general as well as particular.

1. Present :—

εἴ τι ψεύδομαι ἔξεστιν ἐξελέγξαι με. ANTIPH. *de Cher.* 14.
If I am making any false statements, you may confute me.

εἰ θεοί τι δρῶσιν αἰσχρόν, οὐκ εἰσὶν θεοί.
EURIP. *Bell. Frag.* 294.
If the gods do aught immoral they are no gods.

εἰ οὖν τοιοῦτον ὁ θάνατός ἐστι, κέρδος ἔγωγε λέγω.
PLAT. *Apol.* xxxiii.
If therefore death is such a state as this, I for my part count it gain.

2. Past :—

εἰ ἀποστῆναι Ἀθηναίων οὐκ ἠθελήσαμεν, οὐκ ἠδικοῦμεν.
THUC. iii. 55.
If we refused to desert the Athenians, we were doing no wrong.

οὐκ because οὐκ ἐθέλω = nolo.

εἰ μὲν Ἀσκληπιὸς θεοῦ ἦν, οὐκ ἦν αἰσχροκερδής, εἰ δ᾽ αἰσχροκερδής, οὐκ ἦν θεοῦ. PLAT. *Rep.* iii. 408 C.
If Asclepius was the son of a god, he was not covetous; if he was covetous, he was not the son of a god.

εἴ τι ἄλλο ἐγένετο ἐπικίνδυνον, πάντων παρὰ δύναμιν μετέσχομεν. THUC. iii. 54.
If any other danger arose, we took our share in all beyond our strength.

(3.) φράζετε οὖν ἀλλήλοις εἰ πώποτέ τι ἤκουσέ τις.
PLAT. *Apol.* iii.
Explain then one to another, if at any time any one heard anything.

εἴ πού τι ἔπραξα τοιοῦτος φανοῦμαι. PLAT. *Apol.* xxi.
If ever I engaged in any business, I shall be found to be such as I have described myself.

εἰ δὲ δύο ἐξ ἑνὸς ἀγῶνος γεγενῆσθον οὐκ ἐγώ αἴτιος.
ANTIPH. *de caed. Herod.* 84.
If two trials have been made out of one (or instead of one), it is not my fault.

§ 192. Ordinary Future Conditions.

See § **177 A**, 3 (*a*).

Protasis ἐάν (ἤν, ἄν) with the Subjunctive.

ἢν ἀναπείσω τουτονί, σωθήσομαι. ARIST. *Nub.* 77.
If I (shall) persuade this person here, I shall escape.

ἐὰν ἐμοὶ πείθησθε, φείσεσθέ μου. PLAT. *Apol.* xviii.
If you are (will be) persuaded by me, you will spare me.

ἐὰν ἐμὲ ἀποκτείνητε, οὐκ ἐμὲ μείζω βλάψετε ἢ ὑμᾶς αὐτούς.
PLAT. *Apol.*
If you put me to death, you will inflict no greater injury on me than on yourselves.

καὶ παῖδ᾽, ἐάνπερ δεῦρ᾽ ἐμοῦ πρόσθεν μόλῃ, παρηγορεῖτε. AESCH. *Pers.* 529.
And for my son, if he return before me, Comfort ye him.

ORDINARY FUTURE CONDITIONS.

δίδωσ' ἑκὼν
κτείνειν ἑαυτόν, ἢν τάδε ψευσθῇ λέγων.
SOPH. *Phil.* 1342.
Freely he offers himself
To the death if, speaking thus, he lie.

δίδωσι, he offers, practically means, *he says that he will*, is *ready*, and thus implies a future.

παρὰ τὸν ἀγαθὸν θεόν, ἂν θεὸς ἐθέλῃ, αὐτίκα ἰτέον. PLAT.
I must go at once, to the good God, if God will.

ΙΟ. κοὐκ ἄν γε λέξαιμ' ἐπ' ἀγαθοῖσι σοῖς κακά.
ΑΓ. ἢν μή γε φεύγων ἐκφύγῃς πρὸς αἰθέρα.
EUR. *Phoen.* 1215.
Yea, and I would not speak of ill close on thy happiness.
Yea, but thou shalt, unless thou escape in thy flight to the firmament.

Cf. EUR. *Orest.* 1593.

N.B.—A physical impossibility is here spoken of. Observe that it follows an Apodosis with Optative and ἄν: ἢν with the Subjunctive realises vividly the impossibility of the situation.

τί οὖν, ἄν εἴπωσιν οἱ νόμοι κ.τ.λ. PLAT. *Crit.* xii.
What then, if the laws say to us, etc.

A physical impossibility again is brought home as a vivid *argumentum ad hominem*.

§ 193. Less Vivid Future Conditions.

See § 177, A 3 (b).

In English we render εἰ with the Optative in a variety of ways: εἰ ποιήσαιμι, *if I should do, if I were to do, should I do, were I to do, if I did, supposing I were to do*, etc.

οὐ πολλὴ ἂν ἀλογία εἴη εἰ φοβοῖτο τὸν θάνατον ὁ τοιοῦτος.
PLAT. *Phaed.* 68.
Would it not be the height of inconsistency if such a man were to fear death?

εἴ με ἐπὶ τούτοις ἀφίοιτε, εἴποιμ' ἂν ὑμῖν. PLAT. *Apol.* xvii.
If you should dismiss me on these conditions I would reply to you, etc.

οἶκος δ' ἂν αὐτός, εἰ φθογγὴν λάβοι,
σαφέστατ' ἂν λέξειεν. AESCH. *Ag.* 37
Nay, the very house, if gifted with a voice, would tell the tale most plainly.

A physical impossibility represented as supposable; cf. CIC. *Cat.* 1, haec si tecum patria loquatur, nonne impetrare debeat?

ἐγὼ οὖν δεινὰ ἂν εἴην εἰργασμένος εἰ λίποιμι τὴν τάξιν.
PLAT. *Apol.*
I should then be in position of one who has committed dreadful sin, were I to desert my post.

The perfect denotes the state.

§ 194. Most Vivid Future Conditions.

See § 177, A 3 (c).

1. Εἰ with the Future Indicative sometimes refers plainly to the future, and is used much as ἐάν with the Subjunctive, only the latter is more common and less positively and vividly future.[1]

ἀποκτενεῖς γάρ, εἴ με γῆς ἔξω βαλεῖς. EUR. *Phoen.* 1621.
Thou wilt slay me, if thou wilt thrust me from the land.

εἰ μὴ καθέξεις γλῶσσαν, ἔσται σοι κακά.
EURIP. *Aeg. Fr.* 5
If thou wilt not curb thy tongue there will be ills for thee.

ἢν ἐθέλωμεν ἀποθνῄσκειν—εἰ δὲ φοβησόμεθα κινδύνους.
ISOCR. *Archid.* p. 138, *A.* § 107.
If we are ready to die—but if we shall fear dangers.

Observe the co-ordination of the two forms.

εἰ τοῦτο ποιήσομεν, ῥᾳδίως τὰ ἐπιτήδεια ἕξομεν.
If we shall do this we shall easily find supplies.

2. But εἰ with Future Indicative in Protasis is found with a present (or virtual present) in the Apodosis.

εἰ ποιήσεις then = εἰ μέλλεις ποιήσειν, *if you are going to do, if you mean to do, if you are for doing,* and this εἰ with the Future is used of a condition now imminent, and even existing, *e.g. if you're for fighting, I'm your man,* εἰ μαχεῖ ὅδε ἐγώ σοι.

---

[1] Mr. Monro (*Homeric Grammar,* p. 239) considers that εἰ with the Future (in Homer) generally expresses suppositions of an obvious or familiar kind.

αἶρε πλῆκτρον, εἰ μαχεῖ. ARIST. *Av.* 761.
Up with your spur if you mean fighting.
Cf. ARIST. *Ach.* 316.
ἦ νῦν ἐγὼ μὲν οὐκ ἀνήρ, αὕτη δ' ἀνήρ,
εἰ ταῦτ' ἀνατὶ τῇδε κείσεται κράτη. SOPH. *Ant.* 484.
Lo, you now! I am no man, but she is the man, if with impunity these my commands are to count as naught in her eyes.
Si iacebit imperium nostrum, cf. 461.

The periphrasis with μέλλω and Infinitive (Present or Future) is commoner in prose. There is a life about the expression which recommends this εἰ with the Future to poetry.

§ 195. Mixed examples illustrating the connection between and interchangeability of the Subjunctive, Optative, and Future Indicative in Conditional Sentences.

N.B.—This section is supplementary to § 192—§ 194.

πῶς οὖν ἂν ὀρθῶς δικάσαιτε περὶ αὐτῶν ; εἰ τούτους ἐάσετε τὸν νομιζόμενον ὅρκον διομοσαμένους κατηγορῆσαι, κ.τ.λ. πῶς δὲ ἐάσετε ; ἐὰν νυνὶ ἀποψηφίσησθέ μου.
ANTIPH. *de Caede Herod.* 90.
How then would you rightly judge on these points? if you shall allow my prosecutors to take the prescribed oath and accuse me. And how will you allow this? if you acquit me on this present trial.

N.B.—εἰ with the Future Indicative, and ἐάν with Subjunctive, have a modal force, "by permitting."

PLAT. *de Rep.* 359 C (of the ring of Gyges), εἴη δ' ἂν ἡ ἐξουσία ἣν λέγω τοιάδε μάλιστα εἰ αὐτοῖς γένοιτο οἵαν ποτέ φασι δύναμιν τῷ Γύγου τοῦ Λυδοῦ προγόνῳ γενέσθαι.
They would enjoy this liberty which I am speaking of most completely, if they should possess such a power as we are told the ancestor of Gyges the Lydian once possessed.

Compared with

PLAT. *Rep.* 612 B, ποιητέον εἶναι αὐτῇ τὰ δίκαια, ἐάν τ' ἔχῃ τὸν Γύγου δακτύλιον, ἐάν τε μή.
(we concluded, εὕρομεν) that the soul must do what is righteous, whether it possesses the ring of Gyges or no.

οὐδεὶς ἡμῶν τῶν νόμων ἐμποδών ἐστιν, ἐάν τέ τις βούληται
ὑμῶν εἰς ἀποικίαν ἰέναι, εἰ μὴ ἀρέσκοιμεν ἡμεῖς τε καὶ ἡ
πόλις, ἐάν τε μετοικεῖν ἄλλοσέ ποι ἐλθών, ἰέναι ἐκεῖσε
ὅποι ἂν βούληται, ἔχοντα ' ὰ αὑτοῦ. PLAT. *Crit.* xiii.
*None of our laws prevents any of you, if he wishes to go to a
colony, supposing we and the state should not give him
satisfaction, or if he wishes to go and reside anywhere else,
(none prevents him) from going wherever he wishes with all
his belongings.*

The Optative here, Professor Goodwin says, simply marks
a less prominent clause. But, it is to be noticed that ἐάν with
the Subjunctive here, which is thus joined with εἰ and the
Optative, is a general supposition

§ 196. The Optative and Indicative with ἄν without a Protasis.

The Optative with ἄν is freely used without a Protasis in
a variety of modified statements. In some cases it is easy to
supply a Protasis; in others no Protasis appears to have been
thought of. (This is Madvig's *Optativus Potentialis* or *Dubita-
tivus*, § 136.)

1. *As a modified statement in present or future time, very often
drawing an inference from what has preceded.*

ὥρα ἂν ἡμῖν συσκευάζεσθαι εἴη. XEN. *Cyr.* iii. 1. 41.
It is time for us then to be packing up.

Cf. ANTIPH. *Tetral.* B.B. 6, ἐλεγχθείη.

τοῦτ' ἂν εἴη ὃ ἐγὼ φημί σε αἰνίττεσθαι. PLAT. *Apol.* xv.
Herein then would consist what I hold to be your riddling.

Cf. ANTIPH. *de Chor.* 15, οἷός τ' ἂν εἴη.

Often βουλοίμην ἄν, *I could wish, I wish*, velim.

οὐκ ἂν μεθείμην τοῦ θρόνου, μὴ νουθέτει. ARIST. *Ran.* 830.
I'll not resign the throne, don't counsel me.

Cf. ARIST. *Ach.* 1055.

2. *A modified command or prayer,* sometimes put as a question.

σὺ μὲν κομίζοις ἂν σεαυτόν ᾗ θέλεις. SOPH. *Ant.* 444.
Thou may'st betake thee where thou likest, i.e. *get thee gone.*

ἆρ' οὖν ἐθελήσαις ἄν;
Should you feel disposed? Would you mind? Please do so and so.

3. A wish, expressed interrogatively. An interrogation equivalent to a wish.

πῶς ἂν ὀλοίμην; EURIP.
How could I perish? i.e. *would I might perish!*
ARIST. *Ach.* 991.

Similarly, but not so freely, the Imperfect Indicative is used. The time is past.

ἐβουλόμην ἄν.
I could have wished, vellem.

ἦν δ' ἂν οὗτος τῶν ἱππικῶν τις. PLAT. *Apol.* iv.
This man accordingly would be one of those who understand horses.

(ἦν ἄν is Apodosis of an unfulfilled condition.)

§ 197. Unfulfilled Conditions.[1]

See § **177, B** 1 *and* 2.

1. Εἰ with the Imperfect Indicative. The time of the Imperfect Indicative is either present or a past of description, habit, or iteration.

καὶ τόδ', εἴπερ ἔσθενον,
ἔδρων ἄν. SOPH. *El.* 604.
Had I the strength,
I'd do the deed.

The time is present (*I should now have been doing*).

---

[1] We have in English several ways of expressing an unfulfilled condition in present time, some of which resemble the Greek. Thus we may render, εἰ ταῦτα ἐποίεις ᾔδεκεις ἄν, *if you were doing this* (or, *if you had been doing this*), *you would be doing wrong* (or, *would have now been doing wrong*). These are not, however, the forms always used in everyday speech. *E.g.* A tramp, meeting me on the road, asks me for a copper. I put my hand in my pocket, but, finding nothing there, I shake my head and say, "Very sorry, *if I had anything, I would give it*" (εἴ τι εἶχον ἐδίδουν ἄν). A Shaksperean unfulfilled condition, referring to present time, may be given. Constance says to Arthur: "*If thou that bid'st me be content, wert grim,*" etc., "*I would not care, I then would be content, for then I should not love thee,*" etc. "*But thou art fair.*"

εἰ ξένος ἐτύγχανον ὤν, ξυνεγιγνώσκετε δήπου ἄν μοι.
PLAT. *Apol.* i.
If I happened to be a foreigner (which I am not), you would surely pardon me.
The time is present.

εἰ μὴ τότ' ἐπόνουν νῦν ἄν οὐκ εὐφραινόμην. PHILEM. 159.
If I had not been toiling then, I should not be rejoicing now.
The force of the Imperfect Indicative (referring to both kinds of time) is well shown in the above example.

ἐγὼ οὖν ἐκαλλυνόμην καὶ ἡβρυνόμην ἄν, εἰ ἠπιστάμην ταῦτα. ἀλλ' οὐ γὰρ ἐπίσταμαι. PLAT. *Apol.* iv.
I anyhow should plume and pride myself if I possessed this knowledge. But—you see, I don't possess it (or, *I should have been pluming,* etc.)
The time is present, or it may refer to a habit in the past.

δῆλον οὖν ὅτι οὐκ ἄν προέλεγεν εἰ μὴ ἐπίστευεν ἀληθεύσειν.
XEN. *Mem.* i. 1. 5.
It is plain accordingly that Socrates would not have publicly made these statements had he not felt confident that he should speak the truth.
The Imperfect here expresses customary or habitual acts in the past.

Similarly in Latin the Imperfect is used, and not the Pluperfect. The poets are fond of it as a descriptive past. Several instances, not much noticed, occur in HORACE. Ille non inclusus equo Minervae, etc. ; *falleret* aulam, etc. ; sed, etc. ; *ureret* flammis ; *He would not have been deceiving, but burning. Thou hadst not seen Achilles deceiving, but burning.* Non ego hoc ferrem calidus iuventa consule Planco. *I had not brooked this in the heat of youth when Plancus was consul.*

Sometimes ἄν with the Aorist Indicative in Apodosis is joined to εἰ with the Imperfect Indicative, not to denote a past unfulfilled condition, but a single act, *e.g.* PLAT. *Euthyph.* 12 D, εἰ μὲν οὖν σύ με ἠρώτας τι, εἶπον ἄν, *if you were asking me any question I should instantly say.* Here εἶπον ἄν really refers to the present, and denotes the instantaneousness of the single act in a way which the Imperfect could not express.

2. Εἰ with the Aorist or Pluperfect Indicative. The time is past, denoting a single act (Aorist), or a state (Pluperfect).

ἀπέθανον ἂν εἰ μὴ ἡ τῶν τριάκοντα ἀρχὴ κατελύθη.
PLAT. *Apol.* xx.
I should have been put to death if the government of the Thirty had not been overthrown.

εἰ μὴ ἀνέβη "Ανυτος κἂν ὦφλε χιλίας δραχμάς.
PLAT. *Apol.* xxv.
If Anytus had not come into court he would even have incurred a fine of 1000 *drachmae.*

εἰ μὴ ὑμεῖς ἤλθετε ἐπορευόμεθα ἂν ἐπὶ βασιλέα.
XEN. *An.* ii. 1. 4.
If you had not come (past) we should now *be marching against the King* (or *have been now marching*).

Protasis a single act in Past; Apodosis a continued act in the Present.

εἰ τότε ἐβοηθήσαμεν οὐκ ἂν ἠνώχλει νῦν ὁ Φίλιππος.
DEM. 30. 6.
If we had then given help Philip would not be annoying us now.

Here νῦν is added to mark the present.

οὐκ ἂν παρέμεινα εἰ ἐλελύμην. ANTIPH. *Herod.* 13.
I should not have stayed if I had not been set free on bail.

εἰ, ὅ σε ἠρώτων, ἀπεκρίνω, ἱκανῶς ἂν ἤδη ἐμεμαθήκειν.
PLAT. *Euthyph.* 14 C.
If you had answered my question, I should already have finished my learning.

The pluperfect denotes a past state.

§ 198. The omission of ἄν in Apodosis with Indicative.

1. Sometimes a past tense of the Indicative is found in Apodosis without ἄν. Such a construction is necessarily rhetorical. A statement which would have been true if certain conditions had happened is spoken of as actually true. The instances are rare, and many are disputed, but some occur both in poetry and prose.

εἰ δὲ μὴ Φρυγῶν
πύργους πεσόντας ᾖσμεν Ἑλλήνων δορὶ
φόβον παρέσχεν οὐ μέσως ὅδε κτύπος.   EUR. *Hec.* 1111.
(for παρέσχεν ἄν).

*Had we not known
That Phrygia's towers had fallen 'neath the spear
Of Hellas, no slight fear this din had caused.*

Cf. Nec veni nisi fata locum sedemque dedissent.
                                      VERG. *Aen.* xi. 112.

The Imperfect by itself almost bears this meaning without requiring an ἄν. Indeed the intrinsic meaning of the Imperfect (*e.g.* in the following example, "I was not by way of sending,") is closely allied to a conditioned statement.

e.g. καίτοι οὐ δήπου γε κατ' ἐμαυτοῦ μηνύτην ἔπεμπον εἰδώς.
                                      ANTIPH. *de Caed. Herod.* 24.

And yet I surely was not sending an informer against myself with my eyes open (I should not have been sending).

See especially a paragraph too long for quotation in ANDOKIDES *de Myst.* 58. 59. Cf. also EUR. *Bacch.* 1312.

The construction is commoner in Latin (cf. LIV. xxxiv. 29, Difficilior *facta erat* oppugnatio ni T. Quinctius supervenisset. TAC. *Ann.* iii. 14, Effigies Pisonis *traxerant* ac *divellebant* ni iussu principis repositae forent. HOR. *Od.* II. xvii., Me truncus illapsus cerebro *sustulerat* nisi Faunus ictum dextra levasset. VERG. *Georg.* ii. 132, Et, si non alium late iactaret odorem, laurus *erat*.

2. This omission of ἄν is almost the rule with the Imperfect of verbs denoting *necessity, duty, possibility, propriety,* etc.: χρῆν or ἐχρῆν, ἔδει, ἐξῆν, ἐνῆν, εἰκὸς ἦν, προσῆκεν, ἦν or ὑπῆρχεν (*it was possible*), καλὸν ἦν, αἰσχρὸν ἦν, καλῶς εἶχεν, ὤφελον, ἔμελλες, ἐβουλόμην. Also with verbals in -τεος, *e.g.* προαιρετέον ἦν (*satius erat*). All these phrases denote an unfulfilled condition (present or continued past).

This construction is parallel with the Latin—*debebam, decebat, oportebat, poteram,* gerundive with *eram, par, satis, aequum erat,* etc. See MADVIG, *L. G.* § 348 E., and *Obs.* 1.

καλὸν ἦν τοῖσδε, εἰ καὶ ἡμαρτάνομεν, εἶξαι τῇ ἡμετέρᾳ ὀργῇ.
                                      THUC. i. 38.

It would have been well for them, even if we had been wronging them, to give way to our anger.

.ἐβουλόμην μὲν οὐκ ἐρίζειν ἐνθάδε. ARIST. *Ran.* 866.
I could have wished I was not wrangling here.
ἴσον ἦν μοι μὴ ἐλθεῖν (as apodosis to εἰ μηδὲν διέφερε).
ANTIPH. *Herod.* 13.
It would have been all the same to me not to have come.
For ὤφελον, ἐβουλόμην, see *Wishes.*

3. Observe similar constructions of ἔδει and ἐχρῆν (χρῆν).

χρῆν (ἔδει) σε ταῦτα ποιεῖν.
You ought to be doing, or, *to have been doing* (but you are not, or were not, doing the act). Compare ἐποίεις ἄν.

χρῆν (ἔδει) σε ταῦτα ποιῆσαι.
You ought to have done (but you did not do) *the act.*
Compare ἐποίησας ἄν.
Oportebat *and* oportuit facere.
For χρῆν, with Present Infinitive and Aorist Infinitive, see PLAT. *Apol.* xxii., ARIST. *Ach.* 562. ἔδει, DEM. 112. 6. But χρή σε ποιεῖν (ποιῆσαι), *you ought to do this* (of what can still be done), oportet te facere.

οὐκ ἔδει σε ταῦτα ποιεῖν.
You ought not to be doing (what you are doing).
χρῆν, ἔδει, etc., however may take an ἄν.

εἰ μὲν ἠπιστάμεθα σαφῶς, οὐδὲν ἄν ἔδει ὧν μέλλω λέγειν.
XEN. *Anab.* v. 1. 10.
If we had all known for certain, there would be no need for me to say what I am going to say.

So in Latin *possem* may be used and not *poteram, oporteret* and not *oportebat.*

4. κινδυνεύω, μέλλω.

ἡ πόλις ἐκινδύνευσε πᾶσα διαφθαρῆναι, εἰ ἄνεμος ἐπεγένετο.
THUC. iii. 74.
The city was in danger of being entirely destroyed if a wind had not arisen (we might say, *but a wind arose*), a periphrasis for διεφθάρη ἄν.
In eo erat ut consumeretur urbs nisi, etc.

μέλλω in the Imperfect is a periphrasis for an Aorist with ἄν.

οὐ συστρατεύειν ἔμελλον. DEM. *de Fals. Leg.* 391. 11.
They would not have joined forces (οὐκ ἄν συνεστράτευσαν).
Vires non collaturi erant.

§ 199. Ἐάν (ἤν) with the Subjunctive, and Εἰ with the Optative in General or Frequentative Suppositions.[1]

See § 178.

Many of the four forms already given may express general as well as particular suppositions, but to express a supposition which refers not to a particular act, but to customary acts, frequently repeated acts, general truths or maxims, there are two common forms which are given below. They are parallel with Indefinite Relative Sentences, and Frequentative Temporal Sentences (see Index). Ἐάν and εἰ here mean "if ever" (ἐάν ποτε, εἴ ποτε). Ἐάν and εἰ, however, in themselves, with the Subjunctive or Optative, are not Frequentative, but the Tense of the Apodosis (the Principal Sentence) makes the whole compound clause so. It is the Apodosis which distinguishes these uses of ἐάν with the Subjunctive, and εἰ with the Optative from their ordinary uses.

---

[1] The Latin equivalents to Greek General Suppositions should be noticed.

Present.

Si quis eorum decreto non stetit,   sacrificiis interdicunt.
                                                                          CAESAR, *B. G.* vi. 12.
If yet any one does not abide by   *they exclude him from the*
their decree,   *sacrifices.*

Sin autem etiam libidinum intemperantia accessit,   duplex malum est.
                                                                          CIC. *Off.* i. 123.
But if ever in addition there be   *the mischief is doubled.*
want of control over the desires,

(The Present Indicative is also used in Latin.)

Past.

Si a persequendo hostes deterrere nequiverant,   disiectos a tergo circumveniebant. SALLUST, *Iug.* 50.
If ever they could not deter the   *they kept inclosing them in the*
enemy from pursuit,   *rear.*

Si quod erat grande vas,   laeti adferebant. CIC. *Verr.*
If they came across any large   *they used to bring it to him in*
vessel,   *triumph.*

Observe the tenses of the Protasis: the Perfect Indicative in Present Time, the Pluperfect in Past. These are the commonest forms according to the Latin strictness in representing one action as prior to another.

'Εάν (ἤν) WITH THE SUBJUNCTIVE, ETC.

I. Referring generally to present or future time.

PROTASIS.
'Εάν (ἤν, ἄν) with Subjunctive.

Parallel with

ἐάν ποτε
ὅς ἄν
ὅστις ἄν
ὅταν, etc.
} and Subj.

APODOSIS.
Present Indicative or any present Iterative Tense (gnomic Aorist).

II. Referring to past time.
εἰ with Optative.
Parallel with

εἴ ποτε
ὅς, ὅστις
ὅτε, etc.
} with Opt.

Imperfect Indicative, or any past Iterative Tense (Aor. or Imperf. with ἄν).

EXAMPLES OF I.

ἢν ἐγγὺς ἔλθῃ θάνατος οὐδεὶς βούλεται θνῄσκειν. EUR. *Alc.* 671.
If (when) death draws nigh none wish to die.

μέγ' ἐστὶ κέρδος ἢν διδάσκεσθαι θέλῃς. MENAND.
'Tis great gain if thou carest to be taught.

ἅπας λόγος, ἄν ἀπῇ τὰ πράγματα, μάταιόν τι φαίνεται καὶ κενόν. DEM. *Ol.* ii. 21. 20.
All talk, if deeds are wanting, seems idle and empty.

ἢν δ' ἄρα σφαλῶσιν, ἐπλήρωσαν τὴν χρείαν. THUC. i. 70.
If ever by chance they fail, they always make good the loss.

ἐπλήρωσαν, Gnomic Aorist.

Cf. PLAT. *Apol.* ix.; ἄν τινα οἴωμαι. Ibid. xxi.; ἐάν τις βούληται.

EXAMPLES OF II.

εἴ δέ τις καὶ ἀντείποι εὐθὺς ἐτεθνήκει. THUC. viii. 66.
If (as often as, whenever) any one did speak against them, he was promptly put to death.

ἀλλ' εἴ τι μὴ φέροιμεν, ὤτρυνεν φέρειν. EUR. *Alc.* 755.
But if ever we did not fetch him a thing, he would order (i.e. kept ordering) us to fetch it.

εἴ τινες ἴδοιέν πῃ τοὺς σφετέρους ἐπικρατοῦντας ἀνεθάρσησαν ἄν. THUC. vii. 71.

If any of them saw their own side winning in any part of the battle, they would pluck up courage.

ἀνεθάρσησαν ἄν, iterative. For the iterative (or indefinite) use of ἄν with the Imperfect and Aorist Indicative, see § 142. This use must be carefully distinguished from that of ἄν in unfulfilled conditions. The iterative use of ἄν may have arisen from its being used without definite application, *e.g.* ἔλεξε ἄν, *he came—in any given case,* whereas in an unfulfilled condition the ἄν may have been of special application, ἔλεξε ἄν, *he came—in that case, i.e.* he would have come.

Obs.—That here in connection with a past Apodosis, the Optative really refers to past time. It is only when thus used, and in the rare instances in *oratio obliqua* where the Optative represents a Past Indicative of the *recta*, that the Optative denotes past time.

Supplementary Sections, § 200—§ 206.

§ 200. Mixed Examples.

For Examination and Reference.

Not seldom the Protasis and Apodosis do not strictly correspond. No one rule can be laid down for explaining all the irregularities. Sometimes the mind really shifts its ground in the passage between Protasis and Apodosis, making the conclusion depend upon a condition which the expressed Protasis only suggests. But mostly the irregularity is one of expression only. This is chiefly the case with the Optative with ἄν in an Apodosis, connected with a Protasis in the Indicative or Subjunctive. The Optative with ἄν may, as we have seen, express a modified Indicative drawing an inference, or an Imperative, or a Future. Sometimes again there are two Protases actually expressed (Ex. 9). Sometimes Preposition and Case, or a Particle supplies the place of the Protasis (Ex. 11 and 12).

1. εἰ μὲν γὰρ τοῦτο λέγουσιν, ὁμολογοίην ἂν ἔγωγε οὐ κατὰ τούτους εἶναι ῥήτωρ. PLAT. *Apol.* i.

If this is what they mean, I must admit that I am an orator of a far higher order than they.

The Protasis, εἰ λέγουσιν, refers to the present; the Apodosis is partly a remote supposition, and partly an inference.

2. τοῦτό γέ μοι δοκεῖ καλὸν εἶναι, εἴ τις οἷός τ' εἴη παιδεύειν ἀνθρώπους. PLAT. *Apol.* iv.
This does appear to me to be a grand thing—supposing one were able to teach men.

Here, δοκεῖ, a verb of thinking, almost makes the Apodosis like an Optative with ἄν.

3. καὶ ἐγὼ τὸν Εὐηνὸν ἐμακάρισα, εἰ ὡς ἀληθῶς ἔχοι τὴν τέχνην. PLAT. *Apol.* iv.
Lucky Evenus, thought I, if really and truly he were to possess the art.

εἰ ἔχοι is the Protasis to an Apodosis implied in ἐμακάρισα.

4. εἰ τοὺς ἀναιτίους διώκοιμεν . . . δεινοὺς ἀλιτηρίους ἕξομεν, . . . ἔνοχοί τε τοῦ φόνου τοῖς ἐπιτιμίοις ἐσμέν.
ANTIPH. Γ, Α. 4.
If we should indict the innocent, we shall find dread avengers, and we are liable to the penalties for murder.

A series of pictures more and more vividly presented, passing from the Optative to the Future Indicative.

5. πῶς ἂν εἴη δεινότερα μηχανήματα εἰ ὑμῖν κατείργασται ἃ βούλεσθε; ANTIPH. *de Caed. Herod.* 16.
How could there be more terrible practices, if you have (a present ordinary condition) *achieved your object?*

6. εἰ τοίνυν μεγάλων ἀγαθῶν αἴτια ὑμᾶς εἰργάσαντο ἐκεῖνοι, μέρος ἐγὼ οὐκ ἂν ἐλάχιστον δικαίως ταύτης τῆς αἰτίας ἔχοιμι. ANDOK. *de Red. suo.* 12.
If then those men accomplished what secured your great advantages (an ordinary past Protasis), *I might justly claim not the least share of the merit* (a future Apodosis, also marking an inference).

7. εἰ οὖν τινι ὑμῶν γνώμη τοιαύτη παρειστήκει πρότερον περὶ ἐμοῦ, σκοπεῖσθε ἐξ αὐτῶν τῶν γεγενημένων.
ANDOK. *de Myst.* 54.
If, therefore, any of you previously used to entertain such an opinion of me (an ordinary past condition in the Imperfect), *examine the case by the actual facts* (i.e. now in the immediate future).

8. εἰ ἦν δύοιν τὸ ἕτερον ἑλέσθαι, ἢ καλῶς ἀπολέσθαι ἢ αἰσχρῶς σωθῆναι, ἔχοι ἄν τις εἰπεῖν κακίαν εἶναι τὰ γενόμενα.
ANDOK. *de Myst.* 57.
If it had been possible to choose one of two alternatives, either an honourable death or a dishonourable escape, then you might stigmatize my conduct as cowardice (a past unfulfilled condition, a future Apodosis with an inference).

9. ἐγὼ οὖν δεινὰ ἂν εἴην εἰργασμένος, εἰ, ὅτε μέν με οἱ ἄρχοντες ἔταττον . . . τότε μὲν οὗ ἐκεῖνοι ἔταττον ἔμενον . . . τοῦ δὲ θεοῦ τάττοντος . . . λίποιμι τὴν τάξιν. PLAT. *Apol.* xvii.
I accordingly should be in a position of one who is guilty of fearful sin if, when your rulers were assigning me a post, etc.,—if then, I say, I was remaining at the post which they assigned me, but if, when now God is assigning me a post, I were to desert that post.
Here there is one Apodosis, ἂν εἴην εἰργασμένος, and two Protases, εἰ ἔμενον, εἰ λίποιμι. The two Protases make up the combined conditions which produce the Apodosis.

Cf. also ch. xv.

10. εἰ γὰρ οὗτοι ὀρθῶς ὑπέστησαν, ὑμεῖς ἂν οὐ χρεὼν ἄρχοιτε.
THUC. iii. 40.
If they were right in revolting, then your rule is unlawful (it would follow that you are ruling).

11. διά γε ὑμᾶς αὐτοὺς πάλαι ἂν ἀπολώλειτε. DEM. *de Cor.* 242.
So far as you yourselves were concerned, you would have been ruined long ago.
διά γε ὑμᾶς αὐτοὺς = εἰ ὑμεῖς αὐτοὶ μόνοι ἦτε, *if you had been left to yourselves, had it depended on you alone.*

12. οὕτω γὰρ οὐκέτι τοῦ λοιποῦ πάσχοιμεν ἂν κακῶς.
DEM. *Phil.* 1. 44.
For in that we should never again get into trouble.
οὕτω = εἰ ταῦτα γένοιτο.

§ 201. Examples of the Conditional Participle in a Protasis.

ὀλοῦμαι μὴ μαθών. ARIST. *Nub.* 792.
I shall be ruined if I don't learn.
= ἐὰν μὴ μάθω.

CONDITIONAL RELATIVE SENTENCES.

δεῖ γὰρ ἑνὸς οὗ μὴ τυχὼν
ἀπόλωλα. ARIST. *Ach.* 466.
*One thing I need which, if I fail to get,
I'm a lost man.*
οὗ μὴ τυχών = ἐὰν μὴ τύχω . . . ἀπόλωλα being a vivid future.
τὸ ἀποθανεῖν ἄν τις ἐκφύγοι ὅπλα ἀφείς. PL. *Apol.* xxix.
A man might escape death if he were to fling away his arms.
ἀφείς = εἰ ἀφείη.
μεταγνοὺς γάρ (= εἰ μεταγνοίη) ἔτι ἂν ὀρθῶς βουλεύσαιτο.
ANTIPH. *de Caede Herod.* 91.
For if he should repent he yet might come to a right decision.
οὐ γὰρ ἂν ἐβλήθη ἀτρεμίζων καὶ μὴ διατρέχων (= εἰ ἠτρέμιζε
καὶ μὴ διέτρεχε). ANTIPH. 2 *Tetral.* B. B. 5.
*He would not have been struck if he had been standing still,
and not running across.*

§ 202. Examples of Conditional Relative Sentences.

ἃ μὴ οἶδα, οὐδὲ οἴομαι εἰδέναι. PLAT. *Apol.* vi.
What I do not know I do not fancy that I know.
= εἴ τινα μὴ οἶδα..

τῶν δὲ ἄλλων ξένων ὅστις πώποτε ἠθέλησε καταστῆσαι
ἐγγυητάς, οὐδεὶς πώποτε ἐδέθη. ANTIPH. *Herod.* 17.
*Of all the other foreigners who ever at any time chose to furnish
securities, none ever was thrown into prison.*
ὅστις ἠθέλησε = εἴ τις ἠθέλησε, an ordinary past Condition.

ἃ γάρ τις μὴ προσεδόκησεν, οὐδὲ φυλάξασθαι ἐγχωρεῖ.
ANTIPH. *de Caed. Herod.* 19.
*What one does not expect, it is not even possible to guard
against.*
An instructive instance; προσεδόκησεν is a Gnomic Aorist, and
so this is a General Supposition in Present time. The Aorist,
however, may here simply imply priority of time.

ἴσην γε δύναμιν ἔχει ὅστις τε ἂν τῇ χειρὶ ἀποκτείνῃ ἀδίκως
καὶ ὅστις τῇ ψήφῳ. ANTIPH. *de Caed. Herod.* 92.
*The effect is the same whether a man takes life with his hand,
or with his vote.*
A General Supposition again in Present time.

P

§ 203. Relative Conditional Sentences expressing General Suppositions.

(See also the last two examples in the previous section.)

I. PRESENT TIME.

συμμαχεῖν τούτοις ἐθέλουσιν ἅπαντες, οὓς ἂν ὁρῶσι παρε
σκευασμένους.   DEM. *Phil.* i. 42. 1.
All men are ready to be in alliance with those whom ever they see prepared.

= ἐάν τινας = ὅταν, ὁπόταν τινάς.

II. PAST TIME.

οἱ δέ, καιομένου ἄλλου, ἐπιβαλόντες ὃν φέροιεν, ἀπῄεσαν.
                         THUC. ii. 52.
Continually, while one body was burning, they kept throwing on (the funeral pile) any one they were bearing, and then going away.

= εἴ τινα = εἴ ποτέ τινά = ὁπότε τινά.

§ 204. Examples of Infinitive in Apodosis with ἄν.

εἰ Τεγεά σφισι προσγένοιτο, ἐνόμιζον ἅπασαν ἂν ἔχειν
Πελοπόννησον.   THUC. v. 32.
They thought that, if they could get in addition Tegea, they would possess the whole Peloponnese.

ἂν ἔχειν = ἔχοιεν ἄν.

But in the *recta* they would say : ἐὰν ἡμῖν προσγένηται . . . ἕξομεν.

οὐδεὶς ἀντεῖπε διὰ τὸ μὴ ἀνασχέσθαι ἂν τὴν ἐκκλησίαν.
                         XEN. *An.* i. 4. 20.
No one contradicted, because the assembly would not have permitted it.

εἰ ἀντεῖπε—οὐκ ἂν ἠνέσχετο ἡ ἐκκλησία.

ἀλλ' εἰ πέπαυται, κάρτ' ἂν εὐτυχεῖν δοκῶ   SOPH. *Ai.* 263.
Nay, if he hath ceased, methinks all may be well.

εὐτυχοίη ἄν an Optative of inference.

§ 205. Examples of Participle in Apodosis with ἄν.

αἰτεῖ ξένους καὶ μισθὸν ὡς οὕτως περιγενόμενος ἄν τῶν ἀντιστασιωτῶν. XEN. *An.* i. 10.
He asked for mercenaries and pay, representing that thus he would get the better of his opponents.

οὕτω περιγένοιτο ἄν, but as it is in Historical (*Virtual*) *obliqua* the original *recta* would be ἐὰν δέξωμαι ξένους—οὕτω περιγενήσομαι.

ὁρῶν τὸ παρατείχισμα, εἰ ἐπικρατήσειέ τις, ῥᾳδίως ἄν ληφθέν.
THUC. vii. 42.
Seeing that the cross-wall, if any one carried the heights, would easily be captured.

=ῥᾳδίως ἄν ληφθείη. Note the Participle after ὁρῶν, a verb of Perception.

ὦ πάντα τολμῶν, κἀπὸ παντὸς ἄν φέρων
λόγου δικαίου μηχάνημα ποικίλον. SOPH. *O. C.* 761.
*Bold wretch, who out of every cause wouldst bring
Shifty device of righteous argument.*

φέρων = ὅς φέροις ἄν (εἰ καιρὸν λάβοις).

§ 206. Supplementary Note on ἐάν with the Subjunctive, and εἰ with the Optative.

Ἐάν with the Subjunctive is the ordinary form for stating a supposition in future time. By the term *ordinary* it is not meant that this form occurs oftener than εἰ with the Optative, but that if, for instance, we had to say, "*If it is fine to-morrow, we will go for a walk*," we should naturally translate this by ἐάν with the Subjunctive. That is, to say, ἐὰν ταῦτα γένηται means *if this shall happen*. Modern English renders it difficult for us to grasp this very simple explanation, because we equally render εἰ ταῦτα γίγνεται and ἐὰν ταῦτα γένηται by *if this happens*. Εἰ ταῦτα γίγνεται should correctly be translated *if this is (now) happening*, and ἐὰν ταῦτα γένηται, *if this shall happen*. So in the instance first given we ought strictly to say "*If it shall be fine to-morrow.*" In older English it would have been "*if it be fine to-morrow,*" which is an exact parallel to ἐάν with the Subjunctive. The difficulty is aggravated by not bearing in mind that the Apodosis is the

Principal Sentence, and, as such, sets the time of the whole Compound Conditional Sentence. 'Εάν with the Subjunctive (in ordinary particular conditions) is regularly accompanied by an Apodosis in the Future Indicative, e.g. ταῦτα ποιήσω ἐάν τι δέῃ, *I will do this if it is necessary;* ἐάν τι δέῃ thus refers to the future.

Εἰ with the Optative also refers to the future. Εἰ ταῦτα γένοιτο means *if this should happen,* as opposed to ἐὰν ταῦτα γένηται, *if this shall happen.* All scholars now seem agreed that the difference between ἐάν with Subjunctive and εἰ with Optative is the same as that between *if I shall* and *if I should* in English.

In opposition to long-received explanations Professor Goodwin has shown in a series of papers (see especially *Journal of Philology,* Vol. v. No. 10, and Vol. viii. No. 15) that ἐάν with Subjunctive and εἰ with Optative are interchangeable expressions, alternating sometimes in the same paragraph, and when referring to the same condition. There can thus be no fundamental distinction between them, nor, we must add, between them and εἰ with the Future Indicative. All these are variant expressions for a future condition.

The most generally received theory hitherto of ἐάν with Subjunctive has been that of Buttmann, according to which it denotes "an uncertain but possible case with the prospect of speedy decision." Professor Goodwin pertinently asks how we should turn into Greek the proverb, "If the sky falls, we shall catch larks." Of course by ἐάν with the Subjunctive. But what is the "prospect of speedy decision" here? Further he asks whether Demosthenes (*Phil.* i. p. 43, § 11) implies any nearer prospect of decision about Philip's death when he first refers to it in the words ἄν οὗτός τι πάθῃ, than in the very next sentence, when he says εἴ τι πάθοι. Again, ἐάν with Subjunctive has been stated (by Dr. Donaldson and others) to denote "uncertainty with some small amount of probability." This theory, however, is destroyed by such conditions as the following, all with ἐάν and Subjunctive. In PLAT. *Crito,* 50, *of the laws speaking to Sokrates.* In *Euthyd.* 299, *of a man swallowing a cartload of hellebore.* In *Rep.* 612, *of the soul wearing the ring of Gyges.* In EUR. *Phoen.* 1216, and *Orest.* 1593, *of a human being flying on wings to the aether.*

How then do these three Future Conditions differ? 'Εάν with the Subjunctive gives a vivid and distinct representation of a supposition in the future. Εἰ with the Future Indicative is more vivid still; a condition is brought home as of imminent and immediate interest. Εἰ with the Optative, on the other hand, conjures up a future supposition less graphic, vivid, and life-like, a supposition less distinctly conceived, more faintly sketched, a supposition of less immediate concern, one which moves the mind with a more languid interest. We may compare the three forms to three sketches or pictures differing in greater or less distinctness of outline. Or we may say that εἰ with the Future Indicative moves the mind with the immediate interest of the next hour or minute, ἐάν and the Subjunctive with the natural and lively interest of the morrow, εἰ and the Optative with the fainter and remoter interest of next week. But the whole effect in each case is rhetorical, the expression itself does not imply that the fact denoted in the condition is to be decided, or that it is likely or unlikely; it is all a question of realising a conception more or less vividly, or, as Mr. Monro in his *Homeric Grammar* puts it, the **difference depends on the tone assumed by the speaker.**

When, therefore, is ἐάν with the Subjunctive chosen rather than εἰ with the Optative? Professor Goodwin shows that there may be several reasons for choosing the more vivid expression. The following instances are most instructive.

1. *The speaker may have an actual case present to his mind.* In *Rep.* vi. 494, Sokrates is thinking of Alkibiades; in *Rep.* vii. 517, of himself. In both cases ἐάν with the Subjunctive is the form employed.

2. *The speaker may be dreading the fulfilment of his supposition.* DEM. *Aphob.* i. 67 (p. 834), an adverse vote is referred to in these terms, ἐὰν ἀποφύγῃ με οὗτος, ὁ μὴ γένοιτο.

3. *The speaker may be treating an improbable and ridiculous supposition with scorn.* PLAT. *Rep.* x. 610 A, of bodily depravity causing mental depravity (ἐὰν μὴ ἐμποιῇ— τοῦτό γε οὐδείς ποτε δείξει): PLAT. *Gorg.* 470 C, of Polus convicting Sokrates of talking nonsense (ἐάν με ἐλέγξῃς).

There may be other reasons besides the above. Sometimes ἐάν with the Subjunctive seems to single out a supposition for special emphasis: sometimes an unfamiliar conception has been introduced by εἰ with the Optative, which, when we have become familiarised with it, is expressed by ἐάν with the Subjunctive. Or again, and this is a point worth further attention perhaps, different writers, from temperament or style, have a habit of using one expression rather than another. Thus AESCHYLUS very rarely uses ἐάν with the Subjunctive in an ordinary future supposition. He oftener uses εἰ with the Future Indicative; thrice he uses εἰ with the Subjunctive. But his partiality for the Optative is remarkable. THUCYDIDES again often uses εἰ with the Future Indicative.

In all the above cases (1) the time is future, (2) the picture is designedly conceived and drawn in a lively graphic manner. (3) In many cases such as the above ἐάν with the Subjunctive alternates with εἰ and the Optative. Thus in the example from DEM. *Aphob.* the same condition is alluded to later on (ii. § 18, p. 841) by the words εἰ ψηφίσαισθε, then three lines further on by ἐὰν ὀφλωμεν, and yet again (§ 21, p. 842) by εἰ γνώσεσθε. Similarly in PLAT. *Rep.* 517 A, where Sokrates is referring to himself, the Optative is used.

The inferences from the above premises are inevitable.

(1) ἐάν with the Subjunctive, and εἰ with the Optative, both refer to future time.

(2) They are interchangeable, differing only in greater or less clearness of conception and vividness of expression.

(3) As expressions they can in themselves imply no opinion of the writer that the fact denoted by the condition is more or less likely to occur, the one and only thing stated being the dependence of the consequence upon the condition.

The interchangeability of the Subjunctive and Optative is one of the regular and most characteristic features of Greek Syntax. We find it constantly in Indirect Statements and Questions, and throughout the *Oratio Obliqua*, in Temporal, Final Sentences, in Sentences with ὅπως. In all these cases we do not hesitate to accept the explanation that one expression is more or less direct and vivid than the other, and that the two varieties are interchangeable. Conditional Sentences do not stand apart by themselves: they follow the principles which rule Greek Syntax.

Two points may be added :

1. If it is asked whether the writer may not hold an opinion that the fact denoted is more or less probable, we may reply that of course he may, and that holding such an opinion he may choose one form of expression rather than

another. But this covers only some instances and not all. Probability cannot be made the basis of a division, since the fact denoted varies from what is in itself natural and probable to what is physically impossible.

(2) The notion of future time is sometimes very indistinctly marked by εἰ with the Optative, the faintness of the conception being the chief effect intended in such cases. Still εἰ ταῦτα οὕτως εἴη cannot (as sometimes in Homer) be past, *if this had been so;* it cannot be translated, *if it were now so;* it can only be rendered, *if this were to be so, were so, should be so.* The Apodosis also must always be examined in connexion with the Protasis.

CHAPTER III.

§ 207. TEMPORAL SENTENCES.

Temporal Sentences are constantly expressed in Greek by Participles in agreement with the Subject, by the Genitive Absolute, and by the Accusative Absolute.

When the time of the Temporal Sentence is *definite* the Indicative is used; when *indefinite* the Subjunctive and Optative.[1] This is the one clew to the use of the moods in Temporal Sentences.

See § 172, Definite and Indefinite Sentences.

Time is *indefinite* in three ways :—

1. *Indefinite Futurity*, i.e. when the action will occur in the indefinite future.

2. *Indefinite Frequency*, i.e. when the action may recur an indefinite number of times.

3. *Indefinite Duration*, i.e. when the action may continue for an indefinite period.

All Temporal Sentences in the Subjunctive and Optative will fall under *one* of the above three heads, the first,

---

[1] This principle of Indefinite Time may be most usefully applied to the Latin Subjunctive as opposed to the Indicative, e.g.—
Donec labantes consilio patres *firmaret* (HOR.). Indefinite Futurity.
Opperire quoad scire *possis* quod tibi agendum sit. Indefinite Futurity.
Dum Priami Paridisque busto *insultet* armentum. Indefinite Duration.
It is usual to explain many such sentences in Latin (and in Greek) by saying that they express a purpose. So they do, but this is not contained in the Temporal Particle and its Sentence, but in the nature of the principal verb combined with the indefiniteness of time in view. So probably with Temporal Sentences which are described as Conditional (*dum*).
Indefinite Frequency is so differently treated by Latin writers that it is not touched on here.

Indefinite Futurity, being the commonest, and the third, Indefinite Duration, being the rarest. More than one kind of Indefiniteness may be denoted by the same expression.

The Subjunctive is used in Primary, the Optative in Historic sequence, though, as in other Sentences, the Subjunctive occurs in Historic sequence, and sometimes is co-ordinate with the Optative.

A Temporal Particle with the Subjunctive takes ἄν (πρὶν ἄν, ἕως ἄν, ἐπειδάν, ὅταν, etc. etc.).
Thus ἕως ἄν γένηται.

A Temporal Particle with the Optative drops the ἄν (πρίν, ἕως, ἐπειδή, ὅτε, etc. etc.).
ἕως γένοιτο.

For the omission of ἄν in Subjunctive clauses see § 221.

For the retention of ἄν with the Optative see § 222.

§ 208. " WHEN" IN DEFINITE TIME (PAST).

I. ἐπεί, ἐπειδή (ἡνίκα less common), *when, after*, with Indicative Aorist (an action prior to principal sentence), Indicative Imperfect (contemporary with principal sentence).

Latin : *cum* with Pluperfect and Imperfect Subjunctive, *postquam* with Indicative.

ἐπειδὴ δὲ ὀλιγαρχία ἐγένετο, οἱ τριάκοντα μετεπέμψαντό με.   PLAT.
When an oligarchy had been established, the Thirty sent for me.

Cum vero paucorum dominatio constituta esset, Triginta illi me arcessiverunt.

ἐπεὶ ἠσθένει Δαρεῖος, ἐβούλετο οἱ τώ παῖδε ἀμφοτέρω παρεῖναι. XEN. *An.*

When Darius was ill, he wished both his sons to appear before him.

Darius, cum moreretur, filios ambo ad se venire volebat.

For ἡνίκα see PLAT. *Apol.* xxxi., SOPH. *El.* 32, 423, *Ai.* 272.

Note. ὅτε, "when," cannot introduce a clause in Attic Greek like ἐπεί, ἐπειδή. Being a relative it must be connected with some sort of antecedent, though, like all relative sentences, the clause in which it stands may come first. τότε is its strict antecedent.

ἦν ποτε χρόνος, ὅτε θεοὶ μὲν ἦσαν, θνητὰ δὲ γένη οὐκ ἦσαν.
PLAT. *Prot.*

There was a time once when the gods were in existence, but when the races of mortal creatures were not.

ὅτε με οἱ ἄρχοντες ἔταττον, τότε οὗ ἐκεῖνοι ἔταττον ἔμενον.
PLAT. *Apol.*

When the rulers were assigning me a post, then I remained at the post which they assigned me.

§ 209. *"AS SOON AS," "DIRECTLY," IN DEFINITE TIME.*

Ἐπεί, ἐπειδή take τάχιστα when they mean *directly, immediately, as soon as, no sooner—than.*

ὡς (Latin *ut*) has the same meaning even without τάχιστα, but more markedly with τάχιστα.

[Latin : *ubi, ubi primum ; ut, ut primum ; simul, simul ac (atque) ; postquam ;* with the perfect indicative.]

ὡς τάχιστα ἕως ὑπέφαινεν, ἐθύοντο. XEN.

As soon as day began to dawn, they set about taking the auspices.

οἱ τριάκοντα ᾑρέθησαν ἐπεὶ τάχιστα τὰ τείχη καθῃρέθη. XEN.
The Thirty were appointed directly the walls were rased.

In poetry ὅπως has this sense. Cf. AESCH. *Pers.* 200, SOPH. *El.* 736, 749, ὅπως ὁρᾷ (present indicative) *ut vidit.* For ὡς (often with εὐθύς, εὐθέως) see AESCH. *Pers.* 363, ARIST. *Ran.* 504.

§ 210. "WHENEVER," "AS OFTEN AS," IN INDEFINITE TIME.

The same particles, ἐπεί, ἐπειδή, ἡνίκα, ὅτε, and also ὁπότε, denoting Indefinite Futurity, or Indefinite Frequency, take the Subjunctive and Optative.

[Latin: usually a Temporal Conjunction with Future Perfect Indicative. But for Frequentative Sentences see the caution given § 207, footnote.]

A. With Subjunctive in Primary sequence, ἐπειδάν, ὅταν, ὁπόταν (ἡνίκ᾽ ἄν, ἐπήν and ἐπάν rarer).

N.B.—ὡς ἄν is said never to be Temporal, but see SOPH. *Phil.* 1330, *Ai.* 1117, with Jebb's note on the latter passage.

ἐπειδὰν δὲ διαπράξωμαι, ἃ δέομαι, ἥξω. XEN. *An.*
When I have (shall have) accomplished my object I will return. (Indefinite Futurity.)
Cum vero confecero quod in animo est, redibo.

οὐκοῦν, ὅταν δὴ μὴ σθένω, πεπαύσομαι. SOPH. *Ant.* 91.
So, when my power shall fail, I will give o'er.
(Indefinite Futurity.)

αὕτη ἡ φωνή, ὅταν γένηται, ἀεὶ ἀποτρέπει με. PLAT.
This inward voice, whenever it comes, ever checks me.
(Indefinite Frequency.)

μαινόμεθα πάντες, ὁπόταν ὀργιζώμεθα. PHILEMON.
We are madmen all, whenever we are angry.
(Indefinite Frequency.)

Note. For ὅταν (Indefinite Futurity) SOPH. *El.* 386, 1038, (Indefinite Frequency) PLAT. *Apol.* xvi., xxiii., SOPH. *El.* 267, 293, AESCH. *Pers.* 602. ὁπόταν (Indefinite Futurity) SOPH. *Phil.* 146. All these particles may often be rendered, *as soon as, when once,* but the time is still indefinite in the Future.

ὁπόταν (Indefinite Frequency) XEN. *Cyr.* iii. 3. 26, al. ὅπου ἄν) : ἐπειδάν (Frequency) PLAT. *Apol.* xxxii.

For εὖτε ἄν, poetical, SOPH. *El.* 627.

With the Subjunctive expressing Indefinite Frequency compare ἐάν (ἤν) with Subjunctive in General Suppositions.

B. With Optative in Historic Sequence, ἐπεί, ἐπειδή, ὁπότε (ὅτε very rarely).

οἱ ὄνοι, ἐπεί τις διώκοι, προδραμόντες ἂν εἰστήκεσαν.
                                                        XEN.
The asses, whenever any one chased them, would gallop ahead and then halt. (Indefinite Frequency.)

ὁπότ' εὖ πράσσοι πόλις
ἔχαιρε, λυπρῶς δ' ἔφερεν, εἴ τι δυστυχοῖ.
                                    EUR. *Supp.* 897.
*Whene'er the state fared well,
He would rejoice, and mourn if aught it suffered.*

ὁπότε is = εἰ ποτε, as much conditional as temporal. See PLAT. *Apol.* xxxii., ὁπότε ἐντύχοιμι Παλαμήδει. In THUC. i. 99 a good instance.

Note. ἐπεί, ἐπειδή, ὁπότε with the Optative appear always to denote Frequency rather than Futurity, except when they represent an ἐπήν, ἐπειδάν, ὁπόταν, ὅταν turned from Primary to Historic sequence.

Compare εἰ with Optative in General Suppositions.

§ 211. *"SINCE" IN DEFINITE TIME.*

ἐξ οὗ (*ex quo* with Indicative), *since, ever since,* in Definite Time with Indicative.

"WHILST" IN INDEFINITE TIME. 237

ἐξ οὗ τὰ ξενικὰ στρατεύεται, τοὺς φίλους νικᾷ.
DEM.
Ever since mercenaries have been serving, he has been conquering his friends.

ἐξ οὗτε AESCH. Pers. 761, for ὡς (like *ut* in Latin) THUC. iv. 90 (Poppo), ἐξ ὧν, ἀφ' οὗ are also used.
For *ut* in Latin cf. Ov. *Trist.* v. 10. 1, *ut sumus in Ponto*, etc.
This may be expressed participially in the Dative, see § 118, note.

§ 212. "*WHILST*" *IN DEFINITE TIME*.

Ἕως, ἔστε, ἐν ᾧ, ἐν ὅσῳ, ὅσον χρόνον, ἡνίκα (rarely μέχρι), *whilst*, denoting Definite Duration with Indicative.

[Latin : *dum, donec, quamdiu, quoad* with Indicative.]

ἕως ἔτι νέος εἰμί, τὴν ψυχὴν γυμνάζω.
While I am still young, I train my mind.

ῥᾳδίως τὰ ἐπιτήδεια ἕξομεν, ὅσον χρόνον ἐν τῇ πολεμίᾳ ἐσόμεθα.
We shall easily find supplies so long as (during all the time that) we are in the enemies' country.

ἀνὴρ ἐκεῖνος, ἡνίκ' ἦν ἐν τῇ νόσῳ,
αὐτὸς μὲν ἥδετο.   SOPH. *Ai*. 271.
Yon chief, so long as he was set i' the plague, Himself was happy.
Donec morbo versabatur.

ἔστε with past tense, XEN. *An.* iii. 1. 19.

ἕως ἔξεστιν (*dum licet*), PLAT. *Apol.* xxxi.   ἕως ἐλπὶς ἦν (past tense) *dum spes erat*, THUC. viii. 40.   μέχρι, THUC. iii. 10. 2.

§ 213. "*WHILST*" *IN INDEFINITE TIME*.

The same particles denoting Indefinite Duration take
A. Subjunctive in Primary sequence with ἄν.

ἕωσπερ ἂν ἐμπνέω, οὐ μὴ παύσωμαι φιλοσοφῶν.
PLAT.
Just so long as I breathe, I never will give up philosophy.
Dum spirabo haud desinam philosophari.
Cf. AESCH. *Ag.* 1435.

B. Optative in Historic Sequence, without ἄν.
φήσομεν μηδέποτ' ἂν μεῖζον γενέσθαι, ἕως ἴσον εἴη αὐτὸ ἑαυτῷ. PLAT. *Theaet.* 155 A.
We shall admit that it never would become either greater or less, so long as it should remain equal to itself.

[Latin : *dum, donec, quamdiu, quoad*, with Future Indicative, or, when purpose is connoted, Subjunctive.]

§ 214. *"UNTIL" IN DEFINITE TIME.*

ἕως, ἔστε, μέχρι, ἄχρι (μέχρι οὗ, ἄχρι οὗ), *until*, denoting Definite Time with Indicative.

εὖτε poetical, μέχρις, ἄχρις before a vowel in later writers.

[Latin : *donec, quoad*, with past Indicative.]

ταῦτα ἐποίουν, μέχρι σκότος ἐγένετο. XEN.
This they were doing until darkness came on.
quoad *or* donec nox oppressit.

Cf. THUC. i. 109, iv. 4, μέχρι οὗ and μέχρι.

παίουσι τὸν Σωτηρίδην, ἔστε ἠνάγκασαν πορεύεσθαι.
XEN.
They beat Soterides till they compelled him to move on.
quoad progredi coegerunt.

Cf. SOPH. *Ant.* 415.

ἐχώρουν διὰ τῶν Σικελῶν, ἕως ἀφίκοντο ἐς Κατάνην.
THUC. vi. 62. 3.
They marched through the country of the Sicels, till they came to Catane.

παίουσι, κρεοκοποῦσι δυστήνων μέλη,
ἕως ἁπάντων ἐξαπέφθειραν βίον.   AESCH. *Pers.* 466.
*They hack, hew mincemeal the poor wretches' limbs,
Till they had crushed outright the lives of all.*

ἐπισχὼν ἄν, ἕως οἱ πλεῖστοι τῶν εἰωθότων γνώμην ἀπεφή-
ναντο, κ.τ.λ., ἡσυχίαν ἂν ἦγον.   DEM. *Phil.* i. 1.
*I should have waited until most of the regular speakers had
expressed their views, and have been keeping quiet.*

In this example the Indicative denotes Indefinite Futurity thrown back into the past, and consequently now Indefinite only to the original thought of the chief subject. This is parallel with a Final Sentence in the Indicative (see Index).

§ 215. *"UNTIL" IN INDEFINITE TIME.*

The same Particles, denoting Indefinite Futurity, take

A. Subjunctive in Primary Sequence.

μέχρι δ' ἂν ἐγὼ ἥκω, αἱ σπονδαὶ μενόντων.   XEN.
Until I return, let the armistice continue.

ἐπίσχες ἔστ' ἂν καὶ τὰ λοιπὰ προςμάθῃς.   AESCH.
Pause till thou further learn what yet remains.

ἀνάγκη ταῦτα ἀεὶ παρέχειν, ἕως ἂν χώραν λάβῃ.
XEN. *Cyr.* iv. 5. 37.
*It is necessary to furnish continually the same things until he
(shall) take the country.*

εὖτ' ἄν AESCH. *Pers.* 366.

B. Optative in Historic Sequence.

περιεμένομεν ἑκάστοτε, ἕως ἀνοιχθείη τὸ δεσμωτήριον.
PLAT.
*We used to wait about on each occasion, until the
prison was (should be) opened.*

περιεμένομεν is Frequentative, but ἕως ἀνοιχθείη expresses Indefinite Futurity, and expresses indirectly the thought of the chief subject.

σπονδὰς ἐποιήσαντο ἕως ἀπαγγελθείη τὰ λεχθέντα.
XEN.
They made an armistice (to last) till the terms were (should be) announced.

Here again the thought of the chief subject is clearly seen. Their original words would be σπονδὰς ποιούμεθα ἕως ἂν ἀπαγγελθῇ. The moods in the two last examples are thus due to Oratio Obliqua.

Note. It may be generally laid down that ἕως, etc., with the Subjunctive and Optative after Affirmative Sentences correspond to πρίν with the same moods after Negative Sentences. ἕως, etc., *do* occur, but very exceptionally, after Negative Sentences.

οὐκ ἀναμένομεν, ἕως ἂν ἡ ἡμετέρα χώρα κακῶται.
XEN. *Cyr.* iii. 3. 18.
We do not remain until our country is being ravaged.

When πρίν is used with any finite mood the action of its verb will not begin until the action of πρίν with the principal verb has occurred. The difference here consists in the meaning of the verb ἀναμένω, *to continue*.

§ 216. *THE CONJUNCTION* Πρίν.

Πρίν with the Indicative, Subjunctive and Optative is used after Negative Sentences where ἕως, ἔστε, μέχρι, etc., are used after Affirmative Sentences.

Πρὶν ἤ is used like πρίν. πρότερον, πρόσθεν, πάρος, another πρίν (used as an adverb), frequently are used in the Principal Sentence as forerunners of πρίν.

Πρίν differs from other Temporal Particles only in being joined to an Infinitive as well as to other moods. The following table will show the ordinary Attic usage. Exceptions are given subsequently.

A. After Affirmative Principal Sentences. } πρίν with the Infinitive.

B. After Negative Principal Sentences.
{
1. When the Time is Definite, πρίν with the Indicative.
2. When the Time is Indefinite (Indefinite Futurity), πρίν with the Subjunctive and Optative.
}

The order in time of the Principal and Subordinate Sentences in πρίν clauses should be noticed. (1) When πρίν is used with the Infinitive, the action of the Principal Sentence takes place before that of the Subordinate Sentence (the πρίν clause). (2) When πρίν is used with a Finite Mood (Indicative, Subjunctive, Optative) the action of the Principal Sentence had to wait (in the past), or has to wait (in the future) for the decisive occurrence of the πρίν clause.

§ 217. Πρίν WITH THE INFINITIVE.

A. The Principal action takes place before the Subordinate action with πρίν. Πρίν with Infinitive always means *before*. The Infinitive in itself denotes the mere verbal notion rather than a distinct fact, like the English gerundive in *-ing* (before *coming, going, speaking*). But the fact is often implied. Cf. ὥστε with Infinitive.

πρὶν μὲν πεινῆν ἐσθίεις, πρὶν δὲ διψῆν πίνεις.
You eat before being hungry, you drink before being thirsty.

ἔπεμψε πρὶν ἐν Τεγέᾳ αὐτὸς εἶναι. XEN.
He sent before he was himself in Tegea.

Observe the Nominative attraction.

πρὶν γενέσθαι ἡμᾶς ἦν ἡμῶν ἡ ψυχή.   PLAT. *Phaed.* 77.
Before we were created our soul was in existence.
ἡμεῖς Μεσσήνην εἵλομεν πρὶν Πέρσας λαβεῖν τὴν βασιλείαν.
   ISOC. *Archid.* 26.
We conquered Messene before the Persians took the kingdom.
ἐν τῷ πρὶν γενέσθαι ἡμᾶς χρόνῳ.   PLAT. *Phaed.* 88.
In the days before we were born.

§ 218. Πρίν WITH THE INDICATIVE IN DEFINITE TIME (*PAST*).

B 1. *Πρίν* with Aorist Indicative. (The Historic present occurs in THUC. i. 132, πρίν γίγνεται.) Πρίν may equally be rendered *before, until.*

οἱ Λακεδαιμόνιοι οὐ πρότερον ἐπαύσαντο πρὶν Μεσσηνίους ἐξέβαλον ἐκ τῆς χώρας.   ISAEUS 12.
The Lacedaemonians did not leave off until (before) they had expelled the Messenians (and then they did leave off).

οὐ πρόσθεν ἐξενεγκεῖν ἐτόλμησαν πρὸς ἡμᾶς πόλεμον πρὶν τοὺς στρατηγοὺς ἡμῶν συνέλαβον.   XEN. *An.* iii. 2. 29.
They did not dare to make war on us until (before) they seized our generals.

See AESCH. *P. V.* 481.

In ISOCR. *Panegyr.* 19, πρίν ἐδίδαξαν where πρίν διδάξειαν would be expected.

§ 219. Πρίν WITH THE SUBJUNCTIVE AND OPTATIVE IN INDEFINITE TIME.

B 2. *Πρὶν ἄν* with Subjunctive in Primary Sequence, after Negative Sentences, denotes Indefinite Futurity.

οὐ χρή με ἀπελθεῖν πρὶν ἂν δῶ δίκην.
   XEN. *An.* v. 7. 5.
I must not depart before I suffer punishment.

Cf. also AESCH. *P. V.* 165, EUR. *Heracl.* 179.

οὐκ ἀποκρινοῦμαι πρότερον πρὶν ἂν πύθωμαι. PLAT.
I will not answer before (until) I hear.

πρίν alone with Optative may be described as πρὶν ἄν with Subjunctive converted into Historic Sequence by Oratio Obliqua, actual or virtual.

ἀπηγόρευε μηδένα βάλλειν, πρὶν Κῦρος ἐμπλησθείη
θηρῶν.   XEN. *Cyr.* i. 4. 14.
He forbade every one to shoot until Cyrus had had (should have had) his fill of the chase.

The *recta* would be μηδεὶς βαλλέτω πρὶν ἂν ἐμπλησθῇ.

ἐπεχείρουν ἕκαστον πείθειν μὴ πρότερον τῶν ἑαυτοῦ μηδενὸς
ἐπιμελεῖσθαι, πρὶν ἑαυτοῦ ἐπιμεληθείη.
   PLAT. *Apol.* xxvi.
I used to try to persuade each one not to care for any of the things belonging to himself before caring for himself.

Πρίν is also used after another Optative (see *Oratio Obliqua, Assimilation of Optatives*).

ὄλοιο μήπω πρὶν μάθοιμ᾽ εἰ καὶ πάλιν
γνώμην μετοίσεις.   SOPH. *Phil.* 961.
*Perish not ere I learn if yet again
Thou wilt repent thy purpose.*

§ 220. Πρίν with the Infinitive after Negative Sentences, and with the other Moods after Affirmative Sentences.

As stated above, the general Attic rule is that πρίν with Infinitive follows Affirmative Sentences. But the rule is not without exceptions. In Homer πρίν with Infinitive regularly follows either Affirmative or Negative sentences. In the Attic poets it very rarely follows a Negative. In Attic prose, however, several instances occur of πρίν with Infinitive after a Negative.

Instances in the Attic poets occur in AESCH. *Ag.* 1067, SOPH. *Ai.* 1418, EUR. *H. F.* 605, and ARIST. *Av.* 964.

In THUC. some cases occur (i. 68, i. 39) in both of which the οὐ belongs rather to the Infinitive than to the principal verb; in v. 10 the Negative belongs to the principal verb clearly. In all these three cases the abstract verbal notion rather than the fact is stated, *e.g.* v. 10, πρίν τοὺς βοηθοὺς ἥκειν, *before the arrival of his allies.* But in vii. 50 πρίν with the Infinitive is found after a Negative where we should certainly look for an Optative, occurring as it does in the reported words of Nikias.

οὐδ' ἂν διαβουλεύσασθαι ἔτι ἔφη, πρὶν κ.τ.λ., τρὶς ἐννέα ἡμέρας μεῖναι, ὅπως ἂν πρότερον κινηθείη.

He declared that he would not even consider the making of a move until he had waited thrice nine days.

Recta, οὐδ' ἂν διαβουλευσαίμην πρὶν μεῖναι (for πρὶν μείναιμι or πρὶν ἂν μείνω).

Cf. also ANTIPH. *Herod.* 25, ANDOK. *Myst.* 43.

Πρίν, with a Finite Mood (Indicative, Subjunctive, Optative), is found when the Principal Sentence is affirmative *in form,* but *virtually negative.*

ἄφρων νέος τ' ἦν, πρὶν τὰ πράγματ' ἐγγύθεν
σκοπῶν ἐςεῖδον, κ. τ. λ. EUR. *I. A.* 489.

where ἄφρων = οὐκ ἔμφρων.

Similarly in THUC. i. 118. 2, οὔτε ἐκώλυον, ἀλλ' ἡσύχαζον πρὶν δὴ ἡ δύναμις τῶν 'Αθηναίων ᾔρετο, where, besides the true negative οὔτε ἐκώλυον, ἡσύχαζον means, *they did not bestir themselves.* See also THUC. iii. 29, λανθάνουσι πρίν: viii. 105, εἶργον πρίν. But in THUC. vii. 71. 4, πρίν with the Indicative occurs after a principal sentence truly affirmative: παραπλήσια ἔπασχον, πρίν γε δὴ οἱ Συρακόσιοι ἔτρεψαν τοὺς 'Αθηναίους, *they were in the same state of excitement, until at last the Syracusans routed the Athenians* (ἔστε δή might have been expected). With the Subjunctive and Optative πρίν is very rarely found even after quasi-negative sentences:—

τίς ἂν δίκην κρίνειεν ἢ γνοίη λόγον,
πρὶν ἂν παρ' ἀμφοῖν μῦθον ἐκμάθῃ σαφῶς; EUR. *Herac.* 179.

τίς ἄν, however, is almost a real negative.

αἰσχρὸν ἡγοῦμαι πρότερον παύσασθαι πρὶν ἂν ὑμεῖς, ὅτι ἂν βούλησθε, ψηφίσησθε. LYS. 22. 4.

Here αἰσχρόν is a virtually negative word, as its use before μὴ οὐ with an Infinitive shows. (See Negatives.)

Πρὶν ἤ, πρότερον ἤ, πρόσθεν ἤ, ὕστερον ἤ, are used like πρίν with an Infinitive.

τὸν Μῆδον, αὐτοὶ ἴσμεν πρότερον ἐλθόντα ἢ τὰ παρ' ὑμῶν προαπαντῆσαι. THUC. i. 601 (and vi. 58).

For ὕστερον ἢ οἰῆσαι see vi. 4.

§ 221. Ἄν omitted with the Subjunctive, in Temporal and other Subordinate Sentences.

In all sentences with the Subjunctive (Indefinite Relative, Conditional, Temporal), ἄν is sometimes not used even in Attic prose and poetry. It seems quite a mistake to say that ἄν is omitted. It is much more rational to treat this construction (like that of the Optative without ἄν), as a survival of the older usage, so constantly found in Homer, when the mood might or might not at pleasure be modified by the adverb ἄν. Instances of all the constructions are here given, but it must be remembered that they are all exceptional constructions in Attic, except, perhaps, in the case of the Temporal Particles.

Indefinite Relative:—

γέροντα δ' ὀρθοῦν φλαῦρον ὃς νέος πέσῃ. SOPH. O. C. 595.
ἐπιχώριον ὂν ἡμῖν οὐ μὲν βραχεῖς ἀρκῶσι μὴ πολλοῖς χρῆσθαι λόγοις. THUC. iv. 17.

Cf. SOPH. El. 771, 225, 1059; Ai. 496; Ant. 323.

Conditional:—(εἰ with Subjunctive common in Homer, Pindar, several in Herodotus).

δυστάλαινα τἄρ' ἐγώ,
εἰ σοῦ στερηθῶ. SOPH. O. C. 1441.

Cf. 509, Antig. 710, O. T. 198 (Chorus).

Once in THUC. vi. 21, εἰ ξυστῶσιν αἱ πόλεις, according to the best MSS. See Krüger and Poppo.

Temporal :—

πρίν   μὴ πρότερον ἀποκτιννύναι δεῖν πρὶν ἀνάγκην τινὰ ὁ
       θεὸς ἐπιπέμψῃ.   PLAT. *Phaedo*, vi.
       μὴ στέναζε πρὶν μάθῃς.
       SOPH. *Phil.* 917, *Antig.* 619 (Chorus).
μέχρι τὰς σπονδὰς ἐσπεῖσθαι μέχρι οὗ ἐπανέλθωσιν.
       THUC. iv. 16 (also iv. 41 and i. 137), SOPH. *Ai.* 571.
ἕως   ἕως τὸ χαίρειν καὶ τὸ λυπεῖσθαι μάθῃς.
       SOPH. *El.* 555 (*Phil.* 764).
ἐπεί   ἐπεὶ δ' ἁμάρτῃ, κ.τ.λ. SOPH. *Ant.* 1025.

With these Temporal Particles ἄν is commonly used in prose, but it is fairly often omitted. They seem in themselves sufficient to mark the indefiniteness of future time without the addition of ἄν.

§ 222.   Ἄν retained with the Optative.

In a few places ἄν is found with a Relative and Optative, and with a Temporal particle and the Optative, almost as if the writer in changing from the Subjunctive had forgotten to drop the ἄν. ἐλογιζόμην εἰ ταῦτα πρόθυμός σοι συλλάβοιμι, ὡς οἰκεῖός τέ σοι ἐσοίμην, καὶ ἐξέσοιτό μοι διαλέγεσθαί σοι ὁπόσον ἂν χρόνον βουλοίμην, XEN. *Cyr.* vii. 5. 49. Here either ὁπόσον ἂν βούλωμαι or ὁπόσον βουλοίμην would have been expected. Cf. XEN. *Ap.* i. 2. 6, παρ' ὧν ἂν λάβοιεν. So οὐδεὶς ὅστις οὐχ ἡγεῖτο δίκην με λήψεσθαι παρὰ τῶν ἐπιτρόπων, ἐπειδὰν τάχιστα ἀνὴρ εἶναι δοκιμασθείην, DEM. *Onet.* i. 865. 24. Cf. SOPH. *Tr.* 687, ἕως ἂν ἁρμόσαιμι.

§ 223. The Subjunctive instead of the Optative, or co-ordinate with the Optative in Historic Sequence.

ἐβούλευσαν δεσμοῖς αὐτοὺς φυλάσσειν μέχρι οὗ τι ξυμβῶσι.
THUC. iv. 41.

They decided to keep them in prison till some arrangement was come to.

Observe that ἄν is omitted with the Subjunctive, for μέχρι οὗ τι ξυμβαῖεν. Cf. i. 91, πρὶν ἄν Subjunctive after Historic time.

παρήγγειλαν ἐπειδὴ δειπνήσειαν πάντας ἀναπαύεσθαι, καὶ ἕπεσθαι ἡνίκ' ἄν τις παραγγέλλῃ. XEN. *An*. iii. 5. 18.
They issued orders for all to rest as soon as they had dined, and then to follow whenever any one issued orders.
This principle of the return to the Primary Sequence is so common in Greek that it requires no further explanation here.

§ 224. The Participle as a Substitute for a Temporal Sentence.

The Participle is a regular substitute for a sentence expressed by ἐπεί, ἐπειδή, ἡνίκα with Imperfect and Aorist Indicative, but is used still more freely, for it is joined to Present and Future Time, whereas these Particles go with a past Principal Verb.

1. The Present Participle denotes an action contemporary with that of the Principal Verb.

ἅμα and μεταξύ with the Participle bring out more clearly the contemporary time.

ἀπήντησα Φιλίππῳ ἀπιόντι.
I met Philip as he was going away.
ἅμα προιὼν ἐπεσκοπεῖτο. XEN.
As he was going forward he was considering.
τὸ τοῦ θεοῦ σημεῖον πολλαχοῦ δή με ἐπέσχε λέγοντα μεταξύ. PLAT. *Apol.* xxxi.
The sign of the god very often has checked me in the midst of my talk—(while I have been speaking— while the words were on my lips).
ἐπέσχε is here a gnomic aorist.

2. The Aorist Participle denotes an action prior[1] to that of the Principal Verb.

The Perfect Participle would express a completed state before the action of the Principal Verb.

---

[1] Never forgetting that the Aorist Participle does not always denote an action prior to that of the principal Verb. See Participles. Where the Aorist Participle denotes a contemporary action it expresses Circumstance, not Time.

τότε, τότε ἤδη, εἶτα, ἔπειτα, τηνικαῦτα, οὕτως often accompany the Principal Verb. εὐθύς with the Participle is like τάχιστα with a Conjunction.

τυραννεύσας ἔτη τρία Ἱππίας ἐχώρει ἐς Σίγειον.
THUC.
After ruling three years (when he had ruled), Hippias retired to Sigeum, or *he ruled and then retired.*

ἐκέλευσε οὖν διαβάντα τὸν Ἑλλήσποντον ἔπειτα ἀπαλλάττεσθαι. XEN. *An*. vii. 1.
He induced him to accompany him over the Hellespont, and then withdraw (after he had accompanied him, to withdraw).

εὐθὺς γενόμενοι (primo ortu), *immediately after birth.*

εὐθὺς ἀποβεβηκότες, *directly they landed, no sooner had they landed . . . than,* etc.

CHAPTER IV.

§ 225. CONCESSIVE SENTENCES.

The chief Concessive Particle in Greek is καί, with or without the enclitic περ.

Concessive Sentences are most commonly expressed by the Participle, especially with καίπερ (more rarely καί alone). The Negative is οὐ. Ὅμως (tamen) often accompanies the Principal Verb.

τοῦ Κλέωνος, καίπερ μανιώδης οὖσα, ἡ ὑπόσχεσις ἀπέβη. THUC.
Cleon's promise, insane though it was, was fulfilled.
Cf. SOPH. *Ai.* 122.

πείθου γυναιξί, καίπερ οὐ στέργων ὅμως. AESCH.
Listen to women though thou like them not.

The ὅμως belongs to πείθου, though it often is drawn to the Participle.

οὗτος οἴεταί τι εἰδέναι οὐκ εἰδώς. PLAT. *Apol.* vi.
This man thinks he knows something though he knows nothing.

κἀγὼ σ' ἱκνοῦμαι, καὶ γυνή περ οὖσ' ὅμως. EUR. *Orest.* 680.
I too entreat thee, woman though I be.
Here καί and περ are separated, and ὅμως is dislocated from its Verb.

Note 1. οὐδέ, οὐδέ περ, μηδέ, μηδέ περ are also found with Concessive Particles in Negative Concessive Sentences.

οὐκ ἂν προδοίην, οὐδέ περ πράσσων κακῶς. EUR. *Phoen.* 1624.
I'd not betray, not even though in woe.

γυναικὶ πείθου, μηδέ τἀληθῆ κλύων. EUR. *Hipp. Fr.* 443.
Hearken to a woman, even if thou hearest not the truth.

οὐδ' εἰ, οὐδ' ἐάν, μηδ' εἰ, μηδ' ἐάν are used in Negative Concessive sentences (*ne—quidem*).

μὴ θορυβήσητε, μηδ' ἐὰν δόξω τι ὑμῖν μέγα λέγειν.
PLAT. *Apol.* v.
Do not interrupt, even if you shall think that I am speaking presumptuously.
οὐδ' εἰ, *Apol.* xvii. 29.

ἐγὼ μὲν οὖν οὐκ ἄν ποτ', οὐδ' εἴ μοι τὰ σὰ
μέλλοι τις οἴσειν δῶρ' ἐφ' οἷσι νῦν χλιδᾷς,
τούτοις ὑπεικάθοιμι. SOPH. *El.* 360.
*Ne'er then would I, not e'en if one were like
To bring me those thy gifts, wherein thou now
Art glorying, submit to these.*

Note 2. καὶ ταῦτα, and that too, is also used with a participle, and also, but very seldom, καίτοι. For καὶ ταῦτα, PLAT. *Rep.* 404 B, XEN. *Cyr.* ii. 2. 16. For καίτοι, PLAT. *Prot.* 339 C.

ἐγὼ οὐδὲν τούτων ποιήσω, καὶ ταῦτα κινδυνεύων.
PLAT. *Apol.* xxiii.
I will do none of these things, and that too though I am running a risk.

Note 3. The Relative occasionally is used in a concessive sense.

For ὅστις, SOPH. *Ai.* 434, ὅτου πάτηρ : and ARIST. *Ach.* 57, ὅστις ἤθελε : ὃς ἐξέβην, ANTIPH. *Caed. Herod.* 25.

Note 4. εἴπερ, ἐάνπερ, bear a sort of concessive force, or perhaps rather a particularising force, *that is to say,* cf. *if really*, EUR. *Her. Fur.* 1345, LYS. 12. 48; ἐάνπερ, PLAT. *Apol.* xii. (a General Supposition).

§ 226. Note on εἰ καί, καὶ εἰ, etc.

Καί added to the Conditional particles εἰ, ἐάν, ἤν gives the Conditional Sentence a concessive meaning. Καί is thus added to any form of Conditional Sentence, which will therefore follow the rules of Conditional Sentences. A distinction is generally made between εἰ καί and καὶ εἰ. Εἰ καί is said (by Hermann and Kühner) to concede a fact, *although*, καί εἰ a supposition, *even if* (a supposition). It is impossible to support this theory. As καί with εἰ and ἐάν occur with every form of conditional sentence (Indicative, Subjunctive, Optative) with ordinary and general suppositions, καί cannot give the εἰ or ἐάν the power of turning any and every form of supposition into statement of a fact. Hermann's dictum at the most could hold good only of εἰ καί and καί εἰ with the Indicative. And it is equally true here as with ordinary conditions (without καί) that if a fact is stated it is only by virtue of the context. Madvig more cautiously states that εἰ καί sometimes inclines more to the affirmation of the condition, and that it is often only distinguished from καί εἰ by being less emphatic. This is the most we can say, the latter part of his remark being very true. Καί in these phrases is expletive, i.e. it emphasises the word it precedes (as in πρὶν καὶ γενέσθαι ἡμᾶς, PLAT. Phaed. 77. 6, before we came into being at all). It is further clear that καί εἰ with the Indicative often leans to the affirmation of the condition as strongly as εἰ καί. Καί εἰ, being more emphatic, may often mean that even in spite of, under extreme circumstances, the Apodosis holds good.

εἰ καί, with Indic., PLAT. La. 182, SOPH. El. 547, O. T. 302.

καὶ εἰ,   „   PLAT. Apol. xxix., AESCH. Pers. 297, AESCH. Cho. 290 (leans to the fact); SOPH. Aj. 564 (do.); SOPH. Ant. 234 (fut. indic.); PLAT. Apol. xix. (καὶ εἰ μέλλει).

εἰ καί,   „   in unfulfilled conditions, ISOCR. de permut. (33), from Madvig.

καί εἰ,   „   PLAT. Polit. 276 (Apodosis ἔδει); DEM. 21. 199.

ἐὰν καί, with Subj., DEM. 16. 24.

καὶ ἐάν,   „   MENAND. Fr. 19 (a General Supposition); PLAT. Symp. 185, SOPH. El. 25 (a General Supposition).

καὶ εἰ, with Optat., XEN. Hell. vii. 1. 8.

εἰ καί is used concessively with an ellipse of its verb in PLAT. Apol. xviii.

εἰ καὶ γελοιότερον εἰπεῖν.
Though the expression be ridiculous.

εἰ καί, in SOPH. Ant. 90, is not concessive at all; καί emphasises the εἰ.

εἰ καὶ δυνήσει γ'· (ἀλλ' ἀμηχάνων ἐρᾷς).
Ay, if thou wilt be able.

CHAPTER V.

§ 227. FINAL SENTENCES, ὅπως WITH THE FUTURE INDICATIVE, AND VERBS OF FEARING WITH μή, ETC.

Introductory Note.

Three more or less closely connected constructions are here brought into juxtaposition. They are—

A. Final Sentences.

B. Modal Sentences with ὅπως and the Future Indicative.

C. Verbs of Fearing with μή, μὴ οὐ.

These three constructions sometimes run into one another, at other times they widely diverge. Verbs of Fearing with μή deprecate a result. Negative, Modal, and Final Sentences consider or adopt means to avert a result. The connecting links, therefore, are μή and ὅπως. The resemblance is strongest in three such types as the following : A. ταῦτα ποιῶ ὅπως μὴ ἀποθάνω, *I do this that I may not die.* B. ἐπιμελοῦμαι ὅπως μὴ ἀποθανοῦμαι, *I take care that (strive how) I shall not die.* C. φοβοῦμαι μὴ ἀποθάνω, *I fear that I shall die.*[1] The resemblance is even stronger when the construction of B. is ἐπιμελοῦμαι ὅπως μὴ ἀποθάνω, and of C. φοβοῦμαι ὅπως μὴ ἀποθανοῦμαι or ἀποθάνω. On the other hand the divergence is greatest between A. ταῦτα ποιῶ ὅπως μὴ ἀποθάνω (a true Final Sentence), and C. φοβοῦμαι ὡς ἀπορήσεις, *I fear that you will be at a loss,*

---

[1] The term Object Sentence is often applied to the second and third forms of these Sentences. If by an Object Sentence is meant one which stands as an Object to the Principal Sentence, then the term appears too comprehensive to be of practical value. It would include Indirect Statements, Indirect Questions, Indirect Commands, the Infinitive after such verbs as βούλομαι (*e.g.* βούλομαι ἐλθεῖν), besides Sentences with ὅπως, etc. More would be lost. than gained by grouping together constructions so different as οἶδα ἁμαρτών, βούλομαι ἐλθεῖν, and σκόπει ὅπως ταῦτα γενήσεται. Further, if we use the term Object Sentence, why not also Subject Sentence? Syntax must be content sometimes to sacrifice logical system to expediency.

where ὡς ἀπορήσεις is practically a Substantival Sentence of Indirect Statement, or φοβοῦμαι ἀποθανεῖν (τὸ ἀποθανεῖν), which is the same as φοβοῦμαι θάνατον.

It is not easy to give the right name to sentences of class B. They correspond with the Latin construction *curo, enitor, efficio*, with *ut* and the Subjunctive, which Dr. Kennedy assigns to the Indirect Petition. By an extension of the usage of ὅπως, verbs of commanding and of requesting (which introduce a true Indirect Petition) may take ὅπως with a Future Indicative, just as *impero* and *postulo*, etc., take *ut* (or *ne*).

Ὅπως is a Relative Modal Adverb meaning *as, how*, ὥς—ὅπως, (Epic) or οὕτως—ὅπως (Attic) *thus—as* or *how*, ὥς or οὕτως being the Antecedents to ὅπως. It is also used in Questions, κατάλεξον ὅπως ἤντησας (*Od.* iii. 97), *tell me how thou didst meet with*. But one of the most characteristic usages of ὅπως is in Modal Deliberative Questions with the Subjunctive or Optative, after such verbs as φράζομαι, μερμηρίζω, *e.g.* φράζεσθαι ὅππως κε μνηστῆρας κτείνῃς (*Od.* i. 295) *take counsel how thou shalt slay the wooers*. The connection between this and a Final Sentence is obvious, *e.g.* περιφραζώμεθα πάντες νόστον, ὅπως ἔλθῃσι (*Od.* i. 77), *let us all take good counsel touching his return how (so that) he shall reach home*. The Future Indicative is used much in the same way as the Subjunctive, *e.g.* φράζευ ὅπως ἀλεξήσεις κακὸν ἦμαρ (*Il.* ix. 251), *take counsel how thou wilt avert the evil day*.

§ 228. *FINAL SENTENCES.*

Final Sentences denote an *end, purpose*, or *intention* to achieve or avert a result. They are expressed in a variety of ways, chiefly by (1) Final Particles with the Subjunctive and Optative; (2) by the Future Participle; (3) by Relative Sentences; (4) in certain cases by the Infinitive.

§ 229. *FINAL PARTICLES WITH SUBJUNCTIVE AND OPTATIVE.*

The Final Particles are ἵνα, ὡς, and ὅπως (ὄφρα is Epic and Lyric only). In Negative Sentences ἵνα μή, ὡς μή, ὅπως μή, and sometimes μή only. In Primary Sequence the Subjunctive is used, in Historic Sequence the Optative, but the strict Sequence is often disregarded, and the Subjunctive used instead of the Optative.

τὸν κακὸν δεῖ κολάζειν ἵν' ἀμείνων ᾖ. PLAT.
It is necessary to punish the criminal in order that he may be reformed.

ἱκέτευσε τοὺς δικαστὰς μετὰ πολλῶν δακρύων ἵνα ἐλεηθείη. PLAT.
He entreated the jury with many tears in order that he might be pitied.

παρακαλεῖς ἰατροὺς ὅπως μὴ ἀποθάνῃς. XEN.
You call in physicians in order that you may not die.

ἵνα οἱ ἄλλοι τύχωσι τῶν δικαίων, τὰ ὑμέτερ' αὐτῶν ἀνηλίσκετε. DEM.
In order that the rest might obtain their rights, you used to spend your own resources.

For ὡς see EUR. *Tro.* 714. For μή only XEN. *Cyr.* i. 4. 25 (λέγεται εἰπεῖν ὅτι ἀπιέναι βούλοιτο, μὴ ὁ πατήρ τι ἄχθοιτο). Μή truly final is however rare.

Note 1. The Subjunctive and Optative are sometimes found alternating in Historic Sequence.

τὸ ἀπολλύναι ἀνθρώπους ξυμμάχους πολλοὺς δεινὸν ἐφαίνετο εἶναι, μή τινα διαβολὴν σχοῖεν καὶ οἱ στρατιῶται δύσνοι ὦσι. XEN. *Hell.* ii. 1. 2.
To put to death a number of allies was considered a dangerous course, lest they should incur odium and the troops be disaffected.

παρανῖσχον φρυκτοὺς πολλούς, ὅπως ἀσαφῆ τὰ σημεῖα τοῖς πολεμίοις ᾖ, καὶ μὴ βοηθοῖεν πρὶν σφῶν οἱ ἄνδρες διαφύγοιεν. THUC. iii. 22.
They were hoisting many beacons, in order that the enemies' signals might be unintelligible to them, and that they might not bring aid before their own men escaped (should escape).

Dr. Arnold in his well-known note on this passage explains that the Subjunctive expresses the *immediate*, and the Optative the *remote*, consequence (? purpose), the second (Optative) being a consequence upon the first (Subjunctive). Such an explanation, however, clearly cannot apply, as Dr. Arnold thought, to all cases, *e.g.* to passages where the Optative precedes the Subjunctive (see XEN. *Hell.* 1. 2, above, and THUC. vi. 96). This interchange of moods, the graphic Subjunctive and the remoter Optative, is allowable in every variety of Greek subordinate construction.

For other instances cf. HDT. i. 185; viii. 76; ix. 51; THUC. vii. 17. 4; vii. 70. 1.

Note 2. ἄν is sometimes joined to ὡς and ὅπως with the Subjunctive (ὄφρα κε Epic). It adds little, if any, meaning Possibly ἄν may refer to an implied condition, like our English *so* (*in order that so*).

ἄν is not found with the Subjunctive in Negative Final Sentences.

Ἵνα ἄν, when it occurs, is not final but indefinitely local (*wheresoever*).

πατρὶς γάρ ἐστι πᾶσ' ἵν' ἂν πράττῃ τις εὖ.
ARIST. *Plut.* 1151.

The fatherland is any land where'er a man is prospering.

Examples of ὡς ἄν with Subjunctive.

ὡς ἂν μάθῃς, ἀντάκουσον. XEN. *An.* ii. 5.
Listen in return, that you may know.

χώρει δ' ἔνθαπερ κατέκτανες
πατέρα τὸν ἀμόν, ὡς ἂν ἐν ταὐτῷ θάνῃς. SOPH. *El.* 1496.
On to the spot ev'n where thou slew'st my father,
That so on that same spot thou may'st be slain.

Cf. AESCH. *P.·V.* 10; SOPH. *Phil.* 825; PLAT. *Rep.* 567 A, *Symp.* 189 A.

Note 3. When ἄν is found with ὡς or ὅπως and the Optative in a Final Sentence, ὡς and ὅπως are Modal, and the Optative with ἄν is an Apodosis.

ὡς μὲν ἂν εἴποιτε δικαίους λόγους ἄμεινον Φιλίππου παρεσκεύασθε, ὡς δὲ κωλύσαιτ' ἂν αὐτὸν ἀργῶς ἔχετε.
DEM. *Phil.* ii. 66.

As to the means by which you might express just sentiments you are better prepared than Philip, but as to means of checking him you are doing nothing.

βουλευσόμεθα ὅπως ἂν ἄριστα ἀγωνιζοίμεθα. XEN. *Cyr.* ii. 1. 4.
Cf. *Cyr.* i. 2. 5. PLAT. *Symp.* 187, D.

In XEN. *Hell.* iv. 8. 16, ὅπως ἄν, πληρωθέντος ναυτικοῦ κ.τ.λ., προσδέοιντο, we must either explain that ὅπως ἄν προσδέοιντο is the Apodosis (*in order that they might want*), and πληρωθέντος the Protasis, = εἰ πληρωθείη (*if the fleet were manned*): or we must consider that Xenophon is using an Epic construction (ὡς ὅπως ἄν or κεν in Final Sentences with the Optative, *e.g. Od.* ii. 53, xvii. 362).

The Optative with μή ἄν occurs in SOPH. *Trach.* 631, THUC. ii. 93.

Note 4. In a few places ὅπως with a Future Indicative is strictly final rather than modal. And as the verb of *striving*, or *taking precaution*, does not precede in these passages, they are noticed here under Final Sentences. The Future Indicative may be regarded as a vivid form of the Subjunctive.

οὐδὲ δι᾿ ἕν ἄλλο τρέφονται ἤ ὅπως μαχοῦνται.
XEN. *Cyr.* ii. 1. 21.
And they are maintained for no other single purpose except for fighting (lit. *how they shall fight*).

ἔφη χρῆναι ἀναβιβάζειν ἐπὶ τὸν τροχὸν τοὺς ἀπογραφέντας, ὅπως μή πρότερον νύξ ἔσται πρὶν πυθέσθαι τοὺς ἄνδρας ἅπαντας. ANDOK. *de Myst.* 43.
He said that those who had been informed against ought to be put upon the wheel (*to the torture*), *in order to discover all the perpetrators before night-fall.*

Cf. SOPH. *El.* 955; ARIST. *Ecc.* 495.

It is doubtful whether the Future Optative, as the Obliqua of the above, ever occurs. The MSS. appear to favour other constructions where it has hitherto been read. In PLAT. *Rep.* 393 E, μή οὐκ ἐπαρκέσοι occurs as a virtual, rather than literal, obliqua of μή οὐ χραίσμῃ: cf. *Il.* i. 25. See GOODWIN, *Moods and Tenses*, p. 40.

Note 5. In a few places the Optative is found in a Primary Sequence. The Optative carries back the purpose to its original conception in the past; the action, though still continuing in the present, was begun in the past.

τοῦτον δ᾿ ὀχῶ
ἵνα μή ταλαιπωροῖτο. ARIST. *Ran.* 23.
I'm carrying him,
that he mayn't be inconvenienced.
i.e. *I took him on my back* (*and am carrying him*) *that he might not be, etc.*

τοῦτον ἔχει τὸν τρόπον ὁ νόμος, ἵνα μηδὲ πεισθῆναι μηδ' ἐξαπατηθῆναι γένοιτ' ἐπὶ τῷ δήμῳ, DEM. 22. 11 (ANDROT. 596, 17), i.e. *the original intention of the law when first made was, etc.* Cf. XEN. *Cyr.* iv. 2. 45 (ἵνα, εἴ ποτε δέοι, δυναίμεθα, in Primary sequence).

In the same way Cicero uses the Imperfect Subjunctive to recall the original intention :—Homines sunt hac lege generati qui tuerentur illum globum . . . quae terra dicitur, CIC. *Rep.* vi. 15. Sic mihi perspicere videor ita natos esse nos ut inter omnes esset societas quaedam, CIC. *Lael.* 5. Cf. *de Off.* i. § 152, ii. § 1.

Cf. EUR. *El.* 58, and *Hec.* 1138 (Subjunctive followed by Optative in Primary sequence).

§ 230. Final Sentences with Past Tenses of the Indicative.

A Final Sentence with ἵνα (less commonly ὡς and ὅπως) and a Past Tense of the Indicative expresses a purpose unfulfilled either in the Present (Imperfect Indicative), or in the Past (Aorist Indicative). The Principal Sentence is either an unfulfilled Wish, or an unfulfilled Apodosis.

εἰ γὰρ ὤφελον οἷοί τε εἶναι τὰ μέγιστα κακὰ ἐργάζεσθαι, ἵνα οἷοι τέ ἦσαν καὶ ἀγαθὰ τὰ μέγιστα. PLAT. *Crito*, iii.
Would they had been able to do the greatest evil, in order that they might be able (or *might have now been able*) *to do also the greatest good* (which they are not able to do).

καὶ μὴν ἄξιον γ' ἦν ἀκοῦσαι. τί δή; ἵν' ἤκουσας ἀνδρῶν οἱ σοφώτατοί εἰσι. PLAT. *Euthyd.* 304 E.
Well, I assure you it would have been worth hearing. Why so ? In order that you might have heard the ablest men.

ἄξιον ἦν of course=ἄξιον ἂν ἦν, similarly we should say, *It was worth hearing.*

ὡς ὤφελον πάροιθεν ἐκλιπεῖν βίον, κ.τ.λ.
ὅπως θανὼν ἔκεισο τῇ τόθ' ἡμέρᾳ. SOPH. *El.* 1134.
Would God that I had first forsaken life, etc. That death had laid thee low on that far day.

Other well-known examples are AESCH. *P. V.* 152 (after a wish) : *ib.* 766 (after a question equivalent to a wish) : SOPH. *O. T.* 1387, 1391 ; DEM. *Aph.* ii. 837. 11 ; iii. 849. 24.

§ 231. FINAL SENTENCES WITH THE FUTURE PARTICIPLE.

A Final Sentence is often expressed by a Future Participle : ὡς is often added, denoting the *thought*, or the *presumed intention* in the mind of the Subject of the principal verb.

πρέσβεις ἐς Λακεδαίμονα ἔπεμψαν ταῦτά τε ἐροῦντας καὶ Λύσανδρον αἰτήσοντας. XEN.
They sent envoys to Lacedaemon to say this, and to ask for Lysander.

παρεσκευάζοντο ὡς προςβαλοῦντες τῷ τειχίσματι.
THUC.
They were making preparations for an attack on the fort (with the intention of attacking).

Note. Such a Participle is especially common after a verb of motion.

ἤδη ὥρα· ἀπιέναι, ἐμοὶ μὲν ἀποθανουμένῳ, ὑμῖν δὲ βιωσομένοις. PLAT. *Apol.* xxxii.
It is high time to be going, for me that I may die, for you that you may live.

§ 232. RELATIVE FINAL SENTENCES.

A Final Sentence is expressed by ὅστις (less frequently ὅς) with the Future Indicative. In Historic Sequence the Future Optative would strictly be used, but the Future Indicative (the vivid construction) is generally retained. The negative is μή.

πρεσβείαν πέμπετε ἥτις ταῦτ' ἐρεῖ καὶ πάρεσται τοῖς πράγμασιν. DEM.
Send a deputation to bear this message, and to be present at the operations.

Legatos mittite qui haec nuntient rebusque se immisceant.

ἔδοξε τῷ δήμῳ τριάκοντα ἄνδρας ἑλέσθαι οἱ νόμους
ξυγγράψουσι.   XEN.
*The assembly resolved to appoint thirty men who were
to compile laws.*

Cf. XEN. *Cyr.* viii. 6. 3 ; *An.* ii. 3. 6. (οἳ ἄξουσιν). In
THUC. vii. 25, the Subjunctive occurs, οἵπερ φράσωσι (in
Historic sequence).

§ 233. Final Sentences with the Infinitive.

A Final Sentence is expressed by the Infinitive, chiefly after
verbs of *choosing, appointing,* or *assigning.*

Ξενοφῶν τὸ ἥμισυ τοῦ στρατεύματος κατέλιπε φυλάττειν τὸ
στρατόπεδον. XEN.
Xenophon left half his force behind to guard the camp.

οἱ ἄρχοντες οὓς εἵλεσθε ἄρχειν μου. PLAT. *Apol.* xvii.
The rulers whom you chose to rule me.

Cf. THUC. vi. 50, πλεῦσαί τε, κ.τ.λ.

Note 1. As the Infinitive is, in its origin, a Verbal Dative,
we have a natural explanation of this use of it : φυλάττειν, *for
the guarding.* We may, of course, say that the Infinitive is
explanatory (epexegetical).

Note 2. For τοῦ with the Infinitive in a Final Sense, see
Index.

§ 234. Ὅπως, ὅπως μή, *MODAL WITH THE FUTURE INDICATIVE, ETC.*

Ὅπως, ὅπως μή are used with the Future Indicative
(usually the 2d person) after Verbs of taking means to an
end (*considering, striving,* and *contriving*). In Primary
Sequence the Future Indicative is used ; in Historic
Sequence the Future Optative may be used, but the
Future Indicative (the vivid construction) is much commoner.

Such Verbs are:

βουλεύω   μέλει (μοι)   πράσσω
ὁρῶ   μελετῶ   μηχανῶμαι
σκοπῶ (σκοποῦμαι) εὐλαβοῦμαι παρασκευάζω
φροντίζω   προθυμοῦμαι   σπουδάζω
ἐπιμελοῦμαι φυλάσσω   ὠνοῦμαι (*I manage by bribery*).
DEM. *de Cor.* 236. 12.

And periphrases such as πρόνοιαν ἔχω, μηχανή ἐστι, etc.
Cf. Latin *curo*, (*curam, operam, negotium*) *do, studeo, id ago, enitor, efficio, impetro* with *ut* (*ne*) and Subjunctive.

φρόντιζε ὅπως μηδὲν ἀνάξιον σαυτοῦ πράξεις. ISOC.
See that thou do nothing unworthy of thyself.
Vide ne quid te indignum agas.

ἐπιμελητέον ὅπως ὡς ἀρίστη σοι ἔσται ἡ ψυχή.
PLAT.
You must strive that your soul may be as good as possible.
Enitendum est ut tibi quam optimus sit animus tuus.

ἐπεμελεῖτο ὅπως μήτε ἄσιτοι μήτε ἄποτοι ἔσοιντο.
XEN.
He was taking precautions that they should be neither without food nor drink.

ἔπρασσον ὅπως τις βοήθεια ἥξει. THUC.
They were arranging for the arrival of reinforcements.

Note 1. The 1st and 3d person are very rare. In DEM. *Chers.* 99. 14 (ὅπως ἐθελήσουσι); in AR. *Eccl.* (ὅπως καθεδούμεθα).

Note 2. Instead of the Future Indicative the Subjunctive and Optative (Present and Aorist) less often occur, though not uncommonly.

ὅρα ὅπως μὴ παρὰ δόξαν ὁμολογῇς. PLAT. *Crit.*
See that you are not surprised into making an admission.

ἐμεμελήκει αὐτοῖς ὅπως ὁ ἱππαγρέτης εἰδείη οὓς δέοι πέμπειν.
XEN. *Hell.* iii. 3. 9.
They had taken care that the Cavalry-Commissioner should know who should be sent.

In LYS. 12. 44 an Aorist Optative is followed by a Future Indicative (ἐπεβουλεύεσθε ὅπως μήτε ψηφίσαισθε, πολλῶν τε ἐνδεεῖς ἔσεσθε).
Note 3. Variants, of rare occurrence for ὅπως with the Future Indicative are ὅπῃ (THUC. i. 65, γενήσεται); ὅτῳ τρόπῳ (THUC. iv. 128, ξυμβήσεται); ἐξ ὅτου τρόπου (DEM. *Megal.* 207). ὡς is found instead of ὅπως with a Subjunctive or Optative (XEN. *Oec.* xx. 8, AESCH. *P. V.* 203), but seldom with a Future Indicative (XEN. *Cyr.* iii. 2. 13).
Note 4. ἄν is sometimes found with ὅπως and the Subjunctive, cf. PLAT. *Gorg.* 481 A (μηχανητέον ὅπως ἂν διαφύγῃ), but never with ὅπως and the Future Indicative. The Optative (Present or Aorist) with ἄν in this construction is an Apodosis. Cf. XEN. *Oec.* ii. 9 (ἐπιμελεῖσθαι ὅπως ἂν γένοιτο).
Note 5. Μή is found, instead of ὅπως μή, with the Subjunctive (rarely with the Future Indicative) after σκοπῶ, ὁρῶ, εὐλαβοῦμαι, φυλάσσομαι, just as after Verbs of Fearing. Conversely ὅπως μή, instead of the simple μή, is used after Verbs of Fearing. Cf. the next section, page 265. Cf. SOPH. *Phil.* (ὅρα μὴ παρῇς), *O. C.* 1180; PLAT. *Symp.* 213 D. In XEN. *Cyr.* iv. 1. 18 (ὅρα μὴ δεήσει), εὐλαβεῖσθαι μή, PLAT. *Prot.* 321 A; εὐλαβεῖσθαι τὸ μή, PLAT. *Rep.* 539 A; φυλάσσεσθαι μή is fairly common.
Note 6. ἐπιμελοῦμαι is found with an Infinitive in THUC. vi. 54. 6, XEN. *Comm.* iv. 7. 1, APPIAN, *Civ.* v. 73. So *curo* occurs with the Infinitive in CIC. *de Fin.* iii. 19. 62 (*natura . . . diligi procreatos non curaret*). Poppo, THUC. vi. 54. So also φυλάσσομαι μὴ ποιεῖν, τὸ μὴ ποιεῖν, *I guard against doing*, DEM. 773. 1, 313. 6.
Note 7. σκοπῶ is followed by εἰ interrogative (SOPH. *Ant.* 41). See similar construction with Verbs of Fearing, Note, p. 266.
Note 8. In one or two places δεῖ precedes ὅπως with the Fut. Indicative, *e.g.* SOPH. *Ai.* 556, δεῖ σε ὅπως δείξεις : *Phil.* 55, σε δεῖ ὅπως ἐκκλέψεις. Jebb (note to SOPH. *Ai.* 556) quotes CRATINUS (*apud Athenaeum*), δεῖ σ᾽ ὅπως ἀλεκτρυόνος μηδὲν διοίσεις τοὺς τρόπους. There seems to be a confusion between two constructions; δεῖ with the Infinitive, and some verb like ὅρα, σκόπει with ὅπως and the Future Indicative. In ARIST. *Eq.* 926 we have σπεύσω σε ὅπως ἂν ἐγγραφῇς, which however may be regarded simply as an instance of Antiptosis, *i.e.* σε, the Subject to ἐγγραφῇς, is made the Object to σπεύσω, which is a Verb just like σπουδάζω or πράσσω.

§ 235. ELLIPTICAL USE OF ὅπως, ὅπως μή, WITH THE FUTURE INDICATIVE.

Ὅπως, ὅπως μή are used with the Future Indicative in exhortations and prohibitions, when no principal sentence has preceded. All three persons are found, though the second is commonest.

ἀλλ' ὅπως ἀνὴρ ἔσει. EUR. *Cycl.* 595.
Come, be a man!

ὅπως δὲ τοῦτο μὴ διδάξεις μηδενί. AR. *Nub.*
Mind you don't tell this to anybody.

φέρε δὴ ὅπως μεμνησόμεθα ταῦτα. PLAT. *Gorg.* 495 D.
Well, then, let us be sure to remember this.

ὅπως ταῦτα μηδεὶς ἀνθρώπων πεύσεται. LYS. i. 21.
See that not a soul hears of this.

Observe that this construction is generally introduced by a word, ἀλλά, οὖν, δέ, sometimes by ἄγε νυν (AR. *Nub.* 490).

Note. The Subjunctive occasionally is found :
ὅπως γε μὴ ἐξαπατήσῃ ἡμᾶς. PLAT. *Prot.* 313 C.
Mind he does not deceive us.

§ 236. Ὅπως, ὅπως μή WITH VERBS OF COMMANDING AND FORBIDDING.

For this Construction, see Indirect Petition. It is, of course, the same as ὅπως after Verbs of taking means to an end, although an extension of it. There is a natural connexion between, "Take care to do so," and "I bid you do so." But for the sake of convenience the rule and examples are given elsewhere.

§ 237. VERBS OF FEARING WITH μή, AND μὴ οὐ.

Verbs and phrases denoting *fear* are followed by μή and μὴ οὐ with the Subjunctive (in Primary Sequence), and the Optative (in Historic Sequence). The Subjunctive may, by the graphic construction, of course be substituted for the Optative.

δέδοικα μὴ ταῦτα γένηται.
I fear this will happen.
Vereor ne haec fiant.

δέδοικα μὴ οὐ ταῦτα γένηται.
I fear this will not happen.
Vereor ut (ne non) haec fiant.

ἐδεδοίκειν μὴ (μὴ οὐ) ταῦτα γένοιτο or γένηται.
Verebar ne (ut) haec fierent.

Observe that μή does not negative the verb; it expresses a surmise that the result will occur. Οὐ on the other hand is privative and negatives the verb.

δέδοικα μὴ οὐχ ὅσιον ᾖ.
I fear it will not be righteous (i.e. *unrighteous*).

For μή, μὴ οὐ and the Subjunctive, etc., without a principal verb see the Chapter on Negatives.

Verbs of fearing are :—

φοβοῦμαι,   δέος ἐστί   πέφρικα (mostly poet.)
δέδοικα,   δεινόν ἐστι τρέω (mostly poet.)

δέδοικα μὴ ἐπιλαθώμεθα τῆς οἴκαδε ὁδοῦ. XEN.
I fear we shall forget the way home.

οὐκέτι ἐπετίθεντο δεδοικότες μὴ ἀποτμηθείησαν. XEN.
They were no longer attacking from fear of being cut off.

δέδιμεν μὴ οὐ βέβαιοι ἦτε. THUC.
We fear you are not trustworthy.

ἐφοβεῖτο τὸ στράτευμα μὴ ἐπὶ τὴν αὐτοῦ χώραν
στρατεύηται. XEN.
*He was afraid that the army would march against
his own country.*
οὐδὲν δεινὸν μὴ ἐν ἐμοὶ στῇ. PLAT. *Apol.* xv.
*There is no fear (likelihood) of the rule breaking down
in my case.*

Obs. In XEN. *Mem.* i. 2. 7, we have ἐθαύμαζε εἴ τις φοβοῖτο
μὴ ὁ γενόμενος καλὸς κἀγαθὸς μὴ χάριν ἕξοι, instead of μὴ οὐ
χάριν ἕξοι, an abnormal construction not found elsewhere.

Note 1. As these Verbs of Fearing denote doubt and apprehension as much as downright fear, their construction is followed by many Verbs which in other senses take other constructions, but which when denoting *apprehension, anxiety, suspicion lest* or *whether*, are followed by μή and μὴ οὐ.

Such verbs are verbs of *caution* in the sense of *anxiety* (φροντίζω, ἐννοῶ, ὁρῶ, σκοπῶ, εὐλαβοῦμαι, φυλάσσω (-ομαι); ὀκνῶ, *I hesitate* or *scruple* (*from fear, or pity, or shame*); ὑποπτεύω, *I suspect*, ἀπιστῶ (ἀπιστίαν ἔχει, παρέχει) in the sense of *suspecting* rather than *disbelieving*, κίνδυνός ἐστι.

ὑποπτεύομεν μὴ οὐ κοινοὶ ἀποβῆτε. THUC. iii. 53.
We suspect that you will not prove impartial.

ὀκνῶ μή μοι ὁ Λυσίας ταπεινὸς φανῇ. PLAT. *Pol.* 368.

φροντίζω μὴ κράτιστον ᾖ μοι σιγᾶν. XEN. *Mem.* iv. 2. 39.
I am thinking that it may be best for me to say nothing.

Cf. PLAT. *Phaed.* 70 A (ἀπιστίαν παρέχει μὴ οὐδαμοῦ); PLAT.
Theaet. 183 E (αἰσχυνόμενος μή, a very rare construction with
this verb); SOPH. *Tr.* 1129 (εὐλαβεῖσθαι μὴ φανῇς); THUC. iv.
11 (φυλάσσεσθαι μὴ ξυντρίψωσιν).

Consult the Index for other meanings and constructions of these verbs.

Note 2. Instead of the Subjunctive after Verbs of Fearing the tenses of the Indicative are used.

(1) The Future Indicative as a graphic substitute for the Subjunctive.

φοβοῦμαι μη τινας ἡδονὰς ἡδοναῖς εὑρήσομεν ἐναντίας.
PLAT. *Phileb.* 13 A.
I apprehend that we shall find some pleasures opposite to pleasures.

VERBS OF FEARING WITH μή AND μὴ οὔ.

Cf. PLAT. *Rep.* 451 A (φοβερόν τε καὶ σφαλερὸν μὴ κείσομαι). In AESCH. *Pers.* 112, the Subjunctive and Future Indicative are co-ordinate, μὴ πύθηται καὶ ἔσσεται, πέσῃ (δέ). See *Choeph.* 257. So EUR. *H. F.* 1054, AR. *Ecc.* 493.

(2) ὅπως μή with the Future Indicative, Subjunctive, or Optative, as after verbs of taking means to an end in the previous section.

ἀτὰρ τοῦ δαίμονος
δέδοιχ' ὅπως μὴ τεύξομαι κακοδαίμονος.   AR. *Eq.* 112.
*But I'm afraid
This genius will turn out my evil genius*—(Frere).
δέδοιχ' ὅπως μὴ ἀνάγκη γένηται.   DEM. *Phil.* iii. 130. 14.
I fear that a necessity may arise.

(3) ὡς with the Future Indicative. ὡς does not (like ὅπως) appear to have a modal force, but to introduce an Indirect Statement, as if δέδοικα or φοβοῦμαι meant *I fear, thinking that*.
ἀνδρὸς μὴ φοβοῦ ὡς ἀπορήσεις ἀξίου.   XEN. *Cyr.* v. 2. 12.
Do not fear that you will be at a loss for a worthy man.

Cf. SOPH. *El.* 1309, XEN. *Cyr.* vi. 2. 30, DEM. *Phil.* iv. 1. 141.

In EUR. *Heracl.* 248 (ὅπως, as ὅπως is occasionally used in Indirect Discourse).

When ὅτι follows a Verb of Fearing it seems to introduce an ordinary causal (or rather explanatory) sentence.
ὅτι δὲ πολλῶν ἄρχουσι μὴ φοβηθῆτε.   XEN. *Hell.* iii. 5. 10.
Do not be afraid because they rule many.

Though we might translate, *do not be afraid thinking that*.

Note 3. The Infinitive, Future, Present or Aorist is also used.
οὐ φοβούμεθα ἐλασσώσεσθαι.   THUC. v. 105.
We are not afraid that we shall be beaten.

The Future Infinitive is here = the more usual μή with Subjunctive.

φοβοῦμαι διελέγχειν σε μὴ ὑπολάβῃς.   PLAT. *Gorg.* 457 E.
I am afraid to refute you lest you should suppose.

The latter construction (with the Present or Aorist) is common enough, and is the ordinary objective construction common to verbs of fearing with many of the verbs mentioned in *Note* 1, *e.g.* φοβοῦμαι ἀδικεῖν, *I fear to do wrong;* αἰσχύνομαι ἀδικεῖν, *I am ashamed to do wrong;* κινδυνεύω ἀδικεῖν, *I run a risk of doing wrong;* φυλάσσω μηδένα ἀδικεῖν, *I take care that no one does wrong.* Cf. Latin, *culpari metuit fides; penna metuente solvi, etc.*, in HORACE.

Note 4. Observe the following distinctions:—

1. φοβοῦμαι ἀδικεῖν.
I fear to do wrong (and so refrain).

2. φοβοῦμαι μὴ ἀδικῶ.
I fear I shall do wrong.

3. φοβοῦμαι ἀδικήσειν.
I fear I shall do wrong (very rare for 2).

4. φοβοῦμαι τὸ ἀδικεῖν.
I fear wrong-doing (generally, by myself, or by another.)

Note 5. Verbs of Fearing are also followed by εἰ interrogative.

οὐ δέδοικα εἰ Φίλιππος ζῇ. DEM. *Fals. Leg.* 434. 6.
I have no fear whether Philip is alive (i.e. *I have no fear as to that question*).

Cf. EUR. *Herac.* 791, XEN. *Hell.* xi. 1. 4 (ὅποι).

Note 6. ἄν is not used with the Subjunctive after Verbs of Fearing. When the Optative is found with ἄν it is an Apodosis.

§ 238. Verbs of Fearing, etc., with the Indicative.

When the result has actually occurred, or is occurring, the verb with μή is in the Indicative.

Thus : δέδοικα μὴ ἁμαρτάνῃς (or ἁμάρτῃς).
I fear you will make a mistake.

But δέδοικα μὴ ἁμαρτάνεις.
I fear you (actually) are making a mistake.

δέδοικα μὴ ἡμάρτηκας.
I fear you have made a mistake.

So δέδοικα μὴ ἡμάρτανες (*you were making a mistake*); μὴ ἥμαρτες, *that you made a mistake.*

VERBS OF FEARING, ETC., WITH INDICATIVE. 267

1. The Present Indicative :—

φοβεῖσθε μὴ δυσκολώτερόν τι διάκειμαι. PLAT. *Phaed.* xxxv.
You are afraid that I am in a somewhat more fretful state of mind.

ἐπίσχες, ὡς ἂν προὐξερευνήσω στίβον,
μή τις πολιτῶν ἐν τρίβῳ φαντάζεται,
κἄμοι μὲν ἔλθῃ, κ.τ.λ. EUR. *Phoen.* 92.
*Yet stay, that first I may explore the path,
Lest any citizen now is visible
Upon the road, and one shall come to me.*

Cf. *Ion*, 1523, SOPH. *El.* 580. Similarly ὁρῶμεν μὴ Νικίας οἴεται, PLAT. *Lach.* 179 B. εἰσόμεσθα μὴ καλύπτει, SOPH. *Antig.* 1253. διστάζομεν μὴ τυγχάνει, PLAT. *Soph.* 235 A. σκεψώμεθα μὴ λανθάνει, PLAT. *Ly.* 216 C.

2. The Imperfect Indicative :—

ὅρα μὴ παίζων ἔλεγεν. PLAT. *Theaet.* 145 B.
Have a care that he was not speaking in jest.

3. The Perfect Indicative :—

φοβοῦμαι μὴ ἀμφοτέρων ἅμα ἡμαρτήκαμεν. THUC. iii. 53.
I fear that we have missed both objects at once.

Cf. PLAT. *Lys.* 218 D, DEM. 19. 26 (*Fals. Leg.* 372. 1).

4. The Aorist Indicative does not appear to occur in Attic. See HOM. *Od.* v. 300.

5. The Future Indicative may be regarded as a graphic substitute for the Subjunctive (*supra*).[1]

§ 239.   Note on Dawes's Canon.

Dawes laid down the rule that after ὅπως μή and οὐ μή, the First Aorist Passive, and the Second Aorist Active, Middle, and Passive may be used, but not the First Aorist Active or Middle. Instead of the First Aorist Active and Middle, he said that the Future Indicative must be used. Subsequent

---

[1] So at least in Attic. But if the original force of the Subjunctive was imperative (denoting will) rather than future (a point on which it is impossible to speak dogmatically), the Subjunctive in the oldest Greek would mean *shall* rather than *will*, and would be more direct and vivid than the Future. See Monro's *Homeric Grammar*, pp. 231 and 238.

critics extended Dawes's Canon to ὅπως (without μή), and set about changing a First Aorist Active and Middle, wherever they were found in a text, to a Future Indicative. The sole ground for this arbitrary rule of Dawes is the resemblance in form between the First Aorist Active and Middle and the Future Indicative, e.g. ΚΑΤΟΚΝΗCΗΙC (κατοκνήσῃς, SOPH. *El.* 956) and ΚΑΤΟΚΝΗCΕΙC (κατοκνήσεις); ΞΥΛΛΕΞΗΤΑΙ (ξυλλέξηται) and ΞΥΛΛΕΞΕΤΑΙ (ξυλλέξεται). Naturally this resemblance of form might incline a Greek writer to avoid confusion by using a second Aorist (if it existed) rather than a First Aorist. Dawes made no objection to a First Aorist Subjunctive Passive, because it bears no resemblance in form to a Future Indicative. But Dawes's Canon rests on no solid foundation of grammar, and breaks down completely on examination. Instances of the First Aorist Subjunctive Active and Middle in which all the MSS. agree are ὅπως μὴ ἐπιβοηθήσωσι (THUC. iv. 66); ὅπως μὴ βουλεύσησθε (THUC. i. 73); ὅπως μὴ ἐργάσησθε, *Lys.* 138. Secondly, in some cases the First Aorist Active does not resemble in form the Future Indicative, and therefore cannot possibly be changed. *E.g.* SOPH. *Phil.* 381, οὐ μὴ ἐκπλεύσῃς : the Future is ἐκπλευσοῦμαι, and the second person would be ἐκπλευσεῖ not ἐκπλεύσεις. So PLAT. *Rep.* x. 609, ἀπολέσῃ, the Future is ἀπολῶ : SOPH. *El.* 1122, κλαύσω, First Aorist Active, where the Future would be κλαυσοῦμαι. And, lastly, the change made would in some cases spoil the metre.

CHAPTER VI.

§ 240. CONSECUTIVE AND LIMITATIVE SENTENCES.

A Consecutive Sentence may be expressed either by **A.** ὥστε with the Indicative, or **B.** ὥστε with the Infinitive.

A. ὥστε (ὥστε οὐ) with the Indicative states the consequence as an independent fact actually occurring.

ἐγὼ δὴ εἰς τοσοῦτον ἀμαθίας ἥκω ὥστε κακὸν ἑκὼν ποιῶ. PLAT.
I it seems have reached such a pitch of ignorance that I deliberately do wrong.

εἰς τοῦτο ἦλθον ὥστ' οὐκ ἐξήρκεσεν αὐτοῖς ἡ κατὰ γῆν ἀρχή. ISOC.
To such a pitch they came that their empire by land did not satisfy them.

B. ὥστε (ὥστε μή) with the Infinitive expresses merely the consequence which would naturally result from the Principal Verb without affirming or denying its occurrence.

γνώμης γὰρ οὐκ ἄπειρος ὥσθ' ἁμαρτάνειν. SOPH.
He is not void of wit that he should err.

τὰ παραδείγματα τῶν ἁμαρτημάτων ἵκανα τοῖς σώφροσι ὥστε μηκέτι ἁμαρτάνειν. ANDOK.
Examples of errors are sufficient for sensible people that they should no longer err, i.e. *sufficient to keep them from erring.*

270 CONSECUTIVE AND LIMITATIVE SENTENCES.

§ 241. ὥστε with Indicative and Infinitive.

A. ὥστε with the Indicative is parallel with ὅτι and the Indicative, that is to say, it introduces the Indicative as a statement almost, sometimes quite, independent of the Principal Sentence.

Thus: τοσοῦτον σὺ ἐμοῦ σοφώτερος εἶ, ὥστε σὺ μὲν ἔγνωκας— ἐγὼ δὲ ἀγνοῶ. PL. *Apol.* xiii.
So much wiser are you than I, that (and so) you have discovered, while I am ignorant, etc.

This introductory force of ὥστε is best shown by its familiar usage at the beginning of a sentence where it is a synonym for οὖν, τοίνυν, and may be rendered *and so, consequently, therefore.*

εἰς τὴν ὑστεραίαν οὐχ ἧκεν Τισσαφέρνης· ὥσθ' οἱ Ἕλληνες ἐφρόντιζον. XEN. *An.* ii. 3. 25.
On the morrow Tissaphernes did not appear. Consequently the Greeks began to consider, etc.

So with an Imperative.

θνητὸς δ' Ὀρέστης· ὥστε μὴ λίαν στένε. SOPH. *El.* 1172.
Orestes was but mortal. Therefore grieve not too sore.

Occasionally this introductory force of ὥστε is seen even with an Infinitive.

ὥστ' ἐμὲ ἐμαυτὸν ἀνερωτᾶν (after a colon or full stop).
PLAT. *Apol.* viii.
And so I was questioning myself.

As ὥστε, like ὅτι, is merely introductory, it can be followed by any construction which an independent sentence can take, *e.g.* Imperative (supra): ὥστε μὴ ἀποκάμῃς, PLAT. *Crit.* 45. ὥστε ἄν with Optative, ὥστε ἄν διδάσκοιτε, XEN. *Cyr.* iii. 3. 35. ὥστε ἄν ἐτόλμησεν, LYS. 7. 28.

B. ὥστε with Infinitive.

ὥστε with the Infinitive is epexegetical, *i.e.* explanatory of the Principal Verb. It is doubly so, for ὥστε is an explanatory particle, and the Infinitive is in its own nature explanatory. Indeed ὥστε with the Infinitive, as will be seen below, often takes the place of the simple Infinitive. The consecutive use of ὥστε with the Infinitive is only one among several of these explanatory usages. The *result contemplated*, i.e. the *purpose,* may be denoted; the *condition* or *limitation;* the *command* or *advice*. The character of the explanation or definition will depend upon the nature of the Principal Verb or Sentence.

1. *A Purpose, or Contemplated Result.*
πᾶν ποιοῦσιν ὥστε μὴ δίκην διδόναι.
PLAT. *Gorg.* 479 C.
They do anything to avoid punishment.
Cf. PLAT. *Phaed.* 114, ὥστε μετασχεῖν.

2. *Limitation or Condition* (cf. ἐφ' ᾧ, ἐφ' ᾧ τε).
ξυμμαχίαν ἐποιήσαντο ἐπὶ τοῖσδε, ὥστε μὴ στρατεύειν ἐπὶ Πελοποννησίους. THUC. iii. 14.
They made an alliance on these conditions, that they were not to serve against the Peloponnesians.

3. *A Petition or Command.*
πείθουσιν ὥστε ῎Αργει ἐπιχειρῆσαι. THUC. iii. 103.
They try to induce them to attack Argos.
The Infinitive alone would be more usual here.
Cf. THUC. viii. 45, ὥστε ἀποκτεῖναι. SOPH. *O. C.* 969, ὥστε θανεῖν, *ordaining, requiring, to the effect, that he should die.*

4. The *definitive force* (denoting the character, degree, or extent) is well shown in the following:—

πείσομαι γὰρ οὐ
τοσοῦτον οὐδὲν ὥστε μὴ οὐ καλῶς θανεῖν.
SOPH. *Ant.* 97.
*I shall suffer naught
So great as not to die a noble death* (i.e. *nothing which will prevent my dying, etc.*).
For μὴ οὐ see chapter on the Negatives.

5. ὥστε is freely used with the Infinitive, where the Infinitive alone might be used.
πάνυ μοι ἐμέλησεν ὥστε εἰδέναι. XEN. *Cyr.* vi. 3. 19.
I was greatly concerned to know.
πότερα παῖδες εἰσι φρονιμώτεροι ὥστε μαθεῖν ἢ ἄνδρες;
XEN. *Cyr.* iv. 3. 11.
Are boys more sensible at learning than men?

μεῖζον ἢ ὥστε φέρειν.
Too great to bear.
Maius quam quod tolerari possit.
ψυχρὸν ὕδωρ ὥστε λούσασθαι. XEN. *An.* iii. 13. 3.
The water is cold for bathing.
μηχαναὶ πολλαί εἰσιν ὥστε διαφεύγειν θάνατον.
PLAT. *Apol.* xxix.
There are many shifts for escaping death.
ὡς is more rarely so used, cf. XEN. *Cyr.* iv. 5. 15, ὥς ἐγκρατεῖς εἶναι.

Note 1. Can ὥστε with the Infinitive state a fact? The Infinitive, of course, denoting as it does the abstract verbal notion, cannot, like the Indicative, definitely state a fact. ὥστε, with the Infinitive, is parallel with πρίν and the Infinitive, διά with the Infinitive, or any similar substantival use of the Infinitive. The fact, though not stated, is not excluded. More than this, the expression may evidently be a variant for ὥστε with the Indicative, open for a writer to use. This occurs when there is no demonstrative in the Principal Sentence requiring definition. In this way πρὶν ἀπιέναι αὐτόν, *before his departure*, may practically mean, *before he departed;* διὰ τὸ μηδένα παρεῖναι, *because of the presence of no one*, may mean, *because no one was present.*

Κλέαρχος ἤλαυνεν ἐπὶ τοὺς Μένωνος, ὥστε ἐκείνους ἐκπεπλῆχθαι. XEN. *An.* i. 5. 13.
Clearchus was marching against Menon's men, so that they were in a state of amazement.

ἀμφὶ δὲ
κυκλοῦντο πᾶσαν νῆσον, ὥστ' ἀμηχανεῖν
ὅποι τράποιντο. AESCH. *Pers.* 460.
*They round about
Encircled the whole isle, so that the foe
Knew not which way to turn them.*
Cf. EUR. *Hec.* 730.

Note 2. ὥστε with ἄν and the Infinitive. ὥστε with the Infinitive may be an (oblique) Apodosis, and therefore ἄν will go with the Infinitive.

ἐγὼ ἐπὶ τούσδε ἐλῶ ὥστε ἄν ἀναγκασθῆναι, κ.τ.λ.
XEN. *Cyr.* i. 4. 20.
For ὥστε οὐ with the Infinitive, see Negatives.

Note 3. ὡς is sometimes used for ὥστε, generally with the Infinitive.

ὁ ποταμὸς τοσοῦτος τὸ βάθος, ὡς μηδὲ τὰ δόρατα ὑπερέχειν τοῦ βάθους. XEN. *An.* iii. 5. 7.
The river is of so great a depth, that even the spears could not reach the bottom.
(Lit. *rise above the depth*). Cf. XEN. *Cyr.* i. 5. 11. More rarely, if ever in Attic, with an Indicative.

§ 242. Consecutive Sentences in Greek and Latin.

The nearest approach in Latin to the distinction between the Infinitive and Indicative is to be found in the use of the Imperfect Subjunctive and Perfect (Aorist) Subjunctive, e.g. *cecidit ut crus frangeret* (ὥστε καταγνύναι), and *ut crus fregerit* (ὥστε κατέαξε). But the Latin distinction, even supposing it is always observed, a distinction expressed by two tenses of the Subjunctive, is a very different thing from that expressed by two moods, the Infinitive and the Indicative.

§ 243. *RELATIVE CONSECUTIVE SENTENCES.*

Consecutive Sentences are also expressed by Relative Pronouns, οἷος, ὅσος with Infinitive.

For τοιοῦτος ὥστε are used τοιοῦτος οἷος or οἷος alone.
„ τοσοῦτον ὥστε „ τοσοῦτον ὅσον or ὅσον.

The Negative is μή.

τοιοῦτός εἰμι οἷος μηδενὶ ἄλλῳ πείθεσθαι ἢ λόγῳ.
PLAT.
I am of such a character as to yield to nothing but reason.
Is (or eiusmodi) sum ut nulli alii rei nisi rationi paream.

οὐκ ἦν ὥρα οἵα ἄρδειν τὸ πεδίον. XEN. *An.* ii. 3. 13.
It was not the season for irrigating the plain.

νεμόμενοι τὰ ἑαυτῶν ἕκαστοι ὅσον ἀποζῆν. THUC. i. 2.
Each tribe cultivating just enough of its land to obtain a subsistence from it.

Cf. THUC. iii. 49, τοσοῦτον ὅσον ἀνεγνωκέναι

τοιαῦτα εἰπόντες οἷα καὶ τοὺς παρόντας ἄχθεσθαι.
PLAT. *Gorg.* 457.
Saying such things that even the company was annoyed.

"Οστις (more rarely ὅς), with the Indicative, is Consecutive (parallel to ὥστε with Indicative). Negative οὐ.

τίς οὕτως εὐήθης ἐστὶν ὑμῶν ὅστις ἀγνοεῖ ταῦτα ;
DEM.
Who of you is so simple that he is ignorant of this?
Quis vostrum tam stultus est ut (qui) haec ignoret?

οὐδεὶς ἂν γένοιτο οὕτως ἀδαμάντινος ὅς ἂν μείνειεν.
PLAT. *Rep.* ii. 360 B.
No one would prove so steeled against temptation as to remain firm.

ἂν μείνειεν is, of course, an Apodosis. For ὅς see SOPH. *Phil.* 409, 444, *Ai.* 471.

§ 244. *LIMITATIVE OR RESTRICTIVE SENTENCES.*[1]

ὥστε (ὥστε μή), ἐφ' ᾧ, ἐφ' ᾧτε (μή).
On condition that, on the understanding that.

ὥστε (ὥστε μή) with Infinitive.

ἐφ' ᾧ, ἐφ' ᾧτε with Infinitive (Negative μή), or Future Indicative (Negative οὐ or μή).

ἐξῆν αὐτοῖς τῶν ἄλλων ἄρχειν Ἑλλήνων ὥστ' αὐτοὺς ὑπακούειν τῷ βασιλεῖ. DEM. 6. 11.
It was in their power to rule the rest of the Greeks if they themselves would obey the King.

---

[1] With ὥστε Limitative compare the use of *ut* in Latin:
Bonis viris ita fides habetur ut nulla sit iis fraudis suspitio.
CIC. *Off.* ii. 33.
Good men are trusted only when there is no suspicion of dishonesty against them.

LIMITATIVE OR RESTRICTIVE SENTENCES. 275

ἀφίεμέν σε ἐπὶ τούτῳ ἐφ' ᾧτε μηκέτι φιλοσοφεῖν.
PLAT.

We acquit you, on the understanding that you no longer pursue philosophy (ita ut philosophari desinas).

Ξυνέβησαν ἐφ' ᾧτε ἐξίασιν ἐκ Πελοποννήσου ὑπόσπονδοι (καὶ μηδέποτε ἐπιβήσονται αὐτῆς).
THUC.

They surrendered on the condition that they should leave the Peloponnese under truce (and never again set foot on it).

Observe that the Future Indicative is used in Historic Sequence.

Note. The Nominative Attraction is observed:—

ὡς ἂν οὗτος ἐθέλοι τὰ ἀλλότρια ἀποστερεῖν ἐφ' ᾧ κακόδοξος εἶναι. XEN. *Ag.* 4. 1.

CHAPTER VII.

§ 245. CAUSAL SENTENCES.

Causal sentences are expressed in a variety of ways.

A. By Causal Particles and a Finite Mood.
B. By Relative Sentences.
C. By Participles.
D. In various miscellaneous ways.

A. Causal Particles.

The common Causal Particles are also the Temporal Particles, ἐπεί, ἐπειδή, ὡς (cf. Latin *cum*). The negative is οὐ, and the Indicative is the Mood.

τίθημί σε ὁμολογοῦντα ἐπειδὴ οὐκ ἀποκρίνει. PL. *Ap.*
I assume that you consent, since you do not answer.

ἐπεὶ οὐκ ἐδύναντο λαμβάνειν τὸ χωρίον ἀπιέναι ἤδη ἐπεχείρουν. XEN. *Anab.* v. 2. 5.
As they were not able to take the place they were now trying to go away.

For ἐπειδή with Imperfect, THUC. i. 102. For ἐπεί, see XEN. *An.* v. 2. 5. For ὡς, SOPH. *Phil.* 46, 914.

Note 1. When, however, the sentence is explanatory of what has preceded, ὅτι, διότι, διόπερ are used. These particles cannot introduce a Causal Sentence like ἐπεί, etc. (cf. ὅτε Temporal).

τριήρης δὲ σεσαγμένη ἀνθρώπων διά τί ἄλλο φοβερόν ἐστι ἢ ὅτι ταχὺ πλεῖ; διὰ δὲ τί ἄλλο ἄλυποι ἀλλήλοις οἱ ἐμπλέοντες ἢ διότι ἐν τάξει κάθηνται; XEN. *Oec.* viii. 8.
For what other reason is a trireme full of men dangerous, except because it sails fast? And for what other reason do those who are on board occasion no alarm to one another, except because they sit still in their ranks?

Note 2. A Causal Sentence in Historic Sequence is found in the Optative when it expresses the indirect words or thoughts (virtual *oratio obliqua*).

τὸν Περικλέα ἐκάκιζον, ὅτι στρατηγὸς ὤν οὐκ ἐπέξαγοι.
THUC. ii. 21.
They were abusing Pericles, because, though general, he did not lead them out into the field.

ὅτι οὐκ ἐπεξῆγεν would have been the simple explanation of the historian.

In Periclem invehebantur quod, cum praetor esset, non educeret.

Cf. LIV. ii. 7. Matronae annum ut parentem Brutum luxerunt, *quod* tam acer ultor violatae pudicitiae *fuisset*.

ὡς occurs similarly in XEN. *Symp.* iv. 6, οἶσθα ἐπαινέσαντα αὐτὸν τὸν Ἀγαμέμνονα, ὡς βασιλεὺς εἴη ἀγαθός, *because* (as he said) *he was*. Both ὅτι and ὡς may, however, be regarded as introducing an Oblique Statement, the verb of saying being implied in ἐκάκιζον and ἐπαινέσαντα. But in XEN. *Mem.* i. 4. 19, we have ἐπείπερ ἡγήσαιντο, which must be causal or explanatory. And in XEN. *Hell.* vii. 1. 34, we have εἶχε λέγειν ὡς διὰ τοῦτο πολεμήσειαν, ὅτι οὐκ ἐθελήσαιεν, where we have a real blending of ὅτι causal and ὅτι of the Oblique Statement.

Note 3. ὅτε (just like *cum* in Latin) besides being Temporal, is also Causal.

ὅτε τοίνυν τοῦθ' οὕτως ἔχει, προσήκει προθύμως ἐθέλειν ἀκούειν. DEM. *Ol.* i. 9. 3.
Since then this is so, it behoves you to be heartily willing to listen. Quae cum ita sint, etc.

Observe that this Causal ὅτε, unlike the Temporal ὅτε, can begin a sentence.

ὅτ' οὖν τοιόνδε χρησμὸν εἰσηκούσαμεν.
SOPH. *El.* 38, *Phil.* 428, *Ant.* 170, *Ai.* 1231.
Cum vero huiusmodi oraculum accepissemus.

Observe that ὅτι cannot be elided.

ὁπότε is similarly used. THUC. ii. 60, PL. *Leg.* 895 B.

εὖτε causal is poetical (SOPH. *Ai.* 715): ὅπου, causal only in Ionic.

ὁθούνεκα (ὅτου ἕνεκα) in a causal sense occurs in SOPH. *Ai* 123, 153.

B. Causal sentences are also expressed by relatives ὅς, ὅς γε, ὅστις, ὅστις γε, with the Indicative.
Latin *qui* or *quippe qui* with Subjunctive.

πῶς φέρεις γὰρ ὅς γε αὐτὸς ὀχεῖ ; AR.
Why how d'ye bear, when you're being carried yourself ?

θαυμαστὸν ποιεῖς ὃς ἡμῖν οὐδὲν δίδως. XEN.
You are acting strangely in giving us nothing.
= ὅτι οὐδὲν δίδως.
Mirum facis qui nobis nihil des.

πῶς οὐ κάκιστος ὅστις περὶ πλείονος ποιεῖ τοὺς κακούργους ;
Must you not be a scoundrel since you are making much of evildoers ? DEM. 24. 107.
ὅς γε, SOPH. *El.* 911. ὅστις, SOPH. *Ant.* 696.

Note. Other relatives (pronouns and adverbs) are similarly used.

τὴν μητέρα ἐμακάριζον, οἵων τέκνων ἐκύρησε. HDT. i. 31.
They were counting the mother happy in having been blest with such children.
= ὅτι τοιούτων ἐκύρησεν.

εὐδαίμων μοι ἐφαίνετο, ὡς ἀδεῶς ἐτέλευτα. PLAT. *Phaed.* ii.
I deemed him happy, so fearlessly did he meet death.
= ὅτι οὕτως ἀδεῶς, not an uncommon use of ὡς.

C. Participles are frequently used in a Causal Sense. The Negative is οὐ. ἅτε (ἅτε δή), οἷον, οἷα δή often accompany the Participles in this use (also ὥστε in Herodotus).

ὁ Κῦρος, ἅτε παῖς ὤν, ἥδετο τῇ στολῇ. XEN. *Cyr.* i. 3. 3.
Cyrus, boy-like, was charmed with the dress.

οὐδ' ἂν ἕνι ὑπεικάθοιμι δείσας θάνατον. PLAT. *Apol.* xx.
There is not a man to whom I would yield through fear of death.

λέγω δὲ τοῦδ' ἕνεκα, βουλόμενος δόξαι σοὶ ὅπερ ἐμοί.
PLAT. *Phaed.* 102 D.
I speak for the following reason, because I want you to think just as I do.

See also Genitive and Accusative Absolute.

CAUSAL SENTENCES.

D. Causal Sentences are also often expressed by τῷ and the Infinitive.

οὐ πλεονεξίας ἕνεκα ταῦτ' ἔπραξεν ἀλλὰ τῷ δικαιότερα ἀξιοῦν Θηβαίους ἢ ἡμᾶς. DEM. ii. 13.
It was not for sake of greed that he did this, but because the Thebans made a juster demand than we.

Causal Sentences are also very often and very simply expressed by a Preposition and its case, sometimes by a Preposition with the Infinitive, *e.g.*

διὰ τὸ φίλους αὐτοὺς εἶναι.
Because they are friends.

Cf. especially διά and κατά.

CHAPTER VIII.

§ 246. EXPRESSIONS OF A WISH.

I. A Wish that refers to the Future, and which therefore may be fulfilled, is expressed—

A. By the Simple Optative.

B. By the Optative with εἴθε, εἰ γάρ (εἰ and ὡς, πῶς ἄν; in poetry).

The Negative is always μή.

ὦ παῖ, γένοιο πατρὸς εὐτυχέστερος,
τὰ δ' ἄλλ' ὁμοῖος, καὶ γένοι' ἄν οὐ κακός. SOPH.
Boy, mayst thou prove more fortunate than thy father,
Like in all else, so shouldst thou prove not vile.

Observe that γένοιο alone expresses a wish, γενοι' ἄν is an Apodosis.

μὴ ζῴην μετ' ἀμουσίας. EUR.
May I not live without culture!

εἰ γὰρ γενοίμην, τέκνον, ἀντὶ σοῦ νεκρός. EUR. *Hipp.* 1410.
Would to God, my child, I were dead in thy stead.

εἴθ' ὑμῖν ἀμφοῖν νοῦς γένοιτο σωφρονεῖν. SOPH. *Ai.* 1264.
Would that to you twain judgment were granted for discretion

εἴ μοι γένοιτο φθόγγος ἐν βράχιοσι. EUR. *Hec.* 836.
Oh, that a voice were given me in these arms.

ὡς ὁ τάδε πορὼν ὄλοιτο. SOPH. *El.* 126.
Ah, that he who contrived this might perish.

Cf. EUR. *Hipp.* 407.

πῶς ἄν ἀντ' ἐμοῦ τρέφοιτε τήνδε τὴν νόσον;
SOPH. *Phil.* 794.
Would that in my stead ye might hug this plague.

μή πως ἐγώ τοσαύτας δίκας φύγοιμι. PLAT. *Apol.* iii.
May not I be indicted on charges so serious!

II. A Wish which refers to the Past, and which therefore can no longer be fulfilled, is expressed—

A. With εἴθε, εἰ γάρ (μή) $\begin{cases} \text{Imperfect Indicative (of present time, continued or habitual actions).} \\ \text{Aorist Indicative (of single acts).} \end{cases}$

B. ὤφελον (Aorist), sometimes ὤφελλον (Imperfect), from ὀφείλω, *I owe*, with the Infinitive (Present or Aorist).

εἴθε, εἰ γάρ (μή) may accompany ὤφελον, sometimes ὡς in poetry.

εἴθ᾽ εἶχες, ὦ τέκουσα, βελτίους φρένας.
          Eur. *El.* 1061.
Would that thou hadst, O mother, better judgment (but thou hast not).

εἴθε σοι, ὦ Περίκλεις, τότε συνεγενόμην.
          Xen. *Mem.* i. 2. 46.
I wish I had been with you then, Pericles.

ὡς ὤφελον πάροιθεν ἐκλιπεῖν βίον. Soph. *El.* 1131.
Ah, would that I had first forsaken life.

εἴθ᾽ ὤφελες τοιάδε τὴν γνώμην πατρὸς
θνήσκοντος εἶναι. Soph. *El.* 1021.
Would thou hadst been thus minded on the day thy father died.

   μήποτ᾽ ὠφελεῖν λιπεῖν
τὴν Σκῦρον. Soph. *Phil.* 969.
 *Would that I ne'er had left
My Scyros!*

ὡς πρὶν διδάξαι γ᾽ ὤφελες μέσος διαρραγῆναι.
          Arist. *Ran.* 955.
Pity, ere you taught 'em, that you didn't burst asunder in the midst.

Note 1. A wish may be made to depend on a condition which is expressed by οὕτω. Instead of the sentence which logically should follow " so may I . . . *as*," an Indicative or an Imperative is substituted.

οὕτω νικήσαιμί τ' ἐγὼ καὶ νομιζοίμην σοφός,
ὡς ὑμᾶς ἡγοῦμαι εἶναι θεατὰς δεξιούς. AR. *Nub.* 520.
So may I win and be considered wise, as I hold you to be a clever audience.

οὕτως ὀναίμην τῶν τέκνων, μισῶ τὸν ἄνδρ' ἐκεῖνον.
AR. *Th.* 469.
So may I be blest in my children . . . I do hate that fellow.

οὕτως ὄναισθε τούτων, μὴ περιίδητέ με. DEM. *Aph.* ii. 842. 9.
So may you enjoy this . . . do not neglect me.

Instead of saying—*on this condition, namely, that you do not neglect me.*

This is exactly like the well-known Latin idiom :—
Sic te diva potens Cypri
. . . . .
Ventorumque *regat* pater
Navis . .
        Finibus Atticis
Reddas incolumem precor. HOR. *Od.* 1. iii. 1.

Sic venias hodierne . . . tibi *dem* turis honores.
TIBULL. 1. vii. 33.

Note 2. Explanation of expressions of a wish.

(1) Optatives and Indicatives with εἰ, εἰ γάρ, εἴθε are clearly Protases with suppressed Apodoses.

εἰ γὰρ ταῦτα γένοιτο (sc. καλῶς ἂν εἴη).
εἰ γὰρ ταῦτα ἐγένετο (sc. καλῶς ἂν ἦν).

Latin is parallel—
O si haec ita fiant, fierent, facta essent.
With ὡς compare *ut, utinam* in Wishes.

(2) ὤφελον (*I ought,* or *had ought*), on the other hand, is an Apodosis with a suppressed Protasis ; used like χρῆν, ἔδει without an ἄν.

Latin again supplies a parallel—
(Eum) si ulla in te pietas esset, colere *debebas*.
                                           CIC. *Phil.* ii. 38.
Tunc ego *debueram* capienda ad Pergama mitti:
Tunc *poteram* magni, si non superare, morari
Hectoris arma meis.   Ov. *Met.* xii. 445.

CHAPTER IX.

§ 247. RELATIVE SENTENCES.

Relative sentences are introduced by either (1) Relative Pronouns, or (2) Particles of Relative origin, ὡς, ὅτε, εἰ, ὄφρα, etc.
The chief distinction between Relative Sentences is that of Definite and Indefinite, a distinction explained in § 172. It applies to many Relative Particles as well as Pronouns, e.g.

A. DEFINITE—

ἴστε ὁπόθεν ὁ ἥλιος ἀνίσχει, καὶ ὅποι δύεται. XEN.
You knew where (lit. *whence*) *the sun rises, and where* (lit. *whither*) *it sets.*

ὦ γαῖα δέξαι θανάσιμόν μ', ὅπως ἔχω. SOPH.
O Earth! receive me, as I am, in death.
Accipe me, ut sum.

B. INDEFINITE—

ὅποι ἂν στρατηγὸν ἐκπέμψητε, οἱ ἐχθροὶ καταγελῶσι. DEM.
Wheresoever you send out a general, your enemies ridicule you.

ἔξεστι χρῆσθαι ὅπως ἂν βούλωνται. XEN.
You may make whatever use (*of it*) *you please.*

Definite Relative sentences present no difficulty. Indefinite Relative sentences freely form Subordinate sentences of every kind,—Conditional, Temporal, Modal, Consecutive, etc., and will be found under these several heads. Some Relative Particles denote Place (ὅποι, ἵνα, etc.), but a special chapter on Local Sentences is unnecessary.

Other uses of the Relative will be seen by reference to the Index. Especial attention should be paid to the syntax of the Negatives with Relatives; see chapter on the Negatives, Part III.

PART III.

PREPOSITIONS, NEGATIVES, ORATIO OBLIQUA, AND FIGURES.

CHAPTER I.

§ 248. PREPOSITIONS.

Prepositions in Attic are particles which have a double use. Either (1) they are joined in Composition with Verbs; or (2) they serve as links between the oblique case of Nouns or Pronouns and other words, especially Verbs, in the sentence. As such links they denote Place, Time, and various figurative relations, Agency, Cause, Means, etc., more distinctly than could be done by the oblique cases alone. Prepositions also help to form compound adjectives and substantives. Philology and Epic Poetry, however, enable us to trace the origin and usage of Prepositions further back than their Attic uses, and to account for those uses.

§ 249. Introductory Note to Prepositions.

1. Prepositions appear to have been originally caseforms. Thus ὑπό (Ep. ὑπαί) was Locative, meaning *on the under side;* ὑπέρ (Sanskrit *upari*), *on the upper side;* διά (Ep. and Poet. διαί), *in the space between;* ἀντί is Locative, ἄντα Accusative (cf. ἄντην, *coram*); περί Locative; πρός (προτί) Locative; παρά (παραί) Locative; πρό is Ablative. As cases

they must all have been capable of taking a Genitive.[1] Thus ὑπαὶ χθονός, *on the under side of the earth;* πὰρ ποδός (παραί), PINDAR, *P.* 10. 97, *on the near side of the foot;* ἀντὶ ἐμεῖο, *Il.* xxi. 481, *on the opposite side of me.* This is confirmed by the fact that all the quasi-prepositions, which are cases of nouns, are joined to a Genitive, *e.g.* θύραζε, EUR. *Bacch.* 331. This stage, however, is previous to all written literature, and belongs to Philology rather than Syntax.

2. They were used as Adverbs[2] independently of Verb or Noun. Instances still occur frequently in HOMER, *e.g.* μέλανες δ' ἀνὰ βότρυες ἦσαν, *black clusters were throughout, Il.* xviii. 512: περὶ πρὸ γὰρ ἔγχει θῦεν, *around in front he was raging with his spear, Il.* xi. 180 : ἀμφὶ δὲ οἱ βράχε τεύχεα, *on either side for him* (or *near him*) *clashed his arms:* περὶ κῆρι φιλέεσκε, *exceeding much at heart he loved him.* The Adverb qualifies the Verb, but stands apart from it.

3. A transitional period, that of the Homeric poems, succeeds. Originally the Noun went straight with the Verb; the relation between the two might be more particularly defined by an Adverb. Thus ἀγαγεῖν δόμον, *to lead home;* ἀγαγεῖν δόμου, *to lead from home* (Genitive of separation or Ablative): ὤμοις βάλ' αἰγίδα, *on his shoulders* (Locative) *he cast his shield.* Compare these with εἰςῆγον θεῖον δόμον, *Od.* iv. 43 ; ἐκ δ' ἄγαγε κλισίης, *Il.* i. 346 : ἦγεν ἐς κλισίην, *Il.* i. 89 : ἀμφὶ δὲ χαῖται ὤμοις ἀΐσσονται. In the first two of these last four examples the Adverbs εἰς and ἐκ further define the direction of the Verb, and form Compound Verbs which "govern" respectively the Accusative and Genitive. But in the last two the Adverb serves as a link between Noun and Verb, and becomes a Preposition.

4. Prepositions thus come to furnish new analytic cases, the old cases with their blunted and confused suffixes being

---

[1] This is Curtius' view (*Elucidations*, Ch. xvii.) It must apply to Prepositions only when they do not denote *separation* (in which case they would be joined to an Ablative). Such a connection between Prepositions and the Genitive is said not to exist in Sanskrit, and on this ground Delbruck (*Syntaktische Forschungen*, iv. ch. ix. p. 134) only partially accepts Curtius' theory.

[2] No distinction is here intended in speaking of Prepositions as caseforms and as Adverbs. All oblique cases are, of course, adverbial, except the true Genitive, which is adjectival or attributive.

insufficient to express all the new relations between Noun and Verb which were suggested by the expansion of Greek thought and knowledge. When a Preposition links a case to any other word but a Verb, to an Adjective or Noun, a verbal meaning is readily understood. In determining the force of a Preposition we must carefully consider three points: the meaning (1.) of the Preposition, (2.) of the Case, (3.) of the Verb (or verbal word). In the stereotyped phrases with Prepositions which have practically become Adverbs or Adjectives, it will be easy enough to supply the verbal notion which the phrase requires to complete it logically.

5. A few instances may elucidate the foregoing remarks.

a. The noun linked by a preposition to its case has a verbal meaning.

διαλλαγαὶ πρός τινα, *reconciliation with any one,* ISOCR. 60 B, compared with διαλλαχθῆναι πρός τινα, *to be reconciled with any one.*

τοξότης ἀφ' ἵππου, compare with τοξεύειν ἀφ' ἵππου.

b. The Preposition with its Case is a fuller expansion of the Simple Case.

Thus we may say, χρηστοῦ πρὸς ἀνδρός ἐστι, or χρηστοῦ ἀνδρός ἐστί, *it is the part of a good man.*

Lysias writes μνησθῆναί τινος : Thucydides, μνησθῆναι περί τινος : Demosthenes, μνησθῆναι ὑπέρ τινος.

So we may say, εἰρήσεται πρὸς ὑμᾶς, or ὑμῖν, ἡ ἀλήθεια, *the truth shall be told you;* μάχεσθαι τῷ λίμῳ καὶ τῷ δίψει, XEN., *to fight with hunger and thirst;* μάχεσθαι πρὸς ἐπιθυμίας, PLAT., *to fight against desires.*

Similarly, ἡ παρ' ἐμοῦ εὔνοια = ἡ εὔνοια μου, *my goodwill* (Subjective Gen.); τὸ παρ' ἐμοῦ ἀδίκημα = τὸ ἀδίκημά μου, *the wrong done by me* (Objective).

6. Improper or Spurious Prepositions are those which can be joined with Cases, *e.g.* ἄνευ, ἕνεκα with Genitive, ὡς with Accusative, but which are not compounded with Verbs.

7. Tmesis is a late Grammarians' term to denote the separation between Preposition and Verb. The term is unnecessary, for, as we have seen, in early Greek it is not the separation, but the combination, which has to be accounted for. Tmesis in Attic is but a survival of the earlier usage: it is practically confined to poetry and a few colloquialisms,

e.g. δι' ἄρ' ὀλώλαμεν, EUR. *I.T.* 1371, ἀπο' σ' ὀλῶ. It is seldom found except when a particle intervenes. AESCH. *Sept. c. Theb.* 672 forms an exception.

8. Dissyllabic Prepositions are oxytone. They become Paroxytone (*i.e.* Barytone) in certain cases: (1.) When they stand immediately after their Verb or Case, *e.g.* ὀλέσας ἄπο πάντας ἑταίρους, μάχης πέρι. This is called *Anastrophe*. Ἀμφί, ἀντί, ἀνά, διά are not liable to Anastrophe. Monosyllabic Prepositions take the acute accent by Anastrophe, but only when they come at the end of a line. (2.) When they are equivalent to a Compound Verb, generally a Substantive Verb, ἄνα = ἀνάστηθι μέτα = μέτεστι, similarly ἔνι, ἔπι, πάρα, πέρι, and perhaps ὕπο. (3.) ἄπο and πέρι when used as Adverbs.

Oxytone Prepositions with elision lose their accent, *e.g.* παρ' ἡμέραν, ἐπ' αὐτῷ.

§ 250. The Prepositions and the Three Cases.

The Accusative is the case of the Direct Object of the Verb. This, however, implies direction *to*, or *on*, and thus Prepositions with the Accusative denote *motion to*,[1] *extension along* or *over*.

The Genitive is the Case of Connexion and Separation. Prepositions with the Genitive denote *connexion with*, or *separation from*: in the former sense the true Genitive is used, in the latter the old Ablative use has been handed on to the Genitive.

The Dative is connected with Prepositions chiefly in its locative sense. Prepositions with the Dative denote *nearness to*, or *rest at, by, with,* or *near*.

§ 251. Collected usages of Prepositions.

1. The Agent is expressed by the following Prepositions:—

 ὑπό with Gen. (the regular expression to denote the Agent; the others which follow are special.)

---

[1] But it must be remembered that the notion of motion must originally have come from the combined signification of Verb, Preposition, and Case.

πρός (in poetry and Ionic prose) with Gen.
ἐκ   "   "
παρά (the agent as the source) with Gen.
ἀπό (in some special prose uses) with Gen.
διά (the intermediate agent) with Gen.

2. Means by—

διά with Gen. (the regular expression to denote the Means; the others are special).
ἀπό.
ἐκ with Gen.
ἐν with Dat.
ξύν with Dat.

3. The usages of certain Prepositions are closely parallel :—

ἀπό	—	ἐκ
ἀντί	—	πρό
ξύν	—	μετά
ἀνά	—	κατά
ὑπέρ	—	περί (in certain senses).
ἀμφί	—	περί
ἐπί	—	πρός (in certain senses).

4. The usages of certain Prepositions are sharply contrasted :—

εἰς	—	ἐκ	—	ἐν
ὑπέρ	—	ὑπό		
ἀνά	—	κατά, etc.		

5. Synonymous phrases are formed by different Prepositions with Cases, e.g. :—

καθ' ἡμέραν, μέθ' ἡμέραν, πάρ' ἡμέραν.
οἱ ἀμφὶ Πλάτωνα, οἱ περὶ Πλάτωνα.

6. Verbs of rest are used with Prepositions expressing motion. This is known as the *Constructio Praegnans.* See ἀπό, ἐξ, εἰς, ἐν.

7. Prepositions are used, (1) in their literal sense denoting place, or time, (2) in a figurative sense denoting various moral relations.

The Attic use of Prepositions is marked off from the Epic chiefly in two ways : (1) by the disuse of the adverbial senses, (2) by the development of figurative meanings.

§ 252. PREPOSITIONS AND THE CASES.

I. Prepositions with one Case.
  a. Accusative: ἀνά, εἰς (ἐς), ὡς (ἀμφί practically in prose).
  b. Genitive: ἀντί, ἀπό, ἐξ (ἐκ), πρό (ἄνευ, ἕνεκα, ἕκατι, χωρίς, ἄχρι, μέχρι).
  c. Dative: ἐν, σύν (ἅμα, ὁμοῦ).

II. Prepositions with two Cases.
  Accusative and Genitive: διά, κατά, ὑπέρ, μετά.

III. Prepositions with all three Cases.
  ἀμφί, ἐπί, παρά, περί, πρός, ὑπό.

I.—PREPOSITIONS WITH ONE CASE ONLY.

(a.) WITH ACCUSATIVE ONLY.

§ 253. Ἀνά.

Ἀνά, *up to, through*, opposed to κατά (compare the two throughout), Eng. *on*, Gothic *ana*, Germ. *an*. Ἀνά related to ἐνί (ἐν) as *on* and *in*.

Lat. *an-helo, I breathe up*, CURT. *Etymol.* i. 381.

Up along:

τὰ πλοῖα ἀνὰ τὸν ποταμὸν οὐ δύνανται πλέειν.
                                                HEROD.
The boats cannot sail up the stream (cf. κατά).

Throughout or *Among*:

ἀοίδιμος ἀνὰ τὴν Ἑλλάδα ἐγένετο. HEROD.
He became famous in song throughout all Greece.
οἰκεῖν ἀνὰ τὰ ὄρη, XEN. *An*. iii. 5. 16, *to live in the hills.*

Distributively:

ἐπορευθῆσαν ἀνὰ πέντε παρασσάγγας τῆς ἡμέρας.
                                                                    XEN.
They marched at the rate of five parasangs a day.

So ἄνα ἑκατόν, *in bodies of a hundred, in centuries.* Cf. S. Luke ix. 14, S. Matth. xx. 10.

PHRASES:

ἀνὰ κράτος (φεύγειν), *with all one's might* (cf. κατὰ κράτος: ἀνὰ λόγον (φυόμενα δένδρα), PLAT. *Phaed.* lix. *trees growing*) *in proportion;* ἀνὰ στόμα ἔχειν, *to have in one's mouth, at the tip of the tongue.*

N.B. ἄνα has the sense of ἀνάστηθι, *up! arise! sursum!* Cf. SOPH. *Ai.* ἀλλ' ἄνα ἐξ ἑδράνων, *come, up from thy seat!*

Note. ἀνά is also used in Homer, in Lyric poetry (Pindar), and in Choruses of the Tragedians with the Dative (*e.g.* EUR. *I. A.* 754).

IN COMPOSITION:

(1.) *Up,* ἀναβλέπω, *I look up.* (2.) *Reverse action, back,* ἀνανεύω, *I throw the head back.* (3.) *Again,* ἀναβλέπω, *I recover sight.*

§ 254. Εἰς or ἐς.

Εἰς or ἐς, *into, to,* opposed to ἐξ, *out of.* Original form perhaps ἔνς, from ἐνι-ς. In Pindar ἐν means *in* and *into.* Cf. Latin *in* and *inter* with Accusative.

(1) OF PLACE :—

Motion to, into, for:

Σικελοὶ ἐξ Ἰταλίας διέβησαν ἐς Σικελίαν. THUC.
The Sicels crossed over out of Italy into Sicily (or *for Sicily*).

With verbs of rest:

κατακλείειν ἐς τὴν νῆσον. THUC. i. 109.
To shut up in the island. (Constructio praegnans.)

PREPOSITIONS WITH ACCUSATIVE ONLY. 293

(*To speak*) *before* :
λέγειν εἰς τὸ πλῆθος.
To speak before the people.
Cf. εἰσιέναι, στῆναι ἐς.

Looking towards :
τὸ ἐς Παλλήνην τεῖχος. THUC. i. 56.
The wall facing Pallene.

PHRASES :
εἰς ἀκόντιον, εἰς δόρατος πληγὴν (ἀφικνεῖσθαι).
To get within javelin's throw, spear thrust.
Opposed to ἐξ.

(2) OF TIME :—

Up to, until :
εἰς τὴν ἕω, *till dawn* ; ἐς ἐμέ, *up to my time.*

At such a time, by such a date :
εἰς ἑσπέραν, εἰς τρίτην (with or without ἡμέραν), ἐς τὴν ὑστεραίαν (ἥκειν), *to come at even, on the third day* (or *in three days*), *on the morrow.*

PHRASES :
ἐς καιρόν, *in season* ; εἰς αὔριον, *on the morrow* ; εἰς ἔπειτα, *henceforward* ; εἰς ἅπαξ (or εἰσάπαξ), *once for all*, etc.

(3) WITH NUMBERS :—

Denoting limit, up to, amounting to :
ναῦς ἐς τὰς τετρακοσίας. THUC.
Ships to the number of four hundred.
ἐς δραχμὴν διαδοῦναι. THUC.
To pay each man up to (i.e. *as much as*) *a drachma.*

PHRASES :
εἰς ἕνα, εἰς δύο, εἰς τέσσαρας.
One, two, four deep.
εἰς δύναμιν, *to the extent of one's ability* ; εἰς ὑπερβολήν, *in excess.*

(4) OF RELATION TO :—

ἁμαρτάνειν εἴς τινα, *to do wrong to any one.*

Purpose:

ἐς τόδε ἥκομεν, *for this purpose we are come.*
εἰς κάλλος ζῆν, XEN., *to live for show.*

(5) SPECIAL PHRASES :—

ἐς ἄνδρας ("Ελληνας, etc.) τελεῖν, *to come to man's estate* (*to be enrolled among, belong to Greeks*). Cf. ἐγγράφω.
ἔς τι (τ. ὗτο) τελευτᾶν, *to end in a certain way.*
ἔς πᾶν ἀφικέσθαι, *to come to everything,* i.e. *to try every means.*
εἰς Ἀπολλῶνος, Διόνυσου, *to Apollo's, Dionysus' temple,* ad Apollinis, ad Bacchi. So εἰς διδασκάλου, εἰς ἐμαυτοῦ (φοιτᾶν), sc. οἶκον or some such word.

N.B. εἰς is not used in Attic of motion to individual persons; πρός or ὡς must be employed.

IN COMPOSITION:
Into. Examples unnecessary.

§ 255. Ὡς.

ὡς, *to,* with Persons only, not with things.
with πρός, εἰς, ἐπί, and alone.

ὡς Ἆγιν ἐπρεσβεύσαντο. THUC.
They sent an embassy to Agis.

(b.) WITH GENITIVE ONLY.

§ 256. Ἀντί.

ἀντί (original sense, *over against, opposite to*), *instead of, in exchange for;* ἄντα, Epic adv. and prep. *over against, face to face;* ἄντην, Ep. adv. *over against.* Cf. ἐν-αντί-ος ἀντι-κρύ. In Homer ἀντί is still an adverb rather than a preposition. Lat. *ante* (orig. *anted*), cf. Germ. *ant-wort.*

(1) OF PLACE, *opposite to*:
This sense is Epic.

(2) *Instead of*:
κακὰ πράττει ἀντ' ἀγαθῶν. PLAT.
He does evil instead of good.
So μεῖζον, πλέον, ἀντί, instead of Comparative and Simple Genitive, SOPH. *Ant.* 182, *Tr.* 577.

(3) *In return for*:
δεῖ τὰ μὲν ἀντὶ ἀργυρίου ἀλλάξασθαι. PLAT.
We must exchange some things for money.
ἀνθ' ὧν, *wherefore* (also *because*, cf. SOPH. *Antig.* 1068).
Rarely like πρός, *for the sake of* (lit. *over against, in the presence of*), with verbs of entreaty, see SOPH. *O. C.* 1326.

IN COMPOSITION:
Many meanings, (1) *Against*, i.e. *opposite* or *in opposition*, ἀντιβαίνω, *I plant the foot against*, also *I resist*. (2) *Reciprocity, substitution,* or *equality*, ἀντιβοηθῶ, *I help in turn;* ἀνθύπατος, *proconsul;* ἀντίτυπος, *struck*, or *striking back, corresponding;* ἀντίθεος, *godlike*.

§ 257.   Ἀπό.

Ἀπό, *away, off, from.* Sansk. *apa*, away, Lat. *ab*, Germ. *ab*, Eng. *off, of.* Ἀπό (Sansk. *apa*) connected with ἐπί (Sansk. *api*, further, after).

(1) OF PLACE :—
Away from:
ἀπὸ τῆς αὐτῶν ὁρμῶνται. THUC.
They advance from their own country.
With verbs of rest (from the observer's point of view):
ἐβόασεν ἀπὸ πέτρας σταθείς. EUR.
Shouted from the rock, standing (on it).

Hence many phrases: οἱ ἀπὸ τῶν πύργων, *the men on the towers;* ἀπὸ νεῶν, ἀφ' ἵππων μάχεσθαι, *to fight on board ship, on horseback.*

PHRASES:
ἀπὸ σκοποῦ, καιροῦ, *wide of the mark* (cf. ἀπὸ γνώμης, SOPH. *Tr.* 389); ἀπὸ τρόπου (PLAT.), *unsuitably*, opposed to πρὸς τρόπου, κατὰ τρόπον.
ἀπὸ δένδρων καταδεῖν (XEN.), *to tie to trees.*

(2) OF TIME :—
After, since:
ἀπὸ τῶν σίτων διαπονεῖσθαι. XEN.
To work after meals.

PHRASES:
τὸ ἀπὸ τοῦδε, *henceforth;* ἀφ' οὗ, ex quo, *since;* ἀπὸ παλαιοῦ, ἀρχαίου, *of old;* ἀφ' ἑσπέρας (THUC. vii. 29), *at even.*

(3) ORIGIN :—
οἱ μὲν ἀπὸ θεῶν γεγονότες, οἱ δ' ἐξ αὐτῶν τῶν θεῶν
ISOC.
Some descended (remotely) *from gods, others begotten* (directly) *by the gods themselves.*

Material:
κρᾶσις ἀπό τε τῆς ἡδονῆς συγκεκραμένη ὁμοῦ καὶ ἀπὸ τῆς λύπης. PLAT. *Phaed.* ii.
A combination consisting partly of pleasure and partly of pain.

Means:
ζῆν ἀπὸ πολέμου (γεωργίας). THUC. and XEN.
To live by war (husbandry).
Περικλῆς ἀπὸ διακοσίων νεῶν κατεπολέμησεν τὴν Σάμον.
Is. 15. 11.
Pericles with 200 ships reduced Samos.
Cf. THUC. i. 91, ἀπὸ παρασκευῆς.

Cause, in consequence of or for:
ἀπό τινος θαυμάζεσθαι, ἐπαινεῖσθαι, διαβάλλεσθαι.
To be admired, praised, slandered in consequence of anything.
ἀπ' αὐτῶν τῶν ἔργων σκοπεῖτε. THUC. i. 17.
Judge from facts themselves.

Agent, less direct than ὑπό :

ἐπράχθη ἀπ' αὐτῶν οὐδέν. THUC. i. 17.
Nothing was achieved by them.

See Poppo's note.

ἀπό with a case is often a periphrasis for a case alone, *e.g.*
ὁ ἀπὸ τῶν δορφόρων φόβος, *fear of the body guard*, XEN. *Hier.*
x. 3 ; τῶν ἀπὸ τῶν δημοῦ τις, *one of the people*, THUC. iv. 130.
THUCYDIDES's partiality for a free use of ἀπό is remarkable.

(4) PHRASES :—

οἱ ἀπὸ Πυθαγόρου, Πλάτωνος, *the school of Pythagoras, Plato.*
οἱ ἀπὸ τῆς Ἀκαδημείας, Στοᾶς, *the Academics, Stoics (the Academy, the Porch).*
οἱ ἀπὸ σκηνῆς, *actors.*
ἀπὸ σπουδῆς, *earnestly ;* ἀπὸ τοῦ ἴσου (τῆς ἴσης), ἀπ' ἴσης, *equally ;* ἀπὸ τοῦ προφανοῦς, *openly ;* ἀπὸ γλώσσης εἰπεῖν, *to state by word of mouth* (THUC. vii. 10), *to repeat by heart* (XEN. *Symp.* iii. 5), *from hearsay* (AESCH. *Ag.* 813) ; ὀμμάτων ἀπό (EUR. *Med.* 216), *with one's own eyes ;* ἀπὸ τοῦ αὐτομάτου (ταὐτομάτου), *spontaneously,* sponte, casu quodam ; ἀπὸ σημείου, *at a given signal.*

IN COMPOSITION :

(1) *Separation,* hence *completion,* and *ceasing,* ἀπολούω, *I wash off ;* ἀπεργάζομαι, *I finish off,* i.e. *I complete ;* ἀπολήγω, *I leave off, desist.* (2) *Restoration,* ἀποδίδωμι, *I give back.*

Separation also becomes practically privative, *e.g.* ἀπαγορεύω, *I forbid ;* ἀποχρήματος, *without money.*

§ 258. Ἐκ, Ἐξ.

Ἐκ, Ἐξ, *out of ;* opposed to εἰς, *into.* ἐκ and ἀπό run parallel throughout. Lat. *ex, e (cc).*

(1) OF PLACE :—

Out of :

ἐκ Σπάρτης φεύγει.
He is banished from (out of) Sparta.

Denoting change; (cf. ἀντί).

πόλιν ἐκ πόλεως ἀλλάττειν. PLAT.
To change city after city.

With verbs of rest:

ἐκ δένδρων ἀπάγχεσθαι. THUC. iii. 81.
To hang themselves on trees.

PHRASES:

Hence many phrases (observe that the first three or four are instances of Constructio Praegnans): τοὺς ἐκ τῆς ναυμαχίας (οὐκ ἀνελομένους), PLAT. *Apol.* xx., *those in the sea-fight;* οἱ ἐκ νήσων κακοῦργοι, THUC. i. 8, *the evil-doers in (of) the islands;* οἱ ἐκ τῶν πύργων, *those on the towers,* THUC. iii. 22; τὸ ἐξ Ἰσθμοῦ τεῖχος (opposed to τὸ ἐς Παλλήνην), THUC. i. 64, *the wall on the side of the Isthmus;* ἐκ δεξιᾶς, *on the right;* ἐξ ἀριστερᾶς, *on the left;* ἐκ νόμων, *in accordance with the laws;* ὀρθὸς ἐξ ὀρθῶν δίφρων, SOPH. *El.* 742, *erect in chariot erect;* ἐκ τῆς ψυχῆς (ἐκ θυμοῦ, HOM.) *with all one's heart;* ἐκ σαυτῆς (λέγεις), *self-prompted,* SOPH. *El.* 344, cf. ἀπό; ἐκ πολλοῦ, *at a long distance,* XEN.; ἐκ τόξου ῥύματος, XEN., *at bow-shot;* ἐκ χερὸς μάχην ποιεῖσθαι, XEN., *to fight hand to hand.*

(2) OF TIME :—

Since, after:

ἐξ οὗ (χρόνου), *since,* ex quo; ἐκ τοῦ ἀρίστου, *after breakfast.* (So ἀπό.)

ἐκ τούτου, *after this* (ἐκ τούτων gen. *in consequence of this*).
ἐκ τοῦ λοιποῦ (τῶν λοιπῶν) *for the future,* XEN. and PLAT.

After, denoting change:

ἐκ δακρύων γελᾶν. XEN.
To laugh after tears (weeping).

τυφλὸς ἐκ δεδορκότος καὶ πτωχὸς ἀντὶ πλουσίου.
SOPH. *O. T.* 454.
Blind after seeing, and poor instead of (being) rich.

Ever since:

ἐκ νέου, ἐκ παιδός, *from youth, from childhood.*

(3) ORIGIN :—

ἀγαθοί καὶ ἐξ ἀγαθῶν.
       PLAT. (Cf. SOPH. *Ant.* 466.)
Good, and born of good parents.

Material:

τὸ ἄγκιστρον ἐξ ἀδάμαντος. PLAT. *Rep.* 616.
The hook is of adamant.

Agent (HERODOT. *and poetry, rare in Attic*):

ἐκ τῶνδ' ἄρχομαι. SOPH. *El.* 264.
By them am I ruled.

Cf. SOPH. *Ant.* 957. 973, THUC. iii. 69, XEN. *Hell.* iii. 96.

Cause, Consequence, or Means:

ἐκ πολέμου εἰρήνη βεβαιοῦται. THUC. i. 120.
Peace is secured by means of war. (Cf. διά.)

Dependence upon:

παρρησία ἐξ ἀληθείας ἤρτηται. DEM. 1397. 1.
Plain speaking depends on truth (comes of).

Cf. ἀπάγχεσθαι ἐκ, above.

Mixed Phrases:

οἱ ἐξ Ἀκαδημείας, ἐκ τοῦ Περιπάτου (cf. ἀπό).
The Academics, the Peripatetics.

So *N. Test.* οἱ ἐκ πίστεως, *the adherents of the Faith.*

ὁ ἐξ ὑμῶν πόθος, SOPH. *Tr.* 631, *your desire* (like a gen.), so ὕμνος ἐξ Ἐρινύων, *the song of the Erinyes.* AESCH. *Eum.* 344.

Adverbial Phrases:

ἐκ βίας, *by force;* ἐκ τοῦ φανεροῦ (προφανοῖς), *openly* (cf. ex improviso, ex consulto, etc., Latin); ἐκ τοῦ εἰκότος, THUC. iv. 17, *in all likelihood;* ὡς ἐκ τῶν παρόντων, THUC. iv. 17, *so far as present circumstances allow;* ἐξ ἴσων (τοῦ ἴσου) *equally;* ἐκ τοῦ αὐτομάτου, *by chance, or accident,* XEN. (less common than ἀπό).

Periphrasis for a case :
αἱ ἐξ ᾿Αθηνῶν παρθένοι, *the maids of Athens.*

IN COMPOSITION :
(1) *Separation, removal, completion* (cf. ἀπό), ἐκβαίνω, *I go out ;* ἐκπέρθω, *I sack utterly, out and out.*

§ 259. Πρό.

Πρό, *before, in front of.* Cf. πρός. Lat. *prod, pro.*

(1) OF PLACE :—

Before, in front of :

Μινώα ἡ νῆσος κεῖται πρὸ Μεγάρων. THUC.
The island of Minoa lies off (in front of) Megara.

Hence *in defence of, for the sake of.* (Cf. ὑπέρ) :
ἤθελε θανεῖν πρὸ κείνου. EUR. *Alc.* 18.
She willed to die for him.

PHRASE.
πρὸ ὁδοῦ, *forwards, onwards.*

(2) OF TIME :—

οἱ πρὸ ἡμῶν γεγονότες. ISOC.
Those who were born before us (our forefathers).
ὁ πρὸ τοῦ χρόνος, *the former time, aforetime.*

(3) OF RELATION :—

In preference to, cf. ἀντί, περί :

πρὸ τῶν βελτίστων τὰ βραχύτερα αἱρεῖσθαι. PLAT.
To choose more unimportant things in preference to the highest things.

πρὸ πολλοῦ ποιεῖσθαι (τιμᾶσθαι).
To esteem highly, (lit. *in preference to much*).

IN COMPOSITION :
(1) *Forth, forward, in front,* of place and so of *pre-eminence,* of *substitution* or *defence,* προβάλλω, *I put forward ;* πρόθυρον, *front door ;* πρόεδρος, *president ;* πρόμαχος, *champion.* (2) *Before,* of time, προαισθάνομαι, *I learn beforehand.*

§ 260. Ἄνευ.

Ἄνευ, *without*, opposed to σύν.

(1) *Without the help of*, or *order of:* τί βροτοῖς ἄνευ Διὸς τελεῖται; AESCH. *Ag*. 1487, *what comes to pass among men without the will of Zeus?* (*iniussu Iovis, Iove nolente*). Cf. THUC. viii. 52. In PLAT. *Gorg*. 518 D, *without reference to*. (2) *Except, besides* (like χωρίς): πάντα ἄνευ χρυσοῦ, PLAT. *Crit*. 112 C, *all things except gold*, omnia praeter aurum.

In SOPH. *O. C*. 502 ἄνευ comes after its case.

§ 261. Ἕνεκα, ἕνεκεν.

Ἕνεκα, ἕνεκεν (Ion. εἵνεκα, εἵνεκεν), Poet. οὕνεκα.

Generally after its case, sometimes separated from its case (AR. *Ecc*. 105-6). Lat. *gratia, causa*.

(1) *For the sake of:* κολακεύειν ἕνεκα μισθοῦ, XEN. *Hell*. v. 1. 17, *to flatter for the sake of (in order to get) a reward*. (2) *So far as concerns:* ἐμοῦ γε ἕνεκα, *so far as I am concerned;* ἕνεκα τῶν ὀφθαλμῶν, PLAT., *so far as depends on the eyes*.

Note. Sometimes pleonastically with other Prepositions: ἀπὸ βοῆς ἕνεκα, THUC. vii. 92; ἀμφὶ σοῦ ἕνεκα, SOPH. *Phil*. 534; τίνος δὴ χάριν ἕνεκα; PLAT. *Leg*. 701 D.

§ 262. Ἕκατι.

Ἕκατι (Ep. *with the help of*).

(1) *Because of, on account of:* ἀρετῆς ἕκατι, SOPH. *Phil*. 670, *on account of* (i.e. *as a reward for*) *valour*. (2) *So far as concerns* (like ἕνεκα): πλήθους ἕκατι, AESCH. *Pers*. 337, *so far as numbers went*.

§ 263. Χωρίς.

Χωρίς, without.

(1) *Without help of:* πόνου τοι χωρὶς οὐδὲν εὐτυχεῖ, SOPH. *El*. 945; *without toil nothing prospers*. (2) *Far from:* χωρὶς ἀνθρώπων στίβου, SOPH. *Phil*. 487, *far from track of men*. (3) *Without considering, besides:* χωρὶς δόξης, *apart from reputation* PLAT. *Apol*. xxiv. (4) *Different from*, PLAT. *Lach*. 195 A.

Note. χωρίς is also used Adverbially.

§ 264. Besides the Prepositions, a greater number of old Cases, which have become Adverbial, are used like Prepositions with a Genitive.

I. μέχρι and ἄχρι, *as far as.*
(1) Of Place: μέχρι τῆς πόλεως, THUC., *as far as the city.*
(2) Of Time : μέχρι τοσούτου, τούτου, *so far, up to this time.*
(3) μέχρι τοῦ δικαίου (δυνατοῦ), *so far as is right (possible).*

II. χάριν. (1) *For the sake of:* τοῦ χάριν ;= τοῦ ἕνεκα ; *for the sake of what,* or *wherefore ?* (2) *Because of:* χάριν χλιδᾶς= χλιδᾶς ἕκατι, *because of pride,* SOPH. *O. T.* 888. (3) *So far as concerns:* δακρύων χάριν, *if tears could avail,* SOPH. *Fr.* 501.

Note. ἐμὴν χάριν, σὴν χάριν, *for my sake, thy sake,* not χάριν ἐμοῦ, σοῦ, *mea, tua causa, gratia.*

πρὸς χάριν is also redundantly used, *with reference to, for the sake of,* SOPH. *Ant.* 30, 908.

III. Several old Accusatives adverbially used, meaning *like, after the fashion of:* δίκην (lit. *usage*); τρόπον (*way*); δέμας (Epic only, *form* or *body*). Cf. Lat. *instar.*

IV. ἅλις, ἅδην, *enough;* δίχα, *apart;* λάθρα, κρύφα, *secretly.*

V. Many old local cases.

ἐγγύς, *near* (also takes Dative); εἴσω, ἐντός, *within;* ἔξω, ἐκτός, *without;* μεταξύ, *between;* πρόσω, πόρρω, ἄποθεν, *far from;* πρόσθεν, ἔμπροσθεν, *in front of;* ὄπισθεν, κάτοπιν, *behind;* ἀμφοτέρωθεν, ἑκατέρωθεν, ἔνθεν καὶ ἔνθεν, *on both sides of;* πέρα, πέραν, *beyond, across;* ἀντίπερας, καταντίπερας, ἀντικρύ, καταντικρύ, *opposite.*

(c.) *WITH DATIVE ONLY.*

§ 265.   Ἐν.

Ἐν (poet. εἰν, ἐνί, εἰνί), *in, within,* opposed to εἰς, *into,* and ἐξ, *out of.* Lat. *in,* Eng. *in,* Germ. *in.* Cf. ἀνά.

[The old Adverbial usage of ἔν still continues in the phrase ἐν δέ, *and among, and therein, and besides.* Several instances occur in Sophocles.]

(1) OF PLACE (see Dative of Place) :—

At, near, by, on :

Λεωτυχίδης ἡγεῖτο τῶν ἐν Μυκάλῃ ῾Ελλήνων. THUC.
Leotychides commanded the Greeks at Mycale.

Τραπεζοῦς οἰκεῖται ἐν τῷ Εὐξείνῳ πόντῳ. XEN.
Trapezus is built on the Euxine sea.

Among:

νόμοι ἐν πᾶσιν εὐδόκιμοι τοῖς ῞Ελλησιν. PLAT
Laws famous among all the Greeks.

Elliptically (supply οἴκῳ, or some such word), *mostly with proper names in Attic.* Cf. εἰς.

ἐν Ἅιδου, *in Hades.*
ἐν ᾿Αριφρονος, PLAT. *Prot.* 320 A, *in the house of Ariphron;*
ἐν Διονύσου, *in the temple of Dionysus,* DEM. 21. 8.
ἐν παιδοτρίβου, ἐν κιθαριστοῦ, *at (the school) of the gymnastic master, the cithara-player.*

Also an Epic use (the complete construction sometimes occurs, *e.g.* ἐν Ἀιδάο δόμοισι, *Od.* iv. 834).

With Verbs of Motion (Constructio Praegnans). Cf. εἰς, converse construction.

οἱ ἐν τῷ ῾Ηραίῳ καταπεφευγότες. XEN. *Hell.* iv. 5. 5.
Those who had fled to (and were in) the chapel of Hera.

(2) OF TIME (see Dative of Time) :—

Within a space of, during :

ἐν ταῖς σπονδαῖς, *during the armistice,* XEN.
ἐν τούτῳ, *meanwhile;* ἐν ᾧ, ἐν ὅσῳ, *whilst.*

(3) OF RELATION :—

Occupation, Condition :

οἱ ἐν τοῖς πράγμασι, οἱ ἐν τέλει. THUC.
Those who are engaged in public affairs, those who are in office, i.e. *ministers of state, the authorities, the government.*

ἐν φιλοσοφίᾳ, ἐν λόγοις, ἐν τῇ τέχνῃ εἶναι.
To be engaged in philosophy, in oratory, in an art.
εἶναι ἐν φόβῳ, ἐν αἰσχύνῃ, ἐν σιωπῇ, ἐν ἐλπίδι.
To be in a state of fear, shame, silence, hope.

PHRASES:

ἐν ὀργῇ ἔχειν or ποιεῖσθαί τινα, *to feel angry towards any one;* ἐν αἰτίᾳ ἔχειν, *to blame;* ἐν ἡδονῇ εἶναι ἄρχοντες, THUC. 1. 99, *to give satisfaction as rulers;* ἐν καλῷ εἶναι (=καλῶς ἔχειν), EUR. *Heracl.* 971, *to be well;* ἐν δίκῃ δικαίως, *in justice;* ἐν παρασκευῇ εἶναι, *to be in a state of preparation,* THUC. ii. 80; ἐν ὅπλοις εἶναι, *to be under arms* (so ἐν τόξοις, *equipped with arrows;* ἐν φορτίοις τρέχειν, *to run with burdens on the back,* XEN.).

Dependent on:

ἐν ταῖς γυναιξίν ἐστιν ἡ σωτηρία. ARIST.
The safety (of Greece) depends on the ladies.

So, very often, ἔν γ' ἐμοί, ἔν σοίγε, etc., *penes me, quantum in me est, so far as lies, depends on me, thee.*

ἐν τῷ θεῷ τὸ τέλος ἦν, οὐκ ἐν ἐμοί. DEM. 292. 21.
The issue rested with God, not with me.
Cf. SOPH. *O. C.* 1443, *O. T.* 314.

With respect to or at:

γέλωτ' ἔν σοι γελῶ. SOPH. *Ant.* 551.
I laugh a laugh at thee.

A rare use, but found with Compounds, ἐγγελῶ, ἐνυβρίζω.

Instrument, Means, Manner (a special use, originally denoting Place):

ἐν ὀφθαλμοῖς (ὄμμασιν) ὁρᾶν, Hom. and Attic.
To see with the eye (in oculis).

Sophocles is fond of this ἐν. Cf. *Phil.* 60, 102, 1293, *Antig.* 691. Cf. also EUR. *Bacch.* 277, THUC. i. 77 (νόμοις), vii. 11 (ἐπιστολαῖς).

IN COMPOSITION:

(1) *In, at, near,* ἐμβάλλω, *I throw in;* ἐγγελῶ, *I laugh at.* (2) *Of inherent qualities,* ἔμφωνος, *endowed with voice,* cf. ἔννομος.

§ 266. Σύν.

Σύν (ξύν, old Attic form), *with, together with*, opposed to ἄνευ. Lat. *cum.* Compare throughout with μετά.

Together with:

ἐπαιδεύετο σὺν τῷ ἀδελφῷ. XEN.
He was being educated with his brother.

Conformity with (opp. to παρά), *with the help of*:

σὺν τῷ νόμῳ ψῆφον τιθέναι. XEN.
To vote in accordance with the law (παρὰ τὸν νόμον, *contrary to law*).

PHRASES:

σὺν θεῷ, *with God's blessing*, or *help, please God* (*deo favente*). (σὺν θεῷ εἰπεῖν, PLAT., ARIST.)
οἱ σύν τινι, *one's friends, party, followers.* XEN.
σύν τινι μάχεσθαι (εἶναι, γίγνεσθαι), *to fight on one's side* (μετά τινος more usual). XEN.

Accompanying circumstances:

σὺν ναυσὶ προςπλεῖν, XEN. *Hell.* ii. 2. 7, *to sail with ships* (commoner in Epic than Attic).

Expletive use. Cf. Dative:

σὺν τῷ σῷ ἀγαθῷ, *to your advantage,* cum tuo commodo, XEN. *Cyr.* iii. 1. 15. Cp. SOPH. *Ant.* 172.
σὺν τῇ βίᾳ, *with violence* (cf. πρὸς βίαν, βιαίως).
σὺν τῷ χρόνῳ, *at length,* XEN. *Cyr.* viii. 6.

Old Adverbial use:

μὴ ξὺν κακῶς ποιεῖν αὐτούς. THUC. iii. 13.
Not jointly (i.e. *together with the Athenians*) *to injure them.*
Cf. SOPH. *Ai.* 960, AESCH. *Ag.* 586 (=*furthermore*), SOPH. *Ant.* 85 (*moreover*), *El.* 299.

IN COMPOSITION:

(1.) *Together with,* συναγορεύω, *I speak with another.* (2o. *Completely,* συμπληρῶ, *I fill completely,* cf. comple g. With numerals, a distributive force is given, e.) σύντρεις, *three taken together,* i.e. *three apiece.*

§ 267. Note on σύν and μετά.

σύν, *together with*, denotes mere addition.
μετά, *together with, in the midst of, in the company of*, denotes participation with, community of action.

Thus (in Homer):

μετὰ δμώων πῖνε καὶ ἦσθιε. *Od.* x. 140.
He was drinking and eating in the company of the slaves.
ἤλυθε σὺν δίῳ Μενελάῳ. *Il.* iii. 206.
He came with god-like Menelaus (i.e. *both came*).
Cf. SOPH. *Antig.* 115, 116.

So συλλαμβάνω, *I take or get together* (τοὺς στρατιώτας, *the soldiers*).
μεταλαμβάνω, *I take together with others*, i.e. *I share.*
συνέχω, *I hold together, comprise, contain.*
μετέχω, *I have with others, partake, share.*
ἕπεσθαι μετά τινων, *to follow in the midst of others.*
ἕπεσθαι σύν τισι, *to follow with* (as well as) *others.*

In Attic, it is to be observed, that σύν with the Dative is used in Poetry where μετά with the Genitive is used in Prose. XENOPHON, however, apparently following poetical, *i.e.* earlier or Homeric, usage, is the one Attic prose writer who uses σύν with the Dative.

§ 268. One or two old Adverbial Cases, ἅμα and ὁμοῦ, are joined like Prepositions to the Dative.

I. ἅμα, mostly Temporal: ἅμα ἕῳ, ἅμα ἕῳ γιγνομένῃ, *at dawn, daybreak;* but also of accompaniment, οἱ ἅμα Θόαντι, HDT. vi. 138, *those who were with Thoas.* Cf. THUC. vii. 57.

II. ὁμοῦ, *together with;* ὕδωρ ὁμοῦ τῷ πηλῷ, THUC. vii. 84, *water together with the mud;* θεοῖς ὁμοῦ=σὺν θεοῖς, SOPH. *Ai.* 767, *with the help of the gods.*

III. ἐγγύς (see Genitive), *near.* 1. When used of Place is chiefly Epic, and takes a Genitive, but, in EUR. *Herac.* 37, a Dative. 2. Of Time or Numbers, ἐγγὺς ἐνιαυτοῦ, XEN. *Hell.* iii. 1. 28, *near a year.* In THUC. vi. 5, ἔτεσι ἐγγὺς εἴκοσι, *near twenty years;* ἐγγύς is Adverbial, as *post* may be in Latin, *viginti post annis.*

IV. ἐφεξῆς: τὰ τούτοις ἐφεξῆς, PLAT., *what follows.*

II.—PREPOSITIONS WITH TWO CASES.
WITH ACCUSATIVE AND GENITIVE.

§ 269. Διά.

Διά (old and poetical form διαί), *between, apart, through.*
Cf. δύο, δίς, δίχα.

A. WITH GENITIVE.

1. OF PLACE :

Through (right through, and out of):
ἐπορεύθησαν διὰ Χαλύβων. XEN.
They marched through the country of the Chalybes.

All through, along :
θορύβου ἤκουσε διὰ τῶν τάξεων ἰόντος. XEN.
He heard a din passing all along the ranks.

Distributively, intervals of space :
διὰ δέκα ἐπάλξεων πύργοι ἦσαν. THUC.
At every ten battlements were towers.

So διὰ πολλοῦ, διὰ πλείστου, δι' ἐλάσσονος, *at a great distance, greatest distance, short distance.*

Cf. EUR. *Andr.* 1251 (ἄλλον δι' ἄλλου).

2. OF TIME :

Throughout, cf. παρά with Accusative :
ταῦτα δι' ὅλου τοῦ αἰῶνος μοχθοῦσι. THUC.
Thus throughout their whole life they labour.

So διὰ νυκτός, δι' ἡμέρας, etc., διὰ παντός, διὰ τέλους, *continually ;* δι' ὀλίγου, *for a little while.*

Of intervals after :
ἔοικε διὰ πολλοῦ χρόνου σ' ἑωρακέναι. ARIST.
It seems that it is a long while since he has seen you.

Cf. SOPH. *Phil.* 285 (χρόνος διὰ χρόνου, *of succession in time*).

Distributively:

διὰ πέμπτου ἔτους, or διὰ πέντε ἐτῶν, *every fifth year*, quinto quoque anno; δι' ἔτους, δι' ἐνιαυτοῦ, *every year, year by year*.

3. CAUSAL:

The notion is that of a coming between or intervening.

The intermediate agent, through the medium of, by the agency of:

ἔλεγε δι' ἑρμηνέως. XEN.
He was speaking by means of an interpreter.

δι' ἑαυτοῦ ποιεῖν τι, *to do a thing by oneself, all alone*, i.e. *without the intervention of another*.

Cf. ἀπό, ἐξ.

Means or *instrument*. Cf. the Dative (which denotes more direct means):

ἡ διὰ τῶν ὀμμάτων σκέψις. PLAT. *Phaed*. 83.
Examination by means of the eyesight.

διὰ χειρὸς ἔχειν, λαβεῖν τι, *to hold, to take in the hand*.

ADVERBIAL PHRASES:

A great number of Adverbial phrases are formed with διά and the Genitive. In these διά appears to be used sometimes in its local, sometimes in its causal sense.

διὰ μάχης ἰέναι, ἔρχεσθαι (τινι), *to go to, engage in battle with*; δι' ἔχθρας γίγνεσθαι (τινι), *to be hostile to*; διὰ φιλίας ἰέναι (τινι), *to be friendly with*; διὰ λόγων ἰέναι (τινι), *to converse with*; δι' αἰτίας ἔχειν, ἄγειν (τινα), *to hold guilty*; δι' ὀργῆς, φυλακῆς, οἴκτου ἔχειν (τινα, τι), *to be angry with, keep in prison, feel pity for*.

διὰ στόματος ἔχειν, μνήμης, στέρνων, *to have on one's lips, in one's memory, in the breast*.

δι' ὀργῆς, *angrily*; διὰ σπουδῆς, *hastily*; διὰ βραχέων, *shortly*; διὰ μακρῶν, *at length* (e.g. τοὺς λόγους ποιεῖσθαι, *to speak*); διὰ τάχους, *quickly, shortly*.

B. WITH ACCUSATIVE—generally denotes close contiguity.

1. OF PLACE AND TIME :

Throughout, during :
Epic and poetical only. Cf. AESCH. *Supp.* 15, SOPH. *O. T.* 867.

2. CAUSAL :

Of the Antecedent, not the Final Cause. Of the person or thing whose intervention helps towards a result.

Owing to, because of, on account of, with the help of (see note).

οἱ ᾽Αθηναῖοι δι᾽ ἀρετήν, ἀλλ᾽ οὐ διὰ τύχην ἐνίκησαν.
ISAE.
The Athenians conquered through valour, not through chance.

διὰ τοὺς εὖ μαχομένους αἱ μάχαι κρίνονται.
XEN. *Cyr.* v. 2. 35.
Battles are decided by (owing to the conduct of) those who fight well.

Cf. SOPH. *O. C.* 1129 (διά σε).

Through the fault of :

διὰ τοὺς ἀδίκως πολιτευομένους ἐν τῇ ὀλιγαρχίᾳ ἡ δημοκρατία γίγνεται. LYS. 25. 27.
Owing to the unjust administration of rulers in an oligarchy, democracy springs up.

εἰ μὴ διά, *had it not been for, but for :*

εἰ μὴ διὰ τὸν Πρύτανιν ἐνέπεσεν ἄν. PLAT. *Gorg.* 516 E.
Had it not been for the President he would have been thrown into prison. Cf. THUC. ii. 18.

PHRASES :

δι᾽ ἔνδειαν, *because of, owing to poverty* (XEN. *An.* viii. 6) ; δι᾽ ἄγνοιαν, διὰ καῦμα, διὰ χειμῶνα, *because of ignorance, heat, winter ;* διὰ τὸ ξυμμάχους εἶναι, *because they were allies.* Similarly the common expressions διὰ τί, *why? wherefore?* διὰ ταῦτα, *on this account, because of this;* δι' ὅ, δι' ἅ, *on which account.*

Note. For *the sake of this,* denoting a final cause or purpose, would be τούτου ἕνεκα, not διὰ ταῦτα.

For the sake of, in order to :

A very rare use of διά with the Accusative. It occurs seemingly four times in THUCYDIDES, iv. 40, δι' ἀχθηδόνα, *in order to vex;* ii. 40, διὰ τὴν σφετέραν δόξαν, *for their own glory ;* iv. 102, διὰ τὸ περιέχειν αὐτήν, *in order to enclose the city ;* v. 103, διὰ τοῦ θύματος τὴν ἔςπραξιν, *in order to exact the sacrifice.*

Note. It is difficult sometimes to distinguish between the causal uses of διά with Genitive and διά with Accusative. It is extremely difficult to account for the causal use of διά with Accusative. Consult RIDDELL'S *Digest of Platonic Idioms* for instances of διά with Accusative in PLATO and the Orators, meaning *with the help of.*

IN COMPOSITION :

(1) *Through,* and so *throughly* or *thoroughly,* διαβαίνω, *I go through ;* διαφεύγω, *I escape thoroughly.* (2) *Apart,* διασκεδάννυμι, *I scatter asunder.*

§ 270. Κατά.

Κατά, *down,* opposed to ἀνά. Old form καταί, cf. καταιβάτης.

A. WITH GENITIVE.

Note. βῆναι κατὰ πέτρης originally may have meant "to go downwards with regard to the rock," *i.e.* either *down from,* or *down upon.*

1. OF PLACE :

Down from :

ἁλόμενοι κατὰ τῆς πέτρας. XEN.
Leaping down from the rock.

Down, upon or over :

φέρε παῖ ταχέως κατὰ χειρὸς ὕδωρ. ARIST.
Come boy, quickly, pour water on my hand.
Cf. LUCIAN's late use, κατὰ κόρρης πατάξαι, *to box on the head*, for the earlier ἐπὶ κόρρης.
Cf. PLAT. *Rep.* 398 A. In SOPH. *El.* 1433 (κατ' ἀντιθύρων, *towards the vestibule*).

Down into, and under :
ἡ 'Ατλαντὶς νῆσος κατὰ τῆς θαλάττης δῦσα ἠφανίσθη.
PLAT. *Tim.* 25.
The isle of Atlantis sank under the sea and disappeared.

2. FIGURATIVELY :

Against :
οἱ καθ' ἡμῶν λόγοι, DEM. 15. 25, *arguments against us.* Cf. SOPH. *Phil.* 65.
Cf. κατηγορῶ, καταγιγνώσκω τινός, ψεύδομαι κατά τινος.

Concerning, with respect to :
τοῦτο εἴρηται κατὰ πασῶν τῶν πολιτειῶν. AR. *Pol.* v. 7. 11.
This has been asserted of all governments.

So σκοπεῖν, λέγειν, ζητεῖν, κατά τινος, often in PLATO (see RIDDELL, *Digest*, 163).

PHRASES :

κατ' ἄκρας, *utterly* (*Ep.* κατ' ἄκρης, *a culmine*); κατὰ τέκνων ὀμνύναι, DEM., *to swear by one's children;* καθ' ὅλου (later καθόλου, see *Lexicon*), *on the whole.*

B. WITH THE ACCUSATIVE, κατά denotes close proximity.

1. OF PLACE :

Motion down upon or after :
οἱ 'Αθηναῖοι κατὰ πόδας ἔπλεον τῶν Λακεδαιμονίων.
XEN.
The Athenians were sailing in the wake of the Lacedaemonians.

κατὰ ῥόον, *down stream* (cf. ἀνὰ ῥόον).

After, in search of:

ἐσκεδασμένοι καθ' ἁρπαγήν. XEN.
Scattered in quest of plunder.

Over against, opposite:

οἱ Ἀθηναῖοι κατὰ Λακεδαιμονίους ἐγένοντο. XEN.
The Athenians were posted opposite the Lacedaemonians.

Extension throughout:

ἡ εὐλάβεια σκότον ἔχει καθ' Ἑλλάδα. EUR.
Discretion is under a cloud throughout Hellas.
κατὰ γῆν καὶ κατὰ θάλασσαν, *by land and sea.*

In, connected with, belonging to:

κατ' ἀγοράν, *in the market;* αἱ κατὰ τὸ σῶμα (τὴν ψυχὴν) ἐπιθυμίαι, *bodily (mental) desires;* τὰ κατὰ τὴν πόλιν, *public affairs, politics;* τὰ κατὰ τὸν πόλεμον, *military matters.*

2. Hence FIGURATIVELY:

Of fitness, according to:

κατὰ νοῦν λέγεις. PLAT.
You speak to my liking.

Cf. AESCH. *Ag.*, κατ' ἄνδρα σώφρονα, *like a discreet man (with a man's discretion)*; AR. *Av.* 1001, κατὰ πνίγεα, *like an oven;* κατὰ φύσιν, *agreeably to nature* (opposed to παρὰ φύσιν); κατὰ τὸν ἀκριβῆ λόγον, *in strict statement;* PLAT. *Ap.* i., οὐ κατὰ τούτους ῥήτωρ, *an orator of a different stamp from these men;* κατὰ ξυμμαχίαν, *by virtue of an alliance.*

Especially with Comparatives:

εἶδεν νεκρὸν μείζω ἢ κατ' ἄνθρωπον. PLAT.
He saw a corpse of superhuman size.

Cf. THUC. vii. 75, μείζω ἢ κατὰ δάκρυα πεπονθότας.

PREPOSITIONS WITH TWO CASES. 313

3. OF TIME :
Contemporary with :
Θεμιστοκλῆς ὁ τῶν καθ' ἑαυτὸν ἁπάντων ἐνδοξότατος.
                                                    DEM. 20. 73.
Themistocles, the most illustrious man of all his contemporaries.
οἱ κατὰ Πλάτωνα, *Plato and his age ;* κατ' ἀρχήν, *originally ;* κατ' εἰρήνην, *in time of peace.*

4. DISTRIBUTIVELY :
Of Place, Time, Money, etc., a common use :
κατοικοῦνται οἱ Μῆδοι κατὰ κώμας. HEROD.
The Medes live in separate villages.
καθ' ἕνα, *one by one ;* κατὰ μίαν καὶ κατὰ δύο λαβεῖν, DEM. 20. 77, *to take (ships) one and two at a time ;* κατ' ἄνδρα, *man by man.*
καθ' ἡμέραν· (in dies), *day by day ;* κατὰ μῆνα, κατ' ἐνιαυτόν.
κατὰ τὰς πέντε καὶ εἴκοσι μνᾶς πεντακοσίας δραχμὰς εἰσφέρειν.   DEM. 815. 11.
To contribute 500 drachmas on every 25 minae.

5. MISCELLANEOUS PHRASES, *many adverbial :*
καθ' ἑαυτόν, καθ' αὐτούς, *left to themselves,* i.e. *alone or singly ;* κατὰ μόνας, *alone ;* κατὰ μικρόν, κατ' ὀλίγον, *little by little ;* κατὰ δύναμιν, *to the best of one's ability ;* τὸ κατ' ἐμέ, *so far as concerns me ;* κατὰ ταὐτά, *in the same way ;* κατ' Αἴσχυλον, *as Aeschylus has it ;* κατὰ χώραν, *in statu quo, "as you were."*
κατὰ τάχος, *quickly ;* κατὰ κράτος (per vim), *by force ;* κατὰ σπουδήν, *hastily ;* καθ' ἡσυχίαν, *quietly.*
κατὰ τοῦτο, *on this ground ;* κατὰ τί ; *on what ground, wherefore ?* κατὰ τὴν ἀσθένειαν, *on the ground of, by reason of, weakness.*

IN COMPOSITION :
(1) *Down,* καταβαίνω, *I go down.* (2) *Of isolation or abandonment,* καταλείπω, *I leave behind or abandon.* (3) *Against,* κατηγορῶ, *I accuse ;* καταγιγνώσκω, *I condemn.* (4) *All over,* i.e. *completely,* κατακόπτω, *I chop up in pieces.*

§ 271. Ὑπέρ.

Ὑπέρ (poet. ὑπείρ), *above, over, beyond.* Sansk. *upari* (above), Latin *super*, English *over*, German *über.* Ὑπέρ for ὑπέρι is a Comparative of ὑπό.

A. WITH THE GENITIVE.

1. OF PLACE:

   Over, above:

   ὁ θεὸς ἔθηκε τὸν ἥλιον ὑπὲρ γῆς. PLAT.
   God placed the sun above the earth.

   Motion over:

   ἐκκυβιστᾶν ὑπὲρ τῶν ξιφῶν. XEN.
   To turn a somersault over the swords.

   In the interior of a country:

   ἤρξατο ἐξ Αἰθιοπίας τῆς ὑπὲρ Αἰγύπτου. THUC.
   It began in Aethiopia which is beyond Aegypt, i.e. higher up, further inland.

2. FIGURATIVELY:

   To protect, in defence of, cf. πρό:

   νῦν ὑπὲρ πάντων ἀγών. AESCH.
   Now is the contest in defence of our all.

   Joined with πρό, EUR. *Alc.* 690.

   In the interest of:

   οἱ ὑπὲρ τοῦ βελτίστου λέγοντες. DEM. 9. 63.
   Those who speak in the cause of what is best.

   On account of:

   κλαύματα βραδυτῆτος ὑπέρ. SOPH. *Ant.* 932.
   Tears as a punishment for slowness.

   Instead of:

   ἀποκρίνεσθαι ὑπέρ τινος, PLAT. *Rep.* 590, *to answer for one.* Cf. THUC. i. 141, ὑπὲρ ἑαυτοῦ.

With a view to:
ὑπὲρ τοῦ μὴ πράττειν τὸ προςταττόμενον, ISOC. 152 D, *in order not to do what was bidden.* Cf. RIDDELL, *Digest*, p. 167.

B. WITH ACCUSATIVE. Chief signification figurative, *beyond*, i.e. *in excess of*.

1. OF PLACE:

Beyond:
τῶν οὐρέων τῶν ὑπὲρ Μέμφιν πόλιν κειμένων τὸ μεταξύ. HDT.
The space between the hills which lie beyond the city of Memphis.

2. FIGURATIVELY:

In excess of:
οὐκ ἔστιν ὑπὲρ ἄνθρωπον τοῦτο. PLAT.
This is not beyond the power of man.
ὑπὲρ ἐλπίδα, *past, beyond hope;* ὑπὲρ ἡμᾶς, *beyond our power;* ὑπὲρ δύναμιν, *beyond one's ability*.

More than:
ἔπεσον ὑπὲρ τεσσεράκοντα ἄνδρας. HEROD. v. 64.
There fell over more than 40 men.

3. OF TIME:

Before:
ὁ πρὸς τὸν Αἰγινητῶν ὑπὲρ τὰ Μηδικὰ πόλεμον.
THUC. i. 41.
The war with the Aeginetans before the Persian wars.

As an adverb:
Very rarely; cf. EUR. *Med.* 627, ST. PAUL *ad Cor.* II. xi. 23, ὑπὲρ ἐγώ.

IN COMPOSITION:

(1) *Across* or *beyond*, hence of *excess* or *transgression*, ὑπερβαίνω, *I go beyond,. I transgress, omit, surpass.* (2) *For, in defence of,* ὑπεραλγῶ, *I grieve for* (also *exceedingly*) as by (1); ὑπερμαχῶ, *I fight for.*

§ 272. Μετά.

Μετά, *With, among, between, after.* Compare with σύν. Cf. μετα-ξύ, *between,* μέταζε, *afterwards.* Sansk. *mithas* (*alternately*), *mithu* (*together*), German *mit.* CURTIUS (*Etym.* i. p. 258) denies the direct relationship between μετά and μέσος. In Attic, μετά is chiefly used with the Genitive. Compare with σύν.

A. WITH GENITIVE.

With, among :

ἡ ψυχὴ ἀεὶ μετὰ τῶν θεῶν διάγει. PLAT.
The soul lives for ever with the gods (*in their society*).
μετὰ ξυμμάχων κινδυνεύειν, THUC. viii. 23, *to run risk in common with allies.*

On the side of :

οὐκ εἰκὸς τὸ τῆς τύχης οἴεσθαι ἀεὶ μεθ' ὑμῶν ἔσεσθαι.
THUC. iv. 18.
It is not reasonable to suppose that the influence of fortune will ever be on your side. Cf. PLAT. *Apol.* xxii., μετὰ τοῦ νόμου.

Joined to :

ἰσχύς τε καὶ κάλλος μετὰ ὑγιείας. PLAT. *Rep.* 591 B.
Strength and beauty joined to health.

Modal, cf. σύν, and Dative alone :

ἱκέτευσε τοὺς δικαστὰς μετὰ πολλῶν δακρύων.
PLAT. *Apol.* xxiii.
He besought the judges with many tears.

PHRASES :

μετά τινος εἶναι, *to be on one's side ;* οἱ μετά τινος, *one's companions ;* μετ' ἀληθείας, *truly.*

B. WITH ACCUSATIVE (rare in Attic).

Next in order to :

μετὰ θεοὺς ψυχὴ θειότατον. PLAT. *Leg.* 726.
Next to the gods the soul is most divine.

Other usages of μετά with the Accusative, *going among, going in quest* or *search of, according to*, are chiefly Epic. For them the Lexicon should be consulted.

Note 1. With the Accusative μετά denotes either (1) *motion to the midst of*, or (2) *extension over the midst of*. The idiomatic phrases with μετά and Accusative will fall under one of these two heads. Thus (1) μετὰ ταῦτα, *next to, after this* (lit. *going into the midst of*, and so *succeeding*, or *coming next to*); (2) μέθ' ἡμέραν, *interdiu, in the daytime (during, extending over the day)*; μετὰ χεῖρας ἔχειν, *to have in hand.*

Note. 2. In HOMER and in poetry μετά is also used with the Dative to denote *presence among*, one among others, without the close connexion denoted by the Genitive.

μετὰ δὲ τριτάτοισιν ἄνασσεν, *Il.* i. 252, *he was ruler among (in the presence of) the third generation.*
Cf. EUR. *Erechth.* 26.

As an adverb:

Among, amid, next, afterwards, often in HOMER.
In HEROD. also *afterwards*. μετὰ δέ, ὥπλισε κ.τ.λ., i. 128.

IN COMPOSITION:

(1) *Together with*, μετέχω, *I have together with* or *share*.
(2) *Going to, among*, or *extending over,* or *in the midst of*: μεταίχμιον, *the space between armies;* μεθίημι, *I let loose (among)*. (3) Of *succession, alternation, change,* μεταδόρπιος, *after dinner;* μεταγιγνώσκω, *I change my mind;* μετάνοια, *repentance.*

N.B. Coming among implies *following some,* and so *succession* and *alternation*. Thus if a bead is put among or between others in a necklace, it comes after, and alternates with, other beads.

III.—*PREPOSITIONS WITH ALL THREE CASES.*

§ 273. Ἀμφί.

Ἀμφί, *on both sides (about, around)*. Cf. ἄμφω, ἀμφότερος. Sausk. *abhi*, Lat. *amb, (am-, an-), amb-o, amb-io.* Ἀμφί related in form to ἀμφίς as ἐκ to ἐξ. Compare throughout with περί.

Note. In Attic Prose ἀμφί is practically used with the Accusative only.

A. WITH ACCUSATIVE.

About the time of, cf. περί :

ἤδη ἦν ἀμφὶ ἀγορὰν πλήθουσαν. XEN.
It was now already about full market time (forenoon).
ἀμφὶ πεντήκοντα ἔτη, *about* 50 *years.*

(*Employed*) *about* :

ἀσκοῦσι τὰ ἀμφὶ τὸν πόλεμον. XEN.
They practise the arts of war.
ἀμφί τι (*e.g.* ἵππους, ἅρματα, δεῖπνον, etc.) ἔχειν, εἶναι, διατρίβειν, etc., *to engage in, set about, be concerned with anything.*

PHRASES:

οἱ ἀμφὶ Πρωταγόραν (Πλάτωνα), *the school of Protagoras* (*of Plato*). The phrase (especially in later writers) is a periphrasis for Pythagoras himself.
So οἱ ἀμφὶ Ξέρξεα, *the army of Xerxes,* HEROD., but οἱ ἀμφὶ Μεγαρέας καὶ Φλιασίους (HDT. ix. 69) *the Megarians and Phliasians.*

Less common uses :

(Epic and poetical) ἦλθες ἀμφὶ Δωδώνην, AESCH. *P. V.,* 830, *thou camest nigh* (*about*) *Dodona,* cf. 419 ; μερίμνα δ' ἀμφὶ πόλιν, AESCH. *Sept. c. Theb.* 843 (*care about the city*).

B. WITH GENITIVE (the uses are very rare and wholly Epic, Ionic, and Poetic).

Concerning, cf. περί :

ἀμφὶ σῆς λέγω παιδός, EUR. *Hec.* 580 (*I tell thee of thy child*). Cf. SOPH. *Phil.* 554. AESCH. *Ag.* 67, ἀμφὶ γυναικός (*in the cause of*).

Round about :

HDT. viii. 131 (ἀμφὶ πόλιος οἰκέουσι).

C. WITH DATIVE (wholly Epic, Ionic, and Poetic).

Among :

(ἀμφὶ κλάδοις ἑζόμενα, EUR. *Phoen.* 1518 (*seated among branches*).

Concerning :

ἀμφ' ἐμοὶ στένεις, SOPH. *El.* 1180 (*thou sighest for, about me*).

PHRASES, cf. περί :

ἀμφὶ τάρβει (φόβῳ), prae pavore, *for fear.* In poetry.
As an adverb, *on either side.* Homeric use.

§ 274. 'Επί.

'Επί, *on the surface of, upon, by, to.* Cf. ἐπεί, *then.* Sansk. *api, further, after,* Lat. *ob.* See ἀπό.

A. WITH GENITIVE.

1. OF PLACE:

Upon, with verbs of rest :

πᾶς ὅ τ' ἐπὶ γῆς καὶ ὑπό γῆς χρυσός. PLAT.
All the gold on earth and under the earth.
So ἐφ' ἵππου, very often.

With verbs of motion :

ἔπεμψαν αὐτοὺς ἐπὶ τριήρους. XEN.
They sent them away on board a trireme.

And in *Constructio Praegnans,* ἀναβῆναι ἐπὶ πύργων, XEN., *to climb up, and be on towers.*

Towards (a common use):

οἱ ξύμμαχοι ἀνεχώρησαν ἐπ' οἴκου. THUC.
The allies returned homewards.

Cf. i. 60, ἐπὶ Θρᾴκης.

In, by, near, at:

ἐπὶ νήσου, *in the island;* γῆς ἐπὶ ξένης (SOPH. O. C.), *in a foreign land;* ἐν ἀγορᾷ ἐπὶ τῶν τραπεζῶν, PLAT. *Ap.* 1, *in the market at (by) the tables of the banks;* ἐπὶ δικαστηρίου, ISAE., *in court.*

τὰ ἐπὶ Θρᾴκης, THUC. (see Poppo and Krüger) (*the parts in) the neighbourhood or the district of Thrace or Thracewards.* So ἐπὶ τῆς Λακωνικῆς, v. 34. ἐπὶ τῆς αὐτῶν μένειν, *to remain in their own country*, THUC. iv. 118.

In presence of, coram. Cf. παρά.

ἐξελέγχεσθαι ἐπὶ πάντων. DEM. 781. 4.
To be convicted in presence of all.

2. OF TIME (very common):

ἐπὶ Κύρου βασιλεύοντος, *in the reign of Cyrus;* ἐπὶ Θεμιστοκλέους ἄρχοντος, *in the archonship of Themistocles;* ἐπὶ τῶν πατέρων, *in the time of our fathers;* ἐπ' ἐμοῦ, *in my time;* ὡς ἐπὶ κινδύνου, *as in time of danger* (THUC. vi. 34).

3. FIGURATIVELY:

Set over, engaged in:

ἔμενεν ἐπὶ τῆς ἀρχῆς. XEN.
He was continuing in command.

PHRASES:

So μένειν ἐπί τινος, *to abide by a thing;* ἐπὶ τῶν πραγμάτων (τοῦ πολέμου) εἶναι, *to be engaged in business, in war;* ἐπὶ γνώμης γίγνεσθαι, *to come to an opinion*, DEM. 42. 4.
ὁ ἐπὶ τῶν ὁπλιτῶν (ὅπλων), ἐπὶ τῶν ἱππέων, *the commander of the infantry, cavalry;* ὁ ἐπὶ τῆς διοικήσεως, *the controller of the treasury, paymaster-general.*

Resting, dependent upon, ἐφ' ἑαυτοῦ, etc.:

ἐφ' ἑαυτοῦ, *of* or *by oneself, independently* or *separately, spontaneously*, is a common phrase; ἐφ' ἑαυτοῦ πλεῖν, THUC., *to sail by oneself* or *alone;* ἐφ' ἑαυτοῦ οἰκεῖν,

XEN., *to live apart, separately;* ἐφ' ὑμῶν αὐτῶν βάλλεσθαι, HDT., *to consider by yourselves;* ἐφ' ἑωυτῶν διαλέγονται, HDT., *they speak a language* or *dialect of their own, a distinct dialect;* ἐπ' ἀγκυρέων, *at anchor,* HDT. i. 188.

In the case of:

With λέγω, αἰσθάνομαι, σκοπῶ (*I examine* or *consider*), κρίνω, *I decide* or *judge.*

ἃ ἐπὶ τῶν ἄλλων ὁρᾶτε, ταῦτ' ἐφ' ὑμῶν αὐτῶν ἀγνοεῖτε.
Is. viii. 114.
What you see in (the case of) others, that you are ignorant of in your own case.

So ἐπ' ἐμοῦ λέγειν, PLAT. *Rep.* 475, *to speak in my own case, to take myself as an instance;* ἐπὶ πάντων ὁμοίως, *in all cases alike.*

Called after:

κεκλῆσθαι, ὀνομασθῆναι ἐπί τινος (HDT.), *to be named after a person;* ἡ εἰρήνη ἡ ἐπὶ 'Ανταλκίδου, DEM., *the peace of Antalcidas.*
ἐπί ὀνόματος εἶναι, *to bear a name,* DEM. 1000. 21.

Military phrases:

ἐτάχθησαν ἐπὶ τεττάρων. XEN. *An.* i. 2. 15.
They were drawn up four deep.
Generally of the *depth*, sometimes of the *length*, of a line.
ἐπὶ πεντήκοντα ἀσπίδων συνεστραμμένοι.
XEN. *Hell.* vi. 4. 12.
Massed in column fifty shields deep.
τὸ μέτωπον ἐπὶ τριακοσίων, τὸ δὲ βάθος ἐφ' ἑκατόν.
XEN. *Cyr.* ii. 4. 2.
The length of the line was four hundred, its depth one hundred.
ἐφ' ἑνός, *in single file;* ἐπ' ὀλίγων τάσσεσθαι, *to be drawn up in a long line* (or *a shallow column*) (XEN. and THUC.).
πλεῖν ἐπὶ κέρως (cf. Accus.), *to sail in column (towards the wing),* (κατὰ μίαν ἐπὶ κέρως, THUC. ii. 19, *in single file*).

Miscellaneous phrases :

ἐπὶ τοῦ εὐωνύμου, ἐπὶ τῶν πλευρῶν, *on the left, on the flanks.*

ἐπὶ πάντων, DEM., *on all occasions ;* ἐφ' ἑκάστων, PLAT., *on each occasion.*

ἐπὶ τελευτῆς, *at last ;* ἐπὶ σχολῆς, *at leisure, leisurely ;* ἐπ' ἴσης, *equally* (SOPH. *El.* 1061); ἐπὶ προφάσιος, HDT., *as a pretext ;* ἐπὶ ὅρκου, *on oath* (HDT. ix. 11); ἐπὶ προςπόλου μιᾶς, *dependent on one handmaid,* SOPH. *O. C.* 746.

B. WITH THE DATIVE.

[The uses should be compared with those of the Genitive. They often run closely parallel. 'Επί with Dative, meaning *upon,* is commoner in Prose than with the Genitive; the poets use both cases indifferently. 'Επί with the Dative implies closer connection than ἐπί with Genitive.]

1. OF PLACE :

Over, on :

οἱ Θρᾷκες ἀλωπεκίδας ἐπὶ ταῖς κεφαλαῖς φοροῦσι.
XEN.

The Thracians wear fox-skin caps (fitted to) on their heads. Cf. EUR. *Bacch.* 757.

N.B. ἐφ' ἵππῳ must not be used for ἐφ' ἵππον.

τοὺς ὁπλίτας ἐπὶ ναυσὶν ὀλίγαις εὐθὺς πέμπουσιν.
THUC. ii. 80 (cf. iv. 10).
They at once despatch the hoplites in (on board) a few ships.

Against :

αἱ νῆες ἐφ' ἡμῖν τετάχαται. THUC. iii. 13 (cf. iv. 70).
The ships are drawn up against us.

Cf. SOPH. *Ai.* 51, ἐπ' ὄμμασι βάλλειν (Constr. Praegn.).

In, at, near, by :

οἰκέοντες ἐπὶ Στρύμονι, HDT., *living on the shores of,* or *near, the Strymon.*

οἱ τῶν ἀρίστων Περσῶν παῖδες ἐπὶ ταῖς βασιλέως θύραις παιδεύονται. XEN. *An.* i. 9. 3.
The sons of the noblest Persians are brought up at (close by) the king's gate (at the " Sublime Porte ").
Cf. SOPH. *Tr.* 1100, *Phil.* 353.

Next after :

τὰ ἐπὶ τούτοις, *the next step.*
Cf. HOM. *Od.* vii. 216, οὐ γάρ τι στυγερῇ ἐπὶ γαστέρι κύντερον ἄλλο, *naught more blatant next to (than) the belly.*

οἱ ἐπὶ πᾶσιν, *the rear;* ὀλίγοι τῶν ἐπὶ πᾶσιν ὑπὸ τῶν ψιλῶν ἀπέθανον, *few of the rear were slain by the light-armed,* XEN. *Hell.* i. 1. 34.

2. OF TIME (rarely):

Generally of succession, after, or following :

ἕκτῃ ἐπὶ δεκάτῃ or τῇ ἕκτῃ ἐπὶ δέκα.
DEM. 279. 18, 288. 29.
On the 16th of the month (sixth after the tenth).

Near, about (very rare in Attic):

ἦν ἥλιος ἐπὶ δυσμαῖς. XEN. *An.* vii. 3. 34.
It was near sunset (the sun was at his setting).

3. FIGURATIVELY :

Set over and actively engaged in :

τοὺς ἐπὶ τοῖς πράγμασιν ὄντας αἰτιῶνται. DEM.
They accuse those who are engaged in public affairs.

So οἱ ἐπὶ ταῖς μηχαναῖς, ἐπὶ τοῖς καμήλοις, XEN., *those in guard of the engines, the camels,* etc.

Generally at, in, of circumstances :

ἐπὶ τῷ παρόντι, THUC. ii. 36, *on the present occasion (to speak)* ; ἐπὶ τῷ δείπνῳ, XEN., *at supper.*

With : (by no means an infrequent use).

Cf. EUR. *Bacch.*, ἐπ᾽ εὐάσμασι, *with joyous shouts* (cf. 1368).
Cf. also SOPH. *Ant.* 556, ἐπ᾽ ἀρρήτοις λόγοις, *with words unspoken.* ἐπ᾽ ἐξειργασμένοις, *when a deed is done and over,* AESCH. *Ag.* 1379, SOPH. *Ai.* 377, EUR. *Bacch.* 1039.

In reference to, in case of, connected with:

νόμον τιθέναι ἐπί τινι, PLAT., *to make a law for, in the case of, a person* (*for* or *against him*); so νόμος κεῖται ἐπί τινι, DEM.

τὸ ἐπὶ τῷ σώματι κάλλος, PLAT., *beauty of person*.

Upon, i.e. *accumulated on, added to*:

πήματα ἐπὶ πήμασιν πίπτοντα. SOPH. *Ant*. 595.
Woes falling on woes.

So ἐπὶ τούτοις, *thereupon, on this*, very frequently in Attic.

Hence probably phrases connected with meals: ἐπὶ τῷ σίτῳ πίνειν ὕδωρ, XEN., *to drink water with one's food*.

Dependent upon, in power of, with εἰμι *and* γίγνομαι:

εἰ ἐπὶ τοῖς πολεμίοις ἐγένοντο τί ἂν ἔπαθον ;
XEN. *An*. v. 8. 17.
If they had fallen into the hands of the enemy, what would have been their fate ?

τὸ ἐπ' ἐμοί, τὸ ἐπὶ σοί, *so far as in my, thy, power*.
Cf. Acc. τὸ ἐπὶ σφᾶς εἶναι.

(*Be named*) *after, on the ground of*:

ἐπὶ τῇ ἔχθρᾳ στάσις κέκληται, PLAT. *Rep*. 470, see Stallbaum and references there, *sedition is so called from* (*intestine*) *hatred*.

Causal, with words of emotion, at, for, because of:

ἐπί τινι μάλιστα ἀγάλλῃ ; XEN.
In what do you most take delight ?

So with χαίρω, *I rejoice*; σεμνύνομαι, *I pride myself,* δυσχεραίνω, *I am vexed*, etc., and corresponding adjectives, and substantives such as ἔπαινος, φιλοτιμία, etc.
So ζημιοῦσθαι ἐπί τινι, DEM., *to be fined for a thing*.

Condition :
ἐπὶ τούτῳ ὑπεξίσταμαι τῆς ἀρχῆς. HEROD.
On this condition I resign my command.
So very often ἐπὶ τούτῳ, ἐπὶ τούτοις, ἐφ' ᾧ (τε), ἐπ' οὐδενί, ἐπὶ τοῖς εἰρημένοις, *on the conditions expressed.*

Motive :
ψεύδεται τε καὶ ἐπὶ τῇ ἐμῇ διαβολῇ λέγει.
PLAT. *Apol.* v.
He is lying, and is speaking with a view to prejudice you against me.
ἐπὶ κακουργίᾳ, THUC. i. 37, *for knavish purposes;* οὐκ ἐπὶ ὑβρίζεσθαι ἀλλ' ἐπὶ τῷ ἡγεμόνες εἶναι, THUC. i. 38, *not in order to be insulted, but in order to be rulers;* ἐπὶ τῷ κέρδει, XEN. *for gain;* ἐπὶ σοφίᾳ, *to get wisdom,* PLAT.
N.B. In PLAT. *Prot.* 358 B, with Gen., ἐπὶ τοῦ ἀλύπως ζῆν, *with a view to living a painless life;* Liddell and Scott.

The reward or price :
ξυγγενέσθαι Ὁμήρῳ ἐπὶ πόσῳ (sc. μισθῷ) ἄν τις δέξαιτο ;
PLAT. *Apol.* xxxii.
For what price would any of you be willing to meet Homer?
So ἐπὶ δραχμῇ δανείζειν, DEM. 816. 12.
To lend money at twelve per cent. See *Dict. of Antiq.*
ἐπὶ ἀνδραπόδοις δανείζειν. DEM. 822. 8.
To lend money on the security of slaves (i.e. *to hold a mortgage on the slaves*).

PHRASES :
λέγειν ἐπί τινι, *to speak in any one's praise (perhaps over the body of).* AESCH. *Ag.* 1400.

C. WITH ACCUSATIVE (1) *Direction to,* or (2) *Extension over.*

DIRECTION :

Upon :
δεῖ ἀναβῆναι ἐπὶ τὸν ἵππον. XEN.
He must mount (on) his horse.

To :
προτρέπετε τοὺς νεωτέρους ἐπ' ἀρετήν. Is. 3. 57.
Urge the younger to (the pursuit of) virtue.

As far as :
ἡ ἀρχὴ ἡ 'Οδρυσῶν ἐπὶ θάλασσαν καθήκει. Thuc. ii. 97.
The kingdom of the Odrysae stretches as far as the sea.
(See Phrases.)

Against :
οὐκ εἰκὸς ἀρχὴν ἐπὶ ἀρχὴν στρατεῦσαι. Thuc.
It is not likely that empire will advance against empire.

For, for purpose of :
ἔπλεον οὐχ ὡς ἐπὶ ναυμαχίαν. Thuc.
They were sailing not as though for the purpose of a sea-fight.

To fetch :
πέμπουσιν ἐπὶ Δημοσθένην καὶ ἐπὶ τὰς εἴκοσι ναῦς.
Thuc. iii. 105.
They send for Demosthenes and for the twenty ships.
So καλεῖν ἐπὶ δεῖπνον, *to summon to supper.*

Extension :
Over, in space or time :
τὸ ὄμμα δύναται ἐπὶ πολλὰ στάδια ἐξικνεῖσθαι. Xen.
The eye (sight) can reach over many stades.
ἐθύετο ἐπὶ τρεῖς ἡμέρας. Xen.
He was sacrificing for the space of three days.

Phrases: (1) Direction.
ἐπὶ πᾶν ἐλθεῖν, *to come to an extremity, try every means;*
ἐπὶ τὸ μεῖζον κοσμεῖν, *to exaggerate (be extravagant in embellishing),* Thuc. i. 21. (Cf. viii. 74.)

To produce (of a purpose) :
ἐπὶ τὰ γελοιότερα, Plat., *to raise a laugh.* So ἐπὶ τὰ αἰσχίονα (καλλίω, τὸ βέλτιον, τὸ ἀμεῖνον), *changing to, resulting in, something worse (better, etc.).*

PREPOSITIONS WITH ALL THREE CASES. 327

τὸ ἐπί:
τὸ ἐπί τινα, τοὐπ' ἐμέ, τοὐπί σε, Trag., as regards me, thee; τὸ ἐπὶ σφᾶς εἶναι, Thuc. iv. 28, so far as regards them.

Military Phrases:
ἐπὶ δόρυ ἀναστρέψαι, to face to the spear (the right); ἐπ' ἀσπίδα ἀναστρέψαι, to face to the shield (the left); ἐπί πόδα ἀναχωρεῖν, to retire on the foot (with the face to the enemy); ἐπὶ κέρας πλεῖν, to sail towards or on the wing (in column). Cf. Gen.
ἐπὶ δεξιά, ἐπ' ἀριστερά, to the right, to the left; ἐπὶ τάδε, on this side; ἐπ' ἀμφότερα, both ways; ἐπ' ἐκεῖνα (ἐπεκεῖνα), on the yonder side, beyond, ultra; ἐπὶ τὰ ἕτερα, ἐπὶ θάτερα, on the other side.

PHRASES: (2) EXTENSION.

Up to, as far as to:
ἐπὶ διηκόσια ἀποδιδόναι, to yield two hundred fold, Hdt. i. 193; ἐφ' ὅσον δεῖ, so far as is necessary; ἐπὶ σμικρόν, ἐπὶ βραχύ, ἐπ' ὀλίγον, ἐπὶ πλέον, etc., to a slight, to a greater extent, a little way, etc.
ἐπὶ πολύ (ἐπιπολύ), over a large extent or space; ἐπὶ πλεῖστον ἀνθρώπων (extending to or over) the greater part of mankind, Thuc. i. 1. Cf. ἐπὶ πλεῖστον ὁμίλου, ii. 34.
ἐπὶ τὸ πολύ, for the most part, Aristot.

Time:
ἐπὶ πολὺν χρόνον, for a long time; ἐπὶ χρόνον τινά, ἐπὶ τρίς, Act. Ap. x. 16. See Liddell and Scott, τρίς and ἐς τρίς.

IN COMPOSITION:

(1) *Upon, over,* ἐπίκειμαι, *I lie upon;* ἐπιπλέω, *I sail over;* ἐποίχομαι, *I go over, survey.* (2) *To,* i.e. *for,* ἐπινεύω, *I nod assent to.* (3) *To,* i.e. *against,* ἐπιστρατεύω, *I march against.* (4) *In* addition, ἐπιδίδωμι, *I give in addition;* ἐπίτριτος, *with a third added to one,* i.e. 1⅓. (5) *Causally, over, at,* ἐπιχαίρω, *I rejoice at.* (6) *Of* time, *after,* ἐπιγίγνομαι, *I am born after, succeed.* (7) From the joint notion of *advancing* and *addition* such words as ἐπιγαμία, *right of intermarriage;* cf. ἐπινομία, ἐπεργασία.

§ 275. Παρά.

Παρά (παραί, πάρ), *by the side of, to the side of* (the primitive notion being that of *going through* or *crossing*). Sansk. *pará*, *away and towards*, Lat. *per*, Eng. *from* (Goth. *fra, fram*). Παρά and περί are related forms from the root PAR, to *fare* or *go through*.

A. WITH GENITIVE,[1] *coming* or *proceeding from* (but originally *aside, at the side*, or *sideways from*).

Coming from :
> ἐξελθεῖν παρά τινος, *to come from a person's house, or country, or court.*
> γίγνεσθαι παρά τινος, PL. *Symp.* 179 B, *to be born of* or *sprung from.*
> ἔχειν παρά τινος (DEM.), *to receive from;* μανθάνειν παρά (EUR.), *to learn from.*

The Agent with passive verbs :
> παρά τινος δίδοσθαι, λέγεσθαι, συμβουλεύεσθαι, *to be given, said, advised by any one.*

Periphrastically for the Genitive, etc. :
> αἱ παρὰ τῶν δήμων δωρεαί. DEM. 20. 15. *The gifts of democracies.*
> So ἡ παρά τινος εὔνοια, τὸ παρ' ἐμοῦ ἀδίκημα (*the wrong done by me*), XEN.

PHRASES:
> οἱ παρά τινος, *one's friends, dependants, messengers, etc.*, THUC. and XEN.; τὰ παρά τινος, *one's commands, purposes, opinions;* παρ' ἑαυτοῦ διδόναι, *to give of one's resources,* or *spontaneously;* παρ' ἐμοῦ, PL. *Prot.* 322 D, *by my advice.*

---

[1] The Genitive with παρά appears to represent the Ablative; thus παραχωρεῖν τοῦ βήματος would first have meant *to move sideways from the tribune.*

B. With Dative, *by the side of, near, by, with.* (Of persons, seldom of places, παρά σοι, *at your side.*)

Among, with:
παρ' ὑμῖν ἐτράφην, AESCHIN., *I was brought up among you.*
καταλύειν παρά τινι, DEM., *to lodge with any one,* chez quelqu'un.

Belonging to:
τὸ μὲν χρυσίον παρὰ τούτῳ, οἱ δὲ κίνδυνοι παρ' ὑμῖν.
AESCHIN. iii. 240.
This man gets the gold, you the dangers.

In presence of:
εἰς κρίσιν καθιστάναι τινὰ παρά τινι. THUC., DEM.
To bring any one to trial before another.

In the judgment of:
παρὰ τοῖς φρονοῦσιν εὐδοκιμεῖν. Is. 9. 74.
To be in good repute with sensible people.
So παρ' ἐμοί, me iudice. παρὰ σαυτῷ, PLAT.

PHRASES:
οἱ παρ' ἐμοί (ἡμῖν), *my own people;* τὰ παρ' ἐμοί, *my affairs.*

C. With the Accusative:
1. Motion *to* (with persons, παρά σε, *to your side*), with verbs of motion.
2. Motion or extension *alongside,* with verbs of rest.
3. Parallelism and comparison, *side by side,* figuratively.

I. OF PLACE:
1. *Motion to:*
ἔπεμψαν παρ' Ἀθηναίους πρέσβεις. THUC.
They sent envoys to the Athenians.
εἰσιέναι, φοιτᾶν παρά τινα, *to enter, go to any one's house.*
Cf. Genitive and Dative.

2. *Extension along or beside:*
ἡ παρὰ θάλασσαν Μακεδονία. THUC.
The seaboard of Macedonia. Cf. XEN. *An.* iii. 5. 1,
SOPH. *El.* 183.

3. *Parallelism and Comparison:*
Side by side (with verbs of examining):
παρ' ἄλληλα ἔσται φανερώτατα. DEM.
Set side by side they will be most conspicuous.
παρ' ὄμμα, *before one's eyes,* EUR. *Supp.* 484.

Compared with (often implying superiority):
μεγάλη ῥοπὴ ἡ τυχὴ παρὰ πάντα τὰ τῶν ἀνθρώπων
πράγματα. DEM. 2. 22.
Fortune is a mighty makeweight compared with all human influences. Cf. XEN. *Apol.* i. 4. 14 (so used especially with comparatives).

Beyond and contrary to, opposed to κατά:
Many phrases: παρὰ δύναμιν, *beyond one's strength.*
παρὰ τὸ δίκαιον, τὰς σπονδάς, τοὺς νόμους, φύσιν, γνώμην,
δόξαν (λόγον), *contrary to,* or *in violation of, justice, the treaty, the laws, nature, opinion, expectation* (praeter opinionem, spem).

Note. Several peculiar and much debated constructions occur with παρά and the Accusative.

CAUSAL:
Owing to, in consequence of, cf. διά with Accusative.
ἕκαστος οὐ παρὰ τὴν ἑαυτοῦ ἀμελείαν οἴεται βλάψειν τὴν
πόλιν, THUC. i. 141, *each man imagines that he will not in consequence of his own neglect injure the state.* Cf.
DEM. *Phil.* i. 41, παρὰ τὴν ἑαυτοῦ ῥώμην.

Besides, in addition to:

οὐκ ἔστι παρὰ ταῦτ' ἄλλα, ARIST. *Nub.* 698, *there's nothing else besides this;* παρὰ ταῦτα πάντα ἕτερόν τι, PL. *Phaed.* xix., *besides all this something quite different;* πληγὴ παρὰ πληγήν, AR. *Ran.* 643, *blow for blow* (implying alternation).

II. OF TIME :

During :

τὸν δόλιον ἄνδρα φεῦγε παρ' ὅλον τὸν βίον.
MENAND.
Avoid a cunning man thy whole life long.

So παρὰ πάντα τὸν χρόνον, παρὰ πότον, AESCHIN., inter potandum. Cf. Lat. *per totam vitam*.

At the moment of :

παρὰ τοιοῦτον καιρόν, DEM., *at such a moment;* παρ' αὐτὰ τἀδικήματα, DEM. 21. 26, *at the very moment of the wrong-doing*, flagrante delicto. Cf. ἐπ' αὐτοφώρῳ, *in the very act*.

Note 1. παρ' ἡμέραν is generally taken to mean *on each alternate day*. See SOPH. *Ai*. 475. Lobeck and Jebb consider that it rather means *day by day, as each day comes*. The phrase occurs in DEM. viii. 70. In SOPH. *O. C.* 1455, παρ' ἦμαρ αὖθις appears to mean *on the following day*. παρὰ μῆνα τρίτον, ARISTOT., *every third month*.

Note 2. παρά (*motion to*), in certain phrases denoting the limit reached, is used of *excess* or *defect*, and so describes the *difference* of two things.

παρὰ τοσοῦτον ἡ Μυτιλήνη ἦλθε κινδύνου. THUC. iii. 49.
Mitylene came within such a distance of danger.

Cf. THUC. vii. 2, vi. 37 (παρὰ τοσοῦτον γιγνώσκω, *so much within the mark is my opinion*); iv. 106, παρὰ νύκτα ἐγένετο λαβεῖν, *came within a night of taking*, i.e. *one night only stood in the way of taking*.

To this construction belong a great many phrases, *e.g.* παρὰ μικρόν, πολύ, ὀλίγον, βραχύ ἐλθεῖν, γενέσθαι, ἀποφεύγειν, νικᾶν, *to come within a little, to have a narrow etc. escape, to win a narrow or a hollow victory.* Similarly παρ' οὐδέν, μικρόν, ὀλίγον ποιεῖσθαι, ἄγειν, θέσθαι, εἶναι, *to hold of no, little, account, be of little account.*

IN COMPOSITION:

(1) Alongside, παρίστημι, *I set alongside;* παραβάλλομαι, *I expose or stake;* παράλληλος, *beside one another.* Hence (2) of *alternation,* παραλλάσσω, *I make alternate.* (3) *Aside, beside the mark, amiss,* παραβαίνω, *I transgress.*

§ 276. Περί.

Περί, *round about, beyond, over, very* (cf. adverbial use). Cf. πέρι-ξ, *round about;* περισσός, *excessive;*—περ, *however much.* Sansk. *pari, round about,* Lat. *per(magnus).* See παρά.

Compare throughout with ἀμφί.

A. WITH GENITIVE.

In prose the meanings are figurative: the local use is Epic and poetical (cf. EUR. *Tro.* 818).

The Object for *or* about *which :*

ἀγωνίζεσθε πάντες περὶ ἀρετῆς. XEN.
Strive all of you after excellence.

So ὁ ἀγών (ὁ κίνδυνος, etc.) περὶ ψυχῆς (περὶ τῶν μεγίστων) ἐστί, *the struggle is for life (for the highest objects).*

With verbs of caring, thinking, fearing, etc.:

μέλει μοι, βουλεύομαι, φοβοῦμαι περί τινος, *I care etc. for a thing.*

Also of saying and hearing :

ἀγγέλλω, λέγω, ἀκούω, μέμνημαι περί τινος.

The use of these verbs with περί should be compared with the use of the simple Genitive in Epic and in Poetry.

PHRASES:

ἐμπείρως ἔχειν περί τινος, AESCHIN., *to be experienced in a thing.* (Cf. XEN. *An.* vi. 2. 1. Genitive without περί.)

PREPOSITIONS WITH ALL THREE CASES. 333

Periphrastically:

αἱ περὶ Ἡρακλέους πράξεις, PLAT., *the deeds of Heracles.*

ποιεῖσθαι, ἡγεῖσθαί τι περὶ πολλοῦ (σμικροῦ, οὐδένος, παντός), *to esteem a thing highly*, etc. περί here contains the old meaning *beyond*, cf. περιγίγνομαι, *I get beyond,* i.e. *I surpass, excel.*

B. WITH DATIVE.

Comparatively rare in Prose: in a local sense the Dative denotes a closer connexion than the Genitive, cf. ἐπί with Genitive and Dative.

Close round, around and upon ; the literal meaning leads on to the figurative:

εἶδε περὶ τῇ χειρί τοῦ νεκροῦ χρυσοῦν δακτύλιον.
PLAT.
He saw round the finger of the corpse a golden ring.

A good example in XEN. *An.* vii. 4. 4, περὶ τοῖς στέρνοις, etc.

κεῖται δὲ νεκρὸς περὶ νεκρῷ. SOPH. *Ant.* 1244.
He lieth dead, clasping close the dead.

Transfixed by a weapon:

Common in HOMER (so ἀμφί, *Od.* xii. 395).

πεπτῶτα τῷδε περὶ νεορράντῳ ξίφει. SOPH. *Ai.* 828.
Fallen upon this new-reeking sword.

The Object about which, very rare in Prose (cf. Gen.):

περὶ τῇ Σικελίᾳ ἔσται ὁ ἀγών. THUC. vi. 34.
The struggle will be for Sicily.
See Poppo.

περὶ τῷ χωρίῳ ἔδεισαν. THUC. i. 67.
They feared for (about) the place.

Cf. PLAT. *Prot.* 314 A, περὶ τοῖς φιλτάτοις: *Phaed.* 114 D, περὶ τῷ σώματι.

The cause (poetical). Cf. ἀμφί:

περὶ φόβῳ, περὶ τάρβει, περὶ χάρματι. (In Poetry.)
For fear, for terror, for joy.

C. WITH ACCUSATIVE.
[*Motion round about, Epic.*]

1. OF PLACE, the literal meaning sometimes running into the Figurative :

   Rest round about, near, at, by, in :
   οἱ ἔφηβοι κοιμῶνται περὶ τὰ ἀρχεῖα. XEN.
   The Ephebi sleep by (in the neighbourhood of) the town-hall.
   καὶ τῆς κεφαλῆς κατέαγε περὶ λίθον πεσών.
   AR. *Ach.* 1180.
   And he fell on a stone and has cracked his crown.
   Cf. DEM. 21. 4, περὶ αὑτά καταρρεῖν.
   Fall in ruins (lit. *about themselves*).
   So THUC. vii. 23, περὶ ἀλλήλας ταραχθεῖσαι.
   Cf. the Dative, περί ξίφει, etc.
   ἡ περὶ Λέσβον ναυμαχία. XEN. *Hell.* ii. 3. 22.
   The sea-fight off Lesbos.

2. TIME :

   About or *near, with numbers :*
   ἤδη ἦν περὶ πλήθουσαν ἀγοράν. XEN.
   It was now near full-market hour.
   So περὶ τούτους τοὺς χρόνους. THUC.
   About this period, or *time.*
   περί ἑβδομήκοντα, THUC. i. 54, *about seventy.*

3. FIGURATIVELY :

   Be busied about, engaged in. Cf. ἀμφί :
   With εἶναι, γίγνεσθαι, διατρίβειν, σπουδάζειν
   ὄντι αὐτῷ περὶ ταῦτα ὁ Εὐρυμέδων ἀπαντᾷ. THUC. vii. 31.
   While he was engaged in this Eurymedon met him.
   See Phrases below.

   Towards, i.e. *with reference to :*
   περὶ τὸν θεὸν ἀσεβοῦσιν. ANTIPH.
   They are impious with regard to (in *their dealings with,* or *duty towards) the god.*

PREPOSITIONS WITH ALL THREE CASES.

With Verbs:

So εὐσεβεῖν
ἁμαρτάνειν
σωφρονεῖν
σπουδάζειν
} περί τινα, or τι.

With Adjectives:

πονηρός,
ἀγαθός,
etc.,
} περί τι
bad
good
} in the matter of.

ἀγαθός περὶ τὴν πόλιν.
Good as regards the state, i.e. *a patriotic citizen*.

With Substantives, Periphrasis for Genitive or Adjective:

οἱ νόμοι οἱ περὶ τοὺς γάμους, PLAT. *Crito*, 50 D, *the laws which relate to marriage, marriage laws;* οἱ περὶ Λυσίαν λόγοι, PLAT. *Phaedr.* 279 A, *the speeches of Lysias;* ἡ περὶ Φίλιππον τυραννίς, XEN. *Hell.* v. 4. 2, *Philip's despotism;* τὰ περὶ τὰς ναῦς, THUC. i. 3, *naval affairs;* τὰ περὶ Κῦρον, HDT. i. 95, *the deeds* or *history of Cyrus*.

PHRASES:

οἱ περί τινα, *a person's retinue or suite;* οἱ περὶ Ἡράκλειτον, PLAT., *the school of Heracleitus;* οἱ περὶ Ἀρχίαν πολέμαρχοι, XEN., *Archias and his fellow-polemarchs*.

οἱ περὶ μουσικήν, φιλοσοφίαν, τὴν ποίησιν, τοὺς λόγους ὄντες.
Those engaged in music, philosophy, poetry, oratory; musicians, philosophers, poets, orators.

ὁ περὶ τὸν ἵππον. XEN.
The groom.

πέρι, after its case (Anastrophe), is found in THUC. and PLAT. Once in PLATO, *Leg.* 809 E, it is put far from its case, something like a German separable particle. (See Liddell and Scott.)

IN COMPOSITION:

Around, beyond, exceedingly, περιβάλλω, *I put around;* περιπίπτω, *I fall around, embrace, fall foul of, into;* περιγίγνομαι, *I get beyond, excel, survive, escape;* περιχαρής, *exceedingly glad.*

§ 277. Πρός.

Πρός (Ep. and Dor. προτί, ποτί), *towards, to, in front of, before, opposite, beside*. Sansk. *prati, towards*, Eng. *forth-with*. Προ-τί is formed from πρό.
Cf. πρόσ-θεν, *in front*.

A. With Genitive,[1] generally of *direction towards*, or *with reference to*, without implied motion.

Towards:
In presence or in sight of:
  ὅ τι δίκαιόν ἐστι καὶ πρὸς θεῶν καὶ πρὸς ἀνθρώπων
              Xen.
  Whatever is right in the sight of gods and men.

  τὸ πρὸς Σικυῶνος τεῖχος ἐξετείχισαν. Xen.
  They completed the wall which faced Sicyon.

A very common usage in prose and poetry (the verb, such as εἶναι or κεῖσθαι, is readily understood).

So in *entreaties*:
  πρὸς νύν σε πατρός, πρός τε μητρός, ὦ τέκνον,
  ἱκέτης ἱκνοῦμαι.   Soph.
  Now by thy father, by thy mother, boy,
  Suppliant I supplicate thee.

Note. A very common use. Observe (1) that σε is often inserted thus, πρός σε πατρός, cf. *per te deos oro*; (2) the verb is often omitted, πρὸς Διός, πρὸς θεῶν, μὴ πρὸς γενείου, μὴ πρός σε γούνων.

On the side of:
  Ἀλκιβιάδης λέγεται πρὸς πατρὸς Ἀλκμαιοιδῶν εἶναι. Dem.
  Alcibiades is said to have been descended from the Alcmaeonidae on the father's side.

---

[1] Observe that the Genitive with πρός is a genuine Genitive and not a representative of the lost Ablative,—connection, not separation, being denoted.

Cf. SOPH. *Ai.* 1305, τοὺς πρὸς αἵματος, *blood relations.* Cf. SOPH. *El.* 1125 and 1075 (τὰ πρὸς τέκνων).

Belonging to (periphrastically for Genitive alone):

οὐ πρὸς ἰατροῦ σοφοῦ
θρηνεῖν ἐπῳδὰς πρὸς τομῶντι πήματι. SOPH.
*'Tis not a wise physician's part
To mumble spells o'er sore that needs the knife.*

So πρὸς γυναικός, *like a woman,* etc.

And with qualities, πρὸς δίκης, *in accordance with justice.* SOPH. *O. T.* 1014; οὐ πρὸς τῆς ὑμετέρας δόξης, THUC. iii. 59, *it does not accord with your reputation.*

In favour of:

πρὸς τῶν ἐχόντων Φοῖβε τὸν νόμον τίθης. EUR.
Thou makest this law in favour of the rich, Phoebus.

On the part of, at the hand of:

ἐπαίνου τεύξεται πρὸς γοῦν ἐμοῦ. SOPH.
He shall meet with praise at least from me.

The agent with Verbs and Adjectives (very common in Ionic and in poetry):

Κῦρος ὁμολογεῖται πρὸς πάντων κράτιστος γενέσθαι.
XEN. *An.* i. ix. 20.
Cyrus is admitted by all to have been most excellent.

Cf. AESCH. *P. V.* 650, SOPH. *An.* 919 (ἔρημος πρὸς φίλων). Cf. *El.* 562 (with a Substantive).

In poetry also, rarely, of things. SOPH. *El.* 1236.

B. WITH DATIVE.

Near or beside, in rest:

οἱ ποταμοὶ πρὸς ταῖς πηγαῖς οὐ μεγάλοι εἰσίν. XEN
Rivers near their sources are not big.

SOPH. *O. T.* 1169, πρὸς τῷ δεινῷ, *on the brink of horror.*

In presence of:

In Demosthenes: πρὸς τοῖς κριταῖς, *in the presence of the jurymen:* πρὸς τοῖς θεσμοθέταις, etc. (λέγειν).

Engaged in :
πρὸς τῷ εἰρημένῳ λόγῳ ἦν ὁ Σωκράτης.
  PLAT. *Phaed.* xxxv. 84 C.
Socrates was absorbed in the conversation held.
Cf. totus erat in sermone. HOR. *Sat.* i. 9. 2.
Note. A frequent prose usage : εἶναι, γίγνεσθαι, διατρίβειν, τὴν γνώμην ἔχειν πρός τινι.

In addition to :
πρὸς τοῖς παροῦσιν ἄλλα προςλαβεῖν θέλεις.
  AESCH.
In addition to thy present woes thou wouldst add other woes.
πρὸς τοῖς ἄλλοις, *in addition to the rest.*
So constantly πρὸς τούτοις, praeterea, *in addition to, besides this,* seldom πρὸς τούτῳ.

C. WITH ACCUSATIVE :
1. (i) Direction towards, or to, implying motion.
    (ii) Relation to or connection with (a very free and post-Epic usage).

Towards, to, literally and figuratively :
ἔφυγον πρὸς τὴν γῆν. XEN.
They fled to the shore.
ἡ φιλοτιμία παροξύνει πρὸς τὰ καλά. XEN.
Ambition spurs to noble aims.

With verbs of speaking :
εἰρήσεται πρὸς ὑμᾶς πᾶσα ἡ ἀλήθεια. DEM.
The whole truth shall be told you (*spoken out before you*).
Very commonly, εἰπεῖν, λέγειν, φράζειν, ἀποκρίνεσθαι πρός τινα. SOPH. *El.* 640, πρὸς φῶς (to proclaim), *publicly, in broad daylight,* in luce.
  λέγειν πρός τινα, *to speak in reply,* adversus aliquem.
  λέγειν κατά τινος, *to speak against* (in accusation of), in aliquem.

With verbs of considering :
λογίσασθε πρὸς ὑμᾶς αὐτοὺς τί συμβήσεται. DEM.
Consider with yourselves what will happen.
So ἐνθυμεῖσθαι, ἀναμνησθῆναι περί τινος. Cf. SOPH. *El.* 285.
αὐτὴ πρὸς αὐτήν, *alone by myself.*

Of dealings with :
σπονδὰς (συνθήκας) ποιοῦμαι πρός τινα, *I make a truce, treaty with.*
So ξυμμαχία, φιλία, ἔχθρα, ἀπιστία, πόλεμος πρός τινα.
πρὸς τοὺς δικαστάς, *in the presence of the jury.*

Against :
πρὸς τοὺς Μήδους ἐγένοντο ἀγαθοί. THUC. i. 86.
They proved themselves brave men against the Medes.
Cf. XEN. *Cyr.* ii. 3. 13.
πρὸς κέντρα μὴ λάκτιζε. *Prov.*—*Kick not against the pricks.*

Generally, with reference to :
οὐδὲν αὐτῷ πρὸς τὴν πόλιν ἐστί. DEM. 528. 16.
He has nothing to do with the city.
ἀσφαλῶς ἔχειν πρός τι, XEN., *to feel safe or comfortable about.*

MISCELLANEOUS PHRASES :

With a purpose:
χρὴ πρὸς τὸ παρὸν ἀεὶ βουλεύεσθαι. ISOC.
We should ever deliberate with an eye to the present.
So ἕτοιμος, χρήσιμος, ἱκανός πρός τι, *ready, etc., for a purpose.*

According to :
πρὸς ἄλλον ζῆν, DEM., *to live according to the standard of another.*
πρὸς τὴν δύναμιν, *according to one's ability* (pro viribus).
πρὸς τὰς τύχας (EUR. *Hipp.* 701), *suited to one's fortunes.*

In consequence of, on hearing :
χαλεπαίνειν πρός τι. THUC. *To be annoyed on hearing.*
ἀθύμως ἔχειν πρός τι. *To be despondent.*
πρὸς ταύτην τὴν φήμην. HDT. Ad hanc famam.

πρὸς ταῦτα :
πρὸς τί; *wherefore?* πρὸς ταῦτα, *therefore*.

Sometimes introducing a defiance or challenge, *so then* e.g. SOPH. O. T. 455.

Compared with :
πολλὴ ἂν εἴη ἀπιστία τῆς δυνάμεως πρὸς τὸ κλέος αὐτῶν.
THUC. i. 10.
There would be a strong disbelief in their power as compared with their reputation.
Cf. HDT. iii. 34: also iii. 94 (implying superiority), and iii. 94 (τὸ μέσον πρός, *the mean between*).
πέντε πρὸς τρία, ARISTOT. *Five to three.*

Exchange :
ἡδονὰς πρὸς ἡδονὰς καὶ λύπας πρὸς λύπας καὶ φόβον πρὸς φόβον καταλλάττεσθαι. PLAT. *Phaed.* xiii. 69 A.
To exchange pleasures with pleasures, pains with pains, and fear with fear.
Cf. HOM. *Il.* vi. 235.

2. *Of* TIME (a rare use), *towards, near, about :*
πρὸς ἑσπέραν, *drawing towards evening :* πρὸς ἠῶ, *towards daybreak.* PLAT. and XEN.

PHRASES :
τὰ πρὸς τὸν πόλεμον, res militares, *military affairs.*
τά πρὸς τοὺς θεούς (SOPH. *Phil.* 1441); *duty to the gods.*
πρὸς ἡδονὴν λέγειν, *to speak with a view to gratify or please;* so, πρὸς χάριν δημηγορεῖν, *to make a popular speech, talk clap-trap* or *"bunkum";* πρὸς ἔχθραν ποιεῖσθαι λόγον, DEM. (*calculated to inspire dislike);* ἅπαντα πρὸς ἡδονὴν ζητεῖν, *to make pleasure one's sole aim* (omnia ad voluptatem referre).

Adverbial phrases :
πρὸς βίαν (πρὸς τὸ βίαιον, AESCH. *Ag.* 130), *violently, by force;* πρὸς ἀνάγκην, *of necessity* (cf. ὑπ' ἀνάγκης, δι' ἀνάγκην, ἐξ ἀνάγκης, σὺν ἀνάγκῃ).
πρὸς μέρος, *proportionately,* DEM. ; πρὸς εὐσέβειαν, *piously,* SOPH. ; πρὸς ὀργήν, *angrily,* SOPH. and DEM.; πρὸς καιρόν, *seasonably,* SOPH.

PREPOSITIONS WITH ALL THREE CASES. 341

πρὸς χάριν τινος, alicuius gratia, *for the sake of a person.*
πρὸς ἰσχύος χάριν, EUR. *Med.* 538 (*laws not made*) *in support of violence;* cf. SOPH. *Ant.* 30, πρὸς χάριν βορᾶς, *for the sake of food.* In such phrases, πρὸς χάριν is almost like ἕνεκα.
πρὸς αὐλόν, EUR. *Al.* 346, *to the accompaniment of the pipe.*

As an Adverb: in addition, besides :
ἀλογία καὶ ἀμαθία γε πρός, PLAT. *Meno,* 90 E, *absurdity and unreasonableness to boot.* Cf. EUR. *Or.* 622.

IN COMPOSITION :
(1) *Towards,* προsέρχομαι, *I approach.* (2) *Near, beside, besides,* πρόsκειμαι, *I lie near;* προsτίθημι, *I apply, I add.*

§ 278. Ὑπό.[1]

Ὑπό (Epic. ὑπαί), *under,* = Sansk. *upa* (*thither, to, with*). Lat. *sub.*

A. WITH GENITIVE.
1. OF PLACE.

Under :
τὰ ὑπὸ γῆς δικαστήρια. PLAT.
The courts of justice under the earth.

From under :
νεοσσὸν τόνδ᾽ ὑπὸ πτερῶν σπάσας. EUR. *And.* 441.
Drawing from under the wings this chick.
An Epic but rare Attic use.

---

[1] ὑπό, like the Latin *sub*, seems originally to have meant *upwards,* from below towards a place above. Compare ὕπτιος with *supinus, facing upwards,* ὕψι, aloft, surgo (*i.e.* sub-s-rigo), succedo. Hence ὑπό means *going to meet* (ὑπαντιάζω), *supporting,* and so *agency* or *cause.* More generally ὑπό comes to denote *under the power or influence of,* and even *accompanying circumstance,* sometimes almost like ἐπί with a Dative, *e.g.* AESCH. *Sept. c. Theb.* 821, ὑπὸ φόνῳ. With the Genitive ὑπό denoting *separation from,* the Genitive must represent the Ablative ; on the other hand when ὑπό means *under,* the true Genitive, denoting sphere within which anything occurs, whether of place or time, etc., is employed.

2. FIGURATIVELY ; *under the influence of.*
Of Persons:—the Agent, like Lat. *a, ab :*
With Passive Verbs:
οἱ Πέρσαι ἐνικήθησαν ὑπὸ τῶν Ἑλλήνων.
The Persians were defeated by the Greeks.

Of Things:—the cause:
πάντα ὑπὸ δέους ξυνίσταται. THUC.
They all hold together through fear.

A very common use, ὑπὸ νόσου, ὑφ' ἡδονῆς, ὑπ' ὀργῆς, *by, in consequence of, from, for, disease, pleasure, anger.*

ὑπὸ κήρυκος εὐχὰς ἐποιοῦντο. THUC. vi. 32.
At the direction of a herald they were offering prayers, praeeunte praecone.

Hence of accompanying circumstances:
Frequently of music:
ἐστρατεύετο ὑπὸ συρίγγων. HDT. i. 17.
He used to march to war to the sound of the pipe.
Cf. SOPH. *El.* 711. EUR. *Bacch.* 156.
So πίνειν ὑπὸ σάλπιγγος, AR. *Ach.* 1001, *to drink to the trumpet's sound.* ὑπ' εὐφήμου βοῆς θῦσαι, SOPH. *El.* 630, *to sacrifice with auspicious cry.* ὑπὸ φανοῦ πορεύεσθαι, *to march by torchlight.* ὑπὸ πομπῆς, *in procession.* HDT. ii. 45.

Note. ὑπό has this sense with the Dative in early and late Greek, *e.g.* HESIOD and LUCIAN (see Liddell and Scott); also rarely in Attic with the Accusative, PLAT. *Leg.* 670 A, ὑπ' ὄρχησιν καὶ ᾠδήν: XEN. *Sym.* 6. 3, ὑπὸ αὐλόν.

PHRASES:
ὑφ' ἑαυτοῦ (ποιεῖν τι), *to do anything spontaneously, of one-self,* sua sponte. ὑφ' ὑμῶν αὐτῶν καὶ μὴ ὑπὸ τῶν πολεμίων, THUC. iv. 64, *of your own free-will, and not compelled by the enemy.* ὑπό here denotes the Agent.

PREPOSITIONS WITH ALL THREE CASES. 343

B. WITH DATIVE.

ὑπό means *under*, in a local sense, less frequently in Prose than in Poetry.

Under:

εὐκλεὴς θανεῖ
γυνή τ' ἀρίστη τῶν ὑφ' ἡλίῳ μακρῷ. EUR. *Al.* 150.
Glorious thou wilt die,
The noblest woman far beneath the sun.
Cf. XEN. *An.* i. 2. 8, ὑπὸ τῇ ἀκροπόλει εἶναι.

Covered by:
τί ἔχεις ὑπὸ τῷ ἱματίῳ; PLAT. *Phaedr.* 228 D.
What have you concealed under your cloak?
Cf. AESCH. *Ag.* 1030, ὑπὸ σκότῳ.

Under power of persons or things:
ἦν ἔτι ὑπὸ νόμοις καὶ πατρί. PLAT. *Rep.* 574 E.
He was still in subjection to laws and to a father.
ὑφ' ἑαυτῷ ποιεῖσθαι, to bring under one's power; cf.
HDT. vii. 157; THUC. vii. 64 (and see Accusative).

Classed under:
τὰ ὑπὸ ταῖς γεωμετρίαις λέγεις. PLAT. *Rep.* 511 A.
You are speaking of what comes under the head of geometrical pursuits (various branches of geometry).
More rarely with Accusative, see LEXICON.

C. WITH ACCUSATIVE.

Motion under:
ἀνεχώρησαν ὑπὸ τὸ τεῖχος. XEN.
They retired under the walls.
ὑπὸ δικαστήριον, *into* (*under control of*) *a law court.*
HDT. vi. 104.

Extension or position under:
τὸ Πελασγικὸν τὸ ὑπὸ τὴν ἀκρόπολιν ἐξῳκήθη.
THUC. ii. 17.
The Pelasgicum which lies (extends) under the acropolis was crowded.
τὰ ὑπὸ τὴν ἄρκτον. HDT. v. 10, *the northern districts.*

Subjection to:

εἰκὸς αὐτοὺς πάντα πειράσασθαι ὑπὸ σφᾶς ποιεῖσθαι.
                                                    THUC.
It is likely they will try to bring all under their power.
οἱ ὑπό τινα. XEN., *those who are in subjection to any one.*

Cf. Dative.

Of Time : near, about :
ὑπὸ τὸν σεισμόν. THUC.
At the time of the earthquake.
ὑπὸ νύκτα, *towards night, at nightfall*, sub noctem.
ὑπὸ τὴν κατάλυσιν τοῦ πολέμου, *just at the end of the war.*
                                                    XEN. *Mem.* ii. 8. 1.

PHRASES:
ὑπ' αὐγὰς ὁρᾶν τι, *to hold up to the light* (cf. EUR. *Hec.* 1154).
ὑπό τι, PLAT. and ARISTOPH., *to a certain degree*, aliquatenus.

IN COMPOSITION:

(1) *Up to*, ὑπαντιάζω, *I go up to meet, I face*; and so of accompaniment, ὑπᾴδω, *I accompany in song.* (2) *Under*, ὕπειμι, *I am under.* (3) *Secretly, slightly, gradually*, ὑποφαίνω, *I show* or *shine a little;* ὑποβάλλω, *I suggest, suborn, substitute;* ὑπέρυθρος, *reddish.*

CHAPTER II.

THE NEGATIVES.

Introductory Note.

§ 279.   Οὐ *negat*, Μή *infitiatur*.

οὐ *contradicts* or *denies*.[1] The following are typical instances of its use : ταῦτα οὐκ ἐγένετο, *these things did not take place ;* ταῦτα οὐκ ἂν γένοιτο, *these things would not take place ;* οὔ φημι, *I do not assert,* i.e. *I deny.* The statement may take an interrogative form, οὐ ταῦτα ἐγένετο; *did not these things take place?* where an affirmative answer is expected, the person addressed being challenged or dared to say οὐκ ἐγένετο.

Μή on the other hand *deprecates* or *repudiates*. The following instances taken from HOMER are typical : μὴ ἐμὲ λάβοι χόλος, *may not anger seize me!* μή σε κιχείω, *let me not meet thee!* ἦ μή που φάσθε; *what! say ye?* (*be it not that ye say!*) a statement put deprecatingly or repudiated : *Surely no! you don't say, etc.* = *do you say?*

Hence μή naturally expresses a *prohibition*, μή μ' ἐρέθιζε, *provoke me not!* It also naturally expresses *fear, apprehension, surmise* : μή με στίβη δαμάσῃ, *I fear* (or *perchance*) *the frost shall overpower me*. The surmise may be expressed independently, as above, or it may be attached to a verb, and so pass into a Subordinate Sentence : δείδω μὴ γένωμαι, *I fear that I may become*. Again the surmise, or result deprecated, may prove true : δείδω μὴ νημερτέα εἶπεν, *I fear she spake the truth*.[2]

---

[1] Οὐ *denies*, μή *declines*, Curtius.   Οὐ *denies*, μή *rejects*; οὐ is the negative of *fact and statement*, μή of *the will and thought*, Goodwin in *Liddell and Scott*   Οὐ *denies a predication,* μή *forbids* or *deprecates* (further on, *disclaims*), Monro's *Homeric Grammar*.

[2] Μή is identical with the Sanskrit *mâ*. In Sanskrit *mâ* is used with the Conjunctive, Optative of wishing, and Imperative like μή in Greek, Curtius, *Etym.* i. p. 415.   For instances see Delbrück and Windisch, *Syntaktische Forschungen, Der Gebrauch des Conjunctivs und Optativs im Sanskrit und Griechischen*, p. 112 and following.   Max Müller, *Oxford Inaugural Lecture*, Note C., gives an instance (from Wilson) of the prohibitive *mâ* with what may be equally well called an Infinitive or Dative : *mâ kâpalâya*, lit. *not for unsteadiness*, i.e. *do not act unsteadily*.   This seems to trace back μή as far as we can go.

In all the above instances οὐ contradicts downright a statement of fact, whereas μή deals with conceptions or thoughts. A line is thus drawn between the two negatives—a line, on the whole, clearly marked throughout Attic Greek, although subsequently blurred.[1] Μή is thus used with *Wishes, Prohibitions, Conditions*, and *Purposes*. A negative consequence conceived (ὥστε with the infinitive) requires μή, a negative consequence achieved as a fact (ὥστε with the Indicative) requires οὐ.

Μή is used generally with *abstract conceptions* as opposed to *known and definite facts*. Thus οἱ οὐ πιστεύοντες means *those particular (known) persons who do not believe;* οἱ μὴ πιστεύοντες, *all or any persons who do not believe (if any do not believe);* ἐπειδὴ οὐκ ἦλθον, *when, or since* (as a matter of fact), *they did not come;* ἐπειδὴ μὴ ἔλθοιεν, *whenever* (the number of times not being specified) *they did not come;* ἡ οὐκ ἐμπειρία, *the inexperience (of some known person), the fact that some one is inexperienced;* ἡ μὴ ἐμπειρία, *inexperience in the abstract* (without predicating of any particular person); ὁ οὐκ ὤν, *he who is not existing, the dead man;* τὰ μὴ ὄντα, *all things whatsoever are not*, a vast limbo outside of our actual knowledge.

The construction of the sentence may change οὐ to μή, yet even so, if it is necessary to contradict point blank a word or statement, οὐ may be used. See examples at the end of this chapter.

Whatever applies to οὐ and μή applies equally to their compounds, οὐδείς, μηδείς: οὐδέ, μηδέ: οὔτε, μήτε, etc., etc.

§ 280. Οὐ *PRIVATIVE*.

Οὐ prefixed to a word deprives that word of its affirmative meaning and gives it exactly the opposite sense. Hence it is called *privative* (privativum).

Especially noticeable under this head is the idiomatic use of οὐ with verbs of *saying* and *thinking*: οὔ φημι, οὐ φάσκω, οὐ νομίζω, οὐκ οἴομαι, οὐ δοκῶ, οὐκ ἐῶ.

---

[1] As Lucian (second century A.D.) is sometimes read, it may be observed that he uses μή where Attic writers use οὐ: (1) with Participles in a Causal sense, and after ὡς, ὅτι, διότι Causal, (2) after Verbs of Saying and Thinking in Oratio Obliqua.

By this idiom οὐ is used with the principal verb where in English the negative is joined with the following Infinitive.

Οὐ in fact almost coalesces with its word. Compare the use of the Latin negative (*ne* in *nego* (*ne-ig-o*), *nequeo*, *nescio*) which has gone a stage further than οὐ in coalescing.

οὔ φασι θεμιτόν εἶναι. PLAT.
They say it is not right.
negant fas esse.
οὐκ ᾤετο δεῖν λέγειν. AESCHIN.
He thought that he need not speak.
οὔ μοι δοκῶ. PLAT.
I think not.

Note 1. This use of οὐ with the governing Verb seems more ancient than with the Infinitive. See Monro's *Homeric Grammar*, p. 262.

Note 2. This οὐ privative is sometimes retained where the construction requires μή.
ἐὰν οὐ φῆτε ἐάν τε φῆτε. PLAT. *Apol.* xii. 25 B.
Whether you say no or yes.
εἰ μὲν οὐ πολλοὶ ἦσαν. LYS. 13. 72.
If they were few.

Cf. THUC. i. 121 (εἰ οὐκ ἀπεροῦσι); XEN. *An.* i. 7. 18 (εἰ οὐ μαχεῖται); SOPH. *Ai.* 1131, 1242, 1268; *El.* 244: EUR. *Med.* 88.

But generally the μή required by construction is used.
ἐὰν μὴ φῇ ὁ ἕτερος τὸν ἕτερον ὀρθῶς λέγειν. PLAT. *Gorg.* 457 D.

Note 3. Οὐ exerts this privative or contradictory force on any word to which it is prefixed.

(a) Verbs:—
οὐ στέργω, *I hate.*
οὐκ ἐῶ, } *I hinder, forbid.*
οὐ κελεύω, }
οὐκ ὑπισχνοῦμαι, *I refuse.*
οὐ προςποιοῦμαι, dissimulo.

οὐκ ἀξιῶ, *I consider that not* (like οὐ δοκῶ), *I require or expect that not* (THUC. ii. 89), *I disdain or refuse* (AESCH. *P. V.* 285).
οὐ συμβουλεύω, *I advise one not to*, etc. THUC. and HDT.

(b.) Other words :—
τὰ οὐ καλά, *immorality.*
οὐ καλῶς, *immorally ;* οὐκ ὀρθῶς, *wrongly.*
οὐχ εἷς, οὐκ ὀλίγοι = πολλοί, *many.*
οὐκ ἐλάχιστος = μέγιστος.
οὐκ ἥκιστα ἀλλὰ μάλιστα, HDT. iv. 170.
τῆς Λευκάδος ἡ οὐ περιτείχισις, THUC. iii. 95, *the non-investment of Leucas.*
ἡ οὐκ ἐξουσία, THUC. v. 50 ; ἡ οὐ διάλυσις, i. 137 ; ἡ οὐκ ἀπόδοσις, v. 35.
ἐν οὐ καίρῳ, *unseasonably,* EUR. *Bacch.* 1288.

Note 4. In some of these cases the negative doubtless is due to the Greek reserve and abatement of positive assertion (litotes), *e.g.* οὐχ ἥκιστα, *not least,* i.e. (by implication) *most.*

§ 281. Οὐ *AND* μή *WITH ADJECTIVES, PARTICIPLES USED AS ADJECTIVES, ADVERBS, AND SUBSTANTIVES.*

(For Infinitives used as Substantives see § 283.)

Οὐ.

When definite and known individuals or members of a class are spoken of, so that a fact is stated, οὐ is used.

Μή.

When the members of a class are indefinite, so that the expression is virtually *conditional*: (or when certain attributes are thought of, so that it is *consecutive* :) or when the expression is a mere vague *conception*, something thought of rather than known, μή is used.

Instances with μή much outnumber those with οὐ.

οἱ οὐκ ἀγαθοὶ πολῖται.
Those (particular) citizens who are not good.

οἱ μὴ καθαροὶ τὰς χεῖρας.
ANTIPH.
All who are of impure hands.

οἱ οὐ πιστεύοντες.
Those who do not believe.
(Special known persons spoken of.)
ii qui non credunt.

οἱ μὴ πιστεύοντες.
Those, i.e. any (all) who do not believe = if any do not believe.
= οἵτινες μὴ πιστεύουσι.
ὅσοι ἂν μὴ πιστεύωσι.
si qui non credunt.

αἱ οὐκ ὀρθαὶ πολιτεῖαι αὗται. PLAT. Rep.
These wrong forms of government.

τῶν στρατιωτῶν οἱ μὴ δυνάμενοι. XEN.
Such of the soldiers as are unable.

Here, as in many such cases, the οὐ is privative; under which rule are given examples of adverbs and substantives.

τὰ ὁρατὰ καὶ τὰ μή (ὁρατά).
PLAT. Phaed.
The things which are seen and those which are not seen.

ὁ μὴ ἰατρὸς ἀνεπιστήμων.
PLAT. Gorg.
He who is not a physician is inexperienced.

δεινὸν ἐστιν ἡ μὴ ἐμπειρία.
AR. Ecc.
A sad thing is inexperience.

Here no statement is made that any particular person is inexperienced, but the mere conception is spoken of.

Note on Substantives. When οὐ is used with a Substantive, the expression is equivalent to a negative objective sentence. Thus ἡ οὐκ ἐξουσία = *quod non licet*, the fact that it is not permitted. Whereas ἡ μὴ ἐξουσία simply means *the not being able* as an abstract conception, *non licere*. Μή however may be said to be the usual Attic construction with Substantives.

§ 282. Οὐ AND μή WITH PARTICIPLES.

Οὐ.	Μή.
Οὐ is used when the Participle states a fact: the Participle is often Causal.	Μή is used when the Antecedent to the Participle is indefinite, so that the Participle is Conditional.

οὐ πιστεύων.
Since (as, when, etc.) he does not believe.

μή πιστεύων.
If he does not believe.

αἰσχύνομαι οὐ ποιῶν ταῦτα.
I am ashamed because (that) I do not do this.

αἰσχύνομαι μὴ ποιῶν ταῦτα.
I am ashamed if I do not do this.

δηλώσω οὐ παραγενόμενος.
ANTIPH.
I will prove that I was not present.

κἂν ὦφλε χιλίας δραχμὰς οὐ μεταλαβὼν τὸ πέμπτον μέρος τῶν ψήφων.
PLAT. Apol. xxv.
He would even have been condemned to pay a thousand drachmae, because he had not obtained a fifth of the votes.

οὐκ ἂν δύναιο, μὴ καμών, εὐδαιμονεῖν. EUR.
Thou couldst not be happy, unless thou shouldst toil.

οὐκ εὐτυχοῦσαι δόξετ' οὐχὶ δυστυχεῖν.
EUR. Bacch. 1263.
Although not fortunate, ye shall seem not to be unfortunate.

Cf. 270, νοῦν οὐκ ἔχων (void as he is of sense).

Note. ὡς (ὥσπερ) οὐ is more usual with the Participle than ὡς μή. ὡς μή appears to be used when the construction of the Sentence demands μή (*e.g.* when an Imperative or a Conditional particle precedes), though even then ὡς οὐ may be used when a plain statement of fact is intended.

ἐθορυβεῖτε ὡς οὐ ποιήσοντες ταῦτα. Lys. 12. 73 (cf. 27. 16, ὥσπερ οὐ).
Cf. Thuc. iv. 5; vi. 82. 2, Xen. *An.* iv. 4. 15.

For ὡς μή :—

ὡς ἐμοῦ μηδέποτε ἀμελήσοντος, οὕτως ἔχε τὴν γνώμην, Xen. *Cyr.* i. 6. 11.

But,—ἀφίετέ με ἢ μὴ ἀφίετε ὡς ἐμοῦ οὐκ ἂν ποιήσοντος ἄλλα. Plat. *Apol.* xvii. 30 B; Thuc. i. 78. 1. βραδέως βουλεύεσθε ὡς οὐ περὶ βραχέων.

ὡς μή, with the Participle, may denote several characteristics, *e.g.* δίδασκε μ' ὡς μὴ εἰδότα, *as one who knows not*, Soph. *O. C.* 1154.

§ 283. Οὐ AND μή WITH THE INFINITIVE.

Οὐ.   Μή.

Μή is the regular Negative with the Infinitive.

When οὐ is found with an Infinitive, it is chiefly in Indirect Statements after verbs of Saying and Thinking, οὐ being the proper construction in Oratio Obliqua.

An infinitive used as a Substantive with or without the Article regularly takes μή.

ἔφη οὐκ ἐκβῆναί με ἐκ τοῦ πλοίου. Antiph.
He stated that I did not leave the ship = οὐκ ἔφη ἐκβῆναι.

αἰσχρὸν μὴ ἀληθεύειν.
It is wrong not to speak the truth.

ἔλεγον οὐκ εἶναι αὐτόνομοι. Thuc.
They were saying that they were not independent.

χρὴ μὴ καταφρονεῖν τοῦ πλήθους. Isaeus.
We should not despise the multitude.

ἐνόμισεν οὐκ ἂν δύνασθαι μένειν. XEN.
He thought that they would not remain.

τὸ μὴ δικαίως ἀπολέσαι. ANTIPH.
An unjust sentence of death.

ὀμώμοκεν οὐ χαριεῖσθαι.
PLAT. *Apol.* xxiv. 35 C.

A striking instance; verbs of swearing usually are followed by μή, see note 4 below.
For other instances, cf. SOPH. *Ant.* 378, 755 ; PLAT. *Apol.* xvii. 29 B.

Note 1. When οὐ is exceptionally used with the Infinitive, it is generally due either to the *order of* or *emphasis on* a word or sentence. Sometimes οὐ is privative. A positive negation is always made.

οὐδενὸς ἁμαρτεῖν δίκαιός ἐστιν. ANTIPH. iv. Tetr. Γ. α. 6.
There is nothing which he deserves to miss.
= οὐδέν ἐστιν οὗ ἁμαρτεῖν.

ἀξιῶ ἐγὼ ὧν ὀμωμόκατε παραβῆναι οὐδέν.
XEN. *Hell.* ii. 4. 48.
I beg you to violate no single point of your oath.
= οὐκ ἀξιῶ.

Observe that οὐ is used although a Petition strictly requires μή. Cf. THUC. i. 39. 2.

Cf. SOPH. *Phil.* 88, ἔφυν οὐδέν = οὐκ ἔφυν.

κελεύει οὐκ ἐν τῇ ἐκκλησίᾳ ἀλλ' ἐν τῷ θεάτρῳ τὴν ἀνάρρησιν γίγνεσθαι. AESCH. 3. 204.
(*The law) requires the proclamation to be made, not in the Assembly, but in the Theatre.*

Emphasis on the parenthesis.

δοκεῖς χαιρήσειν ἢ οὐκ ἀποθανεῖσθαι; ANDOK. i. 101.
Do you expect to rejoice, or escape death?
οὐκ ἀποθανεῖσθαι is perhaps privative.

Note 2. χρή (χρῆν, ἐχρῆν) are followed by both μή and οὐ with the Infinitive. χρή οὐ may be considered to stand for οὐ χρή.

SOPH. *Phil.* 1363, χρῆν μήτε μολεῖν, κ.τ.λ.
And. 607, χρῆν μὴ κινεῖν.
EUR. *Androm.* 100, χρὴ δ' οὔποτ' εἰπεῖν, so 214.
Hipp. 507, χρῆν οὔ σ' ἁμαρτάνειν.
Med. 294, χρὴ δ' οὐπότ' ἐκδιδάσκεσθαι.

Note 3. Μή is not seldom found with the Infinitive in an Indirect Statement. In some, but not all such instances, the Statement is general, and bears the character of a Conception.

ἀπεκρίνατο μηδενὸς ἥττων εἶναι. XEN. *Hell.* ii. 3. 11.
He replied that he was inferior to none; cf. iii. 2. 31; iv. 4. 5; *Mem.* i. 2. 39.

οἱ μάντεις λέγονται ἑαυτοῖς μὴ προορᾶν τὸ ἐπιόν.
XEN. *Symp.* iv. 5.
Prophets are said not to foresee the future for themselves.

This is not, however, the strict Attic use, and Xenophon is often exceptional. See XEN. *Mem.* i. 2. 39. Οὐ and μή occur in co-ordinate clauses in SOPH. *Phil.* 1058; PLAT. *Prot.* 319 B.

Note 4. Many Verbs which imply an effort of *thought* or *will* prefer μή with the Infinitive. Such are Verbs of *making an admission*, ὁμολογῶ, PLAT. *Phaed.* xlii. 98 D, συγχωρῶ: cf. *conviction*, πιστεύω, XEN. *An.* i. 9. 8; πέπεισμαι, PLAT. *Apol.* xxvii. 37 A: of *witnessing, swearing*, ὄμνυμι, AR. *Vesp.* 1047, 1281 (also an Epic usage), ἐρῶ=ὀμοῦμαι, XEN. *Cyr.* vii. 1. 18; ἐγγυῶμαι, PLAT. *Prot.* 336 D. (For other constructions of ὄμνυμι, see *Lexicon.*)

Verbs of *Perception*, ἐπίσταμαι, are found with μή and the Infinitive in SOPH. *El.* 908, 1092.

§ 284. DIRECT AND INDIRECT STATEMENT.

Οὐ.   Μή.

The Direct Statement takes οὐ.

οὐκ ἐξέβην ἐκ τοῦ πλοίου.
                            ANTIPH.
I did not leave the ship.

Indirect Statement with ὅτι or ὡς takes οὐ.

For the Indirect Statement in the Infinitive, cf. supra.

παρέχομαι μάρτυρας ὡς οὐκ ἐξέβην ἐκ τοῦ πλοίου.
                            ANTIPH.
I produce witnesses (to prove) that I did not leave the ship = οὐκ ἐξέβην.

εἶπεν ὅτι οὐδὲν αὐτῷ μέλοι τοῦ θορύβου.   LYS.
He said he did not care about the disturbance = οὐδέν μοι μέλει.

§ 285. INDIRECT STATEMENT WITH THE PARTICIPLE.

ἤγγειλε τὴν πόλιν οὐ πολιορκηθεῖσαν.   XEN.
He reported that the city had not been besieged.
Recta : οὐκ ἐπολιορκήθη.

Note. But Verbs of Perception sometimes take μή. See SOPH. *Ant.* 1063-64, *O. C.* 65; THUC. i. 76. 1; ii. 17. 2; similarly after δείκνυμι, EUR. *Tro.* 970.

ἔγνωσαν οὐ πραχθεῖσαν τὴν
ξυμμαχίαν. THUC.
They discovered that the alliance had not been concluded.
Recta : οὐκ ἐπράχθη.
Οὐ in both cases is regular, going with an Oblique Statement.

§ 286. *DIRECT QUESTIONS.*

Οὐ expects the answer "yes" (*nonne?*). Μή expects the answer "no" (*num?*). They are often associated with other particles: ἆρ' οὐ; ἆρα μή; οὔκουν; μῶν (i.e. μὴ οὖν); μῶν οὐ; μῶν μή; μῶν οὖν; ἦ οὐ; ἦ μή;

ταῦτ' οὐχὶ καλῶς λέγεται; καλῶς. PLAT.
Is not this rightly said? Yes, rightly.

φῄς ἢ οὔ; πάνυ γε. PLAT.
Do you assent, or do you not (assent)? i.e. *Yes or no? Certainly (I do assent).*

Οὐ interrogative with a Future Indicative is equivalent to an Imperative.
οὐκ ἄξεθ' ὡς τάχιστα;
SOPH. *Ant.* 885.
Will you not lead her away instantly? (i.e. *lead her away*).
Followed by an imperative καὶ ἄφετε.

μή σοι δοκοῦμεν τῇδε λειφθῆναι μάχῃ; AESCH.
Think'st thou we were inferior in this fight?

Note. μή in an oblique question, like *num* in Latin, loses this force of expecting a negative answer. So SOPH. *Ant.* 1253, EUR. *Herac.* 482.

οὔκουν καθεδεῖ δῆτ' ἐνθαδί,
γάστρων; AR. *Ran.* 200.
Sit ye down there, Paunch.
Cf. SOPH. *Ant.* 244, *Ai.* 593,
Phil. 975, *O. C.* 834.

Note. Similarly οὐκ ἄν with
optative, οὐκ ἄν φράσειας;
which is a gentle φράσον,
SOPH. *Phil.* 122. But οὐ in
combination with που and δή
(οὔ που; οὐ τί που; οὐ δή;
οὐ δή που;) means *surely it is
not so?* Cf. SOPH. *Phil.* 900;
AR. *Ran.* 522, 526;—the question here is really outside the
words "*surely not—eh?*"

§ 287. *DELIBERATIVE QUESTIONS.*

Μή is used in Deliberative Questions.

μὴ ἀποκρίνωμαι; PLAT.
Am I not to answer?

λέγετε, εἰσίω ἢ μή; PLAT.
Speak, must I enter or no?

Cf. SOPH. *Ai.* 668, τί μή;

§ 288. *INDIRECT QUESTIONS.*

(*a.*) Indirect Single Question. The Negative is οὐ.

ἠρώτησα, διὰ τί οὐκ ἔλθοι.
*I asked him why he did not
come.*

Πρωταγόρας ἐρωτᾷ εἰ οὐκ
αἰσχύνομαι. PLAT.
*Protagoras asks me if I am
not ashamed.*

Obs. εἰ here is interrogative, not conditional.

(b.) In Indirect Double Questions the usage varies, but οὐ is commoner than μή. There is generally a reason for μή.

σκοπῶμεν, εἰ πρέπει ἢ οὔ.
PLAT.
*Let us consider whether it is
becoming or not.*

ὅπως ἴδῃς
εἴτ᾽ ἔνδον εἴτ᾽ οὐκ ἔνδον.
SOPH.
*That thou may'st see
Whether he be within or not
within.*

ὁ νέος οὐχ οἷός τε κρίνειν ὅ
τι τε ὑπονοία καὶ ὃ μή.
PLAT.
*A child is incapable of deciding what is allegory
and what not.*

Note. Οὐ rather than μή seems to represent simply the original direct double question. Μή seems to import a doubt into the question, or to represent it as a conception. Professor Jebb, in a note to SOPH. *Ai.* 6, and ANTIPHON (*Attic Orators*, p. 161), draws a subtle distinction in every case. Thus, he says σκοπῶμεν εἰ πρέπει ἢ μή means, *let us consider the question of abstract fitness*: but σκοπῶμεν εἰ πρέπει ἢ οὔ ; *let us see whether the matter in hand is fit or no.*

In this passage of ANTIPHON, εἰ ἢ μή—εἰ ἢ οὐ occur in sequent clauses. Similarly in ISAEUS, viii. 9, we have, in three sequent clauses, εἴτε εἴτε μή—καὶ εἰ ἢ οὔ—καὶ εἰ ἢ μή.

§ 289. *INDIRECT PETITION.*

μή is always used whether the Petition is Direct or Indirect.

μὴ κλέπτε or μὴ κλέψῃς.

a. Direct.

μὴ ἀξιοῦτέ με ταῦτα δρᾶν.
Do not require me to do this.

b. Indirect.

ἔλεγον αὐτοῖς μὴ ἀδικεῖν.
THUC.
They were telling them not to do wrong.

ἱκέτευον μὴ στρεβλωθῆναι.
ANDOK.
They were begging not to be tortured.

Note. For exceptions see under οὐ and μή with Infinitive. See also ὅπως μή with Future Indicative (Index).

§ 290.   CONDITIONAL.

Οὐ.

The Apodosis or Principal Sentence takes οὐ.

Μή.

The Protasis or Subordinate Sentence takes μή.

For Examples see Conditional Sentences.

Note 1. Where οὐ is found in a Protasis it is joined privatively to some special word. (Cf. supra, p. 347.)

Note 2. εἰ interrogative, not conditional, takes οὐ not μή.

Note 3. When εἰ is used like ὅτι after verbs of *emotion* (θαυμάζω, κατοικτείρω, δεινόν ἐστι, and the like), οὐ, not μή, follows, for we may either say that a statement of fact is made, or that εἰ is virtually causal. Cf. ISOC. 11 D. μὴ θαυμάσῃς εἰ οὐ πρέπει, DEM. 197 D. οὐκ αἰσχρὸν εἰ οὔ;

Note 4. Also sometimes εἰ οὐ is found when a direct statement is quoted, εἰ, ὡς νῦν φήσει, οὐ παρεσκευάσατο, DEM. 1266. 2, so virtually EUR. Ion, 347.

§ 291. CONCESSIVE.

Οὐ.

Καίπερ (καί, καὶ ταῦτα, καί τοι), with a Participle take οὐ.

Καίπερ ὄντες οὐ δεινοί μεμνῆσθαι μνημονεύετε.
DEM.
Though you are not quick at remembering, you remember.
Cf. SOPH. Phil. 377; EUR. Alc. 352 = even being.

Μή.

Εἰ, ἐάν (ἤν, ἄν), concessive, take μή, being truly Conditional.

§ 292. CAUSAL.

Οὐ.

The regular Negative is οὐ.

ἐπειδὴ οὐκ ἐδύναντο λαμβάνειν τὸ χωρίον ἀπιέναι ἤδη ἐπεχείρουν. XEN.
Since they were unable to take the fort they now were trying to depart.
So διότι, THUC. iv. 11. 2.

Μή.

Note. See Introduction on use of μή in Causal Sentences in late Greek.

§ 293. CONSECUTIVE AND RESTRICTIVE.

Οὐ.
ὥστε with the Indicative takes οὐ.
οὕτω διακείμεθα ὥστε οὐδὲν πρᾶξαι δυνάμεθα. DEM.
We are in such a mood that we are unable to do anything.

Note. οὐ is found with an Infinitive.
δείν' ἐπηπείλει τελεῖν ὥστ' οὔτε νυκτὸς ὕπνον οὔτ' ἐξ ἡμέρας ἐμὲ στεγάζειν ἡδύν.
SOPH. *El.* 782.
She threatened to fulfil a dread revenge, so that, nor day, nor night, did sweet sleep shroud me.
Cf. EUR. *Hel.* 107, *Phoen.* 1357, THUC. v. 40. 2, viii. 70. 6, PLAT. *Apol.* xiv. 26 D.

Note. It is very important to distinguish between the regular and the exceptional use of ὥστε οὐ with the Infinitive. The regular use (*e.g.* PLAT. *Apol.* xiv.) is due to Oratio Obliqua. The example in SOPH. *El.* 782 is excep-

Μή.
ὥστε with the Infinitive takes μή.
οὕτως ἀλόγιστός εἰμι ὥστε μὴ δύνασθαι λογίζεσθαι.
PLAT.
So unreflecting am I that I cannot reflect.
ἀφίεμέν σε ἐφ' ᾧ τε μηκέτι φιλοσοφεῖν. PLAT.
We set you free on the understanding that you no longer pursue philosophy.
Cf. THUC. i. 103. 1. (Fut. Indic.)
For the rule of ἐφ' ᾧ τε, see p. 274.

tional. But in all cases we may perhaps say that there is a negation of fact.

§ 294. TEMPORAL AND LOCAL SENTENCES.

Οὐ.	Μή.
When the Time or Place is definite οὐ is used.	When the Time or Place is indefinite μή is used (*e.g.* with ὅταν, ὁπόταν, ἐπειδάν, ὅπου ἄν, etc., with Subjunctive : or ὅτε, etc., with Optative).
ἐπειδὴ ὁ ἀνὴρ οὐκ ἐφαίνετο ᾠχόμην πλέων. ANTIPH. *When the man was not forthcoming I went on my voyage.*	οὐκοῦν, ὅταν δὲ μὴ σθένω, πεπαύσομαι. SOPH. *So, when I have no strength, I will give o'er.* (ὅταν denotes Indefinite Futurity.)
ἕως μὲν οἱ σύμμαχοι οὐκ εἶχον ὅποι ἀποσταῖεν ἔκρυπτον τὴν πρὸς ὑμᾶς ἔχθραν. XEN. *Hell.* *So long as the allies did not know what side to revolt to, they concealed their dislike to you.*	ὁπότε μὴ φαῖεν ἀπάγοντες ἀπέκτειναν. THUC. *Whenever they said "no," they led them off and executed them.* *Obs.* That ὁπότε changes οὔ φημι to μή φημι.

§ 295. FINAL SENTENCES, ETC.

(*a.*) Final Sentences.
(*b*) ὅπως with Future Indicative.
(*c.*) Verbs of Fearing.

With these Constructions the regular Construction is μή.

§ 296. Οὐ and Μή with Relatives.

Οὐ.

The Relative takes οὐ when the Antecedent is definite, so that a fact is spoken of.

ζητοῦσα φάρμαχ' εὗρον οὐχ ἃ 'βουλόμην. EUR.
ἃ 'βουλόμην, i.e. ἃ ἐβουλόμην.
In seeking drugs I found not what I sought.
Cf. XEN. *An.* ii. 2. 3.

Note. οὐδεὶς ὅστις οὐ, οὐκ ἔστιν ὅστις οὐ take οὐ. THUC. iii. 39; vii. 87; HDT. v. 97. PLAT. *Prot.* 323 C.

In THUC. iii. 81, οἱ δὲ πολλοὶ τῶν ἱκετῶν ὅσοι οὐκ ἐπείσθησαν, the actual fact is perhaps emphasised. With a negative preceding τοιοῦτος, οὐ always follows (MADVIG, § 203, *note*):

νόμον τίθεμεν, οἴκησιν καὶ ταμιεῖον μηδενὶ εἶναι μηδὲν τοιοῦτον, εἰς ὃ οὐ πᾶς βουλόμενος εἴσεισιν.
PLAT. *Rep.* iii. 416 D.
A treasury which not every one who wishes shall enter.

Cf. S. Matt. vii. 21, οὐ πᾶς εἰσελεύσεται.

Μή.

The Relative takes μή when the Antecedent is indefinite. The use of μή with Relatives is the same as its use with εἰ.

ἃ μὴ οἶδα οὐδὲ οἴομαι εἰδέναι. PLAT.
Whatever I know not I do not think that I know.

οἳ ἐμὲ μὴ ἴσασι. PLAT.
Any (all, such as) do not know me.

ὅστις μὴ αὐτάρκης ἐστὶν οὗτος χαλεπὸς φίλος ἐστί. XEN. *Mem.* ii. 6. 2.
Whoever is not self-sufficient is a dangerous friend.

Cf. AESCH. *Eum.* 618, 661, SOPH. *O. T.* 281 (with Subjunctive and Optative with ἄν).

This indefinite or generic use of μή shades off into a Consecutive or Final use.

ψηφίσασθε τοιαῦτα ἐξ ὧν μὴ δεπότε ὑμῖν μεταμελήσει.
ANDOK 3. 41.
Pass such a sentence that you will never repent of.

μέλλουσι γάρ σ'
ἐνταῦθα πέμψειν ἔνθα μή ποθ'
ἡλίου φέγγος προσόψει.
SOPH. *El.* 380.
*They are purposing to send thee
where thou never more shalt
see the glory of the sun.*
Cf. SOPH. *Ai.* 359, 470;
Phil. 408, 588.
Cf. the Restrictive ὅσον μή, ὅσα μή, καθ' ὅσον μή, ὅτι μή.

οὐ and μή are both used with the Relative in a Causal Sense. The analogy of Causal Sentences seems to show that οὐ must be the normal construction; μή is used where perhaps the fact is delicately put, as for instance εἰ is put for ὅτι after θαυμάζω. This use of μή arises from its generic use.

θαυμαστὸν ποιεῖς ὃς οὐδὲν δίδως.
XEN. *Mem.* ii. 7. 13.
You are acting strangely in giving nothing.
So AR. *Nub.* 692 (ἥτις οὐ στρατεύεται), EUR. *Med.* 589.

ταλαίπωρός τις σύ γε ἄνθρωπος εἶ ᾧ μήτε θεοὶ πατρῷοί εἰσι μήτε ἱερά κ.τ.λ. PLAT. *Euth.* 302.
You are a miserable sort of being since you have neither national gods nor sacrifices.

πῶς ἂν ὀρθῶς ἐμοῦ κατεγιγνώσκετε, ᾧ τὸ παράπαν πρὸς τουτονὶ μηδὲν συμβόλαιον ἐστίν;
DEM. *Apat.* 903. 22.
How could you have rightly condemned me, since I have no contract at all with this man?
Cf. AR. *Ran.* 1459.

§ 297. Μή is used in Expressions of a Wish.

Μηκέτι ζῴην ἐγώ.
AR. *Nub.* 1255.
May I no longer live!

μή ποτ' ὤφελον λιπεῖν
τὴν Σκῦρον.
SOPH. *Phil.* 969.
*Would I ne'er had left
My Scyros.*
= *I ought never*, μή like
μή after δεῖ.

ἐγώ θράσυς οὔτ' εἰμὶ μήτε γενοίμην. DEM. 8. 68.
*I am neither bold nor might I
become so.*

ἐγὼ δ' ὅπως σὺ μὴ λέγεις ὀρθῶς
τάδε οὔτ' ἂν δυναίμην μητ'
ἐπισταίμην λέγειν. SOPH.
Ant. 685.
*But that these words thou
speakest are not right I neither
could nor may I learn to say.*

οὔτ' ἂν δυναίμην is an Apodosis, and therefore οὐ is required : μητ' ἐπισταίμην is a
wish ; the μή with ὅπως is far
more difficult to explain, for
it is an Indirect Statement.
But observe that ὅπως μή
depends on a verb of perception, ἐπίσταμαι (see note 4 μή
with Infin.). Also ὅπως μή
expresses doubt, and is much
less positive than ὅτι οὐ.
Moreover the wish μηδ' ἐπισταίμην may throw its shadow
over the previous line.

§ 298. Μή and μὴ οὐ with the Infinitive.

A. After a Principal Sentence containing Verbs and expressions of *denying, hindering, forbidding*, and *avoiding*, μή is used with the Infinitive where in English we use no negative.

φῂς ἢ καταρνεῖ μὴ δεδρακέναι τάδε; SOPH.
Dost own or dost deny that thou hast done this?

ἠναντιώθην μηδὲν πράττειν παρὰ τοὺς νόμους.
PLAT.
I opposed your doing anything contrary to the laws.

ἀπαγορεύω μὴ ποιεῖν ἐκκλησίαν. ARISTOPH.
I forbid your calling an assembly.

ἠπίστουν μὴ εἶναι τοὺς τὰ ὅπλα παραδόντας τοῖς τεθνεῶσιν ὁμοίους. THUC. iv. 40.
They did not believe that those who had given up their arms were like those who had fallen.

θνητούς γ' ἔπαυσα μὴ προδέρκεσθαι μόρον.
AESCH. *P. V.* 248.
Ay, I let mortals from foreseeing their doom.

Note 1.

Such verbs are :—

ἀντιλέγω,
ἀρνοῦμαι (and compounds), } *deny.*

ἀμφισβητῶ,
ἀπιστῶ, } *dispute, doubt.*

ἀπέχομαι,
εὐλαβοῦμαι,
μέλλω,
φεύγω,
φυλάσσομαι, } *abstain, beware of, hesitate, avoid.*

ἔχω (and compounds),
εἴργω (and compounds),
ἐμποδὼν εἶναι, } *hinder.*

κωλύω,
ἀπαγορεύω,
ἀπεῖπον, } *forbid.*

So also ἀπολύομαι, THUC. i. 128; ἀποκρύπτομαι, ii. 53; ἀποστρέφω, viii. 108; ὑπεκτραπέσθαι, SOPH. *O. C.* 565; φυλάσσω, *O. C.* 667.

Note 2.

Μή, however, as in the English idiom, is not seldom omitted.

ὃν θανεῖν ἐρρυσάμην. EUR.
Whom I from death delivered.
τοῦτό τις εἴργει δρᾶν ὄκνος. PLAT.
Some scruple prevents me from doing this.
Cf. SOPH. *O. T.* 129; THUC. i. 62; PLAT. *Phaed.* 108 E.

Note 3.

Other constructions are (1) ὥστε μή with the Infinitive, (2) τὸ μή with the Infinitive, (3) τοῦ or τοῦ μή with the Infinitive.

(1.) ἀγγέλλων ὅτι τὰς ναῦς ἀποστρέψειε ὥστε μὴ ἐλθεῖν.
THUC. viii. 108. 1.
Announcing that he had diverted the ships from coming.

(2.) εἶργον τὸ μὴ κακουργεῖν. THUC. iii. 1.
They prevented them from inflicting damage.
Cf. AESCH. *Eum.* 691; SOPH. *Antig.* 263.

(3.) ἐκώλυσε τοῦ καίειν ἐπιόντας. XEN. *An.* i. 6. 2.
He kept them from advancing and burning.
ἕξει τοῦ μὴ καταδῦναι. XEN. *An.* iii. 5. 11.
It will keep them from sinking.
Cf. THUC. i. 76, ii. 49, iii. 75; XEN. *Cyr.* ii. iv. 23

B. But when the Verbs themselves take a Negative or quasi-Negative, μὴ οὐ and not μή alone is used with the Infinitive.

Here also in English we use no negative in the subordinate sentence.

τίνα οἴει ἀπαρνήσεσθαι μὴ οὐχὶ ἐπίστασθαι τὰ δίκαια; PLAT.
Who do you think will deny that he is acquainted with justice? (= *no* one will deny).

οὐ λήξω μὴ οὐ πᾶσι προφωνεῖν. SOPH.
I will not cease to publish unto all.

τί ἐμποδὼν μὴ οὐχὶ ἀποθανεῖν; XEN.
What is there to hinder us from being put to death?
(= no hindrance).
Cf. AESCH. *P. V.* 627 (τί μέλλεις;); SOPH. *Ai.* 540, 728; XEN. *Symp.* iii. 3 (τὸ μὴ οὔ).

C. Also when the Principal Sentence is negative, μὴ οὐ and the Infinitive is used after expressions denoting what is *impossible, wrong, repugnant*, and the like. Here in English we use a Negative.

ἀδύνατα ἦν μὴ οὐ μεγάλα βλάπτειν. THUC.
It was impossible not to inflict great harm.

οὐδεὶς μ' ἂν πείσειεν τὸ μὴ οὐκ ἐλθεῖν. ARISTOPH.
No one shall persuade me not to go.

ὑπέσχου ζητήσειν ὡς οὐχ ὅσιόν σοι ὃν μὴ οὐ βοηθεῖν δικαιοσύνῃ. PLAT. *Rep.* 427, E.
You promised to search, on the ground that it would be impious for you not to assist justice.

Cf. PLAT. *Symp.* 218 C (ἀνόητον μὴ οὔ).

D. Sometimes μὴ οὐ and the Infinitive follows a Principal Sentence which is not Negative in form.

αἰσχρόν ἐστι σοφίαν μὴ οὐχὶ πάντων κράτιστον φάναι.
PLAT. *Prot.* 352 D.
It is immoral not to assert that wisdom is the highest of all possessions.

In these cases the αἰσχρόν is practically *condemning, blaming, dissuading from* a course.

ὥστε πᾶσιν αἰσχύνην εἶναι μὴ συσπουδάζειν.
XEN. *An.* ii. 3. 11.
So that all were ashamed not to co-operate heartily.

Compare these two examples with XEN. *Cyr.* vii. 7. 16, τίνα αἴσχιον μὴ φιλεῖν ἢ τὸν ἀδελφόν; where a quasi-Negative Principal Sentence is followed by μή only.

See HEROD. i. 187, δεινόν μὴ οὐ λαβεῖν.

§ 299. Μὴ οὐ with the Participle.

Μὴ οὐ is found with the Participle denoting circumstance (*conditionally*, or *restrictively*), after a Principal Sentence expressing what is *impossible* or *repugnant*.
Μὴ οὐ is practically equal to εἰ μή, *except, unless*.

οὐκ ἄρ' ἔστι φίλον τῷ φιλοῦντι οὐδέν, μὴ οὐκ ἀντιφιλοῦν;
PLAT. *Lys.* 212 D.
No creature then is a friend to a friend, unless it love in return, (without loving).

ἥκεις γὰρ οὐ κενή γε, τοῦτ' ἐγὼ σαφῶς
ἔξοιδα, μὴ οὐχὶ δεῖμ' ἐμοὶ φέρουσά τι. SOPH. *O. C.* 359.
Thou comest not empty, this I know full well, unless thou bring'st some horror to mine ears.

δυσάλγητος γὰρ ἂν
εἴην, τοιάνδε μὴ οὐ κατοικτείρων ἕδραν. SOPH. *O. T.* 11.
hard of heart were I,
Compassionating not so sad a session. (Cf. *O. T.* 220.)

Other instances will be found in HEROD. ii. 110, vi. 9. and 106. ISOCRAT. *Laud. Hel.* 47.

So entirely was μὴ οὐ eventually regarded as equivalent to εἰ μή that in DEM. *de Fals. Leg.* 379. 7, we find it used without a participle expressed: αἵ τε πόλεις πολλαὶ καὶ χαλεπαὶ λαβεῖν μὴ οὐ χρόνῳ καὶ πολιορκίᾳ, *the cities were numerous and difficult to take except by long waiting and by siege* (sc. ληφθεῖσαι).

Variant Constructions of B. C. D. (pp. 336, 7).

After a Negative Principal Sentence are used sometimes (1) the Infinitive alone; (2) μή alone instead of μὴ οὐ with the Infinitive; (3) τὸ μὴ οὐ; (4) τοῦ μὴ οὐ.

(1) ταῦτα οὐκ ἐξαρνοῦνται πράττειν. AESCHIN. iii. 250.
They do not deny that they so act.

Φίλιππον παρελθεῖν οὐκ ἠδύναντο κωλῦσαι.
DEM. *de Pac.* 62. 10.
They were not able to prevent Philip advancing.

(2) οὐ πολὺν
χρόνον μ' ἐπέσχον μή με ναυστολεῖν ταχύ. SOPH. *Phil.* 348.
Not long while
they held me from quick setting sail. (Cf. *Antig.* 443.)

(3) οὐκ ἐναντιώσομαι τὸ μὴ οὐ γεγωνεῖν πᾶν.
AESCH. P. V. 786.
I'll not refuse (lit. *oppose thee*) *to declare the whole.*
XEN. Symp. iii. 3.
(4) τίς Μήδων σου ἀπελείφθη τοῦ μὴ ἀκολουθεῖν ;
XEN. Cyr. v. 1. 25.
Who of the Medes failed to follow you ?

Instances of omission of μή and μὴ οὐ are said to be rare. There are however a good many.

1. Μή omitted after an Affirmative Principal Sentence, ANTIPH. Tetr. B. B. 4. and 7. THUC. iii. 39. 3. SOPH. Ai. 70, O. T. 129. EURIP. Or. 263. ARIST. Ach. 127. XEN. Hell. v. 21. PLAT. Apol. xix. 31 D, xxxi. 39 E.

2. Μή for μὴ οὐ after a Negative Principal Sentence, ANTIPH. Tetr. B. B. 3. SOPH. Phil. 349. THUC. iii. 39. ISOCR. Laud. Hel. 47. (Infin. alone after a Negative Sentence.)

§ 300. Μή and μὴ οὐ with the Subjunctive.

Μή with the Subjunctive expresses *anxiety, apprehension, suspicion, surmise,* and so may often be translated *perhaps.*

μὴ τοῦτο ἀληθὲς ᾖ.
Perhaps this is true.

μὴ ἀγροικότερον ᾖ τὸ ἀληθὲς εἰπεῖν. PLAT.
Perhaps it is somewhat blunt to tell the truth.

The addition of οὐ gives the opposite or negative meaning:

μὴ οὐ τοῦτο ἀληθὲς ᾖ.
Perhaps this is not true.

ἀλλὰ μὴ οὐ τοῦτ᾽ ᾖ χαλεπόν, θάνατον ἐκφυγεῖν.
PLAT. Apol.
It looks as if this were not the real difficulty—to escape death.

Cf. Crit. ix. 48 C. Phaed. xi. 67 B.

Note 1. Μή ού is found graphically with the Indicative in questions.

ἀλλ' ἄρα μὴ οὐχ ὑπολαμβάνεις; PLAT. *Prot.* 312 A.
But perhaps then you do not suppose?

Note 2. ὅπως μή, ὅπως μὴ οὐ is similarly used with the Subjunctive and Indicative (Pres. and Future), PLAT. *Crat.* 430 D, *Meno* 77 A, *Phaedo* 77 B; RIDDELL'S *Digest*, p. 140.

Note 3. The same constructions of μή and μὴ οὐ occur even more commonly after a Principal Verb like φράζομαι, ὁρῶ, σκοπῶ, ἀθρῶ, ἐννοοῦμαι, αἰσχύνομαι, ὀκνῶ, κίνδυνός ἐστι, φοβοῦμαι, etc.

(*a.*) With Subjunctive:

φροντίζω μὴ κράτιστον ᾖ μοι σιγᾶν. XEN. *Mem.* iv. 2. 39.
I am considering whether it is not best for me to be silent.
ταῦτα ἀπιστίαν παρέχει περὶ τῆς ψυχῆς μὴ οὐδαμοῦ ἔτι ᾖ.
PLAT. *Phaed.* xiv. 70 A.
This causes a doubt about the soul that possibly it no longer exists.

(*b.*) With Indicative:

a. Present Indicative:

ὁρῶμεν μὴ Νικίας οἴεταί τι λέγειν. PLAT. *Lach.* 196.
Cf. SOPH. *Ant.* 1253; EUR. *Tro.* 178, *Phoen.* 92 (quoted p. 267).

b. Imperfect Indicative:

ὅρα μὴ παίζων ἔλεγεν. PLAT. *Theaet.* 145.

c. Future Indicative:

ὅρα μὴ δεήσει. XEN. *Cyr.* iii. 1. 27.
φοβοῦμαι μὴ εὑρήσομεν. PLAT. *Phileb.* 13. A.
δέδοιχα ὅπως μὴ τεύξομαι. ARIST. *Eq.* 112.
Cf. PLAT. *Crat.* 393 C., *Rep.* 451 A.

d. Perfect Indicative:

φοβούμεθα μὴ ἀμφοτέρων ἡμαρτήκαμεν. THUC. iii. 53.

e. Aorist Indicative:

δείδω μὴ πάντα νημερτέα εἶπεν. HOM. *Od.* v. 300.

οὐ μή *WITH SUBJUNCTIVE, ETC.* 371

§ 301. Οὐ μή WITH SUBJUNCTIVE AND FUTURE INDICATIVE.

A. Οὐ μή with the Subjunctive (generally the Aorist, but sometimes the Present) expresses an emphatic negative future statement.

οὐ μὴ παύσωμαι φιλοσοφῶν.   PLAT. *Apol.* xvii.
I will never give up philosophy.

οὔτοι σ' Ἀχαιῶν, οἶδα, μή τις ὑβρίσῃ.
SOPH. *Ai.* 560.
None of the Achaeans, I know it, shall ever insult thee.

B. Οὐ μή with the Future Indicative has the same meaning.

ἀλλ' εἴσιθ'. οὔ σοι μὴ μεθέψομαί ποτε.
SOPH. *El.* 1052.
Enter within. I ne'er will follow thee.

εἶπεν ὅτι ἡ Σπάρτη οὐδὲν μὴ κάκιον οἰκιεῖται αὐτοῦ ἀποθανόντος.   XEN. *Hell.* i. 6. 32.
He said that Sparta would be governed not one whit the worse after his death.

Observe that the example is in the Graphic Oratio Obliqua.

C. 1. Οὐ μή Interrogative with the Future Indicative (second person singular) expresses a strong prohibition.

ποῖος Ζεύς ; οὐ μὴ ληρήσεις ; οὐδ' ἔστι Ζεύς.
ARIST. *Nub.* 367.
Zeus quotha! don't talk twaddle. There's no Zeus.

ὦ θύγατερ, οὐ μὴ μῦθον εἰς πολλοὺς ἐρεῖς ;
EUR. *Supp.* 1066.
Daughter, tell not the tale among the crowd.

2. Οὐ μή with the Future Indicative (second person) in the first clause is followed by a second clause expressing (a.) an affirmative command (b.) a negative command or prohibition.

(a.) οὐ μὴ διατρίψεις, ἀλλὰ γεύσει τῆς θύρας ;
ARIST. *Ran.* 462.
Don't shilly-shally, but taste the door.

(b.) οὐ μὴ προσοίσεις χεῖρα, μηδ᾽ ἄψει πέπλων ;
EUR. *Hipp.* 606.
Bring not thy hand near, and touch not my robes.

3. Οὐ with the Future Indicative (second person), denoting an affirmative command, is followed by a Future Indicative (with καί μή, μηδέ) denoting a negative command or prohibition.

οὐχὶ συγκλῄσεις στόμα,
καὶ μὴ μεθήσεις αὖθις αἰσχίστους λόγους ;
EUR. *Hipp.* 499.
Set a seal upon thy lips,
and let not fall again most shameful words.

οὐ σῖγ᾽ ἀνέξει, μηδὲ δειλίαν ἀρεῖς ; SOPH. *Ai.* 75.
Keep silence, and awake not cowardice. (Lit. *wilt thou not silently endure?*)

Some make these two separate questions, one with οὐ (*nonne?*), the other with μή (*num?*), *wilt thou not endure silently?* and *wilt thou play the coward?*

§ 302.   Further Examples of οὐ μή.

A. οὐ μή WITH SUBJUNCTIVE.

οὐκέτι μὴ δύνηται βασιλεὺς ἡμᾶς καταλαβεῖν.
XEN. *An.* ii. 2. 12.
There is no longer any likelihood of the King overtaking us.

Obs. The Present Subjunctive is here used. So also in

PLAT. *Rep.* 341 C. (οὐ μὴ οἷός τε ᾖς) : and in SOPH. *O. C.* 1023, (ἐπεύχωνται, one MS. reads ἐπεύξωνται).

τὸ μέγιστον κακὸν ἑκὼν οὐδεὶς μή ποτε λάβῃ.
PLAT. *Leg.* 731 C.
No one is ever likely voluntarily to choose the greatest evil.

οὐ μή σε κρύψω πρὸς ὄντινα βούλομαι ἀφικέσθαι.
XEN. *Cyr.* vii. 3. 13.
I will not conceal from you whom I wish to march against.

See further SOPH. *O. C.* 408, 450, 649, 1024, 1702 ; THUC. v. 67 ; XEN. *Hell.* iv. 2. 3 ; PLAT. *Rep.* 499 B ; AR. *Av.* 461.

οὐ μὴ σκώψῃς, μηδὲ ποιήσῃς ἅπερ οἱ τρυγοδαίμονες οὗτοι, ἀλλ' εὐφήμει. ARIST. *Nub.* 299.
Don't you flout, and don't behave like your poor comedy hacks, but, hold your peace.

Elmsley changes σκώψῃς of the MSS. to σκώψει, Fut. Indic. Mid. Similarly in *Nub.* 505, οὐ μὴ λαλήσῃς has been changed to λαλήσεις. See GOODWIN, *Moods and Tenses*, pp. 186, 187.

If σκώψῃς is right, this is *you won't jest*, a possible way of saying *don't jest:* if σκώψει, ποιήσεις, the construction is interrogative like that of C. 1 above, p. 371.

B. οὐ μή WITH FUTURE INDICATIVE.

οὐ μή σ' ἐγὼ περιόψομαι ἀπελθόντα.   ARIST. *Ran.* 508.
I'll not suffer you to depart.

οὔ τοι μήποτέ σ' ἐκ τῶν ἑδράνων,
ὦ γέρον, ἄκοντά τις ἄξει.   SOPH. *O. C.* 178.
No one, be sure, from these abodes,
Old Sir, shall drag thee hence.

2d person in the same meaning as the above, *i.e.* denoting not a strong prohibition, but a negative statement.

οὔκουν ποτ' ἐκ τούτοιν γε μὴ σκήπτροιν ἔτι
ὁδοιπορήσεις (Schneidewin, ὁδοιπορήσῃς.) SOPH. *O. C.* 848.
Never henceforth, on these props leaning, thou
Shalt journey hence.

τοὺς γὰρ πονηροὺς οὐ μή ποτε ποιήσετε βελτίους.
AESCHIN. *in Cles.* 177.
You will never make the bad better.

The following example may denote either a prohibition or a statement.

οὐ γιγνώσκω σε· οὐ μὴ εἴσει εἰς τὴν οἰκίαν.   ISAEUS, viii. 24.
I do not know you, you shall not enter the house; or οὐ μὴ εἴσει; *don't enter.*

C. οὐκ ἐς κόρακας; οὐ μὴ πρόσιτον;   ARIST. *Ran.* 609.
To the crows with you. Be off!

Observe here that the 2d person dual is used.

ὦ μιαρώτατε, τί ποιεῖς; οὐ μὴ καταβήσει;   ARIST. *Vesp.* 397.
You scoundrel, what are you at? don't come down.

οὐ μὴ 'ξεγερεῖς τὸν ὕπνῳ κάτοχον
κἀκκινήσεις κἀναστήσεις
φοιτάδα δεινὴν
νόσον, ὦ τέκνον;   SOPH. *Tr.* 978.

Observe that ἐκκινήσεις joined by καί is prohibitive co-ordinately with ἐξεγερεῖς.

οὐ μὴ καλεῖς μ',
ὤνθρωπ', ἱκετεύω, μηδὲ κατερεῖς τοὔνομα;   ARIST. *Ran.* 298.
*Don't call me,
Sirrah, I pray thee, nor blab out my name.*

οὐ μὴ δυσμενὴς ἔσει
φίλοις, παύσει δὲ θυμοῦ, καὶ πάλιν στρέψεις κάρα . .
δέξει δὲ δῶρα καὶ παραιτήσει πατρός;   EUR. *Med.* 1151.
*Be not wroth with friends,
Forbear displeasure, turn thy face again,
Accept these offerings, and entreat thy father.*

οὐ μὴ προσοίσεις χεῖρα, βακχεύσεις δ'ἰών,
μηδ' ἐξομόρξει μωρίαν τὴν σὴν ἐμοί;   EUR. *Bacch.* 343.
*Lay not thy hand on me, go play the bacchanal,
Nor smudge me with thy folly.*

οὔκουν καλεῖς αὐτὸν καὶ μὴ ἀφήσεις;   PLAT. *Symp.* 175 A.
Call him, and don't send him away.

οὐ θᾶσσον οἴσεις, μηδ' ἀπιστήσεις ἐμοί;   SOPH. *Tr.* 1183.
Give me thy hand quick, and distrust me not.

3. Οὐ μή is found in the Obliqua with a Future Optative representing a Future Indicative of the Recta.

τά τ' ἀλλὰ πάντ' ἐθέσπισεν
καὶ τἀπὶ Τροίας πέργαμ' ὡς οὐ μή ποτε
πέρσοιεν, εἰ μὴ τόνδ' ἄγοιντο   SOPH. *Phil.* 611.

In the Recta this would be οὐ μὴ πότε πέρσετε ἐὰν μὴ ἄγησθε. A striking instance, for here the 2d person of the Future would clearly be a negative statement.

All the rest he prophesied,
And how they ne'er should sack the towers of Troy
Unless they brought him with them.

οὐ μή is also found with the Future Infinitive.

σαφῶς γὰρ εἶπε Τειρεσίας οὐ μή ποτε
σοῦ τήνδε γῆν οἰκοῦντος εὖ πράξειν πόλιν. EUR. *Phoen.* 1590.
Recta, οὐ μή ποτε εὖ πράξει ἡ πόλις.

Cf. PLAT. *Lach.* 197 D, καὶ γάρ μοι δοκεῖς οὐδὲ μὴ ᾐσθῆσθαι, unless for οὐδὲ μή we substitute οὐδαμῆ as has been suggested.

§ 303. *REPETITION OF THE NEGATIVE.*

I. Where a *simple* Negative follows a Negative in the same clause, two Negatives make one Affirmative, as in English.

οὐδεὶς οὐκ ἔπασχε. XEN.
No one was not suffering (i.e. every one was suffering).

οὐ μόνον οὐ πείθονται.
Not only do they not obey.

οὐ δύναμαι μὴ γελᾶν. AR.
I am not able to keep from laughing.

II. But where a *Compound* Negative follows a Negative in the same clause the first Negation is continued and strengthened.

ἀκούει δ' οὐδὲν οὐδεὶς οὐδενός. EUR. *Cycl.* 120.
No one obeys anybody in anything.

μὴ λανθανέτω σε μηδὲ τοῦτο. XEN. *Cyr.* v. 2. 36.
Let not even this escape you.

θεοὺς φοβούμενοι μήποτ' ἀσεβὲς μηδὲν μηδὲ ἀνόσιον μήτε ποιήσητε μήτε βουλήσητε.
XEN. *Cyr.* viii. 7. 22.
Fear the gods, and never do or intend anything either impious or unholy.

§ 304. Οὐδείς, Μηδείς, Οὐδέν, Μηδέν, etc.

A. Οὐδείς and μηδείς are used as declinable Substantives both in the Singular and Plural, with or without the Article, of persons.
Much more rarely ὁ, ἡ, οὐδέν, ὁ, ἡ, μηδέν.

B. Οὐδέν and μηδέν are used as indeclinable neuter predicates of persons.

C. τὸ μηδέν, an indeclinable substantive, is very freely used both of persons and things.

All these constructions are chiefly poetical with the exception of (**B**), which is also Platonic. Herodotus also uses (**A**) and (**B**).

We may observe with regard to them:—

(1.) That οὐδείς, οὐδέν denotes what is known or proved to be actually non-existent or worthless. (Cf. ἡ οὐκ ἐξουσία under οὐ privative.) Οὐδέν is *actually nothing*.

(2.) Μηδείς, μηδέν denotes an indefinite conception of what is anything non-existent or worthless. (Cf. ἡ μὴ ἐξουσία.) Μηδέν is *abstract nonentity*, hence τὸ μηδέν.

(3.) The two sets often seem to be used indifferently, but though οὐδείς is plainer and blunter, yet μηδείς may be really more contemptuous, "*as nothing,*" "*no better than a mere cipher.*"

(4.) The construction of the sentence (with εἰ or an imperative) may favour μή rather than οὐ.

(5.) Both sets of phrases are the reverse of τὶς (τὶ) εἶναι, *to be somebody.*

EXAMPLES:
ὁ νῦν μὲν οὐδείς, αὔριον δ' ὑπέρμεγας. ARIST. *Eq.* 158.
Nobody now, exceeding great to-morrow.
φρονοῦσι δήμου μεῖζον ὄντες οὐδένες.
  EUR. *Androm.* 700; cf. *I. A.* 371.
ἄγετε μ' ἐκποδὼν
τὸν οὐκ ὄντα μᾶλλον ἢ μηδένα. SOPH. *Ant.* 1326.
*Lead me hence
Who am no more than him that is as nothing.*
οὐ γὰρ ἠξίου τοὺς μηδένας. SOPH. *Ai.* 1114.
τοὺς ζῶντας εὖ δρᾶν· κατθανὼν δὲ πᾶς ἀνὴρ
γῆ καὶ σκιά· τὸ μηδὲν εἰς οὐδὲν ῥέπει. EUR. *Meleager.*
i.e. *what was believed to be nothing now proves to be actually nothing.*
For the sentiment compare the Epitaph on Gay:
  "Life is a jest, and all things show it;
  I thought so once, but now I know it."
(δαίμων) ἡμῖν δ' ἀπορρεῖ κἄπι μηδὲν ἔρχεται. SOPH. *El.* 1000.
Our future is at ebb, and comes to naught.
Compare the μηδέν here with οὐδέν in the *Meleager.*
ἄνδρες ἡμέτεροι εἰσὶν οὐδέν. PLAT. *Rep.* 556 D.; cf. 562 D.
ἐὰν δοκῶσί τι εἶναι μηδὲν ὄντες. PLAT. *Apol.* xxxiii. 41 E.
If they think they are something, when they are nothing.
Here ἐάν favours μηδέν rather than οὐδέν.
ὅτ' οὐδὲν ὢν τοῦ μηδὲν ἀντέστης ὑπέρ.
  SOPH. *Ai.* 1231; cf. 1275
ὑμᾶς τὸ μηδὲν ὄντας ἐν τροπῇ δορός
ἐρρύσατο. SOPH. *Ai.* 1274; cf. EUR. *El.* 369.
κεἰ τὸ μηδὲν ἐξερῶ φράσω δ' ὅμως. SOPH. *Ant.* 234.
τοίγαρ σὺ δέξαι μ' ἐς τὸ σὸν τόδε στέγος
τὴν μηδὲν εἰς τὸ μηδέν. SOPH. *El.* 1165.
Examples in HERODOTUS occur in i. 32, vi. 137, ix. 58, 79.
Note.
οὐδὲν (μηδὲν) λέγειν, *to talk nonsense* or *idly.*
τὸ οὐδ' οὐδέν, PLAT. *Theaet.* 190 A, *the absolute nothing.*
ὁ μηδὲν ὢν γοναῖσι = δυσγενής, SOPH. *Ai.* 1094.
οὐδὲν (μηδὲν) εἶναι, *to be doomed to death, as good as dead.*
  SOPH. *El.* 1166; EUR. *Androm.* 1077.

§ 305. Μή with Oaths and Assertions.

Μή is sometimes found with the Indicative after an oath or a strong assertion.

μὰ τὴν 'Αφροδίτην . . . μὴ 'γω σ' ἀφήσω.
ARIST. *Ecc.* 999, cf. *Av.* 195, *Lysist.* 917.
Cf. also *Il.* x. 330, xv. 41.

This use of μή should be compared with μή and the Infinitive after verbs of swearing and testifying (see μή with Infin. *Note* 4).

The construction is Epic. In HOMER μή is found both with the Infinitive and the Indicative after an oath or protestation. Μή repudiates the charge.

ἴστω νῦν τόδε γαῖα, κ.τ.λ., μή τί σοι κακὸν βουλεύσεμεν.
Od. v. 184.

Be witness earth to this—far from me be it to contrive harm to thee.

ἴστω νῦν Ζεὺς αὐτός, κ.τ.λ., μὴ ἀνὴρ ἐποχήσεται ἄλλος.
Il. x. 329.

Be witness Zeus himself—no other man shall ride.

§ 306. Μή where οὐ might have been expected.

Μή, where οὐ might otherwise have been expected, is used where the structure of the sentence requires or has a natural affinity with μή. Such cases are where (1) an Imperative precedes, (2) where the sentence is Conditional, (3) where the whole cast of the sentence is of the nature of a conception, so that the statement denied is not real fact.

1. ψηφίσασθε τὸν πόλεμον, μὴ φοβηθέντες τὸ αὐτίκα δεινόν.
THUC. i. 124.

Vote the war without fearing the immediate danger.

ταῦτα σκοπεῖτε, ὅτι μὴ προνοίᾳ μᾶλλον ἐγίγνετο ἢ τύχῃ.
ANTIPH. v. 21.

Consider this, that it happened not so much designedly as by accident.

A very exceptional use of μή, hardly explained by the preceding Imperative.

Cf. XEN. *Cyr.* iii. 1. 37, SOPH. *Ant.* 546, DEM. 27. 59

2. ὁ παῖς εἴπερ ἑστὼς φανερὸς ὑμῖν ἐστι μὴ βληθείς, δηλοῦται διὰ τὴν αὑτοῦ ἁμαρτίαν ἀποθανών.
ANTIPH. *Tetr.* B., c. 5.
As to the child, if it is proved to you that he was not struck when he was standing still, it is evident that he was killed by his own fault.

3. οἶμαι μὴ ἂν δικαίως τούτου τυχεῖν ἐπαίνου τὸν μὴ εἰδότα τί ἐστι νόμος.   XEN. *Mem.* i. 2. 41.
I think that one who does not know the meaning of law would not deservedly receive this praise.

The first μή is exceptional, but the example is from Xenophon, an exceptional writer.

ἢ δοκεῖ σοι οἷόν τε εἶναι ἔτι ἐκείνην τὴν πόλιν εἶναι καὶ μὴ ἀνατετράφθαι, ἐν ᾗ αἱ γενόμεναι δίκαι μηδὲν ἰσχύουσιν;
PLAT. *Crit.* xi. 50 B.
Do you really think it possible for a state to continue to exist and not be overthrown, in which verdicts which have been passed have no avail?

This may be regarded as regular, the μή coming after οἷον τε and not after δοκεῖ.

Riddell, *Digest* 135, collects some extreme Platonic instances.

§ 307. Miscellaneous Instances showing the power of οὐ to make a downright Negative Statement. Cf. the use of οὐ in Emphasis, p. 352.

This power is very marked in contrasts:

ξυμβαίνει γὰρ οὐ τὰ μέν, τὰ δ' οὔ.   AESCH. *Pers.* 800.
It is not that some things are happening, while others are not (i.e. *all things are being fulfilled*).

ἦν ὁ ποταμὸς δάσυς δένδρεσι παχέσι μὲν οὔ, πυκνοῖς δέ.
XEN. *An.* iv. 8. 2.
The river was overgrown with trees which, though not big, were numerous.

ἀπώλετο δ' οὐχί, ἀλλ' ἐλύθη.   LYS. vi. 27.
He was not condemned to death, but acquitted.

Of course the construction may change οὐ to μή :—
σκοπεῖτε μὴ τοῦτο, εἰ τάλαντον ἔδωκε, ἀλλὰ τὴν προθυμίαν.
DEM. 470. 26.
Consider not this point, whether he gave a talent, but his will.
Yet even in spite of the construction οὐ may assert itself :
εἰ γνωσθησόμεθα ξυνελθόντες μέν, ἀμύνεσθαι δὲ οὐ τολμῶντες. THUC. i. 124.
If we shall be known to have met together, and yet not to be venturing to protect ourselves.
This power of οὐ to assert itself under difficulties is seen very strikingly in some passages :
μὴ ὅ γε οὐ χρὴ ποίει. PLAT. *Euthyd.* 307 B.
Don't do what is actually wrong.
The generic μή might be expected :
ἐγὼ γάρ, εἰ μὲν μὴ ᾤμην ἥξειν παρὰ θεούς, ἠδίκουν ἂν οὐκ ἀγανακτῶν τῷ θανάτῳ. PLAT. *Phaed.* viii. 63 B.
i.e. *I should be acting wrongly in not grieving, as in reality I do grieve.*
In spite of the Conditional structure :
Cf. SOPH. *O. T.* 551, εἰ νομίζεις οὐχ ὑφέξειν.

§ 308. Note on μή, μὴ οὐ, with the Infinitive and Participle.

1. Μή with the Infinitive. This construction is perfectly natural and intelligible. Indeed the Infinitive without it, though allowable in Greek as in English, may be somewhat ambiguous. Thus ὃν θανεῖν ἐρρυσάμην would in itself mean *whom I rescued for dying.* The addition of μή makes it perfectly clear that the net result is negative.

The negative was thus used in our earlier English :
You may deny that you were not the cause.
SHAKSPERE, *Rich. III.* i. 3.
First you denied you had in him no right.
Comedy of Errors, iv. 2.

Precisely parallel in Greek is the use of οὐ with ὅτι and the Indicative after verbs of denying : ἀντέλεγον ὅτι οὐκ ἐγχωροίη, XEN. *Hell.* ii. 3. 16 ; ἀρνηθῆναι ὡς οὐκ ἀπέδωκε, *Lys.* iv. 1.

---

[1] The double negative is not unknown even in Ciceronian Latin. Cf. CIC. *De Offic.* iii. 102, 118.

2. Μή οὐ with Infinitive. Here it is much more difficult to see the force of each negative, especially as in translating the Greek into English we make no difference between μή and μή οὐ. Thus we translate ὅσιον μὴ βοηθεῖν, *it is pious not to help*; οὐχ ὅσιον μὴ οὐ βοηθεῖν, *it is impious not to help*. But we may be sure that the force of each negative was, originally at least, felt in Greek. Observe that the double negative is only used with the Infinitive when there is a negative, actual or virtual, in the principal clause. Thus there is an additional negative over and above that in the preceding construction (μή with Infinitive). Just as μή with the Infinitive repeats and sums up the net negative result of the principal verb, so when the principal clause is negative, this additional negative is repeated with the Infinitive, and sums up the effect of the principal clause.[1]

That this was not always felt to be necessary is shown by the examples under **B. C. D.**

3. Μή οὐ with Participle must be explained in the same way. *E.g.* in SOPH. O. T. 12, (1) Affirmatively: *I should be kindly*—(net result)—*in refusing pity* (μὴ κατοικτείρων). (2) Negatively: *I should be unkindly*—(net result)—*in not refusing pity* (μὴ οὐ κατοικτείρων). The Participial construction is required either because, as in the three instances from SOPHOCLES, the Participle agrees with the subject of the principal sentence, or because (as in HEROD. vii. 106) it is in the Genitive Absolute. The Participle denotes *circumstance* generally, and more specially *condition, restriction*, etc., which are only kinds of circumstance.

Wünder (Excursus to SOPH. O. T. 12, 13), while pointing out the above reason for the Participle, denies that it is conditional, although in O. T. 221 he translates μὴ οὐκ ἔχων, *unless I had*. In SOPH. O. T. 12, 13, he says that with an impersonal construction we might write δεινὸν ἂν εἴη or αἰσχύνη ἄν μοι εἴη μὴ οὐ κατοικτείρειν. It is true that we might thus give the sense of this one passage, but we could not so analyse the other passages, while the above explanation seems to suit this as well as the others.

---

[1] Mr A. Sidgwick communicates the following note: Just as in κωλύω μὴ δρᾶν the negatived infinitive gives the *total effect* of hindrance, viz.: the *prevented* act, so in οὐ κωλύω μὴ οὐ δρᾶν the doubly negatived infinitive gives the total effect, viz. the *not prevented* act.

To this superfluous μή after verbs of hindering, etc., the French offers an exact parallel : Empêchez qu'il ne se mêle d'aucune affaire. Compare too the redundant *ne* after comparatives :—Ces fruits sont meilleurs que je ne le croyais. With verbs of doubting, denying, etc., used positively, the French idiom follows the English:—je doute qu'il soit ainsi; but with such verbs used negatively the French *ne* corresponds to the Greek μὴ οὐ :—je n'ai jamais nié qu'il ne soit ainsi.

§ 309. Note on μή and μὴ οὐ with the Subjunctive.

The Attic construction is chiefly Platonic and Aristotelian (cf. *Eth. N.* x. 9. 6, *Pol.* iv. 4. 11, ii. 2. 8). But the construction is as old as HOMER, e.g. *Od.* v. 467, μή με στίβη τε κακὴ καὶ θῆλυς ἐέρση δαμάσῃ, *Perchance cruel rime and soft dew shall blast me.* We have here the original deprecatory force of μή, *let it not.* In a writer like PLATO this μή has become simply a suggestion put politely, and with a delicate irony. Closely allied to this is the interrogative use of μή in the example quoted from the Protagoras (312 A). We need not call the construction elliptical any more than μὴ γένοιτο need be called elliptical. When a Principal Verb (such as ὁρῶ) is expressed, the thought is more logically and fully stated, and the clause with μή has become subordinate: but the two constructions are parallel and synonymous.

Μὴ οὐ after a Principal Verb is also found in HOMER, *Il.* xv. 164, φραζέσθω μὴ μ' οὐδὲ κρατερός περ ἐὼν ἐπιόντα ταλάσσῃ μεῖναι, *Let him look to it whether, stout though he be, he endure not to await my coming.* Οὐ is strictly negative or privative here, as in the Attic examples. Thus in the construction of μή and μὴ οὐ both particles exert their legitimate force. Μή οὐ with the Subjunctive occurs also in HEROD. vi. 9.

§ 310. Note on οὐ μή with the Subjunctive and the Future Indicative.

Both constructions are post-Homeric. It is impossible to trace them with historical certainty, and therefore any explanation suggested must be theoretical.

1. οὐ μή with the Subjunctive. This construction is found both in Prose (Herodotus, Xenophon, Isaeus, Plato, Demosthenes), and in Verse (Aeschylus, Sophocles, Euripides, Aristophanes).

Both οὐ and μή appear to exert their proper force. The construction seems to be the negative of μή with the Subjunctive. (See note on that construction, § 309.) Thus μὴ πίθηται would mean *far be it that he obey*; οὐ negatives this apprehension : *it is not a case of such surmise, there is no likelihood of his obeying, he will not obey*. Such a construction in the second person is tantamount to a prohibition, as in the example from the *Clouds* of Aristophanes. If this view is correct, we need no more understand an ellipse of δέος or δεινόν between the οὐ and the μή here than in μή with the Subjunctive.

οὐ δέος, οὐ δεινόν fully expressed occur often enough (HDT. i. 84 ; PLAT. *Apol.* ch. xvi. 28 B, *Phaed.* 84 B, *Rep.* 465 B ; XEN. *Mem.* ii. 1. 25 ; ARIST. *Ecc.* 650).

2. οὐ μή with the Future Indicative is far more difficult. In the first place the construction is almost wholly poetical. It occurs in HDT. iii. 162, Plato, Aeschines, as a rare idiom in each. It is very common in Sophocles, Euripides, Aristophanes.

(*a*) Is the phrase Interrogative ?[1]

In favour of οὐ μή with 2d person of the Future being interrogative are the following considerations : A positive command is commonly expressed by οὐ interrogative with the Future, *e.g.* ARIST. *Lys.* 459, οὐχ ἕλξετ', οὐ ποιήσετ', κ.τ.λ. ; followed by imperatives παύεσθε, κ.τ.λ. Sometimes οὐ μή with the Future (expressing a negative command) appears side by side with οὐ and the Future (expressing a positive command). The juxtaposition is very striking in ARIST. *Ran.* 200-2, a passage which shows that in the time of Aristophanes the two idioms could be used as exact opposites.

Professor Goodwin's objection to the Future being interrogative, derived from the single passage in the *Clouds* (296), where an Imperative and not a Future is joined by ἀλλά to οὐ μή with a Subjunctive (*v. l.* a Future), is not convincing. The inference (supposing that the Future is the true reading) need only be that οὐ μή with the Future had become a stereotyped Imperative. And in ARIST. *Lys.* 459 (above), SOPH. *Ant.* 885 we have the Imperative immediately following οὐ with the Future used interrogatively, though not joined by a conjunction to it.

---

[1] Mr. A. Sidgwick writes : "It is to me quite clear that οὐ μή with the Future is usually interrogative ; when not, it is a form of οὐ μή with the Subjunctive."

Against the phrase being interrogative may be urged that such a theory assigns a different origin not only to οὐ μή with the 2d person of the Future from οὐ μή with Subjunctive, but also from οὐ μή with the 1st and 3d persons of Future. This difficulty is increased by the fact that οὐ μή with the 2d person of the Future *may*, though rarely, express a negative statement, like οὐ μή with Subjunctive.

If, in spite of this, the Interrogative theory is maintained, we should have to assign a different origin to this special idiom; doubtless a serious but not perhaps a fatal objection, for the evolution of popular idioms is as manifold as it is obscure.

(*b*) Οὐ and οὐ μή followed by καί, ἀλλά, καὶ μή, μηδέ:
If οὐ μή is interrogative the explanation is simple. Οὐ throws its force over each connected clause which follows. The simplest case is SOPH. *Tr.* 978, where καί follows. The most complex is EUR. *Bacch.* 343, where the process would be οὐ μὴ προσοίσεις;—οὐ βακχεύσεις; (joined by δέ)—οὐ μὴ ἐξομόρξει; *Will you not avoid bringing near? Will you not play the bacchanal? and will you not avoid wiping off?*

If οὐ μή is not interrogative each subsequent clause will have to be differently explained. EUR. *Bacch.* 343 would run thus—Οὐ μὴ προσοίσεις, *you shall not bring near;* βακχεύσεις δέ, *but you shall play the bacchanal* (like πρὸς ταῦτα πράξεις, SOPH. *O.C.* 956); μὴ ἐξομόρξει could only be explained on the assumption of μή with the Future being prohibitive, a construction which has yet to be established.

The interrogative theory of οὐ μή finds decided support here, not only from the extreme abruptness of each clause thus made independent, but from the grammatical difficulty thus occasioned.

(*c*) Professor Goodwin (*Moods and Tenses*, § 89) considers that in οὐ μή with the Future, οὐ is added (not interrogatively) to μή with the Future Indicative used as a Prohibition. But (1) μή with the Future Indicative thus used is a construction of extreme rarity, if it exists at all. Some of the instances quoted (*Moods and Tenses*, § 25, Note 5 (*b*)), *e.g.* SOPH. *Ai.* 572, are probably not to the point, and in others, assuming the Future Indicative to be the correct reading, a different explanation seems possible. (2) Assuming the existence of μή with the Future Indicative as a Prohibition, it is difficult to see how a prohibition can be got out of οὐ μή with the Future as a statement. An analysis of the phrase οὐ (*you shall not*) μή ποιήσεις (*don't do*) would land us in a meaning precisely opposite to that required. On the other hand, we get the right meaning if the phrase is interrogative, οὐ, *won't you,* μή ποιήσεις; *abstain from doing?*

In οὐ μή with the Subjunctive Professor Goodwin does not attempt to account for the μή. He considers the Subjunctive as "a relic of the common Homeric Subjunctive used as a weak Future."

(*d*) Mr. Riddell (*Digest of Platonic Idioms,* p. 177) explains the double use of the negative on the principle of "simultaneity of force;" *i.e.* both particles, like a double-barrelled gun, concentrate their fire on one verb. It is quite true that in course of time the two particles formed one strong reduplicated negative, their origin being quite lost sight of. Such cases as Soph. *Phil.* 611, Eur. *Phoen.* 1590, clearly show this. Still the question remains, How is it that οὐ and μή, differing as they do, combine their force?

(*e*) Can οὐ and μή be separately explained?
It is μή which requires explanation, not οὐ. Οὐ on any theory exerts its simple contradictory force.

If οὐ μή with the Future is interrogative, οὐ μὴ ποιήσεις; must mean, Won't you *abstain from* or *avoid* doing? It is always objected that this explanation gives μή the privative force of οὐ. Not so, for μὴ ποιήσεις need not represent a privative οὐ ποιῶ, but rather a deprecated future act. The use of μή with the Future Indicative would help us to understand how the idiom might arise. Now the independent use of μή with the Future is extremely uncommon. It occurs, rarely, in questions (*e.g.* Plat. *Rep.* 405 A., ἆρα μή τι μεῖζον ἕξεις λαβεῖν τεκμήριον). Μή interrogative is simply μή denoting an apprehension. It occurs after oaths and similar assertions (*Il.* x. 330, Arist. *Ecc.* 991). But the Future Indicative, graphically substituted for the Subjunctive, is fairly common (φοβοῦμαι μὴ εὑρήσομεν, Plat. *Phileb.* 13, and the Future Indicative is joined co-ordinately to the Subjunctive in several places (*e.g.* Aesch. *Pers.* 124; Soph. *El.* 43; cf. Arist. *Ecc.* 495).

If οὐ μή is not interrogative then it will be a more vivid and graphic substitution of οὐ μή for the Subjunctive. The process would be οὐ μὴ ποιήσῃς, *it is not the case* (οὐ) μὴ ποιήσῃς (*of apprehending that you may do*), or οὐ μὴ ποιήσεις (*that you really will do*). This readily passes into a command (cf. EUR. *Med.* 1320, χειρὶ δ' οὐ ψαύσεις ποτέ, *thou shalt not touch*, i.e. *touch not*).

A list of passages in which οὐ μή occurs with the Future is given for reference.

HDT. iii. 162 (οὐ μὴ ἀναβλαστήσει). AESCHIN. *de Cor.* 79. 12.

XEN. *Hell.* i. 6. 32. ISAEUS, viii. 24.

PLAT. *Symp.* 175 A. (οὔκουν καὶ μή).

SOPH. (*a.*) οὐ μή, 1st or 3d person:
El. 1052; *O. C.* 177; *Phil.* 611 (Optative in Obliqua).

(*b.*) οὐ μή, 2d person:
O. T. 637 (οὐ . . . καὶ μή); *O. C.* 847 (not a prohibition); *Aj.* 75 (οὐ . . . μηδέ); *Trach.* 978 (οὐ μή . . . καί); 1183 (οὐ . . . μηδέ).

EURIPID. *Hipp.* 213; *Ib.* 496 (οὐχί . . . καὶ μή); *Ib.* 1601 (οὐ μή . . . μηδέ); *Androm.* 797; *Supp.* 1066; *Bacch.* 342 (οὐ μή . . . δέ . . . μηδέ).

ARISTOPH. *Ran.* 202 (οὐ μή . . . ἀλλά); *Ib.* 298 (οὐ μή . . . μηδέ); *Ib.* 462 (οὐ μή . . . ἀλλά); *Ach.* 166; *Vesp.* 397; *Nub.* 296, 367, 505 (the subjunctive of the MSS. in these passages has been changed by editors to the future indicative).

CHAPTER III.

ORATIO OBLIQUA.

Introductory.

§ 311. By Oratio Recta is meant the words or thoughts of a person given at first-hand, as from his own lips, *e.g.*—

δώσω ἃ ἔχω.
I will give what I have.

By Oratio Obliqua is meant the words or thoughts of a person given at second-hand by some one else, *e.g.*—

ἔφη   δώσειν   ἃ   ἔχοι.
or
ἔλεγεν ὅτι (ὡς) δώσοι   ἃ   ἔχοι.
He said he would give what he had.

If the words are reported in the following way:—

ἔλεγεν ὅτι (ὡς) δώσω ἃ ἔχω.
He said, "I will give what I have,"

we have no Obliqua at all: ἔλεγεν ὅτι introduces the original words just as in English we put them in inverted commas, as a quotation in fact.

e.g. προσελθόντες δέ μοι τῇ ὑστεραίᾳ Μέλητος καὶ Εὐφίλητος ἔλεγον ὅτι, γεγένηται, ὦ 'Ανδοκίδη, καὶ πέπρακται ἡμῖν ταῦτα. ANDOK. *de Myst.* 63.
Next day Meletus and Euphiletus came to me and said, "It has taken place, Andokides, we have done it."

But the reporter may give the words thus:—

ἔφη   δώσειν   ἃ   ἔχει.
ἔλεγεν ὅτι (ὡς) δώσει   ἃ   ἔχει.

Here we have a kind of Obliqua extremely common in Greek, and often alternating in the same paragraph with the Obliqua given above. From a love of what is graphic and vivid the Greeks keep the original mood while only changing the person. Or we may say that they keep the mood which would be used if the Obliqua were in Primary Sequence:

e.g., λέγει ὅτι δώσει ἅ ἔχει.

Observe then that in Oratio Obliqua—

1. The *person*, whatever it was in the Recta, becomes the 3d in the Obliqua.[1]

2. The *tense* of the Recta never changes. If it did, the Obliqua would not represent faithfully the time and act of the Recta.

3. The *Mood* may either
   (*a.*) be changed to the Optative in the Obliqua (of Historic Sequence),
   (*b.*) be retained as it was in the Recta, or in Primary Sequence.

By Oratio Obliqua is here meant reported speech in Historic Sequence. Oratio Obliqua in Primary Sequence involves (in Greek) no change of Mood in the Adverbial and Relative Sentences, and therefore can at once be dismissed with one brief example by way of illustration.

Oratio Recta:

διαμενῶ   ἕως ἂν ἐπανέλθωσιν   οὓς πέμπω.
I will remain   *until they return*   *whom I am sending.*

Oratio Obliqua:

φησι   } διαμενεῖν
λέγει ὅτι (ὡς) } διαμενεῖ   ἕως ἂν ἐπανέλθωσιν οὓς πέμπει.

He says that he will remain, until they return, whom he is sending.

νομίζω, ἂν τοῦτ' ἀκριβῶς μάθητε, μᾶλλον ὑμᾶς τούτοις μὲν ἀπιστήσειν, ἐμοὶ δὲ βοηθήσειν. DEM. *Onet.* 870. 24.
I consider that, if you learn the truth of this, you will be more likely to distrust them, and help me.

---

[1] Unless the speaker quotes his own words, or those of a person whom he is addressing, *e.g.* "I told you that I knew nothing of the matter:" "You stated that you would lend me ten pounds."

Sub-direct and Sub-oblique.

When Recta is changed to Obliqua, the Principal Sentence (*i.e.* the Substantival Sentence, whether Oblique Statement, Question, or Petition), becomes itself subordinate to the reporter's verb (He *said, asked, requested*). Such a Sentence is technically called *Sub-direct, i.e.* subordinate to Recta.

What were the subordinate sentences of the Recta, *i.e.* Adverbial or Relative Sentences, become subordinate to a Principal Sentence which itself is subordinate. They are now technically called *Sub-oblique, i.e.* subordinate to an Oblique clause. For brevity's sake these terms, Sub-direct and Sub-oblique (*i.e.* Adverbial and Relative Sentences in Oratio Obliqua), will be used in this chapter.

The terms have been explained in the Introductory Chapter, p. 11.

§ 312. Rules for Sub-direct Clauses in Oratio Obliqua.

Such clauses are either (1) *Oblique Statements* with ὅτι and ὡς, or *Oblique Questions*. *Oblique Petitions* take an Infinitive, so that their construction is just like an Oblique Statement in the Infinitive after φημί. Sentences with ὅπως and ὅπως μή (with Future Indicative or Subjunctive) follow the construction of the Oblique Question. The Oblique Statement *in the Participle* presents no difficulty.

Co-ordinate Sentences follow the construction of those to which they are joined.

A. In Primary Sequence, *i.e.* when the Principal Sentence takes a Primary tense, the Mood and Tense of the Sub-direct Sentence undergo no change.

B. In Historic Sequence the Sub-direct Sentence may either

(1.) be just what it was in Primary Sequence, undergoing no change—(this is called *the Graphic Construction*)—or,

(2.) the Verb may be changed to the same tense of the Optative.

But *N.B.* The *Imperfect* and *Pluperfect Indicative* must remain in the Indicative, and not be changed to the Optative. If they were changed we could not distinguish them from Present and Perfect Optatives. Historic Tenses of the Indicative with ἄν must also remain in the Indicative.

A few instances occur where the Present Optative represents an Imperfect Indicative of the Recta. In such cases however no ambiguity exists.

τὰ πεπραγμένα διηγοῦντο, ὅτι αὐτοὶ μὲν πλέοιεν τὴν δὲ ἀναίρεσιν τῶν ναυαγῶν προστάξαιεν. XEN. Hell. i. 7. 5. *They were describing the facts, explaining that they themselves were sailing (against the enemy), and that they had commissioned (proper persons) to pick up the shipwrecked seamen.*

Recta, αὐτοὶ ἐπλέομεν καὶ προσετάξαμεν. Cf. vii. 1. 38, ἐθέλοι, βουλεύοιτο.

Obs. 1. The *Tense* of an Infinitive in a Sub-direct Clause is the same as in the Recta, *e.g.* ἔγραψα, *I wrote ;* ἔφη γράψαι, *he said that he had written ;* λέγε, *speak ;* ἐκέλευεν αὐτὸν λέγειν, *he was ordering him to speak.* The *time* of the Infinitive Tense may therefore be instantly discovered by turning it back to the Recta. So with the *time* of a Participle.

Obs. 2. No verb takes ἄν because of its conversion from Recta to Obliqua. If in the Obliqua a Finite Verb, Infinitive, or Participle takes ἄν, it is because it had an ἄν in the Recta. The tables of converted Conditional Sentences will show this.

§ 313. Types of Sub-direct Clauses in Historic Sequence.

A. I. ORIGINAL RECTA (STATEMENT).

1. ταῦτα μανθάνω.
2. ταῦτα μαθήσομαι.
3. ταῦτα μεμάθηκα.
4. ταῦτα ἐμάνθανον.
5. ταῦτα ἐμεμαθήκη.
6. ταῦτα ἔμαθον.

II. Converted to Obliqua in Historic Sequence.

Principal.
ἔλεξεν ὅτι, ὡς.

Sub-direct.

1. ταῦτα μανθάνει. — Graphic.
   ταῦτα μανθάνοι. — Strict Sequence.
2. ταῦτα μαθήσεται. — Graphic.
   ταῦτα μαθήσοιτο. — Strict Sequence.
3. ταῦτα μεμάθηκε. — Graphic.
   ταῦτα μεμαθηκὼς εἴη. — Strict Sequence.
4. ταῦτα ἐμάνθανε.
5. ταῦτα ἐμεμαθήκει.
6. ταῦτα ἔμαθε. — Graphic.
   ταῦτα μάθοι. — Strict Sequence.

B. I. Original Recta (Question).

1. τί μανθάνεις;
2. τί μαθήσει;
3. τί μεμάθηκας;
4. τί ἐμάνθανες;
5. τί ἐμεμαθήκεις;
6. τί ἔμαθες;

II. Converted to Obliqua.

ἤρετο.
1. ὅτι or τί. μανθάνει. — Graphic.
   μανθάνοι. — Strict Sequence.
2. „ μαθήσεται. — Graphic.
   μαθήσοιτο. — Strict Sequence.
3. „ μεμάθηκε. — Graphic.
   μεμαθηκὼς εἴη. — Strict Sequence.
4. „ ἐμάνθανε.
5. „ ἐμεμαθήκει.
6. „ ἔμαθε. — Graphic.
   μάθοι. — Strict Sequence.

Note. The Aorist Indicative is preferable to the Optative whenever it avoids ambiguity. Thus οὐκ εἶχον ὅτι δράσειαν might mean either *they did not know what to do* (Recta, τί δράσωμεν; a deliberative Subjunctive), or, *they did not know what they had done* (Recta, τί ἐδράσαμεν;). Almost always the first construction is intended.

C. Similarly with ὅπως, ὅπως μή (a much rarer construction after verbs of commanding, etc., than the Infinitive).

Recta: ὅπως μὴ ἔσεσθε ἀνάξιοι ἐλευθερίας.
See that you be not unworthy of freedom.

παρηγγείλεν ὅπως μὴ $\begin{array}{l}\text{ἔσονται}\\\text{ἔσοιντο}\end{array}\Big\}\begin{array}{l}\text{Graphic.}\\\text{Strict Sequence.}\end{array}$

D. With Deliberative Questions.
Recta, ποῖ φύγω;
Obliqua, ἠπόρει ποῖ (ὅποι) $\begin{array}{l}\text{φύγῃ}\\\text{φύγοι}\end{array}\Big\}\begin{array}{l}\text{Graphic.}\\\text{Strict Sequence.}\end{array}$

§ 314. Rules for Sub-oblique Clauses in the Oratio Obliqua.

A. In Primary Sequence they undergo no change of Mood or Tense in passing from the Recta.

B. In Historic Sequence:
1. By the graphic construction they undergo no change, continuing to be what they were in Primary Sequence.
2. The verb is changed to the same tense in the Optative, in Strict Sequence.

But *N.B.* The Imperfect, Pluperfect, and Aorist Indicative must remain in the Indicative and not be changed to the Optative. Exceptions will be noticed further on.

§ 315. Note to accompany the following Tables.

The construction of Sub-oblique as well as Sub-direct Clauses is shown in Conditional Sentences converted from the Recta to the Obliqua. The Recta will be found by referring to Conditional Sentences (page 198), and need not be repeated here. The Apodosis is the Principal Sentence in the Recta and the Sub-direct in the Obliqua. The Protasis is the Sub-direct in the Recta, and the Sub-oblique in the Obliqua. The Protasis may be taken as the type of any Adverbial Sub-oblique Clause by substituting ἐπειδή, ὅτε, ἕως, πρίν, etc., for εἰ or ἐάν. It may equally well stand as the type of any Relative Sub-oblique Clause, but for the sake of completeness a Relative Conditional Table is given converted to the Obliqua.

TYPES OF ORATIO OBLIQUA.

Observe that in the Sub-oblique Clauses, Adverbial or Relative, the Imperfect, Pluperfect, and Aorist Indicative of the Recta are not converted to the Optative but continue in the Indicative.

The conversion of General Suppositions may be thus shown :

Recta : ἢν ἐγγὺς ἔλθῃ θάνατος οὐδεὶς βούλεται θνῄσκειν.
ἀλλ' εἴ τι μὴ φέροιμεν ὤτρυνεν φέρειν.

Obliqua after ἢν ἔλθῃ—βούλεται—Graphic.

ἔλεξε ὅτι εἰ ἔλθοι—βούλοιτο.
εἴ τί μὴ φέροιεν—ὤτρυνεν.

ἔφη ἢν ἔλθῃ—οὐδένα βούλεσθαι—Graphic.
εἰ ἔλθοι—οὐδένα βούλεσθαι.
εἴ τι μὴ φέροιεν—ὀτρύνειν φέρειν.

He said that, if they were not fetching anything, he was ordering them to fetch it.

§ 316. Types of Oratio Obliqua, showing Sub-direct and Sub-oblique Clauses in the Obliqua. The Protasis is the Sub-oblique, the Apodosis the Sub-direct Clause.

If you do this you are doing wrong becomes, when reported by another person, *He said that if he did it he was doing wrong.*

I. With λέγω ὅτι, and a finite mood :

1. PRIMARY SEQUENCE :

Sub-oblique (the Protasis).	Sub-direct (the Apodosis).
εἰ ταῦτα ποιεῖ	ἀδικεῖ
πεποίηκε	
εἰ ταῦτα ἐποίει	ἠδίκει
ἐποίησε	ἠδίκησε
ἐὰν (ἢν) ταῦτα ποίῃ	ἀδικήσει
ποιήσῃ	
εἰ ταῦτα ποιοίη or	ἀδικοίη ἄν or
ποιήσειε	ἀδικήσειεν ἄν
εἰ ταῦτα ποιήσει·	ἀδικήσει
εἰ ταῦτα ἐποίει	ἠδίκει ἄν
εἰ ταῦτα ἐποίησε	ἠδίκησεν ἄν

λέγει ὅτι (ὡς)

ORATIO OBLIQUA.

2. Historic Sequence:

ἔλεξε ὅτι (ὡς)
$\begin{cases} εἰ ταῦτα ποιοίη & ἀδικοίη \\ εἰ ταῦτα ἐποίει & ἠδίκει \\ \quad ἐποίησε & ἀδικήσειε \\ εἰ ταῦτα ποιοίη & ἀδικήσοι \\ \quad ποιήσειε & \\ εἰ ταῦτα ποιοίη & ἀδικοίη ἄν \\ \quad ποιήσειε & ἀδικήσειεν ἄν \\ εἰ ταῦτα ποιήσοι & ἀδικήσοι \\ εἰ ταῦτα ἐποίει & ἠδίκει ἄν \\ εἰ ταῦτα ἐποίησε & ἠδίκησεν ἄν \end{cases}$

In the graphic construction the construction after ἔλεξε ὅτι will be just the same as after λέγει ὅτι. The Future and Perfect Indicative (graphic) are commoner than their corresponding Optatives.

II. With φημί and an Infinitive:

1. Primary Sequence:

I.
φημί or οἶμαί σε
$\begin{cases} \text{A. Present} & εἰ ταῦτα ποιεῖς & ἀδικεῖν \\ \text{B. Past} & εἰ ταῦτα \begin{cases} ἐποίεις \\ ἐποίησας \end{cases} & \begin{cases} ἀδικεῖν \\ ἀδικῆσαι \end{cases} \\ \text{C. Future } a.\ ἐάν\ ταῦτα \begin{cases} ποίῃς \\ ποιήσῃς \end{cases} & ἀδικήσειν \\ \qquad b.\ εἰ\ ταῦτα \begin{cases} ποιοίης \\ ποιήσειας \end{cases} & \begin{cases} ἀδικεῖν ἄν \\ ἀδικῆσαι ἄν \end{cases} \\ \qquad c.\ εἰ\ ταῦτα\ ποιήσεις & ἀδικήσειν \end{cases}$

II.
$\begin{cases} \text{A. Present} & εἰ ταῦτα ἐποίεις & ἀδικεῖν ἄν \\ \text{B. Past} & εἰ ταῦτα ἐποίησας & ἀδικῆσαι ἄν \end{cases}$

Note. An Imperative in Apodosis would of course depend on a Verb of commanding (Indirect Petition), *e.g.* κόπτε τὴν θύραν, *knock at the door;* εἶπε κόπτειν τὴν θύραν, *he told him to knock at the door.*

2. Strict Historic Sequence:

I.
ἔφην or ᾤμην σε
$\begin{cases} \text{A. Present} & εἰ ταῦτα ποιοίης & ἀδικεῖν \\ \text{B. Past} & εἰ ταῦτα \begin{cases} ἐποίεις \\ ἐποίησας \end{cases} & \begin{cases} ἀδικεῖν \\ ἀδικῆσαι \end{cases} \\ \text{C. Future } a.\ εἰ\ ταῦτα \begin{cases} ποιοίης \\ ποιήσειας \end{cases} & ἀδικήσειν \\ \qquad b.\ εἰ\ ταῦτα \begin{cases} ποιοίης \\ ποιήσειας \end{cases} & \begin{cases} ἀδικεῖν ἄν \\ ἀδικῆσαι ἄν \end{cases} \\ \qquad c.\ εἰ\ ταῦτα\ ποιήσοις & ἀδικήσειν \end{cases}$

THE APODOSIS IN THE PARTICIPLE. 395

II. { A. PRESENT εἰ ταῦτα ἐποίεις ἀδικεῖν ἄν
    { B. PAST   εἰ ταῦτα ἐποίησας ἀδικῆσαι ἄν

Note. Εἰ with the Optative in the Strict Historic Obliqua stands for three distinct forms. Thus εἰ ποιοίης may represent (*a*) εἰ ποιεῖς, a present condition; (*b*) ἐάν ποίῃς, an ordinary future condition; (*c*) εἰ ποιοίης, a less graphic future condition.

§ 317. The Apodosis in the Participle.

1. PRIMARY SEQUENCE.

οἶδά σε, εἰ ταῦτα ποιεῖς, ἀδικοῦντα, and so on, the Participle in each case being in the same tense as the corresponding Infinitive.

2. HISTORIC SEQUENCE.

ᾔδη σε, εἰ ταῦτα ποιοίης, ἀδικοῦντα, and so on.

Note. εἰ ταῦτα ποιῶ ἀδικῶ becomes οἶδα εἰ ταῦτα ποιῶ ἀδικῶν.

§ 318. A Relative Sentence in the Sub-oblique Clause.

Recta.

ἃ ἔχει   δίδωσι
ἃ εἶχε or ἔσχε   ἐδίδου or ἔδωκε
ἃ ἔχῃ   δώσει
ἃ ἔχοι   διδοίη ἄν
ἃ ἕξει   δώσει
ἃ εἶχεν   ἐδίδου ἄν
ἃ ἔσχεν   ἔδωκεν ἄν

Note. Observe that ἃ ἄν ἔχῃ becomes in the Obliqua ἃ ἔχοι: whereas ἃ εἶχε remains ἃ εἶχε, and is not converted into ἃ ἔχοι. ἃ ἔχοι represents three forms, ἃ ἔχει, ἃ ἄν ἔχῃ, ἃ ἔχοι, but the Apodosis is in each case sufficient to prevent ambiguity. If, however, ἃ εἶχε ἐδίδου were changed to ἃ ἔχοι διδοίη the ambiguity would be real.

Obliqua.

Note. After ἔλεξε ὅτι or ὡς, by the Graphic Construction the clauses would remain unchanged: but the real Obliqua would be as follows:—

ἔλεξε ὅτι (ὡς) ἃ ἔχοι   διδοίη
               ἃ εἶχε or ἔσχε   ἐδίδου or ἔδωκε (or, instead of
                                  ἔδωκε, δοίη)
               ἃ ἔχοι   δώσοι (more commonly δώσει)
               ἃ ἔχοι   διδοίη ἄν
               ἃ ἔξοι   δώσοι (δώσει)
               ἃ εἶχεν   ἐδίδου ἄν
               ἃ ἔσχεν   ἔδωκεν ἄν

Note. Observe the retention of the Aorist Indicative, which is not changed to the Optative. If we were to write ἔλεξε ὅτι δώσοι (δώσει) ἃ λάβοι, or ἔφη δώσειν ὅ τι λάβοι, we should rightly take this to mean, *he said that he would give whatever he took;* ἃ λάβοι would represent a Recta ἃ ἄν λάβω, and not ἃ ἔλαβον, *what I actually took.*

§ 319. Some real Examples analysed.

PRINCIPAL.	SUB-DIRECT.	SUB-OBLIQUE.
1. ἔφη ἔλεγεν ὅτι (ὡς)	ληπτέον εἶναι ληπτέον ἐστὶ, παρα- στάτας	εἴ τι μάχης δεήσοι.

Adapted from XEN. *Cyr.* viii. 1. 10.

He said that   *he must get comrades*   *if there should be need of a battle.*

Recta: ληπτέον ἐστὶ παραστάτας εἴ τι μάχης δεήσει.
I must get comrades if there shall be need of a battle.

The Obliqua is partly Graphic, partly strict Historic.

2. ἔφη ἔλεγεν ὅτι (ὡς)	οὐδὲν αὐτῷ μέλειν οὐδὲν αὐτῷ μέλοι	ἐπειδὴ εἰδείη. LYS. xii. 74.
He said	*that he cared not*	*since he knew.*

Recta: οὐδέν μοι μέλει ἐπειδὴ οἶδα.

3. ἐβουλεύοντο	ὅπως ἴοιεν	ἐπειδὴ γένοιντο παρὰ τῷ ποταμῷ.

Adapted from THUC. vii. 80.

They were con-   *how they should go*   *when they came to*
sidering   *the river.*

Recta: πῶς ἴωμεν, ἐπειδὰν νενώμεθα; a Deliberative Question.

REAL EXAMPLES ANALYSED. 397

PRINCIPAL.	SUB-DIRECT.	SUB-OBLIQUE.
4. ἐσκόπει	πῶς αὐτῷ ἔσοιτο	ὅστις θάψοι.
		ISAE. ii. 10.
He was considering.	*how he should find one*	*to bury him.*
Recta:	πῶς μοι ἔσται	ὅστις θάψει;
5. Ἄνυτος ἔφη	οὐχ οἷόν τε εἶναι τὸ μὴ ἀποκτεῖναί με	ἐπειδὴ εἰσῆλθον δεῦρο.
		PLAT. *Apol.* xvii. 29 C.
Anytus said that	*it was impossible for you not to sentence me to death*	*when once I had been brought into this court.*
Recta:	οὐχ οἷόν τέ ἐστιν τὸ μὴ ἀποκτεῖναι Σωκράτη	ἐπειδὴ εἰσῆλθε δεῦρο.

Observe that the Aorist Indicative of the Recta is not changed to the Obliqua.

6. λέγουσι δὲ	ὡς ἐν τῇ γῇ ἀπέθανεν ὁ ἀνήρ, κἀγὼ λίθον αὐτῷ ἐνέβαλον εἰς τὴν κεφαλήν,	ὃς οὐκ ἐξέβην τὸ παράπαν ἐκ τοῦ πλοίου.
		ANTIPH. *de Caed. Her.* 26.
They say	*that the deceased was murdered ashore, and that I struck him on the head with a stone,*	*though as a matter of fact I never left the ship at all.*

Observe here that the Aorist Indicative is kept in the Sub-direct Clauses, and also (of course) in the Sub-oblique Clause.

7. ἔφη	μέχρι τούτου δεῖν μανθάνειν	ἕως ἱκανός τις γένοιτο, εἴποτε δεήσειε, κ.τ.λ.
		XEN. *Mem.* iv. 7. 2.
He said	*that it was necessary to go on learning for so long a time*	*until one became capable, if ever it should be necessary, etc.*

Recta: μέχρι τούτου δεῖ μανθάνειν, ἕως ἂν γένηται, ἐάν πότε δεήσῃ.

§ 320. The Infinitive, and ὅτι (ὡς) with Finite Moods in the Sub-direct Sentences.

Both these Constructions occur in the Sub-direct Sentence, i.e. in the Principal Sentence of the Original Recta. But the Infinitive is unquestionably the most common, as it is the most natural, simple, and easy mode of expression. Greek writers seem unconsciously to slide into it, even after an Obliqua has been introduced in the first instance by ὅτι or ὡς. In consequence of this love for the Infinitive, one or two peculiarities should be observed.

1. An Obliqua (indirect words or thoughts) is often suddenly introduced without any introductory Principal Verb. A Particle is the only warning given, *said he, he thought, it was said*, or some such expression was in the writer's mind and can be easily supplied. And in such a case it should be noticed that the Predicate in the Nominative accompanies the Infinitive when referring to the Subject of the Infinitive and of the chief Verb.

Latin and English have the same free and natural usage.

(*a.*) Ἆγις τοὺς πρέσβεις ἐς Λακεδαίμονα ἐκέλευσεν ἰέναι· οὐ γὰρ εἶναι κύριος αὐτός, κ.τ.λ. XEN. *Hell.* ii. 2. 12.
Agis recommended the envoys to go to Lacedaemon (explaining that) he was not himself competent, etc.[1]

(*b.*) Πλάτων δὲ ὅδε, ὦ ἄνδρες Ἀθηναῖοι, καὶ Κρίτων καὶ Κριτόβουλος καὶ Ἀπολλόδωρος κελεύουσί με τριάκοντα μνῶν τιμήσασθαι, αὐτοὶ δ' ἐγγυᾶσθαι.
PLAT. *Apol.* xxviii. 38 B.
Plato here, and Crito, and Critobulus, and Apollodorus, wish me to propose thirty minae (desiring me to say that) they themselves are the securities.

δυοῖν χρησίμοιν οὐ διαμαρτήσεσθαι τὴν πόλιν ἡγούμην πλευσάντων ἡμῶν· ἢ γὰρ Φίλιππον, ἃ μὲν εἴληφει τῆς πόλεως, ἀποδώσειν, τῶν δὲ λοιπῶν ἀφέξεσθαι, ἤ, μὴ ποιοῦντος ταῦτα, ἀπαγγελεῖν ἡμᾶς εὐθέως δεῦρο, κ.τ.λ. DEM. 388. 15.
One of two useful ends I considered the state would not lose. Either Philip would restore the possessions of the state

---

[1] English expresses this just as neatly, with still less warning: "Agis recommended the envoys to go to Lacedaemon. He himself was not competent, etc."

which he had taken, and would hold his hand from the remainder, or, if he were not to do this, we should at once bring back word here, etc.

2. In the same way, but not nearly so often as an Infinitive, an Optative may be introduced by an explanatory γάρ.

(*a.*) ἔλεγον ὅτι παντὸς ἄξια λέγει Σεύθης· χειμὼν γὰρ εἴη, κ.τ.λ. XEN. *An.* vii. 313.

They said that what Seuthes said was quite right: for it was winter, etc.

The whole paragraph 13 is very instructive, and should be carefully read. Observe that the Obliqua ends with a direct indicative of the writer, ἐδόκει.

(*b.*) Or the Optative continues the Obliqua after a preceding Optative with ὅτι or ὡς.

ἀπεκρίναντο αὐτῷ, ὅτι ἀδύνατα σφίσιν εἴη ποιεῖν ἃ προκαλεῖται ἄνευ Ἀθηναίων· παῖδες γὰρ σφῶν καὶ γυναῖκες παρ' ἐκείνοις εἴησαν· δεδιέναι δὲ καί, κ.τ.λ. THUC. ii. 72.

Obs. That after the Optative the writer slides naturally into the Infinitive δεδιέναι.

They answered him that it was impossible for them to comply with their proposals without consulting the Athenians, for their wives and children were with them; moreover they were afraid, etc.

(*c.*) In SOPH. *Phil.* 615, an Optative is still more abruptly introduced.

εὐθέως ὑπέσχετο
τὸν ἄνδρ' Ἀχαιοῖς τόνδε δηλώσειν ἄγων·
οἴοιτο μὲν μάλισθ' ἑκούσιον λαβών.
εἰ μὴ θέλοι δ', ἄκοντα· [καὶ τούτων κάρα
τέμνειν ἐφεῖτο τῷ θέλοντι μὴ τυχών].

*Straightway he promised
To bring and show this man to the Achaeans.
Most like with his consent he thought to take him.
Should he refuse, then in his spite, etc.*

Out of ὑπέσχετο is to be supplied (ἔλεξεν ὡς) before οἴοιτο. And observe, as in the preceding passage of Xenophon, the Direct Indicative ἐφεῖτο is resorted to, relieving the artificial strain of the Optative. Cf. also PLAT. *Phaed.* 95 D, ζῴη ... ἀπολλύοιτο: *Rep.* 420 C, ἐναληλιμμένοι εἶεν. With the last instance compare SOPH. O. T. 1245, ὑφ' ὧν θάνοι ... λίποι. Here, although in a Relative Sentence, the Optative crops up; it is equal to ἔλεξεν ὅτι ὑπὸ τούτων θάνοι, so that the clause is virtually Sub-direct rather than Sub-oblique, being introduced by μνήμην ἔχουσ'. The passage is discussed in Madvig's *Syntax*, p. 116, *note* 2, and Goodwin, *Moods and Tenses*, § 77, 1 (e).

3. The Infinitive and ὅτι (ὡς) with a Finite Mood alternate in the same Obliqua.

οἱ Λακεδαιμόνιοι εἶπον, ὅτι σφίσι μὲν δοκοῖεν ἀδικεῖν οἱ Ἀθηναῖοι, βούλεσθαι δὲ καὶ τοὺς πάντας ξυμμάχους παρακαλέσαντες ψῆφον ἐπαγαγεῖν. THUC. i. 87.

Obs. ὅτι μὲν δοκοῖεν co-ordinate with βούλεσθαί δε.

The Lacedaemonians told them that their own judgment was that the Athenians were in the wrong: they wished, however, to summon all the allies as well as themselves, and to put the matter to the vote.

λέγεις σύ, ὦ πάτερ, ὡς ἐμοὶ δοκεῖ, ὅτι, ὥσπερ οὐδὲ γεωργοῦ ἀργοῦ οὐδὲν ὄφελος, οὕτως οὐδὲ στρατηγοῦ ἀργοῦ οὐδὲν ὄφελος εἶναι. XEN. *Cyr.* i. 6. 18.

You say, father, as I understand you, that, just as an idle husbandman is of no use, so an idle soldier is of no use.

Observe that the verb ἐστι is omitted in the sentence introduced by ὥσπερ, and the finite construction with ὅτι is not carried out at all.

4. And this is the greatest peculiarity. Such is the natural Greek yearning for the Infinitive, that Sub-oblique clauses, both Adverbial and Relative, instead of taking a Finite Mood, are actually followed by an Infinitive. In some cases the writer, after beginning with *if, since, when, which*, etc., seems mentally to throw in a "*said he*," "*it was said,*" "*it was agreed or thought*," and passes to an Infinitive: in others the preceding Infinitive seems to exercise an assimilating influence over the Sub-oblique Verb.

(a.) ἔφη δέ. ἐπειδὴ οὗ ἐκβῆναι τὴν ψυχήν, πορεύεσθαι μετὰ πολλῶν. PLAT. *Rep.* 614 B.

He said that when his soul had gone out of him (i.e. his body), he was journeying with many.

Several similar instances occur from 614 to end of the book after ἐν ᾧ, οὕς, ὅτε, εἰς ὅ, οὗ, ὡς.

(b.) λέγεται καὶ Ἀλκμαίωνι τῷ Ἀμφιάρεω, ὅτε δὴ ἀλᾶσθαι αὐτὸν μετὰ τὸν φόνον τῆς μητρός, τὸν Ἀπόλλω ταύτην τὴν γῆν χρῆσαι οἰκεῖν. THUC. ii. 102.
There is a tradition moreover that Apollo by oracle directed Alcmaeon, the son of Amphiaraus, when he was a wanderer after the murder of his mother, to inhabit this district.

Strictly ὅτε ἠλᾶτο.

(c.) Γύγην φασὶν ἰδόντα τὸ χάσμα καὶ θαυμάσαντα καταβῆναι, καὶ ἰδεῖν ἄλλα τε θαυμαστὰ καὶ ἵππον χαλκοῦν κοῖλον, θυρίδας ἔχοντα, καθ' ἃς ἐγκύψαντα ἰδεῖν ἐνόντα νεκρόν, ὡς φαίνεσθαι, μείζω ἢ κατ' ἄνθρωπον· τοῦτον δὲ ἄλλο μὲν ἔχειν οὐδέν, περὶ δὲ τῇ χειρὶ χρυσοῦν δακτύλιον, ὃν περιελόμενον ἐκβῆναι. PLAT. *Rep.* ii. 359 D.
Gyges, the story runs, seeing the abyss and marvelling at it, descended and saw, among many other marvellous things, a hollow brazen horse, fitted with windows, through which he peeped and saw inside a corpse, so it seemed, of more than human stature. It had nothing but a golden ring on its finger, which Gyges took off, and so made his way out.

καθ' ἃς εἶδεν—ὡς ἐφαίνετο—ἄλλο μὲν εἶχε—ὃν περιελόμενος ἐξέβη.

Though Latin has the same construction of the Relative with the Infinitive, yet Cicero in translating this does not avail himself of the identity of idiom (see *De Offic.* iii. 38).

Note. Latin has, though very rarely, this idiom of the Relative with the Infinitive: the often quoted instance from Liv. xxiv. 3 appears to rest on an incorrect reading, but in Liv. xxx. 42 an undoubted example occurs.

Quorum oratio varia fuit, partim purgantium, quae questi erant missi ad regem legati, partim ultro accusantium socios populi Romani, sed multo infestius M. Aurelium, *quem* ex tribus ad se missis legatis, dilectu habito, *substitisse* et se bello *lacessisse* contra foedus, et saepe cum praefectis suis signis conlatis *pugnasse.*
They spoke on a variety of topics. At one time they endeavoured to clear themselves of the charges brought by the commissioners sent to the king ; at another time they were bringing

countercharges against the allies of the Roman people, with much greater rancour however against M. Aurelius, who (they said), out of the three commissioners sent to them, had levied troops, stayed behind, and had commenced hostilities against them contrary to treaty, and had fought several downright battles with their officers.

§ 321. Assimilation of Optatives.

A. After an Optative in a Principal Sentence it is usual for another Optative to follow in an Adverbial or a Relative Sentence as if in Historic Sequence. As the Optative is not in itself past, but on the contrary almost invariably refers to future time, we can only explain this on the principle of assimilation.

(a.) τεθναίην ὅτε μοι μηκέτι ταῦτα μέλοι.
MIMNERMUS, i. 2.
Then might I die whensoe'er this is no longer my care.
For ὅταν μέλῃ.

(b.) πῶς ἄν τις, ἅ γε μὴ ἐπίσταιτο, σοφὸς ἂν εἴη;
XEN. *Mem.* iv. 6, 7.
How could one be wise in what he does not know for certain?
Instead of ἃ ἐπίσταται, or ἃ ἂν μὴ ἐπίστηται.

(c.) εἰ ἀποθνῄσκοι μὲν πάντα ὅσα τοῦ ζῆν μεταλάβοι, ἐπειδὴ δὲ ἀποθάνοι, μένοι ἐν τούτῳ τῷ σχήματι καὶ μὴ πάλιν ἀναβιώσκοιτο, ἆρ᾿ οὐ πολλὴ ἀνάγκη, τελευτῶντα πάντα τεθνάναι καὶ μηδὲν ζῆν;
PLAT. *Phaed.* xvii. 1. 72.
If all things whatsoever partake of life should die, and when they die, abide in this condition and not come to life again, does it not inevitably follow that in the end all things will be dead and nothing living?
For ὅσα ἂν μεταλάβῃ—ἐπειδὰν ἀποθάνῃ.

But τίς οὐκ ἂν μισήσειεν Φίλιππον, εἰ φαίνοιτο τούτοις ἐπιβουλεύων, ὑπὲρ ὧν ὁ πρόγονος αὐτοῦ προείλετο κινδυνεύειν; ISOC. *Phil.* 77.
Because προείλετο was Aorist Indicative in the Recta.
Who would not detest Philip if he should be proved to be conspiring against those in whose behalf his ancestor deliberately decided to face danger?

ASSIMILATION OF OPTATIVES.   403

Note. After an Optative denoting a wish, the sentence may be assimilated.

θύμον γένοιτο χειρὶ πληρῶσαί ποτε
ἵν' αἱ Μυκῆναι γνοῖεν ἡ Σπάρτη θ' ὅτι
χἠ Σκῦρος ἀνδρῶν ἀλκίμων μήτηρ ἔφυ.   SOPH. *Phil.* 324.

For ἵνα γνῶσι. It is generally stated that a Final Sentence is never assimilated. See SOPH. *Phil.* 961, an often quoted instance. See also SOPH. *Trach.* 955 ; EUR. *Bacch.* 1252 (and consult the note in Sandys' edition).

In EUR. *Bacch.* 1384, we get both constructions, Assimilation and non-Assimilation combined :

ἔλθοιμι δ' ὅπου
μήτε Κιθαιρὼν μιαρός μ' ἐσίδοι
μήτε Κιθαιρῶν' ὄσσοισιν ἐγώ,
μήθ' ὅθι θύρσου μνῆμ' ἀνάκειται·
Βάκχαις δ' ἄλλαισι μέλοιεν.

§ 322. **B.** 1. Occasionally this Assimilation does not take place.

(*a.*) Τίς ἂν δίκην κρίνειεν ἢ γνοίη λόγον
πρὶν ἂν παρ' ἀμφοῖν μῦθος ἐκμάθῃ σαφῶς ;
    EUR. *Her.* 179.
πρὶν ἂν ἐκμάθῃ, and not πρὶν ἐκμάθοι. Cf. *Hel.* 176, *Ion* 672, PLAT. *Rep.* ii. 359 C (ὅ τι ἂν βούληται).

(*b.*) Κῦρος προσκαλῶν τοὺς φίλους ἐσπουδαιολογεῖτο, ὡς δηλοίη, οὕς τιμᾷ.   XEN. *An.* i. 9. 28.
οὕς τιμᾷ, and not τιμῴη.

2. An Indirect Statement with ὅτι or ὡς, an Indirect Question, or a Sentence with ὅπως when following an Optative, is not so assimilated, nor usually a Final Sentence.

(*a.*) οὐ δ' ἂν εἷς ἀντείποι ὡς οὐ συμφέρει τῇ πόλει.
    DEM. 202. 23.
'*Not even one would reply that it is not expedient to the state.*

Here ἂν ἀντείποι is a Principal Sentence in Primary Time.

(b.) εἴ τις λέγοι ἄνθρωπον ἑστηκότα, κινοῦντα δὲ τὰς χεῖράς τε καὶ τὴν κεφαλήν, ὅτι ὁ αὐτὸς ἕστηκέ τε καὶ κινεῖται, οὐκ ἂν ἀξιοῖμεν οὕτω λέγειν δεῖν. PLAT. *Rep.* iv. 436 D.
If one should say of a man who is standing still, but is moving his hands and his head, that the same man is both stationary and in motion, we should not allow this to be a correct mode of expression.

(c.) ὁ πρῳρεὺς τῆς νεὼς ... καὶ ἀπὼν ἂν εἴποι, ὅπου ἕκαστα κεῖται καὶ ὅποσα ἔστιν. XEN. *Oec.* viii. 14.

(d.) ὀκνοίην ἂν εἰς τὰ πλοῖα ἐμβαίνειν, ἃ Κῦρος ἡμῖν δοίη, μὴ ἡμᾶς αὐταῖς ταῖς τριήρεσι καταδύσῃ. XEN. *An.* i. 3. 17.

§ 323. Examples of Mixed Graphic and Strict Obliqua.

(a.) προεῖπον ὑμῖν ὅτι εἰ μὴ παρεσόμεθα συστρασευσόμενοι, ἐκεῖνοι ἐφ' ἡμᾶς ἴοιεν. XEN. *Hell.* v. 2. 13.
I told you beforehand that if we should (shall) not be present to join them, they would march against us.

(b.) ἐφοβεῖτο μὴ οἱ Λακεδαιμόνιοι σφᾶς, ὁπότε σαφῶς ἀκούσειαν, οὐκέτι ἀφῶσιν. THUC. i. 91.
He was afraid that the Lacedaemonians would no longer let them go, whenever they heard of it.

(c.) εἶπον τῇ βουλῇ ὅτι εἰδείην τοὺς ποιήσαντας, καὶ ἐξήλεγξα τὰ γενόμενα ὅτι εἰσηγήσατο μὲν πινόντων ἡμῶν ταύτην τὴν βουλὴν Εὐφίλητος, ἀντεῖπον δὲ ἐγώ, καὶ τότε μὲν οὐ γένοιτο δι' ἐμέ. ANDOK. *de Myst.* 61.
I told the Council that I knew who had committed the act, and I established the facts that Euphiletus had suggested this scheme, and that I had opposed it, and that on that occasion it was not executed owing to my opposition.

... εἰσηγήσατο Εὐφίλητος, ἀντεῖπον δὲ ἐγώ, οὐκ ἐγένετο.

§ 324. Virtual Oratio Obliqua.

Virtual Oratio Obliqua occurs when the words, thoughts, and motives, not of the writer, but of the subject of the sentence, are given rather by implication or allusion than directly introduced.

(a.) τὸν Περικλέα ἐκάκιζον ὅτι στρατηγὸς ὢν οὐκ ἐπεξάγοι.
THUC. ii. 21.
(*The Athenians, οἱ πολλοί, grumbled thus:* στρατηγὸς ὢν οὐκ ἐπεξάγει ἡμᾶς).

(b.) οἱ δ' ᾤκτειρον, εἰ ἁλώσοιντο. XEN. *An.* i. 4. 7.
Others were pitying them if they were to be captured (*felt pity at the thought*).
The thought was οἰκτροί ἔσονται εἰ ἁλώσονται.

(c.) οἶσθα ἐπαινέσαντα Ὅμηρον τὸν Ἀγαμέμνονα ὡς βασιλεὺς εἴη ἀγαθός. XEN. *Symp.* iv. 6.
You know that Homer praises Agamemnon as being a good king.

Cf. laudat Africanum Panaetius quod fuerit abstinens. CIC. *De Offic.* ii. 76.

(d.) τἄλλα, ἤν ἔτι ναυμαχεῖν εἰ Ἀθηναῖοι τολμήσωσι, παρεσκευάζοντο. THUC. vii. 59.
They were making all other preparations in case the Athenians should venture on a battle.

Here, observe, the graphic ἤν τολμήσωσι is used instead of εἰ τολμήσειαν.

(e.) Compare
πρὸς τὴν πόλιν, εἰ ἐπιβοηθοῖεν, ἐχώρουν. THUC. vii. 100.
They were advancing on the city in case the citizens should march out against them.

Εἰ and ἐάν often allude in this way to a thought. See SOPH. *O. C.* 1770, ἐάν πως διακωλύσωμεν: SOPH. *Aj.* 313, εἰ μὴ φανοίην.

§ 325. Past Tenses of the Indicative in Oratio Obliqua.

I. For instances of the Imperfect and Pluperfect Indicative in Sub-direct Clauses, see XEN. *An.* i. 2. 21, *Hell.* vii. 1. 34.

II. For instances of the Imperfect, Pluperfect, and Aorist Indicative in Sub-oblique Clauses, see XEN. *Mem.* ii. 6. 13; THUC. vii. 80 (οὓς μετέπεμψαν); DEM. 869. 9 (ὧν ἀπέδοσαν); XEN. *An.* i. 9. 10 (ἐπεὶ ἐγένετο); *Cyr.* ii. 2. 9 (ἣν ἔγραψα).

The Indicative may be accounted for on the same or analogous principles in the following passages:

(*a*.) ἐχρῆν τοὺς ἄλλους μὴ πρότερον περὶ τῶν ὁμολογουμένων ξυμβουλεύειν, πρὶν περὶ τῶν ἀμφισβητουμένων ἡμᾶς ἐδίδαξαν. Isoc. *Panegyr.* 19.
Here πρὶν διδάξειαν would represent πρὶν ἂν διδάξωσι.

(*b*.) ἡδέως ἄν Καλλικλεῖ ἔτι διελεγόμην, ἕως αὐτῷ τὴν τοῦ Ἀμφίονος ἀπέδωκα ῥῆσιν ἀντὶ τῆς τοῦ Ζήθου.
Plat. *Gorg.* 506 B.
ἕως ἀπέδωκα and not ἕως ἀποδοίην, which would represent ἕως ἂν ἀποδῶ.

§ 326. Apparently Abnormal Obliqua.

Sometimes, but rarely, instead of either the Graphic or the real Obliqua, we get an Indicative. An examination of passages seems to show that the writer throws in the mood and tense from his own point of view instead of giving the mood which would be required if he were quoting words or thoughts.

(*a*.) Κῦρος ὑπέσχετο τοῖς Μιλησίοις φύγασιν, εἰ καλῶς καταπράξειεν, ἐφ' ἃ ἐστρατεύετο, μὴ πρόσθεν παύεσθαι, πρὶν αὐτοὺς καταγάγοι οἴκαδε. Xen. *An.* i. 2. 2.
The Recta would be ἢν καταπράξω, ἐφ' ἃ στρατεύομαι οὐ παύσομαι πρὶν ἂν καταγάγω. ἐφ' ἃ ἐστρατεύετο is really a bit of the writer's narrative.

(*b*.) λέγεται δ' αὐτὸν (Παυσανίαν) μέλλοντα ξυλληφθήσεσθαι ... γνῶναι ἐφ' ᾧ ἐχώρει. Thuc. i. 134.
It is said that Pausanias, when on the point of being arrested, knew for what purpose he (the ephor) was coming.
ἐφ' ᾧ χωροίη or χωρεῖ would be the usual construction; ἐχώρει is the mood and tense of the writer rather than of the subject Pausanias.

(*c*.) ἔλεγον οὐ καλῶς τὴν Ἑλλάδα ἐλευθεροῦν αὐτόν, εἰ ἄνδρας διέφθειρεν, κ.τ.λ. Thuc. iii. 32.
They told him that he was not liberating Greece in the right way, if he was destroying men, etc.

Obliqua would require εἰ διαφθείρει, or διαφθείροι. Cf. Thuc. vi. 29, εἴργαστο (taking διέφθειρεν as Imperfect. It may be Aorist).

Precisely in the same way it is open in Latin for the writer to employ an Indicative or a Subjunctive. Thus we might say, *legati, mirante consule, quod morabantur, venerunt* (or *quod morarentur*); *morabantur* would give the writer's statement (*morarentur* would express the consul's feelings).

(d.) The most peculiar instance perhaps is in ARIST. *Vesp.* 283, λέγων ὡς φιλαθήναιος ἦν καὶ κατείποι, where the λέγων ὡς seems to necessitate a quotation of words (ὡς ἐστί or εἴη).

§ 327. *LONG SPEECHES IN OBLIQUA.*

Long Speeches in the Oratio Obliqua, such as we find in Livy, are rare in Greek. Greek is too lively, too anxious constantly to recur to the present, and cannot bind itself to the formal regularity which characterises a Roman Obliqua. The introductory verb ἔφη, ἔλεξε, ἤρετο, εἶπεν, is repeated, or the writer breaks away suddenly into the Recta.

For longer specimens of the Obliqua see PLAT. *Symp.* 189, *Rep.* 614 B, THUC. vi. 49, XEN. *Cyr.* viii. 1. 10, 11.

A very instructive example occurs in ANDOKIDES *de Mysteriis*, 38, etc., which is here given at length :—

ἔφη γὰρ Διοκλείδης εἶναι μὲν ἀνδράποδον οἱ ἐπὶ Λαυρίῳ, δεῖν δὲ κομίσασθαι ἀποφοράν. ἀναστὰς δὲ πρῲ ψευσθεὶς τῆς ὥρας βαδίζειν· εἶναι δὲ πανσέληνον. ἐπεὶ δὲ παρὰ τὸ προπύλαιον τοῦ Διονύσου ἦν, ὁρᾶν ἀνθρώπους πολλοὺς ἀπὸ τοῦ ὠδείου καταβαίνοντας εἰς τὴν ὀρχήστραν· δείσας δὲ αὐτούς, εἰσελθὼν ὑπὸ τὴν σκιὰν καθέζεσθαι μεταξὺ τοῦ κίονος καὶ τῆς στήλης ἐφ' ᾗ ὁ στρατηγός ἐστιν ὁ χαλκοῦς. ὁρᾶν δὲ ἀνθρώπους τὸν μὲν ἀριθμὸν μάλιστα τριακοσίους, ἑστάναι· δὲ κύκλῳ ἀνὰ πέντε καὶ δέκα ἄνδρας, τοὺς δὲ ἀνὰ εἴκοσιν· ὁρῶν δὲ αὐτῶν πρὸς -ἢν σελήνην τὰ πρόσωπα τῶν

Diokleides stated that he had a slave at Laurium, and that he had occasion to fetch a payment due. Rising early he mistook the time and started : there was a full moon. When he was by the gateway of Dionysus, he saw several persons coming down from the Odeum into the Orchestra. Afraid of them, he withdrew into the shade and crouched down between the column and the pedestal on which stands the Bronze General. He saw some three hundred men standing round about in groups of fifteen and twenty each. As he looked he recog-

πλείστων γιγνώσκειν. καὶ πρῶτον μέν, ὦ ἄνδρες, τοῦθ' ὑπέθετο δεινότατον πρᾶγμα, οἶμαι, ὅπως ἐν ἐκείνῳ εἴη ὅντινα βούλοιτο Ἀθηναίων φάναι τῶν ἀνδρῶν τούτων εἶναι, ὅντινα δὲ μὴ βούλοιτο, λέγειν ὅτι οὐκ ἦν. ἰδὼν δὲ ταῦτ' ἔφη ἐπὶ Λαύριον ἰέναι, καὶ τῇ ὑστεραίᾳ ἀκούειν ὅτι οἱ Ἑρμαῖ εἶεν περικεκομμένοι· γνῶναι οὖν εὐθὺς ὅτι τούτων εἴη τῶν ἀνδρῶν τὸ ἔργον. ἥκων δὲ εἰς ἄστυ ζητητάς τε ἤδη ᾑρημένους καταλαμβάνειν καὶ μήνυτρα κεκηρυγμένα ἑκατὸν μνᾶς.

ἰδὼν δὲ Εὔφημον τὸν Καλλίου τοῦ Τηλεκλέους ἀδελφὸν ἐν τῷ χαλκείῳ καθημένον, ἀναγαγὼν αὐτὸν εἰς τὸ Ἡφαιστεῖον λέγειν ἅπερ ὑμῖν ἐγὼ εἴρηκα, ὡς ἴδοι ἡμᾶς ἐν ἐκείνῃ τῇ νυκτί· οὔκουν δέοιτο παρὰ τῆς πόλεως χρήματα λαβεῖν μᾶλλον ἢ παρ' ἡμῶν, ὥσθ' ἡμᾶς ἔχειν φίλους.

εἰπεῖν οὖν τὸν Εὔφημον ὅτι καλῶς ποιήσειεν εἰπών, καὶ νῦν ἥκειν κελεῦσαι οἱ εἰς τὴν Λεωγόρου οἰκίαν, ἵν' ἐκεῖ ξυγγένῃ μετ' ἐμοῦ Ἀνδοκίδῃ καὶ ἑτέροις οἷς δεῖ. ἥκειν ἔφη τῇ ὑστεραίᾳ, καὶ δὴ κόπτειν τὴν θύραν, τὸν δὲ πατέρα τὸν ἐμὸν τυχεῖν ἐξιόντα, καὶ εἰπεῖν αὐτόν· ἆρά γε σὲ οἵδε περιμένουσι; χρὴ

nised most of their faces by the moonlight. Now in the first place, gentlemen, this story on which he bases his evidence is a most extraordinary thing; his object, I take it, being that it might rest with him to include in this list any Athenian he wished, or to exclude any he did not wish. After seeing this he stated that he went on to Lauri·m, and next day heard of the mutilation of the Hermae. So he knew it was the work of these persons. Returning to town he found the commissioners of inquiry chosen and a reward of a hundred minae offered for information.

Seeing Euphemus the son of Kallias and brother of Telekles sitting in his forge, he brought him up to the Hephaesteum, and told him exactly what I have said to you, how he had seen us that night. Now he did not (so he said) desire to receive money from the state more than from us, if we would be his friends.

Euphemus then told him that he had acted rightly in telling him, and now he asked him to come to the house of Leogoras, to meet me there, said he, with one Andokides and other needful persons. He said that he went next day, and just as he was knocking at the door my father hap-

μέντοι μὴ ἀπωθεῖσθαι τοιούτους φίλους· εἰπόντα δὲ αὐτὸν ταῦτα οἴχεσθαι.

καὶ τούτῳ μὲν τῷ τρόπῳ τὸν πατέρα μου ἀπώλλυε, συνειδότα ἀποφαίνων. εἰπεῖν δὲ ἡμᾶς ὅτι δεδογμένον ἡμῖν εἴη δύο μὲν τάλαντα ἀργυρίου διδόναι οἱ ἀντὶ τῶν ἑκατὸν μνῶν τῶν ἐκ τοῦ δημοσίου, ἐὰν δὲ κατάσχωμεν ἡμεῖς ἃ βουλόμεθα, ἕνα αὐτὸν ἡμῶν εἶναι, πίστιν δὲ τούτων δοῦναί τε καὶ δέξασθαι. ἀποκρίνασθαι δὲ αὐτὸς πρὸς ταῦτα ὅτι βουλεύσοιτο. ἡμᾶς δὲ κελεύειν αὐτὸν ἥκειν εἰς Καλλίου τοῦ Τηλεκλέους, ἵνα κἀκεῖνος παρείη. τὸν δ' αὖ κηδεστήν μου οὕτως ἀπώλλυεν. ἥκειν ἔφη εἰς Καλλίου, καὶ καθομολογήσας ἡμῖν πίστιν δοῦναι ἐν ἀκροπόλει, καὶ ἡμᾶς συνθεμένους οἱ τὸ ἀργύριον εἰς τὸν ἐπιόντα μῆνα δώσειν διαψεύδεσθαι καὶ οὐ διδόναι· ἥκειν οὖν μηνύσων τὰ γενόμενα.

pened to be going out, and said, "Oh, is it you these people are expecting? Well, one ought not to reject such friends." So saying, he was off.

In this way he tried to ruin my father by denouncing him as an accomplice. (According to him) we said that we proposed to give him two talents of silver instead of the hundred minae offered by the Treasury, and that if we gained our object he was (should be) one of our number, and that we exchanged pledges of this. His own reply to this was that he would think it over: we, however, told him to come to the house of Kallias son of Telekles whose presence we desired. Again in this he tried to ruin my relation. He came, so he said, to the house of Kallias, and according to agreement he gave us pledges on the Akropolis, and we, after stipulating to give him the money by the next month, break our promise and refuse to give it. Consequently he is present to inform of the facts.

CHAPTER. IV.

FIGURES OF RHETORIC, Etc.

§ 328. Alliteration.

Alliteration, or the repetition of the same letter.

e.g. Who shall *d*ecide when *d*octors *d*isagree?
Subdola cum ridet placidi pellacia ponti. Luc. ii. 559.
Tympana tenta tonant palmis et cymbala circum
Concava, raucisonoque minantur cornua cantu.
Id. ii. 618

θανάτου θᾶττον θεῖ. Plat. *Apol.* xxix. 39 A.
It (wickedness) fleeth faster than fate.

ἢ τῷ πανώλει πατρὶ τῶν μὲν ἐξ ἐμοῦ
παίδων πόθος παρεῖτο; Soph. *El.* 544.
*Or by thy felon father, for the family
I bore him, was all fondness flung away?*

τὸν δ' ἀγρίοις ὄσσοισι παπτήνας ὁ παῖς
πτύσας προσώπῳ. Soph. *Ant.* 1231.

Cf. Soph. *Ant.* 50, where an initial α occurs seven times.

Instances may easily be collected. Ours is the most alliterative of languages. Shakspere abounds with natural and beautiful examples. As is well known, Early English alliterative poetry consisted of couplets, in which each section contained two or more accented words beginning with the same letter.

In a somer seson,   whan soft was the sonne,
I shope me in shroudes,   as I a shepe were,
In habite as an heremite, unholy of workes,
Went wyde in þis world,   wondres to here.
                      Piers the Plowman

Shakspere ridicules the abuse of Alliteration:
Whereat, with blade, with bloody blameful blame,
He bravely broached his boiling bloody breast.
" Hortatur me frater, ut meos malis miser mandarem natos "
of Accius (CIC. *Tusc.* iv. 77) is little better.

§ 329.   Anakoluthia.

Anakoluthia or Anakoluthon is the term used where the structure of the sentence is not grammatically followed out. It is either natural and unstudied, or artificial and rhetorical. It is natural and unstudied in Herodotus, whose irregular constructions arise from his writing just as if he were talking. It is natural and unstudied again in Aeschylus, whose thoughts and emotions are too big for his words, and in Thucydides, who thinks more of matter than manner. It is rhetorical in Plato, who purposely imitates the easy freedom of ordinary conversation. Sometimes Anakoluthia arises from mere slovenliness, as in Andokides.

During the progress of a sentence a new idea strikes the writer; a new expression is thus introduced and becomes a disturbing influence. Or an explanation may be necessary; and a parenthesis, more or less long, is inserted. The sentence thus may wander far away from its original construction. Generally the writer is aware that he has gone astray, and goes back, not to the grammar, but to the sense of the passage, resuming often in a different construction with a particle δέ, δή, οὖν, *so, then, as I was saying.*

There are many kinds of Anakoluthia, and the figure is constantly recurring. One or two specimens are given just to show what is meant:

ἀνδροῖν δ' ὁμαίμοιν θάνατος ὧδ' αὐτόκτονος,—
οὐκ ἔστι γῆρας τοῦδε τοῦ μιάσματος.
AESCH. *S. c. Theb.* 681.

Here θάνατος, the subject, has no verb (γηράσκει). Instead of the verb the writer solemnly pauses, adding a second sentence nearly complete in itself.

But blood of brothers shed by fellowly hands—
There is no age for such pollution.

τὰ πάντα γάρ τις ἐγχέας ἀνθ' αἵματος
ἑνός, μάτην ὁ μόχθος. AESCH. *Ch.* 521.
*Pour all the atoning offerings in the world
For one life spilt—vain were thy toil.*
Grammatically: μάτην ἂν μοχθοίης.

οἱ Ἀθηναῖοι νόσῳ ἐπιέζοντο κατ' ἀμφότερα, τῆς τε ὥρας τοῦ ἐνιαυτοῦ ταύτης οὔσης, ἐν ᾗ ἀσθενοῦσιν ἄνθρωποι μάλιστα, καὶ τὸ χωρίον ἅμα, ἐν ᾧ ἐστρατοπεδεύοντο, ἑλῶδες καὶ χαλεπὸν ἦν. THUC. vii. 47.
Grammatically it should have been τοῦ χωρίου ἑλώδους καὶ χαλεποῦ ὄντος.

The Athenians were suffering from sickness arising from two causes, first, because this was the time of year when sickness is most prevalent, and next, the ground on which they were encamped was swampy and unhealthy.

Cf. iv. 23, καὶ περὶ Πύλον—τῷ τείχει. HDT. vii. 74, καὶ πολλὰ—ἀμύνασθαι.

One simple instance from Plato may suffice to show how he imitates the freedom of ordinary talk:—

ἦλθον ἐπί τινα τῶν δοκούντων σοφῶν εἶναι ... καὶ διαλεγόμενος αὐτῷ, ἔδοξέ μοι οὗτος ὁ ἀνὴρ δοκεῖν μὲν εἶναι σοφός, κ.τ.λ., εἶναι δ' οὔ. PLAT. *Apol.* vi. 21 B.

I went to see one of those who had the reputation of being wise. And talking with him, this man seemed to me to be considered wise, without being really so.

As if it were διαλεγόμενος αὐτῷ ἐδόξασα, *conversing with him I thought.*

§ 330. Antiptosis.

ANTIPTOSIS. The Subject of the Subordinate Clause is the object of the Principal Clause.

The stock instance is "nosti Marcellum, quam tardus sit" for "nosti quam tardus sit Marcellus." "I know you not, whence ye are."

This is a common construction in Greek, **Latin**, and English.

ἰτέον οὖν σκοποῦντι τὸν χρησμὸν τί λέγει. PLAT. *Apol.* vii. 21 E.

I must go on then examining the oracle, what it means (i.e. *examining what the oracle means, or the meaning of the oracle*).

οἶδε μὲν οὐδεὶς τὸν θάνατον οὐδ' εἰ τυγχάνει πάντων μέγιστον ὂν τῶν ἀγαθῶν. PLAT. Apol. xvii. 29 A.
No one knows (with regard to) death, even whether it is (not) the greatest possible blessing.

We may say that the Accusative and the Subordinate Sentence together become the object of the principal Verb.

Antiptosis is commonly explained as above, but the simpler and more rational account is that the Subordinate Clause expands and explains the Object or Accusative of the Principal Clause.

§ 331. Asyndeton.

Asyndeton, or the omission of Conjunctions, stock instances of which are Shakspere's

                Unhousel'd, disappointed, unanel'd ;

and Cicero's   Abiit, excessit, evasit, erupit.

Cf. Milton's   Unrespited, unpitied, unreprieved.
                Unshaken, unseduced, unterrified.
                Exhaustless, spiritless, afflicted, fallen.

ἄκλαυστος, ἄφιλος, ἀνυμέναιος. SOPH. Ant. 877.
Unwept, unloved, unhymned.

ἄφιλον, ἔρημον, ἄπολιν, ἐν ζῶσιν νεκρόν. SOPH. Phil. 1018.
Friendless, lone, citiless, midst the living dead.

The use of the figure is to set forth each idea separately, and pointedly. It is so common that further instances are unnecessary.

§ 332. Binary Structure.

One conception is stated twice over, so that two aspects of it are given. This double presentment enables the reader to obtain a fuller view of the conception as a whole. Mr. Riddell aptly describes this artifice as giving a rhetorical "binocular vision." It is commonly employed in Similes.

            ἂν δ' Ἀγαμέμνων
ἵστατο δακρυχέων, ὥστε κρήνη μελάνυδρος . . .
ὣς ὁ βαρυστενάχων ἔπε' Ἀργείοισι μετηύδα. Il. ix. 13.
Cf. SOPH. Ai. 840, O. C. 1239.

ταῦτα ἐγὼ δοκῶ ἀκούειν, ὥσπερ οἱ κορυβαντιῶντες τῶν
αὐλῶν δοκοῦσιν ἀκούειν . . . καὶ ἐν ἐμοὶ αὕτη ἡ ἠχὴ . . .
βομβεῖ. PLAT. *Crito*, 54 D.
οὐ ταὐτὸν τοῦτο πεπόνθασιν, . . . ἀκολασίᾳ τινὶ σώφρονές
εἰσιν ; PLAT. *Phaed.* 67 E.
οὑτωσί σοι δοκῶ, οὐδένα νομίζω θεὸν εἶναι;
PLAT. *Apol.* xiv. 26 E.

Binary Structure in giving two descriptions of the same object differs from Apposition, which gives but one description, though in certain forms there is a resemblance between the figures. Asyndeta and Anakoluthia often occur in this structure. The artifice is used by all Greek writers, but it is employed in an almost endless variety of subtle forms by Plato. See Riddell, pp. 196-209, whence the above examples are taken.

Antiptosis is a form of Binary Structure.

§ 333. Brachylogy or Abbreviated Construction.

(Including Zeugma, Constructio Praegnans, Brachylogy of Comparison.)

Brachylogy is a kind of Ellipse; but where Ellipse actually suppresses a word or sentence altogether, Brachylogy leaves them to be supplied from some corresponding expression in the context. Brachylogy is thus more essentially artificial than Ellipse.

ἔφρασας ὑπέρτεραν τῆς τότε χάριτος (sc. ὑπέρτεραν χάριν, the χάριν supplied from χάριτος). SOPH. *El.* 1265.

A Substantive, an Adjective, a Pronoun, a Conjunction, or a Verb may thus be supplied from the context.

τὰ μὲν ἄλλα, ὅσαπερ καὶ πάντες ὑμεῖς ἐποιεῖτε.
XEN. *Cyr.* iv. 1. 3.

i.e. τὰ μὲν ἄλλα (sc. ἐποίει, supplied from ἐποιεῖτε).

In the common phrases οὐδὲν ἄλλο ἤ, τί ἄλλο ἤ, ἄλλο τι ἤ, a different verb of more general meaning is supplied from a special verb in the context.

οἱ Λακεδαιμόνιοι ἄλλο οὐδὲν ἢ ἐκ τῆς γῆς ἐναυμάχουν.
THUC. iv. 14.

i.e. ἄλλο οὐδὲν ἐποίουν ἤ. PLAT. *Apol.* 19 D.

ταῦτα καὶ ποιεῖν καὶ πάσχειν ἃ πάσχει. PLAT. *Phaed.* 98 A, supply καὶ ποιεῖ.

§ 334. Zeugma and Syllepsis.

Zeugma is another form of Brachylogy. There is only one verb in the sentence, but more than one noun. The verb strictly applies only to one of the nouns, but suggests the verb required by the other.

ἀλλ' ἢ πνοαῖσιν ἢ βαθυσκαφεῖ κόνει
κρύψον νιν.
SOPH. *El.* 435 ; cf. *El.* 72, *Ai.* 632, EUR. *Bacch.* 142.
No, or to the winds (sc. μέθες) *or in the deep-dug soil bury them.*

A violent instance of Zeugma :

ἐσθῆτα δὲ φορέουσι τῇ Σκυθικῇ ὁμοίην, γλῶσσαν δὲ ἰδίην.
HDT. iv. 106.
They wear a dress like the Scythian, but (speak) a language of their own.

Cf. the old Tyne ballad : "He wears a blue bonnet, wi' a dimple on his chin."

προθυμίᾳ χρώμενοι καὶ παρακελευσμῷ. THUC. iv. 11.
With energy and with mutual exhortation.

χρώμενοι goes with both nouns not quite in the same sense. This sort of Zeugma is sometimes distinguished as Syllepsis.

1 COR. iii. 2, γάλα ὑμᾶς ἐπότισα οὐ βρῶμα, is a stock instance from the New Testament, ἐπότισα suiting γάλα only. Cf. L. i. 64.

§ 335. Constructio Praegnans.

Constructio Praegnans is a form of Brachylogy. Two sentences are compressed into one.

οὗ ἔδει κακοπαθεῖν τῷ σώματι ἐνταυθοῖ οὐδέν με ὠφέλησεν ἡ ἐμπειρία. ANTIPH. *de Caed. Her.* 2.
Where I ought to have endured personal ill-treatment hither (i.e. *here, whither they have brought me), my experience proved no help to me.*

It is common with certain Prepositions (εἰς, ἐν, ἐξ) and with Relative Adverbs.

e.g. ταῖς ἐν τῇ γῇ καταπεφευγυίαις (sc. ναυσί).
The ships which had fled to the shore, and were on the shore.

κεῖνος δ' ὅπου βέβηκεν, οὐδεὶς οἶδε. SOPH. *Tr.* 10.
Where (for whither) he is gone none knoweth.
ὅπου for ὅποι. Cf. *Phil.* 256.

Constructio Praegnans is very common in the New Testament. A stock instance is Φίλιππος εὑρέθη εἰς Ἄζωτον, ACT. AP. viii. 40. See 2 TIM. iv. 18, MATT. v. 22, ἔνοχος εἰς τὴν γέενναν.

§ 336. Brachylogy of Comparison.

Brachylogy of Comparison, or Comparatio Compendiaria. The stock example is from *Il.* xvii. 51, κόμαι χαρίτεσσιν ὁμοῖαι, *i.e.* κόμαι ὁμοῖαι χαρίτων κόμαισι, *hair like the (hair of) the Graces.*

‛Ηφαίστου δ' ἵκανε δόμον Θέτις ἀργυρόπεζα
ἄφθιτον ἀστερόεντα, μετάπρεπε᾽ ἀθανάτοισιν. HOM. *Il.* xviii.
i.e. μεταπρεπέα δόμοισιν ἀθανάτων. [368.
Silver-footed Thetis came unto the house of Hephaestus Incorruptible, starry, conspicuous among the Immortals.

χεῖρον᾽ ἀρσένων νόσον ταύτην νοσοῦμεν. EUR. *Andron.* 220.
i.e. χείρονα ἀρσένων νόσου νόσον νοσοῦμεν.
Worse than men this plague we are plagued withal.

ὁμοίαν ταῖς δούλαις εἶχε τὴν ἐσθῆτα. XEN. *Cyr.* v. 1. 3.
Cf. REV. xiii. 11, εἶχε κέρατα δύο ὅμοια ἀρνίῳ.

§ 337. Catachresis.

The use of a word not in its strict meaning.

ὑποπτεύω, *I expect;* δαιμόνιος, *extraordinary;* θαυμαστός θαυμάσιος, *strange, eccentric, funny, capital, excellent;* μέγας (sc. λόγος, PLAT. *Phaed.* 62 B), *puzzling;* ὑπερφυῶς ὡς (ὁμολογῶ), *I decidedly do (assent)*; ἀμηχάνως γε ὡς σφόδρα, *most decidedly.*
See Riddell, *Digest,* p. 240.

§ 338. Ellipse and Aposiopesis.

The suppression of a word or sentence.

e.g. ἡ αὔριον (sc. ἡμέρα).
    ἐς κόρακας (sc. βάλλετε, ἔρρετε, οἴχεσθε).
    To the crows!

The suppressed word or sentence can, of course, be easily supplied. The figure is mechanically and unconsciously employed in many common every-day phrases. The object of its artificial use is to give brevity and pith to the expression.

ἡμῖν μὲν εὐχὰς τάσδε (sc. εὔχομαι). AESCH. *Cho.* 142.
For us these prayers—

The omission of the Subject with its Verb, of the copula ἐστι, of the substantive with its epithet or genitive (οἱ ἀγαθοί, ὁ Φιλίππου), are common instances of unconscious Ellipse.

Instances of unconscious Ellipse of Sentences occur in the phrases οὐχ ὅτι, μὴ ὅτι, οὐχ ὅπως, etc., and more or less so in the suppression of a Protasis, or of an Apodosis.

Aposiopesis is a form of Ellipse.[1] In animated and excited expressions the speaker breaks off abruptly, leaving the rest of the sentence to be understood.

μηδὲν πρὸς ὀργήν πρὸς θεῶν (sc. δράσῃς). SOPH. *El.* 369.
By Heaven! naught in anger.

μή τριβὰς ἔτ' (sc. πορίζετε or some such verb). *Antig.* 577.
No longer tarrying!

μή μοι πρόφασιν. AR. *Ach.* 345.
No shuffling!

μή μοί γε μύθους. AR. *Vesp.* 1179.
Come! no tales!

VERGIL'S "quos ego: sed motos praestat componere fluctus," is QUINTILIAN'S stock instance. "Quid multa?" "quid plura?" are common cases.

§ 339. Euphemism.

The substitution of a colourless or an agreeable expression for a strong or disagreeable one. It is the reverse of "calling a spade a spade." The Greeks carefully avoid the mention of death especially, *e.g.* ἔπραξ' ὅπως ἔπραξε.
e.g. ἄλλο τι παθεῖν. PLAT. *Crito,* iv. 44 E, *to suffer something else.*

---

[1] Ἀποσιώπησις. *Reticentia*, CIC. *Obticentia*, CELSUS. *Interruptio al.* QUINT. *Inst.* ix. 2.

So we say " in the event of anything happening."
ἐγὼ γὰρ εἶμ' ἐκεῖσ' ὅποι πορευτέον. SOPH. *Ai.* 690.
For I shall go thither where all must go.
Spoken by Aias when contemplating suicide.

δέδοικ' ἐγὼ
μή μοι βεβήκῃ. SOPH. *Phil.* 494.
Where Philoktetes fears that his father may no longer be alive.

§ 340. Hypallage.

A change of case, so that a word does not agree with the case which logically it qualifies. In such constructions the word agrees with a compound expression, so that the figure is a form of Synesis rather than Hyperbaton. The stock instance is from Horace—

Nec purpurarum sidere clarior
Delenit usus,

where the adjective *clarior*, instead of agreeing with *purpurarum* (purple robes) agrees with the compound substantive *usus purpurarum*.

ὦ πατρῷον ἑστίας βάθρον. SOPH. *Ai.* 860.
Seat of my father's hearth.
For πατρῴας ἑστίας βάθρον.

So *Antig.* 794, νεῖκος ἀνδρῶν ξύναιμον, where νεῖκος ἀνδρῶν forms one word : *Trach.* 817, ὄγκον ὀνόματος μητρῷον.

τὸν δ' ἀθλίως θανόντα Πολυνείκους νέκυν. SOPH. *Ant.* 26.
For θανόντος Πολυνείκους.

In LUCRETIUS, i. 474, we have an instance of true Hypallage : *Ignis Alexandri Phrygio sub pectore gliscens.* Mr. Munro, in his note on the line, collects some striking parallels from other writers.

§ 341. Hyperbaton, Chiasmus, Hysteron-Proteron.

The displacement of the natural order of words. Its chief use is to give emphasis to a word. It also enables language to represent the rapidity of thought, one word instantly catching up another word.

Easy and familiar instances are—

εἰπέ, ὦ πρὸς Διός, Μέλητε. PLAT. Apol. xiii. 25 C.

Like the Latin

Per te Deos oro.

Certain words in particular are thus displaced, especially γέ, μέντοι, ἄν, ἔτι, ἴσως, οὐκ in οὔ φημι, etc.

ἆρ' οὖν ἄν με οἴεσθε τοσαῦτα ἔτη διαγενέσθαι;
PLAT. Apol. xxi. 32 E.

τίς ἦν ἐν ᾗ ματτόμεθα μέντοι τἄλφιτα; ARIST. Nub. 788.

τάχ' ἂν ὀρθῶς ἴσως μέμφοιτο. PLAT. Leg. 640 D.

Chiasmus is a form of Hyperbaton. Chiasmus is the Inverse Parallelism of Clauses and Sentences:

πᾶν μὲν ἔργον πᾶν δ' ἔπος λέγοντας τε καὶ πράττοντας,—

where the outside ἔργον belongs to the outside πράττοντας, and the inside ἔπος to the inside λέγοντας.

οὔτ' ἀδικεῖ, οὔτ' ἀδικεῖται, οὔθ' ὑπὸ θεοῦ, οὔτε θεόν.

Hysteron Proteron (ὕστερον πρότερον) reverses the order in which events occur, e.g. τράφεν ἠδ' ἐγένοντο.

ἔχεις τί κεἰσήκουσας; SOPH. Ant. 9.

ἀλλήλους διδάσκειν τε καὶ φράζειν. PLAT. Apol. iii. 19 D.

αἰσθανόμενος μὲν καὶ λυπούμενος καὶ δεδιὼς ὅτι ἀπηγχανόμην. PLAT. Apol. vi. 21 E.

On the Hyperbaton and its forms see Riddell, p. 228.

§ 342. Litotes.

Litotes or *Meiosis*, smoothing or diminishing a stronger conception by a weaker statement. A common enough figure in all languages, but especially suited to Greek taste, e.g. οὐχ ἧσσον, *not less*, i.e. *more;* οὐ μᾶλλον, *not so much.*

εἰ μὲν γὰρ τοῦτο λέγουσιν, ὁμολογοίην ἂν ἔγωγε οὐ κατὰ τούτους εἶναι ῥήτωρ. PLAT. Apol. i. 17 B.

If this is what they mean, I must admit that I am an orator, not as they are orators (i.e. *an orator of a far higher order than they*).

χαίρουσιν ἐξεταζομένοις τοῖς οἰομένοις εἶναι σοφοῖς, οὖσι δ'
οὔ· ἔστι γὰρ οὐκ ἀηδές.   PLAT. *Apol.* xxii. 33 C.
*They enjoy the cross-examination of those who think they are
wise, without really being so.   It really is not disagreeable*
(i.e. *it is extremely amusing*).

κεῖται θανὼν δείλαιος, οὐ μάλ' εὐτυχῶς.   AESCH. *Pers.* 327.
Lies low in death unhappy, not all fortunately (i.e. *all ingloriously, because unburied:* an euphemism also).

§ 343. Oxymoron.

Oxymoron is the contrast by juxtaposition of opposite
conceptions, e.g. from the *Paradise Lost:*

Our final hope is flat despair.

Dishonest shame
Of Nature's works, honour dishonourable.

A universe of death . . .
Where all life dies, death lives.

In *King John* the despairing and passionate Constance cries:

Death, death ; O amiable, lovely death ! -
Thou odoriferous stench ! sound rottenness !

ἐχθρῶν ἄδωρα δῶρα.   SOPH. *Ai.* 665.
Giftless the gifts of foes.

μαίνεται δ' ὑφ' ἡδονῆς
μήτηρ ἀμήτωρ.   SOPH. *El.* 1154.
She is mad for joy,
A mother, yet no mother.

ὅσια πανουργήσασα.   SOPH. *Ant.* 74.
Daring a holy crime.

ἐξέφθινθ' αἱ τρίσκαλμοι
νᾶες ἄναες ἄναες.   AESCH. *Pers.* 680.
*They are destroyed those three-banked
ships, ships no more, ships no more.*

Cf. Catullus : funera ne funera.

Cf. AESCH. *P. V.* 545, χάρις ἄχαρις.   SOPH. *O. T.* 1214,
γάμος ἄγαμος.

Oxymoron is well caricatured by Shakspere:
A tedious brief scene of young Pyramus
And his love Thisbe, very tragical mirth.
Merry and tragical, tedious and brief!
That is, hot ice, and wonderous strange snow.
How shall we find the concord of this discord?

§ 344. Periphrasis.

Periphrasis or *Circumlocution* is a roundabout way of using two or more words instead of one, e.g. 'Ισμήνης κάρα, *head of Ismene*, for 'Ισμήνη; θρέμματα Νείλου (PLAT. *Leg.* 953), *children of the Nile*, i.e. *Egyptians* (cf. the Hebrew, *children of Israel*, *sons of Belial*, *son of peace*, etc.). The word χρῆμα occurs in one or two phrases: ὑὸς μέγα χρῆμα, HDT.; τὸ χρῆμα. τῶν νυκτῶν, AR. *Nub.* 2.

Very often the Substantive is used for an Adjective or an apposition, e.g. Ποσειδῶνος κράτος, *the might of Poseidon*, for *the mighty Poseidon* (AESCH. *Eum.* 27); παρθενία 'Ιοῦς, *the virgin Io* (AESCH. *P. V.* 898); μητρὸς σέβας, *a revered mother* (*P. V.* 1090). So in Latin, mitis sapientia Laeli, prisci Catonis virtus (HORACE).

Periphrasis is employed in the use of Tenses, e.g. μέλλω ποιήσειν, μέλλω τεθνάναι (PLAT. *Apol.* xviii. 30 C and xix. 32 A), ἀτιμάσας ἔχει, periturus sum, fore *or* futurum esse with a Subjunctive mood.

Very often, again, both in Greek and Latin, a periphrasis is used for a simple verb, especially with ἔχω, e.g. ἐν νῷ ἔχω = διανοοῦμαι: φρονίμως ἔχω = φρονῶ: θαρραλέως ἔχω = θαρρῶ (all in PLAT. *Apol.*): λυπηρῶς ἔχω = λυποῦμαι (SOPH. *El.* 766): ἡδονὴν φέρειν = τέρπειν (SOPH. *El.* 286): φωνὴν λαβεῖν = φωνεῖν, etc.

In fact these periphrastic verbs are of constant use both in prose and poetry.

§ 345. Pleonasm.

Pleonasm or Redundancy is the employment of words apparently superfluous. Apparently, for a second expression may often define or amplify a previous expression, e.g. ὁ στρατηγὸς τῆς στρατιᾶς, μόνον καθ' αὐτὸν κοὐδέν' ἄλλον.

A cognate accusative is a sort of pleonasm, μάχην μάχεσθαι: or an adverb with its adjective, μέγας μεγαλωστί (κεῖτο). Il. xvi. 776, (he lay outstretched) huge with his huge length.

Adverbs are often thus combined : ὡς ἀληθῶς τῷ ὄντι: πάλιν αὖθις, αὖ πάλιν αὖθις: ἔπειτα μετὰ ταῦτα. The repetition of the negative and of ἄν are cases of Pleonasm.

τί δὴ λέγοντες διέβαλλον οἱ διαβάλλοντες ;
          PLAT. *Apol.* iii. 19 B.
ἐπιεικῆ ἄν μοι δοκῶ λέγειν λέγων. PLAT. *Apol.* xxii. 34 D.

Periphrasis is a form of Pleonasm.

§ 346. Prolepsis or Anticipation.

What is intended, or expected to take place, as spoken of, by anticipation, as having already taken place.

It occurs most commonly with a predicative adjective. A good instance is found in Juvenal :
   Paullatim caluerunt mollia saxa.
  i.e. caluerunt ita ut mollia fierent.

A stock instance is—
εὔφημον, ὦ τάλαινα, κοίμησον στόμα. AESCH. *Ag.* 1258.
 i.e. ὥστε εὔφημον εἶναι.
ἐῴα κινεῖ φθέγματ' ὀρνιθῶν σαφῆ. SOPH. *El.* 18.
Awakes to shrillness the birds' matin songs.
       See v. 14, τιμωρόν.

  γονέων
ἐκτίμους ἴσχουσα πτέρυγας
ὀξυτόνων γόων.   SOPH. *El.* 242.
Restraining the wings of shrill-voiced wailings
So that they honour not a parent. Cf. *Antig.* 1200.
Cf. EUR. *Bacch.* 70, 183.

§ 347.   Puns.

   (Paronomasia, Annominatio.)

Occasionally Greek writers indulge in them.

ἀλλὰ γάρ, ὦ Μέλητε . . . σαφῶς ἀποφαίνεις τὴν σαυτοῦ ἀμελείαν, ὅτι οὐδέν σοι μεμέληκε περὶ ὧν ἐμὲ εἰσάγεις.
          PLAT. *Apol.* xii. 25 C
(See xiv. where the pun is repeated.)

Riddell, p. 242, collects many instances from Plato.

ἀπεστέρηκας τὸν βίον τὰ τόξ' ἑλών. SOPH. *Phil.* 931.

where there is clearly a play on βιόν (*bow*) and βίον (*life*).

The grandest instance of punning or playing on words at a solemn moment is in Shakspere. (*Richard* II., Act ii.), where the dying Gaunt dwells on his name :

Old Gaunt indeed, and gaunt in being old, etc.

So of Helen :

ἑλένας, ἕλανδρος, ἑλέπτολις. AESCH. *Ag.* 689.

Helen, the Hell of ships, the Hell of men, the Hell of towns.

Compare the pun made on the rock-built Assus recorded in Athenaeus viii. 352.

"Ἆσσον ἴθ', ὥς κεν θᾶσσον ὀλέθρου πείραθ' ἵκηαι. *Il.* vi. 143.

Paronomasia is the combination of words of similar sound or cognate form.

utrum propter *oves* an propter *aves*; VARRO, *R. R.* iii. 2. 13.
Träume sind Schäume (lit. *dreams are bubbles*).
δόσιν κακὰν κακῶν κακοῖς. AESCH. *Pers.* 1041.
ὠρθοῦθ' ὁ τλήμων ὀρθὸς ἐξ ὀρθῶν δίφρων. SOPH. *El.* 742.

Αὐτὸς ἑαυτόν, αὐτὸς ὑφ' ἑαυτοῦ, etc., would be familiar instances.

ENGLISH INDEX.

Reference is only made to subjects which are not easily found in the Table of Contents.

The numbers refer to the pages of the book.

A

Ablative represented by Genitive, 78-9.
Accusative, see Table of Contents, 66-78.
—— Absolute, 95.
—— with Infinitive,[1] 13, 158, 179.
—— with Infinitive instead of Nominative, 180.
—— in Apposition to Sentence, 25, 74.
—— with Prepositions, 289.
Active Voice, 120.
Adjectives which take a Genitive, 100.
—— which take a Dative, 119.
Adverbs which take a Genitive, 100.
—— which take a Dative, 119.
Adverbial sentences, 9.
Agent, how denoted, 131.
—— denoted by Prepositions, 289-90.
—— Genitive of, 101; Dative of, 111.
Anastrophe, 289.
Aorist, uses of, 145-9.
Sometimes the equivalent of the English, Present, Perfect, or Pluperfect, 147.
Apodosis, meaning of the term, 195, footnote.
—— without ἄν, 217-9.
Apposition, 5; Peculiarities of, 24-26.
Article,[2] see Table of Contents, ch. ii., 27-46.
—— as Personal, Demonstrative, and Relative in Attic, 28.

Article, for Possessive, 30.
—— with words used *materialiter*, 35.
—— not repeated with a second noun, 35.
Asyndeton, 24.
Attraction, 58.
Attributive or Epithet, 5; Peculiarities in Construction, 23-4.

C

Cases, Preliminary Note on, 64.
Causal Sentences, see Table of Contents, 276-9.
Causative Active Voice, 125; do. Middle, 127.
Collective Noun with Plural Predicate, 19.
Comparative and Superlative, 120-3.
—— denoting too great a degree, 97, 120, 121.
Concessive Sentences, see Table of Contents, 249-251.
Conditional Sentences, see Table of Contents, 193-231.
—— Sentences, examples of, 209-231.
Consecutive Sentences, see Table of Contents, 269-275.
Co-ordinate Sentences, 7.
Copula, 1; Verbs used as, 12; omitted, 13.
Construction κατὰ σύνεσιν, 24.

D

Dative, see Table of Contents, 104-119.

Dative of interest in Participial phrases, 107.
—— of circumstance used adverbially (*e.g.* σιγῇ), 114.
—— with Infinitive, 13, 158.
—— as an Oblique Predicate, 45.
Dawes' Canon, note on, 267.
Deliberative or Dubitative, see Questions.
Definite and Indefinite Sentences, 194-5.
Demonstrative Pronouns as Subjects and Predicates, 18.
—— Pronouns preceding a sentence in Apposition, 25.
Deponent Verbs, 131.
Dual Number, 19, 20.

E

Emotion, Verbs of, with Participles, 170.
—— Verbs of, with εἰ for ὅτι, 186.
Epithet, see Attributive.

F

Fearing, Verbs of, with μή, μὴ οὐ, 262-8.
(1) With Subj. or Opt., 262.
(2) With Fut. Indic., 264.
(3) With ὅπως μή and Fut. Indic. Subj. or Opt., 265.
(4) With ὡς and Fut. Indic., 265.
(5) With Infin., 265.
(6) With εἰ Interrogative, 266.

---
[1] For an explanation of this construction, see Monro's *Homeric Grammar*, p. 158.
[2] See Monro's *Homeric Grammar*, where the uses of the Article are arranged under three heads.

ENGLISH INDEX.

Figures of Rhetoric, see Part III., ch. iv., Table of Contents.
Final Sentences, 252, 259.
(1) With ἵνα, ὡς, ὅπως, and Subj. or Opt., 253.
(2) With ὡς, ὅπως ἄν and Subj. (not Opt.), 255.
(3) Rarely with Fut. Indic., 256.
Frequentative, see Iterative.
Future Middle as Passive, 125.
— Perfect, 150.
— Indicative, with ὅπως Final, 256, n. 4; Fut. Opt., as Obliqua of above, 256.

G

Genitive, see Table of Contents, 78-104.
— Absolute,[1] 96, 165-7.
— with Infinitive, 13, 158.
— as Oblique Predicate, 45.
— in Apposition to another Genitive supplied in the Possessive, 26, 49.
Gnomic Tenses, 151.
Graphic (or Vivid) construction, i.e. the Substitution, in a Subordinate Clause in Historic Sequence of the Mood used in the Primary Sequence, 138, 182, etc.
— see also Oratio Obliqua passim, esp. 386, 404.

H

Hoping and Promising, Verbs of, with Pres. and Aor. Infin., 180-1.

I

Imperative Mood, 136-7.
Imperfect Tense, uses of, 143-4.
Indicative Mood—
— states facts or asks questions, 132.
— in the Indirect Statement, 181, etc.

Indicative Mood—
— in the Indirect Question, 188.
— in the Indirect Petition (Fut. Indic.), 192.
— in Definite Sentences, 194-5.
— in Conditional Sentences, see Part II. ch. ii.
(a) Present Conditions.
(b) Future Conditions.
(c) Past Conditions.
(d) Unfulfilled Past or Present Conditions.
— in Temporal Sentences to denote Definite Time, see Part II. ch. iii.
— in Concessive Sentences, see Part II. ch. iv.
— in Final Sentences of Past Purpose, 257.
— in Relative Final Sentences, 258.
— with ὅπως Modal (Fut. Indic.), 259, etc., 262.
— with Verbs of Fearing, 263.
— with Consecutive Sentences, see Part II. ch. vi.
— with Limitative or Restrictive Sentences, 274.
— with Causal Sentences, see Part II. ch. vii.
— with Expressions of Wishes, see Part II. ch. viii.
— with Relative Sentences, see Part II. ch. ix.
— substituted for the Optative by the Graphic or Vivid Construction in Historic Sequence wherever the Recta or the Primary Sequence took an Indicative.
Infinitive, see Table of Contents, 153-162.
— Epexegetical, 155-6.
— compared with Latin Supine, 155.
— after a Comparative with ἤ or ὥστε, 156.
— with ὡς, ὡς γε, Limitative, 156.
— for Imperative,[2] 159.
— denoting surprise, 160.
— personal and impersonal passive construction, 159.

Infinitive, with τοῦ denoting a purpose, 162.
— in Indirect Statement, 178, etc.
— in Indirect Petition, 191.
— with Verbs of Fearing, 265.
— with τῷ, used causally, 279.
— in Oratio Obliqua, introduced without a Principal Verb, 398.
— and Finite Mood alternating in Orat. Obliqua, 400.
— with Adverbial and Relative Sentences in Orat. Obliqua, 400.
— in Latin Orat. Obliqua, 401.
Indefinite Tenses, see Definite.
— Time, three kinds of, 232.
Iterative (Frequentative) Tenses, 151.
See Temporal Sentences.

L

Limitative or Restrictive Sentences, 274-5.
Locative Case, 64-5, 116.

M

Middle Voice,[3] 125-130.
— (and Active) Verbs. Alphabetical List, 127-130.
Modal Sentences with ὅπως, ὅπως μή, 259-262.
(1) Fut. Indic. or Fut. Opt., 260.
(2) Subj. or Opt., 260.
(3) ὅπῃ, ὅτῳ τρόπῳ, ἐξ ὅτου τρόπῳ for ὅπως, 261.
(4) ὅπως with ἄν and Subj., 261.
(5) With μή for ὅπως μή, 261.
Moods, see Table of Contents, 132, 137.

N

Negatives, see Part III.; Ch. ii., Table of Contents.

---

[1] See Monro's *Homeric Grammar*, p. 167.
[2] On the Infinitive as an Imperative see Monro's *Homeric Grammar*, p. 162. The whole of the chapter (see especially the Infin. as Subject, 157, Accus. with Infin., 158, Origin and History of Infinitive, 163), is worth careful perusal.
[3] For the Middle and its uses, see Monro's *Homeric Grammar*, p. 7. The Passive has grown out of the Middle, in fact was originally one of the uses of the Middle.

ENGLISH INDEX.

Neuter Plural, with Verb Singular, 15.
—— Plural, with Verb Plural, 15.
—— Singular Predicate, with Plural Subject, 15.
—— Pronoun, (Adj. or Adv.) with Gen. (like Lat. paullum sapientiae), 85.
Nominative Case, 65.
—— with Infinitive, 13, 158, 179.
—— with Participle, 187.

O

Object, Direct and Remote, 5.
—— Sentence, 252, footnote.
Optative Mood—
—— Introductory Note, 132.
—— in Independent Sentences, 135, etc.
  A. Denoting a Wish (an Exhortation, Command, or Prohibition).
  B. Deliberative Questions.
—— in the Indirect Statement, 181.
—— in the Indirect Question, 188.
—— in Deliberative Indirect Questions, 190.
—— in the Indirect Petition (Fut. Opt.), 191, 262.
—— in Conditional Sentences, *see* Part II. ch. ii.
  (*a.*) In Future Conditions.
  (*b.*) In General or Frequentative Past Conditions.
—— in Temporal Sentences, denoting Indefinite Time (which is of three kinds), *see* Part II. ch. iii.
—— in Concessive Sentences with εἰ καί, καὶ εἰ, 250.
—— in Final Sentences, 252, etc.
—— in Relative Final Sentences, 259.
—— with ὅπως Modal (Fut. Opt.), 259.
—— with Causal Sentences in Virtual Oratio Obliqua, 277.
—— with expressions of a Wish, 280.
—— used in Primary Sequence, 256.

Optative Mood—
—— the Optative with ἄν, found in other Sentences, is always an Apodosis used subordinately.
—— Optative in Oratio Obliqua introduced without a Principal Verb, 399.
—— Assimilation and Non-Assimilation of Optatives, 402-3.
—— Oratio Recta and Obliqua, 10. Virtual Obliqua, 11, 240, 243, 277, etc.
—— *see* Chapter on Oratio Obliqua.
—— Oratio Obliqua, *see* Part III., ch. iii. (Table of Contents).

P.

Participle, *see* Table of Contents, 162-177.
—— Fut. Part. with Article, 163.
—— Neuter or Substantive, 164.
—— with Verbs of Perception, Emotion, etc., 170, etc.
—— in Indirect Statement, 187, etc.
—— Conditional Protasis, 224.
—— Conditional Apodosis, 227.
—— Temporal, 247-8.
—— Concessive, 249.
—— Final, 258.
—— Causal, 278.
Passive Voice, 130-1.
—— Voice, in Greek and Latin, 130.
Perception, Verbs of, with Participle, 186.
—— Verbs with ὅτι, or ὡς, 187.
—— Verbs with Acc. and Gen., 88.
—— Verbs with Preposition, 89.
—— Verbs with Adjectives and Adverbs denoting Perception in Gen., 100.
—— Verbs with μή, and Infin., 353.
—— Verbs with μή, and Particip., 354. *See* 364.
Perfect Tense, uses of, 144.
Person, 2d pers. sing., used impersonally, 122.
Petition Indirect, 191-2.
Plural for Singular, 21-2.

Predicate, 1, 13, contrasted with Attributive, and Apposition, 5. Supplementary, 2, 22; Oblique or Dependent, 43-5.
—— agreement of, with several Subjects, 16-18.
—— with Article, 37.
Prepositions, *see* Table of Contents, Part III., 286, etc.
—— Quasi Prepositions, 288, 301-2, 306.
Present Tense, uses of, 142.
Principal and Subordinate, *see* Sentence.
Promising, *see* Hoping.
Pronouns, *see* Table of Contents, Part I. ch. iii., 47-63.
—— Personal, for Reflexive, 48.
—— Possessive, for a Genitive Subjective, or Objective, 49.
—— in Gen., agreeing with a Personal Pronoun implied in the Possessive, 49.
—— Reflexive, for Reciprocal, 50.
—— as antecedent to the Relative, 52, *n.* 4, 55, *n.* 1.
Protasis and Apodosis, meanings of, 195, footnote.

Q.

Questions, Indirect, 188.
—— Indirect, Deliberative, 190-1.
—— Deliberative, in Subj. and Opt., 134-6.

R.

Recta and Obliqua, 10.
Relative Sentences, 9, 284-5.[1]
Restrictive, *see* Limitative.

S.

Schema Pindaricum, 16.
Sentence, parts of, 1.
—— Simple and Compound, 5.
—— Principal and Subordinate, 6.
—— Co-ordinate, 7.
—— Subordinate classified, 7-10.
Sequence of Moods, 138.
Singular for Plural, 18.
Statement, Indirect, *see* Table of Contents, 178, 187.

[1] On Relative Sentences, *see* Monro's *Homeric Grammar.*

Subdirect and Suboblique, 11, 389 (and Orat. Obl., *passim*).
Subjunctive [1]—
— Introductory Note, 132.
— in Independent Sentences, 134, 135.
 A. In Exhortations.
 B. In Prohibitions.
 C. In Deliberative Questions.
 D. Denoting a future possibility (a very rare Attic construction).
— in Deliberative Indirect Questions, 190.
— in Indefinite Sentences with ἄν, 194.
— in Conditional Questions (see Part II. ch. ii.).
 (*a*.) In Future Conditions.
 (*b*.) In General or Frequentative Present Conditions.
— in Temporal Sentences

denoting Indefinite Time (which is of three kinds), (*see* Part II. ch. iii.).
Subjunctive, in Concessive Sentences with ἐὰν καί, καὶ ἐάν, 250.
— in Final Sentences of Primary Sequence (*see* Part II. ch. v.)
— in Modal Sentences with ὅπως, etc., as a rarer and variant construction, 260.
— with Verbs of Fearing, etc., 263, etc.
— alternating with Optative, 182-184 (*see* Compound Sentence and Oratio Obliqua *passim*, and 254, *n*. 1).
Substituted, by the Graphic or Vivid Construction, for the Optative in Historic Sequence wherever the Recta or the Primary Sequence took a Subjunctive, see Graphic.

Substantive used as Adjective or Attributive, 23.
Superlative and Comparative, 120-123.
Swearing and Witnessing, Verbs of, take μή, 353, *n*. 4, (*see* 352).

T.

Temporal Sentences, *see* Table of Contents, Part II., ch. iii., 232-248.
Tenses, *see* Table of Contents, Part I. ch. vii., 138-152.
Time in the Moods, 139.
Tmesis, 288.
Transitive Verbs become Intransitive, 124.

V.

Vocative, 80.
Voices, *see* Table of Contents, 124-131.

W.

Wish, expressions of, 280-3.

[1] On the Subjunctive and Optative *see* Monro's *Homeric Grammar* (Subjunctive in Principal Clauses, 196; in Subordinate Clauses, 201; Optative in Simple Sentences, 215; in Subordinate, 219; History of Subjunctive and Optative, 229, etc.).

GREEK INDEX.

The numbers refer to the pages of the book.

A

A privative, Adjectives compounded with, take a Gen., *e.g.* ἀμνήμων, ἀνήκοος, 98, 103.
ἀγαθόν (εὖ, κακόν, etc.), λέγω, δρῶ, etc., with double Acc., 72 (for Passive forms, *see* 73, *n*. 2).
ἀγάλλομαι, with Dat., 112.
ἄγαμαι, with Gen., 94.
ἀγανακτῶ, with Dat., 117.
ἄγειν χειρός, 87.
ἁγνός, with Gen., 103.
ἀδελφός, with Gen. or Dat., 119.
ἀδικῶ, with double Acc., 72.
Ἀθηνῶν πόλις, 81.
ἀθυμῶ, with Dat., 112.
αἰδοῦμαι, with Acc., 75.

αἱρῶ, with Gen. of Charge, 95.
αἰσχύνομαι, with Acc., 75.
— with Dat., 112.
— with Infin., 155, 172.
— with μή, 264.
αἰσθάνομαι, with Gen., 86.
— with Particip., 169, 175, 186.
αἰτιῶμαι, with Gen. of Charge, 95.
ἀκολουθός, with Gen. or Dat., 119.
ἀκολουθῶ, with Dat., 118.
ἀκούω, ἀκροῶμαι, with Gen., 86.
ἅλις, with Gen., 82.
ἁλίσκομαι, with Gen. of charge, 95.
ἄλλος, ἀλλοῖος, with Gen., 103.
ἄλλος, meaning *besides*, 62.

ὁ ἄλλος, meaning *in general*, 63.
ἄλλος ὅσος, ἄλλος εἴ τις, 60.
ἀλλότριος, Dat. or Gen., 79, 119.
"Ἀμα, quasi-Prep., 306.
ἅμα, with Dat., 119.
ἁμαρτάνω, with Gen., 86.
ἀμείβομαι, with Gen., 93.
ἀμελῶ, with Gen., 87.
ἀμύνω, with Dat., 116.
ἀμύνομαι, with Acc., 76.
ἀμύνω and ἀμύνομαι, 129.
ἀμφί, Prep., 317-319.
ἀμφιέννυμι, with double Acc., 72.
ἀμφισβητῶ, with Gen and Dat., 117, 118.
— with μή, μὴ οὐ, 365.
Ἄν, see Part II., ch. ii., Table of Contents, 193-231.

GREEK INDEX. 429

Ἄν, with Imperf. and Aor. Indic., denoting a repeated act, 151.
— with Aor. Infin., after Verbs of hoping, etc., 181.
— with Infin., in Indirect Statement, 181.
— with Optat., in Indirect Statement, 185.
— with Particip., in Indirect Statement, 187.
— with Aor. Indic., not denoting an unfulfilled condition, 216.
— omitted with the Subj. in Subordinate Sentences, 245.
— retained with the Optat. in Subordinate Sentences, 246.
— with Final Sentences, 255.
— with ὅπως Modal, 261, *n*. 4.
— with ὥστε Consecutive, 272, *n*. 2.
Ἀνά, Prep., 291, 292.
ἀναγκάζω, with double Acc., 73.
ἀναγκαῖος, construction of, 159.
ἀναμιμνῄσκω τινά τι and τινά τινος, 73, *n*. 3.
Ἄνευ, 301.
ἀνήρ=τις, with Gen., 83.
ἀντέχω, with Dat., 118.
ἀντέχομαι, with Gen., 86.
Ἀντί, Prep., 294.
ἀντιλέγω μή and μὴ οὐ, 365.
ἀντιποιῶ, with double Acc., 72.
ἀντίστροφος, with Gen. or Dat., 119.
ἀνύτω, with Particip., 172.
ἄξιος, construction of, 159.
ἀξιῶ, with Gen., 93, 103.
ἀπαγορεύω (ἀπεῖπον) μή, μὴ οὐ, 365.
ἀπαλλάσσω, -ομαι, with Gen., 99.
ἀπαντῶ, with Dat., 118.
ἀπειθῶ, with Dat., 116.
ἀπεχθάνομαι, with Dat., 117.
ἀπέχω, with Gen., 99.
ἀπέχομαι μή, μὴ οὐ, 363.
ἀπέχω, with Dat., 116.
— (ἀπιστίαν παρέχει) μή, μὴ οὐ, 264, 365.
Ἀπό, Prep., 295-297.
ἀποδέχομαι ταῦτά τινος, 88.
ἀποδιδράσκω, with Acc., 75.
ἀποδίδομαι, with Gen., 93.
ἀποκάμνω, with Particip., 172.

ἀποκρύπτομαι μή, μὴ οὐ, 365.
ἀπολαύω τί τινος, 85, 86.
ἀπολύομαι μή, μὴ οὐ, 365.
ἀπορία, with Gen., 82.
ἀποστερῶ, with double Acc., 72.
ἀποστρέφω μή, μὴ οὐ, 365.
ἀποτρέπω, with Gen., 100.
ἀποτυγχάνω, with Gen., 86.
ἀποφεύγω, with Gen. (of charge), 95.
ἅπτομαι, with Gen., 86.
ἀρήγω, (poet.), with Dat., 116.
ἀρκῶ, ἀρκεῖ, construction, 173.
ἀρνοῦμαι μή and μὴ οὐ, 365.
ἄρτι, with Present, 143.
ἄρχω, ἄρχομαι, with Gen., 86, 88, 98.
— with Infin. and Particip., 171.
ἅτε, Causal.
αὐτοκράτωρ, with Gen., 103.
αὐτός, various uses of, 53-55.
— with Dat. of Circumstance, 114.
— strengthens Reflexives, 49.
— subject to Infinitive, 179.
αὐτο-δικαιοσύνη, etc. (Platonic idioms), 26, 55.
αὑτός and ὁ αὐτός, 42, 53-4.
ὁ αὐτός, constructions of, 110.
ἀφαιροῦμαι τινά τι, and τινά τινος, 72, 73, *n*. 3.
ἀφίημι, with Gen. (of charge), 95.
ἀφίστημι, with Gen., 99.
ἄχθομαι, with Dat., 112, 117.
ἀχρεῖος, ἄχρηστος, with Dat., 119.
Ἄχρι, quasi-Prep., 302.
— temporal Conjunction (see μέχρι).

B

βαίνω πόδα, 77.
βαρέως φέρω, with Dat. 117.
βασιλεύω, with Gen., 98.
βιάζομαι, with Acc., 78.
βλάπτω, with double Acc., 72.
βλαστεῖν, with Gen., 80.
βλέπω νᾶπυ, etc., 78.
βοηθῶ, with Dat., 116.
βούλευω ὅπως, with Fut. Indic., etc., 261-2.

γελῶ, with Acc. 76.

γεύω, with Gen., 84, 86.
γηροτροφῶ, with Acc., 76.
γράφομαι, with Gen. of charge, 95.
— with double Acc., 73.
γυμνός, with Gen., 82, 98, 103.

Δ

δακρύω, with Acc., 76.
δέδοικα, with Infin., 155.
δέρκομαι πῦρ, Ἄρην, etc., 78.
δή, δήποτε, δηποτοῦν, as Suffixes, 58.
δῆλος, δηλῶ, constructions, 172, 174.
δεῖ, constructions, 117.
δεῖ ὅπως, 261, *n*. 8.
δεύτερος, δευτεραῖος, with Gen., 97.
Διά, Prep., 307-310.
διαβάλλω, with double Acc., 72.
διαλλάσσω τινά τινι, 105.
διαλέγομαι, with Dat., 109, 118.
διανέμω, with Acc. and Dat., 105.
διαπλέω, with Acc., 75.
διαφέρω, with Gen., 97.
διαφέρομαι, with Dat., 98, 109.
διαφερόντως ἔχω, with Gen., 97, 103.
διάφορος, with Dat. or Gen., 109, 119.
διδάσκω, with double Acc., 72.
διέχω, with Gen., 99.
δίκαιος, construction of, 159.
διπλάσιος, etc., with Gen., 97.
διψῶ, with Gen., 87.
διώκω, with Gen. of charge (ὁ διώκων), 95.
δοκεῖ, δοκῶ, construction of, 117, 159.
δυοῖν θάτερον, etc., 26.
δυσέρως, with Gen., 103.
δύσνους, with Dat., 119.

E

ἐάν, see Conditional and Concessive Sentences.
— never Interrogative, 191, footnote, 207.
ἑαυτοῦ, for 1st and 2d pers., 50.
— Reciprocal, 50.
ἐγγύς, with Gen. and Dat., 119.
ἐγγυῶμαι, with μή and Infin., 353.

GREEK INDEX.

ἐγώ (σύ) for αὐτός, as Subject of Infin., 180.
ἐγκαλῶ, with Dat., 117.
ἐγκρατής, with Gen., 103.
ἔδει, without ἄν, 144, 218.
εἰ. *See* Conditional and Concessive Sentences.
— Interrogative. *See* Indirect Question.
— Interrogative, with Subj., 291.
— Interrogative, with Verbs of Fearing, 266.
— for ὅτι with Verbs of Emotion, 186.
— with Subj., 245.
εἰ (ἐάν) καί, καὶ εἰ (ἐάν), 250.
εἰ, εἰ γάρ, εἴθε, with Wishes, 280-283.
εἰ δὲ μή, 208.
εἰ (ἐάν)=si forte, 208.
εἰ ἐάν, in Virtual Obliqua, 405.
εἰ οὐ, 347, 358, 359.
εἴπερ (ἐάνπέρ), quasi concessive, 250.
εἰκὸς ἦν (without ἄν), *see* ἔδει.
εἴκω, with Gen., 99, Gen. or Dat., 106.
εἰμί, with Gen., 90.
εἴργω, with Gen., 99.
— μή, μὴ οὐ, 365.
Εἰς, Prep. 292.
εἰς διδασκάλου, Ἅιδου, etc., 79.
εἰς ἀνήρ, with Superlative, 123.
εἴσειμι, with Acc., 75.
Ἐκ, Ἐξ, Prep., 297.
ἕκατι, 301.
ἐκδιδράσκω, with Acc., 75.
ἐκβαίνω, with Gen., 100.
ἐκεῖνος, uses of, 52.
ἐκπλήσσομαι, etc., with Acc., 75.
ἐλαττῶ, ἐλαττοῦμαι, with Gen., 98.
ἐλεύθερος, ἐλευθερῶ, with Gen., 98, 99, 103.
ἐλλιπής, with Gen., 113.
ἕλκος οὐτάσαι, etc., 69.[1]
ἔμμονος (ἐμμένω), with Dat., 119.
ἔμπλεως, with Gen., 82.
ἔμπειρος (ἄπειρος), with Gen., 103.
ἐμποδίζομαι(ἐμπόδών εἶναι), Dat. 116.
— μή, μὴ οὐ, 365.
ἔμφυτος, with Dat., 119.
Ἐν, Prep., 302.
ἐν, when used with Dat. of Time, 115.

ἐνάντιος, with Gen. or Dat., 103.
ἐνδύω (ἐκδύω), with double Acc., 72.
ἕνεκα, ἕνεκεν, 301.
ἐννοῶ μή, μὴ οὐ, 264.
ἐντρέπομαι, with Gen., 87.
ἐντυγχάνω, with Dat., 109, 118.
ἐξ ὅτου τρόπου, 261.
ἐξίστημι, with Acc., 75, with Gen., 100.
ἔοικα, with Dat., 117, constructions of, 159.
ἐπαινῶ, with double Acc., 72.
ἐπαίρομαι, with Dat., 112.
ἐπέξειμι, with Gen. of charge, 95.
ἐπέρχομαι, with Dat., 118.
ἐπήβολος, with Gen., 90, 103.
ἐπηρεάζω, with Dat., 117.
Ἐπί, Prep., 318-327.
— Verbs compounded with, take a Dat., 118.
ἐπιδής, with Gen., 103.
ἐπιδείκνυμι, with Partic., 187 (*see* 174 A.).
ἐπίδοξος, constructions of, 159.
ἐπίκουρος, with Gen., 103.
ἐπικουρῶ, with Dat. 116.
ἐπιμελής, ἐπιλήσμων, with Gen., 103.
ἐπιμελοῦμαι, with ὅπως, Modal, 260-1.
— with Infin., 261, *n.* 6.
ἐπίσταμαι, with Partic., 175.
— with Partic., and with Infin.
— with μή and Infin., 353.
ἐπιτίθεμαι, with Dat., 117.
ἐπιτήδειος, with Dat., 119, constructions of, 159.
ἐπιτυγχάνω, with Dat., 87.
ἕπομαι, with Dat., 109, *see* also 118.
ἔρημος, with Gen., 82, 103.
ἐρίζω, with Dat., 117.
ἐρῶ, with Gen., 87.
— with μή and Infin., 353.
ἐρωτῶ (ἠρόμην), with double Acc., 72.
ἐσθίω, with Gen., 84.
ἐστιν οἵ, εἰσιν οἵ, ἔνιοι, 60.
ἕτερος, with Gen., 97, 103.
εὐδαιμονίζω, with Gen., 94.
εὐλαβοῦμαι, with Acc., 76.
— with Infin., 155.
— with ὅπως, 260, with μή, μὴ οὐ, 264, 365.
εὐλογῶ, with double Acc., 72.
εὔνους, with Dat., 119.

ἐφεξῆς, with Dat., 119.
ἐφ᾽ ᾧ (ᾧ τε), Limitative, 274.
ἐφικνοῦμαι, with Gen., 86, 87.
ἐχθρός, with Dat., 119.
ἔχομαι, with Gen., 86; Meanings of, 90.
ἐχρῆν (χρῆν), without ἄν, 144, 218.
ἔχω, with Gen., 99.
— as a Copulative Verb, 43.
— μή, μὴ οὐ, 365.
ἔχων, in colloquialisms, 165.

Z

ζηλῶ, with Acc., 76; with Gen., 94.

H

ἤδη, with Presen 143.
ἤ τις ἢ οὐδείς, 62.
ἢ κατά, ἢ ὡς (ὥστε), with Comparative, 121.
ἥδομαι, with Dat., 112.
ἡμίσυς (ὁ) τοῦ χρόνου, etc., 85.
ἡμῶν (ὑμῶν) αὐτῶν, Partitively, 51.
ἡττῶμαι, with Gen., 97-98; with Dat., 111.

Θ

θαρρῶ, with Acc., 75.
θαυμάζω, with Gen., 94.
θαυμαστὸς ὅσος, etc., 59.
θιγγάνω, with Gen., 86.

I

ἴδιος, with Gen. or Dat., 79, 119.
ἱερός, with Gen., 79.
ἱκανός, Constructions of, 173.
ἵνα, Final Conjunction, 253.
ἵνα ἄν, not Final, 255.
ἰσόμοιρος, with Gen., 84.
ἰσόρροπος, with Gen. or Dat., 119.
ἴσος, Constructions of, 110, 119.
ἰσῶ, with Acc. and Dat., 117.

K

καθαρός, with Gen., 82, 98, 103.
καί, καίπερ, καί ταῦτα, *see* Concessive Sentences, 242.
καί, joining two Adjectives, 24.

[1] *See* Monro's *Homeric Grammar*, p. 93.

GREEK INDEX. 431

κἄν, κἂν εἰ, 209.
κακοῦργος, with Gen., 103.
καλὸς κἀγαθός, 24.
καλῶ, with double Acc., 71.
Κατά, Prep., 310-313.
κατὰ τοῦτο εἶναι, 157.
κατακρίνω, καταγιγνώσκω, etc., with Gen., 95.
καταπολεμῶ, with Acc., 76.
καταφρονῶ, with Gen., 87.
κείρεσθαι, with Dat., 107.
κελεύω, with Acc. and Dat. also with Acc. and Inf., 116.
κενός, with Gen., 82.
κεφάλαιον (*denique, ad summam*), 26.
κίνδυνός ἐστι μή, μὴ οὐ, 264.
κιχάνω, with Acc., 86.
κλύω ταῦτά σου, 88.
κοινός, with Gen. or Dat., 79, 119.
-κός, Adjectives ending in, with Gen., 113.
κοινωνῶ, with Gen. and Dat. 84.
κρατῶ, with Acc. and Gen., 87, 97, 98.
κρύπτω, with double Acc., 72.
κύριος, with Gen., 103.
κυρῶ, with Gen., 86, 87; with Particip. (poet.), 173.
κωλύω, with double Acc., 72.
— μή, μὴ οὐ, 365.

Λ

λαγχάνω, with Gen., with Acc., 85 *n.* 1; with Acc. and Dat., 116.
λαμβάνω, with Gen. and Acc., 87.
λαμβάνομαι, with Gen., 86.
λανθάνομαι (and Compds.), with Gen., 86.
λανθάνω, with Acc., 76.
λανθάνω, λαθών constructions, 173, 174.
λατρεύω, with Dat., 116.
λείπομαι, with Gen., 98.
λήγω, with Gen., 99.
λοιδορῶ, with Acc., 73, *n.* 3.
λοιδοροῦμαι, with Dat. 73, *n.* 3, and 117.
λυσιτελεῖ, with Dat., 117.

Μ

μά, and similar words, with Acc., 77.
μακαρίζω, with Gen. (and Acc.), 94.
μᾶλλον ἤ, with Compar. and Positive, 121.

μάχομαι, with Dat., 109, 117.
μειονεκτῶ, with Gen., 98.
μέλει μοι τούτου, 87.
μέλει, μεταμέλει, Constructions of, 89, 117.
μέλει μοι, μελετῶ, with ὅπως Modal, 260, 261.
μέλλω, forming Periphrastic Future, 140.
— πῶς (τί) οὐ μέλλω; 150.
— μή, μὴ οὐ, 365.
μέμφομαι, with Acc. and Dat., 73, *n.* 3, and 117.
— also Acc., also Gen., 117.
μέσος, with Gen., 103.
μεστός, with Gen., 82.
Μετά, Prep., 316-317.
μεταδίδωμι, with Gen. and Dat., 84, 105.
μεταλαμβάνω, with Gen., 84.
μεταξύ, with Particip., 165.
μεταποιοῦμαι, with Gen., 84.
μέτειμι, with Acc., 75.
μετέρχομαι, with Acc., 75.
μέτεστι, with Gen. and Dat., 84, 117.
μετέχω, with Gen., 84: with Acc., 85, *n.* 1.
μέτοχος (ἀμέτοχος), with Gen., 84.
μέχρι, Conjunction, 238; quasi-Prep., 302.
Μή, *see* Chapter on Negatives.
μὴ μή for μὴ οὐ, 264.
μή for ὅπως μή, Modal, 261.
μή, omitted after Verbs of denying, and μή for μὴ οὐ, 369.
μηδέ μηδέπερ, Concessive, 249.
μηδ' εἰ, μηδ' ἐάν, Concessive, 250.
μηνύω, with Dat. and Acc., 116.
μηχανῶμαι ὅπως, etc., 260, 261.
μικροῦ, 83.
μιμνήσκομαι, with Gen., 86.
μισῶ, with Acc., 117.
μνήμων (ἀμνήμων), with Gen., 103.

Ν

ναὶ μά (νή), with Acc., 77.
νέμω, with double Acc., 71.
νικῶμαι, with Gen., 97; Dat., 111.
νομίζω, with Dat., 111.

Ξ

ξυνίημι, with Gen., 86.

Ο

ὁ βουλόμενος (ὁ τυχών), 31, 83.
ὅ (ὅπερ) λέγω, 60.
ὅδε, ὁδί, uses of, 51, 53.
ὅζω, with Gen., 86.
ὁθούνεκα, for ὅτι in statements, 185; Causal, 277.
οἶδα (ξύνοιδα), with Partic. with Infin., 175.
οἰκεῖος, with Gen., 79.
οἰκτείρω, with Acc. and Gen., 94.
οἴμοι, with Gen., 94.
οἷον, with Superlative, 123.
οἷος, in Attraction, 60.
οἷός τε, 60.
οἷος, Consecutive, 275; Causal, 278.
οἶσθ' ὃ δρᾶσον; 137.
οἴχομαι, with Partic., 174.
ὀλίγου, ὀλίγου δεῖ, 82; ὀλίγου δεῖν, 157.
ὀλιγωρῶ, with Gen., 87.
ὁμιλῶ, with Dat., 109, 118.
ὄμνυμι, with μή and Infin., 353.
ὅμοιος (ἀνόμοιος), 119.
— Constructions of, 110.
ὁμοιῶ, with Acc. and Dat., 117.
ὁμολογῶ, with Dat., 117, 119; with Partic., 187.
ὁμόσε χωρῶ, with Dat., 117.
ὁμοῦ, with Dat., 119.
ὁμώνυμος, with Dat., 119.
ὅμως, *see* Concessive Sentences, 249.
ὀνομάζω, with double Acc., 71.
ὅπῃ for ὅπως, with Fut., 261.
ὁπότε, Causal, 277.
ὅπως, Final, 253; Modal with Fut., 259, etc.; in Indirect Petition, 262; for ὅτι in Statements, 185; Temporal, 235; ὅπως ἄν, with Opt. not final, 255.
ὀργίζομαι, with Dat. and Gen., 94, 117.
ὀρέγομαι, with Gen., 86.
ὀρφανός, with Gen., 98.
ὁρῶ μή, μὴ οὐ, 264; ὅπως, 260, 261.
ὅς, Personal, 29; Relative, 57; Interrogative, 56; Conditional, 225; Consecutive, 274; Causal, 278.
ὅς γε Causal, 278.
ὅσος, *see* οἷος.
ὅσον γε μ' εἰδέναι, 157.
ὅς περ, 57.
ὅστις, Relative, 57; In-

GREEK INDEX.

terrogative, 56; Conditional, 225, 226; Consecutive, 274; Causal, 278.
ὀσφραίνομαι, with Gen., 86.
ὅτε, Temporal, 234; Causal, 277, *n*. 3.
ὅτι (and ὡς), in Statements, 178, etc.; difference between, 184.
Causal, 276; with Verbs of Fearing, 265.
ὅτι, with Superlative, 123.
ὅτῳ τρόπῳ for ὅπως, 261.
Οὐ, οὐκ, οὐχί, *see* Part III. ch. ii. (Table of Contents), 345, etc.
οὐ μά, with Acc., 79.
οὐ μή, with Fut. Opt. and Infin., 375.
οὐδ' εἰ (ἐάν), Concessive, 250.
οὐδέ (περ), Concessive, 249.
οὗ, οἷ, ἕ, Reflexives, 50.
οὐδεὶς ὅστις οὐ, 59.
οὐκ οἶδ' ἄν εἰ, 203.
οὖν, as a Suffix, 58.
οὕνεκα for ὅτι, 185.
οὗτος, οὑτοσί, Relatives, 57.
οὗτος, *heus tu!* 66.
οὕτω, in Wishes (*sic—ut*), 282.
ὄφρα (Epic and Lyric), final, 253.
ὀψιμαθής, with Gen., 103.

Π

πάλαι, with Present, 143.
πᾶν=*quidlibet*, 63.
πάντα εἶναι, 16.
Παρά, Prep. 318-332.
— Verbs compounded with, take Dat., 118.
παραβάλλω, Constructions of, 118.
παραπλήσιος, with Dat., 119; Constructions of, 110.
παρασκευαστικός, with Gen., 103.
παρασκευάζω ὅπως, etc., 260, 261.
παρατάσσομαι, with Dat., 118.
παραχωρῶ, with Gen., 99.
παύω (Acc.), and Gen., 99; παύομαι, Gen., 99; παύω and παύομαι, with Participle, 163, 170.
πένης, with Gen., 82, 103.
πείθομαι, with Dat., 116.
πείθου and πιθοῦ (μοι), 116.
περ, as a Suffix, 57.
Περί, Prep., 332-335.
— Verbs compounded with,

take a Dat. of reference, 118.
περιβάλλομαι, with double Acc., 72; Constructions of, 118.
περιγίγνομαι, with Gen., 97.
περίειμι, with Gen., 97.
περιέρχομαι, with Acc., 75.
περιπλέω, with Acc., 75.
πίμπλημι, with Gen., 82; Dat., 82.
πίνω, with Gen., 84; Acc., 85.
πιστεύω, with Dat., 116.
πιστεύω (πέπεισμαι), with μή and Infin., 353.
πίσυνος, with Dat., 119.
πλεονεκτῶ, with Gen., 98.
πλέως, with Gen., 103.
πλήρης, with Gen., 82.
πλούσιος, with Gen., 82.
ποιοῦμαι, with Gen., 79.
ποῖος; πόθεν; in Repetitions, 56.
ποιός and ποσός (indefinite), 61.
πολέμιος, πολεμῶ, with Dat., 119, 109.
πολλὴ τῆς χώρας, 85.
πολλοστός, etc., with Gen., 97.
πολλοῦ δεῖ (δέω), 83.
πότερος; and ποτερός, 61.
ποῦ γῆς; etc., 85, *n*. 3.
πρακτικός, with Gen., 103.
πράσσω (πράσσομαι), with double Acc., 72; πράσσω ὅπως, etc. 260, 261.
πρέπει, with Dat., 117.
Πρό, Prep., 300.
προθυμοῦμαι, with Acc., 76; ὅπως, etc. 260, 261.
προκαλοῦμαι, with Gen. of charge, 95.
πρόκειμαι, with Gen., 100.
προσφιλής, with Dat., 119.
προτιμῶ, with (Acc.) and Gen., 100.
Πρός, Prep., 336.
— Verbs compounded with, take a Dat., 118.
προσαγορεύω, with double Acc., 71.
πρόσειμι, with Dat., 118.
προσέρχομαι, with Dat., 109.
πρόσηκεί μοι τούτου, 117.
προσκρούω, with Dat., 118, 119.
προστυγχάνω, with Dat., 87, 109, 118.
προτεραῖος, with Gen., 97.
πυνθάνομαι, with Gen., 86.
πωλῶ, with Gen., 93.
πῶς γὰρ ἄν; 209.

πῶς ἄν; in Wishes, 215, 280, etc.

Σ·

σημεῖον δέ, 26.
σιωπῶ, with Acc., 76.
σκοπῶ εἰ, Interrog., 261; ὅπως, etc. 260, 261; μή, μὴ οὐ, 264.
σπουδάζω ὅπως, etc., 260, 261.
στασιάζω, with Dat., 117.
στερίσκομαι, with Gen., 99.
στεφανοῦμαι, with Dat., 117.
στοχάζομαι, with Gen., 86.
στρατηγῶ, with Gen., 98.
συγγιγνώσκω, with Dat. and Gen., 95.
συγγνώμων, with Gen., 103.
συγχωρῶ, with μή and Infin., 353.
συκοφαντῶ, with Acc., 76.
συλλαμβάνω, Construction, 118.
συμβουλεύω, with Acc. and Dat., 116.
σύμμαχος, with Dat., 119.
σύμφερον, σύμφορος (ἀσύμφορος), with Dat., 119.
συμφωνῶ, with Dat., 117.
Σύν, Prep., 305.
— with Dat. of Circumstance, 114.
σὺν θεῷ εἰπεῖν, 157.
Σύνεσις, *see* Construction κατὰ σύνεσιν (English Index).
— Verbs compounded with, take a Dat., 118.
συνῄδω (διᾴδω), with Dat., 117.
συναλλάσσω, with Acc. and Dat., 117.
σύνειμι, with Dat., 118.
συνελόντι (συντέμνοντι) εἰπεῖν, 107.
σύνοιδα, Construction, 118, 175.
σφάλλομαι, with Gen., 86.
σχεδὸν εἰπεῖν, 157.
σχῆμα καθ' ὅλον καὶ μέρη, 24.

Τ

τὰ πρῶτα εἶναι, 16.
τάδε, τάδε πάντα, 52.
τάσσω, with Gen., 93.
τεκμήριον δέ, 26.
τέμνω, with double Acc., 71.
τῆς αὐτῆς ἡμέρας and τῇ αὐτῇ ἡμέρᾳ, 92.
τί μαθών; τί παθών; (τί ἔχων, τί βουλόμενος), 164.
τίμιος, with Gen., 103.

GREEK INDEX.

τιμῶ, τιμῶμαι, with Gen., 93.
τιμωροῦμαι, with Acc., 76; *see* 129.
τιμωρῶ, with Dat., 116.
τις, idiomatic uses of, 26.
τὸ μή (μὴ οὐ), τοῦ or τοῦ μή (μὴ οὐ), with Infin., after Verbs of denying, etc., 366, 367, 368.
τὸ ποῖον, τὸ τί; 56; τὸ ποιόν, τὸ ποσόν, 63.
τοιοῦτος, followed by οὐ, 362.
τοξεύω, with Gen., 87.
τοῦ, with Infin. Final, 94, *see* 366.
τοῦ λοιποῦ and τὸ λοιπόν, 92.
τυγχάνω, with Gen., 86; with Particip., 173.
τοῦτ' ἐκεῖνο, 52.
τραφῆναι, with Gen., 80.
τρίβων, with Gen., 103.
τυραννεύω, τυραννῶ, with Gen., 98.
τυφλός, with Gen., 103.

Υ

ὑβρίζω, with double Acc., 72.
ὑπακούω, with Gen. and with Dat., 116.
ὑπάρχω, with Particip., 171.
ὑπεκτραπέσθαι μή, μὴ οὐ, 365.
Ὑπέρ, Prep., 314.
ὑπεραλγῶ, with Gen., 100.
ὑπερβάλλω, with Acc., 75.
ὑπερέχω, with Gen., 97.
ὑπερφυὴς ὅσος, etc., 59.
ὑπεύθυνος, with Gen. and Dat., 103.
ὑπηρετῶ, with Dat., 116.
ὑπισχνοῦμαι, with Dat. and with Acc., 116.
Ὑπό, Prep., 341.

ὑποβάλλω, with Dat., 116.
ὑποδύομαι, with Acc., 75.
ὑποπτεύω μή, μὴ οὐ, 264.
ὑποτελής, with Gen., 103.
ὑποτίθεμαι, with Dat., 116.
ὑποφεύγω, with Acc., 75.
ὑστερῶ, ὑστερίζω, ' with Gen., 98.
ὕστερός, ὑστεραῖος, with Gen., 97.
ὑφίσταμαι, with Acc., 75.

Φ

φανερός, φανερόν, φαίνομαι, Constructions, 173, 174.
φείδομαι (φειδωλός), with Gen., 99, 103.
φεῦ, with Gen., 94.
φεύγω δίκην, 81; with Gen. of charge, 95; ὁ φεύγων, 95.
φεύγω μή, μὴ οὐ, 365.
φθάνω, with Acc., 76; with Particip., 171.
φθονῶ, with Gen., 94; with Dat., 117.
φιλικῶς διάκειμαι, etc., with Dat.
φιλόδωρος, with Gen., 103.
φιλομαθής, with Gen., 113.
φοβοῦμαι, with Acc., 76: with Infin., 155; with μή, μὴ οὐ and variant constructions, 266, etc.
φρίσσω, with Acc., 75.
φροντίζω ὅπως, etc., 260, 261; μή, μὴ οὐ, 264.
φυλάσσω, -ομαι ὅπως, etc., 260, 261; μή, μὴ οὐ, 264, 365.
φυλάσσομαι, with Acc. 76; μή, μὴ οὐ, 365.
φῦναι, with Gen., 8:

Χ

χαίρω, with Particip., 170.

χαλεπαίνω, χαλεπῶς φέρω, with Dat., 112-117.
χαρίζομαι, with Dat., 116.
χάριν, quasi-Prep., 302.
χορεύω θεόν, 72.
χρή (χρῆν, ἐχρῆν), with μή and οὐ, 353.
χρῆν, *see* ἐχρῆν.
χρήσιμος, χρηστός (ἄχρηστος), with Dat., 119.
χρῶμαι, with Dat., 111.
χωρίζω, with Gen., 99.
χωρίς, quasi-Prep. 301.

Ψ

ψεύδομαι, with Gen., 86; with double Acc., 72.
ψιλός with Gen., 98, 103; ψιλῶ, with Gen., 99.

Ω

ὠνητός, with Gen., 103; ὠνοῦμαι, with Gen., 93; with ὅπως, etc., 260, 261.
ὡραῖος, with.Gen., 93, 103.
ὡς, Modal, 253; for ὅπως Modal, 261, *n.* 3; Final, 253; with Final Particip., 258; for ὥστε, Consecutive, 275; ὡς ἄν, Final, 255; in Wishes, 280, etc. ; Comparative (also ὥσπερ) with Particip., 165, 167.
ὥς, with Superlative, 123.
ὡς (ὥσπερ) οὐ and μή, 357.
ὡς ἔπος εἰπεῖν, and similar phrases, 157.
ὥσπερ ἄν εἰ, 259.
ὥστε, Consecutive, 269-273; Limitative, 274.
ὥστε μή, with Infin. after Verbs of denying, etc., 366.
ὤφελον, without ἄν, *see* ἔδει; in Wishes, 281-283.

TABLE OF REFERENCES.

Aeschines, B.C. 389-314 (?)
Aeschylus, B.C. 525-456.
Andocides, B.C. 440 (?)—last speech 390.
Antiphon, B.C. 480 (?)-410 (?).
Aristophanes, B.C. 450 (?)—last play 388.
Demosthenes, B.C. 384 (?)-322.
Euripides, B.C. 480-406.
Isaeus, dates of speeches B.C. 389-352.
Isocrates, B.C. 436-338.
Lysias, B.C. 435 (?)-378.
Plato, B.C. 429 (?)-347.
Sophocles, B.C. 496-406.
Thucydides, B.C. 471 (?)-401 (?).
Xenophon, B.C. 429 (?)-356 (?).

The reference to the author is on the left hand, that to the page of the Grammar on the right hand.

LINE	PAGE	LINE	PAGE	LINE	PAGE
AESCHINES.		*Choephorae.*		366,	239
III. In *Ctesiphontem.*		142,	417	384,	77
		200	74	431,	204
86,	39	257,	265	460,	272
177,	373	262,	43	465,	90
204,	352	290,	251	466,	239
333,	49, 122	392,	136	529,	210
		521,	412	680,	420
AESCHYLUS.		705,	92	715,	69
				761,	237
Agamemnon.		*Eumenides.*		793,	87
37,	212	256,	21	800,	379
67,	318	344,	299	1041,	423
130,	340	618,	362		
200,	218	661,	362	*Prometheus Vinctus.*	
225,	74			10,	255
586,	305	*Persae.*		12,	107
642,	29	10,	255	152,	257
689,	423	49,	16	165,	243
788,	77	100,	82	248,	365
813,	297	112,	265	285,	347
930,	206	124,	385	419,	318
1030,	343	162,	26	481,	242
1067,	244	164,	102	627,	367
1258,	422	182,	92	650,	337
1379,	327	297,	251	786,	369
1400,	325	319,	111	830,	318
1438,	40	327,	420	865,	154
1439,	21	331,	74	898,	421
1487,	301	337,	301	904,	74

TABLE OF REFERENCES.

LINE	PAGE	LINE	PAGE	LINE	PAGE
987,	93	17,	122, 225	*L. sistr.*	
1047,	136	19,	225	459,	383
Septem ad Thebas.		21,	378	917,	378
		24,	218	*Nubes.*	
481,	62	25,	244, 250		
513,	206	26,	397	5,	205
553,	778	90,	213	77,	210
672,	289	91,	225	118,	204
681,	411	92,	225	153,	94
821,	note 341			296,	386
843,	318	VI. *De Choreuta.*		299,	373
Supplices.		14,	209	341,	164
15,	309	15,	214	345,	417
594,	74	29,	206	367,	371
				490,	262
ANDOCIDES.		**ARISTOPHANES.**		505,	386
I. *De Mysteriis.*		*Acharnians.*		520,	282
				692,	363
30,	180	1,	41	698,	331
38,	50, 407	12,	41	788,	419
43,	244, 256	57,	250	792,	224
50,	41	94,	78	819,	160
54,	223	106,	56	876,	93
57,	224	166,	386	1027,	150
58, 59,	218	196,	88	1301,	150
61,	404	364,	58	1368,	41
63,	387	384,	123	*Plutus.*	
101,	353	418,	56	438,	136
		466,	225	1133,	172
II. *De Reditu.*		474,	58	1151,	255
10,	41	562,	219	*Ranae.*	
12,	223	675,	120	23,	256
		761,	213	200,	356
III. *De Pace.*		959,	56	202,	386
41,	362	991,	215	298,	374
		1000,	160	456,	158
ANTIPHON.		1001,	312, 342	462,	372
III. *Tetral.* B. β.		1048,	52	504,	235
1,	63	1055,	214	522,	356
2,	41, 48	1078,	122	526,	356
4, 6,	369	1180,	334	609,	374
5,	225	*Aves.*		636,	110
5,	379	54,	137	643,	331
6,	214	195,	278	830,	214
10, 11,	45	461,	373	866,	219
		964,	244	955,	281
IV. *Tetral.* Γ. α.		*Ecclesiazusae.*		1459,	363
4,	223	105,	301	*Thesm.*	
6,	352	115,	349	469,	282
		236,	16	*Vespae.*	
V. *De Caede Herodis.*		493,	265		
1 and *passim*,	45	495,	256	283,	407
2,	415	650,	384	307,	374
7,	122	991,	385	774,	166
11,	50	999,	378	1179,	417
13,	217, 219	*Equites.*			
14,	357	112,	265, 370	* **DEMOSTHENES.**	
15,	205	158,	377	*Olynthiac* I.	
16,	223	926,	261	15, 25,	311

* The references are to the pages of Reiske's edition, 1770. The numbers in brackets are the references as given in the text of this Grammar, in compiling which different editions of Demosthenes have been used. Some of the examples, about eighteen, borrowed from other books, have not been verified in Reiske. They are omitted in this list, but not in the text, as they are evidently authentic, and useful.

TABLE OF REFERENCES.

LINE	PAGE	LINE	PAGE	LINE	PAGE
Olynthiac II.		381, 5,	143	**EURIPIDES.**	
24, 14 [2, 22],	330	381, 10,	160		
		388, 15,	398	*Alcestis.*	
Olynthiac III.		391, 9 [11],	219	18,	300
29, 22 [same construction		395, 8 [§ 190],	206	150,	343
as in text],	70	418, 13,	75	346,	341
		434, 6,	266	662,	172
Philippic I.		In *Leptinem.*		671,	221
40, 1 [Phil. i. 1],	239			690,	314
42, 4,	320	460, 2 [20, 10],	75	741,	94
44, 12 [Phil. i. 44],	224	470, 26,	380	755,	221
45, 1 [Phil. i. 18],	206	478, 25 [20, 73],	313		
45, 11 [iv. 19],	108	In *Midiam.*		*Andromache.*	
49, 14 [Phil. i. 9],	43			134,	68
51, 27 [Phil. i. 10],	90	527, 3,	321	168,	18, 52
54, 20 [Phil. i. 54],	150	528, 16,	339	220,	416
		530, 21 [21, 51],	209	441,	341
De Pace.		582, 25,	206	700,	377
61, 17 [de Pace iv.]	76	In *Androtionem.*		797,	386
				946,	114
Philippic II.		596, 17,	257	1077,	377
66, 12 [Phil. ii. 66],	255	In *Aristocratem.*		1251,	307
De Chersoneso.		660, 7 [23, 120],	16	*Bacchae.*	
107, 8 (viii. 70),	331	In *Timocratem.*		1,	71
		734, 2 [24, 107],	278	5,	71
Philippic III.		734, 5 [37, 28],	34	29,	74
112, 7,	219	763, 15 [24, 203],	76	70,	422
119, 8 [9, 31],	23	In *Aristogit.* I.		142,	415
124, 19 [same construction				156,	342
as in text],	314	773, 1,	261	183,	422
129, 19 [129, 72],	17	In *Aphobum* I.		250,	74
130, 14,	265			270,	350
		815, 11,	313	277,	304
Philippic IV.		816, 12,	325	331,	287
141, 3 [1, 141],	265	822, 8,	325	342,	386
		834, 23,	229	343,	374
De Rhod. Libertat.		In *Aphobum* II.		757,	322
197, 8,	359			847,	71
Pro Megalop.		837, 13 [11],	572	1039,	323
		841, 17,	230	1134,	114
202, 23,	403	842, 9,	282	1263,	350
207, 4,	261	*Pro Phano in Aphob.*		1288,	348
De Corona.		(*Aphob.* III.)		1312,	218
				1353,	71
229, 16 [21, 26],	331	849, 24,	257	1368,	323
236, 10 [12],	260	In *Onetor.* A.		*Cyclops.*	
242, 10 [242],	224				
243, 17,	115	865, 24,	246	120,	375
246, 10,	41	869, 9,	405	131,	137
263, 28 [18, 124],	135	870, 24,	388	595,	262
269, 19 [18, 127],	23	In *Stephanum.*		*Electra.*	
274, 28,	207				
278, 15 [21, 117],	24	1113, 4 [45, 38],	164	231,	25
279, 18,	323	In *Polyclem.*		369,	377
288, 29,	323			939,	62
292, 21,	304	1206, 12 [Meid.],	206	1035,	16
301, 1,	77	In *Cononem.*		1061,	281
301, 27 [18, 220]	39			1165,	377
313, 6,	261	1266, 2,	359	*Hecuba.*	
De Fals. Legat.		In *Neaeram.*		580,	318
343, 19 [19, 8],	106	1360, 20 [viii. 70],	331	730,	272
372, 1,	267	*Epitaphium.*		836,	280
379, 7,	368	1397, 1,	299	1085,	111

TABLE OF REFERENCES.

LINE	PAGE	LINE	PAGE	LINE	PAGE
1111,	218	*Orestes.*		v. *Philippus.*	
1138,	257				
1154,	344	263,	369	77,	402
1275,	147	380,	54	vi. *Archidamus.*	
Helena.		418,	18	13,	269
		497,	101	24,	122
107,	360	529,	23	25 [120],	206
176,	403	622,	341	26,	242
825,	206	680,	249	89,	26
885,	93	936,	172	107 [138 A],	212
1358,	16	1098,	25		
Heracleidae.		1320,	149	vii. *Areopagiticus.*	
37,	306	1593,	211, 228	64 [152 D],	315
130,	24	*Phoenissae.*		viii. *De Pace.*	
179,	243, 403	92,	267, 370		
248,	265	518,	319	114,	321
482,	355	710,	169	ix. *Evagoras.*	
699,	23	838,	23	74,	329
800,	23	1215,	211		
971,	304	1216,	228	x. *Helenae Laud.*	
Hercules Furens.		1357,	360	28,	99
		1590,	375	47,	368
1054,	265	1621,	212		
1435,	250	1624,	249	xii. *Panathenaicus.*	
Hippolytus.		*Rhesus.*		97,	20
213,	386	5,	131	xv. *Antid. s. ve de Permutatione.*	
407,	280	415,	25		
496,	386	*Supplices.*		33,	251
499,	372				
606,	372	484,	330	LYSIAS.	
659,	13	897,	836		
701,	339	1066,	371, 386	i. 4,	49
1103,	22	*Troades.*		21,	262
1410,	280			iv. 1,	380
1425,	107	178,	370	vii. 27,	270
1601,	386	214,	254	xii. 44,	261
Ion.		662,	55	48,	250
347,	359	735,	24	73,	351
672,	403	818,	332	74,	396
1074,	75	905,	176	xiii. 83,	88
1523,	267	970,	354	xix. 39,	97
Iphigenia in Aul.		ISAEUS.		49,	59
436,	171	iii. *De Pyrrhi Hered.*		xxii. 4,	245
489,	244			18,	180
754,	292	32,	107	xxv. 27,	30
1025,	55	v. *De Dicaeog. Hered.*		xxvii. 16,	351
1047,	77	26,	74	xxx. 13,	62
Iphigenia in Taur.		vi. *De Philoct. Hered.*		PLATO.	
534,	71	6,	20	*Apology.*	
1203,	137			i. 17 A,	184
1371,	289	viii. *De Ciron. Hered.*		17 B, 62, 222, 312,	419
Medea.		9,	357	17 C,	320
88,	347	24,	374	17 D,	276, 320
216,	297			ii. 18 A,	95, 159
233,	93	ISOCRATES.		18 B,	74
334,	82	i. *Ad Demonicum.*		18 C,	37
627,	315	15,	60	18 D,	44, 210
753,	58			iii. 19 B,	422
1018,	112	iv. *Panegyricus.*		19 C,	280
1151,	374	19,	242, 406	19 D,	210, 414, 419
1271,	135			iv. 19 E,	22
				20 A,	109

TABLE OF REFERENCES.

LINE	PAGE	LINE	PAGE	LINE	PAGE
20 B,	29, 215, 223	xxxii. 40 D,	204	835 D,	17
20 C,	216	40 E,	209	895 B,	277
v. 20 E,	44, 250, 325	41 A,	325	948 C,	19
21 A,	68	xxxiii. 42 A (in text xxxii.),	258	942 C,	135
vi. 21 B,	187, 412			*Lysis.*	
21 D,	225, 249	*Cratylus.*			
21 E,	419			212 D,	368
vii. 22 A,	68	393 C,	370	216 C,	267
22 B (in text viii.),	151	430 D,	370	218 D,	267
22 C (in text vi.),	13	*Crito.*			
viii. 22 D,	187			*Meno.*	
22 E,	270	iii. 44 D,	257	70 A,	370
ix. 23 A,	209	iv. 44 E,	417	70 C,	59
23 B,	221	45 A,	159	73 B,	70
xii. 25 B,	203, 250, 347	45 B,	191, 270	90 E,	341
25 C,	422	v. 45 D,	129		
xiii. 25 C,	419	ix. 48 C,	208, 369	*Phaedo.*	
25 D,	270	xi. 50 B,	379	58 E,	278
xiv. 26 D,	360	xii. 50 C,	211, 228	60 C,	148
26 E,	414	50 D,	335	61 B,	369
xv. 27 D,	214	51 A,	174	62 B,	416
xvi. 28 B (in text xv.),	264, 383	xv. 53 D,	205	68 B,	211
28 C,	236	xvi. 54 B,	120	69 A,	340
xvii. 28 D,	212, 224	*Euthydemus.*		70 A,	264, 370
28 E,	234, 259	299 B,	228	72 C,	402
29 A,	413	302 C,	16	77 B (in text 77 6),	242
29 B,	100, 165, 352	304 E,	257		251, 370
29 C,	205, 211	307 B,	380	84 B,	383
29 D (in text xviii.),	26			84 C,	338
30 B,	351	*Euthyphro.*		84 E,	267
30 C,	205	12 D,	216	85 A,	91, 100
30 C (in text xxix.),	25	14 C,	217	87 E,	136
xviii. 30 A,	251	*Gorgias.*		88 A,	38, 242
30 C,	421			93 B (Phaedr. in text),	25
30 D,	105, 156	457 D,	274, 347	95 A,	399
31 A,	204, 210	457 E,	265	98 A,	414
xix. 31 D,	369	459 D,	349	98 D,	353
32 A,	251, 278, 421	477,	26	102 D,	278
xx. 32 A,	68	479 C,	271	108 E,	366
32 B (in text xxiii.),	298, 316	479 D,	91	*Phaedrus.*	
xxi. 32 D,	203	489,	90		
33 A,	210	495 D,	262	227 B,	205
33 B,	221	499,	25	228 D,	343
xxii. 33 C,	420	506 B,	406	229 A,	40
33 D,	219	514 A,	48	239 D,	75
33 E,	40	516 E,	309	242 C [Phaedo],	16
34 A,	219	*Laches.*		260 B,	23
34 D,	422	180 C,	251	279 A,	335
xxiii. 34 C,	250, 316	180 E,	24	*Philebus.*	
34 D,	203	195 A,	301	13 A,	264, 370
35 A,	236	196,	370	27 E,	42
xxiv. 35 B,	301	*Leges.*		*Politicus.*	
35 C,	352	640 D,	419	276 C [καὶ εἰ],	251
xxv. 36 A,	350	679 C,	21	303 A,	103
xxvi. 36 C,	243	698 C,	113	303 D,	32
xxvii. 37 D,	88	701 D,	301		
xxviii. 38 A,	205	715 E,	122	*Protagoras.*	
38 B,	398	719 E,	205	309 D,	70
39 A,	225, 272, 410	721 A,	81	313 C,	262
39 C (εἰ καὶ, in text καὶ εἰ),	251	726 A,	316	320 A,	303
xxxi. 39 E,	237, 369	731 C,	373	321 A,	261
40 B,	234	737 E,	71	322 D,	328
41 E,	377	809 E,	335	323 C,	362

TABLE OF REFERENCES. 439

LINE	PAGE	LINE	PAGE	LINE	PAGE
326 D,	24	615 D,	205	586,	147, 148
329 B,	206	616 C,	299	593,	356
336 D,	353			632,	415
352 D,	367	*Sophistes.*		659,	85
358 B,	325	235 A,	267	665,	420
Republic.		254 A,	38	674,	151
				680,	418
329 B,	100	*Symposium.*		690,	418
337 E,	192	175 A,	374	692,	147
338 D,	24	179 B,	328	715,	277
339 E,	192	185 E,	251	725,	59
344 D,	45	186 B,	22	728,	367
345 E,	177	187 D,	255	767,	114, 306
348 E,	186	189,	407	803,	100
352 C,	136	213 D,	261	807,	101
354 A and B,	32	222 A,	205	816,	106
358 B,	208			828,	335
359 C,	213, 403	*Theaetetus.*		840,	413
360 B,	274	145,	370	960,	305
360 D,	121	145 B,	267	1094,	377
362 D,	55	155 A,	238	1114,	337
362 D (O in text),	136	169 B,	21	1121,	44
393 E,	256	183 E,	264	1131,	347
398 A,	311	190 A,	377	1231,	277, 377
404 B,	250			1242,	347
405 A,	385	*Timaeus.*		1264,	280
406 C,	25	25 D,	311	1268,	347
408 C,	211	31 B,	145	1274,	377
412 A,	150	86 D,	23	1275,	377
416 D,	362			1340,	123
424 D,	86	SOPHOCLES.		1418,	244
427 E,	363				
428 C,	25	*Aias.*		*Antigone.*	
434 B,	112	6,	357	9,	419
436 D,	404	27,	114	20,	171
451 A,	265, 370	42,	49	25,	106
459 B,	101	44,	71	26,	418
461 B,	75	51,	322	28,	82
463 D,	102	70,	369	30,	302, 341
465 B,	383	75,	372	41,	261
470 A,	101	122,	249	42,	85
470 B,	324	123,	277	43,	40, 52
472 B and C,	38	153,	112, 277	48,	154
475 A,	371	263,	226	50,	410
478 B,	21	271,	237	69,	204
494 D,	229	272,	234	74,	420
499 B,	102, 373	275,	42	85,	305
511 E,	343	285,	92	91,	235
517 A,	229, 230	313,	405	97,	271
518 C,	180	318,	89	100,	122
539 A,	261	359,	363	115,	114
545 A (in text 535),	38	367,	94	152,	71
549 E,	192	377,	323	170,	277
562 C,	89	403,	135	172,	305
567 A,	255	434,	250	182,	120, 295
574 E,	343	470,	363	212,	77
579 B,	82	474,	113, 171	223,	185
579 B,	85	475,	331	234,	251, 377
590 A,	314	496,	245	239,	189
591 B,	316	536,	204	242,	172
606 B,	25	540,	367	244,	356
607 C,	20	557,	189	260,	177
610 A,	229	560,	371	263,	366
612 B,	213, 228	564,	91, 251	265,	155
614 B,	400	567,	192	323,	245
615 B,	407	572,	384	378,	352

TABLE OF REFERENCES.

Electra.

LINE	PAGE	LINE	PAGE	LINE	PAGE
400,	159			627,	94, 236
411,	25	9,	160	630,	342
415,	238	14,	422	640,	338
443,	368	18,	422	668,	89, 147
444,	214	24,	173	676,	143
460,	176	25,	250	677,	147
466,	204, 209	32,	189, 234	679,	189
470,	106	38,	277	682,	100
484,	213	43,	184, 385	690,	92
492,	90	49,	115	705,	113
538,	73	58,	257	707,	62
546,	378	66,	106	711,	342
547,	173	72,	415	736,	235
551,	304	84,	104	742,	298, 423
556,	45, 323	85,	104	749,	235
589,	113	121, etc.,	77	766,	421
595,	324	123,	69, 101	771,	245
605,	136	141,	87	782,	360, 361
618,	106	174,	115	811,	91, 104
619,	246	183,	330	817,	92
633,	102	188,	100	875,	104
675,	69	193,	115	908,	353
680,	22, 204	225,	245	920,	94
685,	185	244,	347	945,	301
691,	304	248,	147	950,	19
696,	278	264,	299	955,	256
710,	245	267,	236	956,	268
718,	106	269,	110	974,	189
751,	62	272,	108	977,	20
755,	352	285,	339	979,	106
789,	74	286,	421	996,	73
794,	418	293,	236	1000,	377
877,	413	299,	305	1022,	205
884,	204	305,	62	1038,	236
885,	355, 383	317,	102, 177	1052,	371
904,	106	337,	63	1054,	80
908,	302	338,	80	1059,	245
919,	337	344,	101, 298	1061,	322
932,	314	360,	250	1092,	353
957,	299	364,	156	1095,	102
973,	69, 299	369,	417	1117,	94
994,	76	372,	104	1122,	268
997,	75	380,	363	1131,	281
1025,	245	381,	268	1134,	257
1033,	87	384,	99	1154,	420
1063,	354	386,	236	1165,	377
1065,	88	390,	85	1166,	377
1068,	295	399,	22	1172,	270
1080,	160	404,	85	1180,	319
1084,	87	415,	67	1195,	91
1152,	77	423,	234	1210,	94
1156,	306	424,	88	1214,	101
1169,	24	435,	415	1236,	337
1178,	45	447,	99	1262,	93
1182,	102	478,	92	1265,	414
1190,	189	479,	99	1274,	70
1199,	29	496,	106	1308,	185
1200,	422	547,	251	1309,	265
1206,	81	549,	112	1334,	96
1212,	122	555,	246	1343,	113
1229,	85	556,	77	1348,	189
1231,	410	562,	337	1433,	311
1244,	333	571,	93	1451,	87
1253,	267, 355, 370	580,	267	1460,	102
1295,	44	604,	215	1476,	185
1326.	377	612,	83	1496,	255

TABLE OF REFERENCES. 441

LINE	PAGE	LINE	PAGE	LINE	PAGE
Oed. Col.		65,	311	10,	31, 340
38,	79	88,	352	12,	175
65,	354	102,	304	17,	296, 297
118,	261	122,	356	21,	326
178,	373	169,	185	23,	120
305,	62	197,	94	24,	107
317,	162	244,	71	36,	101
337,	63	285,	307	37,	325
359,	368	289,	151	38,	218, 244, 325
408,	373	348,	368	39,	352
450,	373	349,	369	41,	161, 315
502,	301	353,	323	44,	115
509,	245	377,	359	45,	120
556,	171	408,	363	54,	334
565,	365	409,	274	56,	293
595,	245	427,	277	58,	15
649,	373	444,	274	60,	319
667,	365	487,	301	62,	366
707,	62	494,	418	64,	298
746,	322	523,	68	65,	261
761,	227	534,	301	67,	333
834,	356	554,	318	68,	244
848,	373	588,	363	70,	221
956,	149, 384	611,	375, 385	71,	145
969,	271	674,	164	73,	268
996,	73	764,	246	74,	166
1023,	372	825,	255	76,	354, 366
1024,	373	900,	356	77,	304
1154,	351	914,	276	78,	351
1239,	413	917,	245	86,	339
1441,	245	931,	423	87,	400
1443,	304	961,	243	89,	59
1455,	331	969,	281	91,	13, 296, 404
1513,	39	975,	356	95,	112
1702,	373	1030,	107	96,	60, 91
		1079,	19	97,	45
Oed. Tyr.		1171,	122	99,	236
11,	368, 381	1224,	70	100,	99
129,	366, 369	1289,	147	102,	276
198,	245	1293,	304	103,	360
220,	368	1314,	147	104,	29
255,	144	1363,	353	107,	170
281,	362	1441	340	109,	238, 292
302,	251			112,	68
314,	304	*Trachiniae.*		116,	166
442,	154	389,	296	118,	85, 244
446,	208	545,	154	120,	299
544,	410	577,	295	121,	121, 347
551,	380	631,	256, 299	123,	23
454,	298	687,	246	124,	373, 380
867,	309	817,	418	125,	168
888,	302	978,	374, 384	126,	131, 168
1129,	309	1100,	323	128,	115, 365
1214,	420	1122,	102	131,	90
1267,	207	1129,	264	132,	242
1326,	295	1183,	374	134,	406
1380,	123	1342,	211	137,	246, 348
1387,	257			140,	91
1391,	257	**THUCYDIDES.**		41,	314, 330
1437,	101	*Book* I.			
1770,	405	1,	36, 85, 327	*Book* II.	
Philoctetes.		2,	85, 273	3,	107
26,	44	3,	335	4,	85, 191
46,	276	4,	94, 162	5,	23
60,	304	8,	293	15,	19, 321
				17,	343, 354

TABLE OF REFERENCES.

LINE	PAGE	LINE	PAGE	LINE	PAGE
18,	309	38,	83	50,	123, 244
20,	115	40,	310	57,	306
21,	277, 405	41,	246	59,	405
32,	162	47,	92	64,	343
36,	323	60,	92	70,	255
38,	111	64,	342	71,	151, 222, 244
40,	310	66,	268	74,	55
41,	18	70,	322	75,	121, 312
49,	107, 366	90,	237	77,	52
52,	226	102,	310	80,	396, 405
53,	365	106,	331	81,	34
60,	277	118,	320	87,	362
61,	121	125,	168	92,	301
72,	399	128,	261	100,	405
76,	45	130,	85, 297		
80,	304, 322			**Book VIII.**	
89,	347	**Book V.**		1,	37
92,	147	9,	160	23,	316
93,	256	10,	244	36,	39
95,	105	17,	76	40,	237
97,	326	32,	175	66,	196, 221
102,	401	33,	92	70,	360
		34,	320	72,	34
Book III.		35,	348	74,	326
1,	366	37,	131	85,	30
10,	237, 322	40,	360	86,	34, 5
12,	121	46,	90	89,	
13,	305, 322	50,	348	108,	365, 366
14,	271	55,	109		
15,	31	67,	373	**XENOPHON.**	
22,	254	74,	20	*Anabasis.*	
29,	107, 244	103,	310	i. 1, 1, .	20
32,	406	105,	265	1, 3, .	147, 184
37,	120	111,	76	1, 10,	227
39,	362, 369			2, 2, .	406
40,	224	**Book VI.**		2, 5, .	255
41,	246	4,	245	2, 8, .	343
46,	123	5,	306	2, 15,	321
49,	273	21,	245	2, 21,	186, 405
53,	264, 267, 370	32,	342	2, 23,	15
54,	51, 210	34,	160, 320, 333	2, 31,	21
55,	209	37,	331	3, 17,	404
59,	337	39,	58, 105	4, 7, .	405
64,	111	49,	407	4, 20,	226, 272
69,	299	50,	259	5, 5, .	62
74,	219	54,	261	5, 13,	272
75,	366	58,	245	6, 2, .	366
81,	298, 362	62,	114, 238	6, 10,	87
88,	184	76,	75	7, 18,	347
95,	348	77,	18	8, 12,	150
96,	299	82,	351	9, 3, .	323
103,	271	100,	208	9, 10,	405
105,	326			9, 20,	337
		Book VII.		ii. 1, 4, .	217
Book IV.		2,	331	1, 6, .	19
1,	76, 104	10,	297	1, 15,	25
4,	238	11,	304	1, 16,	17
5,	351	17,	255	2, 3, .	362
11,	264, 359, 415	21,	60	3, 11,	367
14,	414	22,	76	3, 13,	273
16,	242	23,	334	3, 25,	270
17,	36, 43, 245, 299	29,	296	4, 22,	163
18,	316	31,	334	5, 13,	205
28,	327	34,	91	iii. 1, 19,	237
29,	39	42,	227	2, 6, .	259
33,	192	47,	412		

TABLE OF REFERENCES.

LINE	PAGE	LINE	PAGE	LINE	PAGE
2, 29,	242	3, 9, .	74	v. 1, 17,	301
3, 18,	240	3, 18,	240	2, 13,	404
4, 9, .	81	3, 35,	206, 270	4, 2, .	335
5, 1, .	330	3, 51,	121	vi. 4, 12,	34
5, 7, .	273	iv. 1, 3, .	414	vii. 1, 8, .	251
5, 11,	366	1, 18,	261	1, 34,	277, 405
5, 16,	291	1, 21,	180		
5, 18,	247	2, 25,	257	*Memorabilia.*	
13, 3, .	272	3, 11,	271	(*Apomnenmata*).	
iv. 2, 6, .	40	4, 21,	59		
4, 15,	351	5, 15,	272	i. 1, 4, .	277
4, 23,	75	5, 37,	239	1, 5, .	216
4, 24,	24	6, 8, .	93	2, 6, .	246
8, 2, .	379	v. 1, 25,	369	2, 7, .	264
8, 4, .	18	2, 12,	265	2, 35,	121
8, 5, .	96	2, 35,	309	2, 39,	353
v. 1, 10,	219	2, 36,	376	2, 41,	379
2, 5, .	276	vi. 2, 30,	265	2, 46,	281
3, 35,	81	3, 19,	271	4, 14,	336
4, 16,	166	4, 16,	156	ii. 1, 8, .	344
4, 30,	92	vii. 1, 18,	358	1, 25,	383
7, 5, .	242	3, 13,	373	2, 39,	264
8, 17, .	324	4, 4, .	333	3, 3, .	168
vi. 1, 21,	55	5, 13,	71	3, 18,	220
2, 1, .	232	5, 49,	246	6, 2, .	362
3, 17,	90	7, 16,	367	7, 11,	104
3, 20,	177	viii. 1, 10,	396	7, 13,	363
3, 26,	24	1, 10, 11, .	407	9, 8, .	109
vii. 1, 4, .	248	1, 48,	22	iii. 1, 6, .	177
3, 13,	399	3, 40,	113	5, 1, .	37
3, 34,	323	4, 16,	191	5, 17,	121, 156
6, 4, .	76	6, 3, .	258	11, 1, .	97
*8, 6, .	309	6, 13,	48	13, 3, .	121, †272
8, 22,	54	7, 19,	152	iv. 1, 3, .	38
		7, 22,	376	2, 36,	17
Cyropaedia.				2, 39,	370
i. 2, 1, .	80	*Hellenica.*		4, 12,	207
2, 5, .	255	i. 1, 16,	166	6, 7, .	402
2, 11,	20	1, 28,	306	7, 2, .	397
3, 3, .	278	1, 34,	323		
3, 9, .	29	6, 32,	371	*Agesilaus.*	
4, 14,	243	7, 5, .	390	ii. 15, .	107
4, 18,	166	ii. 1, 2, .	254	iv. 1, .	275
4, 20,	272	1, 25,	75		
4, 25,	254	2, 7, .	305	*Hiero.*	
5, 11,	273	2, 13,	398	x. 3, .	297
6, 4, .	94	3, 11,	353		
6, 18,	400	3, 16,	380	*Oeconomicus.*	
ii. 1, 4, .	255	3, 22,	334	ii. 9, .	261
1, 21,	256	iii. 1, 28,	306	23, .	13
2, 9, .	114, 405	2, 31,	353	iii. 5, .	59
2, 22,	83	3, 9, .	260	vii. 3, .	71
3, 13,	339	3, 19,	168	viii. 8, .	276
4, 2, .	301	5, 10,	265	x. 1, .	41
4, 7, .	147	iv. 1, 33,	207		
4, 23,	366	1, 41,	58	*Symposium.*	
iii. 1, 15,	305	2, 3, .	373	ii. 3, .	367
1, 37,	378	4, 5, .	353	iii. 5, .	297
1, 41,	214	5, 5, .	303	iv. 5, .	353
2, 3, .	85	8, 4, .	13	6, .	277 405
2, 37, .	136	8, 16,	256		

* Misprint, viii. 6.   † On 272, read Ap. for An.

www.ingramcontent.com/pod-product-compliance
Lightning Source LLC
Chambersburg PA
CBHW022136300426
44115CB00006B/211